QUICK START GUIDE

Welcome to your SAT Premier LIVE Online Program!

1 REGISTER YOUR ONLINE COMPANION

DOUBLE CHECK!

The serial number on the inside back cover of your book is your key to the online companion. *Enter it carefully* and make sure all of the numbers and letters match exactly!

2 TAKE THE ONLINE DIAGNOSTIC QUIZ AND ESSAY PROMPT

3 GET TO KNOW THE SAT, AND CREATE YOUR STUDY PLAN

4 WATCH THE FAST FACT VIDEOS

5 JOIN A LIVE ONLINE SESSION

6 TAKE A NEW PRACTICE QUIZ EVERY MONTH

1 REGISTER YOUR ONLINE COMPANION

The Online Companion gives you access to SAT Premier LIVE Online components that are not included between the covers of this book, including the Fast Fact Videos, registration for a LIVE Online Event, the Diagnostic Quiz, fresh new quizzes every month, and more!

Register your Online Companion using these simple steps:

1. **Locate your serial number in the book.** It's on the inside back cover.

2. **Go to Kaptest.com/SAT/booksonline.**

3. **Enter your serial number.** Make sure to enter it exactly as it appears in the book.

74NDA-WU35W-ZHW8L-SJSET-9TDXE

You can return to your Online Companion 24/7! Enter **Kaptest.com** in any Internet Browser and select the "My Page" link.

2 # TAKE THE ONLINE DIAGNOSTIC QUIZ

After logging in to your Online Companion, go to the "Diagnostic Quiz" session on your syllabus, and click on the "SAT Diagnostic Quiz" link that appears. This will prompt a separate window to appear with the quiz.

- The SAT Diagnostic Quiz is half the length of the real test. After you complete the Diagnostic Quiz, you will receive a percentage-based score that you can access in the "My Score" section of your syllabus.

■ Use this score as a baseline, and compare how well you improve in each content area as you go through the lessons, skill-building practice, quizzes, and tests in your program.

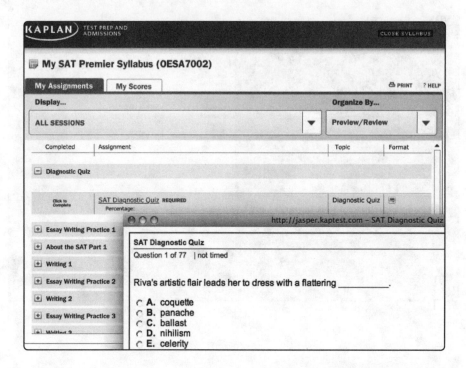

The Diagnostic Quiz will help you to do the following:

■ **Identify your strengths and weaknesses.** The Diagnostic Quiz will help you identify your test strengths and weaknesses for each section of the SAT exam. This will help you target your practice time.

■ **Develop your SAT study plan.** Once you review the results of your Diagnostic Quiz, you can understand where you went wrong and focus your study time based on your needs and schedule. This will help you develop a study plan that targets the concepts and question types you need to work on most.

• When reviewing the results of your Diagnostic Quiz, check your answers carefully, noting how many questions you got right and how many you got wrong.

- Look for patterns. Did you ace the reading comprehension? Did the advanced math trip you up? Do you need to work on test pacing and time management?

■ **Know what to expect on Test Day.** This half-length SAT provides you with a sample of each question type, so you'll know just what's waiting for you on Test Day.

■ **Reinforce key concepts and sharpen your skills.** Read all of the answer explanations—even those you got right—to reinforce key concepts and sharpen your test skills.

▶ Online Essay Prompt

Your Online Companion also includes **essay prompts** similar to those you'll see on Test Day.

■ **Choose an essay prompt.** Allow yourself 25 minutes to write your essay. Review your work. When you're finished, compare it to the model essays provided and check it against the scoring rubric to get a good sense of how you're doing.

■ **Review your work.** Based on the results of your essay, include time in your study plan to work on improving your writing score. There are additional essays prompts online to help get you ready for Test Day.

■ **How'd you do?** Based on the results of your essay, include time in your study plan to work on improving your writing score. Make a list of your personal strengths and weaknesses by identifying:

- If your argument was coherent
- If your writing flowed fluently from one paragraph to the next
- If your use of grammar and spelling was correct
- If you finished the essay in the allotted time

③ GET TO KNOW THE SAT AND CREATE YOUR STUDY PLAN

Remember, your SAT Premier LIVE Online Program is designed to meet your individual needs.

What does that mean?

■ **You're in control.** You control the variety and amount of study that best suits you. Use the results of your diagnostic quiz and sample essay to design a study plan that will help you achieve maximum results.

■ **You customize your study.** To make sure that you don't get bored with a big book of lessons and tests, we made your SAT program interactive—you get to mix things up by jumping between the book and the online resources.

After choosing a test date and registering for the SAT exam, figure out exactly what areas you need to concentrate on and how much time you have to prepare. Use the following tips to help you create an effective study plan that works for you.

Take some time to familiarize yourself with some of the key components of your SAT Premier Program. It's got all the tools you'll need to conquer the SAT exam on Test Day.

▶ Your SAT Premier LIVE Online Program Book

Kaplan's SAT Premier LIVE Online Program book is packed with resources to help you get ready for Test Day.

Like what? We're glad you asked! It's got:

■ a targeted review of key SAT terms and concepts

■ tips and strategies for each exam section and question type

■ lots of test practice (including 4 full-length exams)

▶ Tips for Customizing your Study Plan

The most effective study plan will adapt to your individual needs. Here are some helpful tips:

○ Start with a review of the content you're weakest in and include quizzes on these weaker topics to boost your skills and understanding.

○ Devote time to reinforcing content strengths through lesson reviews and practice quizzes.

○ Use full-length practice tests as milestones. There are 10 full-length practice tests in the program—don't plan on saving them all for the final weeks. Test yourself periodically and chart your progress.

○ Think about the topics on which you need to focus. Plan to read those lessons in the book, take practice sets, and review answer explanations.

○ As time permits, go back to the question types that you aced so you can keep the material sharp.

○ Take time to practice your essay writing. Understanding the essay requirements and practicing your writing will help you deliver a great essay on Test Day.

○ Reevaluate your strengths and weaknesses regularly. If they change, adjust your plan accordingly.

▶ Take Advantage of Additional Kaplan Exclusives

In addition to our Fast Fact Videos and LIVE Online Events, there are additional Kaplan exclusives that make *this* the most effective SAT test-prep product available.

Take advantage of these powerful tools. They'll help you score higher on Test Day!

SAT Premier Tutor Tips

Throughout the book, you'll see the following talk blurbs:

Inside each you'll find proven test tips provided by Kaplan's expert SAT instructors. Let this helpful and encouraging advice guide you through the book and get you ready to conquer the SAT.

SAT Perfect Score Tips

As you work your way through the book, you'll also see the following blurbs:

Inside each of these you'll find advice and strategies from a Kaplan student who earned a perfect score on the SAT. As you prep for the exam, who's better to listen to then someone who actually got a perfect score?

▶ SmartPoints™

SmartPoints rank the skills and topics that are tested and utilized most often on the SAT. They help you focus your test prep on the areas that will earn you the most points on Test Day.

How does it work? We ranked the most tested topics and crucial SAT skills using our exclusive SmartPoints bars system. The more SmartPoint bars an item has (from 1 bar to 5 bars), the more important it likely will be on Test Day.

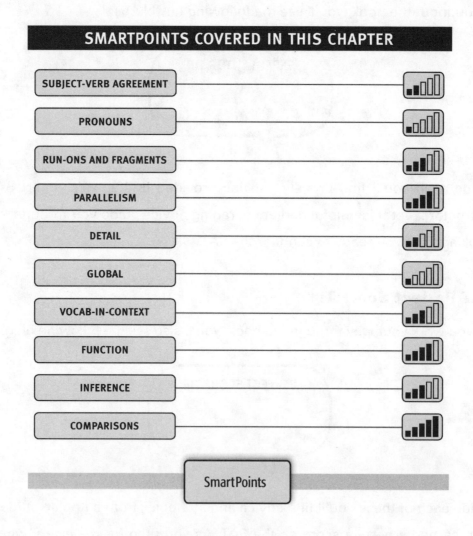

As you go through this book, you'll see SmartPoints skills and topics discussed throughout.

Look for the SmartPoints bars as you study:

 Equations

Use SmartPoints to prioritize your SAT studies:

■ Customize your study plan according to your strengths and weaknesses, giving extra time to items with higher SmartPoints rankings.

■ If you're short on time, focus your study on items with higher SmartPoints rankings first, and review items with lesser rankings as time allows.

4 WATCH THE FAST FACT VIDEOS

In Fast Fact Videos, one of Kaplan's experienced, highly rated SAT tutors explains and reinforces the most important concepts from each chapter. No long, drawn-out, boring tutorials here! With these quick video sessions, you get the effective, streamlined SAT info and strategies that will help you reach your target score.

Fast Fact Videos can only be accessed through your Online Companion. Here's how:

1. Once you've signed into your student home page, open your Syllabus.

2. In the Syllabus window, go to the "Fast Fact Videos" menu option.

3. Click on the link for the video you'd like to see. A separate window will appear with your video.

⑤ JOIN A LIVE ONLINE SESSION

While working your way through your book and the Online Companion, you may need extra clarification on an SAT question type, a Kaplan strategy, or any other SAT Premier LIVE Online component.

Kaplan's SAT LIVE Online Sessions are interactive, instructor-led SAT prep lessons that you can participate in from anywhere you can access the Internet.

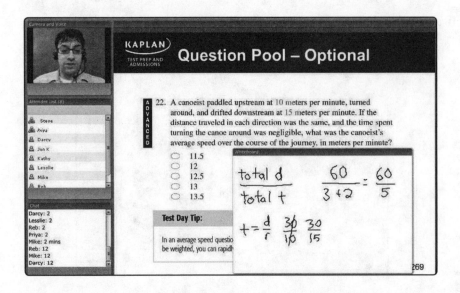

SAT LIVE Online Sessions are held in a state-of-the-art virtual classroom—actual lessons in real time, just like a physical classroom experience. Interact with your teacher and other classmates using audio, instant chat, whiteboard, polling, and screen-sharing functionality. And just like courses at Kaplan Centers, an SAT LIVE Online Session is led by an experienced Kaplan instructor.

To register for an SAT LIVE Online event:

1. Once you've signed into your student home page, open your Syllabus.

2. In the Syllabus window, go to the "LIVE Online Registration" menu option.

3. Click on the link. A separate window will appear with registration instructions.

There are two SAT LIVE Online events available. One event will take place in each of the following months:

- September 2009

- November 2009

Please check your online companion for dates and times!

Please note: Registration begins one month before the session date. Be sure to sign-up early, since spaces are reserved on a first-come, first serve basis.

6 TAKE A NEW PRACTICE QUIZ EVERY MONTH

You'll find a new quiz in your Online Companion each month, so you can continue to target your strengths and opportunities, and assess your progress.

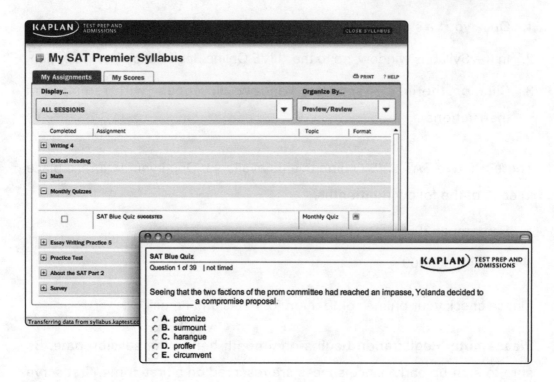

➡ NAVIGATING AROUND YOUR ONLINE SYLLABUS

Here are some quick tips for navigating around the features of your SAT Premier LIVE Online Companion:

▶ To Add Completion Dates for All Activities

1. Go to the corresponding session.

2. Click on the box to the left of the task you completed.

3. A pop-up will appear allowing you to select the date.

▶ To Start a Quiz, Test, or Online Essay Prompt

1. When you roll your mouse over the name of the quiz, test, or prompt, it will turn into a hyperlink.

2. Click on the hyperlink, and a separate window will appear.

3. Read the explanation of the activity and click "Next" or "Click Here to Start…" to begin.

▶ To Suspend a Quiz at Any Time

Click on the "Suspend" button at the bottom left side of the quiz window.

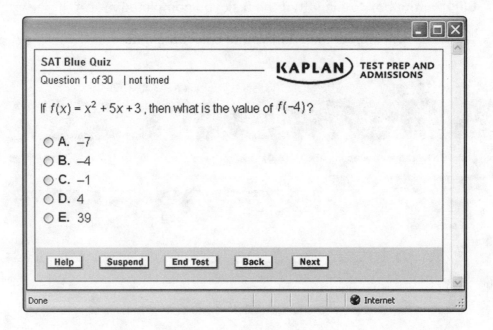

▶ To Suspend a Test at Any Time

Click on the "Quit Section" button at the bottom left side of the quiz window.

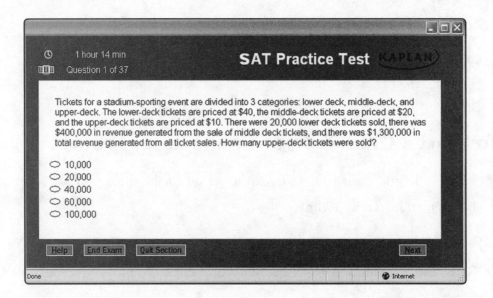

▶ To Resume a Quiz or Test

1. Select the quiz from the corresponding session.

2. A pop-up will appear with a table showing the status.

3. Click the "Resume" button in the right-hand column of the table.

▶ To Start a Quiz or Test over Again

1. Select the quiz from the corresponding session.

2. A pop-up will appear with a table showing the status.

3. Click the "Click Here to Start…" link.

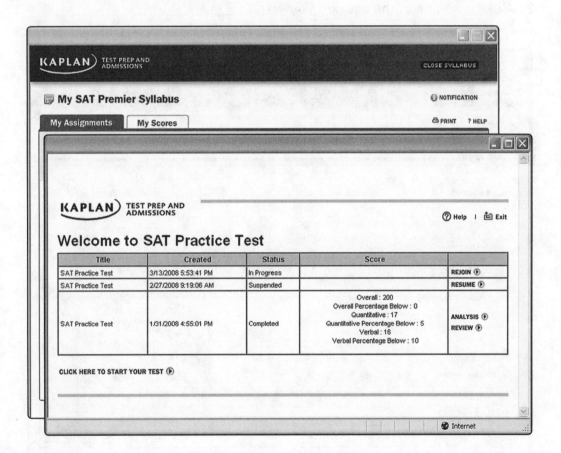

→ CUSTOMIZING THE ORGANIZATION OF YOUR ONLINE SYLLABUS

After logging in to your Online Companion, you will arrive at your student homepage. When you click on the "GO" button to access your online syllabus, the default "My Assignments" page will appear with the default "Preview/ Review" category. This option presents all the assets for every session.

To see all the assets of just one session:

1. Go to the "Display" pull-down menu.

2. Click on the "ALL SESSIONS" option.

3. Select the title of the session you want.

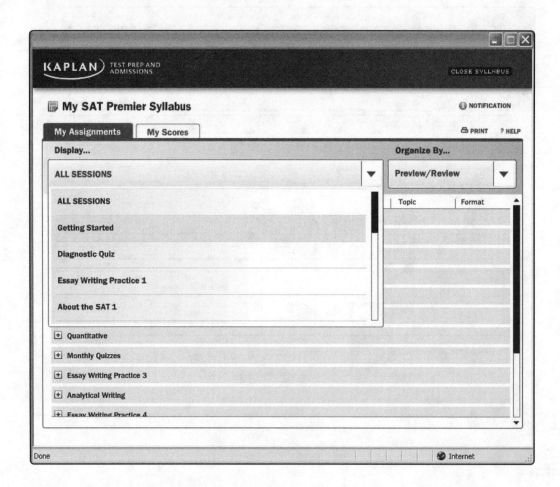

▶ Reorganize Your Syllabus by Category

There are six categories in the online syllabus: Preview/Review, Requirement Level, Completion Status, Assignment Name, Topic, and Format.

Requirement Level

1. Go to the "Organize by..." pull-down menu.

2. Select the "Requirement Level" option.

3. Each asset will be listed by a requirement level: Required (in red); Strongly Encouraged (in green); Suggested (in blue).

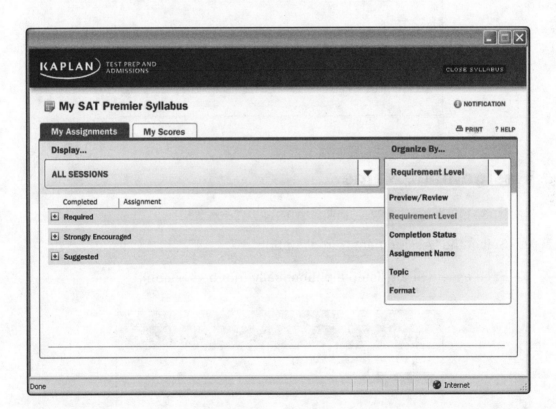

Completion Status

1. Go to the "Organize by..." pull-down menu.

2. Select the "Completion Status" option.

3. Each asset will be listed by a completion status: Completed; In Progress; Incomplete.

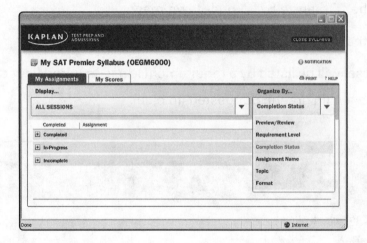

Assignment Name

1. Go to the "Organize by..." pull-down menu.

2. Select the "Assignment Name" option.

3. Each asset will be listed alphabetically (not by session).

Topic

1. Go to the "Organize by..." pull-down menu.

2. Select the "Topic" option.

3. Each asset will be listed by topic, such as "Review," "Skillbuilding, or "Practice Test."

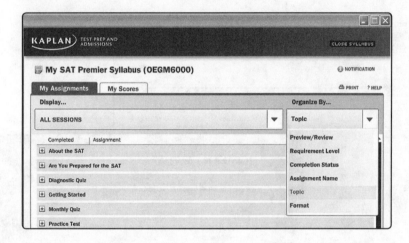

Format

1. Go to the "Organize by..." pull-down menu.

2. Select the "Format" option.

3. Each asset will be listed by format.

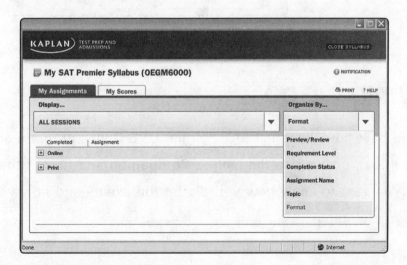

▶ View Your "My Scores" Page

Click on the "My Scores" tab next to the "My Assignments" tab.

The scores from the online features will automatically appear here. Scores you fill once you have completed your in-book practice sets will appear here as well.

➡ HOW DID WE DO?

After you have completed the SAT Premier LIVE Online program and have taken the test, go back to the Online Companion and fill out the online survey. We want to know how you did on the exam—and how we did in helping you to prepare.

Good luck!

SAT UPDATE: CHANGES TO SCORE-REPORTING POLICY

The College Board has decided to make an important change to the SAT score-reporting policy. The following information will tell you everything you need to know about this new change and how you can use it to your advantage.

WHAT'S CHANGING?

The new SAT score-reporting policy gives you the ability to select which scores by sitting (test date) that you wish to send to colleges. This is a completely **optional** feature and will first be available during the **March 2009** SAT test administration. You can use this new score-reporting feature on any score report you plan on sending, and you can send one, several, or all of your test scores to a college on a single report—with no difference in cost.

If you've taken an SAT prior to the start of this new policy or have already registered for the March 2009 exam, you will still be able to take advantage of this new option. For those who choose not to use this feature, all scores will be sent automatically.

It's important to note that only scores from an entire SAT exam can be sent to schools—you cannot select individual test sections from exams you've taken at different times. Please visit the official College Board website at www.collegeboard.com for complete details.

HOW DOES THIS CHANGE AFFECT ME?

This new policy gives you a real boost of empowerment in the college admissions process. It gives you more control over what colleges see and lets you show schools the SAT score that you feel best represents your test-taking ability. Because choosing to send sectional scores from different testing dates is not an option, you should make sure that you are well prepared for each and every SAT exam you take.

Although you should be aware of the score-reporting requirements of each college that you plan on applying to, the bottom line is that **this score-reporting change is good news for students**—use it to lower your anxiety and stress level as you prepare for Test Day.

STAY ON TOP OF THE LATEST SAT DEVELOPMENTS

You can depend on Kaplan to provide you with the most accurate, up-to-the-minute test information. You can get updates by visiting us at **kaptest.com/SAT.**

Good Luck!

SAT®

PREMIER LIVE ONLINE

2010 EDITION

The Staff of Kaplan Test Prep and Admissions

 PUBLISHING

New York

© 2009 Kaplan, Inc.

Published by Kaplan Publishing, a division of Kaplan, Inc.
1 Liberty Plaza, 24th Floor
New York, NY 10006

Printed in the United States of America

10 9 8 7 6 5 4 3 2 1

ISBN-13: 978-1-4195-5302-8

Kaplan Publishing books are available at special quantity discounts to use for sales promotions, employee premiums, or educational purposes. Please email our Special Sales Department to order or for more information at kaplanpublishing@kaplan.com, or write to Kaplan Publishing, 1 Liberty Plaza, 24th Floor, New York, NY 10006.

Table of Contents

PARENTS' GUIDE

PARENTS' GUIDE TO SURVIVING THE SAT

For many parents, the SAT was a long time ago, in a galaxy far, far away. In particular, it was a galaxy where you took the SAT once, got your score, and went to college. Prepping for the SAT probably involved sharpening your pencils the night before and brushing your teeth before leaving in the morning.

Today, the SAT is a bit more complicated, and the competition to get into a top college and get financial aid to cover the steep costs is tougher than ever! The test now includes an essay. The score is out of 2400. And what about all those other exams you may have heard about? Your child can now take the SAT, the PSAT, or SAT Subject Tests. Are they the same? Different? Does your son or daughter need to take all of them? What about the ACT? What does your son or daughter need to do in order to get into a good college?

These questions, as well as many others, probably fill your mind, your child's mind, and possibly your dinner table conversations and Internet searches as well! Fear not—Kaplan is here to help your family get through this important exam successfully!

Use the following guide to learn everything you need to know about the SAT, discover ways you can help your child prepare for this important exam, and manage your family's SAT stress.

After reviewing this section, we recommend that you and your child visit the official College Board website at www.collegeboard.com for additional SAT details and information. It's a great way to get involved and stay informed!

FREQUENTLY ASKED QUESTIONS

Kaplan gets a lot of questions from parents about the SAT exam. The following FAQs should help you get up to speed on SAT basics:

Q: What is the SAT and why should my child take it?

A: The SAT is a standardized test administered by the College Board and taken by millions of high school students annually. It measures students' critical thinking, math, and writing skills and is used by college admissions officers to determine their ability to do college-level work. Many colleges look at SAT scores in conjunction with GPA and extracurricular activities when deciding about admissions acceptance.

Q: What is the SAT exam like?

A: The SAT is a 3 hour and 45 minute test broken into three sections: Critical Reading, Math, and Writing. Most of the exam is composed of multiple-choice questions, although 1/3 of the Writing section score is based on the 25-minute essay students write in the first section of the exam.

Q: When should my child take the SAT exam?

A: Most students take the SAT as juniors or seniors, and many take the exam more than once.

Q: How is the SAT exam scored?

A: The highest score possible on the SAT is a 2400, computed from 800 in each section, Critical Reading, Math, and Writing.

Q: How can my child register for the SAT?

A: Your child can register online or by mail. Visit the official College Board website at www.collegeboard.com for complete registration rules and requirements.

Q: How much does the SAT exam cost?

A: The basic test fee is $45. Families who cannot afford this fee can request a fee waiver from their school counselor.

Q: How is the SAT different from other college admissions exams?

A: The Preliminary SAT/National Merit Scholarship Qualifying Test (PSAT/NMSQT®) is also administered by the College Board in conjunction with the National Merit Scholarship Corporation. The PSAT can help your child prepare for the SAT and enter the competition for a National Merit Scholarship—but taking the PSAT is not a requirement for taking the SAT.

SAT Subject Tests are different from the SAT because they are subject-specific (Literature, U.S. History, French, etc.), whereas the SAT is a general knowledge exam. Some colleges may require these exams, but they are not required for all schools. Check the admissions requirements of the schools your child is applying to.

The ACT is a general-knowledge exam similar in scope to the SAT. It also includes an essay component, English, Reading, and Math sections, but it includes a Science section as well. Many schools throughout the country accept either the SAT or the ACT. Because the tests are different, some students feel more comfortable taking one exam versus the other. It really is a matter of personal preference and college admissions requirements.

COMMON SAT MISCONCEPTIONS

There's a lot of inaccurate information floating around about the SAT. Let's clear up some common sources of confusion:

THE SAT IS NOT CURVED.

Theoretically, every student who takes the SAT this October could get a 2400. Your child is not competing against his classmates and friends to get his score. The tests are scaled prior to Test Day. The scaled score is what colleges use to compare scores from different test administrations.

THERE IS A PENALTY FOR WRONG ANSWERS.

For each question a student answers correctly, she gains 1 point. For each question a student misses on the test, the student loses $\frac{1}{4}$ of a point. If a student skips a question, no points are gained or lost.

STUDENTS WHO RECEIVE ACCOMMODATIONS FOR A DISABILITY ARE NOT PENALIZED.

Parents sometimes fear that applying for accommodations for disabilities will cause their child to be penalized—that their score reports will indicate the accommodation received, be it additional time, computer assistance, extended breaks, etc. If your child has a documented disability, contact your school's guidance counselor or visit www.collegeboard.com for more information.

WHEN IT COMES TO COLLEGE ADMISSIONS, THE SAT ISN'T EVERYTHING!

Yes, college admissions are becoming more and more competitive each year. But the SAT is just one component of your child's full application. Help your child—and yourself—by keeping the SAT in perspective. Your child's SAT score goals should align with his or her college choices. Know the target score range of the schools your child is applying to and set reasonable goals. Having a defined goal will help your child see what she's working toward, measure success along the way, and feel a strong sense of accomplishment when he or she reaches that goal. Remember: a 2400 is a great score, but NO school requires a 2400 for admission!

HELPING YOUR CHILD SUCCEED ON THE SAT

There are lots of SAT test-prep options available, from courses to self-study guides like this one. Your study choices should align with your child's needs and resources. Buying this book is a great option! By giving your child access to Kaplan's expert resources, you are helping her build an excellent foundation for SAT success. You can also assist your child by keeping the following things in mind:

HELP REDUCE TEST ANXIETY BY EMPATHIZING

Whether your child is the nonchalant "Mom, don't worry about it" type or the up-until-midnight crammer, your child is probably nervous about the SAT. It's an important exam, and if your child has already taken the PSAT, he could be worried about whether his SAT score will be better. Or maybe he's worried he won't be able to do as well as he did on the PSAT and won't get into his dream school? Perhaps you've bought this book because your child has already taken the SAT and wants to do better than the first time around. Maybe your child has never taken the PSAT or the SAT before, and the fear of the unknown is causing anxiety. Whatever the case, for most people, just saying "SAT" will send shivers down their spines, and for your child, the pressure is on. One of the biggest ways you can help is by empathizing.

You probably took the SAT, but even if you didn't, you can remember some time when you had to prepare for an important event—a test, a presentation at work, or a job interview. All of these events are daunting because, to some degree, they shape the course of our lives. You might not remember what you got on the SAT, but saying, "Oh, in 15 years, no one will care what you got on the SAT " WILL NOT HELP. This test matters to them right now, a lot. Recognize that, and make sure your kids know that *you know* how important this test is and that their anxiety isn't abnormal or strange.

Most of all, talk to them about this anxiety—gently! Know when it's the right time to approach your child and start a casual discussion. Try sharing a time when you were worried about a big life event over dinner. Then let your child open up on his terms and share his thoughts and feeling. Let him know you believe in succeeding at this together, and no matter what happens, life will continue after the SAT.

SET MEASURABLE GOALS AND INCREASE YOUR CHILD'S CONFIDENCE

A good first step is to determine some target schools. Offer to help your child with this, serving as a sounding board for their thoughts and offering helpful advice. Keep in mind that your goals and theirs might be completely different. Even if you don't have a sense of where your child's SAT scores are right now, consider things like size, location, academic competitiveness, and academic majors. Having a realistic list of schools will help the unmotivated student see the point of studying for the SATs and will help the super-motivated student keep things in perspective.

By setting goals, you can reward steps along the way. If your daughter learned 25 new vocabulary words this week, reward her—an iTunes download or snack perhaps?—even if she hasn't shown a 20-point increase on her Practice Test yet. If your child continually sees how proud of you are, she'll be more likely to be proud and confident herself on Test Day. Successes along the way will make Test Day feel much less like a "make or break" event and more like a "I'm going to conquer this test" opportunity!

LEAD BY EXAMPLE AND MANAGE YOUR OWN STRESS

If you want your child to stick to his or her study schedule, lead the way. Share some tricks that you use to help with time management, and most importantly, use them! If you say you're going to be home at 5:00 to drive them to hockey practice, be home at 5:00, not 5:30. If you say you're going to exercise three times per week, then exercise. We've all had that boss who tells you to respond to his emails within 24 hours, but who only responds to yours after three follow-up emails. You know what you think when he says, "Please respond within 24 hours to all emails." You think, *if you don't do it, then why should I?* Your kids think this too.

Also, manage your own stress about the SAT by keeping these things in mind.

- With commitment and dedication, it will all work out. Your son or daughter's confidence may waver, they may have moments while preparing for the SAT where they feel as if they're fighting a losing battle, but stay positive and believe that in the future, it all works out.

- Your child gets to focus on their SAT score; you get to focus on praising your child for their effort and encouraging them to succeed in a healthy and positive way.

- Stay calm and supportive and your child will come to you for help.

- By choosing Kaplan, you have a lot of resources to guide you through this process.

LISTEN TO KAPLAN—THE SAT EXPERTS

You don't have to have all the answers for the SAT, but keep in mind that you and your child have a larger support network than you might realize. By choosing Kaplan you get the benefit of nearly 70 years of experience and the wisdom from Kaplan's SAT experts. We asked a veteran Kaplan Premier tutor for some SAT advice for parents. Here's what she had to say:

1. **Keep everything in perspective.** The SAT gets a lot of press nowadays, but you have to keep in mind that the SAT is simply a piece of your child's college application—not the whole story. Keeping the SAT in perspective will help you and your child keep your cool while preparing for Test Day.

2. **Don't get caught up on the "SAT treadmill."** I always encourage my students to set a realistic score goal that they will be satisfied with on Test Day. Sure, if they score higher than that great, but you don't want them to be caught on the treadmill of "Oh, I only got a

630 in Math; why didn't I get a 650 or a 670?" I always tell my students, "Know what your goal is and work toward it, and most of all: be happy when you reach it and proud that you tried!"

3. **Utilize the accommodations the College Board provides.** If your child has a documented disability, he or she will not be stigmatized for it, because the use of accommodations is not indicated on SAT score reports. Just make sure to start arranging for accommodations several months before your child will actually take the SAT.

4. **Don't expect a miracle on Test Day.** I sometimes have students who will take a Practice Test a week before Test Day and still be 80 or 100 points shy of their score goal. You can just imagine how disheartening this can be. Unless this is their last possible opportunity to take the test, review the option of taking a later test with your child. That way, your child can study more and wait until his or her Practice Test scores are solidly in score goal range. Remember, even with the SAT's new "Score Choice" option, you still send the scores from an ENTIRE test. In other words, you can't pick and choose the Math score from the October test, the Writing score from the December test, and the Critical Reading score from the March test. Know your options and make the most of them!

5. **Keep an optimistic eye on your child's future.** Remember, college is great. Your child just has to get through the SAT to get there. No matter what your child's SAT score is, stay positive and know that he or she will get into college and have a positive experience. Everyone I know loved college, but virtually no one I know loved the SAT. Just help your child choose a range of colleges, set a target score, and make a study plan—and be that positive motivating force until Test Day. Freshman move-in day will be here before you know it!

Best of luck and success!

SAT STUDY GROUP GUIDE

SAT STUDY GROUP GUIDE

W e've all heard the phrase "two heads are better than one." Well, that also can be true when you're studying for the SAT!

You might feel that SAT prep is a lone experience, because when Test Day comes around, it'll just be you, your calculator, and your number 2 pencils. If this is the case, that's okay—your test prep should be based on how *you* learn best.

However, if you feel as if you'd benefit from preparing for the SAT with the help of a study group, then keep reading. The following section is designed to show you the benefits of group study, how to get the most out of your study buddy or study group, and what pitfalls to avoid when studying in groups.

STUDY GROUPS CAN BE GREAT FOR SAT PREP

One of the best reasons to get together with other people to prep for the SAT is that you'll have the opportunity to work with others who complement your strengths and weaknesses. Also, having someone to explain a difficult concept directly to you can help you sort out the areas that are causing you the most confusion. This strategy works well with a buddy as well as in a larger study group.

Study buddies can be helpful in lots of ways:

- Working with a study buddy or group will help keep you on track and force you to stick to your study plan. Good study buddies don't want to waste time watching you goof off or send emails, so if you have a study buddy—or better yet a whole study group—you can keep procrastination to a minimum.

- Study buddies are there to support you when you're struggling and can share in your success when you make progress and reach your score goal.

- Study buddies can help you vent your frustrations—because they are frustrated too! Get together, listen to each other talk about your SAT challenges, and celebrate when you all reach your score goals.

- Study groups are great for simulating real test conditions. Get together with your group and take practice sections or full-length tests under timed, test-like conditions. Not only can the tick of the clock simulate the pressure of Test Day, but also having to concentrate in the same room as other test takers can help you prepare for the pressure of Test Day.

WHY STUDY WITH A BUDDY?

- If you're quite facile with vocabulary but you're wary of geometry, you can find a study buddy who can teach you the Pythagorean theorem after you drill him on vocabulary flash cards.

- If you're a math whiz but couldn't finish a crossword puzzle if it came with a million-dollar prize, study the Critical Reading and Writing sections with a word nerd and let her benefit from your Math section genius.

STUDY BUDDIES: THE DARK SIDE AND WHAT TO DO ABOUT IT

Now that you're ready to call up every SAT taker in your area code and form your study group, let's talk about potential pitfalls so that you'll know how to avoid them. If you've ever had to do a group project before, the dangers often found in group study situations are probably no secret to you. Beware of the following:

MORE CHATTY = LESS WORKY

The biggest potential danger in a study group is, well, not studying. If you get a group of your friends together, your first reaction might be to rehash all of the newsworthy events that happened during the day. Doing this completely invalidates the whole study portion of study group.

What can you do to avoid it?

The best way may be the most shocking piece of advice in this whole chapter. Are you sitting down? Ready? **Don't** pick your friends as study buddies.

Consider looking for study buddies among people with whom you won't run the risk of excessive socializing. Choose those who share a common goal: succeeding on the SAT. Sure, your friends want you to do well on the SAT, too, but if you don't stick closely to your study schedule, they'll more than likely cut you some slack, which doesn't help you much. If you have some friends that will keep you on task, then by all means make them your study buddies, but save your favorite procrastinators for blowing off steam *after* you've taken a Practice Test.

NO TIME TO MEET

Does this sound familiar: You have soccer at 7:00 A.M. Monday, Wednesday, and Friday; school until 3:30 every day; cello lessons on Tuesdays and Thursdays after school, but it takes 30 minutes to get there, plus you have to eat dinner. On Saturdays, you go to visit your grandmother, who lives an hour away, and every other Sunday in months ending in *y* you volunteer for the local free-range hamster rescue. And now you have to work around someone else's schedule. With everything else in your life going on, how can you and your study buddies make time to meet?

What can you do about it?

First, look for people who share a similar schedule to your own:

KAPLAN STUDY GROUP STRATEGY

• Try having each member prepare a brief lesson on one of his strengths, and take turns sharing it with the rest of the group.

• Make time for questions and answers during each mini-tutorial. This way, not only do you reinforce something you're already feeling confident about, but you can also learn from experts in the areas where you can improve.

- Who else on your soccer team is taking the SAT this year?
- Maybe someone at the hamster rescue can meet with you on every *other* Sunday to take Practice Tests?

Often, students form study groups and then think about when everyone can get together, but Kaplan recommends choosing study groups based on schedules, particularly if your schedule is extremely full.

Treat your SAT study schedule as seriously as your soccer team or those cello lessons. Remember, one of the best reasons to study with others is because it keeps you from procrastinating, or even worse, failing to study altogether. You would never just skip a practice the day before your big soccer game, because you know your team is counting on you. Your SAT team is counting on you just as much.

KNOW-IT-ALLS AND SLACKERS

The purpose of the study group is for everyone to benefit from each other. Two personality types that violate this covenant are know-it-alls and slackers:

1. The know-it-all often dominates the teaching portion of the study session. He has to be right and will often fight about it. If proven wrong, know-it-alls often sulk or become passive aggressive, wasting everyone's time and ruining your mood.
2. Slackers, if they even show up, often have nothing to contribute. They'll probably just coast along and let everyone else talk through tough problems without adding any insights. Slackers might be really fun to hang out with on the weekend, but if you have one in your study group, you'll probably just end up feeling resentful that she is doing all taking and no giving.

Although slackers and know-it-alls represent opposite ends of the spectrum, both can ruin a study partnership or group.

What can you do about it?

This is your study group. Don't invite people who might end up being know-it-alls or slackers. Just because someone has a lot to contribute does not necessarily make him a know-it-all, so be willing to listen to others in their areas of expertise. Still, if all this expertise is getting in the way of you actually preparing for the SAT, you might be in the presence of a know-it-all.

We all might be prone to a little "slackerism," but your SAT group is there to keep you honest and working hard. At your first group meeting, have everyone agree to hold each other accountable for doing what they say they will do. One of the most unproductive types of groups is the one in which no one holds anyone else accountable because everyone knows that they didn't do what they were supposed to do either! Be on the lookout for signs of slackerism, and be ready to stomp it out!

STUDY GROUP BEST PRACTICES

Now that you know some of the things to avoid when forming your study group, we thought we'd offer some of the best things TO DO.

PICK SMART

Choose those who will complement your strengths and weaknesses, best match your schedule, and keep you on track for SAT success. Remember, you can always test-drive a study buddy. If you think you want to work with someone, but you think she might be a know-it-all, set up *one* study session. If things go well, you can continue working with her. If she turns out to be a know-it-all, then you can be glad you didn't commit to working with her until Test Day!

ASSIGN ROLES

If you want to have a study group rather than a study partner, assigning roles to group members is a good practice:

- One person can be the Scheduler and keep track of meeting times and locations.
- Another person can be the Break Maker, making sure that there's some study food to enjoy after a particularly challenging set of Critical Reading paired passages.
- Another person can be the Lesson Planner, assigning who will present which section or which practice sections the group should do for timed, testlike practice.

Many different roles are available, but making sure each group member has a stake in the overall success of the group is an important factor.

SHARE GOALS

Aligning around each other's successes is the best way to have a strong study partnership or team. If you don't feel comfortable at first sharing the fact that your Math score is a 380, you can always share that you want to raise your Math score 70 points. You should always have measureable goals, and you should encourage your study buddies to have clear goals too. Checking in with your study partners along the way is a great way to support the group's success. After taking a practice test, compare group members' results from this test to the last one. Celebrate each other's successes.

STUDY GROUPS—KEEP THEM IN PERSPECTIVE

Sure, you can succeed on the SAT without forming study partnerships, but for some students, study groups can be a great asset in preparation for Test Day. In addition, the experience you get building and working with a team right now has far-reaching benefits for the future. Now more than ever, the world functions in groups and teams. As you go on to college and eventually embark upon your career, the opportunities to work in teams will abound, and quite often teamwork will not be optional. The ability to create and work in successful teams will serve you long after you've taken the SAT. In the short term, however, it can be a highly effective tool for achieving your goal score.

Whether you study on your own, with a buddy, or in a study group, best of luck on Test Day!

| Part One |

KNOW THE SAT

CHAPTER 1: SAT Basics

CHAPTER 2: SAT Strategies

Knowing the SAT inside and out will gain you points on *every section*. Those extra points could mean a lot to a college admissions officer reviewing your score. Part 1 of this book is an overview of the SAT and Kaplan's strategies for doing your absolute best on the exam!

CHAPTER 1: SAT BASICS

GET READY FOR TEST DAY

The first two chapters in this book cover basic information on the SAT and Kaplan's overall strategies for approaching the test—the fundamentals you need to be ready for the exam and improve your score. Knowing this information will make you feel more confident when you walk into the testing room, and the more confidence you have, the more success you will have in attaining a top score.

SAT DATES AND HOW TO REGISTER

SAT TEST DATES

These days, more students are taking the SAT earlier in high school. Many are applying to early-decision programs, and many are taking the SAT more than once.

> **PERFECT SCORE TIP**
>
> " I decided to take the PSAT in the 10th grade. It was good prep for the SAT and helped set me up for success. "

2009 TEST DATES

Please visit the official College Board website at www.collegeboard.com for a complete list of test dates.

Dates & Registration | Format | Scoring | Ground Rules | Chapter Highlights

SAT REGISTRATION

There are a few different ways to register for the SAT exam. Check out the College Board website at www.collegeboard.com for complete information about registering for the SAT and for the most up-to-date information concerning changes in dates, fees, etc.

> **PERFECT SCORE TIP**
>
> " I made sure to schedule the SAT on a weekend where I didn't have much else going on. That way, I could focus on one thing: doing well on the SAT! "

REGISTER EARLY

Try to register early to secure the test center of your choice and to avoid late registration fees.

> **EXPERT TUTOR TIP**
>
> " Study smart—schedule realistic study sessions on a regular basis, and be conscious of how much you are learning. You're not a robot, so don't study like one! "

HOW TO REGISTER

- **To register by mail,** you'll need to get a Registration Bulletin from your high school guidance counselor and follow the instructions.

- **To register online,** you'll need to visit www.collegeboard.com. The website contains easy, step-by-step instructions for electronically submitting your registration. Read the instructions and requirements carefully.

- **Students with disabilities** can call (609) 771-7137 (TTY: Domestic 888-857-2477/International (609) 882-4118) for more information regarding special testing accommodations.

OTHER IMPORTANT REGISTRATION INFORMATION

- **The basic fee for the SAT is $45** in the United States. This price includes reports for you, your high school, and up to four colleges and scholarship programs. There are additional fees for late registration, standby testing, international processing, changing test centers or test dates, rush reporting, and for additional services and products.

- **Make sure to bring proper identification and admission ticket with you to the test center.** Some acceptable forms of identification include photo IDs, such as a driver's license, a school identification card, or a valid passport. Unacceptable forms of identification include a Social Security card, credit card, or birth certificate.

Dates & Registration   Format   Scoring   Ground Rules   Chapter Highlights

ALSO . . .

- You might be wondering whether to take the ACT in addition to the SAT. For more information on the ACT, go to the ACT website at www.act.org.

- SAT scores will be available online approximately three weeks after the test. If you can't wait that long, you can get your scores eight days earlier with Scores by Web or Scores by Phone. Please visit www.collegeboard.com for more information.

- Check your online companion or log onto the College Board for all the latest information on the test. Every effort is made to keep the information in this book up to date, but changes may occur after the book is published.

TEST FORMAT

The SAT is 3 hours and 45 minutes long, and there are two 10-minute breaks. The exam is mostly multiple-choice, and it's divided into three Math, three Critical Reading, and three Writing sections. There is also an experimental section, but we will discuss that section later. The essay section is always first. The multiple-choice sections can appear in *any order* on Test Day. The order is random, and your test will be different from that of the person sitting next to you.

The SAT sections are broken down like this:

SECTION	LENGTH	CONTENT	TYPE
Critical Reading	25 minutes	Sentence Completion and Reading Comprehension	Multiple-choice questions
Critical Reading	25 minutes	Sentence Completion and Reading Comprehension	Multiple-choice questions
Critical Reading	20 minutes	Sentence Completion and Reading Comprehension	Multiple-choice questions
Math	25 minutes	High School Geometry and Algebra, Numbers and Operations, Statistics, Probability, and Data Analysis	Multiple-choice questions and student-produced responses

PERFECT SCORE TIP

❝ It was easier for me to study the sections one at a time, instead of jumping around between sections. The material seemed to really fit together in my head this way. ❞

EXPERT TUTOR TIP

❝ Don't play the comparison game; everyone is different. Don't dwell on what you don't know; think about all you do know, and know you're going to conquer the SAT! ❞

Dates & Registration | Format | Scoring | Ground Rules | Chapter Highlights

Math	25 minutes	High School Geometry and Algebra, Numbers and Operations, Statistics, Probability, and Data Analysis	Multiple-choice questions and student-pro-duced responses
Math	20 minutes	High School Geometry and Algebra, Numbers and Operations, Statistics, Probability, and Data Analysis	Multiple-choice questions
Writing	25 minutes	Student-Written Essay	Long-form essay
Writing	25 minutes	Identifying Sentence Errors, Improving, Sentences, Improving Paragraphs	Multiple-choice questions
Writing	10 minutes	Improving Sentences	Multiple-choice questions
Experimental	25 minutes	Math, Writing, or Critical Reading	(Anything is fair game)

SAT COMPONENTS

Now it's time for brief summaries of each of the SAT's three components: Writing, Critical Reading, and Math.

THE WRITING COMPONENT

The SAT has three Writing sections: one essay and two multiple-choice sections.

THE ESSAY

The essay directions ask you to write a persuasive essay answering the assigned question, which typically asks you to respond to a quotation. Here is an example of a quote and essay prompt that you might see on the test:

> "My future starts when I wake up every morning . . . Every day I find something creative to do with my life."
>
> —Miles Davis

Assignment: Are there more advantages to planning for the future than living in the moment?

> **PERFECT SCORE TIP**
>
> When practicing for the essay, I used as many of Kaplan's prompts as I could and had my parents read and comment on my work.

Dates & Registration | **Format** | Scoring | Ground Rules | Chapter Highlights

We know what kind of essay the SAT graders are looking for, and we'll tell you exactly how to write one in chapter 4.

MULTIPLE-CHOICE QUESTIONS

Multiple-choice questions test your ability to spot errors in grammar, sentence structure, and paragraph structure or organization. Here's an example of a sentence structure question:

Directions: Part of the sentence below is underlined; beneath it are five ways of phrasing the underlined material. Choice (A) repeats the original phrasing; the other four choices are different. If you think the original phrasing produces a better sentence than any of the alternatives, select choice (A); if not, select one of the other choices.

> The lawyer advised her client to wear a suit, shave, <u>and stopping crying.</u>
>
> (A) and stopping crying
> (B) and crying is stopped
> (C) also stopping crying
> (D) and they should stop crying
> (E) and stop crying

We go into detail on the Writing component's multiple-choice questions in chapter 5.

THE CRITICAL READING COMPONENT

There are two kinds of questions in the Critical Reading component of the SAT. Both are multiple-choice.

SENTENCE COMPLETION QUESTIONS

These questions test your ability to determine how words or ideas work together to create meaning in a sentence. About half have one word missing from a sentence; the other half have two words missing. Both types test vocabulary and reasoning skills.

Here is a sample question:

Directions: The sentence that follows has two blanks, each blank indicating that something has been omitted. Beneath the sentence are five sets of words labeled A through E. Choose the word or set of words that, when inserted in the sentence, *best* fits the meaning of the sentence as a whole.

> **PERFECT SCORE TIP**
>
> " I planned the time I spent studying for the SAT so that it didn't interfere with my activities at all. The SAT doesn't have to take over your whole life! "

> **EXPERT TUTOR TIP**
>
> " Real life doesn't stop for the SAT. There are a lot of problems that might come up, but don't let them keep you from the score you want.

The king's ------- decisions as a diplomat and administrator led to his legendary reputation as a just and ------- ruler.

(A) quick . . . capricious
(B) equitable . . . wise
(C) immoral . . . perceptive
(D   generous . . . witty
(E) clever . . . uneducated

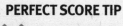
Remember, Sentence Completion questions are arranged in order of difficulty. The first few questions in a set will be fairly easy. The middle few questions are harder, and the last few are the most difficult. Keep this in mind as you work through this section of the exam.

Answer (B). Focus on clue words *diplomat* and *just*.

READING COMPREHENSION QUESTIONS

These questions test your ability to understand a piece of writing. Some passages are short (100–150 words), others are long (400–850 words), and at least one passage contains two related readings. Most Reading Comprehension questions test how well you understand the information in the passage, some ask you to draw conclusions, and some test your vocabulary or your ability to determine the meaning of words in context. More about these in part 3.

Reading Comprehension questions are not arranged by difficulty. Whenever you find yourself spending too much time on a question in these sections, you should skip it and return to it later. We recommend you circle it in your test booklet so you can find it later.

THE MATH COMPONENT

There are two kinds of Math questions on the SAT, broken down as follows:

MATH MULTIPLE-CHOICE QUESTIONS

These are straightforward multiple-choice questions with five answer choices.

Here is a sample question:

At a diner, Joe orders three strips of bacon and a cup of coffee and is charged $2.25. Stella orders two strips of bacon and a cup of coffee and is charged $1.70. What is the price of two strips of bacon?

(A) $0.55
(B) $0.60

(C) $1.10

(D) $1.30

(E) $1.80

Answer: (C).

GRID-IN QUESTIONS

Grid-in questions are not multiple-choice. Instead of picking an answer choice, you write your response in a grid like the one below.

Here is a sample Grid-in answer:

Both question types cover *the same* math concepts across the full range of difficulty. Either one can ask you a geometry, algebra, or statistics question. However, Grid-ins are more challenging because you don't have answers to choose from, as in the multiple-choice questions; you are totally on your own to come up with the correct answer.

You should answer all Grid-in questions since you've got nothing to lose.

HOW MATH QUESTIONS ARE SCORED

A wrong multiple-choice answer loses you 1/4 point. A wrong Grid-in loses you *nothing*.

Dates & Registration | **Format** | Scoring | Ground Rules | Chapter Highlights

SAT Math is covered in detail in the SAT Premier Program's part 4.

EXPERIMENTAL SECTION

Every SAT has an experimental section. The experimental section is used by the test developers to try out new questions before including them in upcoming SATs.

DID YOU KNOW?

The experimental section DOES NOT COUNT in your score.

PERFECT SCORE TIP

“ I always tried to remember that I wasn't defined by my SAT score, it was simply one part of my application. This helped me keep the SAT in perspective. ”

It can show up anywhere on the exam and will look just like a normal section. You shouldn't try to figure out which SAT section is experimental. You will fail to do so. Just treat all the sections as if they count toward your score.

THE BOTTOM LINE

These are the basics you need to know about the structure of the SAT before you take it. You'll get more familiar with the format and setup of the SAT question types and sections as you work your way through the rest of the book.

SCORING

Here's a rundown of how the SAT is scored:

EXPERT TUTOR TIP

“ The wrong answer penalty exists to discourage *random* guessing. But if you can eliminate at least one answer choice you *know* is wrong, it's in your best interest to guess! ”

- You gain one point for each correct answer on the SAT and lose a fraction of a point (1/4 point, to be exact) for each wrong answer (except with Grid-ins, where you lose *nothing* for a wrong answer).

- You do *not* lose any points for questions you leave blank.

- The totals for the Critical Reading, Writing, and Math questions are added up to produce three raw scores. These raw scores equal the number you got right minus a fraction of the number you got wrong.

- These scores are converted into scaled scores, with 200 as the lowest score and 800 the highest.

SCORE BREAKDOWN

The three scaled scores are added together to produce your final score of 600–2400, as follows:

Scaled Scores:	Writing	Math	Critical Reading	Total
	200–800	200–800	200–800	600–2400

ORDER OF DIFFICULTY

On the SAT, some sections will have their multiple-choice questions arranged in order of difficulty. Here's a breakdown:

	TEST SECTION	ARRANGED EASIEST TO HARDEST?
Math	Regular Math	Yes
	Grid-ins	Yes
Critical Reading	Sentence Completion	Yes
	Short Reading Comprehension	No
	Long Reading Comprehension	No
Writing	Essay	N/A
	Identifying Sentence Errors	No
	Improving Sentences	No
	Improving Paragraphs	No

As you work through a set that is organized by order of difficulty, *be aware of where you are in a set*. When working on the easy problems, you can generally trust your first impulse—the obvious answer is likely to be right. As you get to the end of the set, you need to be more suspicious of *obvious* answers, because the answer should not come easily. If it does, look at the problem again. It may be one of those distracters—a wrong answer choice meant to trick you.

> **EXPERT TUTOR TIP**
>
> " Don't rush through easier questions and make careless errors on your way to the harder ones. They're all worth the same points! "

SAT GROUND RULES

These are SAT rules you can use to your advantage. Knowing these rules will keep you from asking questions and wasting precious time and from committing minor errors that result in serious penalties.

- You are NOT allowed to jump back and forth between sections.

- You are NOT allowed to return to earlier sections to change answers.

- You are NOT allowed to spend more than the allotted time on any section.

- You CAN move around within a section.

- You CAN flip through your section at the beginning to see what types of questions are coming up.

| Dates & Registration | Format | Scoring | **Ground Rules** | Chapter Highlights |

IF YOU LEARN ONLY THREE THINGS IN THIS CHAPTER . . .

1. TEN SECTIONS IN 3 HOURS, 45 MINUTES

- Three Critical Reading sections
- Three Math sections
- Three Writing sections
- One Experimental section (Critical Reading, Math, or Writing multiple-choice)

2. HOW TO HANDLE QUESTIONS FROM EASY TO HARD

- Be sure to get to all the questions you can answer easily.
- Don't spend too long on any one question.
- Answer all Math Grid-in questions. There's no penalty.

3. SCORING FACTS

- You gain 1 point for every question you get right.
- You lose 1/4 point for every multiple-choice question you get wrong.
- Grid-in questions are "free," as in "feel free to guess."
- Each section is worth 200–800 points. These scores are added to get your total score of 600–2400.

Dates & Registration   Format   Scoring   Ground Rules   **Chapter Highlights**

CHAPTER 2: SAT STRATEGIES

SAT FUNDAMENTALS

The SAT is different from the tests you're used to taking in school. The good news is you can use the SAT's particular structure to your scoring advantage!

Learn the following SAT rules—they'll really help you on Test Day:

- The directions *never* change. Each section is completely predictable, so you don't have to waste time reading them.

- Skipping hard or time-consuming questions in order to have time for easier ones is often a good idea.

- The scoring machine doesn't care about your methods. It only cares if you bubble in your answer correctly—so be careful!

- All questions are worth the same, whether easy or hard, *if* you get them right.

STRATEGIES FOR SCORING HIGHER

Kaplan's exclusive strategies for scoring higher on the SAT are based on decades of proven test-prep experience. Use the following information to conquer the exam on Test Day!

KNOW THE DIRECTIONS BEFORE TEST DAY

One of the easiest things you can do to help your performance on the SAT is to understand the directions before taking the test. Because the directions are always exactly the same, knowing them in advance will help you save time.

> **PERFECT SCORE TIP**
>
> " I casually talked to my friends about the SAT. We swapped tips and it was great to pick up some new strategies and techniques from them. "

> **EXPERT TUTOR TIP**
>
> " As you prep for the SAT, offer yourself rewards for achievements. After your first chapter, have a tasty treat. After your first practice test, treat yourself to a movie. "

We provide sample SAT directions in parts 2, 3, and 4. Learn them as you go through this book so you can just skim them during the test. Save your time on Test Day for the questions!

USE ORDER OF DIFFICULTY TO YOUR ADVANTAGE

Not all of the questions on the SAT are equally difficult. Some question types are ordered easiest to hardest.

As you work:

- Always be aware of where you are in the set.
- When working on the easy problems, you can generally trust your first impulse—the obvious answer is likely to be right.
- As you get to the end of the set, you need to become more suspicious. The answers probably *shouldn't* come easily. If they do, look at the problem again because the obvious answer is likely to be wrong.
- Watch out for the answer that *just looks right*. It may be a *distracter*—a wrong answer choice meant to entice you. (We'll go into detail on the most common kinds of distracters later.)

YOU DON'T HAVE TO ANSWER THE QUESTIONS IN ORDER

You are allowed to skip around within each section of the SAT. High scorers know this and use their test time wisely. They move through the test efficiently. They don't dwell on any one question, even a hard one, until they've tried every question at least once.

DON'T GET STUCK

When you run into questions that look tough, circle them in your test booklet and skip them. Go back and try again after you have answered the easier ones. Remember, you don't get more points for answering hard questions. If you get two easy ones right in the time it would have taken you to get one hard one right, you just improved your score.

There's another benefit to coming back to hard ones later. On a second look, troublesome questions can turn out to be simple. By answering some easier questions first, you can come back to a harder question with fresh eyes, a fresh perspective, and more confidence.

KEY SAT ANSWER STRATEGIES

Kaplan has gathered some important SAT answer strategies to help you conquer the exam on Test Day. Use the following helpful tools to your advantage!

TAKE A GOOD GUESS

If you have come back to a tough question and still can't find the correct answer the second time around, consider a different approach. Begin eliminating choices that are absolutely wrong. If you can whittle the choices down to two, your chances of guessing the correct answer just increased from 20 percent to 50 percent.

ANSWER ALL GRID-INS

If you get an answer wrong on a Grid-in math question, you lose nothing. So you should write in an answer for every Grid-in. The worst that can happen is that you get zero points for the questions you guessed on. If you get just one right, that's an extra 10 points.

AVOID ANSWER SHEET TROUBLE

It sounds simple, but it's extremely important: don't make mistakes filling out your answer grid. When time is short, it's easy to get confused going back and forth between your test book and your grid. To avoid mistakes on the answer grid, try some of these methods:

CIRCLE THE QUESTIONS YOU SKIP

Perhaps the most common SAT disaster is filling in all of the right answers—in the wrong spots. Put a big circle in your test book around any question numbers you skip to help you locate these questions when you are ready to go back to them. Also, if you accidentally skip a box on the grid, you can always check your grid against your book to see where you went wrong.

CIRCLE YOUR ANSWERS IN YOUR TEST BOOK

Circling your answers in the test book makes it easier to check your grid against your book. It also makes the next grid strategy possible.

GRID SETS OF ANSWERS AT ONCE

To save time and make sure you are marking your answers in the correct bubbles, transfer your answers after every five questions, or at the end of each reading passage, rather than after every question. That way, you won't keep breaking your

PERFECT SCORE TIP

" I didn't fill in my answer grid until I had answered all the questions on a page. It helped me stay focused and keep up my momentum. "

EXPERT TUTOR TIP

" Although there are lots of strategies and theories for how best to tackle the SAT, you should find a test pace and plan that works for *you*—and stick to it! "

SAT Fundamentals | Strategies for Scoring Higher | **Key Answer Strategies** | Chapter Highlights

concentration to mark the grid. You'll end up with more time and less chance to make a mistake on your answer sheet.

WEAR A WATCH TO KEEP TRACK OF TIME

Throughout the test it is important to keep track of time. The test monitor will alert you at certain time intervals, usually at a halfway point and "five minutes left," but you might want to be more aware of how the time is passing.

- You don't want to have your answers in the test booklet and run out of time before you're able to transfer them to your answer grid.
- This is also true when you are gridding your answers in groups. Toward the end of each section you should grid each answer one at a time.

WRITE YOUR ESSAY—EVEN IF YOU'RE SHORT ON TIME

If you write a terrible essay, you still get two raw points, no matter how bad it is. (We go into essay scoring in detail in chapter 3.) If you freeze and skip the essay, you get zero. So write *something*. The essay is worth one-third of your total 800-point Writing score. Even if you get the lowest possible score that you can get on your essay, that's 44 more points than zero!

DON'T GET DISTRACTED BY TRICK ANSWERS

On the SAT, there will always be distracters among the answer choices. Distracters are answer choices that look right but aren't, and they are easy to choose if you haven't read the question carefully. If you jump right into the answer choices without thinking first about exactly what you're looking for, you're much more likely to fall into one of these traps.

LOCATE EASIER QUESTIONS IF YOU'RE RUNNING OUT OF TIME

In sections that are not ordered from easy to hard, you can skip ahead when time runs short. For example, in a multiple-choice Writing section, you may be able to find questions you know you can answer correctly. Don't leave any of these unanswered.

READ QUESTIONS CAREFULLY

Look for keywords or symbols; rephrase them in simple words. *You won't be able to find the right answer if you don't know what you are looking for.*

PERFECT SCORE TIP

" Try avoiding on-and-off studying. If I didn't study on a regular schedule, I frequently forgot some tricks and strategies and had to relearn them. "

EXPERT TUTOR TIP

" Wear a watch on Test Day. I've had students tell me that they couldn't see the room clock on Test Day and couldn't keep track of time. Don't let this happen to you! "

SAT Fundamentals   Strategies for Scoring Higher   **Key Answer Strategies**   Chapter Highlights

USE BACKDOOR STRATEGIES

There are usually a number of ways to get to the right answer on an SAT question. Most of the questions on the SAT are multiple-choice. That means the answer is right in front of you—you just have to find it. This makes SAT questions open to several different ways of finding the answer.

If you can't figure out the answer in a straightforward way, try other techniques. We'll talk about specific Kaplan methods such as back-solving and picking numbers in upcoming Math chapters.

SAT
Fundamentals

Strategies for
Scoring Higher

Key Answer
Strategies

Chapter Highlights

IF YOU LEARN ONLY THREE THINGS IN THIS CHAPTER . . .

1. EASY WAYS TO MAKE THE TEST WORK FOR YOU

- Know the directions for each section of the test cold.

- Locate the easier questions in each section and answer them first.

- Always write the essay, even if you are struggling to come up with examples or a good answer to the question.

- Always answer the Math Grid-in questions.

2. TACKLING TOUGH QUESTIONS

- Make a good guess by eliminating two or more obviously wrong answers and then choose.

- Write the essay even if you are not sure what stance to take or have trouble with the examples. A few sentences are better than none.

- Don't be distracted by a trick answer. If it seems too easy (and you are in a "hard" question area), take a closer look.

- Use backdoor strategies. In a multiple-choice question, the answer is in front of you. Remember, there are often several ways to get to an answer, especially in the Math section.

3. MANAGING TIME AND AVOIDING CARELESS ERRORS

- Wear a digital watch to help you keep track of time.

- When running out of time, locate the easier questions to add quick points.

- Circle your answers in the test booklet, so you can easily check your answers on the answer grid.

- Bubble in your answer sheet after answering every five questions.

SAT Fundamentals   Strategies for Scoring Higher   Key Answer Strategies   Chapter Highlights

Part Two

HOW TO ATTACK THE WRITING COMPONENT

Chapter 3: SAT Writing Basics
Chapter 4: The Essay
Chapter 5: The Multiple-Choice Questions

Welcome to the Writing component of the SAT. Part 2 of this book covers this component in depth. From the essay to the three multiple-choice question types, Kaplan's got the prep you need to ace the Writing component.

CHAPTER 3: SAT WRITING BASICS

SMARTPOINTS COVERED IN THIS CHAPTER

ESSAY

WHAT TO EXPECT ON TEST DAY

There are three Writing sections on the SAT:

- Improving Sentences
- Identifying Sentence Errors
- Improving Paragraphs

The essay will be the first section of the test and will count for one-third of your 800-point Writing score. Your essay and multiple-choice section scores will be combined into a single scaled score that reflects the weight given to each section. This new scaled score will then be converted into a final score ranging from 200–800 points.

 ## THE ESSAY

For the essay portion of the test, your task is to write a short, persuasive essay on an assigned topic.

The keywords here are *persuasive*, *specific*, and *relevant*. Your essay must convince the grader of your point of view using concrete and pertinent examples. If any of these elements are missing, or if you repeat statements without adding new insight or new information, your score will suffer.

> **PERFECT SCORE TIP**
>
> " Whenever an essay asked me to take a position on an issue, I made sure to take a position very clearly and stick with it. "

SmartPoints · Ready for Test Day · **The Essay** · Multiple-Choice Questions · Chapter Highlights

You are required to write about the topic you are given, but you don't need any specific knowledge to complete the SAT essay, and you do have a lot of freedom in what you actually write. Because the topic will be very broad in scope, you can write about what you know and what you are interested in.

ESSAY SCORING

Your essays will be scored holistically by two readers. *Holistically* means your essay gets a single score—a number—that indicates its overall quality. This nu mber takes into account a variety of essay characteristics, including organization and development of ideas, sentence structure, vocabulary, and grammar and usage. Thus, a highly persuasive and eloquent essay that has several run-ons or other minor errors could still earn a top score because of its overall effectiveness and impact.

HOW WILL MY ESSAY BE SCORED?

Each reader will assign your essay a score ranging from a high of 6 to a low of 1. These two scores are added together to get a total score ranging from a high of 12 to a low of 2. The essay score accounts for one-quarter of your final Writing section score.

The following chart shows the main criteria that the graders use to score your essay.

THE ESSAY SCORING CHART

SCORE	PROMPT	SUPPORT AND ORGANIZATION	LANGUAGE
6	**Understanding:** clear **Focus:** clear **Critical thinking skills:** insightful	**Examples:** developed, specific, relevant **Paragraphs:** organized **Logic:** strong **Transitions:** clear	**Language use:** good **Vocabulary:** varied, appropriate **Sentence structure:** varied, effective **Errors:** few, if any, small
5	**Understanding:** reasonably clear **Focus:** clear **Critical thinking skills:** strong	**Examples:** generally specific and relevant, developed **Paragraphs:** generally organized **Logic:** strong **Transitions:** effective	**Language use:** competent **Vocabulary:** appropriate, sometimes varied **Sentence structure:** somewhat varied, effective **Errors:** few, small

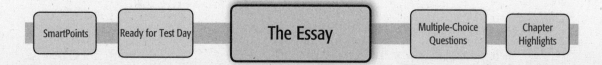

SmartPoints | Ready for Test Day | **The Essay** | Multiple-Choice Questions | Chapter Highlights

4	Understanding: some Focus: generally good Critical thinking skills: competent	Examples: adequate with adequate development Paragraphs: generally clearly organized Logic: generally good Transitions: used sporadically	Language use: adequate Vocabulary: somewhat appropriate, sometimes varied Sentence structure: somewhat varied Errors: some, may be distracting
3	Understanding: some Focus: inconsistent Critical thinking skills: developing	Examples: may be irrelevant and/or inadequate with inconsistent development Paragraphs: limited organization Logic: inconsistent Transitions: limited	Language use: limited Vocabulary: developing, but inconsistent Sentence structure: lacks variety Errors: numerous, may affect readability, clarity
2	Understanding: vague or limited Focus: poor Critical thinking skills: weak	Examples: may be irrelevant and/or inadequate with very limited development Paragraphs: poorly organized Logic: not presented well Transitions: weak	Language use: little facility Vocabulary: limited, may be incorrect Sentence structure: frequent problems Errors: many, sometimes affect readability, clarity
1	Understanding: little or none Focus: fails to do so Critical thinking skills: lacking	Examples: limited or nonexistent with poor development Paragraphs: poorly organized Logic: not presented well Transitions: not used well	Language use: no facility Vocabulary: little or no mastery Sentence structure: seriously flawed Errors: many, often affect readability, clarity

The next chapter will show you Kaplan's strategies for writing a top-scoring essay.

MULTIPLE-CHOICE QUESTIONS

The multiple-choice portion of the Writing section consists of 49 questions, 35 in the 25 minute section and 14 in the second 10 minute section. They are divided into three types:

- 18 Identifying Sentence Errors questions
- 25 Improving Sentences questions
- 6 Improving Paragraphs questions

SmartPoints   Ready for Test Day   The Essay   **Multiple-Choice Questions**   Chapter Highlights

The Identifying Sentence Errors and Improving Sentences questions are based on single, unrelated sentences on a variety of topics. The Improving Paragraphs questions are based on a brief passage. The sentences and passages upon which the questions are based will usually (but not always) contain one or more grammar, usage, or organizational error. Your task is to spot (and sometimes fix) the mistakes in as many of the multiple-choice questions as you can in 25 and 10 minutes, respectively.

HOW MULTIPLE-CHOICE QUESTIONS ARE SCORED?

- If you get a multiple-choice question right, you earn 1 point. If you get a multiple-choice question wrong, you lose 1/4 of a point. If you omit a multiple-choice question, you neither gain nor lose any points.

- Your raw score for the multiple-choice questions is converted into a scaled score ranging from 200–800.

- This scaled score will account for two-thirds of your total Writing score.

SmartPoints | Ready for Test Day | The Essay | **Multiple-Choice Questions** | Chapter Highlights

IF YOU LEARN ONLY THREE THINGS IN THIS CHAPTER . . .

1. OVERVIEW OF THE WRITING SECTIONS

The Writing component is 60 minutes long and includes three sections:

- The essay—a persuasive essay that requires concrete support/examples

- Two multiple-choice sections—separate, unrelated sentences and paragraphs

2. ESSAY CRITERIA AND SCORING

- Writing an off-topic essay results in a score of 0.

- You must respond to a general topic phrased as a question, backed with specific examples and explanations.

- Two graders score the essay from 1 to 6; your final essay score is the total of the two scores.

- The essay is worth about one-quarter of your total Writing score.

3. MULTIPLE-CHOICE QUESTIONS

- These questions test your grammar, vocabulary, and to some extent, your reading skills.

- Some questions require you to find the error (if any) among choices (Identifying Sentence Errors).

- Some questions offer a list of multiple-choice "fixes" in addition to a "no change" option (Improving Sentences and Improving Paragraphs).

- You lose 1/4 point for each question you answer incorrectly.

CHAPTER 4: THE ESSAY

SMARTPOINTS COVERED IN THIS CHAPTER

ESSAY —————————————————————

WHAT TO EXPECT ON TEST DAY

There are three important elements to master in order to succeed on the essay.

The SAT essay is a *persuasive* essay that you write in response to a particular question, also called a *prompt*. The essay is the first section you tackle on the test and many students are glad to get it out of the way.

CONTENT

You will be given a quote, or a pair of quotes, and a prompt that is related to the content of the quote. It is the prompt that will guide your essay topic; the quote is there just to get your creative juices flowing. The graders will be looking for whether your subject matter is relevant to the prompt, whether your stance is insightful, and whether your essay is persuasive. It is very important that you take a firm stance in your essay and stick to it.

> **PERFECT SCORE TIP**
>
> ❝ I found that I didn't need to be overly creative to get a good score on the essay. Simply following Kaplan's rough format is enough to get you a good score. ❞

WRITING A PERSUASIVE ESSAY

> If you remember nothing else, remember that your essay needs to be *persuasive*. You are trying to convince your reader to see something from your point of view, and the bulk of your essay should be used to explain *why* you have taken your chosen stance.
>
> Also, if the topic allows, it's a good idea to include references to current events, history, and literature in your essay. You don't have to do this to get a high score, but it couldn't hurt either.

SmartPoints | **Ready for Test Day** | Write a Great Essay | Essay Grading | Essay Practice

Essays are graded by high school teachers and college professors. They want to know if the things they have taught you are sinking in. They'll be impressed by an essay that goes beyond your personal experience to make interesting and meaningful connections.

Please also note that grammar and punctuation are a part of a successful essay and will be looked at by the graders, but errors in these areas will not be the most important factors influencing your grade. Naturally, you want as few errors as possible, but you can still achieve a high score with some mistakes, so don't stress yourself out worrying about grammar and punctuation if they are not your strongest skills.

DEVELOP AN EXTENSIVE EXAMPLE BANK

You should have a ready stable of examples, ones that can easily be trotted out to answer whatever essay you get on Test Day. By assembling a wide variety of specific instances on a wide variety of topics, you'll be ready to tackle any prompt.

EXAMPLE BANK #1: BRAINSTORM ON PAPER

Step 1: Take several sheets of blank or lined paper and write a favorite topic in the center of each page. Be sure your topic isn't too narrow or too broad. (WWII—too broad; my dog—too narrow)

Step 2: Draw a few lines, similar to bicycle wheel spokes, extending from the word(s). At the end of the lines, write subtopics. From the subtopics you can draw more lines for sub-subtopics.

Step 3: Repeat steps 1 and 2 at least *nine more times*. More is better here.

So, if your main topic for a page is "Getting into College," you might write the names of some colleges you are interested in, the SAT, getting organized, college trips, and more.

Note: All the words you write on these pages are examples that would work for any essay, as long as they are relevant to the topic you are asked to discuss.

SmartPoints | Ready for Test Day | Write a Great Essay | Essay Grading | Essay Practice

EXAMPLE BANK #2: ANSWER QUESTIONS AND PROMPTS ON INDEX CARDS

Answering the following five questions or topics should help you get started building your example bank (feel free to make up more questions). Use one card for each.

1. What book changed your mind about something and why?

2. What non-school subject do you know the most about and why?

3. List three people—whether real or fictional, living or dead, famous or personal friends/family—whom you respect and admire. Why did you choose them?

4. Think of an event that changed your life. What happened? Where? When? How and why did it happen? What happened after that that demonstrates its importance?

5. What major historical event is the one you know most about? Why did you learn about it? Does it have any significance for your own life?

Along with being concrete and relevant, the best examples are those that are interesting to the person who is writing the essay. This will allow your passion to shine through to the reader. For example, if you only know about music, concentrate on that. If you love movies, that works too. Nothing is off limits (except obscenities).

Here are two ways to create an Example Bank. Either one is equally effective. Just pick the one that appeals to you and be thorough in your efforts.

LENGTH

It's true that the content and quality of your essay are two important aspects of achieving a high score, but there is also a certain expectation from the essay graders concerning the length of a well-written essay. Specifically, your essay should range between 300–400 words if you want to receive a 5 or 6.

If your essay is too short, no matter how well written, it could mean the difference between a low 3 or 4 and a 5 or 6, which would have a considerable impact on your overall Writing score. That is not to say that a wordy essay will grab the top score either or that you should spend time counting each word. You will have to use your judgment as to which parts of your essay actually help and which parts are there to fill space. Just keep in mind that your essay should at least be *long enough* to put you in the running for a good score.

SmartPoints   Ready for Test Day   Write a Great Essay   Essay Grading   Essay Practice

Another aspect of length is the space in which you will write your essay. You will only receive two pages with 46 lines, and you must use a pencil.

DON'T FORGET

When you begin to write your essay, try to remember the following:
- A high-scoring essay will be approximately 300–400 well-written words.
- Small, yet legible, handwriting will conserve space.

NEATNESS

EXPERT TUTOR TIP

" Keep in mind that essay graders particularly remember the first and last things they see in your work, so start strong and finish the same way. And write legibly! "

Your essay must be readable. If you edit what you've written, do it neatly. If you add a word, change a phrase, or cross out a sentence, do it carefully. It may sound silly, but neatness matters—a lot.

Why? The graders have tons of essays to read and grade in a short amount of time. That means they don't have much time to spend reading your essay (about a minute, on average), and they aren't going to read an essay three or four times in order to decipher illegible handwriting. So if the handwriting in your essay is messy and hard to follow, graders may conclude that the content itself is, too. A good essay may not get the score it deserves because it is shabbily presented.

A NOTE ON . . . HANDWRITING SIZE

How large or small you write will affect the length of your essay. You get two pages on which to write—no more. Just filling up the lines with large letters and not focusing on writing a well-developed argument will not earn you more points. Practice using smaller handwriting before the test so you don't run out of space and waste time rewriting on Test Day.

You're not expected to produce a perfect piece of writing. The graders know that you only have 25 minutes to think about, write, and proofread your work. What they expect is an organized and readable piece of writing that makes an argument supported by real examples. The rest of this chapter will show you how to accomplish this worthy task.

SmartPoints — **Ready for Test Day** — Write a Great Essay — Essay Grading — Essay Practice

HOW TO WRITE A HIGH-SCORING SAT ESSAY

The directions for the essay are as follows:

The essay gives you an opportunity to show how effectively you can develop and express ideas. You should, therefore, take care to develop your point of view, present your ideas logically and clearly, and use language precisely.

Your essay must be written in your Answer Grid Booklet—you will receive no other paper on which to write. You will have enough space if you write on every line, avoid wide margins, and keep your handwriting to a reasonable size. Remember that people who are not familiar with your handwriting will read what you write. Try to write or print so that what you are writing is legible to those readers.

You have 25 minutes to write an essay on the topic assigned below.
DO NOT WRITE ON ANOTHER TOPIC. AN OFF-TOPIC ESSAY WILL RECEIVE A SCORE OF ZERO.

Think carefully about the issue presented in the following excerpt and the assignment below.

> "When I played pro football, I never set out to hurt anybody deliberately . . . unless it was, you know, important, like a league game or something."
>
> –Dick Butkus
>
> "Pro basketball has turned into Wrestlemania, which is why I like college basketball and high school basketball. Actually, it's why I like baseball."
>
> –Frank Layden

Assignment: Have professional sports influenced the values of American society? Plan and write an essay in which you develop your point of view on this issue. Support your position with reasoning and examples taken from your reading, studies, experience, or observations.

DO NOT WRITE YOUR ESSAY IN YOUR TEST BOOK.
You will receive credit only for what you write in your Answer Grid Booklet.

PERFECT SCORE TIP

" When choosing examples, I found it better to choose from a variety of sources (one from history, one from personal experience, and one from a book). That way, my essays were more interesting. "

KAPLAN'S TARGET STRATEGY FOR ESSAY WRITING

We have developed a system that we think will make writing the essay that much easier—Kaplan's 4 Ps Strategy.

Prompt—read and understand it.

Plan—collect and organize your ideas and examples.

Produce—write your essay.

Proofread—check for consistency and errors.

SmartPoints | Ready for Test Day | **Write a Great Essay** | Essay Grading | Essay Practice

PERFECT SCORE TIP

" Kaplan's essay strategy gives you enough time to write a great essay, but you definitely have to write fast! Keeping track of time helped me avoid rushing at the end. "

You have 25 minutes to write your essay. Here is a minute-by-minute rundown of Kaplan's 4 Ps Strategy:

MINUTES 1–2: PROMPT—READ AND UNDERSTAND IT

Take one minute to read the quote and think about the prompt (you'll be surprised how long a minute is). Begin to think about your stance and possible examples that pop into your head. Start to jot some notes as ideas and instances come to you.

DON'T QUOTE THE QUOTE!

It is *not* desirable to refer to the quotation, or to quote it, in your essay. Use it as inspiration and come up with your own examples—that is what the graders are looking for. The quotation should only be used as a last resort.

Let's say that you get the following quote and assignment:

> "A man walking down a crowded street noticed a dog lying by the side of the road that looked like it might be injured; but since everyone else just passed by, the man was satisfied to assume that the dog was fine. The next day he learned that the dog had been hit by a car and lay injured for two hours before a concerned man stopped and took it to the vet. The animal recovered, but the man never forgave himself for leaving it for someone else to help."
>
> —Narawhal Bherundi, *Autobiography*

Assignment: What is your view on individual responsibility in a situation in which many people could have reacted?

Then the assignment asks you to take a specific example from your personal experience, from current events, or from history, literature, or any other discipline and develop it to support your persuasive argument, using the quote as a guidepost.

CAN'T CHOOSE A SIDE?

If you can't decide which stance to take, draw a large "T" on the page and label the sides *Pro* and *Con*. Then write each supporting example under the side it belongs on. The side with the most wins.

SmartPoints | Ready for Test Day | **Write a Great Essay** | Essay Grading | Essay Practice

The most important aspect of this step is to fully understand what you need to write about and how you will develop your essay based on that.

MINUTES 2–5: PLAN—COLLECT AND ORGANIZE YOUR IDEAS AND EXAMPLES

You have already started to do this in *Minute 1*. Now your job is to zero in on getting organized as you continue to brainstorm examples and decide your position on the issue. Before the test, practice using your first five minutes effectively; they are the keys to a successful essay!

GATHER YOUR EXAMPLES FIRST

Because it doesn't matter which stance you take, choose the one for which you have the more concrete and relevant examples. Now is the moment when all your Example Bank work comes in handy. If you have done your job, you should have at least two, if not three, good supporting instances to write about.

NO EXAMPLES?

Pick keywords—*responsibility* and *reacted* in this chapter's prompt—then ask yourself:

- **Who hasn't taken responsibility, but should have?** (Witnessing a cheating incident at school, observing a bully in action)

- **Who reacts well?** (Firemen, parents)

If need be, you can create a concrete example or two from these ideas. Just be sure the examples you make up are plausible.

EVALUATE YOUR EXAMPLES

Take the time to be sure that the examples relate to the topic. Ask yourself the following questions:

- Are they concrete *and* relevant?

- How does each of your examples relate to the topic?

If any examples don't measure up, be ruthless and toss them out. If you have the luxury of more than three, choose the ones that are the most varied and interesting.

FINE-TUNE YOUR STANCE AND WRITE YOUR THESIS SENTENCE

Once you have your examples lined up, you can work on a statement that expresses your stance. It is the heart of your first paragraph.

SmartPoints | Ready for Test Day | Write a Great Essay | Essay Grading | Essay Practice

COMPARE AND CONTRAST YOUR EXAMPLES

When you were evaluating your examples, you were to think about how they related to the topic. Now, you'll need to think about this again. Make a few notes about each example in relation to the others you have on your list. Then make a few notes on how each example relates *back to the topic*.

These notes become the transitions between paragraphs that will round out and add interest—*and prevent you from repeating yourself*.

CREATE A BRIEF OUTLINE FOR YOUR FIVE-PARAGRAPH ESSAY

Ideally, SAT essays have five paragraphs:

- An introduction with your thesis statement or stance
- A paragraph for each of three examples
- A conclusion

If you have only one example, you would have three paragraphs; a two-example essay would have four paragraphs.

Here's one possible outline for the Bherundi prompt in this chapter:

SAMPLE ESSAY OUTLINE

Paragraph 1: Introduction—People have a responsibility to help others, especially when others have ignored those in need. (Should help, power of individual and groups of individuals)

Paragraph 2: Example #1—Saw bully pick on a kid in school/felt badly/was the only person to report it to the teacher. *Transition:* Anybody can/should fix a small injustice.

Paragraph 3: Example #2—Mother Teresa started own charity order/helped outcasts, those whom no one else would help. *Transition:* A very dedicated person can make a huge difference.

Paragraph 4: Example #3—Doctors Without Borders/doctors who could make a lot of money at home go to dangerous places and help others/no one else there would help. *Transition:* Group of individuals can be dedicated to a larger cause, can be effective.

Paragraph 5: Conclusion—It is easy to ignore the needs of others, but people have the responsibility to react/respond to need. Small to large efforts are important; a group of organized people is very powerful.

Note: To save time, your outline will be briefer, using abbreviations and shorthand notes that you understand.

SmartPoints | Ready for Test Day | **Write a Great Essay** | Essay Grading | Essay Practice

MINUTES 6–23: PRODUCE—WRITE YOUR ESSAY

The writing step of your essay should take about 18 minutes. That's plenty of time to write solid paragraphs using your outline and notes.

HAVE A PLAN

> When you have a good plan, writing the essay is just a matter of turning your notes into full, descriptive sentences.

To write your strongest essay, follow your outline. You spent five minutes learning the prompt and planning your essay, so stick to it! Don't panic and write from the opposing point of view. However, if you come up with the perfect example halfway through your essay, replace it in your outline, see how it works, then continue. But *try try try* not to erase and rewrite any big chunks of text. Trust yourself.

You also need to write clearly, write concisely, write complete sentences, and use proper grammar. But you only have 18 minutes. So write fast. Here is a quickly written essay (a draft version, you might say) about responsibility:

An individual can have a major effect on another individual or situation. In the example above, an individual save a dog's life. A group of people ignored the situation but an individual man actually did something. He stepped out of the mob mentality. Everyone else conformed to each other and walked by. This man stopped and saved the dog.

However, the primary man in the example did not do so. He conformed and walked by. He shirked his responsibility. This is like that one time my sister needed help and didn't get it. On her way home from college, she had car trouble and was stranded on the side of the road at night. Many cars passed by but no one stopped to see if they could give her a hand. After waiting for forever, she ended up having to walk to the nearest gas station two miles away, which is not safe for a young girl to do by herself. Here, no individual took responsibility to help her, and this refusal of responsibility could have led to more severe consequences.

On a lighter but related note, I had personal experience with individual responsibility. At the beginning of last year, I was walking to first period science class when I noticed a confused, nervous girl standing in the hallway. She looked like she was about to cry as everyone rushed past her. She was

> **EXPERT TUTOR TIP**
>
> " Don't be afraid to use *I/me/mine*, especially if you're writing about a personal experience. Using *one* can make your essay sound formal or stilted. "

SmartPoints · Ready for Test Day · **Write a Great Essay** · Essay Grading · Essay Practice obviously lost, but no one who knew the way took responsibility to help her. I felt badly so approached her and asked if I could help. It turned out that she had just moved from another part of the country and knew no one at my high school. She couldn't find her science class, which turned out to be my science class, and was too shy to ask for help. I walked with her to science class, made a new friend, and took the responsibility to help someone.

At the end of the day, everyone has the responsibility not to conform in a situation in which many people can react. Each person should be the individual who takes action and helps. No one should assume that someone else will take responsibility, because maybe no one will.

MINUTES 24–25: PROOFREAD—CHECK FOR CONSISTENCY AND ERRORS

This step takes two minutes. It involves reading your essay carefully and fixing errors you find. Hopefully, all you'll need to do is fix minor grammatical or spelling errors, change a few words here and there, and maybe add a sentence or two for clarity's sake.

If you spend the bulk of the 25 minutes thinking about, planning, and writing the essay, the repair step should entail nothing more than putting the finishing touches on an already strong essay.

Here is our edited essay with changes underlined:

An individual can have a major effect on another individual or situation. In the example above, an individual <u>saved</u> a dog's life. A group of people ignored the <u>situation, but</u> an individual man actually did something. He stepped out of the mob mentality. Everyone else conformed to each other and walked by. This man stopped and saved the dog.

However, <u>the man</u> in the example did not do so. He conformed and walked by. He shirked his responsibility. <u>This relates to a situation that my sister experienced</u>. On her way home from college, she had car trouble and was stranded on the side of the road at night. Many cars passed <u>by, but</u> no one stopped to see if they could give her a hand. After waiting for <u>over an hour</u>, she ended up having to walk to the nearest gas station two miles away, which is not safe for a young girl to do by herself. Here, no individual took responsibility to help her, and this refusal of responsibility could have led to more severe consequences.

On a lighter but related note, <u>I had a personal</u> experience with individual responsibility. At the beginning of last year, I was walking to first period science class when I noticed a confused, nervous girl standing in the hallway. She looked like she was about to cry as everyone rushed past her. She was obviously lost, but no one who knew the way took responsibility to help her. <u>I felt badly for her, so I approached</u> her and asked if I could help. It turned out that she had just moved from another part of the country and knew no one at my high school. She couldn't find her science class, which turned out to be my

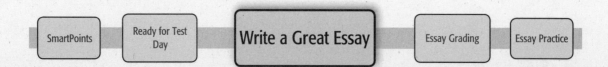

science class, and was too shy to ask for help. I walked with her to science class, made a new friend, and took the responsibility to help someone.

At the end of the day, everyone has the responsibility not to conform in a situation in which many people can react. Each person should be the individual who takes action and helps. No one should assume that someone else will take responsibility, because maybe no one will.

Okay, now it's your turn. Let's go through each of the steps.

PRACTICE PLANNING PROMPTS

Below are three sample statements. Look at your watch (a digital one, if possible, or use a digital kitchen timer). Spend exactly five minutes understanding the prompt and planning essays for each one as described above. Working without quotes is harder, but helps you think more independently. See how you do:

ESSAY PROMPT ONE: TWO MINUTES

Is financial status the most important factor governing an individual's quality of life?

ESSAY PROMPT TWO: TWO MINUTES

Do you have to be brave to do something courageous?

ESSAY PROMPT THREE: TWO MINUTES

Does the media have too much influence on the young adult population?

ESSAY PLANNING PRACTICE

Read the essay directions below and try to outline an essay based on the prompt. In your outline, you will want to try to include the stance you're taking, the evidence that supports your stance, and how this information will be arranged.

The essay gives you an opportunity to show how effectively you can develop and express ideas. You should, therefore, take care to develop your point of view, present your ideas logically and clearly, and use language precisely.

Your essay must be written in your Answer Grid Booklet—you will receive no other paper on which to write. You will have enough space if you write on every line, avoid wide margins, and keep your handwriting to a reasonable size. Remember that people who are not familiar with your handwriting will read what you write. Try to write or print so that what you are writing is legible to those readers.

You have twenty-five minutes to write an essay on the topic assigned below.

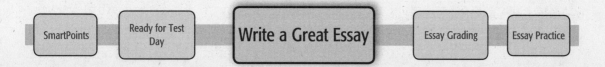

DO NOT WRITE ON ANOTHER TOPIC. AN OFF-TOPIC ESSAY WILL RECEIVE A SCORE OF ZERO.

Think carefully about the issue presented in the following excerpt and the assignment below.

> "A man walking down a crowded street noticed a dog lying by the side of the road that looked like it might be injured; but since everyone else just passed by, the man was satisfied to assume that the dog was fine. The next day he learned that the dog had been hit by a car and lay injured for two hours before a concerned man stopped and took it to the vet. The animal recovered, but the man never forgave himself for leaving it for someone else to help."
>
> –Narawhal Bherundi, *Autobiography*

Assignment: What is your view on individual responsibility in a situation in which many people could have reacted? Plan and write an essay in which you develop your point of view on this issue. Support your position with reasoning and examples taken from your reading, studies, experience, or observations.

DO NOT WRITE YOUR ESSAY IN YOUR TEST BOOK.
You will receive credit only for what you write in your Answer Grid Booklet.

Plan your paragraphs on a separate sheet of paper. Remember that on the SAT you will plan your essay by using space on the test booklet, and your essay MUST be written on the lined pages of your answer sheet.

I. Introduction

    A. General argument: A person should take responsibility, as a member of a community, in a group situation to help those in need.

    B. Examples:

        1. Given example of man and injured dog.

        2. My mom's experience in the grocery store.

II. Body

    A. Given example of man and injured dog.

        1. Man assumes that others would help if it was really needed.

        2. Ignores his instinct to help and conforms to others' actions.

        3. Feels guilty for not acting.

    B. My mom's experience in the grocery store.

        1. People assumed she was crazy and weird.

        2. Others didn't help because no one else was.

        3. Not helping could have been matter of life or death.

III. Conclusion

    A. It's easy to just walk by and do what everyone else does.

    B. As a part of a community, everyone is responsible for the well-being of others.

SmartPoints | Ready for Test Day | **Write a Great Essay** | Essay Grading | Essay Practice

CREATE A GOOD ESSAY OUTLINE

A good outline will help you write a better essay and save time. Always take the time to prepare a detailed outline.

PRODUCING PRACTICE

This outline is more in-depth than the previous outline and may lead to a more complete and organized essay. It is also a little different from the first way we went about answering this question. This proves our point—there is not *one way* to write these essays. You have to use *your* knowledge and *your* experiences.

Now that you're done with your outline, you're ready to start writing. Start your practice with the essay topic that you just outlined. Write your essay on separate sheets of paper.

PROOFREADING PRACTICE

When you are done, take two minutes to proofread for spelling, grammar, and any other glaring errors. Some things to look for are comma splices, run-on sentences, misspelled or skipped words, ideas that are not sufficiently developed, vague references to the elements in the essay (e.g., *this* is a good example, *that* is important because, etc.) and making sure you have taken a clear stance and have explained that stance persuasively.

HOW YOUR ESSAY IS GRADED

To help you get a sense of how your essay might be graded, we have included a sample high-scoring essay. Compare your essay to the one that follows using the following criteria, and you'll get a sense of how well you've done.

- My essay has a clear stance on the given issue.
- I provided specific support using examples and evidence.
- I have logical organization.
- I have used appropriate transitions between ideas.
- I have used variety in my sentence structure and vocabulary.
- My sentences are clear and have an even tone.

Now let's look at a Grade 6 essay:

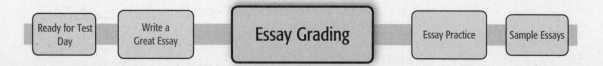

Ready for Test Day | Write a Great Essay | **Essay Grading** | Essay Practice | Sample Essays

GRADE 6 ESSAY (ALMOST PERFECT)

A person should take responsibility in a group situation. A group is made up of individuals, after all. People hide too much behind others' actions and don't think for themselves. Rather than hiding, they should be proactive.

The first man in the example had a responsibility, as did everyone on the sidewalk, to help the dog. He saw the dog, the potential bad situation, and instead of following his instinct to check out the problem, he decided to walk by because no one else was helping. He consciously decides to walk by, assuming that if the dog were really that hurt, someone else would take care of it. It doesn't occur to him that everyone is thinking the same thing and doing nothing. He feels badly because he knows he was persuaded by the actions of others and ignored his responsibility toward another living creature.

Something similar happened to my mother in a grocery store. There was a puddle of something in one of the aisles, and she slipped, fell to the ground, and hit her head. Unfortunately, no one saw what happened, so when people came around the corner and saw her lying on the floor, they just kept going past thinking that she was crazy or weird. Others came down the aisle, too, but did nothing because they saw that the people in front of them did nothing. She remained dizzy and injured on the floor until her husband came down the aisle and found her on the ground. It is sad that no one took the responsibility to help an injured woman. Someone should have called for help or at least asked her if she was OK, especially because it could have been a matter of life or death.

It's very easy to just walk by, to do what everyone else in the group does. Everyone could just look the other way and not listen to the pleas for help. But that is not how a community is run, and as humans who share this planet, we are entitled to act as a community, and that entails having a responsibility to help.

ESSAY PRACTICE

This is your chance to put the 4 Ps to work. Give yourself 25 minutes to go through this target strategy:

Prompt—read it and understand it.

Plan—collect and organize your ideas and examples.

Produce—write your essay.

Proofread—check for consistency and errors.

After you finish, read the three sample essays—a strong essay, a mediocre essay, and a weak essay—and the sample grader comments. Use these essays and comments to judge the quality of your own essays.

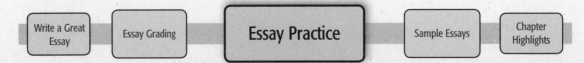

The essay gives you an opportunity to show how effectively you can develop and express ideas. You should, therefore, take care to develop your point of view, present your ideas logically and clearly, and use language precisely.

Your essay must be written in your Answer Grid Booklet—you will receive no other paper on which to write. You will have enough space if you write on every line, avoid wide margins, and keep your handwriting to a reasonable size. Remember that people who are not familiar with your handwriting will read what you write. Try to write or print so that what you are writing is legible to those readers.

You have twenty-five minutes to write an essay on the topic assigned below. DO NOT WRITE ON ANOTHER TOPIC. AN OFF-TOPIC ESSAY WILL RECEIVE A SCORE OF ZERO.

Think carefully about the issue presented in the following excerpt and the assignment below.

> "Don't flatter yourself that friendship authorizes you to say disagreeable things to your intimates. The nearer you come into relation with a person, the more necessary do tact and courtesy become. Except in cases of necessity, which are rare, leave your friend to learn unpleasant things from his enemies; they are ready enough to tell them."
>
> –Oliver Wendell Holmes,
> *The Autocrat of the Breakfast-Table*
>
> "A good friend can tell you what is the matter with you in a minute. He may not seem such a good friend after telling."
>
> –Arthur Brisbane, *The Book of Today*

Assignment: Should friends be honest with each other, even if a truthful comment could be hurtful? Plan and write an essay in which you develop your point of view on this issue. Support your position with reasoning and examples taken from your reading, studies, experience, or observations.

DO NOT WRITE YOUR ESSAY IN YOUR TEST BOOK.
You will receive credit only for what you write in your Answer Grid Booklet.

Organize your paragraphs and write your essay on separate sheets of paper.

SAMPLE ESSAYS

GRADE 6 ESSAY

One of the defining qualities of a good friendship is that both friends can be completely honest with each other. This does not mean that the two friends don't consider each others feelings or blurt out comments without thinking, but it does mean that each person can rely on the

EXPERT TUTOR TIP

" This essay does something really important: it frames the issue in the introduction. She clearly defines the scope of her argument in her intro paragraph. "

Write a Great Essay · Essay Grading · Essay Practice · **Sample Essays** · Chapter Highlights

other to tell the truth, even if the truth can sometimes be awkward or hurtful.

My sister and I have always been close friends, even when we were younger. When my sister was in junior high school and I was in elementary school, she decided to get her hair permed because all of her friends were doing the same thing. Unfortunately, the treatment didn't work well on her hair and she ended up with a big, frizzy clump of curls that stuck out on the sides. Most of her friends didn't have the courage to tell her that it didn't look good. Instead, they just made fun of her behind her back. So it was up to me to tell her the truth. I was a bit scared to confront my older sister, because I knew that she would be upset. But I also knew that she would be more upset if no one dared to be honest with her. A few years earlier, we were in the opposite roles, and she had gently but firmly advised me against a choice that I later realized would have been embarrassing for me when I started school.

Although my sister was hurt when I told her that the perm didn't look good, she was more hurt to learn that some of her other friends had thought the same thing but hadn't said anything to her. She was angry with me at first for making a negative comment, but in the end she was glad I had told her so that she could go back to the hair stylist to fix the problem. Since my sister was very concerned about her appearance and personal style at that time in her life, she appreciated my honesty because it helped her get through a tough situation and our friendship grew stronger as a result of this experience.

In the years since this incident, my sister and I have both continued to be honest and upfront with each other, and we value this aspect of our relationship. After all, friendly honesty is far better than hostile honesty, so being a good friend involves telling the truth, no matter what the circumstances. Honesty truly is an essential component of a good friendship.

(388 words)

Grader's Comments: The author begins this essay with a clear statement based on the prompt, showing that she has clearly understood the topic. The remainder of the essay presents and develops an example to support her opinion. The example provided is relevant to multiple aspects of the prompt—the importance of honesty in friendship as well as the possibility that being honest can be difficult in certain situations.

The essay is well organized, with a clear narrative flow framed by a cohesive introduction and conclusion. The structure of the essay reflects that the author took

> **EXPERT TUTOR TIP**
>
> " Avoid hypotheticals! Your essay will be much stronger if you use real examples and experiences rather than "imagine that . . . " ones. "

Write a Great Essay | Essay Grading | Essay Practice | **Sample Essays** | Chapter Highlights time to plan before writing and carefully followed her plan as she composed her essay. Although the vocabulary used in the essay is not very sophisticated, the author's ideas are communicated effectively. Finally, there are few grammatical or spelling errors—*others* instead of *other's* in the first paragraph—and a couple of sentences lacking commas in the second and third paragraphs. This author clearly managed her time effectively so that she could proofread her essay.

GRADE 4 ESSAY

Being honest is part of being a good friend. However, their are times when you shouldn't be completely honest because what you say might hurt your friend's feelings.

For example, imagine that your best friend tells you his parents are getting divorced. He is obviously upset by this even though you know his parents haven't been getting along well because he constantly complained about their fights and even joked about hoping they'd get a divorce so he wouldn't have to listen to them anymore. In this situation, reminding your friend of his earlier comments or pointing out that his parents will be happier apart isn't the right thing to do because at a time like this you're friend doesn't need you to tell him the harsh truth, he needs you to by sympathetic and supportive. It's pretty likely that he'll hear all about the negative things from other people or even from his parents, so your job as his best friend is to try not to say or do anything unpleasant.

Another example could be if you're friend has bought something that she's really excited about. You might not agree that she's made a good choice or you might not like what she bought, but you don't need to spoil her enthusiasm by making a negative comment. Again, this is a time when you should keep quiet about your own opinion so that your friend can be happy.

There are certain situations when it's okay not to tell the complete truth to your friends. You should never lie to your friends, but an important part of being a good friend is knowing when to be totally honest and when to keep silent because a truthful comment could do more harm than good.

(292 words)

Grader's Comments: The author introduces his essay with a clear statement of his opinion, showing that he has understood the prompt. His two examples provide decent support for the topic, but the second example is vague and not well developed. The author would have a stronger essay if he expanded upon the prompt and provided additional details for the first example rather than trying to include a weak second example. Having a clear plan could help to accomplish this change in structure.

The essay is fairly well organized, with several keywords *(However, For example, Another example, Again)* that add structure to the author's argument. The weakest parts of this essay are some simplistic language and awkward sentences: in the second paragraph, the second sentence is long and wordy, and the third sentence is a run-on sentence and is very difficult to follow, so the author's meaning almost gets obscured by the effort it takes to decipher his thoughts. There are also a few usage/spelling errors: *their* instead of *there* in the first paragraph; *you're* instead of *your* in the second and third paragraphs. The author needs to be more deliberate when writing the essay and needs to proofread to catch these spelling errors and prevent run-on sentences or awkward sentence structure.

GRADE 2 ESSAY

No matter what, friends should tell each other the truth. That's the whole point of having friends, so you have some people around you that you can trust and talk to and that you know will tell you everything.

Friends can tell you negative things in a kind way so you can here the truth even if its not so good. Enemies tell you the same negative things in a mean way because their trying to hurt you. But friends can accomplish this in a nicer way.

Its important to know and learn the truth even if its about yourself or its something you don't want to face. You need honest friends to tell you the truth, because they do it out of love not hate like enemies.

(128 words)

Grader's Comments: This author starts strongly with a clear statement of her opinion, which is directly related to the topic of the prompt. However, the author continues with a series of generalizations, none of which are specific examples to support her opinion. She needs to spend more time planning her essay to make sure that she's got at least one strong example to include to support her argument.

This essay does not follow an organized structure, and it lacks good transitions and keywords. To improve this part of her writing, the author should make an outline during her planning stage and should focus on using several keywords while she writes, which will give her essay a stronger and clearer structure.

The author's language is simplistic and repetitive. The essay contains several grammatical and spelling errors: *that* twice instead of *whom/who* when referring to *people* in the first paragraph; *here* and *their* are misused for *hear* and *they're* in the second paragraph; *its* is misused numerous times for *it's* in the second and third paragraphs. The author should study the SAT grammar materials to improve this aspect of her writing and should also be sure to proofread to avoid careless errors.

> **EXPERT TUTOR TIP**
>
> " What's the biggest problem with this essay? No support! This writer goes on and on telling us her opinion but never supports it with any facts. "

IF YOU LEARN ONLY FOUR THINGS IN THIS CHAPTER . . .

1. **THE ELEMENTS OF A HIGH-SCORING ESSAY**

   - A clear stance on the essay topic

   - Three relevant, concrete examples

   - Developed, organized paragraphs (five, if three examples)

   - Good transition phrases and sentences that compare and contrast the examples

   - Easy-to-read handwriting (a grader won't score high what the grader can't read)

   - Concise language with varied sentence structure and only a few errors

2. **KAPLAN'S FOUR STEPS FOR THE ESSAY**

   1. **P**rompt—read and understand it.

   2. **P**lan—collect and organize your ideas and examples.

   3. **P**roduce—write your essay.

   4. **P**roofread—check for consistency and errors.

3. **SKILLS TO BUILD FOR THE ESSAY**

   - Learn to think up relevant and concrete examples.

   - Learn to organize ideas in a timed setting.

   - Learn to write "short" so your ideas will fit on 51 lines.

   - Make sure your handwriting is easily read. An essay that is hard to read won't score well, *even if it follows all the guidelines*.

4. **THE KEY TO SUCCESS ON THE SAT ESSAY**

   - Practice! The more you practice and sharpen your essay skills, the more prepared you'll be on Test Day.

| Write a Great Essay | Essay Grading | Essay Practice | Sample Essays | **Chapter Highlights** |

CHAPTER 5: THE MULTIPLE-CHOICE QUESTIONS

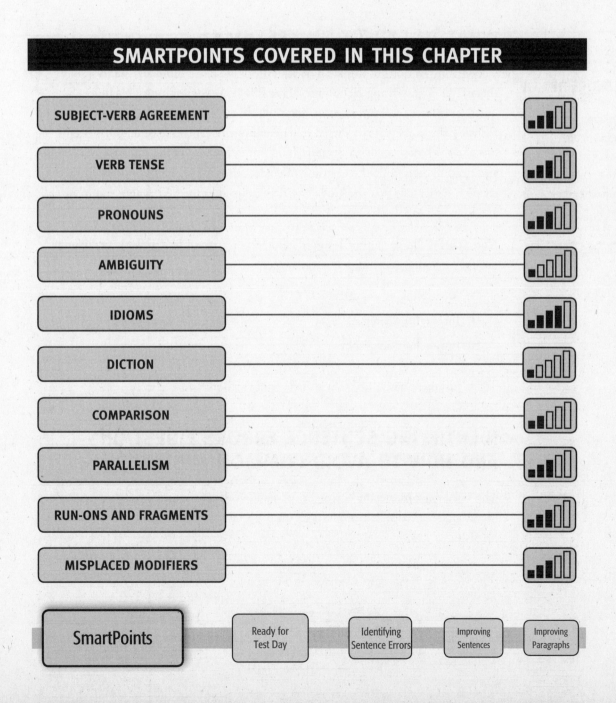

SMARTPOINTS COVERED IN THIS CHAPTER

- SUBJECT-VERB AGREEMENT
- VERB TENSE
- PRONOUNS
- AMBIGUITY
- IDIOMS
- DICTION
- COMPARISON
- PARALLELISM
- RUN-ONS AND FRAGMENTS
- MISPLACED MODIFIERS

SmartPoints | Ready for Test Day | Identifying Sentence Errors | Improving Sentences | Improving Paragraphs

PASSIVE VS. ACTIVE VOICE

PARALLELISM

TRANSITIONS

WORDINESS

WHAT TO EXPECT ON TEST DAY

The Writing section's multiple-choice questions are like a mini-SAT all to themselves. The Writing section uses three different types of multiple-choice questions to test three different writing skills, but each question type works basically the same way: you need to determine what mistake (if any) has been made in the sentences or paragraphs in question. For two of the three types, you will also need to determine the best way to correct those mistakes. Throughout this chapter, we'll show you the kinds of writing mistakes the SAT wants you to catch and how you can catch them.

Note: This is a long chapter. It might be helpful to treat it like three short chapters, one for each multiple-choice question type:

- Identifying Sentence Errors
- Improving Sentences
- Improving Paragraphs

Tackle just one question type in a single study session.

IDENTIFYING SENTENCE ERRORS QUESTIONS AND HOW TO AVOID COMMON MISTAKES

The word *usage* means the customary or standard way in which words are used. The Identifying Sentence Errors questions on the SAT cover four main areas of written English:

- Basic grammar
- Sentence structure

PERFECT SCORE TIP

" To boost my word skills, I brought vocab flashcards on car trips and I tried to get the rest of my family involved whenever possible. "

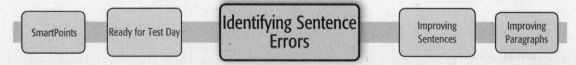

SmartPoints — Ready for Test Day — Identifying Sentence Errors — Improving Sentences — Improving Paragraphs

- Idiomatic expressions
- Choice of words (diction)

That sounds like a lot of ground to cover, but as you'll see, most Identifying Sentence Errors questions only test a few key grammar and usage concepts. We'll show you the kind of grammar the SAT usually tests and help you become an expert at the SAT's spot-the-mistake questions.

Remember, the Writing section measures your ability to recognize acceptable and unacceptable uses of *written* English. Standard *written* English is a bit more formal than the average person's spoken English, and it is what professors will expect you to use on college papers. That's why it is being tested on the SAT.

KAPLAN'S TARGET STRATEGY FOR IDENTIFYING SENTENCE ERRORS

To tackle Identifying Sentence Errors questions, Kaplan's test experts have devised a Target Strategy that will guide you in answering these types of questions. The four steps are as follows:

- **Step 1.** Read the whole sentence, listening and watching for an error.
- **Step 2.** If you clearly hear the error, choose it and move on.
- **Step 3.** If not, read each underlined choice, and eliminate choices that contain no errors.
- **Step 4.** Choose from the remaining choices.

Try this out on the following example. Start by reading it to yourself.

Although the number of firms declaring
    A

bankruptcy keep growing, the mayor claims that the
        B   C

city is thriving. No error
    D   E

Did you hear the error? If so, your work is done. Fill in the appropriate oval, and move on. If you didn't hear the error on the first reading, go back, read each underlined part, and start eliminating underlined parts that are right.

The word *although* seems fine in this context. The word *keep* is a plural verb, but its subject is *number*, which is singular. That seems to be an error. The phrase

SmartPoints | Ready for Test Day | **Identifying Sentence Errors** | Improving Sentences | Improving Paragraphs

claims that sounds all right; it has a singular verb for a singular subject, *mayor*. Similarly, *is thriving* sounds all right, and it too provides a singular verb for the singular subject *city*. Choice (B) contains the mistake, so (B) is the correct answer.

This is a classic example of subject-verb agreement, which is a common question type in the Writing section. You'll learn more about the most common errors in the following pages, which offer a quick reference to the most frequently made and tested grammatical mistakes. It's much easier to spot errors when you know what to look for.

NO ERROR?

Please keep in mind that not all the Identifying Sentence Errors questions on the Writing section contain errors. Some will be choice (E), or No Error. These are often the hardest to pick because you must be confident that there's nothing wrong with the sentence. Knowing the most common errors used on the test—and therefore knowing that those aren't in a given sentence—will make choosing (E) easier.

PERFECT SCORE TIP

"At first, I worried about the number of (E) answers I had as I went through the section—and that was very stressful. I found it better not to worry about them until the end, when I went back over each question that I thought had no error."

AVOID COMMON MISTAKES FOR IDENTIFYING SENTENCE ERRORS QUESTIONS

Although the SAT Writing questions will test your knowledge of grammar and usage, you won't have to recite any rules on the exam. In fact, you don't have to know all the rules *per se*; you just have to be able to recognize when something is *not* correct. So instead of trying to review all of the rules, we'll show you the top 16 errors you need to watch out for on the SAT. Once you are used to seeing these Identifying Sentence Errors in practice, you'll have an easier time spotting them on Test Day.

REMEMBER!

Being familiar with the most common mistakes that test takers make will help you tackle Identifying Sentence Errors questions.

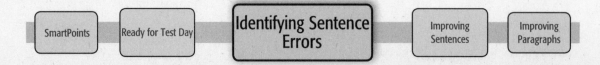

SmartPoints   Ready for Test Day   **Identifying Sentence Errors**   Improving Sentences   Improving Paragraphs

SUBJECT-VERB AGREEMENT

- **Rule: Singular** subjects call for **singular** verbs. **Plural** subjects call for **plural** verbs.

COMMON ERROR 1: WHEN THE SUBJECT FOLLOWS THE VERB

In this situation, it is hard to find the subject of the verb because it comes later in the sentence. "There is" is a common sentence construction of this sentence error. For example:

> Despite an intensive campaign to encourage conservation, there is many Americans who have not accepted recycling as a way of life.

This sentence demonstrates one of *the most common* of all subject-verb agreement errors found on the Writing section. It generally occurs once or twice on each test. Words such has *there* or *here* can not be subjects of sentences. The subject of the sentence is not *there*. The subject is *Americans*, which is plural. Therefore, the singular verb is incorrect; *is* should be replaced by the plural verb *are*.

Here's another example in which the subject follows the verb:

> High above the Hudson River rises the gleaming skyscrapers of Manhattan.

The sentence is tricky because a prepositional phrase with a singular noun, *Hudson River*, comes before the verb *rises*. Because the object of a preposition cannot be the subject of a sentence, a noun even later in the sentence, skyscrapers, is the subject. Think about it. What's doing the rising? Not the river, the *skyscrapers*. The subject is plural, and so the verb should be *rise*.

> **EXPERT TUTOR TIP**
>
> " Don't waste time trying to figure out how many "No error" questions there are in your section. However, if you have several "No error" answers in a row, you should double-check your work. "

WHAT'S A PREPOSITION?

It is a small word that (usually) tells where something is: *above* the door, *over* the hill, *under* a tree, and more. The SAT uses very small ones most often: *in, at, on, of,* and *to.*

COMMON ERROR 2: WHEN THE SUBJECT AND VERB ARE SEPARATED

The SAT has another way to complicate a subject-verb agreement. They insert some additional information about the subject before the verb appears.

PERFECT SCORE TIP

Identifying the subject and action was definitely the easiest way for me to answer questions where the subject and verb were separated. I didn't have to think about the whole sentence, just about those two pieces of information.

EXPERT TUTOR TIP

Get in the habit of matching underlined verbs with their subject. You'll start to see patterns in what the test makers use to separate subjects and verbs.

Consider the following sentences:

> The local congressman, a reliable representative of both community and statewide interests, are among the most respected persons in the public sector.

What is the subject of this sentence? You see several nouns before the verb: *congressman, representative, community*, and *interests*. So which is it? *Congressman*. If you thought any of the others was the subject, here's what to do: take a pencil and put parentheses where the pair of commas are. This is your tip-off that this is "oh-by-the-way" descriptive information. You can do without it and still have a complete sentence.

Another tip-off is the presence of a small preposition, such as *of, in, to*, and *at*. Look at the following sentence.

> The collection of paintings entitled "Clammy Clam Clams" are one of the most widely traveled exhibits in recent years.

Again, more nouns to consider before the verb: *collection, paintings,* and *Clammy Clam Clams*. Find the subject? It is *collection*. If you thought it was *paintings*, you overlooked the little preposition *of. Paintings* is the object of that little preposition and isn't eligible for the job. The subject is singular and the verb should be *is*, not *are*.

The SAT writers like this type of question because the intervening modifying phrases or clauses can cause you to lose track of the subject. These phrases simply modify the subject they follow, without changing its number. Don't be fooled by the placement of these intervening phrases.

ALWAYS FIND THE SUBJECT

When you see an underlined verb, automatically look for its subject. Draw parentheses around any prepositional phrases and modifiers that stand between subject and verb. Do this routinely to build speed, confidence, and accuracy in your answering process, a *win-win-win* situation.

Rule: Only the conjunction *and* can form a plural verb. The word pairs *neither . . . nor* and *either . . . or* take singular verbs, if each side of the pair is singular.

SmartPoints   Ready for Test Day   Identifying Sentence Errors   Improving Sentences   Improving Paragraphs

COMMON ERROR 3: WHEN THE SUBJECT SEEMS PLURAL (BUT ISN'T)

Sometimes the sentence includes what seems to be, but in fact is not, a plural subject. Here's an example.

> Neither ambient techno nor trance were a part of mainstream listening habits in the United States 10 years ago.

This sentence is tough because it has two singular subjects (*ambient techno* and *trance*), but with *neither* and *nor* in the mix, they don't add up to a plural subject. The verb should be *was*.

Note: If the nouns in a *neither … nor* or *either … or* sentence are plural on their own, then the verb should be plural. The SAT doesn't usually bother with these. It's too easy!

 ## VERB TENSE AND SENSE

Make it a habit to examine all verbs in every sentence and remember the following rules:

- **Rule:** Tenses must be as simple as possible (most often, present, past, and future) and make sense in context.

- **Rule:** Verbs must be complete, with *to be* predicate helpers (*am thinking*).

- **Rule:** If a sentence has more than one complete verb in it, be consistent. Don't change tenses unless it makes sense to do so.

COMMON ERROR 4: WRONG TENSES

Here's a sentence with a verb in the wrong tense.

> Over the last half-century, the building of passenger airliners had grown into a multibillion-dollar industry.

In a one-verb sentence like this one, time-descriptive phrases help you determine what the time frame of a sentence is. The action being described is a process that began during the last half-century and that is continuing to the present day. Any action starting in the past and continuing today is expressed by a verb in the present perfect tense. The present perfect form of this verb is *has grown*. Using the verb *had* makes it seem that passenger airliners aren't being made anymore. That can't be! The key is to pay attention to the time cues in the sentence. With practice, you'll be able to spot mistakes like this with confidence.

PERFECT SCORE TIP

❝ Knowing whether a construction produces a singular or plural subject was the easiest way for me to avoid this type of mistake. It let me answer the related questions quickly and confidently. ❞

EXPERT TUTOR TIP

❝ In an *either/or neither/nor* construction, if one of the nouns is plural and the other singular, remember that the verb should agree with the *closest* noun. ❞

SmartPoints | Ready for Test Day | **Identifying Sentence Errors** | Improving Sentences | Improving Paragraphs

Another type of sentence might have two verbs and an unnecessary or confusing shift in tense. Here's an example.

> Many superb tennis players turn professional at an alarmingly early age, but because of their lack of physical stamina, suffered early in their careers.

When there are two verbs in a sentence, first study the time relation between the verbs, and determine whether it is logical as presented. In this sentence, the verb in the first clause of this sentence is *turn*, a present tense verb. The action is not occurring at any specified occasion but in the general present. The verb *suffered* is in the simple past, but it should remain in the general present, even though the phrase *early in their careers* may suggest a past time. Be sure that there is a logical relation between the verbs when two are presented in the same sentence.

COMMON ERROR 5: INCORRECT USE OF PAST PARTICIPLES AND INCOMPLETE VERBS

A typical error tested on the Writing section is confusion between the simple past tense and the past participle forms of a verb. The error is to put the past participle form where the simple past tense should be. Consider the following sentence.

> Several passersby seen the bank robber leaving the scene of the crime.

The verb form *seen* is the past participle and should be used only with a helping verb, such as *have* or *be*. This sentence requires the simple past form *saw*.

 ## PRONOUN USE

Like verbs, all pronouns in a Writing multiple-choice sentence should be examined carefully. Remember the following rules:

- **Rule:** A pronoun must agree in number and gender with the noun it replaces (called an *antecedent*).

- **Rule:** A pronoun must be in the proper case (*subjective, objective, possessive*).

- **Rule:** The antecedent must be clear. If it could refer to more than one thing or person, or if there is no antecedent, you have found an SAT error.

COMMON ERROR 6: PRONOUN IN THE WRONG NUMBER

You'll be tested on your ability to tell whether or not a noun and the pronoun that refers to that noun agree in number. A singular pronoun should be used to refer to a singular noun; a plural pronoun should be used with a plural noun. In the

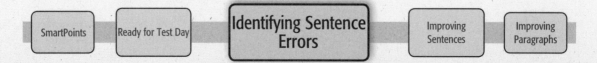

following examples, the pronoun does not match the noun to which it refers in number.

> The typical college student has difficulty adjusting to academic standards much higher than those of their school.

The pronoun *their* should refer to a plural noun, but in this sentence, it refers back to *student*, a singular noun. Therefore, the pronoun should be the singular form *his* or *hers*, and not the plural form *their*. Look for the same kind of mistake in the next sentence.

> Most infants, even unusually quiet ones, will cry with greater intensity when it begins teething.

The error in this sentence is just the opposite of that in the first example. The subject is *infants*, a plural noun. But the pronoun that refers back to this plural noun is *it*, a singular form. The correct form of the pronoun is *they*, referring back to the plural subject. Be sure that a pronoun agrees with its antecedent in number.

COMMON ERROR 7: WRONG CASE

Errors involving word case tend to appear on the SAT. Remember that pronouns must be in their proper case:

- **Subjective pronouns:** *I, you, he, she, it, we, they*
- **Objective pronouns:** *me, you, him, her, it, us, them*
- **Possessive pronouns:** *my, your, his, her, its, our, their*

COMMON ERROR 8: PRONOUN SHIFT

Pronoun shift is a switch in pronoun person or number within a given sentence. Here's an example.

> One cannot sleep soundly if you exercise vigorously before retiring to bed.

The subject in the first clause is *one*, and the subject in the second clause is *you*. These two pronouns refer to the same performer of two actions, so they should be consistent in person and number. The sentence should not shift to the second person *you* form.

Look for another kind of pronoun shift in the next sentence.

> If someone loses his way in the airport, they can ask any employee for directions.

The subject is *someone* in the first clause, but *they* in the second clause. Clearly, both pronouns refer to the same agent; the performer of both actions, losing and asking,

> **EXPERT TUTOR TIP**
>
> " Watch out for some commonly tested "wrong words": *affect/effect*, *raise/rise*, and *accept/except*. "

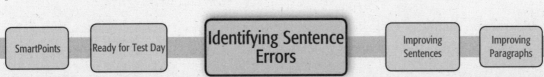

SmartPoints | Ready for Test Day | **Identifying Sentence Errors** | Improving Sentences | Improving Paragraphs

is the same. This switch in number from singular to plural is not grammatical. In creating such a sentence, SAT writers play on a common logical confusion. In English, singular words like *one*, *someone*, and *a person* can represent people in general. So can plural words like *people* or *they*. Be on the lookout when general statements use pronouns because this is one of the most common mistakes made in the English language, and consider whether these pronouns are consistent.

COMMON ERROR 9: PRONOUN WITH AMBIGUOUS REFERENCE

There are two ways the Writing section might test your ability to recognize an ambiguous pronoun reference. First, a sentence may be given in which it is impossible to determine what noun the pronoun refers to. Take a look at this example.

> The United States entered into warmer relations with China after its compliance with recent weapons agreements.

To which country does the pronoun *its* refer? Grammatically and logically, either country could be the antecedent of the pronoun. With the limited information provided by this sentence alone, you simply can't determine which country the pronoun stands in for. The reference is ambiguous.

Pronoun reference can also be ambiguous if the pronoun's antecedent is not explicitly stated in the sentence.

> After the derailment last month, they are inspecting trains for safety more often than ever before.

The question to ask about this sentence is *who* is *they*? There is no group of people identified in this sentence to whom the pronoun could refer. You can logically infer that *they* refers to agents of a railroad safety commission, but because these inspectors are not explicitly mentioned in the sentence, the personal pronoun cannot be clear. Be sure to locate the antecedent of any pronoun in Identifying Sentence Errors sentences.

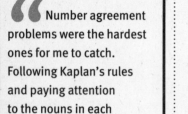 ## IDIOMS

An idiom, also called an *idiomatic expression*, is a term that refers to a wide range of commonly accepted combinations of words. This is the one area where your language "ear" will be very helpful. While there is no definitive list to memorize, some general rules and guideposts are helpful:

- **Rule:** Listen for the wrong verb combination (infinitive vs. gerund).
- **Rule:** Watch for an odd sounding preposition after a verb.

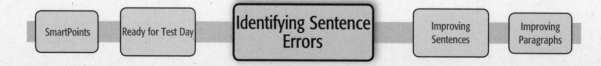

SmartPoints   Ready for Test Day   **Identifying Sentence Errors**   Improving Sentences   Improving Paragraphs

COMMON ERROR 10: CONFUSION OF INFINITIVE AND GERUND

Some questions test your sense of idiomatic use of English. *Idiomatic use* means combinations of words that sound right or words that sound right in particular contexts.

For example, there is generally at least one Identifying Sentence Errors question in which the infinitive is used where a gerund would be appropriate, or vice versa, as in the following example.

> Team officials heralded Cap Day as an attempt at attracting a larger turnout of fans.

This sentence is not idiomatic. There's no grammar rule that explains why it's wrong to say *an attempt at attracting*. But if you have a good sense of idiom, your ear tells you it should be *an attempt to attract*. This sentence confuses the *-ing* gerund form with the *to + verb infinitive* form. Here's another sentence.

> Surveillance cameras are frequently placed in convenience stores to prevent customers to shoplift.

After *prevent* you don't use the infinitive but rather the word *from* plus the gerund. The sentence should end *to prevent customers from shoplifting*.

Why? There's no real grammatical reason. That's just the way we say and write it in English. You have to trust yourself on these. Whereas there are some general patterns, there are no hard and fast rules that determine when to use an infinitive or gerund, and there are so many possible combinations that there's no way to list all that could possibly appear on the Writing section. But don't worry. You don't need to see every possible combination in advance. Just remember to prick up your ears whenever an infinitive or gerund is underlined on the test.

COMMON ERROR 11: WRONG PREPOSITION AFTER VERB

The Writing section also tests your recognition of prepositions that idiomatically combine with certain verbs. Here's a sentence that uses the wrong preposition.

> City Council members frequently meet until the early morning hours in order to work in their stalemates.

It's not always wrong to write *work in*. You might use it to speak about the field one *works in* or the place one *works in*. But this combination does not correspond to the meaning of this sentence. The writer means to say *work through* or *work out*—that is, overcome—the stalemates.

SmartPoints   Ready for Test Day   **Identifying Sentence Errors**   Improving Sentences   Improving Paragraphs

Here's another sentence with the wrong preposition.

> The rapper's new CD was frowned at by many parents because of
> its violent lyrics.

That's just not the way we say it in English. The preferred verb-preposition combination is
frowned upon. That's the idiomatic expression. Once again, this is an area where you'll have to trust
your ear. Just remember to pay attention and think for a moment when you see an underlined
preposition after a verb.

 ## DICTION

Diction is a cousin of idiom in that it often sounds wrong and the right word is dictated by
accepted use or meaning. It too covers a range of issues, such as *sit* vs. *set*, *lie* vs. *lay*, and *rise*
vs. *raise*, as well as expressions of quantity and often confused words. Any or all of these will
be tested in the SAT multiple-choice Writing sections.

- **Confused Verb Rule:** *Sit, lie,* and *rise,* the "I" verbs, have no objects. *Set, lay,* and *raise,* the
  no "I" verbs, are action verbs with objects.

- **Quantity Rule:** Use amount words *when referring to an uncountable noun*. Use number
  words to refer to a countable one.

- **Similar Sounding Words Rule:** Be on the lookout for often confused words. They sound
  very similar, but don't mean the same thing.

DON'T FORGET

> You may see a question about the pronoun *one* on the SAT; be sure this pronoun
> and all other pronouns are used consistently.

COMMON ERROR 12: WRONG WORD IN CONTEXT

Some verbs are often used interchangeably and incorrectly, especially in spoken English. The
correct use should be as follows:

"I" verbs:		No "I" verbs:	
	I sit down.		I set the table.
	I lie down.		I lay the book on the table.
	The sun rises.		I raise my hand.

Here are two sentences that misuse these verbs:

> **Wrong:** I am working so hard that my grade point average raises
> every semester.

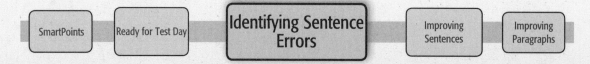

Right: I am working so hard that my grade point average rises every semester.

A grade point average *rises* (no object).

Wrong: I set with my neighbors on the front porch until dark.

Right: I sit with my neighbors on the front porch until dark.

With my neighbors is a prepositional phrase, so the verb should be *sat*, which is the past tense of *sit*.

Quantity issues: How much coffee have you had? How much sugar did you put in your tea? It depends if you can count the units or not. You can't count coffee, but you can count the cups. The same is true for *sugar, sand, information, time*, and more.

- Many cups of coffee, but much coffee
- A few teaspoons of sugar, but too little sugar

Often confused words: The list is nearly endless; thus, they are hard to catch as you work your way through a test. For example:

- *Imply*: to suggest; *implicate*: to accuse or charge (with a crime)
- *Accept*: receive willingly (verb); *except*: not including (preposition)
- *Affect*: create a result (verb); *effect*: the result (noun)

The examples above are among the most common. So on the test you might see: I *excepted* his invitation to the prom. Be on the lookout for these "hidden" errors.

 ## COMPARISON ISSUES

There are three areas to think about here (and thus three different traps):

1. What's being compared
2. Parallel (similar) phrasing
3. Number of items in the comparison

Remember the following rules for comparison issues:

- **Rule:** Compare similar things and use similar wording.
- **Rule:** Use comparative (*better*) for comparing two things; use superlative (*best*) for comparing more than two.

> **PERFECT SCORE TIP**
>
> " Kaplan's method of isolating the pronoun was definitely the most effective way to catch pronoun case errors. I never made mistakes when I used it! "

PERFECT SCORE TIP

❝ Kaplan's method of finding the antecedent of each pronoun in a sentence was very effective for me. It took some time to locate all the antecedents at first, but with practice, it actually became a huge time-saver. ❞

EXPERT TUTOR TIP

❝ We often use an ambiguous *they* in conversation, so you might not catch the error. It is another time to be very cautious when you see *they* underlined. ❞

COMMON ERROR 13: FAULTY COMPARISON

Most faulty comparisons happen when two things that logically cannot be compared are compared. A comparison can be faulty either logically or grammatically. Look for the faulty comparison in the following sentence.

> A Nobel Peace Prize winner and the author of several respected novels, Elie Wiesel's name is still less well known than last year's Heisman Trophy winner.

In every sentence, you should first identify what things or actions are being compared. In this sentence, Elie Wiesel's *name* is compared to last year's Heisman Trophy winner. This comparison is faulty because a person's name is compared to another person. If the first item were *Elie Wiesel,* then the comparison would be valid.

Try to identify the faulty comparison in the next sentence.

> To lash back at one's adversaries is a less courageous course than attempting to bring about reconciliation with them.

The comparison in this sentence is logically correct in that two actions are compared. But the problem lies in the grammatical form of the words compared. An infinitive verb, *to lash*, expresses the first action, but a gerund, *attempting*, expresses the second action. These verb forms should match to make the comparison parallel. If *lashing* replaced *to lash*, the comparison would be grammatically parallel and logically valid. Check all comparisons for logic and grammatical consistency.

EASY-TO-OVERLOOK ISSUES

Hidden in the Identifying Sentence Error questions are three other errors to be aware of. Because they are usually small errors (and may only have a missing letter or an extra small word inserted), it pays to know what they are. We'll look at them one at a time.

BE CAREFUL!

Be wary of vague subject references such as *its*, *their*, *they*, and *those*. If you can't tell what the pronoun refers to, something is missing from the sentence.

COMMON ERROR 14: NUMBER AGREEMENT PROBLEMS

The Writing section also tests number agreement between the singular or plural noun and the phrase or word describing it. For instance, a noun may be plural

SmartPoints   Ready for Test Day   **Identifying Sentence Errors**   Improving Sentences   Improving Paragraphs

while a phrase describing the noun belongs with a singular noun. That sounds complicated, but fortunately, you don't need to be able to explain the grammar involved; you just need to be able to spot this type of mistake. Here's an example.

> The advertisement in the newspaper requested that only persons with a high school diploma apply for the position.

Nouns in a sentence must have logical number relations. The noun in question, the subject of the second clause of this sentence, is *persons*, a plural noun. However, the noun *diploma* is singular. Because the phrase *with a high school diploma* is singular, it seems to say that *persons* share one diploma, when in fact each person has his own diploma. The phrase should read *with high school diplomas*.

Here's an example of number disagreement in which a singular noun is coupled with a plural subject.

> Mary's rose gardens are considered by many to be the symbol of beauty in the neighborhood.

Again, identify the subject of the sentence, *gardens*. The noun that corresponds to the subject is *symbol*, a singular noun. There is no agreement in number between *gardens* and *symbol*. Each individual garden is a symbol; many gardens would not be a single symbol. The plural form, *symbols*, makes this sentence grammatically correct. Make sure that the nouns in a sentence logically agree in number.

COMMON ERROR 15: MISUSE OF ADJECTIVE OR ADVERB

Remember the following rules regarding the misuse of adjectives and adverbs:

- **Rule:** An adjective can only describe a noun or pronoun.

- **Rule:** An adverb modifies everything else and answers the question *How?*

These questions test your ability to recognize misuses of one-word modifiers. Keep in mind that adjectives modify nouns and adverbs modify verbs, adjectives, and other adverbs. Now ask yourself what the underlined word is intended to modify as you look at the sentence below.

> The applicants for low-interest loans hoped to buy decent built houses for their families.

The word *decent* is an adjective. However, this modifier describes an adjective, explaining how the houses were built. A word that modifies an adjective like *built* is an adverb. So the word needed in this sentence is the adverb *decently*. Notice also that this adverb ends in *-ly*, the most common adverbial ending.

PERFECT SCORE TIP

" Identifying exactly what was being compared (I underlined everything!) was by far the easiest method to use—and it never failed! "

EXPERT TUTOR TIP

" Remember: *-er*, the comparative, compares two things and has two letters; *-est*, the superlative, compares three or more things and has three letters. "

SmartPoints | Ready for Test Day | **Identifying Sentence Errors** | Improving Sentences | Improving Paragraphs

Now take a look at the second sentence.

> The critics who reviewed Dave Eggers's novels like
> the second one best.

The word *best* is a superlative modifier. Superlative adverbs and adjectives (adverbs and adjectives ending in *-est* (such as *biggest, loudest, fastest,* etc.) should express comparisons between three or more things or actions. Comparative adverbs and adjectives end in *-er* (*bigger, louder, faster,* etc.) and express comparisons between two things or actions. This sentence compares critics' responses to only two novels by Dave Eggers. Thus, instead of the superlative *best,* this sentence needs the comparative modifier *better.*

Remember that some adjectives and adverbs, usually those of two or more syllables, form the comparative with *more* instead of the *-er* ending, and *most* instead of the *-est* ending converts some modifiers to superlatives.

Trust your ear to distinguish adjectives from adverbs in Writing section Identifying Sentence Errors questions, but do *listen* carefully. Pay close attention when you decide whether a sentence needs a comparative or superlative modifier.

COMMON ERROR 16: DOUBLE NEGATIVE

When dealing with double negatives, remember the following rule:

- **Rule:** Don't use two negatives in a sentence unless the intention is to have one cancel out the other.

On the Identifying Sentence Error portion of the SAT, a double negative is wrong. Double negatives can be correct in certain circumstances, but they won't be in the Writing sections. Notice the two negative words in this sentence.

> James easily passed the biology exam without hard-
> ly studying his lab notes.

Without is a negative, as is any word that indicates absence or lack. *Hardly* is a less familiar negative; it also denotes a scarcity of something, but perhaps not a total absence. With these two negatives, the sentence is incorrect.

Now look at the next sentence.

> In the history of the major leagues, barely no one
> has maintained higher than a .400 batting average
> for an entire season.

Clearly, *no one* is a negative, but so is *barely.* Just like *hardly* does, this word indicates a scarcity of something or an almost total absence. In Identifying Sentence Errors

PERFECT SCORE TIP

Whenever I got frustrated about the SAT, I told myself that it wasn't the end of the world and that I had the option to retake it if I wanted to.

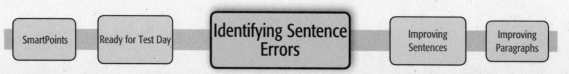

SmartPoints · Ready for Test Day · **Identifying Sentence Errors** · Improving Sentences · Improving Paragraphs

questions, be on the lookout for negatives that are not obviously negative, such as *hardly*, *barely*, and *scarcely*.

IMPROVING SENTENCES QUESTIONS AND HOW TO AVOID COMMON MISTAKES

Just like Identifying Sentence Errors questions, most Improving Sentences questions relate to a small number of grammatical issues. Here's the main difference between the two question types: whereas the errors in the Identifying Sentence Errors questions consist of single words or short phrases, the errors in the Improving Sentences questions generally involve the structure of the whole sentence. As a result, they can be a little harder to identify than the errors in the Identifying Sentence Errors section.

KAPLAN'S TARGET STRATEGY FOR IMPROVING SENTENCES

Step 1. Read the sentence carefully, and look and listen for an error.

Step 2. Identify the error or errors.

Step 3. Look for the most correct, concise, and relevant answer. Don't forget it could be correct as written (choice A).

Let's use the method on the following example.

The Emancipation Edict freed the Russian serfs in 1861; <u>that being four years</u> before the Thirteenth Amendment abolished slavery in the United States.

(A) in 1861; that being four years

(B) in 1861 and is four years

(C) in 1861 and this amounts to four years

(D) in 1861, being four years

(E) in 1861, four years

STEP 1. READ THE SENTENCE CAREFULLY, AND LOOK AND LISTEN FOR AN ERROR

The stem sentence (sentence part in question) in the example doesn't sound right. The semicolon might be wrong.

STEP 2. IDENTIFY THE ERROR OR ERRORS

The semicolon and phrase *that being* sound like the wrong way of joining the two parts of the sentence.

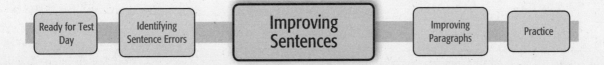

The semicolon and the phrase *that being* seem unnecessary. Joining the two sentence fragments with a simple comma would probably work. (Plus, as you'll learn later, answer choices that contain the word *being* are usually wrong.) Plug in your choice to be sure it sounds best.

STEP 3. LOOK FOR THE MOST CORRECT, CONCISE, AND RELEVANT ANSWER

Choice (E) has just a comma. Is that enough? All the answer choices begin with *in 1861* and end with *four years*, so you have to look at what comes in between to see what forms the best link. Scan the choices, and you'll find that *and is* in (B), *and this amounts to* in (C), and *being*, preceded by a comma, in (D) are no better than (A) because they are wordy and awkward phrases.

Choice (E) is the best way to rewrite the underlined portion of the sentence, so (E) is the correct answer.

Remember, not every sentence contains an error. Choice (A) is correct about one-fifth of the time. In any event, because you should begin by reading the original sentence carefully, you should never waste time reading choice (A).

AVOID COMMON MISTAKES FOR IMPROVING SENTENCES QUESTIONS

As you work through the Improving Sentences section, *read each sentence carefully*. We can't say that often enough. The error, if there is one, will often be obvious to you in the first reading.

If it isn't, remember that only a rather limited range of grammar rules is tested. Once your ear has become attuned to the Improving Sentences section's favorite grammar mistakes, you'll have an easier time spotting them on Test Day.

Remember the following rules:

- **Rule:** An independent clause has a subject and a complete verb and can stand alone as a sentence.

- **Rule:** A dependent, or subordinate, clause has a subject and a complete verb but needs an independent clause to become a sentence.

- **Rule:** To combine two independent clauses correctly, you must do one of three things:

1. Insert a semicolon

2. Make one clause dependent/subordinate

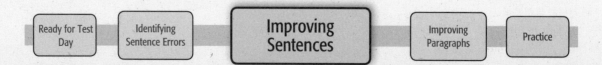

Ready for Test Day   Identifying Sentence Errors   **Improving Sentences**   Improving Paragraphs   Practice

3. Use one of the following conjunctions with a comma: **F**or, **A**nd, **N**or, **B**ut, **O**r, **Y**et, **S**o (FANBOYS)

Here are five classic Improving Sentences mistakes.

COMMON ERROR 1: RUN-ON SENTENCES

The Improving Sentences questions on the Writing section always includes run-on sentences. In a typical run-on sentence, two independent clauses, each of which could stand alone as a complete sentence, are erroneously joined together, either with no punctuation or, most often, with just a comma.

Here's an example.

> Even the town's most apathetic citizens rallied behind the cause, this support resulted in the passage of the law.

Both clauses in this sentence are independent; each could stand alone as a sentence. So it's incorrect to join them with a comma. There are several ways to correct run-on sentences. One way is to change the comma into a semicolon, so you would see the following.

> Even the town's most apathetic citizens rallied behind the cause; this support resulted in the passage of the law.

Another common way to fix a run-on is to keep the comma and add a FANBOYS conjunction (see list). This type of change can affect the meaning of the sentence, so be careful here—you don't want to change the meaning of the sentence. You might see the following.

> Even the town's most apathetic citizens rallied behind the cause, and this support resulted in the passage of the law.

Yet another way to fix a run-on sentence is to make one of the independent clauses dependent. To correct the original sentence in this way, you could see the following answer choice.

> Because even the town's most apathetic citizens rallied behind the cause, this support resulted in the passage of the law.

Adding *because* to the first clause makes it a dependent or subordinate clause. Now the comma is fine. Be sure, as stated above, that the "fix" does not change the meaning of the sentence.

PERFECT SCORE TIP

" Identifying run-on sentences was difficult at first. But paying special attention to long sentences, especially those with commas, helped me catch many of the run-on errors. "

EXPERT TUTOR TIP

" When trying to choose between two choices for Improving Sentences questions, look at the shortest answer choice first. Shorter is usually better. "

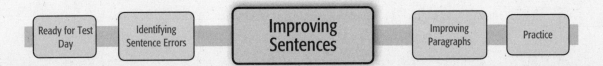

Ready for Test Day | Identifying Sentence Errors | **Improving Sentences** | Improving Paragraphs | Practice

SUSPICIOUS COMMAS

> When you see a long sentence with just a comma in the middle, suspect a run-on sentence. Then look to see which answer choice the test makers have chosen as a fix.

COMMON ERROR 2: SENTENCE FRAGMENTS

The Improving Sentences section usually includes one or two sentence fragments. Sentence fragments come in many forms, but they all share the same problem: they cannot stand alone because they have no independent clauses.

KEY POINT

> A sentence must contain a subject and verb (a clause) *and* express a complete thought (be independent).

PERFECT SCORE TIP

> " I caught most of the sentence fragment errors when I read the sentences out loud. Even if I didn't know exactly what was wrong, I usually noticed that something didn't sound right. "

What looks like a sentence on the Writing section may actually be merely a fragment. Take a look at the following example.

> Whereas many office managers are growing more and more dependent on facsimile machines, others resisting this latest technological breakthrough.

This just sounds wrong, doesn't it? Here's why. This is a sentence fragment because it has no independent clause. The first clause begins with the subordinating conjunction *whereas*, and the phrase following the comma contains the incomplete verb form *resisting*. Plus, a sentence must always have at least one clause that could stand alone, and here neither of the clauses can do that. The easiest way to repair this sentence is to insert the helping verb *are*.

> Whereas many office managers are growing more and more dependent on facsimile machines, others are resisting this latest technological breakthrough.

Here's another sentence fragment.

> In the summertime, the kindergarten class that plays on the rope swing beneath the crooked oak tree.

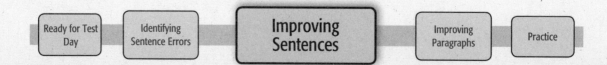

| Ready for Test Day | Identifying Sentence Errors | **Improving Sentences** | Improving Paragraphs | Practice |

Once again, the sentence clause cannot stand alone. Here we have a fragment not because something is missing, but because something is included that makes the clause dependent. The word *that* makes everything after the comma a dependent clause. Simply remove the word *that*, and look at what you get.

> In the summertime, the kindergarten class plays on the rope swing beneath the crooked oak tree.

Now you have a grammatically complete sentence that is shorter than the fragment.

 ## COMMON ERROR 3: MISPLACED MODIFIERS

A modifier is a word or group of words that gives the reader more information about a noun or verb in the sentence.

> **PERFECT SCORE TIP**
>
> " By matching up modifiers with the noun that they modified, I easily caught any misplaced modifiers. "

KEY POINT

To be grammatically correct, the modifier must be positioned so it is clear which word is being modified.

The best place to put a modifier is as close as possible to the word it modifies. Here is an example of a misplaced modifier like those you may see on the Writing section.

> Flying for the first time, the roar of the jet engines intimidated the small child, and he grew frightened as the plane roared down the runway.

The modifying phrase above is found at the beginning of the sentence: *Flying for the first time.* A modifying phrase that begins a sentence should relate to the sentence's subject. Usually, a comma sets off this kind of introductory modifier, and then the subject immediately follows the comma.

> **EXPERT TUTOR TIP**
>
> " Be careful: If your sentence starts with a gerund (an *-ing* verb), you could have a misplaced modifier to fix. "

Logically, in this example, you know that it is the child who is flying for the first time. But because of the grammatical structure of the sentence (the placement of the modifier), the sentence actually states that it is the *roar* that is flying for the first time. Of course, this doesn't make sense: roars don't fly for the first time (or the second time or the third time). The sentence needs to be revised so that the modifier is as close as possible to the noun it modifies.

> Flying for the first time, the small child was intimidated by the roar of the jet engines and grew frightened as the plane roared down the runway.

Here's another example of a sentence with a misplaced modifying modifier.

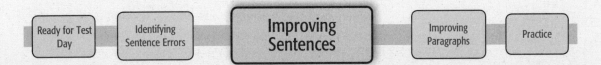

Ready for Test Day | Identifying Sentence Errors | **Improving Sentences** | Improving Paragraphs | Practice

> An advertisement was withdrawn by the producer of the local news program that was considered offensive by the city's minority communities.

Grammatically, the phrase *that was considered offensive by the city's minority communities* refers to *the local news program*, because this is the nearest noun. Is that what the writer means? Is it the local news program or the advertisement that was offensive to the minority communities? If the writer means to say that the advertisement was deemed offensive, she should rewrite the sentence as follows to make her idea clear.

> The producer of the local news program withdrew an advertisement that was considered offensive by the city's minority communities.

Note: There is no one way to fix a modifier that's in the wrong place. You can add a subject and verb to the modifying phrase and create a dependent clause, or rearrange the words. Look at the following examples.

- **Wrong:** Being a good athlete, the team was glad to have Maria on the team.
- **Right:** Because she was a good athlete, the team was glad to have Maria on the team.
- **Right:** Because she was a good athlete, Maria was welcomed *by* the team. (Note passive voice here—weaker than the first right answer, but correct all the same.)

The first right answer transforms the modifying phrase *Being a good athlete* into a dependent clause with a subject *she* and the verb *was*. The second turns *Maria* into the subject and makes the verb construction passive, *was welcomed by*.

 ### PASSIVE VS. ACTIVE VOICE

Avoid, if possible, sentences with passive voice verbs. What are these?

- **Passive verbs** are weak and wordy, and focus on who/what receives the action.
- **Active verbs** are stronger and use fewer words. Active voice emphasizes the action.

Consider the following examples:

- **Passive:** The panic button was pushed *by* me.
- **Active:** I pushed the panic button.

If you see *by*, think passive voice. When you can, choose sentences with the active voice.

 ### COMMON ERROR 4: FAULTY PARALLELISM

Certain sets of words in a sentence, or the general design of a sentence, often require a parallel construction—that is, the words or phrases must share the same grammatical structure. If they don't, the sentence will be off balance.

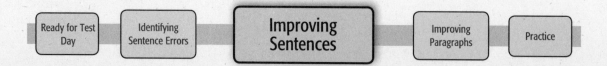

Ready for Test Day | Identifying Sentence Errors | **Improving Sentences** | Improving Paragraphs | Practice

KEY POINT

Sentences with two or more similar elements must be worded similarly. Lists or series of items, comparisons, and connective pairs are examples that require similar wording.

Use parallel structure with connective phrases such as *neither . . . nor, either . . . or, not only . . . but also*, and lists whether long or short.

For example:

- I looked for the dog *under the sofa, in the garage*, and *in the backyard.*

- I asked my mother for a snack, went to my room, and started to study.

Remember the following rules:

- **Rule:** A conjunction is a connective word joining two clauses or phrases.

- **Rule:** Two independent clauses in a sentence must be connected logically.

- **Rule:** Phrases and clauses in a sentence must be connected logically.

For example, compare these two sentences.

> My hobbies include swimming, gardening, and to read science fiction.

> My hobbies include swimming, gardening, and reading science fiction.

In the first sentence, two of the hobbies use the *-ing* gerund form, but the third uses a different structure—the infinitive. The sentence is not parallel. In the second version, all three hobbies correctly use the same *-ing* form, creating a balanced sentence.

PERFECT SCORE TIP

" Taking the first item in a list and then comparing it to the others was an easy way for me to catch parallel structure problems. "

PARALLEL STRUCTURE

Use parallel structure with connective phrases such as *neither . . . nor* and lists.

Two kinds of parallel construction errors are used over and over again on the Writing section. The first occurs in sentences with pairs of connective words that require parallelism. These connective words include those in the following list.

> neither . . . nor
>
> either . . . or
>
> both . . . and

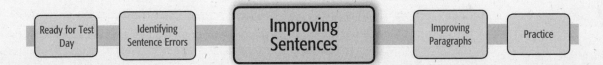

the better . . . the better

the more . . . the more (or less)

not only . . . but also

In the sentence below, look at that first pair of words, *neither . . . nor*, and the phrases that follow both words.

> Nineteenth-century nihilists were concerned with neither the origins of philosophical thought nor how societal laws developed.

The phrases following the words *neither* and *nor* must be parallel in grammatical structure. That is, if a noun phrase (*the origins of philosophical thought*) follows *neither*, then a noun phrase must follow *nor* too. But here *nor* is followed by *how societal laws developed*—a dependent clause. The two parts of the sentence are not grammatically parallel.

In this example, the dependent clause must be rewritten as a noun phrase (*nor the development of societal laws*) to make the sentence parallel. Now both connective words are followed by a noun and a prepositional phrase. The sentence now has proper parallel construction.

 ## COMMON ERROR 5: FAULTY TRANSITIONS IN CLAUSES AND PHRASES

These errors occur when sentence clauses are joined incorrectly. The FANBOYS appeared in Identifying Sentence Errors (page 69). They are back because they can be incorrect in context. The SAT may insert a *but* into a sentence that should have an *and* instead. You'll need to be on the lookout for these situations. Identify the conjunction in the following sentence. Why does it fail to connect the clauses logically?

KEY POINT

> Don't forget the conjunctions that connect two independent clauses. Don't pick one that doesn't make sense in context (for example, *and* instead of *but*).

Besides the FANBOYS conjunctions, other things connect phrases and dependent clauses to their independent neighbors. You must be alert to a poor connection in these cases as well.

Some of the most common connectors are:

- **Similarity:** *like, as, as if, as though, just as, as well as*
- **Continuation:** *plus, in addition*
- **Cause and Effect:** *because, since, due to, as a result of, as a consequence*
- **Contrast:** *while, though, although, nevertheless, rather than, despite*
- **Emphasis:** *in fact, indeed*

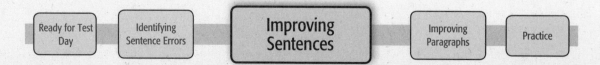

Ready for Test Day | Identifying Sentence Errors | **Improving Sentences** | Improving Paragraphs | Practice

Faulty coordination and faulty subordination are closely related, but they require separate explanations.

Coordination between two clauses is faulty if it doesn't express the logical relation between the clauses. Often, this error involves a misused conjunction. A conjunction is a connective word joining two clauses or phrases in one sentence. The most common conjunctions are:

> and
>
> but
>
> because
>
> however
>
> for
>
> or

Identify the conjunction in the following sentence. Why does it fail to connect the clauses logically?

> Ben Franklin was a respected and talented statesman, and he was most famous for his discovery of electricity.

To identify and correct the faulty coordination, determine what the relationship between the sentence's two clauses really is. Does the conjunction *and* best express the relationship between the two facts the writer states about Ben Franklin? *And* normally expresses a consistency between two equally emphasized facts. However, the fact that Franklin is best known for his discovery of electricity is presented in contrast to the fact that he was a talented statesman. Thus, the use of *and* is an error in coordination.

A better way to connect these two contrasting ideas would be to use the conjunction *but*, which indicates some contrast between the two clauses. In this sentence, *but* points to a common expectation. An individual usually distinguishes herself or himself in one field of accomplishment—in politics or in science—but not in both. So Franklin's distinction in two diverse fields seems to contradict common expectations and calls for a *but*.

Faulty subordination is most often found on the Writing section in a group of words that contains two or more subordinate, or dependent, clauses but no independent clause. There are several connective words that, when introducing a sentence or clause, always indicate that the phrase that follows is dependent, or subordinate. They are as follows:

> since
>
> because

EXPERT TUTOR TIP

" Most often these types of questions are testing *contrast* vs. *continuation/conclusion*. If you see one of these phrases or clauses underlined, ask yourself: Is this contrast or continuation? Do I need to make it the other? "

PERFECT SCORE TIP

" Kaplan's method of taking out the conjunction made it easier to see what the relationship between two clauses was. It was really easy to pick the best conjunction after doing that! "

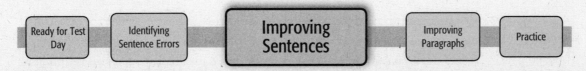

so that

if

Whenever a dependent clause begins a sentence, an independent clause must follow somewhere in the sentence. Look at the group of words below and identify the faulty subordination.

> Since the small electronics industry is one of the world's fastest growing sectors, because demand for the computer chip continues to be high.

Since indicates that the first clause in the group of words is subordinate and needs to be followed by an independent clause. But *because* in the second clause indicates that the second clause is also subordinate. The sentence is faulty because there is no independent clause to make the group of words grammatically complete. Result: two sentence fragments. The second connective word *because* should be eliminated to make the group of words a complete and logical sentence. With this revision, the *since* clause expresses a cause, and the independent clause expresses an effect or result.

 ## WORDINESS: IT'S EVERYWHERE

One of the most important concepts in the Improving Sentences (and Improving Paragraphs) section is wordiness. You'll find this style problem everywhere you look: in the questions themselves and in many wrong answers. As such, wordiness isn't a stand-alone error. It's an invasive weed that wends its way through these two parts of the multiple-choice section and into Improving Paragraphs too.

KEY POINT

> A sentence that uses more words than necessary to make its point may not contain any *grammatical* errors, but it does contain a *style* error: wordiness.

For example, can you find three areas that can be trimmed in the following sentence?

> At this point in time, we are meeting for the purpose of deciding that we have the ability to choose a charity.

At this point in time = now
for the purpose of deciding = to decide
have the ability to = can

| Ready for Test Day | Identifying Sentence Errors | **Improving Sentences** | Improving Paragraphs | Practice |

In this concise version, 4 words replace 14 in the above example. Elsewhere in the SAT you may find sentences that *take into consideration*, instead of *consider*, or discuss an *annual* parade that takes place *every year*.

Take care as you go through the multiple-choice questions that you avoid all redundancies (e.g., the *parade* example) and excessive wordiness, such as the following example. As you read these, note how much easier it is to understand the concise version.

WORDY:

I am of the opinion that the aforementioned managers should be advised that they will be evaluated with regard to the utilization of responsive organizational software for the purpose of devising a responsive network of customers.

CONCISE:

We should tell the managers that we will evaluate their use of flexible computerized databases to develop a customers' network.

IMPROVING PARAGRAPHS QUESTIONS AND HOW TO AVOID COMMON MISTAKES

As the title implies, these questions (a total of six on the test) follow a single, short essay. You don't need to worry much about the content to answer the questions correctly:

- About three will be standard grammar and style questions presented in the previous Improving Sentences section.

- The other three will test your understanding of the overall paragraph(s). Here, context is critical and you'll need to know the gist of the passage:

  - What is the best transition sentence to start a new paragraph?

  - What is the best way to combine two poorly worded sentences or fragments?

You'll face the following question types:

- Content-related Wording questions

- Sentence Revision questions

- Combining Sentences questions

- Paragraph Transition questions

> **EXPERT TUTOR TIP**
>
> " Don't assume that wordy, hard to understand sentences are correct because they sound "smarter." Proofread multiple-choice questions for wordiness just like you would proofread your essay for wordiness. "

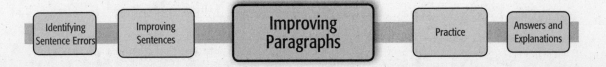

Identifying Sentence Errors | Improving Sentences | **Improving Paragraphs** | Practice | Answers and Explanations

KAPLAN'S TARGET STRATEGY FOR IMPROVING PARAGRAPHS

Kaplan's Target Strategy works for all three kinds of Improving Paragraphs questions.

Step 1. Read the passage for the overall idea and tone.

Step 2. Read the question.

Step 3. Reread (if necessary) relevant portion and its context.

Step 4. Predict the correction.

Step 5. Check for a match that doesn't introduce a new error.

STEP 1. SKIM THE PASSAGE FOR THE OVERALL IDEA AND TONE

Read the entire essay quickly. Get a sense of the essay's overall main idea, as well as the main idea of each paragraph. This will come in handy when you're asked to answer questions about the essay as a whole.

STEP 2. READ THE QUESTION

Now read the question closely. Make sure that you understand exactly what you're asked to do. Questions that require you to revise or combine sentences will supply you with the sentence numbers. Questions that ask about the entire essay generally won't refer to specific sentences.

STEP 3. REREAD THE RELEVANT PORTION AND ITS CONTEXT

Go back and reread that sentence or two that the question is about. But don't stop there. This next part is very important! Also *reread the sentences before and after the target sentence(s).* This will provide you with the context (the surrounding ideas or information) for the sentence(s). Context helps you to choose the best answer from the answer choices.

Note: For those questions about the essay as a whole, skim quickly over the entire essay to refamiliarize yourself with its contents.

STEP 4. PREDICT THE CORRECTION

Say in your head what you think the correct sentence or answer should be.

STEP 5. CHECK FOR A MATCH THAT DOESN'T INTRODUCE A NEW ERROR

Go to the answer choices and pick the choice that best matches the sentence or idea in your head. Make sure the one you pick doesn't introduce a new mistake if you are correcting a sentence.

EXPERT TUTOR TIP

 If you're looking to save some time, read the passage quickly and jump right to the questions, which often repeat the key piece you need.

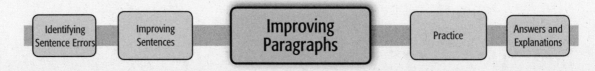
Identifying Sentence Errors | Improving Sentences | **Improving Paragraphs** | Practice | Answers and Explanations

So, to summarize: read the essay quickly; read the question; reread the target sentences and the sentences that surround them; make up a sentence that would eliminate the mistake; and choose the answer choice that best matches your sentence.

The practice set at the end of this chapter will help you get a handle on this approach.

EXPERT TUTOR TIP

"Keep in mind that errors often have multiple possible corrections. Don't be so intent upon finding the correction that you predicted that you miss other valid corrections."

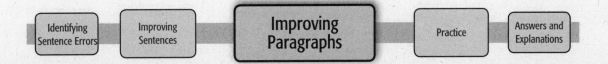

Identifying Sentence Errors — Improving Sentences — **Improving Paragraphs** — Practice — Answers and Explanations

PRACTICE

Use everything you have learned about Identifying Sentence Errors questions, Improving Sentences questions, and Improving Paragraphs questions to answer the questions in the practice set that follows. All of the questions are similar to the ones that will be on the SAT.

For the questions you get wrong, reread the part of this chapter that covers the specific question type. Make sure you understand all the strategies from this chapter.

1. Since the government <u>was</u> bankrupt, many of
                A

   the soldiers <u>which</u> were sent <u>to quell</u> the riots
            B   C

   had <u>not been</u> paid in months. <u>No error</u>
        D   E

2. Although <u>they had been</u> political rivals on
          A

   <u>more than one</u> occasion, John Quincy Adams
     B

   <u>remained</u> one of Thomas Jefferson's closest
     C

   friends until <u>his</u> death. <u>No error</u>
           D   E

3. Even <u>those who</u> profess <u>to care</u> about "green"
        A   B

   issues often fail to consider <u>how</u> their daily
                     C

   choices <u>effect</u> the environment. <u>No error</u>
         D   E

4. Ants, <u>which</u> have inhabited the earth for at
       A

   least 100 million years, <u>are without doubt</u> the
                    B

   <u>more successful</u> of all the social insects of the
       C

   Hymenoptera, an order <u>that also</u> includes
                 D

   wasps and bees. <u>No error</u>
               E

5. For my sister and <u>I</u>, the trip to Paris was the
               A

   <u>fulfillment</u> of a lifelong wish we <u>had scarcely</u>
       B   C

   <u>dared to express</u>. <u>No error</u>
      D   E

6. The volunteers, <u>upon discovering</u> that
               A

   <u>a large number</u> of the village children <u>were</u>
       B   C

   infected by parasites <u>from</u> unclean drinking
                 D

   water, decided to make the well-digging

   project their highest priority. <u>No error</u>
                        E

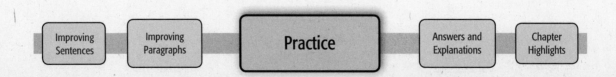

7. Although farmers complained that the
   company's new product was expensive,
   malodorous, and <u>dangerous to handle,</u>
                              A
   <u>there was</u> few who <u>would dispute</u> its
        B   C
   effectiveness <u>as</u> an insecticide. <u>No error</u>
                     D   E

8. In the wake <u>of</u> recent thefts, the town's
                    A
   wealthier residents <u>have installed</u> gates, alarm
                              B
   systems, and even video surveillance
   equipment in their neighborhoods, hoping
   <u>that it will</u> prevent <u>further burglaries</u>. <u>No error</u>
        C   D   E

9. <u>To repair</u> the damage <u>that</u> time and the
      A   B
   elements <u>had wrought</u> on the ancient fresco,
                  C
   the restorer used a simple mixture <u>from</u>
                                            D
   plaster, pigment, and a little water. <u>No error</u>
                                              E

10. Opponents of the act <u>argued that</u> the
                              A
    legislation <u>was not only</u> vaguely formulated
                     B
    and unconstitutional, but also impossible
    <u>to enforce</u> in an international <u>and virtually</u>
        C   D
    unregulated arena. <u>No error</u>
                            E

11. One reason that a growing number of people
    <u>have no</u> family doctor <u>may be that</u> fewer and
        A   B
    fewer medical students <u>are choosing to train</u> as
                                  C
    <u>a general practitioner.</u> <u>No error</u>
              D   E

12. <u>That</u> J. L. Solomon's first novel <u>was selected for</u>
      A   B
    several major literary prizes <u>was surprising to</u>
                                        C
    no one who had read his <u>previous</u> collections
                                  D
    of short stories, poems, and essays. <u>No error</u>
                                              E

13. Citizens <u>protesting</u> the planned demolition of
                  A
    the historic YMCA building claim <u>that without</u>
                                            B
    the YMCA, many young people in the town
    <u>would of</u> grown up <u>with no</u> access to sports
        C   D
    facilities and no place for after-school
    recreation. <u>No error</u>
                     E

14. When questioned, <u>a surprising</u> number of
                          A
    fifth-graders said that telling the truth—even
    <u>if it</u> meant <u>being</u> punished—was preferable
        B   C
    <u>than living</u> with a lie. <u>No error</u>
        D   E

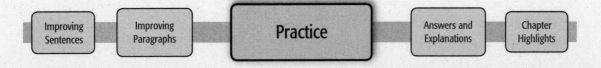

Improving Sentences | Improving Paragraphs | **Practice** | Answers and Explanations | Chapter Highlights

15. <u>Though</u> Patricia's résumé was <u>not nearly as</u>
    A   B

    long and impressive as <u>the other applicant,</u>
                           C

    her personal charisma was <u>so great that</u>
                              D

    Mr. Alvarez hired her on the spot. <u>No error</u>
                                       E

16. <u>Under</u> the proposed law, which many <u>deem</u>
    A   B

    too harsh, any motorist <u>convicted of</u> drunk
                            C

    driving would spend thirty days in prison and

    lose <u>their license</u> for five years. <u>No error</u>
         D   E

17. When <u>it became apparent</u> to Clive that not one
         A

    of the remaining jurors <u>were going to</u> believe
                            B

    his <u>client's</u> alibi, he began to reconsider the
        C

    district attorney's <u>offer of a</u> plea bargain.
                        D

    <u>No error</u>
    E

18. <u>If only</u> the factory owners <u>had conducted</u>
    A   B

    regular safety inspections <u>of</u> their equipment,
                               C

    the horrible accident of 1969 <u>may have been</u>
                                  D

    averted. <u>No error</u>
             E

19. The symphony <u>had not</u> hardly begun <u>when</u> a
                 A   B

    group of schoolchildren, who <u>had been forced</u>
                                 C

    to attend, began irritating the rest of the

    audience <u>by talking loudly</u> and kicking the
             D

    seats. <u>No error</u>
           E

20. The gods of Greek mythology, who

    <u>were neither</u> omniscient nor <u>particularly</u>
    A   B

    ethical, amused themselves <u>by taking on</u>
                               C

    disguises and <u>meddling</u> in the affairs of
                  D

    mortals. <u>No error</u>
             E

21. Fast food chains are <u>among the most</u> ubiquitous
                        A

    restaurants in our town; <u>they welcome</u> everyone
                             B

    with no <u>distinction between</u> <u>you and me</u>, teachers
            C   D

    and students, or parents and kids. <u>No error</u>
                                       E

22. <u>Like other gourmet restaurants</u>, M. Dubois
    A

    creates magnificent meals <u>in which</u> <u>he likes</u>
                              B   C

    <u>to use</u> only the finest ingredients. <u>No error</u>
    D   E

23. *High Fidelity*, a successful book and film, <u>became</u>
                                                    A

    <u>successful</u> as a cult classic because of its sharp wit
       B

    and <u>by presenting</u> a quirky main character,
           C

    Rob, <u>as a common man</u>. <u>No error</u>
              D   E

24. Often <u>believed to be</u> <u>dangerous and dirty places</u>
               A   B

    where tourists <u>were</u> always mugged, New York
                     C

    City <u>has been reforming</u> its image radically with
          D

    dropping crime rates over the past few years.

    <u>No error</u>
     E

25. <u>To understand</u> the current Russian government,
     A

    <u>we have to be</u> <u>highly aware</u> of the theory and
        B   C

    history of communism, whether or not one

    <u>agrees with</u> its tenets. <u>No error</u>
     D   E

26. Bill <u>had hoped</u> to go to the baseball game
          A

    <u>that night,</u> but as the afternoon wore on, he
     B

    realized he <u>would have to work</u> late <u>to meet</u> his
                 C   D

    deadline. <u>No error</u>
                E

27. The process <u>of learning new languages</u> <u>require</u> a
                      A   B

    commitment to memorization and

    pronunciation practice, <u>even if</u> progress
                             C

    <u>seems slow</u>. <u>No error</u>
     D   E

28. Jane Eyre <u>could not marry</u> Mr. Rochester <u>until</u>
                 A   B

    the <u>fateful</u> night when Grace Poole <u>set</u> the
         C   D

    mansion ablaze. <u>No error</u>
                     E

29. <u>Widely divergent</u> opinions <u>could be heard</u> from
     A   B

    the audience as the planning commission

    unveiled <u>their</u> proposal <u>for a remodeled</u>
              C   D

    city square. <u>No error</u>
                  E

30. The advisory board <u>cautioned</u> employees that
                        A

    the <u>existing</u> program of <u>health benefits</u> <u>were</u>
         B   C   D

    likely to be eliminated. <u>No error</u>
                              E

31. <u>The runners coming this far, they</u> decided to
    push through the very strenuous final miles
    of the marathon.

    (A) The runners coming this far, they
    (B) Although they came this far, the runners
    (C) Having come this far, the runners
    (D) To come this far, the runners
    (E) The runners came this far; so that they

Improving Sentences   Improving Paragraphs   **Practice**   Answers and Explanations   Chapter Highlights

32. Our English teacher handed out the worksheet, and we started filling in the answers quickly, and we continued to do so until the bell rang.

   (A) Our English teacher handed out the worksheet, and we started filling in the answers quickly, and we continued to do so until the bell rang.
   (B) Upon starting to fill in the answers quickly after we were given the worksheet by our English teacher, we continued to do so until the bell rang.
   (C) Following our English teacher's giving us the worksheet, we started filling in the answers quickly and continued doing just that until the bell rang.
   (D) After our English teacher gave us the worksheet, we filled in the answers quickly until the bell rang.
   (E) We filled in the answers quickly until the bell rang when the worksheet had been given to us by our English teacher.

33. Some of the classes taught in American classrooms are interpretations of lessons used worldwide, particularly those in European history.

   (A) classrooms are interpretations of lessons used worldwide, particularly those in European history
   (B) classrooms, there are interpretations of lessons used worldwide, particularly European history
   (C) classrooms, and in particular European history, is an interpretation of lessons used worldwide
   (D) classrooms, particularly in European history, are interpretations of lessons used worldwide
   (E) classrooms being interpretations, European history in particular, of those used worldwide

34. Olga Korbut, a Soviet gymnast, whose fame as an athlete on the Olympic stage almost equals that of Nadia Comaneci.

   (A) Olga Korbut, a Soviet gymnast, whose fame as an athlete
   (B) Olga Korbut, who was a Soviet gymnast and whose fame as an athlete
   (C) A Soviet with fame as an Olympic athlete, Olga Korbut
   (D) Olga Korbut was a Soviet gymnast whose fame as an athlete
   (E) A Soviet, Olga Korbut who was a gymnast and whose fame

35. Many parents believe that extreme sports are too dangerous, consequently, some of those parents do not allow their children to bungee jump.

   (A) dangerous, consequently, some of those parents do not allow
   (B) dangerous, therefore, some of those parents do not allow
   (C) dangerous; consequently, some do not allow
   (D) dangerous, some people do not allow
   (E) dangerous, and therefore not allowing

36. Although its being fictional in form, the new book on America raises many historical questions.

   (A) Although its being fictional in form
   (B) Despite its fictional form
   (C) Whereas it was fictional in form
   (D) Its form being fictional
   (E) Even though fictional form was there

37. The novels of Louisa May Alcott are sought out by each new generation of readers <u>considering that her books blend both wild youthfulness and a rational side</u>.

   (A) considering that her books blend both wild youthfulness and a rational side

   (B) considering that her books blend both wild youthfulness and rationality

   (C) because her books blend wild youthfulness and rationality

   (D) because her books will blend not only wild youthfulness but also a rational side

   (E) being that her books will blend both wild youthfulness and rationality

38. Joann, the newest student at Leon Blum High School, has been portrayed as <u>the brightest student and also the most unruly of them</u>.

   (A) the brightest student and also the most unruly of them

   (B) not only the brightest student, but also more unruly than any

   (C) the brightest student at the same time as she is the most unruly student

   (D) at once the brightest and also the most unruly of them

   (E) the brightest and yet the most unruly of students

39. Anaelle's parents explained that she was promoted to head journalist <u>for the reason that her articles were mindful always for both sides of the issues</u>.

   (A) for the reason that her articles were mindful always for both sides of the issues

   (B) since her articles for issues were always mindful of both sides

   (C) because her mindfulness of both sides of the issues was always in her articles

   (D) for the fact being that her articles were always mindful about both sides of the issues

   (E) because her articles were always mindful of both sides of the issues

40. Of all the countries in the UN Security Council, <u>the representative of China was the only one to speak</u> to the General Assembly today.

   (A) the representative of China was the only one to speak

   (B) making the representative from China the only one to speak

   (C) China's representative only spoke

   (D) China's governor spoke only

   (E) China was the only one whose representative spoke

41. Patients with Alzheimer's disease typically exhibit symptoms such as confusion, memory loss, <u>and their language skills are impaired</u>.

   (A) and their language skills are impaired

   (B) and it also impairs their language skills

   (C) and impaired language skills

   (D) besides their language skills being impaired

   (E) in addition to their language skills being impaired

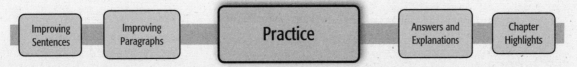

Improving Sentences | Improving Paragraphs | **Practice** | Answers and Explanations | Chapter Highlights

42. <u>Upon entering the jail, the prisoners' personal belongings are surrendered to the guards.</u>

   (A) Upon entering the jail, the prisoners' personal belongings are surrendered to the guards.
   (B) Upon entering the jail, the prisoners surrender their personal belongings to the guards.
   (C) The prisoners' personal belongings having been surrendered to the guards upon entering the jail.
   (D) Upon entering the jail, the guards are to whom the prisoners surrender their personal belongings.
   (E) Upon entering the jail, the prisoners will have been surrendering their personal belongings to the guards.

43. <u>The albatross has a broad wingspan, it is graceful in the air but ungainly on dry land.</u>

   (A) The albatross has a broad wingspan, it is graceful in the air but ungainly on dry land.
   (B) The albatross, with its broad wingspan, is graceful in the air but ungainly on dry land.
   (C) Having a broad wingspan, the albatross is graceful in the air, however it is ungainly on dry land.
   (D) The albatross, which has a broad wingspan, graceful in the air but ungainly on dry land.
   (E) The albatross, although having a broad wingspan, is graceful in the air but ungainly on dry land.

44. King John of England is remembered not so much for his administrative successes <u>but for failing in</u> <u>military engagements</u>.

   (A) but for failing in military engagements
   (B) but more for the fact that he failed in military engagements
   (C) than he was for having failed militarily
   (D) the reason being that he failed in military engagements
   (E) as for his military failures

45. According to older fishermen, cod and haddock were once plentiful in the North Sea, but years of overfishing and pollution have <u>had a negative overall impact on the fish stocks</u>.

   (A) had a negative overall impact on the fish stocks
   (B) impacted the fish stocks negatively
   (C) the result that the fish stocks are diminished
   (D) depleted the fish stocks
   (E) been depleting the fish stocks overall

46. <u>During the winter months, several feet of snow cover the narrow mountain pass, which is the only route to the monastery.</u>

   (A) During the winter months, several feet of snow cover the narrow mountain pass, which is the only route to the monastery.
   (B) The only route to the monastery, several feet of snow cover the narrow mountain pass during the winter months.
   (C) Several feet of snow cover the narrow mountain pass during the winter months which is the only route to the monastery.
   (D) Several feet of snow cover the narrow mountain pass, which is the only route to the monastery during the winter months.
   (E) During the winter months, covering the narrow mountain pass which is the only route to the monastery is snow.

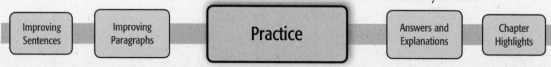

Improving Sentences · Improving Paragraphs · **Practice** · Answers and Explanations · Chapter Highlights

47. The Townshend Acts, a piece of British legislation enacted on June 29, 1767, <u>were intended for the raising of revenue, to tighten customs enforcement, and assert</u> imperial authority in America.

   (A) were intended for the raising of revenue, to tighten customs enforcement, and assert

   (B) were intended to raise revenue, tighten customs enforcement, and assert

   (C) were with the intention of raising revenue, tightening customs enforcement, and assert

   (D) had for their intention the raising of revenue, tightening of customs enforcement, and asserting

   (E) were intended to raise revenue, also to tighten customs enforcement and assert

48. The border crossing proved more unpleasant than the two American reporters had <u>expected, having their cameras seized</u> and their tape recorders smashed by belligerent soldiers.

   (A) expected, having their cameras seized

   (B) expected, their cameras being seized

   (C) expected: their cameras were seized

   (D) expected; when their cameras were seized

   (E) expected and so their cameras had been seized

49. <u>Without the warming effects of the Gulf Stream, England's climate would resemble that of Greenland.</u>

   (A) Without the warming effects of the Gulf Stream, England's climate would resemble that of Greenland.

   (B) Had the Gulf Stream not such warming effects, England's climate would resemble Greenland.

   (C) Without the warming effects of the Gulf Stream, England's climate were resembling Greenland's.

   (D) If not for the warming effects of the Gulf Stream, therefore England's climate would have resembled that of Greenland.

   (E) If the Gulf Stream would not have had its warming effects, England's climate would resemble that of Greenland.

50. Perhaps best known for his portrayal of T. E. Lawrence in the film *Lawrence of Arabia*, <u>Peter O'Toole's distinguished acting career spans nearly five decades</u>.

   (A) Peter O'Toole's distinguished acting career spans nearly five decades

   (B) Peter O'Toole has a distinguished acting career spanning nearly five decades

   (C) Peter O'Toole spans nearly five decades in his distinguished acting career

   (D) Peter O'Toole's distinguished acting career will have spanned nearly five decades

   (E) nearly five decades have been spanned by Peter O'Toole's distinguished acting career

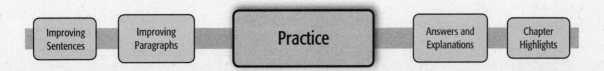

Improving Sentences | Improving Paragraphs | Practice | Answers and Explanations | Chapter Highlights

51. In their haste to complete the new stadium before the Olympic games, the contractors disregarded safety <u>codes, thereby they endangered the lives of thousands of spectators</u>.

    (A) codes, thereby they endangered the lives of thousands of spectators

    (B) codes they have endangered the lives of thousands of spectators

    (C) codes and thus endangered the lives of thousands of spectators

    (D) codes; thus the lives of thousands of spectators endangered

    (E) codes, they endangered the lives of thousands of spectators as a result

52. When Dr. Park presented an abridged version of his paper at the conference, <u>several tantalizing theories about the origins of life on earth were introduced, but these were not fully developed by him</u>.

    (A) several tantalizing theories about the origins of life on earth were introduced, but these were not fully developed by him

    (B) he introduced several tantalizing theories about the origins of life on earth but they had not been fully developed

    (C) several tantalizing theories about the origins of life were introduced by him and not fully developed

    (D) several tantalizing theories about the origins of life on earth were introduced, but he did not fully develop these

    (E) he introduced, but did not fully develop, several tantalizing theories about the origins of life on earth

Questions 53–57 are based on the following essay, which is a response to an assignment to write a letter to a local newspaper protesting cuts in funding for after-school sports programs.

(1) I disagree with the editor's view that after-school sports programs should be cut in our city government's search for ways to reduce spending. (2) The editor argues that extracurricular sports play a less important role than academic studies, distracting students from the opportunity to increase their knowledge after school is out. (3) However, I myself believe that playing sports enhances students' academic performance. (4) Why is sports so effective in this regard? (5) The main reason is that sports teaches people to excel. (6) It gives students the chance to strive for greatness. (7) It shows them that it takes courage and discipline to succeed in competition with others. (8) Top athletes such as Michael Jordan become role models for young people everywhere, inspiring them with his brilliant individual performances. (9) In addition to these personal attributes, playing in team sports show young people how to interact with each other, achieving shared goals. (10) Such principles have a direct impact on how students perform in their academic studies. (11) I know that being selected for the school lacrosse team taught me many valuable lessons about working with others. (12) Not only that, friendships which I have made there were carried into the rest of my school life. (13) In summary, I would urge the editor to strongly reconsider his stance on extracurricular sports. (14) There are doubtless other ways of city government saving the money they require.

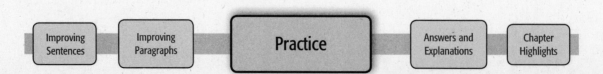

53. Which of the following is the best way to revise the underlined portion of sentence 3 (reproduced below)?

    However, I myself believe that playing sports enhances students' academic performance.

    (A) However, I myself believe that playing sports should enhance
    (B) Playing sports, however, I believe enhances
    (C) However, I personally believe that playing sports enhances
    (D) I believe, however, that playing sports enhances
    (E) However, I myself believe that to play sports is to enhance

54. Which of the following is the best way to revise and combine sentences 6 and 7 (reproduced below)?

    It gives students the chance to strive for greatness. It shows them that it takes courage and discipline to succeed in competition with others.

    (A) Although it gives students the chance to strive for greatness, it also shows them that it takes courage and discipline to succeed in competition with others.
    (B) While it gives students the chance to strive for greatness, also showing them that it takes courage and discipline to succeed in competition with others.
    (C) It gives students the chance to strive for greatness, showing them that it takes courage and discipline to succeed in competition with others.
    (D) Because it gives students the chance to strive for greatness, they are shown that it takes courage and discipline to succeed in competition with others.
    (E) It gives students the chance to strive for greatness and show them that it takes courage and discipline to succeed in competition with others.

55. In the context of the second paragraph, which of the following is the best version of the underlined portion of sentence 8 (reproduced below)?

    Top athletes such as Michael Jordan become role models for young people everywhere, inspiring them with his brilliant individual performances.

    (A) (As it is now)
    (B) inspiring him with their
    (C) inspiring them with their
    (D) to inspire them with his
    (E) inspiring him with his

56. Which of the following is the best way to revise the underlined portion of sentence 12 (reproduced below)?

    Not only that, friendships which I have made there were carried into the rest of my school life.

    (A) And,
    (B) Moreover,
    (C) Nevertheless,
    (D) Sequentially,
    (E) Finally,

57. The author could best improve sentence 14 (reproduced below) by

    There are doubtless other ways of city government saving the money they require.

    (A) making an analogy to historical events
    (B) taking alternative points of view into account
    (C) including a personal anecdote about her participation in team sports
    (D) speculating about the motivations of those advocating cuts
    (E) providing examples of other areas in which spending could be reduced

Improving Sentences | Improving Paragraphs | **Practice** | Answers and Explanations | Chapter Highlights

Questions 58–61 are based on the following passage.

(1) Until recently, I was convinced I had no musical ability whatsoever. (2) In grade school, I could hardly keep my voice in tune with other singers around me. (3) I thought that I would never play a musical instrument or become a rock star. (4) I really enjoyed music, just no one thought I had any talent at all.

(5) When I entered junior high I took music classes with our teacher, Mr. Daniels. (6) At first he seemed really stern and strict. (7) He gave us lots of warnings that even though he had a reputation for being harsh around school, the reality was ten times worse. (8) But after a couple of weeks, he started encouraging us to get into musical ensembles. (9) At first I was disinterested, thinking that I would be ridiculed as to my contribution. (10) Mr. Daniels kept insisted that everyone had to play some kind of instrument, so I chose his handbell choir. (11) Other kids thought handbells were stupid, but I liked the sound they made—it was so much purer than the electric guitar. (12) Mr. Daniels coached us regular after school. (13) Not only did the group actually start to sound good, but also I discovered that I had some rhythmic talents that no one had suspected. (14) Maybe I will be a rock star yet! (15) The whole experience showed me that with encouragement and a sense of adventure you can overcome your limitations. (16) As our former First Lady Eleanor Roosevelt once said, sometimes "you must do that which you think you cannot do."

58. Which of the following versions of sentence 4 (reproduced below) is best?

    I really enjoyed music, just no one thought I had any talent at all.

    (A) (As it is now)
    (B) Even though I really enjoyed music, just no one thought I had any talent at all.
    (C) I really enjoyed music, and therefore no one thought I had any talent at all.
    (D) Although I really enjoyed music, no one thought I had any talent at all.
    (E) The music was enjoyable to me, however no one thought I had any talent at all.

59. Which of the following sentences, if added after sentence 4, would best link the first paragraph with the rest of the essay?

    (A) As a result, I learned that other people's opinions are irrelevant.
    (B) However, I soon met an inspiring person who disproved this assumption.
    (C) This was why no one thought I would become a rock star.
    (D) Nevertheless, I knew all along that I possessed a form of musical genius.
    (E) I have held these beliefs about my musical ability for many years.

60. In the context of the second paragraph, which of the following is the best version of the underlined portion of sentence 11 (reproduced below)?

    Other kids thought handbells were stupid, but I liked the sound they made—it was so much purer than the electric guitar.

    (A) (As it is now)
    (B) it was so much more pure than the electric guitar
    (C) the sound of it was so much purer than the electric guitar
    (D) compared to the electric guitar, its sound was so much purer
    (E) it was so much purer than the sound of the electric guitar

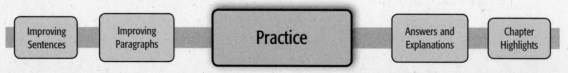

Improving Sentences   Improving Paragraphs   **Practice**   Answers and Explanations   Chapter Highlights

61. Which of the following is the best version of the underlined portion of sentence 13 (reproduced below)?

    Not only did the group actually start to sound good, but also I discovered that I had some rhythmic talents that no one had suspected.

    (A) (As it is now)
    (B) The group actually started
    (C) While the group actually started
    (D) Not only was the group actually starting
    (E) Although the group was actually starting

Questions 62–67 are based on the following passage.

(1) Despite his early death at 35, Austrian composer Wolfgang Amadeus Mozart is one the most famous musicians in history for three reasons. (2) He was extraordinarily talented, he was exposed to music at an early age, and his love of it. (3) Mozart's talent showed early. (4) At age seven, he was already writing sonatas for the harpsichord. (5) He could improvise music at the keyboard and played any piece of music in any style—even when blindfolded!

(6) Mozart was always encouraged and even driven by his father. (7) Leopold Mozart was a composer, and Wolfgang learned to play and read music when he was a small child. (8) To establish his son early and build a path for his future career, he lost no time showing him off to audiences. (9) He arranged for six-year-old Wolfgang to play in the palaces of most of the major European cities. (10) Leopold Mozart determining that his gifted son should reap the rewards his talent deserved.

(11) And Mozart loved music. (12) As a child, Leopold was often surprised with tunes his son had written. (13) Some of these little pieces were so technically challenging that although Wolfgang could play them easily, his father's adult friends and colleagues could not play them at all! (14) He once wrote that composing music was such

a delight to him that he could not describe it in words.

62. In context, what is the best way to revise and combine sentences 1 and 2 (reproduced below)?

    Despite his early death at 35, Austrian composer Wolfgang Amadeus Mozart is one the most famous musicians in history for three reasons. He was extraordinarily talented, he was exposed to music at an early age, and his love of it.

    (A) Despite his early death at 35, Austrian composer Wolfgang Amadeus Mozart is one the most famous musicians in history for three reasons: he was extraordinarily talented, he was exposed to music at an early age, and he loved it.
    (B) Despite his early death at 35, Austrian composer Wolfgang Amadeus Mozart is one the most famous musicians in history for three reasons, this is because he was extraordinarily talented, he was exposed to music at an early age, and his love of it.
    (C) Despite his early death at 35 years of age, Austrian composer Wolfgang Amadeus Mozart is one the most famous musicians in history for the following three reasons: he was extraordinarily talented, he was exposed to music at an early age, and he loved it.
    (D) Despite his death at 35, which was early, Austrian composer Wolfgang Amadeus Mozart is one the most famous musicians in history for three reasons: that he was extraordinarily talented, that he was exposed to music at an early age, and that he had a love of it.
    (E) Despite his early death at 35, Austrian composer Wolfgang Amadeus Mozart is one the most famous musicians in history for three reasons: he was extraordinarily talented, he was exposed to music at an early age, and his love of it.

Improving Sentences · Improving Paragraphs · **Practice** · Answers and Explanations · Chapter Highlights

63. In context, which revision is needed in sentence 5?

    (A) No revision is needed.
    (B) Replace "He" with "Mozart."
    (C) Replace "could improvise" with "could have improvised."
    (D) Replace "played" with "play."
    (E) Eliminate the phrase "in any style."

64. In context, which is the best version of sentence 8 (reproduced below)?

    To establish his son early and build a path for his future career, he lost no time showing him off to audiences.

    (A) (As it is now)
    (B) To establish his son early and build a path for his future career, Leopold Mozart lost no time showing him off to audiences.
    (C) To establish Wolfgang early and build a path for his future career, he lost no time showing him off to audiences.
    (D) To establish his son early and build a path for his future career, he lost no time showing Wolfgang off to audiences.
    (E) To establish his son early and build a path for his future career, Mozart lost no time showing him off to audiences.

65. In context, what revision is necessary in sentence 10?

    (A) No revision is necessary.
    (B) Change "determining" to "determines."
    (C) Change "determining" to "determined."
    (D) Change "determining" to "having determined."
    (E) Change "should reap" to "should be reaping."

66. In context, what is the best version of sentence 12 (reproduced below)?

    As a child, Leopold was often surprised with tunes his son had written

    (A) As a child, the tunes his son had written often surprised Leopold.
    (B) As a child, his son often surprised Leopold with tunes he had written.
    (C) As a child, surprising Leopold with tunes he had written was his son.
    (D) Leopold was often surprised with tunes that, as a child, his son had written.
    (E) Tunes written by his son as a child often surprised Leopold.

67. Sentence 14 would make the most sense if placed after

    (A) sentence 1
    (B) sentence 2
    (C) sentence 11
    (D) sentence 12
    (E) sentence 13

Improving Sentences   Improving Paragraphs   **Practice**   Answers and Explanations   Chapter Highlights

ANSWERS AND EXPLANATIONS

IDENTIFYING SENTENCE ERRORS QUESTIONS

1. B
SMARTPOINT CATEGORY: PRONOUNS

The relative pronoun *which* refers to the soldiers, but *which* cannot be used to refer to people, only to things. The sentence should use the word *who* instead.

2. D
SMARTPOINT CATEGORY: PRONOUNS

Another pronoun error: in this sentence, it is not clear whether *his* refers to Adams or to Jefferson; hence this sentence contains a vague pronoun reference.

3. D
SMARTPOINT CATEGORY: DICTION

Affect and *effect* are commonly confused words. Here, *affect* (meaning *to influence* or *to have an effect on*) would be the correct word, not *effect*.

4. C
SMARTPOINT CATEGORY: COMPARISONS

Faulty comparison: ants are being compared to all the other social insects in the *Hymenoptera* order. Since this order includes far more than two insect species, the superlative *most successful* should be used instead of the comparative *more successful*.

5. A
SMARTPOINT CATEGORY: PRONOUNS

Take out the words *my sister and*, and the error of pronoun case becomes obvious—you wouldn't say *for I*. Since this pronoun is the object of the preposition *for*, it should be in the objective case: for my sister and *me*.

Improving Paragraphs | Improving Sentences | Practice | **Answers and Explanations** | Chapter Highlights

6. E

SMARTPOINT CATEGORY: FINDING NO ERROR

The sentence contains no error.

(A) is a correct use of a verb gerund, (B) and (D) are correct idiomatically, and (C) agrees with its subject *volunteers*.

7. B

SMARTPOINT CATEGORY: SUBJECT-VERB

In the second half of the sentence, the verb *was* does not agree with its subject, *few. Few* is a plural noun, so the sentence should read *there were few*.

8. C

SMARTPOINT CATEGORY: PRONOUNS

If you look for the antecedent of the pronoun *it* here, you won't find it—this is a case of ambiguous pronoun reference.

9. D

SMARTPOINT CATEGORY: IDIOMS

This is an example of an idiom error. The correct preposition should be *a mixture of, not a mixture from.*

10. E

SMARTPOINT CATEGORY: FINDING NO ERROR

The sentence contains no error.

(A) verb is correct; (B) verb agrees with its subject *legislation.* (C) is a correct idiomatic use of the infinitive *to enforce,* and (D) is a proper use of adverb.

11. D

SMARTPOINT CATEGORY: PARALLELISM

Number agreement problems: since *students* is a plural noun, the second part of the sentence should also be plural: *as general practitioners.*

12. E

SMARTPOINT CATEGORY: FINDING NO ERROR

The sentence contains no error, although the phrasing may have sounded strange to your ear.

(A) *That* may sound odd as a beginning of a sentence, but it is grammatically correct. (B) and (C) are correct as singular verbs with proper idiomatic uses of prepositions *for* and *to*. (D) is correct use of adjective.

13. C

SMARTPOINT CATEGORY: IDIOMS

Nonidiomatic preposition after verb: *would of* is not standard written English, and it makes no sense. The sentence should read *would have grown up.*

14. D

SMARTPOINT CATEGORY: IDIOMS

The correct idiom here should be *preferable to,* not *preferable than.*

15. C

SMARTPOINT CATEGORY: COMPARISONS

The way it's written, *Patricia's résumé* is being compared to the *other applicant*, which is not parallel. *Patricia's résumé* should be compared to the *other applicant's résumé.*

16. D

SMARTPOINT CATEGORY: PRONOUNS
TOPICS: IDIOMS

The pronoun *their* is plural and does not agree in number with its singular antecedent, *motorist.* The sentence should read *his or her license.*

17. B

SMARTPOINT CATEGORY: SUBJECT-VERB

The subject *one* takes a singular verb: *not one* of the jurors *was* going to believe the alibi.

Improving Paragraphs | Improving Sentences | Practice | **Answers and Explanations** | Chapter Highlights

18. D

SMARTPOINT CATEGORY: VERB TENSE

The context makes it clear that the accident was *not* averted; hence the sentence is describing a situation that is contrary to fact. When you know that something *did* happen (but would likely have been avoided if things had been different), *might* is the correct word to use. *May have* suggests that you are not sure whether a thing happened or not: e.g., "I will try Dr. Miller's office, but she may have left already."

19. A

SMARTPOINT CATEGORY: DICTION

Not hardly is a double negative.

20. E

SMARTPOINT CATEGORY: FINDING NO ERROR

The sentence contains no error.

(A) has a plural verb to match *gods* and *neither* that must accompany the *nor* later in the sentence. (B) is a correct use of adverb, and (C) and (D) are parallel and correct use of verb gerunds.

21. E

SMARTPOINT CATEGORY: FINDING NO ERROR

(A) properly uses *among* and *most* in a comparison of more than two items. (B) is the appropriate plural pronoun with the antecedent *fast food chains*. (C) correctly uses *between* to compare two items. (Each compound object of this preposition is separate. Remember, only the conjunction *and* can form a compound; *or* cannot.) (D) correctly uses the objective pronoun form.

22. A

SMARTPOINT CATEGORY: COMPARISONS

Here, *M. Dubois* is being compared to *other gourmet restaurants*. To form a correct comparison, (A) should read *Like chefs in other*. (B) uses the correct pronoun form as the object of the preposition. In (C), *he* is the proper pronoun to refer to M. Dubois, and the verb agrees with its singular subject. (D) makes appropriate use of the infinitive verb form.

Improving Paragraphs | Improving Sentences | Practice | **Answers and Explanations** | Chapter Highlights

23. C

SMARTPOINT CATEGORY: PARALLELISM

Its sharp wit and *by presenting* should have parallel structures, so (C) is incorrect. *High Fidelity* is already a classic, so (A) is correctly in the past tense. (B) properly uses an adjective to modify *High Fidelity*, and (D) is appropriate idiomatic usage.

24. B

SMARTPOINT CATEGORY: PARALLELISM

Dangerous and dirty places in (B) refers to the singular subject in the second clause, *New York City*. Therefore, *places* should also be singular. (A) is correct usage of both the past tense and the infinitive in context. (C) agrees with its plural subject *tourists*. (D) is the appropriate verb tense, since the action is in the recent past and is still occurring (*over the past few years* indicates this).

25. B

SMARTPOINT CATEGORY: PRONOUNS

The singular pronoun *one* is used in the third clause and, since it is not underlined, it cannot be changed. Therefore, the underlined pronoun *we* must be changed because it is inconsistent; the error is in (B). (A) is appropriate use of the infinitive. (C) properly uses an adverb to modify an adjective. (D) uses the appropriate preposition in context.

26. E

SMARTPOINT CATEGORY: FINDING NO ERROR

(A) is correct use of the past perfect to refer to one past action (*Bill had hoped*) that preceded another (*he realized*). (B) is correct idiomatic usage. (C) is an appropriate verb phrase in context. (D) is proper use of the infinitive.

27. B

SMARTPOINT CATEGORY: SUBJECT-VERB

Even though *languages* is closer to the verb *require*, its subject is actually the singular *process*; the error is in (B). (A) and (C) are correct idiomatic usage. (D) is consistent present tense verb use and properly uses the adjective *slow* to modify the noun progress.

Improving Paragraphs · Improving Sentences · Practice · **Answers and Explanations** · Chapter Highlights

28. E

SMARTPOINT CATEGORY: FINDING NO ERROR

This sentence is correct as written. (A) is an appropriate verb phrase in context. (B) is correct preposition usage. (C) properly uses an adjective to modify *night*. (D) agrees with its singular subject *Grace Poole*.

29. C

SMARTPOINT CATEGORY: PRONOUNS

Although a commission is made up of a number of people, the noun itself is singular; (C) should be *its*. (A) appropriately uses an adverb to modify an adjective and an adjective to modify the noun *opinions*. (B) is an appropriate verb phrase in context. (D) uses the idiomatically correct preposition and an adjective to describe *city square*.

30. D

SMARTPOINT CATEGORY: SUBJECT-VERB

Although *benefits* is the closest noun to the verb *were*, the subject of the verb is actually the singular *program*; (D) should be *was*. (A) uses an appropriate verb tense in context. (B) appropriately modifies the noun *program*. (C) is a correctly used prepositional phrase.

IMPROVING SENTENCES QUESTIONS

31. C

SMARTPOINT CATEGORY: RUN-ONS AND FRAGMENTS

As written, this is a run-on sentence. (C) corrects this by making the first clause subordinate. (B) and (D) use transition words that are inappropriate in context. (E) misuses the semicolon splice.

32. D

SMARTPOINT CATEGORY: WORDINESS

As written, this sentence is unnecessarily wordy, and the conjunction *and* merely strings the ideas together, without relating them in any way. (D) corrects both errors. (B) is awkward and introduces the passive voice unnecessarily. (C) is even wordier than the original sentence. (E) is awkward and still too wordy.

33. D

SMARTPOINT CATEGORY: MODIFIERS

As written, it is unclear what noun *particularly those in European history* is intended to modify. (D) corrects this error without adding any other ones. (B) is grammatically incorrect. The singular verb *is* in (C) does not agree with its subject *Some*, which is grammatically plural. (E) is a sentence fragment.

34. D

SMARTPOINT CATEGORY: RUN-ONS AND FRAGMENTS

As written, this sentence is a fragment. (D) adds a predicate verb without introducing any additional errors. (B) and (E) do not address the error. (C) is incorrect grammatical structure.

35. C

SMARTPOINT CATEGORY: RUN-ONS AND FRAGMENTS

As written, this is a run-on sentence. Both clauses are independent, so a comma cannot join them. (C) corrects this error by using a semicolon splice. (B) and (D) do not address the error. (E) leaves the meaning of the second clause incomplete.

36. B

SMARTPOINT CATEGORY: WORDINESS

The underlined selection here is awkward and wordy. (B) expresses the same idea more clearly and concisely. (C) introduces an inconsistent verb tense. (D) does not express the correct relationship between the clauses. (E) is awkward and unnecessarily wordy.

37. C

SMARTPOINT CATEGORY: TRANSITIONS

The transition words *considering that* do not accurately express the cause and effect relationship between the clauses. Both (C) and (D) correct this error with the *because*. However, (D) uses a verb tense that is incorrect in context; *will blend* indicates a future action, but Louisa May Alcott's books were written in the past. (B) does not address the error. (E) also uses the future tense.

38. E

SMARTPOINT CATEGORY: PARALLELISM

The preposition *as* here has a compound object; (E) is the only choice that puts *brightest and . . . most unruly* in parallel form. (B), (C), and (D) do not address the error.

39. E

SMARTPOINT CATEGORY: WORDINESS

As written, this sentence is overly wordy. Additionally, *mindful . . . for* is idiomatically incorrect; in English, we are *mindful of.* (E) corrects both errors. In (B), *for* is the incorrect preposition in context. (C) and (D) are even wordier than the original sentence, and *for the fact being* in (D) is incorrect grammatical structure.

40. E

SMARTPOINT CATEGORY: MODIFIERS

As written, this sentence calls *the representative of China* one of *the countries on the UN Security Council.* Although it's slightly longer than some of the other choice, only (E) is correct in context. (B), (C), and (D) do not address the error.

41. C

SMARTPOINT CATEGORY: PARALLELISM

For the sake of parallelism, all three things in this list must be in the same grammatical form. *Confusion* and *memory loss* are both nouns, so *impaired language skills* is the best choice to complete the sentence.

42. B

SMARTPOINT CATEGORY: MODIFIERS

Upon entering the jail is an introductory phrase that describes the prisoners (they are the ones entering the jail). As the sentence is worded, it sounds as though the prisoners' personal belongings are entering the jail. (B) and (E) are the only two choices that place *the prisoners* right next to the phrase that describes them. (B) is the best choice; (E) puts the verb in an awkward and incorrect tense.

43. B

SMARTPOINT CATEGORY: RUN-ONS AND FRAGMENTS

Choice (B) is the best way to rephrase this run-on sentence; it expresses, in an economical and graceful way, the logical connection between these two pieces of information about the albatross.

Improving Paragraphs | Improving Sentences | Practice | **Answers and Explanations** | Chapter Highlights

44. E

SMARTPOINT CATEGORY: IDIOMS

So much should be followed by the preposition *as*. (E) completes the comparison and conforms to the rules of parallelism; *administrative successes* (an adjective-noun pair) is balanced by *military failures*.

45. D

SMARTPOINT CATEGORY: WORDINESS

The underlined portion of the sentence is wordy and awkward. (D) is a concise and correct rephrasing (note that it is also the shortest answer choice).

46. A

SMARTPOINT CATEGORY: CORRECT AS WRITTEN

The sentence contains no error. Choices (B) through (E) are all awkward or grammatically incorrect.

47. B

SMARTPOINT CATEGORY: PARALLELISM

The three items in this list should be in parallel grammatical form. The best way to correct the error is to rephrase all three as infinitive verbs. (Note, again, that the correct answer is also the shortest and most concise.)

48. C

SMARTPOINT CATEGORY: RUN-ONS AND FRAGMENTS

The second half of the sentence is an explanation of the first half, and a colon best expresses this logical connection. (A), (B), and (D) all introduce sentence fragments, and (E) uses the wrong verb tense and incorrectly presents the camera seizure as a consequence (not an explanation) of the first half of the sentence.

49. A

SMARTPOINT CATEGORY: CORRECT AS WRITTEN

The sentence contains no error and is not wordy or awkward. The introductory phrases in (B) and (E) are awkward. (C) has a wrong verb tense, and (D) has an awkward introductory phrase, an incorrect verb tense, and is wordy.

Improving Paragraphs | Improving Sentences | Practice | **Answers and Explanations** | Chapter Highlights

50. B

SMARTPOINT CATEGORY: MODIFIERS

The sentence contains a misplaced modifier: it sounds as though O'Toole's *career* is known for his portrayal of T. E. Lawrence. The introductory phrase describes *Peter O'Toole* (the man, not his career); hence, Peter O'Toole should come directly after it. Only choices (B) and (C) begin correctly, and (C) is poorly worded.

51. C

SMARTPOINT CATEGORY: RUN-ONS AND FRAGMENTS

The best way to repair this run-on sentence while preserving the logical relationship between the two halves of the sentence is with choice (C), which correctly presents the second half of the sentence as a consequence of the first. (A), (B), and (E) are all run-ons, and (D) makes *spectators* the subject of *endangered*.

52. E

SMARTPOINT CATEGORY: WORDINESS

The underlined portion of this sentence is passive, wordy, and awkward. A good rephrasing will begin with *he* and will be in the active voice. (B) and (E) are possibilities, but (B) is still somewhat awkward and puts the verb into the past perfect for no apparent reason. (E) is clear and concise.

IMPROVING PARAGRAPHS QUESTIONS

53. D

SMARTPOINT CATEGORY: WORDINESS

The key to this problem is realizing that *I myself* is redundant—if the author has already used *I*, there's no need to add *myself* to clarify. (D) provides the best fix here—notice that it's also the shortest, most straightforward answer. Choices (A) and (E) still include *myself*. (C) substitutes another redundancy—the word *personally*. (B) is unnecessarily convoluted and is missing a comma following *I believe*.

54. C

SMARTPOINT CATEGORIES: TRANSITIONS

WORDINESS

The context here suggests a strong link between the two sentences—the idea is that sports provide students with the chance to strive for greatness by showing them it takes courage. Choice (C) is the best answer. (A) introduces an illogical contrast. (B) creates a sentence fragment. (D) uses the passive voice unnecessarily. In (E), the verb *show* doesn't agree with the subject *it*.

Improving Paragraphs | Improving Sentences | Practice | **Answers and Explanations** | Chapter Highlights

55. C

SMARTPOINT CATEGORY: PRONOUNS

The key to this sentence is spotting a subject-verb agreement problem—the subject in the sentence is *top athletes*, not *Michael Jordan*—he's only introduced as an example of a top athlete. So the underlined pronouns should be *them* (to agree with *young people*) and *their* (to agree with *top athletes*).

56. B

SMARTPOINT CATEGORIES: TRANSITIONS

To fix this ambiguous introductory phrase, you're looking for a conjunction that expresses the idea of listing an *additional benefit* of participation in team sports. (B) *moreover* does this effectively. (A)'s *and* is not an idiomatic conjunction with which to begin a sentence. (C) creates an unnecessary contrast. In (D), *sequentially* means in order, not *consequently*. (E), *finally*, is wrong because this sentence describes the second item in a list of two.

57. E

SMARTPOINT CATEGORY: READING COMPREHENSION

Sentence 14 provides a weak ending to the passage because it refers to *other ways of the city government saving money*, without suggesting what these might be. So the best improvement to sentence 14 might be (E), to provide examples of alternative areas for cuts. (A) would be an odd solution—historical events haven't been mentioned thus far in the passage. (B) would weaken the essay just at the point at which the author needs to strengthen it. (C) would be repetitive—the author has already included a personal anecdote. Finally, (D) would simply offer a digression at this point.

58. D

SMARTPOINT CATEGORY: RUN-ONS AND FRAGMENTS

The word *just* creates a run-on sentence here that needs fixing. To combine both clauses in a logical manner, you need to remove *just* and add conjunctions that express the idea of *contrast—in spite of* the author's enjoyment of music, everyone thought he had no talent. (D) is the best answer here. (B) is wrong because it still includes *just*. (C) is not logical—why would people conclude the author was talentless if he enjoyed music? (E)'s *however* is the wrong conjunction—it expresses contrast, but it doesn't link the two phrases to fix the run-on.

Improving Paragraphs | Improving Sentences | Practice | **Answers and Explanations** | Chapter Highlights

59. B

SMARTPOINT CATEGORIES: TRANSITIONS

A good setup for paragraph 2 would be a sentence that leads into the author's discovery that he had musical ability and introduces Mr. Daniels. (B) accomplishes this. (A) is illogical because Mr. Daniel's opinion soon persuades the author to try playing music. (C) and (E) are non sequiturs—they don't lead into paragraph 2 in any way. (D) is too extreme and a bit premature—the author doesn't discover his talent until mid-paragraph 2.

60. E

SMARTPOINT CATEGORY: COMPARISONS

The key here is realize that sentence 11 contains an illogical comparison. The *sound of the handbell* cannot be purer than the *electric guitar*—it has to be purer than the *sound of the electric guitar*, as (E) suggests. None of the other choices fixes this problem.

61. A

SMARTPOINT CATEGORY: CORRECT AS WRITTEN

There is no error in this sentence—*Not only . . . but also* is a common and perfectly correct idiomatic expression.

62. A

SMARTPOINT CATEGORY: PARALLELISM

There are two problems here. The sentences are choppy as written, and the items in the second sentence's list are not parallel. (A) does the best job of combining the sentences and corrects the parallelism error. (B) creates a run-on sentence: two independent clauses combined with a comma splice. (C) and (D) address the errors but unnecessarily add additional words and phrases, making the sentence wordier than it needs to be. (E) correctly combines the sentences but fails to address the parallelism problem.

63. D

SMARTPOINT CATEGORY: PARALLELISM

The conjunction *and* requires that the two verbs in the compound predicate be in parallel form, which they are not here (*He could improvise . . . and played . . .*). (D) makes the two verbs parallel. (B) is unnecessary—the pronoun *He* clearly refers to Mozart. (C) introduces an inconsistent verb tense. (E) alters the meaning of the sentence.

Improving Paragraphs   Improving Sentences   Practice   **Answers and Explanations**   Chapter Highlights

64. B

SMARTPOINT CATEGORY: AMBIGUITY

This sentence uses the pronouns *his*, *he*, and *him*. Sometimes the pronoun refers to the elder
Mozart, sometimes it refers to Wolfgang, so the reader is likely to lose track of which person is
being referred to. (B) is best because none of the pronouns are ambiguous. (C) and (D) still leave
some pronoun usage unclear. (E) is confusing because *Mozart* could refer to either of the men.

65. C

SMARTPOINT CATEGORY: RUN-ONS AND FRAGMENTS

As written, this sentence is actually a fragment. (Remember, the-*ing* verb form can never be a
predicate verb.) Changing *determining* to *determined* corrects the problem. (B) and (E) introduce
verb tenses that are inappropriate in context. (D) does not correct the error.

66. B

SMARTPOINT CATEGORY: MODIFIERS

Leopold was not a child when he was surprised by his son's tunes; his son was. (B) corrects the error
without introducing any additional issues. In (A), the phrase *As a child* is modifying *tunes*. (C) and
(E) introduce the passive voice unnecessarily. (D) is awkwardly worded.

67. C

SMARTPOINT CATEGORY: READING COMPREHENSION

The best choice here is (C), because the pronoun *he* in sentence 14 refers to *Mozart*, and the
ideas make sense in sequence. (A) is incorrect because sentence 14 does not give the three reasons
referred to in sentence 1. Placing it after sentence 2, as (B) suggests, does not make sense in
context. (D) is wrong because sentences 12 and 13 deal with the same specific detail and should
not be separated. (E) is incorrect because the pronoun reference would be unclear and the ideas in
sentence 14 do not follow as logically from sentence 13 as they do from sentence 11.

Improving Paragraphs | Improving Sentences | Practice | **Answers and Explanations** | Chapter Highlights

IF YOU ONLY LEARN SEVEN THINGS IN THIS CHAPTER . . .

1. **KAPLAN'S STRATEGY FOR IDENTIFYING SENTENCE ERRORS**

    *   **Step 1.** Read the whole sentence, listening and watching for an error.

    *   **Step 2.** If you clearly hear the error, look for a rule it breaks. If you find the rule, choose the answer.

    *   **Step 3.** If no rule is found, check each underlined choice carefully, eliminating each in order.

    *   **Step 4.** Choose from the remaining choices (including No Error).

2. **THE 16 MOST COMMON IDENTIFYING SENTENCE ERRORS**

    *   When the subject follows the verb

    *   When the subject and verb are separated

    *   When the subject seems plural (but isn't)

    *   Wrong tenses

    *   Incorrect use of past participles and incomplete verbs

    *   Wrong pronoun number

    *   Wrong pronoun case

    *   Incorrect use of past participles and incomplete verbs

    *   Ambiguous pronoun reference

    *   Confusion of infinitives and gerunds

    *   Wrong preposition after verb

    *   Wrong word in context

    *   Faulty comparison (subjects, wording, how many)

    *   Number agreement pronouns

    *   Misuse of adjectives and adverbs

    *   Double negatives

3. KAPLAN'S STRATEGY FOR IMPROVING SENTENCES

- **Step 1.** Read the sentence carefully, looking and listening for an error.

- **Step 2.** Identify the error or errors.

- **Step 3.** Look for an answer that is the most correct, concise, and relevant one.

4. THE FIVE MOST COMMON ERRORS:

- Run-on sentences

- Sentence fragments

- Misplaced modifiers

- Faulty parallelism

- Faulty transition between clauses and phrases

5. WORDINESS WATCH IN QUESTIONS AND ANSWERS

- No extra words

- No redundancies (saying the same thing twice)

- Consider the shortest answer: it may be the right one to pick

6. KAPLAN'S STRATEGY FOR IMPROVING PARAGRAPHS

- **Step 1.** Read the passage for the overall idea and tone.

- **Step 2.** Read the question.

- **Step 3.** Reread (if necessary) the relevant portion and its context.

- **Step 4.** Predict the correction.

- **Step 5.** Find a correct answer that doesn't introduce a new error and isn't wordy.

8. IMPROVING PARAGRAPH QUESTION TYPES

- Content-related wording questions

- Sentence Revision questions

- Combining Sentences questions

- Paragraph Transition questions

Improving Paragraphs · Improving Sentences · Practice · Answers and Explanations · **Chapter Highlights**

HOW TO ATTACK THE CRITICAL READING COMPONENT

Part 3 of this book covers the two Critical Reading question types on the exam: Sentence Completion questions and Reading Comprehension questions. The Reading Comprehension questions are based on two kinds of reading passages—short passages and long passages.

CHAPTER 6: SAT CRITICAL READING BASICS

SMARTPOINTS COVERED IN THIS CHAPTER

- DEFINITION
- CONTRAST
- CAUSE AND EFFECT
- DETAILS
- FUNCTION
- INFERENCE
- GLOBAL
- VOCABULARY-IN-CONTEXT

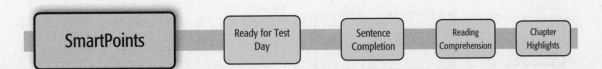

SmartPoints | Ready for Test Day | Sentence Completion | Reading Comprehension | Chapter Highlights

WHAT TO EXPECT ON TEST DAY

There are three Critical Reading sections on the SAT.

LENGTH	CONTENT	TYPE
25 minutes	Sentence Completion and Reading Comprehension (short and long)	Multiple-choice
25 minutes	Sentence Completion and Reading Comprehension (short and long)	Multiple-choice
20 minutes	Sentence Completion and Reading Comprehension (short and long)	Multiple-choice

The Critical Reading component of the SAT is designed to test three basic skills:

- **Vocabulary**—both the breadth of your vocabulary and your ability to determine meaning from context

- **Reasoning skills**—including your ability to determine the relationship between words and ideas

- **Reading skills**—how well you understand what you read (main idea, tone, etc.)

The Critical Reading section of the SAT includes two types of questions.

1. Sentence Completion questions
2. Reading Comprehension questions

To do well on SAT Critical Reading, you need to be systematic in your approach to each question type. We'll describe each type in more detail in a moment.

QUICK SCORING TIP

Sentence Completion questions are the fastest question type of the three because there is no passage to read—just a sentence with one or two blanks that you need to fill in. You can earn points faster on these questions than on Reading Comprehension questions, which require you to read anywhere from one to three paragraphs.

SmartPoints | **Ready for Test Day** | Sentence Completion | Reading Comprehension | Chapter Highlights

You might want to do the Reading Comprehension questions based on the shorter passages right after that. Why? It takes less time to read a short passage than it does to read a long one, so the short passage points can be accumulated faster. By working on the long passage questions last, you won't run the risk of getting bogged down on the longer passages and leaving yourself only a few minutes for the short passages and Sentence Completion questions.

Now that you know what order to work through the Critical Reading section, let's take a look at the question types. (We go into detail in the chapters that follow.)

SENTENCE COMPLETION QUESTIONS

The Sentence Completion sections test your vocabulary—both the extent of your word knowledge and your ability to determine meaning from the context of a particular sentence. These sentences are the quickest ones to answer in the section. You only have to read one sentence and plug in the right answer.

Sentence Completions fall into three main categories:

- Definition/Similar Meaning
- Contrast
- Cause and Effect/Make Sense in Context

The Sentence Completion question sets are arranged in order of difficulty. The first few questions in a set might be fairly straightforward and manageable. The middle few questions will be a little harder, and the last few questions should be the most difficult. Keep this in mind as you work.

Sentence Completion questions look like this:

> Although this small and selective publishing house is famous for its ------ standards, several of its recent novels have appealed to the general population.
>
> (A) proletarian
> (B) naturalistic
> (C) discriminating
> (D) imitative
> (E) precarious

> **PERFECT SCORE TIP**
>
> 66 Getting the Sentence Completion questions out of the way early really reduced my stress and let me focus on the passage-based questions for the rest of the time. 99

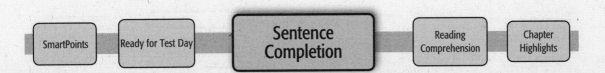

To answer this type of question, you must choose the word that best completes the sentence. We have specific strategies for tackling this question type in chapter 7. In case you're curious, the answer for this question is (C), *discriminating*.

READING COMPREHENSION QUESTIONS

As we mentioned, there are two kinds of Reading Comprehension passages: short and long. Short passages are approximately 100–150 words long. They are typically followed by two questions. Long passages are approximately 400–850 words long and are typically followed by 8–13 questions.

The passages and questions are predictable. The topics are drawn from the following:

- Humanities
- Social sciences
- Natural sciences
- Fiction

The questions ask about the overall tone and content of a passage, the details used, and what the author's overall meaning may be. You will also have one or more *paired-passage* question sets consisting of two related excerpts. Those questions will ask you to compare and contrast the two passages.

DON'T FORGET!

Reading Comprehension questions are not arranged by difficulty. That means easy, medium, and hard questions can appear in any order. Any time you find yourself spending too much time on a question, skip it and return to it later.

Reading Comprehension questions are covered in detail in chapters 8 and 9.

LEARN TO READ ACTIVELY

A key skill to master for the Reading passages is active reading. What does this mean? It means you take an active role as you read. You ask yourself questions as you read:

- Why did the author write this?
- What is the purpose of this paragraph?
- Why include this detail?

Compare this style of reading to the casual way you read a magazine. When you read casually, you don't take special care; you know it doesn't really matter what you understand. On the SAT

SmartPoints | Ready for Test Day | Sentence Completion | **Reading Comprehension** | Chapter Highlights

Reading section, however, you need to be on your toes. It will pay to remember the following two rules:

THE 3 Ws OF ACTIVE READING

- *Why* is more important than *what*.
- Keep straight *who* said *what*.

As you read a passage you'll want to look for the author's motivation and keep track of the various opinions and points of view. The author's view is likely to be different than any of the people the author mentions in the paragraphs. And the opinion of the characters in the text may well differ from each other. Why? These are some of the concerns to keep an eye out for.

MAPPING THE PASSAGE

The best way to understand (and keep focused on) a passage is to map it. This means marking up the passage with your own notes and highlighting marks.

Note: Keep underlining to an absolute minimum. Some students go into "autopen" mode and underline everything, thinking they are going to remember what the passage is about. But when the time comes to look for answers, everything—and nothing—stands out in the text.

ABCs OF ACTIVE READING

An easy mnemonic to keep in mind when reading actively:

A = Abbreviate margin notes

B = Bracket key sentences

C = Circle keywords and phrases

SHORT PASSAGES STRATEGY

Short passages have about 100 words and are followed by one or two questions. Long passages have 500–800 words and have 5–13 questions.

These questions test how well you understand and can identify:

- **Details** in the passage
- The **Function** or role of certain words, details, and paragraphs in the passage

- Small **Inference** statements that can be made from the passage
- The **Global** or main idea/purpose of the passage
- **Vocabulary-in-Context**

Because a short passage has only a few lines to read, you can keep the one or two question stems in mind as you read. Predicting an answer while you read will save time in the section.

Remember to read the question stem (not the answers) first and underline words and phrases you are likely to see in the passage. They often use the same, or similar, words in the stems and in the body of the passage. These flags will speed you up as you gather points.

IF YOU LEARN ONLY FIVE THINGS IN THIS CHAPTER . . .

1. EASY-TO-HARD QUESTIONS

- The Sentence Completion questions ARE arranged by difficulty.

- The Reading Comprehension questions ARE NOT arranged by difficulty.

2. SENTENCE COMPLETIONS

- Have one or two blanks to fill

- Test vocabulary knowledge and understanding of words in context

- Fall into three main categories: Definition, Contrast, and Cause and Effect

3. READING COMPREHENSION QUESTIONS

- Have topics in four areas: humanities, social sciences, natural sciences, and fiction

- Require skilled *active reading* (see below)

- Have questions that determine how well you can identify various aspects of the passage, including:

  - Details in the passage

  - Functions of various elements in the passage

  - Logical Inference statements

  - Global or main idea of the passage

  - A word in context

4. KAPLAN'S 3 Ws OF ACTIVE READING

- *Why* is more important than *what*.

- Keep straight *who* said what.

5. ABCs MNEMONIC FOR ACTIVE READING

- A = Abbreviate margin notes

- B = Bracket key sentences

- C = Circle keywords and phrases

SmartPoints · Ready for Test Day · Sentence Completion · Reading Comprehension · **Chapter Highlights**

CHAPTER 7: SENTENCE COMPLETION STRATEGIES

SMARTPOINTS COVERED IN THIS CHAPTER

DEFINITION

CONTRAST

CAUSE AND EFFECT

WHAT TO EXPECT ON TEST DAY

Sentence Completion questions are probably the Critical Reading section's most student-friendly question type. Unlike the Reading Comprehension questions that make up the bulk of this section, Sentence Completion questions require you to pay attention to just one sentence at a time.

ONE-BLANK SENTENCE COMPLETIONS

The word you are looking for to fill the blank will have one of three types of relationships to the sentence as a whole:

- **Definition** (similar meaning to a keyword in the sentence)
- **Contrast** (a contrasting word to a keyword in the sentence)
- **Cause and Effect** (make sense in the context of the sentence)

PERFECT SCORE TIP

I always approached Sentence Completion questions with Kaplan's Target Strategy. Doing so helped me be much more consistent and accurate with my predictions.

SmartPoints | Ready for Test Day | Steps for Test Day Success | Tackling Hard Questions | Practice

TWO-BLANK SENTENCE COMPLETIONS

The relationships between these words will *relate to each other* in three ways:

 1. Definition

 2. Contrast

 3. Cause and Effect (both make sense in the context of the sentence)

Note: Both words must fit in the sentence. If one word fits and the other doesn't, the answer is wrong.

FOUR STEPS TO TEST DAY SUCCESS

KAPLAN'S TARGET STRATEGY FOR SENTENCE-COMPLETION QUESTIONS

Here's Kaplan's powerful Target Strategy for tackling Sentence Completion questions.

- **Step 1.** Read the sentence for clue words.
- **Step 2.** Predict the answer.
- **Step 3.** Select the best match.
- **Step 4.** Plug your answer choice back into sentence.

> **PERFECT SCORE TIP**
>
> " I found that predicting the answers to Sentence Completion questions was helpful. I usually found a synonym in the answer choices, and occasionally I would even predict the correct answer. "

STEP 1. READ THE SENTENCE FOR CLUE WORDS

Read the sentence. Now think about the sentence for five seconds. Take special note of the clue words. A clue word like *but* tells you to expect a CONTRAST in the next part of the sentence; a clue word like *moreover* tells you that what follows is a CONTINUATION of the same idea. Clue words such as *and, but, such as, however,* and *although* tell you how the parts of the sentence will relate to each other.

STEP 2. PREDICT THE ANSWER

Decide what sort of word should fill the blank or blanks. Do this before looking at the answer choices. You don't have to guess the *exact* word; a rough idea of the *kind* of word you'll need will do. It's often enough to simply predict whether the missing

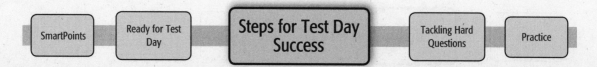

SmartPoints | Ready for Test Day | **Steps for Test Day Success** | Tackling Hard Questions | Practice

word is positive or negative. But often you will be able to go farther. For example, you may be able to predict whether you need a pair of synonyms to fill in the blanks or two words that contrast.

STEP 3. SELECT THE BEST MATCH

Compare your prediction to each answer choice. Read every answer choice before deciding which answer best completes the sentence.

STEP 4. PLUG YOUR ANSWER CHOICE INTO THE SENTENCE

Put your answer choice in the blank (or blanks). Only one choice should really make sense. If you've gone through the four steps and more than one choice still looks good, eliminate the choice(s) that you can, guess from the remaining choices, and move on. If all of the choices look great or all of the choices look terrible, circle the question and come back to it when you've finished the section.

USING KAPLAN'S TARGET STRATEGY FOR SENTENCE COMPLETION

Let's unleash the powers of Kaplan's Target Strategy for Sentence Completion questions on a sample question.

> The king's ------- decisions as a diplomat and administrator led to his legendary reputation as a just and------- ruler.
>
> (A) quick . . . capricious
> (B) equitable . . . wise
> (C) immoral . . . perceptive
> (D) generous . . . witty
> (E) clever . . . uneducated

STEP 1. READ THE SENTENCE FOR CLUE WORDS

The clues here are the phrase *led to* and the word *just*. You know that the kind of decisions the king made *led to* his having a reputation as a just and ------- ruler. So whatever goes in both blanks must be consistent with *just*.

> **EXPERT TUTOR TIP**
>
> " Get in the habit of predicting quickly. Each Sentence Completion question should only take between 30 and 45 seconds. "

AND & BUT

And is a clue for a definition. *But* is a keyword for contrast. Keep your eyes out for these.

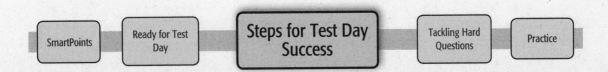

SmartPoints   Ready for Test Day   **Steps for Test Day Success**   Tackling Hard Questions   Practice

STEP 2. PREDICT THE ANSWER

The word *and* means that the second blank must be similar to *just*. Now the key is to know what *just* means. (It means *fair*.) If you didn't know for sure what *just* means, you could also rely on the word *diplomat*, which is also a positive word (one who keeps peaceful relations between countries). Between these two context words, you'd be able to predict that the king was a careful or good ruler. Now, write a + sign in each blank.

A NOTE ON . . . TWO-BLANK QUESTIONS

Another approach for two-blank Sentence Completion questions is to take them one blank at a time. Choose the easier blank, cross out any choices that clearly don't fit, and finish by checking ONLY the remaining choices for the other blank.

STEP 3. SELECT THE BEST MATCH

Check each answer to see which pair has two positive words—and are synonyms—as descriptive words for the king.

PERFECT SCORE TIP

" Instead of forcing myself to follow a study schedule that was too demanding or easy, I adjusted according to the difficulty of the material and how quickly I grasped the concepts. "

Choice (A): *Quick* and *capricious* are not necessarily positive, and they are not similar in meaning (*capricious* means erratic or fickle).

Choice (B): *Equitable* means fair. *Equitable* and *wise* are similar, and they're both positive. This is the best choice so far, but check the rest.

Choice (C): *Immoral* is a negative word, so eliminate this choice right away.

Choice (D): *Generous* and *witty* are positive, but they are not similar and don't make sense in the sentence.

Choice (E): *Uneducated* is negative, so eliminate this choice.

Don't stop until you have checked out all five answers. The best choice may well be the last one!

STEP 4. PLUG YOUR ANSWER CHOICE INTO THE SENTENCE

The king's equitable decisions as a diplomat and administrator led to his legendary reputation as a just and wise ruler. Choice (B) is the correct answer.

ONE BLANK AT A TIME

Many times the second blank is easier to fill than the first, especially when the first comes early in the sentence. Lean heavily on the second blank prediction and eliminate the ones that don't fit. Chances are, you'll be down to two choices. Now look at the first-blank choices and go from there.

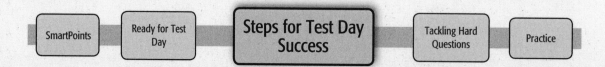

SmartPoints | Ready for Test Day | **Steps for Test Day Success** | Tackling Hard Questions | Practice

TECHNIQUES FOR TACKLING THE HARDEST QUESTIONS

Sentence Completion questions will go from easiest to hardest, though some sections will start with medium-difficulty questions. The higher the question number, the harder the question, so the last few Sentence Completion questions in a set will be the most difficult.

IF YOU GET STUCK

If you find yourself getting stuck, we have a few techniques to pull you through:
- Avoid tricky wrong answers.
- Take apart tough sentences.
- Work around tough vocabulary.
- If all else fails—guess.

AVOID TRICKY WRONG ANSWERS

Toward the end of a set, watch out for tricky answer choices. Avoid the following:

- Opposites of the correct answer

- Words that sound right just because they're hard

- Two-blankers in which one word fits but the other doesn't

DECODE TRICKY SENTENCES

Sometimes a sentence may seem to mean one thing, but a word or two turns it into the opposite meaning.

Take a look at the following example.

> Granted, Janyce is extremely --------; still, it is difficult to imagine her as a professional comedian.
>
> (A) dull
> (B) garrulous
> (C) effusive
> (D) conservative
> (E) witty

Read this sentence carefully or you may get tricked. If you read too quickly, you might think, "If Janyce is hard to imagine as a comedian, she's probably extremely dull or conservative. So I'll pick either (A) or (D)." But the sentence is saying something else.

PERFECT SCORE TIP

" Stay calm and don't get thrown off or flustered while answering Sentence Completion questions. That way, you won't miss important sentence clues. "

SmartPoints | Ready for Test Day | Steps for Test Day Success | **Tackling Hard Questions** | Practice

Remember to pick up the clues:

- One key here is the clue word *granted*, which is another way of saying "Sure, Janice is extremely_____."
- The words *still* and *difficult* might also throw you off.
- Taken all together, the clues means that she is *funny*, but not really a stand-up comedian.

Choice (E) is correct. If you read this sentence quickly, you might have thought she was extremely *dull* (A).

HELPFUL WORD TOOLS

Remember the following:
- **Word charge:** This is the positive, negative, or neutral feeling of words.
- **Foreign language:** English words are sometimes similar.
- **Word roots:** The meaning of Latin and Greek roots connect large families of words in English.
- **Similar words:** These are often related (example: *antique* and *antiquarian*: *old*).

TAKE APART TOUGH SENTENCES

Some sentences are difficult because they seem to lack the context you need to determine the correct answer. Let's look again at a previously used example.

> Although this small and selective publishing house is famous for its -------
> standards, several of its recent novels have appealed to the general public.

(A) proletarian
(B) naturalistic
(C) discriminating
(D) imitative
(E) precarious

In this sentence, the parts of the sentence surrounding the blank seem a little vague, and the word choices are advanced adjectives. What sort of publishing house is it? The answer here is not clear right off the bat. But what if you were stumped and had no idea which word to pick or what the meaning of all of the words were? Sometimes the only thing to do in this situation is to plug in the answer choices and make the best guess based on which word you think gives the most information. Here, we are looking for a word that describes standards that would keep them from publishing books that appeal to the general public.

(A) *Proletarian* standards? Hmmm . . . doesn't seem appropriate. *Proletarian* means characteristic of the average citizen or working class, so in fact, it's the opposite of what we need.

(B) *Naturalistic* standards? Not great. It doesn't seem to contrast with the idea of popular appeal.

(C) *Discriminating* standards? Seems to fit. If they are discriminating, they are very selective and would probably not publish books that are popular with the general public.

(D) *Imitative* standards? Sounds weird and doesn't really make sense.

(E) *Precarious* standards? Nope. Again, it doesn't make sense in the context of the sentence, whatever kind of publisher it is.

Choice (C) sounds best and is correct. Although the small publishing house has *discriminating*, or picky, standards, several of its recent novels appeal to a general audience.

> **PERFECT SCORE TIP**
>
> " If I couldn't predict an answer accurately, and rereading didn't help, I immediately plugged in the answer choices—trial and error takes time but works. "

TIME MANAGEMENT

> Sentence Completions are easy to come back to at the end of a 25-minute section. Reading passages, especially the long ones, are not. Plan your timing with this in mind.

TWO-BLANK SENTENCE PRACTICE

Now try a medium-difficulty sentence with two blanks, in the following order in conjunction with Kaplan's Target Strategy:

> These latest employment statistics from the present administration are so loosely documented, carelessly explained, and potentially misleading that even the most loyal senators will ------- the ------- of the presidential appointees who produced them.
>
> (A) perceive . . . intelligence
> (B) understand . . . tenacity
> (C) recognize . . . incompetence
> (D) praise . . . rigor
> (E) denounce . . . loyalty

It's not so easy to see what goes in the first blank, so try the second blank. You need a word to describe presidential appointees who produced the *loosely documented, carelessly explained,* and *misleading* statistics. Based on these keywords, we know

SmartPoints   Ready for Test Day   Steps for Test Day Success   **Tackling Hard Questions**   Practice

that the second blank must be negative. The only second-word answer choice that's definitely negative is (C), *incompetence*, or inability to perform a task. Now try *recognize* in the first blank. It fits too. (C) must be correct. See how much time you save? This step safely eliminates all choices except the correct answer.

WORK AROUND TOUGH VOCABULARY

Fortunately, you can often figure out enough context to get the correct answer, even if you don't know all of the vocabulary words in the sentence. That's because test developers often provide other clues to help you figure out the intended meaning. Look at the following sentence as an example.

> Despite her ------- of public speaking experience, the student council member was surprisingly cogent, and expressed the concerns of her classmates persuasively.
>
> (A) hope
> (B) depth
> (C) method
> (D) lack
> (E) union

If you don't know what *cogent* means, work around it. From the sentence, especially the clue word *and*, you know that *cogent* goes with *expressed the concerns of her classmates persuasively*. So you don't have to worry about what *cogent* means. All you need to know is that the student council member was persuasive despite a ------- of speaking experience. *Surprisingly* is another clue. It suggests that the student was not expected to express herself so effectively because she did not have much public speaking experience. Further, two of the answer choices don't really make sense if you insert them in the blank—a *method* or *union* of speaking experience? Can't be.

Only (D), *lack*, fits the context. *Despite her lack of public speaking experience, the student council member expressed the concerns of her classmates persuasively.* (By the way, *cogent* means convincing, believable, roughly the same as *expressing concern persuasively*.)

IF ALL ELSE FAILS—GUESS!

If you're really stumped, don't be afraid to guess. Eliminate all answer choices that can't possibly be right, and guess from the remaining choices. If you have eliminated at least one or two choices, the chance to gain points outweighs the possibility of losing points for incorrect answers.

Now take a deep breath before you go on to practice the strategies you've learned on this Sentence Completion problem set.

SmartPoints | Ready for Test Day | Steps for Test Day Success | **Tackling Hard Questions** | Practice

PRACTICE

Select the lettered word or set of words that best completes the sentence.

1. The stranger was actually smaller than I thought; his stature was ------- by the alarm he caused as he loomed up suddenly in the dark alley.

    (A) worsened
    (B) magnified
    (C) disparaged
    (D) disfigured
    (E) admonished

2. Although the risk of a major accident remained -------, the public's concern about such an accident gradually -------.

    (A) steady . . . waned
    (B) acute . . . persisted
    (C) unclear . . . shifted
    (D) obvious . . . endured
    (E) pressing . . . remained

3. Prior to the American entrance into World War I, President Woodrow Wilson strove to maintain the ------- of the United States, warning both sides against encroachments on American interests.

    (A) involvement
    (B) belligerence
    (C) versatility
    (D) magnanimity
    (E) neutrality

4. The graceful curves of the colonial-era buildings that dominated the old part of the city contrasted sharply with the modern, ------- subway stations and made the latter appear glaringly out of place.

    (A) festive
    (B) grimy
    (C) angular
    (D) gigantic
    (E) efficient

5. The discovery of the Dead Sea Scrolls in the 1940s quickly ------- the popular imagination, but the precise significance of the scrolls is still ------- by scholars.

    (A) impressed . . . understood
    (B) alarmed . . . obscured
    (C) troubled . . . perceived
    (D) sparked . . . disputed
    (E) eluded . . . debated

6. In Kafka's characteristically surreal story "The Hunger Artist," the main character "entertains" the public by starving himself until he is too ------- to survive.

    (A) glutted
    (B) lachrymose
    (C) emaciated
    (D) superfluous
    (E) satiated

Ready for Test Day | Steps for Test Day Success | Tackling Hard Questions | **Practice** | Answers and Explanations

7. Recent editions of the Chinese classic *Tao Te Ching*, based on manuscripts more authoritative than those hitherto available, have rendered previous editions -------.

   (A) incomprehensible
   (B) interminable
   (C) inaccessible
   (D) obsolete
   (E) illegible

8. Despite their outward resemblance, the brothers could not be more ------- temperamentally; while one is quiet and circumspect, the other is brash and -------.

   (A) inimical . . . timid
   (B) passionate . . . superficial
   (C) dissimilar . . . audacious
   (D) different . . . forgiving
   (E) alike . . . respectful

9. Her scholarly rigor and capacity for ------- enabled her to undertake research projects that less ------- people would have found too difficult and tedious.

   (A) fanaticism . . . slothful
   (B) comprehension . . . indolent
   (C) analysis . . . careless
   (D) negligence . . . dedicated
   (E) concentration . . . disciplined

10. It was difficult to tell what the auditor was thinking, as his expression was -------.

   (A) palpable
   (B) salient
   (C) titular
   (D) impassive
   (E) bilious

11. As a result of being confined to the rim of the excavation site, the archeologist found it difficult to surmise exactly what the ------- chamber might hold.

   (A) potable
   (B) fulsome
   (C) insensate
   (D) beatific
   (E) subterranean

12. Casey's creative writing teacher praised his story but said it was somewhat ------- and suggested that he ------- it a bit.

   (A) adept . . . declaim
   (B) gauche . . . filibuster
   (C) verbose . . . pare
   (D) contiguous . . . diffuse
   (E) abortive . . . abscond

13. Dr. Fowler's compact disc collection clearly revealed his ------- for early jazz recordings.

   (A) penchant
   (B) tenet
   (C) confluence
   (D) phalanx
   (E) hegemony

14. If all world leaders were to ------- violent solutions to problems, there would soon be a ------- of war.

   (A) emulate . . . tutelage
   (B) condole . . . paean
   (C) eschew . . . cessation
   (D) becloud . . . demagogue
   (E) mitigate . . . recidivism

Ready for Test Day | Steps for Test Day Success | Tackling Hard Questions | **Practice** | Answers and Explanations

15. The austere life of a medieval monk required sleeping in a ------- cell.

    (A) variegated
    (B) specious
    (C) Spartan
    (D) inchoate
    (E) intransigent

16. The corrupt judge's ------- insistence on his honesty was belied by his ------- unfair rulings.

    (A) colloquial . . . amorphously
    (B) disingenuous . . . blatantly
    (C) macabre . . . morosely
    (D) saturnine . . . stringently
    (E) opprobrious . . . truculently

17. The chess-playing computer Big Blue is a ------- opponent, as it never makes a careless mistake.

    (A) illusory
    (B) formidable
    (C) circuitous
    (D) novel
    (E) temporal

18. The leader of the minority party met with members of the business ------- to devise an economic reform package.

    (A) caucus
    (B) aerie
    (C) milieu
    (D) rostrum
    (E) interregnum

19. Because of her ------- the cat burglar was finally caught, when she showed a neighbor her ------- of stolen jewels.

    (A) hubris . . . cache
    (B) pseudonym . . . fodder
    (C) yen . . . vernacular
    (D) calumny . . . onus
    (E) kismet . . . platitude

20. One who betrays the trust of a close-knit group is likely to be shunned by his former compatriots, as when, for example, a whistle-blower becomes a ------- within her organization.

    (A) exponent
    (B) pariah
    (C) sybarite
    (D) potentate
    (E) paragon

21. Gerald felt his history assignment was not well defined; in fact, he found it rather -------.

    (A) prosaic
    (B) importunate
    (C) epochal
    (D) nebulous
    (E) febrile

22. Just as a criminal could ------- honesty in order to dupe a victim, likewise a superhero might fake------- in order to trick a villain.

    (A) burnish . . . histrionics
    (B) ingratiate . . . aplomb
    (C) feign . . . duplicity
    (D) aver . . . sinecure
    (E) thwart . . . convergence

23. By choosing to live in a relatively impoverished country, Mr. Jones enjoyed a ------- lifestyle, despite having a rather ------- income by European standards.

   (A) replete . . . squalid
   (B) lavish . . . paltry
   (C) licentious . . . obstinate
   (D) cumulative . . . complacent
   (E) winsome . . . tortuous

24. Later, it was hard for Maia to say which had been more frightening: the tyrant's ------- stare or his ------- words.

   (A) mawkish . . . wry
   (B) gamely . . . imperious
   (C) tenuous . . . sanctimonious
   (D) incarnadine . . . implacable
   (E) malevolent . . . virulent

ANSWERS AND EXPLANATIONS

1. B

SMARTPOINT CATEGORY: CONTRAST

The clue here is the phrase *was actually smaller than I thought.* The missing word has to mean *made larger* or *made to seem larger.* Choice (B), *magnified,* is the answer. *Disparaged* (C) means belittled. *Admonished* (E) means scolded. (A) and (D) do not make sense in the context. The stranger's stature cannot be *worsened* because it was never suggested that it was bad in the first place, and a *disfigured* stature would cause alarm, not be caused by alarm.

2. A

SMARTPOINT CATEGORY: CONTRAST

The word *although* indicates contrast. The contrast is between the risk and the public's concern. Choice (A) is the only one that presents a clear contrast: the risk didn't decrease, but the public's concern did.

3. E

SMARTPOINT CATEGORY: DEFINITION

The phrase *warning both sides against encroachments on American interests* indicates that Wilson was attempting to prevent each side from taking an action that would force the United States to get involved in the war. Choice (E), *neutrality,* gets this point across. *Involvement* (A) suggests the opposite of the correct answer. *Belligerence* (B) is the quality of being warlike; *versatility* (C) means being able to handle a variety of different situations; *magnanimity* (D) is generosity.

4. C

SMARTPOINT CATEGORY: CONTRAST

You're specifically told that there's a contrast between the buildings and the subway stations. Checking the answer choices for a word that contrasts in meaning with *graceful curves,* you find that the answer is (C), *angular,* which means *jagged* or *angled.*

5. D

SMARTPOINT CATEGORY: CAUSE AND EFFECT

The word *but* indicates contrast. If you plug in the answer choices, (D) makes the most sense with the word *imagination* and completes the contrast: the public became quickly excited about the issue, but agreement among experts as to the significance of the scrolls has been slower in coming. None of the other choices provides a clear contrast of ideas. In addition, *still* suggests a lack of understanding, so (A) and (C) cannot be correct.

6. C

SMARTPOINT CATEGORY: CAUSE AND EFFECT

The missing word describes people who starve themselves and become malnourished. Choice (C), *emaciated*, which means extremely thin, is the only choice that really fits. (A) and (E) are the exact opposites of what's needed, and *lachrymose* (B) means tearful. (D), *superfluous*, means unnecessary, which would be a comment on the person's social, not physical, status.

7. D

SMARTPOINT CATEGORY: CONTRAST

If new editions of this book are based on *more authoritative*, or more accurate, manuscripts, previous editions would be rendered out-of-date, or *obsolete* (D)—scholars wouldn't use the old editions because the new ones are markedly superior. However, the new edition wouldn't render the old edition *incomprehensible* (A), *interminable* (B), *inaccessible* (C), or *illegible* (E).

8. C

SMARTPOINT CATEGORY: CAUSE AND EFFECT

The clue word *despite* indicates that the brothers must have different temperaments—making *dissimilar* (C) and *different* (D) both possibilities. The second word has to contrast with *quiet and circumspect* and be similar in tone to *brash*; *audacious*, or bold, is the only choice that makes sense, so (C) is correct.

9. E

SMARTPOINT CATEGORY: SIMILAR MEANING/DEFINITION

It's easier to start with the second blank. You need a word that goes with *rigor* and contrasts with finding things *difficult and tedious*. *Slothful* (A) and *indolent* (B) both mean *lazy*, so they're the opposite of what you need. Only *dedicated* (D) and *disciplined* (E) fit. Eliminate the other choices and try (D) and (E) in the first blank. The correct choice will be a quality held by a dedicated, rigorous scholar, so *concentration* (E) is the answer. *Negligence* (D) is the opposite of what you're looking for.

10. D

SMARTPOINT CATEGORY: DEFINITION

The key to this question is the word *as*, which signals a definition. You must look for a word that tells you why "it was difficult to tell what the auditor was thinking." *Impassive* means expressionless, revealing nothing. (A), *palpable*, means obvious or easily perceived. *Salient*, (B), means prominent. Choice (C), *titular*, refers to having a title, often in name only. *Bilious* (E) means sickly or ill-humored, both with a connotation of too much bile.

Steps for Test Day Success | Tackling Hard Questions | Practice | **Answers and Explanations** | Chapter Highlights

11. E

SMARTPOINT CATEGORY: CAUSE AND EFFECT

The logical relationship within this sentence is cause and effect, signaled by the phrase *as a result of*. The archeologist cannot determine what the chamber holds because of being *confined to the rim of the excavation site*. On the rim of a hole, one could not see what is underground, the meaning of *subterranean* (*sub*, below, and *terranean* from *terre*, meaning earth). (A), *potable*, means fit to drink. *Fulsome* (B) means abundant, often with a connotation of insincerity, as in the phrase *fulsome praise*. (C), *insensate*, means unconscious or lacking awareness. *Beatific* (D) means showing joy and calmness.

12. C

SMARTPOINT CATEGORY: CONTRAST

The second part of the sentence, after *but*, contrasts with the first part, in which Casey's teacher praises his story. Therefore, you are looking for a word for the first blank that denotes a flaw in the writing. The keyword for the second blank is *suggested*. That means you are looking for a second word that will correct the flaw noted in the first blank. *Verbose* means wordy, while to *pare* is to trim or cut, in this case words. (A) is incorrect, as *adept* is a positive word meaning skilled. To *declaim* is to recite or speak, usually vehemently. In (B), *gauche* means lacking in social polish, though it's an adjective appropriate to a human, not to writing. To *filibuster* is to delay through speechmaking. (D), *contiguous* and *diffuse* are in the relationship of possible flaw and remedy, but *contiguous* means touching or adjacent without a break, while *diffuse* means to spread out; so the choices don't fit the sentence. (E)'s choices, *abortive* and *abscond*, mean fruitless or imperfectly developed (*abortive*) and to flee and hide oneself (*abscond*), which are extreme choices for a bit of good, though somewhat flawed writing.

13. A

SMARTPOINT CATEGORY: CAUSE AND EFFECT

The word *revealed* is the key to this question. It directs you to look for the word that connects *Dr. Fowler's compact disc collection* to *early jazz recordings*. *Penchant* means a definite liking. (B), *tenet*, refers to a belief of doctrine or principle. *Confluence*, choice (C), means a gathering or flowing together, either literal or figurative. (D), *phalanx*, is a close-knit group of people, often used in reference to troops or guards. (E), *hegemony*, refers to the dominance of one nation over others.

Steps for Test Day Success | Tackling Hard Questions | Practice | **Answers and Explanations** | Chapter Highlights

14. C

SMARTPOINT CATEGORY: CAUSE AND EFFECT

The logical relationship in this sentence is cause and effect, an *if . . . then* relationship, although in this case the *then* is implied. To *eschew* is to forego or avoid. *Cessation* refers to stopping or ceasing. Avoiding violence, the sentence says, would stop war. (A) is incorrect because to *emulate* is to strive to equal or surpass through imitation, while *tutelage* is instruction or guardianship, from the same root as *tutor*. The words in (B), *condole* and *paean*, are incorrect because *condole* means to feel or express sympathy for another, while *paean* means joyful praise, as a hymn. In (D), *becloud* and *demagogue* mean to obscure or cover, as with clouds (becloud), and a popular leader who appeals to the emotions of the people (demagogue). At first, (E) seems as though it could be correct: to *mitigate* is to alleviate or moderate; but *recidivism* is a relapse into previous bad behaviors, often applied to repeat criminals, and so does not fit the sense of the sentence.

15. C

SMARTPOINT CATEGORY: DEFINITION

The verb *required* is the key to this sentence. The *austere life* of a monk *required sleeping in* what kind of cell? *Spartan*, from the Greek city of Sparta, means simple or frugal, in other words, austere. (A), *variegated*, means characterized by variety, especially of color. *Specious* (B) refers to something that is false, though it has the appearance of truth. (D), *inchoate*, means in an early, imperfect, state of development. (E), *intransigent*, means extreme and uncompromising.

16. B

SMARTPOINT CATEGORY: CONTRAST

The correct answer can be determined by the context of the sentence. *Corrupt* is a keyword, as are *honesty* and *belied* (shown to be false, and thus a relationship of contrast), so look for words that relate to honesty or corruption. *Disingenuous* means not straightforward; *blatantly* means obviously offensive, without any effort to conceal. In other words, the judge misrepresented his honesty but his obviously unfair rulings showed his representation to be false. In (A), *colloquial* means conversation-like in its informality, and *amorphously* means shapeless or lacking form. In (C), *macabre* means gruesomely horrifying or reminiscent of death, and *morosely* means in a sullen or melancholy manner. *Saturnine* in (D) means tending to be bitter or sardonic in manner, while *stringently* means rigorous or severe. In (E), *opprobrious* means either scornful and abusive, or disgraceful and shameful, so it could possibly fit in the first blank. *Truculently*, however, means bitterly or violently opposed and does not fit the sentence.

17. B

SMARTPOINT CATEGORY: DEFINITION

This sentence includes a logical restatement in its structure, signaled by the word *as*. Ask yourself what kind of opponent never makes a careless mistake. *Formidable* means difficult to defeat, thus inspiring awe and dread. (A), *illusory*, means deceptive, as in the word *illusion*. (C), *circuitous* means roundabout, as in *circuit*. *Novel* (D) means new and different, when it's not referring to a literary form. (E), *temporal*, means limited by time, as is the material world.

18. A

SMARTPOINT CATEGORY: CAUSE AND EFFECT

This question must be answered by looking at context. First, note the words that are clues, such as *minority party*, *members*, and *business*, as well as *economic reform package*. You are looking for a term that is used in politics to apply to a group with members. *Caucus* means a group with a special focus within a larger group or party. *Aerie* (B) is a nest or a house built on a high place. (C), *milieu*, is an environment or setting. *Rostrum*, (D), is an elevated platform for public speaking. (E), *interregnum*, refers to the interruption of the usual functions of government.

19. A

SMARTPOINT CATEGORY: CAUSE AND EFFECT

This sentence contains a cause and effect relationship, signaled by the word *because*. The second part of the sentence sheds more light on the chain of cause and effect. *Hubris* is another word for excessive pride. It was the cat burglar's pride that led her to show her neighbor her *cache*, her concealed store, of jewels. In (B), *pseudonym* means alias or assumed name. *Fodder* is food or raw material. *Yen* (C) means desire; and *vernacular* means everyday, informal language. (D), *calumny* and *onus*, mean slander or false statements and burden or blame, respectively. *Kismet* and *platitude* (E) mean fate or fortune (*kismet*) and cliché statement (*platitude*).

20. B

SMARTPOINT CATEGORY: DEFINITION

The logical form of this question is one of comparison, as the phrase *for example* tells you. A *pariah* is a social outcast, one who is shunned by a community. (A), *exponent*, in the nonmathematical sense, is one who advocates or speaks for. (C), *sybarite*, refers to a person devoted to pleasure. *Potentate* (D) means one who exercises extensive power. *Paragon* (E) refers to a model of excellence, even perfection.

21. D

SMARTPOINT CATEGORY: DEFINITION

The sentence requires a definition. The logical form of this sentence directs you to look for a restatement of the phrase *not well defined*. *Nebulous* means vague, i.e., not well defined. (A), *prosaic*, from the same root as the word *prose*, means straightforward, lacking in imagination. *Importunate* (B) means urgent and persistent in requesting. (C), *epochal*, means significant or momentous. *Febrile* (E) means feverish, either literally or figuratively.

22. C

SMARTPOINT CATEGORY: SIMILAR MEANING/DEFINITION

The relationship signaled in this sentence by *just as* and *likewise* is one of comparison. The comparison is inverted by the choice of the two subjects, the criminal and the superhero. The words *dupe* and *trick* are synonyms that help you see the comparison. When inserted into the blanks, the words *feign* and *duplicity* work by aligning with their counterparts *fake* (feign) and *honesty* (duplicity). Though *fake* and *feign* are synonyms, *honesty* and *duplicity* (deception) are antonyms, which makes sense because a criminal and a superhero would be faking, or feigning, opposite traits. In (A), *burnish* means to make smooth or glossy by rubbing, and *histrionics* is exaggerated emotional behavior. *Ingratiate* in (B) means to seek the good graces of another, and *aplomb* is self-confidence or assurance. To *aver* (D) is to declare or affirm, and a *sinecure* is a job that requires little or no effort to secure or maintain. In (E), to *thwart* is to frustrate or prevent the realization of plans, and *convergence* means meeting or coming together from different directions.

23. B

SMARTPOINT CATEGORY: CONTRAST

The logical relationship in this sentence is one of contrast, signaled by the word *despite*. You want to make sure that the first word, an adjective describing *lifestyle*, contrasts with the adjective that describes *income*. Then you also want to look at the introductory clause that tells you Mr. Jones has chosen to live in an impoverished country and ask yourself why someone would make that choice in relation to lifestyle and income. The word *lavish* means abundant, even extravagant; while *paltry* means lacking in worth or trivial. In (A), *replete* means abundantly supplied and *squalid* means dirty and wretched, as from poverty. These words fit the general sense of the sentence but their use is idiomatically incorrect here. *Licentious* in (C) means lacking restraint, especially in sexual connotations, and *obstinate* means stubborn. *Cumulative* (D) means enlarged by successive additions, and *complacent* means unconcerned due to self-satisfaction. *Winsome* (E) means charming, often in a childish way, and *tortuous* means devious and not straightforward, either literally or figuratively.

24. E
SMARTPOINT CATEGORY: SIMILAR MEANING/DEFINITION

In this sentence, the colon indicates an elaboration on the word *frightening*. The word *tyrant* reinforces this concept, so you are looking for words that could express frightening qualities of a tyrant's stare and words. *Malevolent* means exhibiting ill will, and *virulent* means hostile, harmful, or poisonous. The other answer choices can be eliminated, as they do not have the same connotations. *Mawkish* (A) means sickeningly sentimental, and *wry* means dryly humorous. In (B), *gamely* means bravely and *imperious* means arrogantly overbearing. *Tenuous* (C) means having little substance, literally or figuratively, and *sanctimonious* means feigning righteousness. In (D), *incarnadine* means flesh or blood colored, and *implacable* means impossible to appease or satisfy.

IF YOU LEARN ONLY FIVE THINGS IN THIS CHAPTER . . .

1. KAPLAN'S STRATEGY FOR SENTENCE COMPLETION QUESTIONS

Step 1. Read the sentence looking for clue words.

Step 2. Predict the answer.

Step 3. Select the best match.

Step 4. Plug your answer choice back into the sentence.

2. VALUABLE TOOLS FOR SENTENCE COMPLETIONS

- **Clue words:** Clue words are important keys to help you predict the correct answer: the relationship of one blank to the sentence or of two blanks to each other.

- **Word roots:** Prefixes and roots help you identify the word "family" a word relates to.

- **Foreign language:** French, Spanish, and Italian can help you define an English word.

- **Word charge:** The positive, negative, or neutral feeling of words help in elimination.

- **Similar words:** Similar sounding words **often** (not always) have similar meanings.

3. ONE-BLANK SENTENCES

In context, the right answer will:

- Define

- Contrast

- Show cause and effect/make sense in context

4. TWO-BLANK SENTENCES

In context, the right answers will:

- Have similar meanings

- Be in direct contrast to one another

- Show cause and effect/make sense together

Steps for Test Day Success · Tackling Hard Questions · Practice · Answers and Explanations · **Chapter Highlights**

5. OTHER HELPFUL STEPS

- Focus on whichever blank is easiest to predict.

- Eliminate all obviously wrong answers first.

- Remember that an unfamiliar word isn't correct *unless you are sure the others are wrong*.

- If you *know* four answers are wrong, pick the fifth, even if you have no idea what it means!

CHAPTER 8: READING COMPREHENSION STRATEGIES— SHORT PASSAGES

SMARTPOINTS COVERED IN THIS CHAPTER

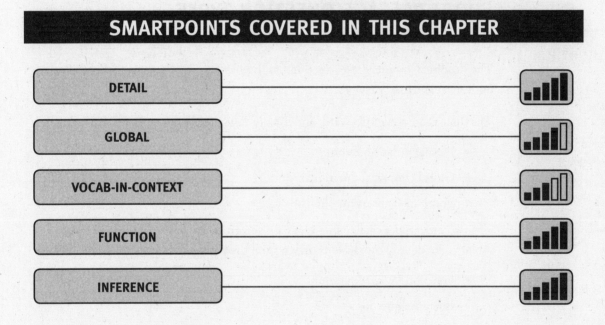

DETAIL

GLOBAL

VOCAB-IN-CONTEXT

FUNCTION

INFERENCE

SmartPoints | Ready for Test Day | Short Passage Questions | Practice | Answers and Explanations

WHAT TO EXPECT ON TEST DAY

The Reading Comprehension questions are divided into two types—short passages and long passages. We'll cover the short passages in this chapter and then look at the longer passages in chapter 9. Just remember that the two types are more alike than they are different. Everything you learn in this chapter will also help you tackle the longer passages.

As we have mentioned, the topics you will see will be based on the humanities, social sciences, natural sciences, and fiction. In order to do well on these, you must read actively and analyze information. You will not, however, need to have any previous knowledge about a topic to answer the questions. Everything you need to know will be right there in front of you.

SHORT PASSAGE QUESTION TYPES AND STRATEGIES

The Reading Comprehension section has five basic types of questions that follow both short and long passages.

The three more straightforward, and usually easier, questions are:

- Detail (What?) questions
- Global (Big Idea) questions
- Vocab-in-Context questions

The two often more challenging types ask you either to understand the author's intent or to identify conclusions drawn from the passage. They are:

- Function (Why?) questions
- Inference questions

Let's look at these in order of difficulty, starting with the easiest.

DETAIL QUESTIONS

These *What?* questions ask about specific facts or details in the passage and often provide you with a line reference or at least indicate the paragraph where the detail is located.

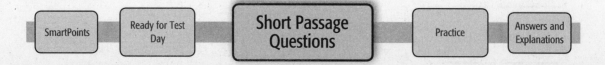

Detail questions test:

- Whether you understand significant information that's stated in the passage
- Your ability to locate information within a text
- Your ability to differentiate between main ideas and specific details

BE SMART!

Little Picture questions are usually easier to answer than Big Picture questions. Keep this in mind if you're short on time.

Sometimes the answer to a question will be directly in the line or lines that are referenced. Other times, you might need to read a few sentences before or after the referenced line(s) to find the correct answer. When in doubt, use the context (surrounding sentences) to confirm the right choice.

GLOBAL QUESTIONS

Global questions test how well you understand the passage as a whole. They ask about:

- The main point or purpose of a passage or individual paragraphs
- The author's overall attitude or tone
- The logic underlying the author's argument
- How ideas relate to each other in a passage

If you are stumped on a Global question, even after reading the passage, do the Detail questions first. They can often help you understand the big idea (and even some of the other, harder questions).

VOCABULARY-IN-CONTEXT QUESTIONS

Vocabulary-in-Context questions ask about the usage of a single word. These questions do not test your ability to define hard words like *archipelago* and *garrulous*. Instead, they test your ability to infer the meaning of a word from context.

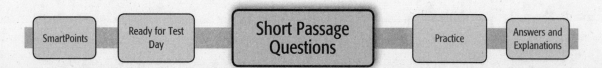

Words tested in SAT questions are usually fairly common words with more than one definition. But that's the trick! Many of the answer choices will be definitions of the tested word, but only one will work in context. Vocabulary-in-Context questions almost always have a line reference, and you should always use it!

Sometimes one of the answer choices will jump out at you. It will be the most common meaning of the word in question—but it's RARELY right. You can think of this as the *obvious* choice. Say *curious* is the word being tested. The obvious choice is *inquisitive*. But curious also means *odd*, and that's more likely to be the answer.

Using context to find the answer will help keep you from falling for this kind of trap. But you can also use these obvious choices to your advantage. If you get stuck on a Vocabulary-in-Context question, you can eliminate the obvious choice and guess from the remaining answers.

KAPLAN'S STRATEGY FOR VOCABULARY-IN-CONTEXT QUESTIONS:

Step 1. Reread the sentence containing the word and the sentences nearby.

Step 2. Treat it as you would a Sentence Completion sentence.

FUNCTION QUESTIONS

These *Why?* questions are a little tricky because they require you to take an extra step *beyond* the *What?* of the passage. To answer these questions effectively you must put yourself in the author's place.

A Function question will ask you:

- Why include this detail?
- Why include this word?
- Why include this sentence?
- Why include this quote?
- Why include this paragraph?

Your job is to look back in the passage using the line references or other hints the question stem gives you. There you will discover clues to the answer. Most often, you have to read around any lines they give you to find the answer.

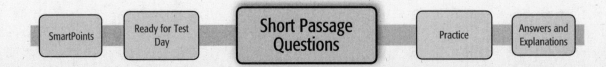

SmartPoints · Ready for Test Day · **Short Passage Questions** · Practice · Answers and Explanations

This question type brings the second pair of Kaplan's Golden Rules to the foreground:

- Function questions are easy to spot because they have distinctive phrasing. You'll see the following phrases in the question stem: *serves to, in order to, is meant to, is used to,* or *functions as.*

- Be careful as you go through the answers. Sometimes you'll see an answer that is really a Detail/What answer, and a perfectly good answer—for a different question.

INFERENCE QUESTIONS

To *infer* is to draw a conclusion based on reasoning or evidence. For example, if you wake up in the morning and there's three feet of fresh snow on the ground, you can infer that school will be canceled.

Often, writers will use suggestion or inference rather than stating ideas directly. But they will also leave you plenty of clues so you can figure out just what they are trying to convey. Inference clues include word choice (diction), tone, and specific details. For example, say a passage states that a particular idea *was perceived as revolutionary*. You might infer from the use of the word *perceived* that the author believes the idea was not truly revolutionary but only *perceived* (or seen) that way.

Thus, Inference questions test your ability to use the information in the passage to come to a logical conclusion. The key to Inference questions is to stick to the evidence in the text. Most Inference questions have pretty strong clues, so avoid any answer choices that seem far-fetched. If you can't find any evidence in the passage, then it probably isn't the right answer.

DON'T FORGET!

Make sure you read Inference questions carefully. Some answer choices may be true, but if they can't be inferred from the passage, then they can't be the correct answer.

Inference questions ask you to read between the lines. The correct answer will be a small step from what is directly said in the passage. They are easy to spot because they have distinctive phrasing.

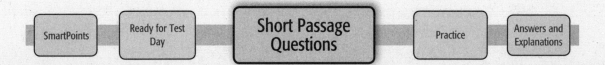

You'll see one of the following phrases in the question stem:

- *Suggests, implies, infers, would regard as, most directly supports the conclusion that*

STRATEGIES FOR ANSWERING SHORT PASSAGE QUESTIONS

You'll find the following strategies helpful when answering Reading Comprehension questions. You must be able to identify the type of question being asked, do research, make predictions, and identify trick answers.

The SAT is an open-book test, and focusing on details is a waste of time, especially on long passages. Instead, concentrate only on the main focus of each paragraph.

The key is to know where to read closely *once you have begun to answer the questions*. Begin by reading the entire passage quickly, knowing that you are going to come back in search of answers—and points.

KAPLAN'S TARGET STRATEGY FOR READING COMPREHENSION QUESTIONS

Serious skimming is a vital component of Kaplan's Target Strategy for attacking Reading Comprehension questions. Once you have seriously skimmed the passage, here's how to attack the questions:

Step 1. Read the question stem.

Step 2. Locate the material you need.

Step 3. Predict the answer.

Step 4. Select the best answer choice.

STEP 1. READ THE QUESTION STEM

This is the time and place to read very carefully. Make sure you understand exactly what the question is asking.

Keep the following in mind:

- Look for the following flag words and phrases: *in order to, implies, because*, etc.

- Are you looking for a main idea or specific information?

- Are you trying to determine the author's attitude or *why* someone did something?

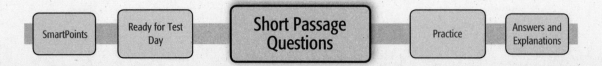

STEP 2. LOCATE THE MATERIAL YOU NEED

If you are given a line reference, read the material surrounding the line mentioned. It will clarify exactly what the question is asking and provide you with the context you need to answer the question correctly.

If you're not given a line reference, scan the text to find the place where the question applies, and quickly reread those few sentences. Keep the main point of the passage in mind.

STEP 3. PREDICT THE ANSWER

Don't spend time making up a precise answer. You need only a general sense of what you're after so you can recognize the correct answer quickly when you read the choices.

STEP 4. SELECT THE BEST ANSWER CHOICE

Scan the choices, looking for one that fits your idea of the right answer. If you don't find an ideal answer, quickly eliminate wrong choices by checking back to the passage. Rule out choices that are too extreme or go against common sense. Get rid of answers that sound reasonable but don't make sense in the context of the passage or the question. Don't pick far-fetched inferences, and make sure there is evidence for your inference in the passage. Remember, SAT inferences tend to be strongly implied in the passage.

WRONG ANSWER TRAPS

It is as important to read the answers as it is the question stems in the Reading Comprehension section. The test makers often set traps throughout the section. Don't worry, once you know where trouble lies, you won't be fooled!

These are the most common wrong answer traps:

- **Out of Scope:** The answer lies outside the passage topic or is only vaguely connected to it.
- **Extreme:** If it's strong, it's wrong. Beware of answer choices with words such as *all, only, never, always, most, least,* or *unique.*
- **Opposite:** Small syllables (*unusual* vs. *usual*) or a small word, such as *not,* change everything.
- **Distortion:** An answer starts out promising but turns into a wrong answer with the addition of a single word or two.
- **Misused Detail:** This is an answer that is true, but refers to a different section of the text.

> **EXPERT TUTOR TIP**
>
> " Remember to select the answer that best matches your prediction. Don't get swayed by a wrong answer that is too extreme or out of the scope of the passage. "

> **PERFECT SCORE TIP**
>
> " Knowing why the incorrect answer choices were wrong really let me understand the traps that come up frequently, which helped raise my score. "

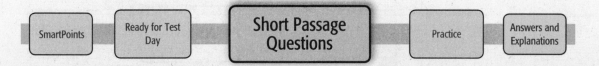

SmartPoints — Ready for Test Day — **Short Passage Questions** — Practice — Answers and Explanations

The bottom line: Remember to read the question stems *before* you read short passages. Underline the words that you'll likely see while reading the passage. This short, preliminary step will save you time and help you find the right answers.

PRACTICE

Try Kaplan's Target Strategy on the passage and question that follow.

Question 1 refers to the following passage.

Recently, at my grandmother's eightieth birthday party, my family looked at old photographs. In one of them, I saw a scared little boy holding tightly to his mother's skirt, and I scarcely recognized myself. My foremost memory of that
(5) time is simply being cold—the mild Vietnamese winters that I had known couldn't prepare me for the bitter winds of the American Midwest. The cold seemed emblematic of everything I hated about my new country—we had no friends, no extended family, and we all lived together in a
(10) two-room apartment. My mother, ever shrewd, remarked that selling heat in such a cold place would surely bring fortune, and she was right. My parents now own a successful heating supply company.

1. The author's attitude toward the "scared little boy" mentioned in line 3, indicates that the author

    (A) is unsure that the photograph is actually of his family
    (B) believes that the boy is likely overly dependent on his mother
    (C) feels that he has changed considerably since childhood
    (D) regards his mother's strategy to sell heating supplies as clever
    (E) regrets his family's move to the United States

STEP 1. READ THE QUESTION STEM

In this case, the question is straightforward: what does the author think about the little boy? It asks you to make an inference about the author's attitude.

STEP 2. LOCATE THE MATERIAL YOU NEED

You're given a line reference, so be sure and go back to that line. But don't read just that specific line—read the line or two before and after as well. When you do, you see that the author says that he scarcely recognizes himself. From this, you know that the boy in the picture is the author when he was younger.

STEP 3. PREDICT THE ANSWER

Why would the author say that he scarcely recognizes himself? The implication is that the author (now grown) is so different from that frightened little boy that it's hard to believe they're the same person. So look for an answer choice that matches this prediction.

STEP 4. SELECT THE BEST ANSWER CHOICE

(A) is too literal—the author is speaking figuratively when he says he scarcely recognizes the boy.

(B) goes too far in making an inference. Although the boy is sticking close to his mother in the picture, there's no evidence that the author thinks this is a bad thing.

(C) is a great match for your prediction and is the correct answer.

(D) might be a true statement, but it comes later in the passage. It has nothing to do with the author's attitude toward the boy in the picture.

(E) like (B), is too great a leap and can't safely be inferred from the information in the passage.

Now try Kaplan's Target Strategy on the remaining questions for the passages. Question 2 uses the same passage that we used for question 1; we've reprinted the passage on the following page. (Answers are on page 160. We also show you there how to apply the Target Strategy to questions 3 and 4.)

> **EXPERT TUTOR TIP**
>
> " Predict an answer before looking at the choices; otherwise, you'll see several choices that sound plausible and have to decide between them. "

SmartPoints | Ready for Test Day | Short Passage Questions | **Practice** | Answers and Explanations

Question 2 refers to the following passage.

Recently, at my grandmother's eightieth birthday party, my family looked at old photographs. In one of them, I saw a scared little boy holding tightly to his mother's skirt, and I scarcely recognized myself. My foremost memory of that
(5) time is simply being cold—the mild Vietnamese winters that I had known couldn't prepare me for the bitter winds of the American Midwest. The cold seemed emblematic of everything I hated about my new country—we had no friends, no extended family, and we all lived together in a
(10) two-room apartment. My mother, ever shrewd, remarked that selling heat in such a cold place would surely bring fortune, and she was right. My parents now own a success-ful heating supply company.

2. Lines 10–14 ("My mother . . . heating supply com-pany") suggest that the author's mother regarded the cold of the American Midwest as

   (A) more drastic than that of Vietnam
   (B) an opportunity for economic success
   (C) an obstacle to familial happiness
   (D) symbolic of other challenges and problems
   (E) unimportant to the family's future

Questions 3–4 refer to the following passage.

Many mammals instinctively raise their fur when they
are cold—a reaction produced by tiny muscles just under
the skin which surround hair follicles. When the muscles
contract, the hairs stand up, creating an increased air space
(5) under the fur. The air space provides more effective insulation for the mammal's body, thus allowing it to retain more
heat for longer periods of time. Some animals also raise
their fur when they are challenged by predators or even
other members of their own species. The raised fur makes
(10) the animal appear slightly bigger, and, ideally, more powerful. Interestingly, though devoid of fur, humans still retain
this instinct. So, the next time a horror movie gives you
"goosebumps," remember that your skin is following a
deep-seated mammalian impulse now rendered obsolete.

3. The "increased air space under the fur" mentioned
   in lines 4–5 serves primarily to

   (A) combat cold
   (B) intimidate other animals
   (C) render goosebumps obsolete
   (D) cool overheated predators
   (E) make mammals more powerful

4. Based on the passage, the author would most likely
   describe "goosebumps" in humans as

   (A) an unnecessary and unexplained phenomenon
   (B) a harmful but necessary measure
   (C) an amusing but dangerous feature
   (D) a useless but interesting remnant
   (E) a powerful but infrequent occurrence

Questions 5–6 refer to the following passage.

Elizabeth Barrett Browning, a feminist writer of the
Victorian Era, used her poetry and prose to take on a wide
range of issues facing her society, including "the woman
question." In her long poem *Aurora Leigh*, she explores this
(5) question as she portrays both the growth of the artist and
the growth of the woman within. Aurora Leigh is not a traditional Victorian woman—she is well educated and self-
sufficient. In the poem, Browning argues that the limitations
placed on women in contrast to the freedom men
(10) enjoy should incite women to rise up and effect a change
in their circumstances. Browning's writing, including
Aurora Leigh, helped to pave the way for major social
change in women's lives.

5. It can be inferred from the passage that the author
   believes the traditional Victorian woman

   (A) wrote poetry
   (B) was portrayed accurately in *Aurora Leigh*
   (C) fought for social change
   (D) was not well educated
   (E) had a public role in society

6. As used in line 10, "effect" most nearly means

   (A) imitate
   (B) result
   (C) cause
   (D) disturb
   (E) prevent

Questions 7–8 refer to the following passage.

Each passing evening brings more frustration. Tonight I spent an hour in front of the typewriter staring at the silent keys, listening to the girl upstairs play the piano and sing. I'd never noticed her ability before; she is remarkable. It
(5) seems everything she plays is of her own spontaneous creation, an absolute movement of feeling. Her music is a painting, the lines so intense and coloring that it manages to exist above the realm of the material, impressing a desolate image of the pianist upon my mind. But even the
(10) beauty of this pure work of art failed to inspire me, and after she stopped I was again without refuge.

7. In lines 2–3 the phrase "silent keys" implies that the narrator

   (A) can't play the piano
   (B) is suffering from writer's block
   (C) is tone deaf
   (D) is searching for clues
   (E) is annoyed by the girl upstairs

8. The narrator uses the description of the girl's playing in lines 4–6 (It seems . . . feeling) mainly to

   (A) contrast it with his inability to write
   (B) illustrate her talents as a musician
   (C) compare it with painting
   (D) criticize her lack of skill
   (E) indicate his inferiority as an artist

Questions 9–10 refer to the following passage.

Bear Mountain State Park opened in 1916 and rapidly became a popular weekend destination for many New Yorkers looking for an escape from the city grind. The ensuing unnaturally high volume of visitors to the area
(5) caused an upsurge in traffic, and it was soon apparent that the ferry services used to cross the Hudson were insufficient. In 1922, the New York State Legislature introduced a bill that authorized a group of private investors led by Mary Harriman to build a bridge across the river. The
(10) group, known as the Bear Mountain Hudson Bridge Company, was allotted thirty years to construct and maintain the bridge, after which the span would be handed over to New York State.

9. In context, "volume," (line 4) most closely means

   (A) loudness
   (B) pollution
   (C) resentment
   (D) capacity
   (E) quantity

10. According to the passage, which is true about the bridge?

   I. It was originally constructed by New York State

   II. It opened to the public in 1916

   III. It was necessitated by inadequate ferry services

   (A) Statement II
   (B) Statement III
   (C) Statements I and II
   (D) Statements I and III
   (E) Statements II and III

Questions 11–12 refer to the following passage.

Like the writers of the Beat Generation almost a half-century before, many of the original grunge musicians who helped give birth to a movement were horrified at the final result of their efforts. Grunge music and culture was
(5) spawned in Seattle in the late 1980s as an underground revolt against the shallow values of the time. But with Nirvana's 1991 release of *Nevermind*, and the successive popularity of other Seattle bands like Pearl Jam and Soundgarden, the once-countercultural grunge movement
(10) skyrocketed into popular consciousness. Many aspects of the culture that were originally forms of rebellion, such as the hairstyles and fashions worn by grunge musicians, found their way into the most mainstream of places.

11. In lines 1–2, the author invokes the Beat Generation in order to

   (A) detail an earlier movement in music
   (B) introduce the topic by illustrating a similarity
   (C) imply the insignificance of grunge
   (D) recall an important time in American cultural history
   (E) emphasize grunge's influence upon today's music

12. As used in line 3, "movement" most closely means

   (A) an organized attempt at change
   (B) a specific manner of moving
   (C) the changing of location or position
   (D) a rhythmic progression or tempo
   (E) a mainstream belief

Questions 13–14 refer to the following passage.

Bovine spongiform encephalopathy (BSE) is a fatal, transmissible, neurological disorder found in cattle that slowly attacks a cow's brain cells, forming what resembles sponge-like holes in its brain. As the disease progresses, the
(5) cow begins to behave abnormally, hence BSE's more common name, "Mad Cow Disease."

On December 23, 2003, the first case of BSE in the U.S. was detected in a cow from Washington State. The ensuing national hysteria was largely unfounded; years earlier, in response to the previous epidemics abroad, the USFDA had
(10) implemented preventative measures to contain an outbreak of the disease before it could spread. These measures were in place for a good reason: there is a causal link between eating BSE-infected meat and the development of a fatal human brain disorder known as new variant Creutzfeldt-
(15) Jakob Disease (nvCJD).

13. The first paragraph mostly serves to

    (A) explain the origin of the term "Mad Cow Disease"

    (B) introduce background information on BSE

    (C) warn of BSE's transmissibility to humans

    (D) dissuade people from eating meat

    (E) provide in-depth description of BSE's different stages

14. Which of the following best describes the "national hysteria" in line 9 of the passage?

    (A) totally justified

    (B) necessary for USFDA policy change

    (C) rooted in misinformation about BSE's harmfulness

    (D) completely inexcusable

    (E) understandable, but unnecessary

SmartPoints | Ready for Test Day | Short Passage Questions | **Practice** | Answers and Explanations

Questions 15–16 refer to the following passage.

Ann's footsteps crunching upon the fallen leaves are
amplified by the pre-dusk serenity that is quickly setting
upon the forest. The path before her is quickly dissolving
into the growing shadows, yet the fear that would normally
(5) be creeping into her chest is absent. Somewhere secretly
inside she finds the prospect of disappearing into the
woods exhilarating. Liberated, all her daily burdens would
go as the daylight goes, only the empty night, spattered
with benevolent stars. But as the trail opens onto her back-
(10) yard, Ann is surprised to find herself breaking into
a trot, eager to return to the familiar warmth of her home.

15. Ann's absence of fear (lines 4–5) suggests that she

   (A) is brave in the face of danger
   (B) doesn't realize she is lost
   (C) is an apathetic person
   (D) longs for a change in her life
   (E) knows exactly where she is

16. In line 8, "the empty night" is symbolic of

   (A) everyday life
   (B) a lack of responsibility
   (C) being lost
   (D) loneliness
   (E) death

SmartPoints | Ready for Test Day | Short Passage Questions | **Practice** | Answers and Explanations

ANSWERS AND EXPLANATIONS

1. C

SMARTPOINTS CATEGORIES: INFERENCE

GLOBAL

Explanation on pages 150–151.

2. B

SMARTPOINTS CATEGORY: INFERENCE

The word *suggests* indicates that this is an Inference question.

Context clues from lines 10–13 include the word *shrewd* and the inference that selling heat would *surely bring fortune*. Although choice (A) is certainly true of the passage, it is not specifically referred to in the lines cited. There was no mention of the cold being an obstacle (C) or of it being unimportant (E), so choice (B) is the correct answer.

3. A

SMARTPOINTS CATEGORY: FUNCTION

Here's how you could solve this question using Kaplan's strategy:

STEP 1. READ THE QUESTION STEM

Because the question has the words *serves primarily to*, you know it is a Function question.

STEP 2. LOCATE THE MATERIAL YOU NEED

When you read around the lines given (meaning lines 3–7), you see that the air space *provides more effective insulation for the mammal's body*. This leads directly to a good prediction, and Step 3.

STEP 3. PREDICT THE ANSWER

It looks like the increased air space helps keep the animal warm.

STEP 4. SELECT THE BEST ANSWER CHOICE

(B) can be tempting because raised fur also intimidates other animals. However, that point is made later in the passage and is a Misused Detail. Your prediction is about combating cold.

You are left with (A) as your choice. It is the only one that fits. Note that if you had not followed the Four-Step Method, you could have been easily sidetracked by (B) or (E).

4. D

SMARTPOINTS CATEGORY: INFERENCE

The phrase *would most likely describe* in question 4 flags this as an Inference question. Here's how you might answer it with Kaplan's Four-Step Method:

STEP 1. READ THE QUESTION STEM

Seems simple enough: what does the author think about goosebumps?

STEP 2: LOCATE THE MATERIAL YOU NEED

This question doesn't cite the lines where *goosebumps* are discussed, but because you underlined the keyword *goosebumps* in the question stem before reading the passage, you know where to look. In addition, you know to read around the lines given, so you probably would begin rereading at line 9.

STEP 3. PREDICT THE ANSWER

You might say something like, "Goosebumps are left over from when people had fur."

STEP 4: SELECT THE BEST ANSWER CHOICE

(D) looks very good. Note that the *word interesting* in the answer echoes *Interestingly* in the passage—another clue that it is the right answer.

5. D

SMARTPOINTS CATEGORY: INFERENCE

The answer to this question can be found in lines 6–8. The author writes, *Aurora Leigh is not a traditional Victorian woman—she is well educated and self-sufficient.* This statement sets up the contrast between Aurora, who is well educated, and the traditional Victorian woman, who is not well educated.

6. C

SMARTPOINTS CATEGORY: VOCAB-IN-CONTEXT

The word *effect* is both a noun and a verb, so you must look at its use in the sentence to determine its part of speech and meaning. The word is used in the phrase *to rise up and effect a change*. If you are unclear of the meaning, try inserting the answer choices in the sentence to see if they make sense: to *imitate* a change, to *result* a change, to *cause* a change, to *disturb* a change, to *prevent* a change. Although you may have been tempted to choose (B), *result*, thinking that effect is a noun, the only answer choice that makes sense in the context of the sentence is choice (C), *cause*.

7. B

SMARTPOINTS CATEGORY: INFERENCE

The word *implies* shows that this is an Inference question. The *silent keys* referred to in the passage are the keys of a typewriter, and the fact that they are described as *silent* implies that they are not in use. Using what the author offered you in the first sentence about his mounting frustration, you are looking for the choice that best reflects what conclusions can be drawn from this phrase. (A) is a distortion; the silent keys are those of a typewriter, not a piano. The author never mentions whether or not he can play the piano. (C) is the opposite of what you're looking for. The author's detailed description of the music upstairs proves that he is obviously not *tone deaf*. (D) is out of scope. The narrator may be searching for clues to break his writer's block, but this implication makes no sense within the scope of the paragraph. (E) is also opposite. The girl's playing does not annoy the narrator; in fact, in the paragraph's final sentence he admits that he found *refuge* in it. (B) is the best answer.

8. A

SMARTPOINTS CATEGORY: FUNCTION

This is a Function question. The narrator's description of the piano player has one overarching function in the paragraph—the ease with which she plays the piano offers a stark contrast to the narrator's writer's block, thus highlighting his frustration. (B) and (C) are distortions. Although the description does serve to *illustrate her talents* (B), it's true function in the paragraph is to emphasize the author's frustration with his own writer's block. Also, the author compares the piano player's music to a painting (C) in the sentence that follows the one in question. (D) is the opposite of what you're looking for. The narrator describes the girl's playing as *remarkable*. (E) is out of scope; nowhere in the passage does the author offer a critique of his own skills, he simply tells of his frustration at not being able to employ them. (A) is a solid match with your prediction.

9. E

SMARTPOINTS CATEGORY: VOCAB-IN-CONTEXT

Often, the simplest way to answer a Vocabulary-in-Context problem is to replace the word in question with each of the given answer choices to see which fits best in the context of the sentence. Look for the word that could best be linked to *an upsurge in traffic* and *insufficient*. (A) is a distortion; this synonym of volume might have been a product of *the upsurge in traffic*, but it is unlikely to have been the cause of it. (B) and (C) are both out of scope. *Pollution* is an effect of traffic, but this makes no sense in context, and *resentment* is never alluded to in the passage. (D) is also a distortion. Although exceeding the *capacity* for cars in an area is the cause of traffic, this definition of *volume* does not work in terms of the sentence's structure. (E) is an excellent match for your prediction.

10. B

SMARTPOINTS CATEGORY: DETAIL

Don't let the Roman numeral statements affect your approach, this is a simple Detail question whose answer is specifically based in the facts of the passage. Verify each given statement, and find the answer choice that corresponds with the statement or statements that you validated. (A) is a distortion. Bear Mountain State Park opened in 1916. The bridge opened later, but the date is not mentioned. You can thus assume that (C) and (E) are incorrect, as well. (D) is also a distortion. Statement III is true, but I is false: New York State did not build the bridge, "it introduced a bill that authorized a group of private investors" to build it. (B) is the best answer.

11. B

SMARTPOINTS CATEGORY: FUNCTION

The phrase in the question stem *in order to* lets you know that this is a Function question. The author uses the similar experiences of the Beat writers and grunge musicians to establish the main idea of the passage. Look for the choice that best illustrates this statement. (A) is a distortion. The first sentence clearly establishes that the Beats were writers, not musicians. (C) is out of scope. The author never implies that the grunge movement was insignificant. By invoking the Beats, the author is recalling *an important time in American cultural history* (D), but this is not the purpose for the author's doing so. (E) is also out of scope. The author only mentions *grunge's influence* upon mainstream culture of the early '90s.

12. A

SMARTPOINTS CATEGORY: VOCAB-IN-CONTEXT

In line 4, the author describes the movements of the Beat writers and grunge musicians as *efforts*, and then in line 6 characterizes the grunge movement as a *revolt*. Look for the choice that contains the best definition of what both of these words could imply. (B) is out of scope. This alternate definition of *movement* makes no sense in the context of the passage. (C) is also out of scope. Again, this definition makes no sense in context. (D) is a distortion. The definition of *movement* used in the passage refers to the efforts of musicians, not a *rhythmic progression or tempo* in music. (E) is the opposite of what you're looking for. A movement is usually an organized effort by an individual or group to change a *mainstream belief*. (A) is the best choice.

13. B

SMARTPOINTS CATEGORY: FUNCTION

The phrase *serves to* lets you know that this is a Function question. The author uses the first paragraph to brief the reader on the basic facts about BSE, and then uses the second paragraph to explore the subject a bit further. You are looking for the choice that best fits the first paragraph's role in the author's use of structure. (A) is a distortion. This is only a supporting detail of the first paragraph—you are looking for the paragraph's overall purpose in the passage. (C) and (E) are also distortions; the transmissibility of BSE to humans (C) is not established until the second paragraph, and the quick summary of BSE's stages hardly amounts to *in-depth description* (E). (D) is out of scope. Although this first paragraph certainly may dissuade some from eating meat, that is not the intended function of the paragraph or the passage. (B) is an excellent match for your prediction.

14. E

SMARTPOINTS CATEGORIES: INFERENCE
GLOBAL

The phrase *best describes* denotes that this is an Inference question. You are looking for a phrase that best captures the author's point of view about the nation's reaction to BSE. The answer to this question lies in one important detail of the passage: the use of the word *largely* (line 9). The author describes the *national hysteria* as *largely* unfounded because while the USFDA was well prepared for such a scenario, the dire consequences of the disease should not be overlooked. (A) is the opposite of what the answer is. By definition, the word *hysteria* implies going a bit overboard in terms of response or emotion. (B) and (C) are distortions; the details of the passage clearly state that the USFDA had effected BSE policy change (B) long before the first case in the country, and (C) suggests that the hysteria was largely unfounded because BSE is not particularly harmful. (D) is too extreme; BSE is a fatal, transmissible disease. (E) is the best choice.

15. D

SMARTPOINTS CATEGORY: INFERENCE

The word *suggests* alerts you that this is an Inference question. The passage states that rather than fear, Ann secretly feels exhilarated by the *prospect of disappearing into the woods* because she would be *liberated* from *all her daily burdens*. You are looking for the choice that best conveys what these statements suggest about Ann. (A) is a distortion; the passage states that *normally*, Ann would be scared by the prospect of being lost in the woods at night. (B) is also a distortion. Ann is not lost; the passage deals only with the prospect of her losing her way in the woods. (C) is the opposite of the correct answer. The fact that Ann could find something *exhilarating* (line 7) proves that she is not *apathetic*. The fear would come from the prospect of Ann losing her way on the path as the darkness sets in, but the author never suggests that she does not know where she is on the path (E). (D) is the best choice.

16. B

SMARTPOINTS CATEGORY: VOCAB-IN-CONTEXT

Like the *daylight* (line 8), Ann wants her burdens to disappear into the night. Using this comparison, the answer is the choice that best expresses what the empty night represents with respect to her *daily burdens*. (A) is the opposite of the best answer; in the passage, *the empty night* is symbolic of what Ann hopes would replace in her *everyday life*. (C) and (D) are distortions. Don't be fooled by (C); *being lost* could be a literal representation of the empty night, but you're looking for the symbolic meaning. Although *empty night* may invoke images of *loneliness* (D), the author never suggests that Ann is lonely. (E) is also opposite of the correct choice. The passage deals with themes of life, not *death*. (B) is a solid choice.

IF YOU LEARN ONLY SIX THINGS IN THIS CHAPTER . . .

1. FIVE TYPES OF READING QUESTIONS

- **Detail:** *What* questions

- **Global:** Big Idea questions

- **Vocab-in-Context:** Word in a sentence questions

- **Function:** *Why* questions

- **Inference:** Read-between-the-lines questions

2. KAPLAN'S STRATEGY FOR READING COMPREHENSION QUESTIONS

Step 1. Read the question stem.

Step 2. Locate the material you need. The answer is in the passage. Read around the lines given.

Step 3. Predict the answer.

Step 4. Select the best answer choice.

3. WRONG ANSWER TYPES

- **Out of Scope:** The answer is beyond the passage.

- **Extreme:** If it's strong, it's wrong.

- **Opposite:** Beware of small syllables and the word *not*.

- **Distortion:** This is a word or two that ruins an answer.

- **Misused Detail:** This is an answer referring to a different section of the text.

4. ACTIVE READING

- Understand the big picture of each passage with the ABCs:

    - A Abbreviate margin notes

    - B Bracket key sentences

    - C Circle keywords

- *Why* is more important than *what*.

- Keep straight *who* said what.

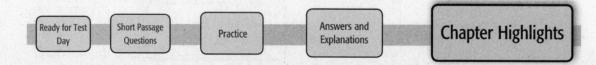

Ready for Test Day | Short Passage Questions | Practice | Answers and Explanations | Chapter Highlights

5. SHORT PASSAGES AND QUESTIONS

- Remember to read the question stems *before* you read short passages.

- Underline the words that you'll likely see *while* reading the passage.

6. LONG PASSAGES AND QUESTIONS

- The questions are not arranged from easy to hard, so make sure you get to them all.

- Skip a question if you need to and come back to it (before moving to another passage).

- Answering Detail questions can help you choose the answers to Global questions.

CHAPTER 9: READING COMPREHENSION STRATEGIES— LONG PASSAGES

SMARTPOINTS COVERED IN THIS CHAPTER

| DETAIL |
| FUNCTION |
| INFERENCE |
| GLOBAL |
| VOCAB-IN-CONTEXT |
| COMPARISONS |

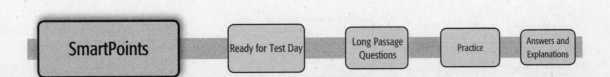

SmartPoints · Ready for Test Day · Long Passage Questions · Practice · Answers and Explanations

WHAT TO EXPECT ON TEST DAY

You use the same skills and strategies to tackle long passages as you do short passages—**Active Reading** and **Kaplan's Strategy for Reading Comprehension Questions.**

In addition, the passages cover similar topics—humanities, social sciences, natural sciences, and prose fiction.

What's the difference? With longer passages, you need to work harder to stay focused and organized. You might have been able to cut some corners in the short passages. Not with these—you need all your skills sharpened and ready.

LONG PASSAGE QUESTION TYPES AND STRATEGIES

There are a few things to keep in mind when you read the long passages. Consider these as strategies that will help you master the section.

QUESTION ORDER

Although Reading Comprehension questions are not arranged by degree of difficulty, they do have a specific order for longer passages. In general, the questions correspond to the passage, so the first few questions ask about the beginning of the passage, the middle questions about the middle, and the last few questions about the end. The last couple of questions are likely to be Big Picture questions that ask you about the overall main idea of the passage.

INTRODUCTION

Each long passage begins with a brief introduction that tells you what the passage is about. This is an important part of the question set and should not be skipped. The introduction helps you focus your reading by preparing you for the kind of information and ideas to come.

MAP IT

Longer passages cover many aspects of a topic. For example, the first paragraph might introduce the subject, the second paragraph might present one viewpoint, and the third paragraph might argue for a different viewpoint. Within each of these paragraphs, there are several details that help the author convey a message.

> **PERFECT SCORE TIP**
>
> " Knowing the topic and opinion in each paragraph helped me eliminate incorrect answer choices easily, especially if they were too narrow or contradicted part of the passage. "

> **EXPERT TUTOR TIP**
>
> " Don't skip the introduction! This is usually where the author states the main point of the passage. "

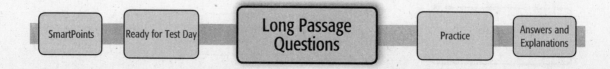

SmartPoints · Ready for Test Day · **Long Passage Questions** · Practice · Answers and Explanations

Long passages cover many aspects and, because there is a lot to keep track of, you need to confront them as follows:

- **Write** the simplest notes possible in the margin—abbreviations work well, but be sure you understand them.

- **Note** the summary purpose of each paragraph—such as *backgrd, opin, pro, con*, etc.

- **Bracket or circle** key points (keep underlining to a minimum).

- **Mark** places where opinion and point of view are expressed—the chance of seeing questions on these points is nearly 100 percent.

- **Pay attention** to all contrasting elements—one person thinks one thing, while another thinks another. *Keep these, along with what the author thinks, straight.*

These notes are your *passage map*. The passage map helps you find the part of the passage that contains the information you need. The process of creating your passage map also forces you to read actively. This is especially helpful in the SAT's second and third hour when your energy is flagging. Because you are constantly trying to identify the author's viewpoint and the purpose of each sentence and paragraph, you will be working hard to understand what's happening in the passage. This translates into points on the test.

> **EXPERT TUTOR TIP**
>
> " Writing down the main idea of each paragraph is the most valuable part of mapping the passage, yet it is the part that most students skip. Don't skip it! "

PASSAGE MAPS

A good passage map:
- Contains short words or phrases
- Uses clear marks like underlines and circled words
- Concentrates on viewpoints and opinions
- Notes opinions other than the author's
- Avoids too-specific details

READING RATE

How you mark a passage often depends on how fast or slowly you read.

- Some students read quickly and have time to make fairly detailed notes.

- Others read more slowly and have to keep their notes to a minimum.

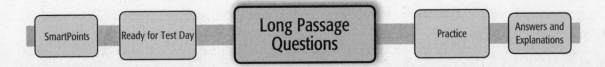

SmartPoints | Ready for Test Day | **Long Passage Questions** | Practice | Answers and Explanations

You know what kind of reader you are and how fast you can go without losing all understanding?

Note: The effective skimming of text, known as Active Reading, is important to work on. The time allowance for each Reading section in the test means that you need to read long passages in two or three minutes, at most. But you *don't* get points for reading, just for answering questions correctly.

What's the bottom line? The better you are at Active Reading, the more time you'll have for point-gathering.

READING RECAP

In addition to Kaplan's Strategy for Answering Reading questions, don't forget:

- **In Active Reading:**
  - *Why* is more important than *what*.
  - Keep straight *who* said what.

- **In answering questions:**
  - Predict before you peek.
  - The answer is in the passage. Read around the lines given.

PASSAGE MAP PRACTICE

Write a passage map of this sample SAT passage using the guidelines we just provided.

What a marvelous and celestial creature was Leonardo da Vinci. As a scientist and engineer, his gifts were unparalleled. But his accomplishments in these capacities were hindered by the fact that he was, before all else, an artist. As one conversant with the perfection of
(5)   art, and knowing the futility of trying to bring such perfection to the realm of practical application, Leonardo tended toward variability and inconstancy in his endeavors. His practice of moving compulsively from one project to the next, never bringing any of them to completion, stood in the way of his making any truly useful technical advances.
(10)   When Leonardo was asked to create a memorial for one of his patrons, he designed a bronze horse of such vast proportions that it proved utterly impractical—even impossible—to produce. Some historians maintain that Leonardo never had any intention of finishing this work in the first place. But it is more likely that he simply became so
(15)   intoxicated by his grand artistic conception that he lost sight of the fact that the monument actually had to be cast.
       Similarly, when Leonardo was commissioned to paint the *Last Supper*, he left the head of Christ unfinished, feeling incapable of investing it with a sufficiently divine demeanor. Yet, as a work of art rather than
(20)   science or engineering, it is still worthy of our greatest veneration, for

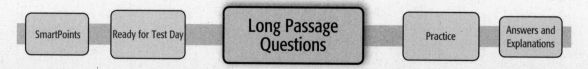

Leonardo succeeded brilliantly in capturing the acute anxiety of the Apostles at the most dramatic moment of the Passion narrative.

Such mental restlessness, however, proved more prob-
(25) lematic when applied to scientific matters. When he turned his mind to the natural world, Leonardo would begin by inquiring into the properties of herbs and end up observing the motions of the heavens. In his technical studies and scientific experiments, he would generate an
(30) endless stream of models and drawings, designing complex and unbuildable machines to raise great weights, bore through mountains, or even empty harbors.

It is this enormous intellectual fertility that has suggested to many that Leonardo can and should be regarded
(35) as one of the originators of modern science. But Leonardo was not himself a true scientist. "Science" is not the hundred-odd principles or *pensieri* that have been pulled out of his *Codici*. Science is comprehensive and methodical thought.
(40) Granted, Leonardo always became fascinated by the intricacies of specific technical challenges. He possessed the artist's interest in detail, which explains his compulsion with observation and problem solving. But such things alone do not constitute science, which requires the work-
(45) ing out of a systematic body of knowledge—something Leonardo displayed little interest in doing.

Before you turn the page to see how we marked up this passage, remember that there is no *one* way to mark up a passage. Students should develop their own style within the guidelines we have set up.

Now take a look at our passage map notes on the next page. Did you highlight similar parts of the passage? Did you concentrate on the author's views? Look carefully at your mark up. How would you summarize the author's main idea?

> **PERFECT SCORE TIP**
>
> " It's incredibly important to read actively. Whenever I broke my concentration, I couldn't remember anything and wasted time having to reread the passage. "

> **EXPERT TUTOR TIP**
>
> " The author usually gives the reader the main idea of each paragraph in his topic sentences. Pay close attention to these when creating your passage map. "

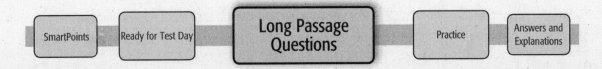

SmartPoints | Ready for Test Day | **Long Passage Questions** | Practice | Answers and Explanations

PERFECT SCORE TIP

" Mapping really helped me get through some of the more difficult passages. Underlining key sentences and writing down the topic of each paragraph helped me understand what the passage was actually saying. "

What a marvelous and celestial creature was Leonardo da Vinci. As a scientist and engineer, his gifts were unparalleled. But his accomplishments in these capacities were hindered by the fact that he was, before all else, an artist. As
(5) one conversant with the perfection of art, and knowing the futility of trying to bring such perfection to the realm of practical application, Leonardo tended toward variability and inconstancy in his endeavors. His practice of moving compulsively from one project to the next, never bringing
(10) any of them to completion, stood in the way of his making any truly useful technical advances.

OP– L is great

MainPoint—L is genius, but never stuck w/1 thing long enuf 2B a "scientist"

OP – L underachieved

When Leonardo was asked to create a memorial for one of his patrons, he designed a bronze horse of such vast proportions that it proved utterly impractical—even
(15) impossible—to produce. Some historians maintain that Leonardo never had any intention of finishing this work in the first place. But it is more likely that he simply became so intoxicated by his grand artistic conception that he lost sight of the fact that the monument actually had to
(20) be cast. Similarly, when Leonardo was commissioned to paint the *Last Supper*, he left the head of Christ unfinished, feeling incapable of investing it with a sufficiently divine demeanor. Yet, as a work of art rather than science or engineering, it is still worthy of our greatest veneration,
(25) for Leonardo succeeded brilliantly in capturing the acute anxiety of the Apostles at the most dramatic moment of the Passion narrative.

Ex #1 – horse

alt. opinion

OP – L is a genius but impractical

Ex #2 – last Sup

MainPoint L gets caught up in idea, forgets actual work

Such mental restlessness, however, proved more problematic when applied to scientific matters. When he turned
(30) his mind to the natural world, Leonardo would begin by inquiring into the properties of herbs and end up observing the motions of the heavens. In his technical studies and scientific experiments, he would generate an endless stream of models and drawings, designing complex and unbuild-
(35) able machines to raise great weights, bore through mountains, or even empty harbors.

OP – switching from art to science here

Ex #1 – Natural

Ex #2 – technical

MainPoint: L's short attention span bad for science

It is this enormous intellectual fertility that has suggested to many that Leonardo can and should be regarded as one of the originators of modern science. But Leonardo
(40) was not himself a true scientist. "Science" is not the hundred-odd principles or *pensieri* that have been pulled out of his *Codici*. Science is comprehensive and methodical thought. Granted, Leonardo always became fascinated by the intricacies of specific technical challenges. He possessed
(45) the artist's interest in detail, which explains his compulsion with observation and problem solving. But such things

alt. opinion

OP

back?

MainPoint—L is genius and a compulsive problem-solver, but no scientist

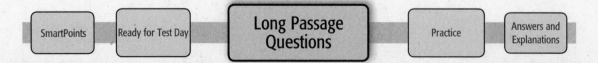

SmartPoints | Ready for Test Day | **Long Passage Questions** | Practice | Answers and Explanations

alone do not constitute science, which requires the working out of a <u>systematic body of knowledge</u>—something ⎯⎯ L not good
Leonardo displayed little interest in doing.   at

PAIRED PASSAGES

The SAT will include at least one long paired passage and one short paired passage.
Paired passages are two separate passages that relate to the same topic. Questions
following paired passages are generally ordered the same way. The first few questions
relate to the first passage, the next few to the second passage, and the final questions
ask about the passages as a pair.

Don't let the paired passages intimidate you—they're not twice as hard as the
single-passage reading selections. In fact, students often find the paired passages
the most interesting selections on the test.

> **EXPERT TUTOR TIP**
>
> " A challenging part of paired passages is keeping straight *who* says *what*. Kaplan's method makes this much easier because you consider each passage individually. "

KAPLAN'S TARGET STRATEGY FOR PAIRED PASSAGES

Follow the Reading Comprehension strategies given and use the following systematic
approach for paired passages:

- **Step 1:** Read Passage 1 and answer the questions about it.
- **Step 2:** Read Passage 2 and answer the questions about it.
- **Step 3:** Answer the questions asking about both passages.

Because you have to keep track of two different viewpoints with paired passages, it's
especially important to read actively and create a map for each passage.

Ask yourself as you read the *first* passage:

- What is the author's main point?

When you read the *second* passage, ask yourself:

- How is this different or similar to the first passage?

TIMING STRATEGIES FOR THE READING SECTION

What's the best way to use your time in the Reading sections?

Leave as much time as possible for reading and answering the long passage questions.
These take more time than either the short reading or the Sentence Completions.

> **PERFECT SCORE TIP**
>
> " It definitely helped to do the questions that related to both passages last. After answering the other questions, I understood the purposes and themes of each really well. "

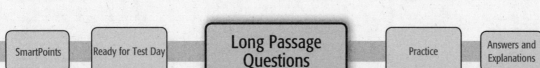

SmartPoints | Ready for Test Day | **Long Passage Questions** | Practice | Answers and Explanations

Here is a possible plan for a 25-minute section:

- Spend only two or three minutes on the Sentence Completions.

- Save a minute or two at the end to come back to the harder Sentence Completion questions.

- Short passages should take no more than 5 minutes, less if possible.

- Two long passages (paired or not) usually follow; you'll want *at least* 15 minutes for reading and answering the questions, more if possible.

Note: The shorter 20-minute section has 19 questions and often has no short passages, so you'll be able to adapt the above timing strategy to fit.

Also, remember to skip around within the section if you need to. You can tackle the passages in any order you like within the same section. So if you can see from the introductions that one passage will be much easier for you than the others, work through that one first. But don't skip around after you've already read most or all of a passage. You've already invested your time reading, so try all the questions that go with it before you move to another text.

PERFECT SCORE TIP

" Whenever I took a practice test, I read all the answer solutions carefully. The explanations made the problems clearer and helped me avoid mistakes in the future. "

SmartPoints | Ready for Test Day | **Long Passage Questions** | Practice | Answers and Explanations

PRACTICE

Test your reading skills on the following sample long passage, keeping our tips in mind. Remember to read actively and construct a passage map. Then, use the Target Strategy to answer the questions that follow. Answers and explanations are on page 190.

Questions 1–8 refer to the following passage.

In this essay, the author writes about her childhood on a Caribbean island that was an English colony for many years.

When I saw England for the first time, I was a child in school sitting at a desk. The England I was looking at was laid out on a map gently, beautifully, delicately, a very special jewel; it lay
(5) on a bed of sky blue, its yellow form mysterious, because though it looked like a leg of mutton*, it could not really look like anything so familiar as a leg of mutton because it was England. England was a special jewel all right, and only
(10) special people got to wear it. The people who got to wear England were English people. They wore it well and they wore it everywhere: in jungles, in deserts, on plains, in places where they were not welcome, in places they should not
(15) have been. When my teacher had pinned this map up on the blackboard, she said, "This is England"—and she said it with authority, seriousness, and adoration, and we all sat up. We understood then—we were meant to under-
(20) stand then—that England was to be our source of myth and the source from which we got our sense of reality, our sense of what was meaningful, our sense of what was meaningless—and much about our own lives and
(25) much about the very idea of us headed that last list.

At the time I was a child sitting at my desk seeing England for the first time, I was already very familiar with the greatness of it. Each
(30) morning before I left for school, I ate a breakfast of half a grapefruit, a bowl of oat porridge, bread and butter and a slice of cheese, and a cup of cocoa. The can of cocoa was often left on the table in front of me. It had written
(35) on it the name of the company, the year the company was established, and the words "Made

in England." Those words, "Made in England," were written on the box the oats came in too. The shoes I wore were made in England; so
(40) were my socks and cotton undergarments and the satin ribbons I wore tied at the end of two plaits of my hair. My father, who might have sat next to me at breakfast, was a carpenter and cabinet maker. The shoes he wore to work
(45) would have been made in England, as were his khaki shirt and trousers, his underpants and undershirt, his socks and brown felt hat. Felt was not the proper material from which a hat that was expected to provide shade from
(50) the hot sun should be made, but my father must have seen and admired a picture of an Englishman wearing such a hat in England. As we sat at breakfast a car might go by. The car, a Hillman or a Zephyr, was made in England.
(55) The very conception of the meal itself, breakfast, and its substantial quality and quantity was an idea from England; we somehow knew that in England they began the day with this meal called breakfast and a proper breakfast was a big
(60) breakfast.

At the time I saw this map—seeing England for the first time—I did not say to myself, "Ah, so that's what it looks like," because there was no longing in me to put a shape to those three
(65) words that ran through every part of my life, no matter how small; for me to have had such a longing would have meant that I lived in a certain atmosphere, an atmosphere in which those three words were felt as a burden. But I did not
(70) live in such an atmosphere. My father's brown felt hat would develop a hole in its crown, the lining would separate from the hat itself, and six weeks before he thought that he could not be seen wearing it—he was a very vain man—he
(75) would order another hat from England. And my mother taught me to eat my food in the English way: the knife in the right hand, the fork

in the left, my elbows held still close to my side.
When I had finally mastered it, I overheard her
(80) saying to a friend, "Did you see how nicely she
can eat?" But I knew then that I enjoyed my
food more when I ate it with my bare hands,
and I continued to do so when she wasn't looking. And when my teacher showed us the map,
(85) she asked us to study it carefully, because no test
we would ever take would be complete without
this statement: "Draw a map of England."

I did not know then that the statement "Draw
a map of England" was something far worse than
(90) a declaration of war. I did not know then that
this statement was part of a process that would
result in my erasure, not my physical erasure,
but my erasure all the same. I did not know
then that this statement was meant to make
(95) me feel in awe and small whenever I heard
the word "England": awe at its existence, small
because I was not from it. I did not know very
much of anything then—certainly not what a
blessing it was that I was unable to draw a map
(100) of England correctly.

*the flesh of a sheep

1. According to the author, England could not
    really look like a leg of mutton (lines 6–8)
    because

    (A) maps generally don't give an accurate
         impression of what a place looks like

    (B) England was too grand and exotic a
         place for such a mundane image

    (C) England was an island not very different
         in appearance from her own island

    (D) the usual metaphor used to describe
         England was a precious jewel

    (E) mutton was one of the few foods familiar
         to her that did not come from England

2. The author's reference to felt as "not the proper
    material" (line 48) for her father's hat chiefly
    serves to emphasize her point about the

    (A) extremity of the local weather

    (B) arrogance of island laborers

    (C) informality of dress on the island

    (D) weakness of local industries

    (E) predominance of English culture

3. The word "conception" as used in line 55
    means

    (A) beginning

    (B) image

    (C) origination

    (D) notion

    (E) plan

4. The word "substantial" in line 56 means

    (A) important

    (B) abundant

    (C) firm

    (D) down-to-earth

    (E) materialistic

5. In the third paragraph, the author implies that
    any longing to put a shape to the words "Made
    in England" would have indicated

    (A) a resentment of England's predominance

    (B) an unhealthy desire to become English

    (C) an inability to understand England's
         authority

    (D) an excessive curiosity about England

    (E) an unfamiliarity with English customs

SmartPoints   Ready for Test Day   Long Passage Questions   Practice   Answers and Explanations

6. The author cites the anecdotes about her father and mother in lines 70–81 primarily to convey their

(A) love for their children
(B) belief in strict discipline
(C) distaste for anything foreign
(D) reverence for England
(E) overemphasis on formal manners

7. For the author, the requirement to "Draw a map of England" (lines 88–90) represented an attempt to

(A) force students to put their studies to practical use
(B) glorify one culture at the expense of another
(C) promote an understanding of world affairs
(D) encourage students to value their own heritage
(E) impart outmoded and inappropriate knowledge

8. The word "erasure" (line 92) as used by the author most nearly means

(A) total annihilation
(B) physical disappearance
(C) sense of insignificance
(D) enforced censorship
(E) loss of freedom

Questions 9–15 refer to the following passage.

The following is adapted from a biology textbook.

Blood, a connective tissue, is a sticky fluid that has multiple functions. It transports oxygen, nutrients, and other solutes to cells; carries away metabolic wastes and secretions; and
(5) helps stabilize internal pH. Plasma, red blood cells, white blood cells, and platelets are its components.

Plasma, which is mostly water, functions as a transport medium for blood cells and
(10) platelets. It also serves as a solvent for ions and molecules, including hundreds of different kinds of plasma proteins. Some of the plasma proteins transport lipids and fat-soluble vitamins through the body. Others have roles in
(15) blood clotting or in defense against pathogens. Collectively, the concentration of plasma proteins affects the blood's fluid volume, for it influences the movement of water between blood and interstitial fluid.
(20) Erythrocytes, or red blood cells, are biconcave disks, like doughnuts with a squashed-in center instead of a hole. They transport the oxygen used in aerobic respiration and carry away some carbon dioxide wastes. When oxygen
(25) diffuses into blood, it binds with hemoglobin, the iron-containing pigment that gives red blood cells their color.

Mature red blood cells no longer have their nucleus, nor do they require it. They have
(30) enough hemoglobin, enzymes, and other proteins to function for about 120 days. At any time, phagocytes are engulfing the oldest red blood cells or the ones already dead, but ongoing replacements keep the cell count fairly stable.
(35) Leukocytes, or white blood cells, arise from stem cells in bone marrow. They function in daily housekeeping and defense. Many patrol tissues, where they target or engulf damaged or dead cells and anything chemically recognized
(40) as foreign to the body. Many others are massed together in the lymph nodes and spleen. There

they divide to produce armies of cells that battle specific viruses, bacteria, and other invaders.

(45) White blood cells differ in size, nuclear shape, and staining traits. There are five categories: neutrophils, eosinophils, basophils, monocytes, and lymphocytes. The neutrophils and monocytes are search-and-destroy cells. The monocytes follow chemical trails to

(50) inflamed tissues where they develop into macrophages that can engulf invaders and debris. Two classes of lymphocytes, B cells and T cells, make highly specific defense responses.

Some stem cells in bone marrow give rise

(55) to giant cells called megakaryocytes. These shed fragments of cytoplasm enclosed in a bit of plasma membrane. The membrane-bound fragments are platelets, which initiate blood clotting. Each platelet only lasts five to nine

(60) days, but hundreds of thousands are always circulating in blood.

9. The passage is primarily concerned with

(A) blood function
(B) plasma and platelets
(C) blood components
(D) blood
(E) the circulatory system

10. According to the passage, plasma is

(A) a biconcave disk
(B) composed of ions and molecules
(C) interstitial fluid
(D) mostly water
(E) hemoglobin

11. In line 19, "interstitial" most nearly means

(A) situated within an organ
(B) within the blood
(C) small space
(D) erythrocytes
(E) a lattice

12. According to the passage, what gives blood its red color?

(A) hemoglobin
(B) oxygen
(C) iron
(D) the nucleus
(E) hemoglobin, enzymes, and other proteins

13. The author's use of the words "defense" and "patrol" (line 37) and "armies" and "battle" (line 42) implies that

(A) white blood cells serve as protection against invaders
(B) white blood cells differ in size, shape, and traits
(C) white blood cells are violent
(D) B and T cells are highly specific
(E) phagocytes attack old red blood cells

14. In line 50, "inflamed" most nearly means

(A) on fire
(B) under attack
(C) engulfed
(D) irritated
(E) healthy

15. Megakaryocytes are

(A) plasma
(B) giant cells that shed cytoplasm
(C) giant cells that are platelets
(D) giant cells that initiate blood clotting
(E) platelets that last five to nine days

SmartPoints | Ready for Test Day | Long Passage Questions | Practice | Answers and Explanations

Questions 16–22 refer to the following passage.

A renaissance is a rebirth. The Harlem Renaissance of the 1920s was a time when African-American art and literature flourished. Blacks migrating from the South brought with
(5) them a key element to the thriving Harlem area; jazz. The rhythms of this music set the stage for a new kind of literature and a new kind of art. But the vitality was not just exhibited in the fine arts; it was also present in
(10) the politics of the era. Inevitably, it changed African-Americans and America through the power of its legacy.

Inspired by the freedom that jazz construction provided, poet Langston Hughes began
(15) writing riffs that contained the elements of jazz and blues but maintained the structure of poetry. However, it was the language in his writing that was truly revolutionary. Instead of the highly stylized, theatrical black voice
(20) used at the time, Hughes wrote in the everyday language he heard around him. It was the language of musicians, workers, and servants and it became a poetic revolution.

Likewise, African-American art was revitalized.
(25) The works of Aaron Douglas could be seen throughout New York City. He was a prolific muralist and graphic illustrator. His subjects were rendered in the art deco style that was popular at the time. His murals depicted jazz
(30) musicians and singers posing heroically above the cityscape. No major literary work from the Harlem Renaissance was published without his design gracing its cover. Other notable artists, like Archibald Motley Jr. and Malvin Gray Johnson,
(35) gave African-American subjects dignity and grace that were considered radical in the America of 1920.

At the same time, African-American scholars, like W.E.B. Du Bois, urging racial pride,
(40) were publishing magazines. Activist Marcus Garvey campaigned against the colonization of Africa and started an organization called the Universal Negro Improvement Association to further the goal of racial pride.

This was a reformation; an intellectual rebel-
(45) lion shouting out that the black voice in America would be heard.

And heard it was, not just in America but around the world. Paris, considered the cultural capital of the world, was quick to assimi-
(50) late the sounds, textures and words that were coming out of Harlem. The sound of Duke Ellington and the songs of Bessie Smith swung from the Cotton Club in Harlem to the nightclubs of Paris. The world was taking notice
(55) of the artists, activists, and writers of Harlem. This meant that the world was also taking note of black Americans, their struggles and their achievements.

1920s Harlem, with its intellectuals and art-
(60) ists, its activists and musicians, inspired generations. Its influence can be seen in the novels of Toni Morrison, the music of Wynton Marsalis, the films of Spike Lee and, perhaps most importantly, the politics of Malcolm X and Martin
(65) Luther King Jr. Inspired by the art and politics of the time, African-Americans redefined themselves and the world had to take notice.

16. Renaissance and rebirth are synonymous. Why were the intellectuals and artists of 1920s Harlem considered to be part of a renaissance?

(A) They studied the revival of art and learning from the 14th, 15th, and 16th centuries in Europe.

(B) They underwent a religious transformation.

(C) Their work is the basis of all African-American art and politics today.

(D) Their works are still considered masterpieces today.

(E) Their collective works of art and thought were instrumental in changing the perception of African-Americans at the time and continue to influence attitudes today.

17. What impact did the migration of blacks from the South have on the Harlem Renaissance?

   (A) More black people in New York City allowed Harlem to flourish.

   (B) Southern thought and art was superior to that found in the north.

   (C) African-Americans from the South brought their musical sensibilities which influenced the writings, art, and thought of the 1920s.

   (D) Southern African-Americans were not interested in music so more time could be spent on writing, painting and politics.

   (E) Duke Ellington played in Paris, thus allowing African-American music to gain acceptance.

18. In paragraph 2, lines 18–21, the author describes Langston Hughes as writing in a voice very different than the *highly stylized, theatrical* style accepted at the time. What characterized the difference between the two styles?

   (A) Shakespearean English was the only acceptable literary voice of the time.

   (B) Langston Hughes wrote in the language of ordinary people instead of the artificial voice that identified the style of the time.

   (C) Southern dialects became important in Langston Hughes's work but were not important to the elite New Yorker of the 1920s.

   (D) The use of literary devices like similes and metaphors were common in the poetry of Langston Hughes but not in mainstream America.

   (E) The preferred voice of the time was less affected than that of Langston Hughes.

19. In paragraph 2, line 15, the author states that Langston Hughes was writing *riffs*. This word is not normally associated with writing. Why would the author choose this particular word?

   (A) The use of this word indicates that Langston Hughes was an angry poet.

   (B) *Riff* is a term for a passage in a jazz performance. The author used the word to illustrate the close connection between Hughes's poetry and jazz.

   (C) The word *riff* is actually synonymous with verse.

   (D) This is a shortened version of the word *riff-raff*, which further illustrates his revolutionary poetic voice.

   (E) The use of this word indicates that his poetry was vital and teeming with imagery of the Harlem of his day.

20. In the last sentence of paragraph 3, the author states that the subjects of African-American artists were depicted with dignity and grace. This would indicate which of the following?

   (A) That previous depictions of African-American subjects were largely based on stereotypical biases present at the turn of the century.

   (B) All African-American artwork prior to the Harlem Renaissance was unflattering.

   (C) African-American artists were working with inferior supplies and were unable to create artwork that reflected their subjects in a respectful manner.

   (D) Art Deco, by virtue of the stylistic approach, created an air of nobility and culture to the subject matter.

   (E) The artistic atmosphere created by the Harlem Renaissance allowed for a more realistic portrayal of African-Americans, which resulted in a more dignified and tasteful depiction of the subject.

21. In paragraph 4, line 44, the word *reformation* is used. Which of the following is the best description of the meaning of this word in the context of the passage?

(A) The act of reshaping an object or thing

(B) An act of civil disobedience to further a cause

(C) A decision made by a group of people to form a committee to investigate a community need

(D) A vote taken directly to the people to decide an issue

(E) A transformation that corrects and betters the current condition

22. The author states that the Harlem Renaissance changed the political climate of the time and that both Martin Luther King Jr. and Malcolm X were influenced by the activists of the 1920s. In what way might these two very different leaders have been affected?

(A) The pioneers of racial political activism infused their message with pride in one's heritage.

(B) Both W.E.B. DuBois and Marcus Garvey organized large numbers of like-minded people, both black and white, in demonstrations across the country.

(C) W.E.B. DuBois and Marcus Garvey instructed Malcolm X and Martin Luther King Jr.

(D) The Harlem Renaissance was an intellectual movement that resulted in a large body of work of which Martin Luther King Jr. and Malcolm X must surely have been aware.

(E) Marcus Garvey organized a bus strike in New York City that Martin Luther King later emulated in the South.

Questions 23–29 refer to the following passage.

The following passage is about a form of expression called conceptual art.

Conceptual "art" is a relatively recent artistic movement that began in the 1960s. After abstract impressionism and minimalism, artists were left at a dead end as far as finding new
(5) inroads into abstraction; there was nowhere left to go with traditional artistic media. Those who wished to further pursue abstraction to its absurd end became conceptual artists.

Conceptual artists were heavily influenced by
(10) the French dadaist/surrealist artist Marcel Duchamp, who maintained that the most important part of a work of art is its idea, rather than its physical expression. A 1970s bumper sticker capitalized on this idea and made fun
(15) of it: "If you like conceptual art, think about honking."

Conceptual art, for the most part, completely left behind a physical representation and relied only on the concept of the work that might (or
(20) might not) result. For example, Sol LeWitt created a *Wall Drawing* series that was composed only of a set of instructions for creating the drawings—that is to say, a blueprint for the eventual work. No physical representation of the
(25) ideas ever resulted. On a slightly different track, the contemporary conceptual artist Adib Fricke deals with language; his company The Word Company produces and distributes "words that do not yet exist" (*protonyms*). Similarly, per-
(30) formance art was a natural outgrowth of the idea of conceptual art, and visual one-time events became popular in the 1960s. They were often documented by pictures or narrative statements, but the actual work could not be preserved:
(35) only its idea.

This type of "art" stretches the limits of credibility; the bumper sticker referenced previously shows the slanted light in which many view conceptual art. Abstract art blurs the
(40) boundaries between "art" and "not art" nearly

to unrecognizability, but conceptual art obliterates this distinction completely. It is thus a way to avoid having to undertake the effort and exhibit the skill necessary to produce a lasting
(45) physical work of art. The author Leo Tolstoy created intricate plot outlines on the walls of the room in which he wrote. If he had left only the outlines and had never made them into books, would he still receive the same acclaim he now
(50) receives for works such as *War and Peace*?

23. In lines 1–2 "Conceptual 'art' is a relatively recent artistic movement that began in the 1960s," the quotation marks around *art* serve to

    (A) show that the author is about to define *art*
    (B) no purpose
    (C) set the tone for the passage
    (D) indicate that the author is especially fond of conceptual art
    (E) emphasize the importance of art

24. In line 11, the word "maintained" most nearly means

    (A) repaired
    (B) asserted
    (C) kept up
    (D) argued
    (E) disputed

25. An appropriate title for this passage might be

    (A) "Conceptual Art: An Important Advance"
    (B) "Marcel Duchamp: Life and Times"
    (C) "Bumper Stickers and Art"
    (D) "Conceptual Art: A Negative Opinion"
    (E) "All Art Is Absurd"

26. *Protonyms* are

    (A) words that do not yet exist
    (B) subatomic particles
    (C) words that sound alike
    (D) prototypical sounds
    (E) a type of visual art

27. All of the following statements are true EXCEPT

    (A) Adib Fricke uses language as a medium for conceptual art
    (B) Leo Tolstoy's outlines are an example of conceptual art
    (C) a work of conceptual art can exist with no physical representation
    (D) according to the author, conceptual art is the lazy way out
    (E) conceptual art is an extension of abstract art

28. The author of this passage would probably view a work of art that consisted only of a description of how to create a sculpture (rather than of an actual sculpture)

    (A) with sadness
    (B) with architectural curiosity
    (C) with anger
    (D) with joy
    (E) with disdain

29. This passage serves mainly to

    (A) provide a history of conceptual art
    (B) describe Leo Tolstoy's literary methods
    (C) convince the reader that conceptual art is unimportant
    (D) introduce the work of Adib Fricke
    (E) compare and contrast conceptual and abstract art

SmartPoints | Ready for Test Day | Long Passage Questions | Practice | Answers and Explanations

Questions 30–33 refer to the following passages.

Passage 1

In 1984, great fanfare and optimism accompanied the funding of an ecosystem research project called "Biosphere 2." The project's mission was to create an airlock-sealed habitat that
(5) could support a human crew for several years without contact with or resources from the outside world. Less than a decade later, however, enthusiasm for the project had almost entirely eroded after serious questions were raised about
(10) adherence to that mission. Media scrutiny began with reports that the mission's managers had quietly supplied the crew with goods from the outside, and this scrutiny intensified when these same administrators denied having
(15) tampered with the project. As an unfortunate result, doubts regarding the integrity of all the scientific data generated by the project began to surface.

Passage 2

Consistently propped up by the press since
(20) its inception, Biosphere 2 came to be regarded during the late 1980s as an indicator of the possibility of human habitation in space. Even as many scientists worked to quench such lofty goals, the press was dubbing Biosphere 2 the
(25) most exciting scientific project undertaken since the moon landing. Then, as the project's first crew emerged from a supposed two-year isolation to be greeted by a swirl of negative attention and controversy, the publications that had
(30) trumpeted the project quickly reversed direction. Frustrated with their conception's failures, the project's financiers fired their management team and, in a reversal of their own, lashed out at the same press they had once courted.

30. The word "quietly" as it is used in line 12 most nearly means

   (A) gingerly
   (B) easily
   (C) meekly
   (D) secretly
   (E) carelessly

31. In the second sentence of Passage 2 (lines 21–26), the author implies that

   (A) the media's expectations for the project were probably unrealistic
   (B) many scientists thought that aeronautical projects should not have ambitious goals
   (C) some scientists found the Biosphere 2 project more exciting than the moon landing
   (D) the project's management team should have heeded the advice of scientists
   (E) few could have predicted how controversial the project would become

32. Both authors agree that the Biosphere 2 project

   (A) failed to produce any useful data
   (B) became more scientifically valuable over time
   (C) neglected to supply the crew properly
   (D) was comparable to the moon landing
   (E) resulted in disappointment

33. The two passages differ in their approaches to the topic of the Biosphere 2 project in that

(A) Passage 1 emphasizes both the successes and failures of the project, while Passage 2 focuses primarily on the project's disappointments

(B) Passage 1 indicates that the goal of the project was to create a self-sufficient habitat, while Passage 2 states that the project was only intended to explore space habitation

(C) Passage 1 is supportive of the financiers, while Passage 2 is critical of the financiers' anger with the media

(D) Passage 1 focuses on how excitement for the project declined, while Passage 2 focuses largely on the media's relationship to the project

(E) Passage 1 concludes that the management team ruined the project, while Passage 2 indicates that the media caused its failure

Questions 34–45 refer to the following passages.

Passage 1

There are approximately 90 different elements that occur naturally, but most of the things we encounter are made up of combinations of only about one-third of them. Like most things in
(5) life, elements are each unique and, yet, can be grouped into classifications with other elements because of similarities. Thus, elements can be grouped according to whether they are highly reactive, somewhat reactive, or inert.
(10) Each element is made up of atoms. Within each atom is a certain number of protons and a matching number of electrons. This balance is necessary to keep each atom electrically neutral. An atom contains a nucleus with shells around
(15) it. The inner shell contains a maximum of two electrons. The next shell contains a maximum of eight electrons. Large atoms have a third shell

that can contain a maximum of 32 electrons. As a general rule, if the outer shell is complete, it
(20) will seldom react with anything. If the outer shell still has room for several electrons, it is considered somewhat reactive. However, an atom that only needs one or two electrons to fill its outer shell will grab an electron or two from another
(25) atom. It is then considered highly reactive.

Table salt, which is the combination of sodium and chlorine, is an example of two highly reactive elements coming together. Sodium loses an electron from its outer shell, and chlorine
(30) gains that electron. This makes an ionic bond. One is negatively charged, the other is positively charged. This "opposites attract" bond is very strong.

Another kind of bond is a covalent bond.
(35) This is a bond in which elements come together and share electrons. Oxygen has six electrons in its outer shell. It thus needs two more. Hydrogen has one in its outer shell. So, when two hydrogens meet one oxygen, the one elec-
(40) tron in the outer shell of each hydrogen fills in the two missing in oxygen to complete it to eight. However, they simply share the electrons. It is a nice sharing bond.

There are six elements that usually do not
(45) combine with others. These are called inert gases. They have the maximum number of electrons in their outer shells so they are not looking to find another element to bond with. Four of these elements are helium, argon, neon, and
(50) krypton.

Passage 2

It is often said that all is fair in love and war. That is used to explain the seemingly unlikely pairings done in the name of love. From years of observing couples, I have found that they can
(55) be classified into three main types. One pairing I call the sharing the relationship type. Another I term separate, but equal. The final type is what I call the odd couples.

In the first type, the people are true partners.
(60) They are together because they choose to share resources, space, and their lives. Sometimes, she is in charge. Sometimes, he is in charge. They take turns being the caregiver and the receiver. Some months, he writes out the bills. Other
(65) months, she does.

The second type is separate, but equal. Each member of the couple lives a separate life. They may have married because of society's expectation or because of a particular need, such as
(70) having children. They may live in the same household. But, overall, they have not bonded in an emotional sense.

The third type, the odd couples, fall into the "opposites attract" category. She is attracted to
(75) him because he has characteristics she doesn't see in herself. Likewise, he is attracted to her because she displays traits he knows he will never have. Examples of this type of couple are the shy, quiet, studious librarian who is mar-
(80) ried to the life of the party.

34. What is the main idea of Passage 1?

(A) one-third of the elements are common
(B) the ninety elements
(C) the classification of elements according to bonding preference
(D) bonds versus elements
(E) the periodic table

35. According to Passage 1, most common items are composed of

(A) approximately thirty separate elements
(B) combinations of approximately thirty separate elements
(C) approximately ninety different elements
(D) combinations of approximately ninety different elements
(E) the passage does not address this

36. The author of Passage 1 uses the phrase *As a general rule* (lines 18–19) to indicate

(A) that most elements will combine with other elements given the right environment
(B) that most elements have two missing electrons in their outer shell
(C) that elements with full outer shells are not reactive
(D) how table salt is made
(E) the reactivity of hydrogen

37. In looking at Passage 1, which of the following is true?

(A) There are only four inert gases.
(B) Inert gases are elements that do not combine with other elements easily.
(C) The six inert gases are helium, argon, neon, and krypton.
(D) Verification of inert gases has never been done.
(E) Inert gases are more readily able to combine with other elements than are sodium and chlorine.

SmartPoints Ready for Test Day Long Passage Questions **Practice** Answers and Explanations

38. What is the main idea of Passage 2?

    (A) People choose strange partners because of love.
    (B) All is fair in love and war.
    (C) Pairings of people can be classified into three types.
    (D) True partners versus infatuation.
    (E) Couples can be observed.

39. The sentence, *Other months, she does* (lines 64–65), in Passage 2 is used

    (A) to show that the woman is in charge in this type of pairing
    (B) as a part of an example demonstrating the true partners type
    (C) to indicate that women can have equal rights in a relationship
    (D) to introduce one of the types of pairings
    (E) to allow the reader into the insight of the author

40. According to Passage 2, which of the following statements is true?

    (A) The odd couples are the same as the opposites attract pairings.
    (B) The separate but equal pairings are similar to the true partners.
    (C) The opposites attract couples usually evolve into becoming separate but equal pairings.
    (D) The opposites attract pairings often become true partners over time.
    (E) Most of the odd couples end up being in failed marriages.

41. In Passage 2, the term *resources* (line 61) most likely refers to

    (A) land, air, and water
    (B) emotional closeness
    (C) children and pets
    (D) relatives, including the extended family
    (E) shelter, money, and possessions

42. In terms of person, which is true concerning these two passages?

    (A) Passage 1 is first person; Passage 2 is third person.
    (B) Both are in first person.
    (C) Both are in third person.
    (D) Passage 1 is in third person; Passage 2 is in first person.
    (E) Passage 1 is in first person; Passage 2 is in second person.

43. The ionic bonds in Passage 1 are most like

    (A) the odd couples in Passage 2
    (B) the couples who share resources, but do not share their emotions in Passage 2
    (C) the separate but equal partners in Passage 2
    (D) the true partners described in Passage 2
    (E) the partners who are unhappily married, as described in Passage 2

44. The passages differ in tone in that Passage 1 is

    (A) informational but Passage 2 is not

    (B) expository but Passage 2 is not

    (C) less formal than is Passage 2

    (D) more formal in its presentation of material while Passage 2 is more informal in its presentation

    (E) friendly and Passage 2 is businesslike

45. The reason for pairing these two passages is to show that

    (A) couples are made up of elements like everything else in life

    (B) elements can be classified in similar classifications to those of people

    (C) people combine into couples in ways that are similar to the ways that elements combine

    (D) ionic bonds are different from covalent bonds

    (E) true partners in life cannot be separated once they have combined, be they either elements or people

ANSWERS AND EXPLANATIONS

1. B

SMARTPOINTS CATEGORY: DETAIL **.ııll**

Here's how you might use your passage map and the Four-Step Method to answer question 1.

STEP 1. READ THE QUESTION STEM

The word *because* shows that this is a Detail question. There's no mystery about what the question is asking: why couldn't England really look like a leg of mutton? (Notice that mutton is defined at the end of the passage—you aren't expected to know the meaning of unfamiliar terms.)

STEP 2. LOCATE THE MATERIAL YOU NEED

Here's where active reading and your passage map come into play. In the margin by the first paragraph, you might have written "England = impt." You might also have bracketed *England was to be our source of myth and the source from which we got our sense of reality*. All that information around the cited lines helps you make a prediction.

STEP 3. PREDICT THE ANSWER

A good prediction might be "England was too special to look like a familiar leg of mutton."

STEP 4. SELECT THE BEST ANSWER CHOICE

Choice (B) comes close to the ideal—it might have jumped out. But if you weren't sure, you could have quickly eliminated the other choices. Thinking of the main idea would have helped you eliminate (A) and (C)—ideas that are not discussed in the passage. England was precious—like a jewel—but the author doesn't imply that England was usually compared to a *jewel* (D), and you never learn where mutton *comes from* (E). Choice (B) is the only one that works here. By reading the material surrounding the line reference and putting an answer into your own words, you should have been able to choose (B) with confidence.

2. E

SMARTPOINTS CATEGORY: FUNCTION **.ııll**

The phrase *chiefly serves to* indicates a Function question. Reading around lines 44–47 tells you that the things her father wore could have been made in England, and that her father must have

Ready for Test Day | Long Passage Questions | Practice | **Answers and Explanations** | Chapter Highlights

admired a picture of an Englishman wearing a felt hat (lines 51–52). This supports choice (E). Choices (B) and (C) might be tempting (if you had not done the research). The same is true for choice (A), which references the weather. (D) is off the point of the passage.

3. D

SMARTPOINTS CATEGORY: VOCAB-IN-CONTEXT

Use context clues to determine the answer. Refer back to the passage and, if necessary, replace *conception* with the answer choices to find the best meaning of the word. *The very conception of the meal itself, breakfast . . .was an idea from England.* Although *beginning* and *origination* seem to fit in the context of the sentence, only *notion*, or idea, most nearly means *conception*.

4. B

SMARTPOINTS CATEGORY: VOCAB-IN-CONTEXT

For this question, try replacing *substantial* as it is used in the sentence, with each of the answer choices. For example, *its substantial quality and quantity was an idea from England*: its *important* quality, its *abundant* quality, its *firm* quality, its *down-to-earth* quality, or its *materialistic* quality. Even if you don't know the meaning of the word *abundant*, this answer choice makes the most sense in the context of the sentence.

5. B

SMARTPOINTS CATEGORY: INFERENCE

The word *implies* tells you this is an Inference question. You are only told to look in paragraph 3, so you'll need to rely on a margin note that the narrator had negative thoughts about England (*au = neg about being Eng*) and bracketed or circled words *there was no longing in me, I did not live in such an atmosphere*, and *I enjoyed my food more when I ate with my bare hands*. These all indicate you are looking for a negative attitude toward England. While (A), (C), (D), and (E) all have some negative meaning, only (B) captures the author's attitude toward *Made in England* that she first discusses in paragraph 2.

6. D

SMARTPOINTS CATEGORY: FUNCTION

Throughout the passage, the author is commenting on her parents' love for England and its traditions. The anecdotes refer to their behavior relating to English custom, so the author is conveying her parents' *reverence* for England.

7. B

SMARTPOINTS CATEGORY: INFERENCE ▪▪▪▫

The phrase *For the author* tells you to think like the author. You must have the entire passage in mind as you consider what she thinks about drawing a map of England. Drawing a map of England did not promote an understanding of world affairs, encourage students to value their own heritage, or give them inappropriate knowledge. Although you might be tempted by choice (A), within the context of the passage, drawing a map of England was a way of glorifying one culture at the expense of another.

8. C

SMARTPOINTS CATEGORY: VOCAB-IN-CONTEXT ▪▪▫▫

Read the lines referenced in the question. The author talks about a *process that would result in my erasure, not my physical erasure, but my erasure all the same.* The context eliminates choices (A) and (B) since she is not *being destroyed* or *physically disappearing*. The context mentions nothing of *censorship* or *freedom*. Therefore, the best choice is (C), *her sense of insignificance.*

9. C

SMARTPOINTS CATEGORY: GLOBAL ▪▪▪▫

Carefully read the opening paragraph and notice that the topic becomes more detailed as the paragraph progresses. The topics mentioned are blood, blood attributes, blood function, and blood components. (A) is a misused detail; although the *function* of blood is discussed, the overall passage focuses on the components of blood and the attributes of those components. (C), although similar, is a better answer. *Plasma and platelets* (B) are discussed, but they are not the main concern of the entire passage. (D) and (E) are both out of scope. The passage is concerned with *blood* (D) but focuses on a more detailed topic, and although blood is a component of *the circulatory system* (E), this is never mentioned in the passage. (C) is the best choice.

10. D

SMARTPOINTS CATEGORY: DETAIL ▪▪▪▫

The detail of plasma being *mostly water* (D) is set apart by commas, which should alert the reader that the author recognizes this attribute as important and wants it to be noted. (A) is a misused detail; red blood cells, not plasma, are biconcave disks. (B) is a distortion; plasma serves as a solvent for ions and molecules, but the passage does not state that it is composed of them. (C) and (E) are both too extreme; plasma interacts with the movement of water between blood and *interstitial fluid* (C) but is not itself *interstitial fluid*. Likewise, the passage does not say that plasma is *hemoglobin* (E), which is mentioned in the next paragraph pertaining to red blood cells. (D) is the only answer supported in the passage.

Ready for Test Day | Long Passage Questions | Practice | **Answers and Explanations** | Chapter Highlights

11. A

SMARTPOINTS CATEGORY: VOCAB-IN-CONTEXT

While *interstitial* is not explicitly defined in the passage, you can gather from the context that it is separate from blood: the sentence says *blood and interstitial fluid.* Where would other fluids be located in the body? (B) is opposite of what you are looking for; plasma affects the water between blood and interstitial fluid, thus signifying that blood is not the same as this fluid. (C) and (E) are misused details; (C) relies on the assumptions of the reader and not the context of the passage. Interstices are indeed *small spaces*, but interstitial in this context is descriptive of the fluid. (E) relies on the assumption of the reader. Although *a lattice* is often used as a metaphor for interstitial space, this metaphor is not mentioned in the passage at hand. (D) is too extreme. *Erythrocytes* are red blood cells, which are not related to the topic of plasma in this sentence. (A) is the best answer choice.

12. C

SMARTPOINTS CATEGORY: DETAIL

Notice that many elements are responsible for eventually coloring blood red. Oxygen must bind with hemoglobin, and the *iron* (C) in hemoglobin is mentioned as giving "red blood cells their color," making choice (A) a distortion of what is stated in the passage. (B) is also a distortion; *oxygen* binds with hemoglobin and plays a part in coloring red blood cells, but the passage provides more details than that. (D) is too extreme; mature red blood cells no longer have their nucleus, and the nucleus does not color them. *Hemoglobin, enzymes, and other proteins* (E) help in red blood cell function, but this fact is not detailed enough to discern what colors the red blood cells.

13. A

SMARTPOINTS CATEGORY: INFERENCE

As always, the word *implies* denotes an Inference question. Writers use metaphor to better illustrate their argument. Consider what patrols and armies do, and picture what that role would be within the blood system and body. (B) is a misused detail; these are attributes of white blood cells, but the author's metaphors do not apply to them. (C) is too extreme because although white blood cells may be considered violent by the invader's standpoint, the passage implies that they must be provoked before acting. Indeed, *B and T cells are highly specific* (D) combative cells, but this is too detailed an answer given the broad range of the question. Like (C), (E) is also too extreme; phagocytes engulf old red blood cells, and these metaphors do not pertain to red blood cells but rather white blood cells. (A) is the best choice.

14. B

SMARTPOINTS CATEGORY: VOCAB-IN-CONTEXT

The sentence states that macrophages *engulf invaders and debris* at the site of *inflamed tissues*. It can therefore be inferred that *inflamed* describes the state of being attacked, or choice (B). (A) is out of scope; although flame can be found in inflamed, this answer solely relies on the assumptions of the reader and not the context of the sentence. (C) and (D) are distortions; macrophages engulf the invaders, which are responsible for inflaming the tissue, and *irritated* (D) is often synonymous with *inflamed*. However, the reader should extricate the meaning of inflamed from the context of the sentence, which points out that inflammation is the result of invaders and debris. (E) is too extreme; an inflamed tissue is clearly not healthy but is one in need of rescue.

15. B

SMARTPOINTS CATEGORY: DETAIL

The introduction to the passage names platelets as a blood component that would be discussed. Carefully read the paragraph on platelet production, and find the role megakaryocytes play in their development. (A) is a misused detail; megakaryocytes work with *plasma* to produce platelets. (C) and (D) are distortions; megakaryocytes are giant cells responsible for the development of *platelets* (C), but they are not platelets. Likewise, megakaryocytes are giant cells indirectly responsible for *blood clotting* (D), which is the role of platelets. (E) is opposite of the correct answer; megakaryocytes are responsible for the development of platelets, and their life span is not mentioned in the passage. (B) is the best choice.

16. E

SMARTPOINTS CATEGORY: GLOBAL

To answer this question, you need to understand the passage as a whole, and thus it is a Global question. A rebirth indicates a dramatic and lasting change. With that in mind, how did the intellectuals and artists of the 1920s make dramatic or lasting changes? (A) and (B) are out of scope; the author never talks about the European Renaissance (A) or a religious transformation (B). (C) is too extreme; the author does not say that all contemporary African-American artists and politicians were influenced by the Harlem Renaissance. (D) is a distortion; the artists and intellectuals of 1920s Harlem certainly created some masterpieces, but this would not constitute a renaissance. (E) speaks of a lasting change that would characterize a *rebirth* or *renaissance*, and thus is the correct answer.

Ready for Test Day | Long Passage Questions | Practice | **Answers and Explanations** | Chapter Highlights

17. C

SMARTPOINTS CATEGORY: DETAIL

The first two paragraphs of this passage are describing the musical influence inherent in the roots of the Harlem Renaissance. Where did these musical styles originate? (A) is a distortion; it could be inferred that there were more black people living in New York, but this does not explain the flourishing of arts and ideas that characterized the Harlem Renaissance. (B) is out of scope; there is nothing in the passage that would indicate that Southern thought and art was superior. (D) is opposite of what the correct answer should be. The first paragraph clearly states that African-Americans from the South brought jazz to the North, which clearly influenced the works of the Harlem writers, artists, and intellectuals. (E) is a misused detail; Duke Ellington is mentioned in the passage, but this is unrelated to the question being asked. (C) most closely reflects the author's intention.

18. B

SMARTPOINTS CATEGORY: DETAIL

The author is asking you to contrast two styles. Which answer best shows a contrast? (A) is out of scope; there is no mention of Shakespeare in this passage. (C) is a distortion; it could be inferred that Southern dialects were present in the Harlem of 1920, but there is nothing in the passage to indicate that Hughes was influenced by them or that the elite found the dialects unimportant. (D) is also out of scope; there is no mention of similes or metaphors in the passage. (E) is opposite; a voice that is *highly stylized and theatrical* would be more affected than the voice of ordinary people used by Hughes. (B) best contrasts two different styles: the voice of ordinary people versus the accepted artificial voice.

19. B

SMARTPOINTS CATEGORIES: INFERENCE
VOCAB-IN-CONTEXT

This is a souped-up Vocab-in-Context question in that you must connect the jazz influence mentioned previously in lines 5–6 to Langston Hughes's work. The question states that this word is not normally associated with writing. Which of the answers would show an association to another area or art form? (A) cannot be correct because the passage never speaks to his mental state or any thematic anger. (C) If *riff* were synonymous with verse, it would certainly be associated with writing and is, therefore, incorrect. (D) does not make sense in the context of the sentence. (E) would not meet the criteria that it was a word that was not normally associated with writing. (B) meets all the qualifications of the question and is, therefore, correct.

Ready for Test Day | Long Passage Questions | Practice | **Answers and Explanations** | Chapter Highlights

20. E

SMARTPOINTS CATEGORY: INFERENCE

The phrase *would indicate* means that this is an Inference question. The author talks about Langston Hughes's poetry as revolutionary because it used the language of the people he encountered instead of the stylized voice common at the time. Can you make any assumptions about other art forms based on this theme? (A) is out of scope; while this may be true, it is not addressed in the passage. There is no indication in the passage that African-American art was *unflattering* (B). (C) is also out of scope; there is no mention in the passage about what kind of art supplies were used by the artists of the time. *Art Deco* (D) is mentioned as a style used by one of the artists. It does not indicate that all Art Deco works were, by virtue of the style, imbued with an air of dignity and grace. (E) best fits the overall mood of the Harlem Renaissance that allowed for a more realistic depiction of the African-American life of the 1920s.

21. E

SMARTPOINTS CATEGORIES: VOCAB-IN-CONTEXT

Even though this question is long and out of the usual Vocab-in-Context *most nearly means* mold, it is still a Vocab-in-Context question. *Reformation* has been used to describe any movement that alters the status quo and moves a group toward a specified goal. Which of the definitions best fits with the historical use of the word? While *reform* can mean to reshape something (A), this definition does not make sense in the context of the passage. There is no indication of *civil disobedience* (B) being a part of the Harlem Renaissance, so this answer cannot be correct. (C) does not make sense in the context of the sentence or passage. Community need does not come into play here. (D) is the definition of a referendum, not a reformation. (E) is the best fit in the context of the sentence. It is used to show that social reform was necessary to bring about change and better the current conditions.

22. A

SMARTPOINTS CATEGORY: DETAIL

There are a couple of answers that may be correct, but only one answer is directly addressed by the author. (A) is the only answer that is directly written about in the passage. (B) is out of scope; there is no mention of either man organizing demonstrations in this passage. Also, the passage does not substantiate the claim that Martin Luther King Jr. and Malcolm X ever met W.E.B. Dubois or Marcus Garvey (C). (D) is a distortion; it is probably true that both Martin Luther King Jr. and Malcolm X were aware of the works from the Harlem Renaissance. This awareness does not answer the question of how they might have been influenced by what they read. Finally, the passage does not state that there was any such bus strike mentioned in answer choice (E).

23. C

SMARTPOINTS CATEGORY: FUNCTION

The phrase *serve to* marks this as a Function question, in this case asking about the role of quotation marks around *art*. To answer this question, decide what the overall goal of the passage is. How does this introductory sentence serve to further this goal? How do the quotation marks around *art* help with this goal? (A) seems possible, but the author never attempts to define art itself. (B) is incorrect because it is usually good to assume that in test question passages, literary and typographical devices do serve a purpose. (C) is correct because the quotation marks around *art* indicate that the author questions the classification of conceptual art as art (this is an *ironic* use of quotation marks). This indicates a negative view toward conceptual art, and because in the passage the author states the opinion that conceptual art is not a worthwhile medium, this minimal typographical detail alerts the reader about what is likely to follow. (D) is opposite of what you're looking for; the passage indicates that the author is NOT fond of conceptual art. (E) is out of scope; the importance of art in general is not discussed in this passage.

24. B

SMARTPOINTS CATEGORY: VOCAB-IN-CONTEXT

Several wrong answer choices reflect a more common meaning of *maintain*. Eliminate these, and try the others in the sentence, paying close attention to the surrounding context; can you guess which is the best answer? The correct answer is (B), *asserted*. *Maintain* most often means "repair" or "keep up," but as always, don't reactively select the first answer choice that looks as if it might be correct. Choices (D) and (E) make sense in the sentence, but not with its surrounding context (no dispute or argument is involved).

25. D

SMARTPOINTS CATEGORY: GLOBAL

INFERENCE

Skim the passage, and try to understand how the author seems to feel about the topic. Is there an answer choice that reflects your impression? (A) is opposite; the author clearly does not believe that conceptual art is important and, in fact, calls it *absurd*. (B) is a misused detail; Marcel Duchamp is mentioned in the passage but only as a supporting detail. It would therefore be inappropriate to title the passage accordingly. (C) is also a misused detail; one bumper sticker is referenced in the passage, but again, this is only a supporting detail and not worthy of inspiring a title for the passage. (E) is too extreme; the word *all* should alert you that this may be an extreme answer choice, but in addition, the passage does not attempt to describe *all art* or make any value judgments about it. The passage is written to explain what conceptual art is and why the author dislikes it. The last paragraph, in particular, makes it very clear that the author holds a negative opinion of this type of art, which makes (D) correct.

Ready for Test Day | Long Passage Questions | Practice | **Answers and Explanations** | Chapter Highlights

26. A

SMARTPOINTS CATEGORY: DETAIL

This is not a Vocab-in-Context question because it directly asks you what a word means. However, it doesn't give you a line reference to go to, so you'll have to rely on skimming the passage to find the word, or better yet, find the word you circled as you were reading. This word is defined immediately before it appears. The correct answer is (A) (lines 28–29: "*words that do not yet exist*").

27. B

SMARTPOINTS CATEGORY: DETAIL

The EXCEPT question is a time-consuming one, because you have to systematically eliminate the four that are true before you can pick the one you are looking for. If time is short, save this one to the end of the passage group of questions. Answering this question requires you to make several inferences and then exclude each answer choice that can be supported by the passage. (A) is supported by lines 26–27, "the contemporary conceptual artist Adib Fricke deals with language." (C) is supported by lines 17–20, "Conceptual art, for the most part, completely left behind a physical representation . . ." (D) is supported by the lines 42–45, "It is thus a way to avoid having to undertake the effort and exhibit the skill necessary to produce a lasting physical work of art." (E) is supported by lines 6–8, "Those who wished to further pursue abstraction to its absurd end became conceptual artists." Tolstoy's outlines are actually given as an example that is NOT conceptual art, and thus choice (B) is the correct answer.

28. E

SMARTPOINTS CATEGOR-Y: INFERENCE

The author . . . would view is a clause that indicates an Inference question about the author's opinion of conceptual art. To answer this question, you must first use your inference skills to determine how the author feels about this type of art. The correct answer is (E), *with disdain*. This inference can be made on the basis of the author's example about Leo Tolstoy; the rhetorical question in the last sentence, as well as the clearly stated opinion about this type of art, show that the author's main feeling toward conceptual art is disdain.

Ready for Test Day | Long Passage Questions | Practice | **Answers and Explanations** | Chapter Highlights

29. C

SMARTPOINTS CATEGORIES: FUNCTION

GLOBAL

This question combines understanding the passage as a whole (Global) and knowing the author's intent (Function), as shown by the phrase *serves to*. The author has a strongly negative opinion on the topic of the passage, as discussed in the previous question (28).

The author has a strong opinion on the topic of the passage. What is it? (A) is a distortion; the middle paragraphs do describe the history of conceptual art, but this is not the main point of the passage. (B) is a misused detail; Tolstoy's literary methods are described in order to support the author's opinion about conceptual art; however, this is not the main subject or goal of the passage. From the first line of the passage (in which *art* is placed in quotation marks to cue the reader that the author has a disparaging opinion of the subject matter) to the last paragraph (in which the author states outright that conceptual art is "a way to avoid having to undertake the effort and exhibit the skill necessary to produce a lasting physical work of art", lines 42–45), the author attempts to convince the reader that conceptual art is undeserving of attention as a real art form. (D) is also a misused detail; Adib Fricke's work with The Word Company is treated in the passage as a way to clarify what conceptual art consists of. Still, this is a supporting detail and is not the main point of the passage. (E) is out of scope. Abstract art is mentioned, but it is neither compared nor contrasted with conceptual art.

30. D

SMARTPOINTS CATEGORY: VOCAB-IN-CONTEXT

Because the cited line describes an act that caused people to question the project's adherence to its mission of self-sufficiency, you can infer that the managers would probably have tried to be secretive about any supplies they were providing to the crew. Look for a choice that reflects the undercover or illicit nature of the activity. Doing something *gingerly* (A) means doing it in a cautious, tentative way. While this comes close to capturing the meaning of the cited word, it does not express the idea that the managers' actions were not intended to be seen or discovered. The context of the passage does not indicate how difficult it was for the managers to supply the crew with outside goods, thus (B) is incorrect. Whereas a quiet person might be meek or submissive, *meekly* (C) does not fit the context. Whereas you might infer that the managers were careless because they got caught, (E) is not a meaning of the cited word. (D) nicely matches your prediction.

31. A

SMARTPOINTS CATEGORY: INFERENCE

The phrase *implies that* signals an Inference question. The sentence tells you that many scientists were trying to suppress or extinguish the *lofty goals* or overly high expectations for the project, suggesting that the scientists thought such goals were unrealistic. Since it was the press that was *dubbing* the project as so exciting, this indicates that the unrealistic expectations were put forth or perpetuated by the media. (B) is out of scope; the passage only discusses the Biosphere 2 project, not projects dealing with aircraft or flight. (C) is a distortion; the passage only suggests that the *press* believed the project was *as* exciting as the moon landing, not that scientists found it more exciting. The author makes no recommendations regarding what the management team (D) should or should not have done, and the passage does not mention whether the management team consulted scientists. While (E) may be accurate given all the hype about the project, the cited sentence does not support this statement.

32. E

SMARTPOINTS CATEGORIES: GLOBAL

COMPARISONS

When tackling Comparison questions, think only of one passage at a time. Choose whichever passage you understand best and scan the answers with that one in mind. You should be able to eliminate one to four answers this way. Then analyze the remaining answer(s) thinking only of the other passage. Generally, Passage 1 states that it began with *great fanfare and optimism* that later became *almost entirely eroded*, and Passage 2 notes that the project was initially seen as *exciting* but eventually caused frustration. Both passages, then, discuss how high expectations were let down. (A) is too extreme; both passages suggest that the project failed to achieve its main goal, but they do not rule out the possibility that some useful data was produced. (B) is out of scope; neither passage explores changes over time in the scientific value of the project. (C) misinterprets a statement in Passage 1 about managers sneaking outside supplies to the crew. (D) is also out of scope; Passage 1 does not mention the moon landing. (E) is the best answer choice.

33. D

SMARTPOINTS CATEGORIES: GLOBAL

COMPARISONS

As with all Comparison questions, think of only one passage at a time. The pattern of the answers is Passage 1 says . . ., while Passage 2 says . . . Go down the answers with either passage in mind, eliminating as you can; then repeat with the other one in mind.

Passage 1 focuses on how and why enthusiasm for the project declined, while Passage 2 focuses on the media's role in portraying the project. You are looking for a choice that captures this difference. (A) is out of scope; neither passage emphasizes successes of the project. (B) is a distortion; Passage 2 does not state that exploring space habitation was the project's only goal. (C) is also a distortion; Passage 1 does not express an opinion of the financiers, and Passage 2 describes but does not evaluate the financiers' anger with the media. (E) is too extreme; both characterizations are too strong given the rather objective tone of the passages. Thus, (D) is the best answer.

34. C

SMARTPOINTS CATEGORY: GLOBAL

This passage describes the fact that elements can be classified into three types based on their likelihood of forming bonds. Although (A) and (B) are both mentioned in the first paragraph, these are simply establishing details. They are not the main ideas of the passage. (D) is not accurate because of the *versus*. This passage discusses elements and bonds, but they are not in a *versus* relationship. Although the periodic table is indeed where the classification of the elements could be found, the table itself is not the main idea of the passage. Thus, (E) is not correct.

35. B

SMARTPOINTS CATEGORY: DETAIL

The passage states that there are approximately 90 elements, but most things are made up of combinations of approximately one-third of those. That would be approximately 30. Answers (A) and (C) are not correct because most things are not made up of single elements. (D) is not correct because most common things involve only about one-third of the 90 elements. (E) is not correct because, whereas the passage does not say it directly, it can be inferred using the evidence from the passage that there are approximately *90 elements* and *most things* are made up of combinations of *one-third* of them.

36. C

SMARTPOINTS CATEGORY: FUNCTION

The phrase *uses . . . to indicate* means that this is a Function question. As in all Function questions, you must read around the lines given. This question requires you to reread the entire paragraph. Here, the author is focusing on how the relative number of protons and electrons makes an atom reactive or nonreactive, and that reactivity relates to balance (lines 10–13). You can further see that *as a general rule*, a complete atom is a balanced one—one that doesn't react. This leads only to (C); the other answers are off topic.

37. B

SMARTPOINTS CATEGORY: DETAIL

This is a specific Detail question answered by the evidence offered in the first two sentences in the last paragraph. Although there are only four inert gases listed, there are actually six inert gases. Thus, answer (A) is not correct. Answer (C) is not correct because it uses the number six, but then only lists four. Answer (D) is not correct because it is not addressed in the passage, and it is not true. Answer (E) is not correct because inert gases, as stated in the final paragraph, do not combine readily with other elements.

38. C

SMARTPOINTS CATEGORY: GLOBAL

This entire passage is about the idea of classifying couples into three distinct types. (A) is not correct because it does not address the entire passage. (B) is simply a statement that is used to introduce the topic but certainly is not the main idea of the entire passage. (D) is not accurate because infatuation is not discussed in the passage at all. (E) is not correct because, whereas indeed the couples had to be observed in order for the author to come to the conclusions she did, the idea that this observation took place is not the main idea being expressed.

39. B

SMARTPOINTS CATEGORY: FUNCTION

The phrase *is used to* denotes a Function question and reading around the lines is required. This sentence corresponds with the sentence before it and is a part of the example that explains how a couple classified as true partners conduct their relationship. (A) is not accurate because the woman in this type of pairing is in charge some of the time, but at other times, she is not. (C) is not correct because the purpose of the statement is simply to exemplify the type, not to make a political statement about male/female relationships. (D) is not correct because the statement is a part of an example, rather than a part of an introduction of a classification. (E) is not correct because the statement is simply showing an example rather than insight into the thinking of the author.

40. A

SMARTPOINTS CATEGORY: DETAIL

In the first sentence of the final paragraph, the author names couples in the third classification as both odd couples and as opposites who are attracted to one another. (B) includes one type from the second classification and one type from the first classification. They are not similar. (C) and (D) are not accurate because the passage does not state anything about one classification type evolving into another type. (E) is not accurate because the passage does not discuss any aspect of failed marriages.

41. E

SMARTPOINTS CATEGORY: VOCAB-IN-CONTEXT

Because the passage is discussing couples and the things they share, it can be inferred that the resources are shelter, money, and possessions. (A) is about natural resources, but it would not make sense to choose it in this context. (B) is not correct because the author chooses to include *their lives* in the same series. The emotional closeness is probably inferred there rather than in the term *resources*. (C) and (D) are not correct because they do not describe items that are normally thought of as resources.

42. D

SMARTPOINTS CATEGORIES: DETAIL
COMPARISONS

Passage 1 is written using the objective voice of third person. Because of the usage of *I* in Passage 2, we can determine that it is written in first person. The other answers are not accurate because none of them indicate this correct identification.

43. A

SMARTPOINTS CATEGORIES: INFERENCE
COMPARISONS

This is a Reasoning question that requires you to relate the concepts of the two passages. This is also an Inference question asks you to consider how the three classifications in the first passage correlate with the three classifications in the second passage. The correlations are: (1) ionic bonds correlate with the odd couples; (2) covalent bonds correlate with the true partners; and (3) inert gases correlate with the separate but equal partners. Thus, (A) is the only one that shows the correct correlation.

44. D

SMARTPOINTS CATEGORIES: INFERENCE
GLOBAL
COMPARISONS

An easy way to tackle this question is to read the answers with (only) Passage 1 in mind, eliminating wrong answers as you go. Thus, you can eliminate (C) because it has a formal third person manner, and (E) for the same reason. Then, with Passage 2 in mind, you see that (A) and (B) are out because Passage 2 is both informational and expository. This leaves (D), and the right answer.

45. C

SMARTPOINTS CATEGORIES: FUNCTION ▁▃▅▇

GLOBAL ▁▃▅▇

COMPARISONS ▁▃▅▇

The word *reason* in the question stem asks for a Function comparison; because the question refers to the passages as a whole, it is also a Global one. (A) is not correct because, whereas the statement is true, it does not show the correlation of the passages. (B) is not correct because the second passage is not about classification of people, but rather is about classification of couples. (D) is not correct because it only mentions bonds discussed in Passage 1. (E) describes only one type of bond in each passage. However, there are two other types of bonds in each of the passages.

IF YOU LEARNED ONLY SIX THINGS IN THIS CHAPTER . . .

1. MAPPING THE PASSAGES

- *Why* is more important than *what*.

- Keep straight *who* said what.

- Use Abbreviations (margin notes), Brackets (key sentences), and Circles (keywords and phrases).

- Focus on opinions, contrast, and varying points of view.

- Practice makes perfect in honing Active Reading skills.

- How extensive your notes are may depend on how fast you read.

2. ANSWERING QUESTIONS

- Predict before you peek.

- The answer is in the passage. Read around the lines given.

- Once you have read a passage, answer its questions before moving on.

3. KAPLAN'S STRATEGY FOR PAIRED PASSAGES

- **Step 1.** Read Passage 1 and answer the questions about it.

- **Step 2.** Read Passage 2 and answer the questions about it.

- **Step 3.** Answer the questions asking about both passages.

4. COMPARISON QUESTIONS

- Simplify Comparison question stems, restating them in simple words.

- Read answers twice. Think about only one passage at a time. You'll be able to eliminate two or more choices, and then decide among the rest.

5. TIMING STRATEGIES FOR THE READING SECTION

- You can move between passages in a section, but answer (or decide to omit) all questions before leaving any one passage.

- Don't spend more than three minutes on the sentence Completion section. Leave a minute at the end of the time for the harder ones.

Ready for Test Day | Long Passage Questions | Practice | Answers and Explanations | **Chapter Highlights**

- Spend four to five minutes or less on short reading passages.

- Leave plenty of time for long passage reading and questions—at least 15 minutes in a 25-minute section, more if at all possible.

6. KAPLAN'S STRATEGY FOR READING COMPREHENSION QUESTIONS

- **Step 1.** Read the question stem to determine what kind of question it is.

- **Step 2.** Locate the material you need. (Read around the lines; the answer is in the passage.)

- **Step 3.** Predict the answer.

- **Step 4.** Select the best answer choice.

CHAPTER 10: VOCABULARY-BUILDING STRATEGIES

SMARTPOINTS COVERED IN THIS CHAPTER

DEFINITION	
VOCAB-IN-CONTEXT	

WHAT TO EXPECT ON TEST DAY

A good score on the Critical Reading component depends, in part, upon your ability to work with unfamiliar words. You will often need to have a sense of their meaning to answer both the Sentence Completion and Reading Comprehension questions.

- What are the types of words I'm going to see on the SAT?
- What strategies will help me learn the right vocabulary words?
- What skills will help me succeed with the tough SAT vocabulary words?

MASTERING SAT VOCABULARY

There are two types of hard SAT words:

- Unfamiliar words
- Familiar words with secondary meanings

| SmartPoints | Ready for Test Day | **Mastering SAT Vocabulary** | Chapter Highlights |

EXPERT TUTOR TIP

" One of the best ways to prep for SAT vocabulary is by reading. Literature is great, but news articles can be more manageable for busy schedules. "

Some words are hard because you haven't seen them before. The words *scintilla* and *circumlocution*, for instance, are probably not part of your everyday vocabulary. But they might pop up on your SAT.

Easy words, such as *recognize* or *appreciation*, can also trip you up on the test because they have secondary meanings that you aren't used to. Reading Comprehension, in particular, will throw you familiar words with unfamiliar meanings.

KAPLAN'S TARGET STRATEGY FOR LEARNING VOCABULARY

A great vocabulary can't be built overnight, but it can be improved in a relatively short period of time with a minimum amount of pain.

Here's our three-step plan for building your vocabulary for the SAT:

Step 1. Learn words strategically.

Step 2. Learn word roots, prefixes, and word families.

Step 3. Personalize your vocabulary study.

EXPERT TUTOR TIP

" Review your vocabulary words more than once. One of the worst feelings on Test Day is realizing the definition you can't remember is one you've studied before. "

STEP 1. LEARN WORDS STRATEGICALLY

The best words to learn are words that have appeared often on the SAT. The test makers are formulaic in test creation, so the test is consistent from one administration to the next, thus words that have appeared frequently are likely bets to show up again.

STEP 2. LEARN WORD ROOTS, PREFIXES, AND WORD FAMILIES

Most SAT words are made up of prefixes and roots that can get you at least part way to a definition. Often, that's all you need to get a right answer. Target these words in your vocabulary review. Learn a few new roots a day, familiarizing yourself with their meaning.

Word families may also be of some use. A word family is a group of words that shares a similar meaning. For example, *loquacious, verbose*, and *garrulous* all mean *wordy*, *talkative. Taciturn, laconic, terse, concise,* and *pithy* all mean *not talkative, not wordy.* Instead of learning just one of these words, learn them all together—you get eight words for the price of just two definitions.

STEP 3. PERSONALIZE YOUR VOCABULARY STUDY

- There isn't just one *right* way to study vocabulary. Figure out a study method that works best for you and stick to it.

- Use flash cards. Write down new words or word groups and run through them whenever you have a few spare minutes. Put one new word or word group on one side of a 3 × 5 index card and a short definition on the back.

- Make a vocabulary notebook. List words in one column and their meanings in another. Test yourself. Cover up the meanings, and see what words you can define from memory. Make a sample sentence using each word in context.

- Think of hooks that lodge a new word in your mind. Create visual images of words. For example, to remember the verb form of *flag*, you can picture a flag drooping or losing energy as the wind dies down.

- Use rhymes and other devices that help you remember the words. For example, you might remember that a *verbose* person uses a lot of verbs.

It doesn't matter which techniques you use, as long as you learn words steadily and methodically. Doing so over several months with regular reviews is ideal.

> **PERFECT SCORE TIP**
>
> " Knowing prefixes and roots really helped me determine the meanings of challenging words. "

WORD ASSOCIATION

Associating words together really can help sharpen your vocabulary skills.

Take the word *gregarious*:

- If you think of your friend Greg as a sociable sort, then you'll long remember the meaning of the word *gregarious*.

- Now add the word root: if you know that the root *greg* means *crowd*, you'll be able to remember the following:

  - *Segregate* means to separate a *crowd*.

  - *Integrate* means to *crowd* together.

  - *Aggregate* means a *crowd* of different elements.

Now you have four new words firmly stuck in your head!

DECODING STRANGE WORDS ON THE TEST

Trying to learn every word that could possibly appear on the SAT is like trying to memorize the license plate number of every car on the road. There are just too many to commit to memory.

No matter how much time you spend with flash cards or word lists, you're bound to face some mystery words on your SAT. Just as you can use your basic multiplication skills to find the product of even the largest numbers, you can use what you know about words to focus on likely meanings of tough vocabulary words.

REMEMBER WHERE YOU'VE HEARD THE WORD BEFORE

If you can recall a phrase in which the word appears, that may be enough to eliminate some answer choices or even zero in on the right answer.

Between the two villages was a ---- through which passage was difficult and hazardous.

(A) precipice

(B) beachhead

(C) quagmire

(D) market

(E) prairie

To answer this question, you need to know whether or not to eliminate the word *quagmire*. You may remember *quagmire* from news reports referring to "a foreign policy *quagmire*" or "a *quagmire* of financial indebtedness." If you can remember how *quagmire* was used, you'll have a rough idea of what it means, and you'll see it fits. You may also be reminded of the word *mire*, as in "We got *mired* in the small details and never got to the larger issue." Sounds something like stuck, right? You don't need an exact definition. A *quagmire* is a situation that's difficult to get out of, so (C) is correct. Literally, a *quagmire* is a bog or swamp.

REMEMBER

Prefixes and roots can suggest a word's charge. *Mal, de, dis, un, in, im, a,* and *mis* often indicate a negative, whereas *pro, ben,* and *magn* are often positives.

DECIDE WHETHER THE WORD IS POSITIVE OR NEGATIVE

Simply knowing that you're dealing with a positive or negative word can earn you points on the SAT. For example, look at the word *cantankerous*. Say it to yourself. Can you guess whether it's positive or negative? Often words that sound harsh (such as *irk*) have a negative meaning, whereas smooth-sounding words (such as *benevolent*) tend to have positive meanings. If *cantankerous*

sounded negative to you, you were right. It means *ill-tempered*, *disagreeable*, or *difficult to handle*.

Not all words sound positive or negative; some sound neutral. But if you can define the charge, you can probably eliminate some answer choices on that basis alone. Here's an example.

> He seemed at first to be honest and loyal, but before long it was necessary to ---- him for his ---- behavior.
>
> (A) admonish . . . steadfast
> (B) extol . . . conniving
> (C) reprimand . . . scrupulous
> (D) exalt . . . insidious
> (E) castigate . . . perfidious

All you need to know to answer this question is that negative words are needed in both blanks. Then you can scan the answer choices for one that contains two clearly negative words. Even if you don't know what all the words mean, you can use your sense of positive or negative charge to eliminate answers. Choice (E) is right. *Castigate* means punish or scold harshly, and *perfidious* means treacherous.

USE YOUR FOREIGN LANGUAGE SKILLS

Many of the roots you'll encounter in SAT words come from Latin. Spanish, French, and Italian also come from Latin and have retained much of it in their modern forms. English is also a cousin to German and Greek. That means that if you don't recognize a word, try to remember if you know a similar word in another language. Look at the word *carnal*. Unfamiliar? What about *carne*, as in *chili con carne*? *Carn* means meat or flesh, which leads you straight to the meaning of *carnal*—pertaining to the flesh.

You could decode *carnivorous* (meat-eating) in the same way. You can almost always figure out something about strange words on the test. Chances are that few words on the SAT will be totally new to you, even if your recollection is more subliminal than vivid.

WHEN ALL ELSE FAILS

If you feel totally at a loss in determining the exact meaning of the word, eliminate choices that are clearly wrong and make an educated guess from the remaining choices. A wrong answer won't hurt you much, but a right answer can help you a lot.

> **PERFECT SCORE TIP**
>
> " For answering two-blank Sentence Completions with really tough vocab, I used compare/contrast clues to eliminate incorrect answer choices. "

> **PERFECT SCORE TIP**
>
> " If I didn't feel totally confident in an answer, I would make a note to review it at the end if there was time, instead of wasting time dwelling on it. "

SmartPoints | Ready for Test Day | **Mastering SAT Vocabulary** | Chapter Highlights

IF YOU ONLY LEARN THREE THINGS IN THIS CHAPTER . . .

1. HOW TO LEARN SAT WORDS

- Use study aids (flash cards, study lists) that work best for you.

- Concentrate on word roots, prefixes, and word families.

- Make associations between words and between roots and their related words.

- Don't forget that many words have more than one meaning. The SAT may use a less familiar meaning for a word you think you know.

2. KAPLAN'S STRATEGY FOR LEARNING VOCABULARY

Step 1. Learn words strategically.

Step 2. Learn word roots, prefixes, and word families.

Step 3. Personalize your vocabulary study.

3. OTHER TOOLS FOR WORKING WITH UNFAMILIAR WORDS

- Think of where you might have heard the word before, in a different context perhaps.

- Determine if the word is positive or negative.

- Use your knowledge of foreign language.

- Eliminate other answers if you can, and make an educated guess.

- Don't forget: you can omit without penalty. Don't guess wildly.

SmartPoints   Ready for Test Day   Mastering SAT Vocabulary   **Chapter Highlights**

| Part Four |

HOW TO ATTACK THE MATH COMPONENT

Many students fear the Math section more than they do the Writing and Critical Reading sections. But there is no reason to feel that way. Just as in the other sections, there are proven Kaplan strategies for approaching the different kinds of SAT Math questions.

CHAPTER 11: SAT MATH STRATEGIES

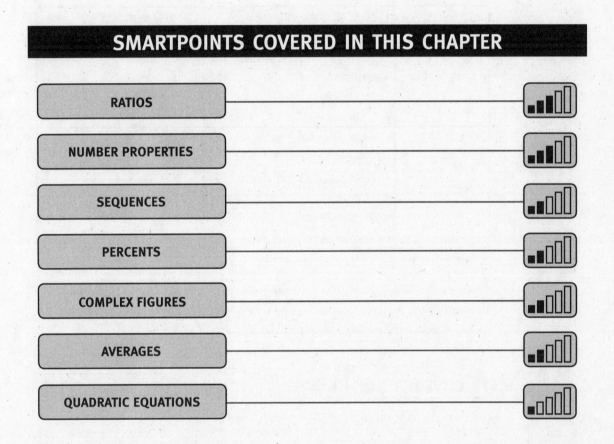

SMARTPOINTS COVERED IN THIS CHAPTER

RATIOS

NUMBER PROPERTIES

SEQUENCES

PERCENTS

COMPLEX FIGURES

AVERAGES

QUADRATIC EQUATIONS

SmartPoints | Ready for Test Day | Multiple-Choice Questions | Grid-in Questions | Using Your Calculator

WHAT TO EXPECT ON TEST DAY

There are three Math sections on the SAT. They can appear anywhere during the test, except section 1, in any order. They are:

LENGTH	CONTENT	TYPE
25 minutes	• High school geometry • Algebra • Numbers and operations • Statistics • Probability • Data analysis	• Multiple-choice • Student-produced responses*
25 minutes	• High school geometry • Algebra • Numbers and operations • Statistics • Probability • Data analysis	• Multiple-choice • Student-produced responses*
20 minutes	• High school geometry • Algebra • Numbers and operations • Statistics • Probability • Data analysis	• Multiple-choice

*Grid-ins will appear in one of the two 25-minute sections.

Questions in the Math sections are arranged to gradually increase in difficulty. Be aware of the difficulty level as you go through a question set. The harder the question seems, the more traps you will have to avoid.

MATH COVERED ON THE SAT

The tested math concepts on the SAT are as follows:

• Numbers and operations

• Algebra I, II, and functions

• Geometry

• Statistics, probability, and data analysis

SmartPoints — **Ready for Test Day** — Multiple-Choice Questions — Grid-in Questions — Using Your Calculator

MULTIPLE-CHOICE QUESTIONS

The multiple-choice question setup in the Math section is the same as in the other two sections. You will be given five answers from which to choose the best one. Thus, certain techniques will help you eliminate answer choices and make the problems more manageable. We will go over those techniques later in this chapter.

DIRECTIONS

Read these directions through carefully. By Test Day, you will want to know these directions by heart so you won't waste precious time trying to decipher their meaning.

Directions: For this section, solve each problem and decide which is the best of the choices given. Fill in the corresponding oval on the answer sheet. You may use any available space for scratchwork.

Notes:

(1) Calculator use is permitted.

(2) All numbers used are real numbers.

(3) Figures are provided for some problems. All figures are drawn to scale and lie in a plane UNLESS otherwise indicated.

(4) Unless otherwise specified, the domain of any function f is assumed to be the set of all real numbers x for which $f(x)$ is a real number.

$A = \frac{1}{2}bh$ $c^2 = a^2 + b^2$ Special Right Triangles $A = \pi r^2$ $V = \ell wh$ $V = \pi r^2 h$ $A = \ell w$
$C = 2\pi r$

The sum of the degree measures of the angles in a triangle is 180.
The number of degrees of arc in a circle is 360.
A straight angle has a degree measure of 180.

GRID-IN QUESTIONS

The Grid-in section on the SAT is more like the math tests you're used to taking at school. Rather than choosing your answer from five choices provided by the test makers, you have to work through the problem and write whatever answer you came up with in grid boxes on the answer sheet. Some Grid-in questions only have one correct answer, whereas others have several correct answers. *There is no penalty for wrong answers on the Grid-in section.*

PERFECT SCORE TIP

Gridding my answers starting in the first column let me immediately see if my answer was too large, and helped me avoid rounding and decimal place mistakes.

SmartPoints | Ready for Test Day | Multiple-Choice Questions | **Grid-in Questions** | Using your Calculator

EXPERT TUTOR TIP

" Think of Grid-in questions as a safe space to show off the math skills you've learned. And there aren't any pesky answer choices to confuse you! "

DIRECTIONS

Each Grid-in question provides four boxes and a column of ovals, or bubbles, to write your answer in. The elements of your answer, that is, the digits, decimal points, or fraction signs, should be written in a separate box for each part. The corresponding bubbles underneath should be shaded in to match the box at the top of the column. There are limitations to what you may grid and what will not be counted.

Each of the remaining 10 questions requires you to solve the problem and enter your answer by marking the ovals in the special grid, as shown in the example below. You may use any available space for scratchwork.

Answer: 1.25 or $\frac{5}{4}$ or 5/4

Write answer in boxes.

Grid-in result →

Fraction line
Decimal point

Either position is correct.

You may start your answers in any column, space permitting. Columns not needed should be left blank.

- It is recommended, though not required, that you write your answer in the boxes at the top of the columns. However, you will receive credit only for darkening the ovals correctly.

- Grid only one answer to a question, even though some problems have more than one correct answer.

- Darken no more than one oval in a column.

- No answers are negative.

- Mixed numbers cannot be gridded. For example: the number $1\frac{1}{4}$ must be gridded as 1.25 or 5/4.

(If 1 1 / 4 is gridded, it will be interpreted as $\frac{11}{4}$ not $1\frac{1}{4}$.)

- Decimal Accuracy: Decimal answers must be entered as accurately as possible. For example, if you obtain an answer such as 0.1666..., you should record the result as .166 or .167. Less accurate values such as .16 or .17 are not acceptable.

Acceptable ways to grid $\frac{1}{6}$ = .1666...

You **cannot** grid:

- Negative answers
- Answers with variables (x, y, w, etc.)
- Answers greater than 9,999
- Answers with commas (write 1000, not 1,000)
- Mixed numbers (such as $2\frac{1}{2}$)

A NOTE ON . . . GRID-INS AND MIXED NUMBERS

To grid a mixed number, you must first convert it to an improper fraction or decimal and then grid that new value. For example, $2\frac{1}{2}$ will be read as $\frac{21}{2}$ if gridded as a mixed number. Thus, gridding it as $\frac{5}{2}$ or 2.5 will ensure that your answer will be correct.

We discuss Grid-ins more in this chapter and other chapters in this section.

It is not enough to know about the types of math questions on the test and how many you will have to answer. If it were, we could end this section right now. To maximize your score on the Math section, you will need to work systematically. Just like the Critical Reading and Writing questions, the key to working systematically on Math questions is to think about the question before you look for the answer.

On the more basic questions, you may find that you know the answers right away and are able to work through them quickly. However, when working through the harder problems, a few extra seconds spent looking for traps, thinking about your approach, and deciding whether to work on the problem immediately or to come back to it later is very important and will help you accrue more points.

PERFECT SCORE TIP

" Knowing my strengths improved my time management. I like algebra, so I tended to do all the algebra problems the first time I went through a section. "

KAPLAN'S TARGET STRATEGY FOR THE MATH COMPONENT

Kaplan's Target Strategy is a good system for tackling *all* SAT Math problems.

Step 1. Estimate the question's difficulty.

Step 2. Read the question.

Step 3. Skip or do.

Step 4. Look for the fastest approach.

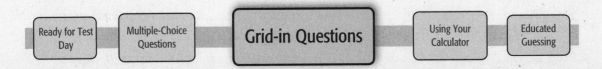

Ready for Test Day | Multiple-Choice Questions | **Grid-in Questions** | Using Your Calculator | Educated Guessing

We will now show you how our Target Strategy works as we use it to answer this sample SAT question:

> At a diner, Joe orders three strips of bacon and a cup of coffee and is charged $2.25. Stella orders two strips of bacon and a cup of coffee and is charged $1.70. What is the price of two strips of bacon?
>
> (A) $0.55
> (B) $0.60
> (C) $1.10
> (D) $1.30
> (E) $1.80

STEP 1. ESTIMATE THE QUESTION'S DIFFICULTY

SAT Math questions are arranged in order of difficulty. Keep this in mind as you work through a set. In a Math set, the first few questions are basic, the middle few are moderately difficult, and the last few are hard. The question above is a moderately difficult word problem.

On difficult questions, watch out for math traps (see chapter 14). Hard questions are often written to be misleading, containing one or two answers that will seem to be right at first glance. Be careful of these easy answers for hard questions. They are there specifically to trick you. Make sure you always know what's being asked.

STEP 2. READ THE QUESTION

If you try to start solving the problem before reading the question all the way through, you may end up doing unnecessary work. The question above looks straightforward, but read through it carefully, and you will see a slight twist.

You're asked to find the cost of two strips of bacon, not one. Many people will find the price of a single bacon strip and forget to double it. Don't make this mistake.

STEP 3. SKIP OR DO

If a problem renders you clueless, circle it in your test booklet and move on. Spend your time on the problems you can solve; if there's still time at the end of the section, come back to the ones you had trouble with then. It is better to get two points from two less challenging problems than spend the same amount of time on one tricky question you are unsure of.

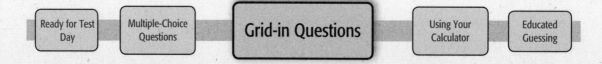

Ready for Test Day   Multiple-Choice Questions   **Grid-in Questions**   Using Your Calculator   Educated Guessing

STEP 4. LOOK FOR THE FASTEST APPROACH

On an easy question, all the information you need to solve the problem may be provided in the question stem or in a diagram. Harder questions often hide the information that will help you solve the problem.

For instance, for a question like the one on the previous page that would appear in the middle of the question set, you would want to be suspicious of easy answers and cautious in your approach to it. If you get the answer too easily, you may have missed something. (In this case, you're asked to find the price of two strips of bacon, not one.)

> **PERFECT SCORE TIP**
>
> " When I was practicing for the SAT, I noticed that familiarity with a question type helped me solve it much faster. Practice makes perfect! "

LOOK FOR SHORTCUTS!

> Sometimes the obvious way of doing a problem is the long way. If the method you choose involves lots of calculating, look for another route. There's usually a shortcut you can use that won't involve tons of arithmetic.

Again, in the sample question, the cost of bacon and coffee could be translated into two distinct equations using the variables b and c. You could find c in terms of b, and then plug this into the other equation. But if you think carefully, you'll see there's a quicker way:

The difference in price between three bacon strips and a cup of coffee and two bacon strips and a cup of coffee is the price of one bacon strip. So one bacon strip costs $\$2.25 - \$1.70 = \$0.55$.

(Remember, you have to find the price of two strips of bacon: $2 \times \$0.55 = \$1.10$.)

Chapters 12 and 13 provide strategies for specific problem types that help you get to the right answer fast. You can also use Kaplan's alternate techniques, such as picking numbers and back-solving, which we will get to in this chapter.

> **EXPERT TUTOR TIP**
>
> " Have you ever been lost in an abstract math problem with lots of variables? Find your way out by using concrete examples: pick actual numbers! "

TWO EFFECTIVE TECHNIQUES

Kaplan's Target Strategy for the Math Component will help you save time and avoid mistakes on the SAT. But sometimes you won't know how to do the math needed to find the answer or doing so would simply be too time-consuming. Luckily, there are several methods for working through Math problems.

Ready for Test Day | Multiple-Choice Questions | **Grid-in Questions** | Using Your Calculator | Educated Guessing

There are two techniques, in particular, that can be useful when you don't know where to start: picking numbers and back-solving.

PICKING NUMBERS

Sometimes you get stuck on a Math question just because it's too general or abstract. A good solution to this problem is to substitute particular numbers for the equation variables.

WHEN TO PICK NUMBERS

The picking numbers strategy works especially well with **even/odd questions**.

If a is an odd integer and b is an even integer, which of the following must be odd?

(A) $2a + b$

(B) $a + 2b$

(C) ab

(D) a^2b

(E) ab^2

Rather than trying to wrap your brain around abstract variables, simply pick numbers for a and b. When you are adding, subtracting, or multiplying even and odd numbers, you can generally assume that what happens with one pair of numbers generally happens with similar pairs of numbers.

Let's say, for the time being, that $a = 3$ and $b = 2$. Plug those values into the answer choices, and there's a good chance that only one choice will be odd:

(A) $2a + b = 2(3) + 2 = 8$

(B) $a + 2b = 3 + 2(2) = 7$

(C) $ab = (3)(2) = 6$

(D) $a^2b = (3^2)(2) = 18$

(E) $ab^2 = (3)(2^2) = 12$

Choice (B) is the only odd answer for $a = 3$ and $b = 2$; thus, it is fair to assume that it must be the only odd answer choice, no matter what odd numbers you plug in for a and b. The answer is (B).

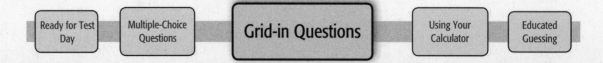

Ready for Test Day | Multiple-Choice Questions | **Grid-in Questions** | Using Your Calculator | Educated Guessing

ANOTHER TIME TO PICK NUMBERS

> **Percent problems** are great for picking numbers. If you see answers with percent signs in them, choose 100 and get started.

Look at the following example.

> From 1985 to 1990, the berry production of bush x increased by 20 percent. From 1990 to 1995, the berry production increased by 30 percent. What was the percent increase in the berry production on the bush over the entire ten-year period from 1985–1995?
>
> (A) 10%
> (B) 25%
> (C) 50%
> (D) 56%
> (E) 60%

Rather than attempting to solve this problem in the abstract, choose a number for the berry production in 1985 and see what happens. There's no need to pick a realistic number. You're better off picking a number that's easy to work with. In percent problems, the number that's easiest to work with is almost always 100.

Now that we have our number, let's plug it into the problem:

- The number of berries on the bush in 1985 was 100. What would the 1990 berry production be?

- Twenty percent more than 100 is 120.

- Now, if 1990's berry production was 120, what would the number of berries in 1995 be?

- What's 30 percent more than 120?

- Be careful. Don't just add 30 to 120. You need to find 30 percent of 120 and add that number on.

- Thirty percent of 120 is $(.30)(120) = 36$.

- Add 36 to 120, and you get 156 berries in 1995.

- What percent greater is 156 than 100? That's easy—that's why we picked 100 to start with.

- It's a 56 percent increase. The answer is (D).

PERFECT SCORE TIP

" Picking numbers was something that I got better at the more I practiced. I tried to determine the number that would make each problem as simple as possible. "

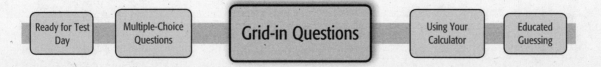

YET ANOTHER TIME TO PICK NUMBERS

A third problem ideal for picking numbers is when the answer choices to a word problem are **algebraic expressions**.

Consider the following example.

If n sunglass lenses cost p dollars, then how many dollars would q sunglass lenses cost?

(A) $\dfrac{nq}{q}$

(B) $\dfrac{nq}{p}$

(C) $\dfrac{pq}{n}$

(D) $\dfrac{n}{pq}$

(E) $\dfrac{p}{nq}$

The hard thing about this question is it uses variables instead of numbers. So make it real. Pick numbers for the variables. Pick numbers that are easy to work with. Let's say that $n = 2$, $p = 4$, and $q = 3$.

The question then becomes: "If two sunglass lenses cost \$4, how many dollars would three sunglass lenses cost?" That's easy—\$6. When $n = 2$, $p = 4$, and $q = 3$, the correct answer should equal 6. Plug those values into the answer choices and see which ones yield 6:

(A) $\dfrac{np}{q} = \dfrac{(2)(4)}{3} = \dfrac{8}{3} = 2\dfrac{2}{3}$

(B) $\dfrac{nq}{p} = \dfrac{(2)(3)}{4} = \dfrac{6}{4} = \dfrac{3}{2} = 1\dfrac{1}{2}$

(C) $\dfrac{pq}{n} = \dfrac{(4)(3)}{2} = \dfrac{12}{2} = 6$

(D) $\dfrac{n}{pq} = \dfrac{2}{(4)(3)} = \dfrac{2}{12} = \dfrac{1}{6}$

(E) $\dfrac{p}{nq} = \dfrac{4}{(2)(3)} = \dfrac{4}{6} = \dfrac{2}{3}$

Choice (C) is the only one that yields 6, so it must be the correct answer.

Ready for Test Day | Multiple-Choice Questions | **Grid-in Questions** | Using Your Calculator | Educated Guessing

When picking numbers for an abstract word problem like this one, try all five answer choices. Sometimes more than one choice will yield the correct result. When that happens, pick another set of numbers to eliminate the coincidences. *Avoid picking 0 and 1.* These often give several *possibly correct* answers.

BACK-SOLVING

Sometimes it is not possible simply to pick numbers and solve the problem. In these cases, the answer choices become your tools, and you can work backward to find the right choice. We call this back-solving, which essentially means plugging the choices back into the question until you find the one that fits.

Back-solving works best when:

- The question is a complex word problem, and the answer choices are numbers
- The alternative is setting up multiple algebraic equations

Back-solving is not ideal:

- If the answer choices include variables
- On algebra questions or word problems that have ugly answer choices, such as radicals and fractions (plugging them in takes too much time)

> ### PERFECT SCORE TIP
>
> 66 When using back-solving, Kaplan's method of starting with answer choice (C) was by far the best way for me to use back-solving. 99

A NOTE ON . . . WHY BACK-SOLVING WORKS

The answer choices on the SAT are arranged in order, either descending or ascending, from (A) to (E). Choosing choice (C) first will guide your next step in solving the problem. For example, if plugging choice (C) into the equation gives you too small of a value, then either (A) and (B) or (D) and (E) can be eliminated, depending on which values are smaller than (C).

COMPLEX QUESTION, SIMPLE ANSWER CHOICES

Sometimes back-solving is faster than setting up an equation. For example:

A music club draws 27 patrons. If there are seven more musicians than singers in the club, how many patrons are musicians?

(A) 8
(B) 10
(C) 14
(D) 17
(E) 20

> ### EXPERT TUTOR TIP
>
> 66 Back-solving can save time and energy, especially when you can avoid remembering and setting up equations. 99

The five answer choices represent the possible number of musicians in the club, so try them in the question stem. The choice that gives a total of 27 patrons, with seven more musicians than singers, will be the correct answer.

When back-solving, start with answer choice (C). For example, plugging in (C) gives you 14 musicians in the club. Because there are seven more musicians than singers, there are seven singers in the club. But $14 + 7 < 27$. The sum is too small, so there must be more than 14 musicians; thus, you can eliminate answer choices (A), (B), and (C) just like that.

Either (D) or (E) will be correct. Plugging in (D) gives you 17 musicians in the club; $17 - 7$ equals 10 singers, and $17 + 10 = 27$ patrons total. Answer choice (D) is correct.

Algebra problems with multiple equations:

If $a + b + c = 110$, $a = 4b$, and $3a = 2c$, then $b =$

(A) 6

(B) 8

(C) 9

(D) 10

(E) 14

You're looking for b, so plug in the answer choices for b in the question and see what happens. The choice that gives us 110 for the sum $a + b + c$ must be correct.

Start with the midrange number, 9, choice (C).

If $b = 9$, then $a = 4 \times 9 = 36$.

$2c = 3a = 3 \times 36 = 108$

$c = 54$

$a + b + c = 36 + 9 + 54 = 99$

Because this is a smaller sum than 110, the correct value for b must be larger. Therefore, eliminate answer choices (A), (B), and (C). Now, plug in either (D) or (E), and see which answer works.

GUESSING UNDER THE GUN

If you are short on time and have two answers left, choose a number that makes the most sense after your back-solving work.

Ready for Test Day | Multiple-Choice Questions | **Grid-in Questions** | Using Your Calculator | Educated Guessing

Short on time? Try guessing between (D) and (E). But guess intelligently. Because (C) wasn't that far off the correct answer, you want to choose a number just slightly bigger than 9. That's choice (D).

GRID-IN STRATEGIES

The Grid-in section is special. Grid-in questions are not multiple-choice, and there is no penalty for wrong answers. You have to solve the equation in the question yourself and fill in your answer on a special grid.

WRITE YOUR ANSWERS IN THE NUMBER BOXES

This doesn't get you points by itself, but you will make fewer mistakes if you write your answers in the number boxes. You may think that gridding directly will save time, but writing first then gridding helps guarantee accuracy, which means more points.

ALWAYS START YOUR ANSWER IN THE FIRST COLUMN BOX

Of course you can start in any column you choose, but if you go in order, you will avoid any confusion. If you always start with the first column, even if your answer has only one or two figures, your answers will always fit. However, there is no oval for 0 in the first column, so you will need to grid an answer with 0 in any other column.

EXPERT TUTOR TIP

Here's some advice for Grid-ins: measure twice—write your numbers in the boxes and grid in your answer as an extra measure.

GRID SMARTLY!

If your answer is .7, don't grid 0.7!

IN A FRACTIONAL ANSWER, GRID (/) IN THE CORRECT COLUMN

The sign (/) separates the numerator from the denominator. It appears only in columns two and three. A fractional answer with four digits—like $\frac{31}{42}$—won't fit and will need to be converted.

NEVER GRID A MIXED NUMBER

Always change mixed numbers to decimals or fractions before you grid.

PERFECT SCORE TIP

I found it better to stay consistent with my grid-in answers. Unless a question specified otherwise, I would also convert fractions to decimals.

If you try to grid a mixed number, it will be read as a fraction and be counted wrong. For example, $4\frac{1}{2}$ will be read as the fraction $\frac{41}{2}$, which is $20\frac{1}{2}$. So first change mixed numbers to fractions or decimals, then grid in. In this case:

- Change $4\frac{1}{2}$ to $\frac{9}{2}$ and grid in the fraction OR

- Change $4\frac{1}{2}$ to 4.5 and grid in the decimal.

PLACE DECIMAL POINTS CAREFULLY

A few pointers:

- For a decimal less than 1, such as .127, enter the decimal point in the first column.

- Only grid in a zero before the decimal point if it is part of the answer, as in 20.5—don't put one there (if your answer is, say, .5) just to make your answer look more accurate. Don't begin an answer with a zero in the first column.

- Never grid a decimal point in the last column.

HOW TO HANDLE LONG OR REPEATING DECIMALS

Grid the first three digits only, and plug in the decimal point where it belongs. Say three answers are .45454545, 82.452312, and 1.428743:

- Grid .454, 82.4, and 1.42, respectively.

- You could round 1.428743 up to the nearest hundredth (1.43), but it's not required, and you could make a mistake.

- Note that rounding to an even shorter answer —1.4—would be incorrect.

MORE THAN ONE RIGHT ANSWER? CHOOSE ONE AND ENTER IT

Say you're asked for a two-digit integer that is a multiple of 2, 3, and 5. You might answer 30, 60, or 90. Whichever you grid would be right.

SOME GRID-INS HAVE A RANGE OF POSSIBLE ANSWERS

Suppose you're asked to grid a value of m where $1 - 2m < m$ and $5m - 2 < m$. Solving for m in the first inequality, you find that $\frac{1}{3} < m$. Solving for m in the second inequality, you find that $m < \frac{1}{2}$. So, $\frac{1}{3} < m < \frac{1}{2}$. Grid in any value between $\frac{1}{3}$ and $\frac{1}{2}$. (Gridding in $\frac{1}{3}$ or $\frac{1}{2}$ would be wrong.) When the answer is a range of values, it's often easier to work with decimals: $.333 < m < .5$. This way, you can quickly grid .4 (or .35 or .45, etc.) as your answer.

USING YOUR CALCULATOR (OR NOT)

You've read about all of our techniques for finding the answers to Math questions using just your pencil and your mind. However, there are times when you can get some extra help and make life a little easier.

You are allowed to use a calculator on the SAT. However, that doesn't mean that you should always use your calculator on the SAT. Yes, you can do computations faster, but you may be tempted to waste time using a calculator on questions that shouldn't involve lengthy computation.

Remember, you never need a calculator to solve an SAT problem. If you ever find yourself doing extensive calculations—elaborate division or long drawn-out multiplication—stop. You probably missed a shortcut.

SHOULD I JUST LEAVE MY CALCULATOR AT HOME?

No. Bring it. By zeroing in on the parts of problems that need calculation, you can increase your score and save yourself time on the SAT by using your calculator.

WHAT KIND OF CALCULATOR SHOULD I BRING?

One that you're comfortable with. If you don't have a calculator now, buy one right away, and practice using it between now and Test Day. You can use just about any small calculator; however, there are a few restrictions you must abide by.

You may not bring:

- Calculators that print out your calculations
- Handheld minicomputers or laptop computers
- Any calculators with a typewriter keypad
- Calculators with an angled readout screen
- Calculators that require a wall outlet
- Calculators that make noise

WHEN SHOULD I USE MY CALCULATOR?

Calculators help the most on Grid-ins. Because Grid-ins don't give you answer choices to choose from, it's especially important to be positive about your results, and calculators can help you check your work and avoid careless errors.

Remember, a calculator can be useful when used selectively and strategically. Not all parts of a problem will necessarily be easier with a calculator. Consider this problem:

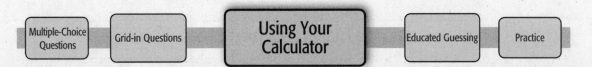

Multiple-Choice Questions | Grid-in Questions | **Using Your Calculator** | Educated Guessing | Practice

> If four grams of peanuts can make 32 Peanut Joy
> candy bars, how many Peanut Joy candy bars could
> be produced from 86 grams of peanuts?

This word problem has two steps. Step one is to set up the following proportion:

4 g of peanuts = 32 bars

A little algebraic engineering tells you that:

1 g of peanuts = 8 bars

Here's where you whip out that calculator. This problem has now been reduced down to pure calculation:

$86 \times 8 = 688$

WHEN SHOULD I AVOID MY CALCULATOR?

You may be tempted to use your calculator on every problem, but many questions will be easier without it. Look at this example:

If $x \neq \dfrac{1}{3}$ and $\dfrac{51}{3x-1} = \dfrac{51}{29}$, then what is the value of x?

One way of answering this question would be to cross-multiply and then isolate x:

$$(51)(29) = (3x - 1)(51)$$
$$1{,}479 = 153x - 51$$
$$1{,}530 = 153x$$
$$\frac{1{,}530}{153} = x$$
$$10 = x$$

Notice how much more quickly you'll arrive at the answer if, rather than reflexively reaching for your calculator, you invest a few moments in thinking about the question—specifically what you're given and what you're asked for. Notice that after you cross-multiplied the equation above, you were left with $(51)(29) = (3x - 1)(51)$ Simply cancel out 51 from both sides. You are now left with the following equation:

$$3x - 1 = 29$$
$$3x = 30$$
$$x = 10$$

TWO COMMON CALCULATOR MISTAKES

Be aware of the two following common calculator mistakes. Learning how to avoid them now will help you from losing points on Test Day:

EXPERT TUTOR TIP

Don't rely too much on your calculator—you might not find the answer you need. Use it only to save time.

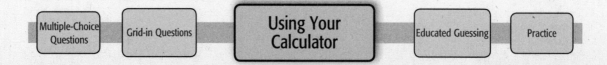

Multiple-Choice Questions — Grid-in Questions — **Using Your Calculator** — Educated Guessing — Practice

COMMON CALCULATOR MISTAKE #1: CALCULATING BEFORE YOU THINK

On the Grid-in problem below, how should (and shouldn't) you use your calculator?

> The sum of all the integers from 1 to 44, inclusive, is subtracted from the sum of all the integers from 7 to 50, inclusive. What is the result?

The Wrong Approach:

1. Grab calculator.
2. Punch in all the numbers.
3. Put down answer and hope you didn't hit any wrong buttons.

You might be tempted to punch in all the numbers from 1 to 44, find their sum, do the same for the numbers 7 through 50, and then subtract the first sum from the second. But doing that means punching 252 keys. The odds are you'll hit the wrong key somewhere and get the wrong answer. Even if you don't, punching in all those numbers takes too much time.

The Kaplan Approach:

1. Think first.
2. Decide on the best way to solve the problem.
3. Only then, use your calculator.

The right approach is to *think first*. The amount of computation involved in directly solving this tells you that there must be an easier way. You'll see this if you realize that both sums contain the same number of consecutive integers. Each integer in the first sum has a corresponding integer 6 digits greater than it in the second sum:

$$1 \quad 7$$
$$+\,2 + 8$$
$$+\,3 + 9$$
$$\ldots$$
$$\ldots$$
$$\ldots$$
$$+\,42 + 48$$
$$+\,43 + 49$$
$$+\,44 + 50$$
$$=\quad\ =$$

> **PERFECT SCORE TIP**
>
> " If I couldn't think of a reason why using a calculator would make a problem easier or quicker to solve, I didn't use it. "

Multiple-Choice Questions — Grid-in Questions — **Using Your Calculator** — Educated Guessing — Practice

EXPERT TUTOR TIP

" Memorization tricks, like PEMDAS, can help you remember important concepts. Try creating other catchy mnemonic devices to help you on Test Day. "

As you'll see in the Math Traps chapter, the way to find the number of integers in a consecutive series is to subtract the smallest from the largest and add:

$1 (44 - 1 = 43; 43 + 1 = 44$ or $50 - 7 = 43; 43 + 1 = 44)$.

So there are 44 pairs of integers that are 6 apart.

Therefore, the total difference between the two sums will be the difference between each pair of integers times the number of pairs. Now take out your calculator, punch $6 \times 44 =$, and get the correct answer of 264 with little or no time wasted.

COMMON CALCULATOR MISTAKE #2: FORGETTING THE ORDER OF OPERATIONS

Even when you use your calculator, you can't just enter numbers in the order they appear on the page—you have to follow the order of operations. This is a very simple error, but it can cost you lots of points. The order of operations is PEMDAS, which stands for:

Parentheses first, then deal with

Exponents, then

Multiplication and

Division(from left to right), and finally

Addition and

Subtraction (from left to right)

PERFECT SCORE TIP

" If my calculations involved parentheses in any way, I would always make sure that they were correct before pressing "Enter." I avoided a lot of errors this way! "

For example, say you want to find the value of the expression $\dfrac{x^2+1}{x+3}$ when $x = 7$.

If you just punched in $7 \times 7 + 1 \div 7 + 3 =$, you would get the wrong answer.

The correct way to work it out is:

$$(7^2 + 1) \div (7 + 3) = (7 \times 7 + 1) \div (7 + 3) = (49 + 1) \div 10 = 50 \div 10 = 5$$

Combining a calculator with an understanding of when and how to use it can help you boost your score.

PUNCH WISELY!

Don't just grab your calculator, punch in all the numbers, and put down an answer. You'll have to hope you didn't hit any wrong keys. If you have time, always check your answers.

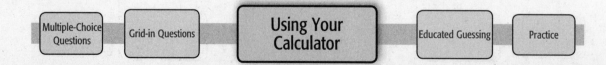

Multiple-Choice Questions   Grid-in Questions   **Using Your Calculator**   Educated Guessing   Practice

FOUR STRATEGIES FOR EDUCATED GUESSING

EXPERT TUTOR TIP

Only guess if you can follow one of Kaplan's four strategies for educated guesses. Avoid guessing randomly.

You *can* and *should* make *educated* guesses on the Math section of the SAT. If you can eliminate one or more wrong answer choices, it increases your odds of guessing correctly. This increases your score, which is a good thing. We'll show you how.

The exception to the guessing penalty rule is the Grid-in section. You lose no points for wrong answers on Grid-in questions; therefore, you should ALWAYS fill something in the grid on these questions.

To make an educated guess, you need to eliminate answer choices that you know are wrong and guess from what's left. The more answer choices you can eliminate, the better chance you have of guessing the correct answer from what's left over. You do this by:

1. Eliminating unreasonable answer choices
2. Eliminating the obvious answers on hard questions
3. Eyeballing lengths, angles, and areas on geometry problems
4. Finding the range on Grid-ins—then guessing

ELIMINATING UNREASONABLE ANSWER CHOICES

Before you guess, think about the problem, and decide which answers don't make sense.

The ratio of celebrities to agents in a certain room is 13:11. If there are 429 celebrities in the room, how many agents are there? ___

(A) 143
(B) 363
(C) 433
(D) 507
(E) 792

The ratio of celebrities to agents is 13:11, so there are more celebrities than not. Because there are 429 celebrities, there must be fewer than 429 agents. You can eliminate choices (C), (D), and (E). The answer must be either (A) or (B), so guess. The correct answer is (B).

ELIMINATING THE OBVIOUS ON HARD QUESTIONS

On the hard questions late in a set, obvious answers are usually wrong. So eliminate them when you guess.

This strategy does not hold true for easier questions that may appear at the beginning of the Math set, when the obvious answer could be right.

In the following difficult problem, found late in a question set, which obvious answer would you eliminate?

> A number x is increased by 30 percent, and then the result is decreased by 20 percent. What is the final result of these changes?
>
> (A) x is increased by 10 percent
> (B) x is increased by 6 percent
> (C) x is increased by 4 percent
> (D) x is decreased by 5 percent
> (E) x is decreased by 10 percent

If you picked (A) as the obvious choice to eliminate, you'd be right. Most people would combine the decrease of 20 percent with the increase of 30 percent, getting a net increase of 10 percent. That's the easy, obvious answer, but not the correct answer. If you must guess, avoid (A). The correct answer is (C).

EYEBALLING LENGTHS, ANGLES, AND AREAS ON GEOMETRY PROBLEMS

Use diagrams that accompany geometry problems to help you eliminate wrong answer choices.

First, double-check for specific instructions involving whether or not the diagram is drawn to scale. Diagrams are always drawn to scale unless there's a note like this: Note: Figure not drawn to scale. If it's not drawn to scale, you cannot use this strategy. If it is, estimate quantities or eyeball the diagram, then eliminate answer choices that are way too large or too small.

Length—When a geometry question asks for a length, use the given lengths to estimate the unknown length. Measure off the given length by making a nick in your pencil with your thumbnail. Then hold the pencil against the unknown length on the diagram to see how the lengths compare. Try it.

In the figure, what is the length of BC?

(A) $\sqrt{2}$

(B) 2

(C) $2\sqrt{2}$

(D) 4

(E) $4\sqrt{2}$

- *AB* is 2, so measure off this length on your pencil.

- Compare *BC* with this length.

- *BC* appears almost twice as long as *AB*, so *BC* is approximately 4.

- Because $\sqrt{2}$ is approximately 1.4, and *BC* is clearly longer than *AB*, choices (A) and (B) are too small.

- Choice (E) is greater than 4, so eliminate that.

- Now guess between (C) and (D). The correct answer is (C).

Angles—You can also eyeball angles. To eyeball an angle, compare the angle with a familiar angle, such as a straight angle (180 degrees), a right angle (90 degrees), or half a right angle (45 degrees). The corner of a piece of paper is a right angle, so use that to see if an angle is greater or less than 90 degrees.

In the figure above, if $\ell_1 \parallel \ell_2$, what is the value of *x*?

(A) 40

(B) 50

(C) 80

(D) 100

(E) 130

- You see that *x* is less than 90 degrees, so eliminate choices (D) and (E).

- Because *x* appears to be much less than 90 degrees, eliminate choice (C).

- Now pick between (A) and (B). In fact, the correct answer is (A).

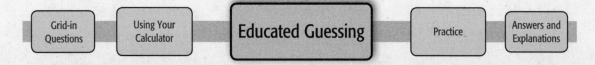

Areas—Eyeballing an area is similar to eyeballing a length. You compare an unknown area in a diagram to an area that you do know.

In square *ABCD* above, what is the area of the shaded region?

(A) 4

(B) 6

(C) 8

(D) 9

(E) 10

Because *ABCD* is a square, it has the area 4^2, or 16. The shaded area is less than one-half the size of the square, so its area must be less than 8. Eliminate answer choices (C), (D), and (E). The correct answer is (B).

FINDING THE RANGE ON GRID-INS—THEN GUESSING

On Grid-ins, there are no answer choices to eliminate, but you won't lose points for guessing. So if you are stuck, try to estimate the general range of the answer and guess.

PRACTICE

REGULAR MATH

1. A certain pump can drain a full 375-gallon tank in 15 minutes. At this rate, how many more minutes would it take to drain a full 600-gallon tank?

    (A) 9
    (B) 15
    (C) 18
    (D) 24
    (E) 25

2. A gardener plants flowers in the following order: carnations, daffodils, larkspurs, tiger lilies, and zinnias. If the gardener planted 47 flowers, what kind of flower did he plant last?

    (A) carnation
    (B) daffodil
    (C) larkspur
    (D) tiger lily
    (E) zinnia

3. How many different positive two-digit integers are there such that the tens' digit is greater than 5 and the units' digit is odd?

    (A) 10
    (B) 12
    (C) 15
    (D) 20
    (E) 25

4. If a and b are positive integers, what is a percent of b percent of 200?

    (A) $\dfrac{ab}{100}$
    (B) $\dfrac{ab}{50}$
    (C) ab
    (D) $50ab$
    (E) $100ab$

5. A 7.5-L mixture of water and molasses is 60 percent molasses. If 1.5 L of water is added, approximately what percent of the new mixture is molasses?

    (A) 40%
    (B) 50%
    (C) 63%
    (D) 64%
    (E) 68%

6. The figure above is formed from a square and a right triangle. What is its area?

    (A) $\dfrac{a(a+b)}{2}$
    (B) $\dfrac{a^2+b^2}{2}$
    (C) $\dfrac{a(b-a)}{2}$
    (D) a^2+b^2
    (E) $a^2+\dfrac{ab}{2}$

GRID-INS

7. If the three-digit number $11Q$ is a prime number, what digit is represented by Q?

8. The sum of five consecutive odd integers is 425. What is the greatest of these integers?

9. A triangle has one side of length 3 and another of length 7. If the length of the third side is a solution to the equation $x^2 - 2x = 63$, what is the length of the third side?

ANSWERS AND EXPLANATIONS

1. A
SMARTPOINTS CATEGORY: RATIOS

You are given that the pump drains 375 gallons in 15 minutes and asked for the number of additional minutes it would take to drain a 600-gallon tank. Because we are dealing with the *additional* minutes, we're really just looking for the amount of time that it'd take to drain $600 - 375 = 225$ gallons. 225 gallons is less than 375, so it should take less than 15 minutes. The only choice *less than 15* is (A).

2. B
SMARTPOINTS CATEGORY: SEQUENCES

You're looking for the 47th flower in a repeating pattern. Since there are five different flowers in the pattern, the last flower in the pattern corresponds to a multiple of 5. So the 5th, 10th,..., and 45th flowers will be zinnias. But there will also be two *remainders*, and so the 46th will be the first flower in the pattern and the 47th will be the second flower, which is a daffodil.

3. D
SMARTPOINTS CATEGORY: NUMBER PROPERTIES

We want two-digit numbers with a tens' digit greater than 5 and a units' digit that's odd, so we're looking for odd two-digit numbers greater than 60. From 60 to 99, there are $99 - 60 + 1 = 39 + 1 = 40$ numbers. Half of these are even and half are odd, so the answer is $40 \div 2 = 20$.

4. B
SMARTPOINTS CATEGORY: PERCENTS

Multiple percents with variables *look* scary but they're really not that bad if you remember to pick numbers. In even the scariest, most abstract math problem on the SAT, there will always be at least one concrete spot for you to work from. In this problem, that's the number 200. Working backwards in that sentence, we're looking for b percent of 200, then a percent of the result. So pick 100 for b and 50 for a. Now the problem becomes: "What's 50 percent of 100 percent of 200?" Well, 100 percent of 200 is 200 and 50 percent of that is half of 200, or 100, so the correct choice needs to evaluate to 100 when $a = 50$ and $b = 100$. Right away, you may have noticed that (C), (D), and (E) would be way too large. Both (A) and (B) involve 50×100 in the numerator. (A) divides that by 100, leaving you with 50, while (B) divides it by 50 and leaves you with 100, so (B) is correct.

Using Your Calculator | Educated Guessing | Practice | **Answers and Explanations** | Chapter Highlights

5. B

SMARTPOINTS CATEGORY: PERCENTS

First find the amount of molasses in the original mixture. There are 7.5 L of the mixture, of which 60% is molasses, so there are $\dfrac{60}{100} \times 7.5 = 4.5$ L of molasses. An additional 1.5 L of water is added, so now the mixture is $7.5 + 1.5 = 9$ L, of which 4.5 L is molasses. Percent $= \dfrac{\text{Part}}{\text{Whole}} \times 100\%$, so in this case, $\dfrac{4.5}{9} \times 100\% = .5 \times 100\% = 50\%$.

If you were low on time and needed to guess, you may have noticed that we're *diluting* a mixture that was originally 60% molasses, so the resulting mixture must be less than 60% molasses. That allows you to eliminate (C), (D), and (E) right off the bat.

6. A

SMARTPOINTS CATEGORY: COMPLEX FIGURES

With all those variables in the answer choices, this problem is perfect for picking numbers. First, relabel the diagram as follows:

Let's pick some numbers for a and b. Because b is clearly greater than a, try $a = 3$ and $b = 5$. The area of a square is the square of its side, so the area of this square is $3^2 = 9$. The area of a right triangle is $\dfrac{1}{2} \times$ base $\times$ height, so the area of this triangle is $\dfrac{1}{2} \times 2 \times 3 = 3$. So the combined area when $a = 3$ and $b = 5$ is $9 + 3 = 12$.

Now plug those values into each of the choices and see which ones return a value of 12:

(A) $\dfrac{a(a+b)}{2} = \dfrac{3(3+5)}{2} = \dfrac{3(8)}{2} = \dfrac{24}{2} = 12.$

(B) $\dfrac{a^2 + b^2}{2} = \dfrac{3^2 + 5^2}{2} = \dfrac{9 + 25}{2} = \dfrac{34}{2} = 17.$ Eliminate.

(C) $\dfrac{a(b-a)}{2} = \dfrac{3(5-3)}{2} = \dfrac{3(2)}{2} = 6.$ Eliminate.

(D) $a^2 + b^2 = 3^2 + 5^2 = 9 + 25 = 34.$ Eliminate.

(E) $a^2 + \dfrac{ab}{2} = 3^2 + \dfrac{3(5)}{2} = 9 + \dfrac{15}{2} = \dfrac{18}{2} + \dfrac{15}{2} = \dfrac{33}{2} = 16\dfrac{1}{2}$. Eliminate.

Only (A) works, so it must be correct.

7. 3

SMARTPOINTS CATEGORY: NUMBER PROPERTIES

This problem may be a Grid-in but you *can* actually back-solve it. Begin by narrowing down your list of possible values for Q to back-solve from. Q is a digit, so it must be one of the integers from 0 through 9. Because a prime number is a number that cannot be divisible by anything other than 1 and itself, eliminate digits that would make the number violate this property. We can begin by eliminating all the even digits, as they would produce numbers divisible by 2. Eliminate 1 and 7, as they would produce numbers divisible by 3 (a number is divisible by 3 if the sum of its digits is a multiple of 3.) Eliminate 5, as that produces a number divisible by 5. You are now left with 3 and 9, and the only divisibility under 10 that we haven't checked is 7.

Dividing 113 and 119 by 7 reveals that $119 = 7 \times 17$, so the answer is 3.

8. 89

SMARTPOINTS CATEGORY: AVERAGES

The middle integer of an odd number of consecutive integers will be equal to their average. Five consecutive odd integers sum to 425, so the middle integer is $425 \div 5 = 85$. This is the third integer in the set, so the fourth integer is $85 + 2 = 87$, and the fifth (and greatest) integer is $87 + 2 = 89$, the correct answer.

9. 9

SMARTPOINTS CATEGORY: QUADRATIC EQUATIONS

The Triangle Inequality Theorem states that any side of a triangle is always shorter than the sum and longer than the difference of the other two sides. The two given sides are 3 and 7, so the third side must be shorter than $3 + 7 = 10$ and longer than $7 - 3 = 4$. SAT quadratic solutions tend to be integers, so we're really dealing with the integers 5, 6, 7, 8, or 9 as possible "choices."

That allows us to back-solve for the answer. Begin with 7, the middle value:

$$x^2 - 2x = 63$$

$$7^2 - 2(7) = 63$$

$$49 - 14 = 63$$

$$35 \neq 63$$

Using Your Calculator | Educated Guessing | Practice | **Answers and Explanations** | Chapter Highlights

So 7 is much too small. Eliminate 5, 6, and 7. Let's try 9:

$$x^2 - 2x = 63$$

$$9^2 - 2(9) = 63$$

$$81 - 18 = 63$$

$$63 = 63$$

That works, so the answer is 9.

IF YOU LEARN ONLY SIX THINGS IN THIS CHAPTER . . .

1. SAT MATH FACTS

- Math questions are arranged by order of difficulty.

- Look for two types of questions on the test: Multiple-Choice and Grid-ins.

- Don't automatically reach for the calculator to solve an equation. Often, there is an easier path to the answer.

- All figures are drawn to scale unless otherwise indicated.

2. MULTIPLE-CHOICE QUESTIONS

- You lose $\frac{1}{4}$ point for each incorrect multiple-choice answer.

- The right answer is in front of you, waiting to be chosen.

3. GRID-IN QUESTIONS

- You don't lose any points for incorrect Grid-in answers.

- You have to calculate and write out (carefully) your own answers for them.

- Mixed numbers must be converted to improper fractions or decimals and gridded in. Otherwise, the answer will be wrong.

4. KAPLAN'S FOUR BASIC MATH STEPS

- Estimate the question's difficulty

- Read the question.

- Skip or do.

- Look for the fastest approach.

5. EFFECTIVE PROBLEM-SOLVING TECHNIQUES

- Picking numbers is a good strategy for abstract questions.

- Back-solving works well for solving complex word problems or questions requiring numerous algebraic equations.

6. HOW TO MAKE AN EDUCATED GUESS

- Eliminate unreasonable answer choices.

- Eliminate the obvious answers on hard questions.

- Eyeball lengths, angles, and areas.

- Find the range on Grid-in questions.

Using Your Calculator — Educated Guessing — Practice — Answers and Explanations — **Chapter Highlights**

CHAPTER 12: BASIC MATH CONCEPTS

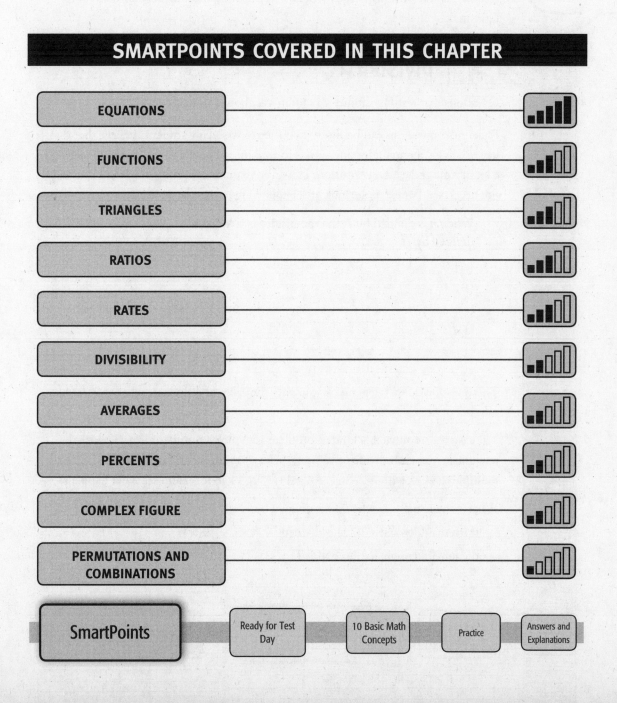

SMARTPOINTS COVERED IN THIS CHAPTER

EQUATIONS

FUNCTIONS

TRIANGLES

RATIOS

RATES

DIVISIBILITY

AVERAGES

PERCENTS

COMPLEX FIGURE

PERMUTATIONS AND COMBINATIONS

SmartPoints

Ready for Test Day

10 Basic Math Concepts

Practice

Answers and Explanations

WHAT TO EXPECT ON TEST DAY

The SAT Math section has always tested certain topics of basic math. When you are confident that you understand these basic math concepts, the SAT Math section gets a whole lot easier.

THE TEN MOST TESTED BASIC MATH CONCEPTS

This chapter reviews these basic math concepts and explains how the SAT tests them. We also teach you our techniques for solving these problems and how these techniques will work with both types of SAT Math questions: regular math and Grid-ins.

 ## DIVISIBILITY

Questions that test Divisibility will often ask about a remainder.

Remainder questions can be easier than they seem. Many students believe that the key to solving a remainder question is to find the value of a variable, which takes up a lot of time and causes confusion. However, that type of problem solving is usually not necessary. For example, look at the following remainder problem.

> When n is divided by 7, the remainder is 4. What is the remainder when $2n$ is divided by 7?
>
> (A) 0
> (B) 1
> (C) 2
> (D) 3
> (E) 4

This question doesn't depend on knowing the value of n. In fact, n has an infinite number of possible values.

The easy way to solve this kind of problem is to pick a number for n. Because the remainder when n is divided by 7 is 4, pick any multiple of 7 and add 4. The easiest multiple to work with is 7. So $7 + 4 = 11$. Plug 11 in for n and see what happens:

What is the remainder when $2n$ is divided by 7?

. . . the remainder when 2(11) is divided by 7?

. . . the remainder when 22 is divided by 7?

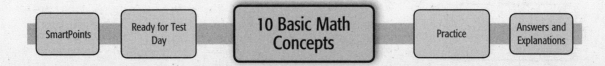

SmartPoints | Ready for Test Day | **10 Basic Math Concepts** | Practice | Answers and Explanations

$\frac{22}{7} = 3$, remainder 1

The remainder is 1 when $n = 11$. So the answer is (B). The remainder will also be 1 when $n = 18, 25,$ or 46.

 ## AVERAGES

Instead of giving you a list of values to plug into the average formula $\frac{\text{Sum of Terms}}{\text{Number of Terms}}$, SAT average questions often put a spin on the problem. The following problem tells you the average of a group of terms and asks you to find the value of a missing term.

Work with the sum to get the answer:

> The average weight of five amplifiers in a guitar shop is 32 pounds. If four of the amplifiers weigh 25, 27, 19, and 35 pounds, what is the weight of the fifth amplifier?
>
> (A) 28 pounds
> (B) 32 pounds
> (C) 49 pounds
> (D) 54 pounds
> (E) 69 pounds

This problem tells you the average of a group of terms and asks you to find the value of a missing term. To get the answer, you need to work with the sum. Let the variable $x =$ the weight of the fifth amplifier. Plug this into the average formula:

$$\text{Average} = \frac{\text{Sum of Terms}}{\text{Number of Terms}}$$

$$32 = \frac{25 + 27 + 19 + 35 + x}{5}$$

$$32 \times 5 = 25 + 27 + 19 + 35 + x$$

The average weight of the amplifiers times the number of amplifiers equals the total weight of the amplifiers. The new formula is:

$$\text{Average} \times \text{Number of Terms} = \text{Sum of Terms}$$

PERFECT SCORE TIP

" For questions with averages, I found that writing out all the terms and expressions to evaluate reduced the number of calculator mistakes I made. "

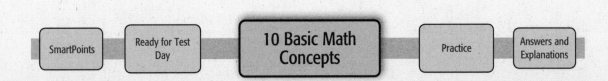

SmartPoints | Ready for Test Day | **10 Basic Math Concepts** | Practice | Answers and Explanations

Remember this version of the average formula so you can find the total sum whenever you know the average of a group of terms and the number of terms. Now you can solve for the weight of the fifth amplifier as follows:

$$32 \times 5 = 25 + 27 + 19 + 35 + x$$

$$160 = 106 + x$$

$$54 = x$$

The weight of the fifth amplifier is 54 pounds, choice (D).

BACK SOLVING FOR AVERAGES

If you forget how to set up an average problem, try back solving the choices. This can help you earn some crucial extra points on Test Day.

 RATIOS

SAT test makers often write ratio questions in a way that tricks you into setting up the wrong ratio. For instance, try to work through the question below.

> Out of every 50 CDs produced in a certain factory, 20 are scratched. What is the ratio of unscratched CDs produced to scratched CDs produced?
>
> (A) 2:5
> (B) 3:5
> (C) 2:3
> (D) 3:2
> (E) 5:2

PERFECT SCORE TIP

" When solving ratio problems, I always circled what the question was asking and made sure to find all the parts and the whole so I didn't make any silly mistakes. "

You need to find the parts and the whole in this problem. In this case, the total number of CDs is the whole, and the numbers of unscratched CDs and scratched CDs, respectively, are the parts that make up this whole. You're given a part-to-whole ratio (the ratio of scratched CDs to all CDs) and asked to find a part-to-part ratio (the ratio of unscratched CDs to scratched CDs).

If 20 CDs of every 50 are scratched, the remaining 30 CDs must be okay. So, the part-to-part ratio of good-to-scratched CDs is 30:20, or 3:2, choice (D). If you hadn't

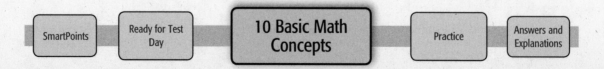

SmartPoints | Ready for Test Day | **10 Basic Math Concepts** | Practice | Answers and Explanations

identified the part and the whole first, it would have been easy to become confused and compare a part to the whole, like the ratios in answer choices (A), (B), and (E).

Part: part ratio problems give you the whole number and one part number. Using simple math, you can usually figure out the quantity of the other part of the whole.

This approach also works for ratio questions where you need to find actual quantities. Here's an example.

> Of every 5 CDs produced in a certain factory, 2 are scratched. If 2,200 CDs were produced, how many were scratched?

(Note: This is a Grid-in, so there are no answer choices.)

Here you need to find a quantity: the number of defective CDs. If you're looking for the actual quantities in a ratio, set up and solve a proportion. You're given a part-to-whole ratio (the ratio of scratched CDs to all CDs) and the total number of CDs produced. You can find the answer by setting up and solving a proportion:

$$\frac{\text{Number of scratched CDs}}{\text{Total number of CDs}} = \frac{2}{5} = \frac{x}{2,200}$$

x = number of scratched CDs

$5x = 4,400$ (by cross-multiplying $\frac{2}{5} = \frac{x}{2,200}$)

$x = 880$ (by dividing both sides by 5)

RATIOS

Remember that ratios compare only relative size; they don't tell you the actual quantities involved. Distinguish clearly between the parts and the whole in ratio problems.

 ## RATES

A rate is a ratio that compares quantities represented by different units. In the following problem, the units are dollars and the number of headphones. **Pick numbers for the variables** to find the context of the relationship.

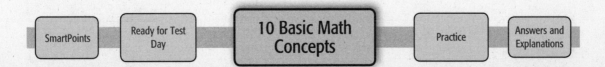

If 8 headphones cost a dollars, b headphones would cost how many dollars?

(A) $8ab$

(B) $\dfrac{8a}{b}$

(C) $\dfrac{8}{ab}$

(D) $\dfrac{a}{8b}$

(E) $\dfrac{ab}{8}$

This rate problem at first seems difficult because of the variables. It's hard to get a clear picture of what the relationship is between the units. You need to pick numbers for the variables to find the context of that relationship.

Pick numbers for a and b that will be easy for you to work with in the problem.

Let $a = 16$. Then 8 headphones will cost \$16. So the cost per headphone at this rate is $\dfrac{\$16}{8 \text{ headphones}} = \$2$ per headphone. Let $b = 5$. Therefore, the cost of 5 headphones at this rate will be 5 headphones $\times$ \$2 per headphone $=$ \$10.

Now plug in $a = 16$ and $b = 5$ into the answer choices to see which one gives you a value of 10.

(A) $8 \times 16 \times 5 = 640$. Eliminate.

(B) $\dfrac{8 \times 16}{5} = \dfrac{128}{5}$. Eliminate.

(C) $\dfrac{8}{16 \times 5} = \dfrac{1}{10}$. Eliminate.

(D) $\dfrac{16}{8 \times 5} = \dfrac{2}{5}$. Eliminate.

(E) $\dfrac{16 \times 5}{8} = 10$

Because (E) is the only one that gives the correct value, it is the correct answer.

DEALING WITH VARIABLES

Don't let a problem with lots of variables throw you off. If a problem has variables and plenty of them, picking numbers *will* work!

SmartPoints   Ready for Test Day   **10 Basic Math Concepts**   Practice   Answers and Explanations

PERCENTS

In percent problems, you're usually given two pieces of information and asked to solve for a third value, as in the following question.

> Last year Aunt Edna's annual salary was $20,000. This year's raise brings her to an annual salary of $25,000. If she gets a raise of the same percentage every year, what will her salary be next year?
>
> (A) $27,500
> (B) $30,000
> (C) $31,250
> (D) $32,500
> (E) $35,000

PERCENT FORMULAS

When you see a percent problem, remember the following formulas:

If you are solving for a percent: $\dfrac{\text{Part}}{\text{Whole}} = \text{Percent}$

If you need to solve for a part: $\text{Percent} \times \text{Whole} = \text{Part}$

This problem asks for Aunt Edna's projected salary for next year—that is, her current salary plus her next raise. You know last year's salary ($20,000), and you know this year's salary ($25,000), so you can find the difference between the two salaries: $25,000 − $20,000 = $5,000 = her raise.

Now, your next step is to find the percent this raise represents by using the formula. $\text{Percent} = \dfrac{\text{Part}}{\text{Whole}}$. Because Aunt Edna's raise was calculated on last year's salary, divide by $20,000. Be sure you know which *whole* to plug in. Here, you're looking for a percentage of $20,000, not of $25,000.

$$\text{Percent} = \frac{\$5,000}{\$20,000} = \frac{1}{4}, \text{ or } 25\%$$

You know Aunt Edna will get the same percent raise next year, so solve for the part. Use the formula Percent × Whole = Part. Make sure you change the percent to either a fraction or a decimal before beginning calculations.

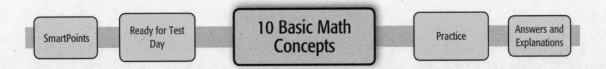

Her raise next year will be $25\% \times \$25{,}000 = \frac{1}{4} \times 25{,}000 = \$6{,}250$. Add that amount to this year's salary and you have her projected salary: $\$25{,}000 + \$6{,}250 = \$31{,}250$, or answer (C).

WHICH WHOLE NUMBER?

Be sure you know which whole number to plug in when using a percent formula. Using the wrong whole number will give you a wrong answer.

PERMUTATIONS AND COMBINATIONS

Combination problems ask you to find the different possibilities that can occur in a given situation. The order of events *is not* important.

Permutation problems ask for the number of possible arrangements among a given set of entities. The order of events *is* important.

> If Alice, Betty, and Carlos sit in three adjacent empty seats in a movie house, how many different seating arrangements are possible?
>
> (A) 3
> (B) 4
> (C) 5
> (D) 6
> (E) 8

PERFECT SCORE TIP

" I tried to set up my area to make studying as enjoyable as possible. I usually had some music in the background. Finding out what works best for you is the key! "

To solve this question, you need to find the number of possibilities by listing them in a quick but systematic way. Let the first letter of each name stand for that person. First, find all the combinations with Alice in the first seat as follows:

    ABC

    ACB

Use the same system, putting Betty in the first seat, and then Carlos. You get the combinations:

    BAC

    BCA

    CAB

    CBA

At this point, we've exhausted every possibility. There are six possible arrangements, so (D) is the correct answer.

CONSIDER THE POSSIBILITIES

Some problems set up conditions that limit the possibilities somewhat. Some may ask for the number of distinct possibilities, meaning that if the same combination shows up twice in different forms, you should count it only once.

Consider the following problem.

Set I: {2, 3, 4, 5}

Set II: {1, 2, 3}

If x is a number generated by multiplying a number from Set I by a number from Set II, how many possible values of x are greater than 5?

(A) 3
(B) 4
(C) 5
(D) 6
(E) 7

PERFECT SCORE TIP

"Although I was familiar with some complicated equations for combinations and permutations, I found it faster most of the time just to list out all the possible cases."

Again, list the possibilities in a systematic way, pairing off each number in the first set with each number in the second set, so every combination is included. The following list is a good example of how this strategy works.

$2 \times 1 = 2$ $4 \times 1 = 4$

$2 \times 2 = 4$ $4 \times 2 = 8$

$2 \times 3 = 6$ $4 \times 3 = 12$

$3 \times 1 = 3$ $5 \times 1 = 5$

$3 \times 2 = 6$ $5 \times 2 = 10$

$3 \times 3 = 9$ $5 \times 3 = 15$

STAY ORGANIZED

Always write down the possibilities as you organize them so you can count them accurately and so you don't count the same combination twice.

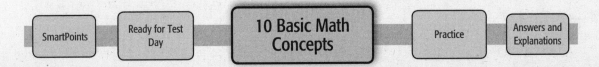

How many of these values are greater than 5? Going down the list: 6, 6, 9, 8, 12, 10, and 15. Although there are seven answers for x that are greater than 5, two of them are the same. There are six different values of x greater than 5, not seven. The answer is (D).

Here, it would have been very easy to quickly take 7 as the correct answer and miss the last step. Be sure you carefully consider every possibility before moving on. We will teach you how to recognize and avoid traps like this one in chapter 14.

 ## EQUATIONS

Equation problems can involve things as simple as $3 + 4 = 7$ or as complex as $15x^5z + 23yz^3 \div 13x^4y = 4$. Sometimes the SAT will even ask for the value of a variable derived from a set of equations, known as simultaneous equations.

To get a numerical value for each variable in a simultaneous equation, you need as many different equations as there are variables. So, if you have two variables, you need two distinct equations. Let's look at the following example.

$$\text{If } p + 2q = 14 \text{ and } 3p + q = 12, \text{ then } p =$$

(Note: This is a Grid-in, so there are no answer choices.)

You could tackle this problem by solving for one variable in terms of the other and then plugging this expression into the other equation. But the simultaneous equations that appear on the SAT can usually be handled in an easier way.

Combine the equations, by adding or subtracting them, to cancel out all but one of the variables. You can't eliminate p or q by adding or subtracting the equations in their present forms. But if you multiply the second equation by 2, you'll have this equation:

$$2(3p + q) = 2(12)$$
$$6p + 2q = 24$$

With this new equation, subtracting one equation from the other is easier because the q's will cancel out, so you can solve for p:

$$6p + 2q = 24$$
$$\underline{-[p + 2q = 14]}$$
$$5p + 0 = 10$$

If $5p = 10$, $p = 2$. On the answer sheet, you would grid in the answer 2.

> ### PERFECT SCORE TIP
>
> " Whenever I was confronted with simultaneous equations, I made sure to list them vertically. It made it easier to find out how to eliminate variables and add and subtract the equations. "

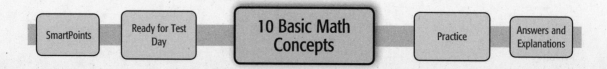

DIFFERENT IS NOT DISTINCT

Two equations are considered distinct *only* if one cannot simplify into the other.
$A + B = 4$ and $2A + 2B = 8$ may look *different*, but they aren't *distinct*.

 FUNCTIONS

A common type of Function question on the SAT is one that uses symbols. You should be quite familiar with the arithmetic symbols $+$, $-$, $\times$, and $\div$. Finding the value of $10 + 2$, $18 - 4$, 4×9, or $96 \div 16$ is easy. However, on the SAT, you may come across bizarre symbols. You may even be asked to find the value of $10 \star 2$, $5 \ast 7$, $10 \bullet 6$, or $65 \heartsuit 2$.

BE READY FOR STRANGE SYMBOLS

The SAT puts strange symbols in questions to confuse or unnerve you. Don't it them succeed. The question stem always tells you what the strange symbol means. Although this type of question may look difficult, it is really an exercise in plugging in numbers.

Look at the following example:

If $a \star b = \sqrt{a+b}$ for all nonnegative numbers, what is the value of $10 \star 6$?

(A) 0

(B) 2

(C) 4

(D) 8

(E) 16

To solve, just plug in 10 for a and 6 for b into the expression $\sqrt{a+b}$. That equals $\sqrt{10+6}$, or $\sqrt{16} = 4$, choice (C). Don't get confused by the symbol; just plug in the numbers, and you'll be fine.

 TRIANGLES

Look for the special triangles in geometry problems. Special triangles contain a lot of information. For instance, if you know the length of one side of a 30-60-90 triangle, you can easily work out the lengths of the others. Special triangles allow you to transfer one piece of information around the whole figure.

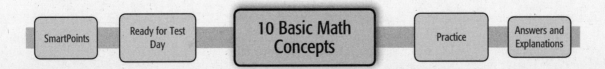

SmartPoints | Ready for Test Day | **10 Basic Math Concepts** | Practice | Answers and Explanations

KNOW THE TRIANGLES

The SAT instructions list the properties of many triangles in the test book for easy referral. However, if you know them by heart, you'll save a lot of time on Test Day.

PERFECT SCORE TIP

❝ I almost always found special triangles in more complicated geometry figures. Knowing their properties usually eliminated all calculations I would have otherwise needed. ❞

The following are the special triangles you should look for on the SAT. You don't have to memorize the ratios (they're listed in the instructions), but you'll need to be able to recognize them when you see them.

EQUILATERAL TRIANGLES

All interior angles are 60 degrees, and all sides have equal length.

ISOSCELES TRIANGLES

Two sides have equal length, and the angles facing these sides are equal.

RIGHT TRIANGLES

These contain a 90-degree angle. The sides are related by the Pythagorean theorem: $a^2 + b^2 = c^2$, where a and b are the legs and c is the hypotenuse.

$$a^2 + b^2 = c^2$$

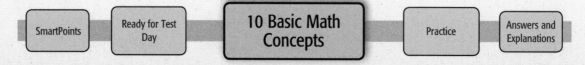

SmartPoints | Ready for Test Day | **10 Basic Math Concepts** | Practice | Answers and Explanations

THE *SPECIAL* RIGHT TRIANGLES

Many triangle problems contain *special* right triangles in which the side lengths always come in predefined ratios. If you recognize them, you won't have to use the Pythagorean theorem to find the value of a missing side length.

THE 3-4-5 RIGHT TRIANGLE

(Be on the lookout for multiples of 3-4-5 as well.)

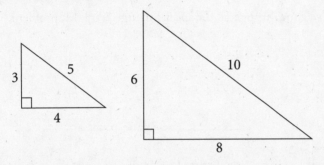

> **PERFECT SCORE TIP**
>
> " Knowing the ratios of special right triangles and being able to find all their sides quickly made these problems really easy! "

TRIANGLE INEQUALITY THEOREM

When you add the lengths of any two sides of any triangle, the result must be *greater* than the length of the third side.

THE ISOSCELES RIGHT TRIANGLE

(Note the side ratio: 1 to 1 to $\sqrt{2}$.)

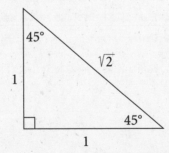

THE 30-60-90 RIGHT TRIANGLE

(Note the side ratio: 1 to $\sqrt{3}$ to 2, and which side is opposite which angle.)

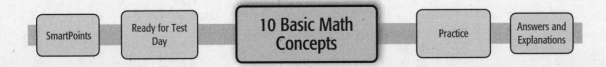

SmartPoints | Ready for Test Day | **10 Basic Math Concepts** | Practice | Answers and Explanations

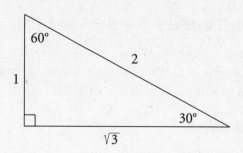

Now that we've gone through all the special triangles, try this problem.

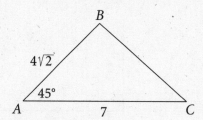

Note: Figure not drawn to scale.

In the triangle above, what is the length of side *BC*?

(A) 4

(B) 5

(C) $4\sqrt{2}$

(D) 6

(E) $5\sqrt{2}$

You can drop a vertical line from *B* to line *AC*. This divides the triangle into two right triangles. That means you know two of the angles in the triangle on the left: 90° and 45°. The third angle must also be 45°, so this is an isosceles right triangle, with sides in the ratio of 1 to 1 to $\sqrt{2}$.

The hypotenuse here is $4\sqrt{2}$, so both legs have length 4. Filling this in, you have the following:

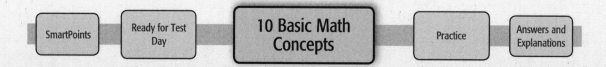

Now you can see that the legs of the smaller triangle on the right must be 4 and 3, making this a 3-4-5 right triangle, and the length of hypotenuse *BC* is 5. So choice (B) is correct.

 ## COMPLEX FIGURES

In a problem that combines figures into more complex ones, you have to look for the relationship between the figures. Look for pieces the figures have in common. For instance, if two figures share a side, information about that side will probably be the key.

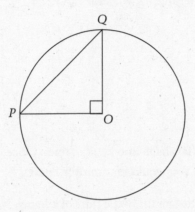

In the figure above, if the area of the circle with center *O* is 9π, what is the area of triangle *POQ*?

(A) 4.5

(B) 6

(C) 9

(D) 3.5π

(E) 4.5π

In this case, the figures don't share a side, but the triangle's legs are important features of the circle—they are radii. You can see that $PO = OQ =$ the radius of circle *O*. The area of the circle is 9π. The area of a circle is πr^2, where $r =$ the radius. So $9\pi = \pi r^2$, $9 = r^2$, and the radius $= 3$.

The formula for the area of a triangle is $\mathbf{a = \frac{1}{2}(base \times height)}$.

Therefore, the area of $\triangle POQ$ is $\frac{1}{2}(\text{leg}_1 \times \text{leg}_2) = \frac{1}{2}(3 \times 3) = \frac{9}{2} = 4.5$, answer choice (A).

> **PERFECT SCORE TIP**
>
> " For problems with multiple figures, I'd determine what information was necessary to answer the question and think about how to use the multiple figures to find out what I needed. "

> **EXPERT TUTOR TIP**
>
> " On questions that combine more than one figure, try to take each part on its own. On those with unfamiliar figures, break them down into manageable pieces. "

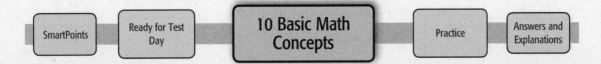

SmartPoints | Ready for Test Day | **10 Basic Math Concepts** | Practice | Answers and Explanations

But what if, instead of a number of familiar shapes, you are given something like this?

What is the perimeter of quadrilateral *WXYZ*?

(A) 680

(B) 760

(C) 840

(D) 920

(E) 1,000

Try breaking the unfamiliar shape into familiar ones. Once you do this, you can use the same techniques that you would for multiple figures.

Perimeter is the sum of the lengths of the sides of a figure, so you need to find the length of *WZ*.

Drawing a perpendicular line from point *X* to side *YZ* will divide the figure into a right triangle and a rectangle. Call the point of intersection *A*.

Opposite sides of a rectangle have equal length, so *WZ* = *XA* and *WX* = *ZA*.

WX is labeled as 180, so *ZA* = 180.

Because *YZ* measures 300, *AY* is 300 − 180 = 120.

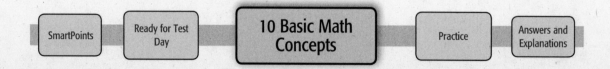

In right triangle XYA, hypotenuse $XY = 200$, and leg $AY = 120$; you should recognize this as a multiple of a 3-4-5 right triangle.

The hypotenuse is 5×40, one leg is 3×40, so XA must be 4×40, or 160. (If you didn't recognize this special right triangle, you could have used the Pythagorean theorem to find the length of XA.)

Because $WZ = XA = 160$, the perimeter of the figure is $180 + 200 + 300 + 160 = 840$, answer choice (C).

TRIANGLES, RECTANGLES, AND CIRCLES

Unfamiliar geometric figures on the SAT can always be broken down into familiar shapes. If a complex figure has you stumped, look for triangles, rectangles, or circles.

PRACTICE

We have labeled the following questions by the math concept they test. If you get stumped, go back to the appropriate part of this chapter and refresh your memory on how to solve that kind of problem. There is no time limit for this practice set.

DIVISIBILITY

1. When z is divided by 8, the remainder is 5. What is the remainder when $4z$ is divided by 8?

    (A) 1
    (B) 3
    (C) 4
    (D) 5
    (E) 7

RATIOS

2. The ratio of right-handed pitchers to left-handed pitchers in a certain baseball league is 11:7. What fractional part of the pitchers in the league is left-handed?

    (A) $\dfrac{6}{7}$

    (B) $\dfrac{6}{11}$

    (C) $\dfrac{7}{11}$

    (D) $\dfrac{7}{18}$

    (E) $\dfrac{11}{18}$

FUNCTIONS

3. If $x \neq 0$, let $\neg x$ be defined by $\neg x = x - \dfrac{1}{x}$. What is the value of $\neg 2 - \neg \dfrac{1}{2}$?

PERMUTATIONS AND COMBINATIONS

4. A three-digit code is made up of three different digits from the set $\{2, 4, 6, 8\}$. If 2 is always the first digit in the code, how many three-digit codes can be formed if each digit is used only once?

    (A) 6
    (B) 8
    (C) 10
    (D) 12
    (E) 16

AVERAGES

5. The average (arithmetic mean) of six numbers is 16. If five of the numbers are 15, 37, 16, 9, and 23, what is the sixth number?

   (A) −20
   (B) −4
   (C) 0
   (D) 6
   (E) 16

COMPLEX FIGURES

6. What is the value of x in the figure above?

   (A) 4
   (B) $3\sqrt{3}$
   (C) $3\sqrt{5}$
   (D) $5\sqrt{3}$
   (E) 9

RATES

7. If David paints at the rate of h houses per day, how many houses does he paint in d days, in terms of h and d?

   (A) $\dfrac{h}{d}$
   (B) hd
   (C) $h + \dfrac{d}{2}$
   (D) $h - d$
   (E) $\dfrac{d}{h}$

PERCENTS

8. What is 25 percent of 25 percent of 72?

EQUATIONS

9. If $x + y = 8$ and $y - x = -2$, then $y =$

   (A) −2
   (B) 3
   (C) 5
   (D) 8
   (E) 10

TRIANGLES

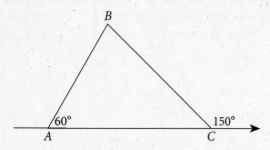

Note: Figure not drawn to scale.

10. In triangle ABC above, if $AB = 4$, then $AC =$

   (A) 6
   (B) 7
   (C) 8
   (D) 9
   (E) 10

DIVISIBILITY

11. When n is divided by 12, the remainder is 0. What is the remainder when $2n$ is divided by 6?

AVERAGES

12. Bart needs to buy five gifts with $80. If two of the gifts cost a total of $35, what is the average (arithmetic mean) amount Bart can spend on each of the remaining three gifts?

   (A) $10
   (B) $15
   (C) $16
   (D) $17
   (E) $45

RATIOS

13. In a group of 24 people who are either homeowners or renters, the ratio of homeowners to renters is 5:3. How many homeowners are in the group?

   (A) 8
   (B) 9
   (C) 12
   (D) 14
   (E) 15

RATES

14. Bill has to type a paper that is p pages long, with each page containing w words. If Bill types an average of x words per minute, how many hours will it take him to finish the paper?

   (A) $60wpx$

   (B) $\dfrac{wx}{60p}$

   (C) $\dfrac{60wp}{x}$

   (D) $\dfrac{wpx}{60}$

   (E) $\dfrac{wp}{60x}$

PERCENTS

15. Eighty-five percent of the members of a student organization registered to attend a certain field trip. If 16 of the members who registered were unable to attend, resulting in only 65 percent of the members making the trip, how many members are in the organization?

TRIANGLES

16. In the coordinate plane, point R has coordinates $(0, 0)$ and point S has coordinates $(9, 12)$. What is the distance from R to S?

EQUATIONS

17. If $4a + 3b = 19$ and $a + 2b = 6$, then $a + b =$

FUNCTIONS

18. If $r \heartsuit s = r(r - s)$ for all integers r and s, then $4 \heartsuit (3 \heartsuit 5)$ equals

(A) -8

(B) -2

(C) 2

(D) 20

(E) 40

PERMUTATIONS AND COMBINATIONS

19. Five people attend a meeting. If each person shakes hands once with every other person at the meeting, what is the total number of handshakes that take place?

SmartPoints   Ready for Test Day   10 Basic Math Concepts   **Practice**   Answers and Explanations

COMPLEX FIGURES

20. In the figure above, square *PQRS* is inscribed in a circle. If the area of square *PQRS* is 4, what is the radius of the circle?

    (A) 1
    (B) $\sqrt{2}$
    (C) 2
    (D) $2\sqrt{2}$
    (E) $4\sqrt{2}$

AVERAGES

21. The average (arithmetic mean) of five numbers is 8. If the average of two of these numbers is −6, what is the sum of the other three numbers?

    (A) 28
    (B) 34
    (C) 46
    (D) 52
    (E) 60

RATES

22. If Seymour drove 120 miles in *x* hours at constant speed, how many miles did he travel in the first 20 minutes of his trip?

    (A) $60x$

    (B) $3x$

    (C) $\dfrac{120}{x}$

    (D) $\dfrac{40}{x}$

    (E) $\dfrac{6}{x}$

FUNCTIONS

23. $c \star d = \dfrac{(c-d)}{c}$, where $c \neq 0$.

    $12 \star 3 =$

    (A) -3

    (B) $\dfrac{1}{4}$

    (C) $\dfrac{2}{3}$

    (D) $\dfrac{3}{4}$

    (E) 3

RATIOS

24. Magazine *A* has a total of 28 pages, 16 of which are advertisements and 12 of which are articles. Magazine *B* has a total of 35 pages, all of them either advertisements or articles. If the ratio of the number of pages of advertisements to the number of pages of articles is the same for both magazines, then Magazine *B* has how many more pages of advertisements than Magazine *A*?

    (A) 2
    (B) 3
    (C) 4
    (D) 5
    (E) 6

DIVISIBILITY

25. A bracelet is made of colored beads in the repeated sequence red, orange, yellow, green, blue, indigo, and violet. If the first bead in the bracelet is red and the last is yellow, then the total number of beads in the bracelet could be

    (A) 48
    (B) 49
    (C) 50
    (D) 51
    (E) 52

EQUATIONS

26. If $m - n = 5$ and $2m + 3n = 15$, then $m + n =$

    (A) 1
    (B) 6
    (C) 7
    (D) 10
    (E) 15

PERCENTS

27. If a sweater sells for $48 after a 25 percent markdown, what was its original price?

    (A) $56
    (B) $60
    (C) $64
    (D) $68
    (E) $72

TRIANGLES

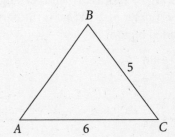

28. If the perimeter of triangle *ABC* above is 16, what is its area?

    (A) 8
    (B) 9
    (C) 10
    (D) 12
    (E) 15

COMPLEX FIGURES

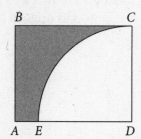

Note: Figure not drawn to scale.

29. In the figure above, the quarter circle with
     center D has a radius of 4 and rectangle $ABCD$
     has a perimeter of 20. What is the perimeter of
     the shaded region?

     (A) $20 - 8\pi$

     (B) $10 + 2\pi$

     (C) $12 + 2\pi$

     (D) $12 + 4\pi$

     (E) $4 + 8\pi$

FUNCTIONS

30. $x \star y = \dfrac{(x - y)}{x}$, where $x \neq 0$.

     If $9 \star 4 = 15 \star k$, then $k =$

     (A) 3

     (B) 6

     (C) $\dfrac{20}{3}$

     (D) $\dfrac{25}{3}$

     (E) 9

PERMUTATIONS AND COMBINATIONS

31. Three people stop for lunch at a hot dog
     stand. If each person orders one item and
     there are three items to choose from, how
     many different combinations of food could be
     purchased? (Assume that order doesn't matter;
     e.g., a hot dog and two sodas are considered
     the same as two sodas and a hot dog.)

     (A) 6

     (B) 9

     (C) 10

     (D) 18

     (E) 27

ANSWERS AND EXPLANATIONS

1. C
SMARTPOINTS CATEGORY: DIVISIBILITY

Let $z = 13$, as 13 divided by 8 produces a remainder of 5. Plug in $4z = 4(13) = 52$, which leaves a remainder of 4 when divided by 8.

2. D
SMARTPOINTS CATEGORY: RATIOS

The parts are the number of right-handed pitchers (11) and the number of left-handed pitchers (7). The whole is the total number of pitchers (right-handed + left-handed), which is $11 + 7$, or 18. So:

$$\frac{\text{Part}}{\text{Whole}} = \frac{\text{Left-Handed}}{\text{Total}} = \frac{7}{11+7} = \frac{7}{18}$$

3. 3
SMARTPOINTS CATEGORY: FUNCTIONS

Identify the value of $\neg 2$ and then of $\neg\frac{1}{2}$, and then subtract the second value from the first:

$$\neg 2 = 2 - \frac{1}{2} = 1\frac{1}{2} = \frac{3}{2}$$

$$\neg\frac{1}{2} = \frac{1}{2} - \frac{1}{\frac{1}{2}} = \frac{1}{2} - 2 = -1\frac{1}{2} = -\frac{3}{2}$$

$$\neg 2 - \neg\frac{1}{2} = \frac{3}{2} - \left(-\frac{3}{2}\right) = \frac{3}{2} + \frac{3}{2} = \frac{6}{2} = 3$$

4. A
SMARTPOINTS CATEGORY: PERMUTATIONS AND COMBINATIONS

Every code starts with 2, so the last two digits determine the number of possibilities. The last two digits could be: 46, 48, 64, 68, 84, and 86. That makes six combinations that fit the conditions.

5. B

SMARTPOINTS CATEGORY: AVERAGES

Average × Number of Terms = Sum of Terms

$$16 \times 6 = 15 + 37 + 16 + 9 + 23 + x$$
$$96 = 100 + x$$
$$-4 = x$$

6. D

SMARTPOINTS CATEGORY: COMPLEX FIGURES

Draw a straight line from point H to point F to divide the figure into two right triangles.

ΔEFH is a 3-4-5 right triangle with a hypotenuse of length 10. ΔFGH has a right angle and its hypotenuse is twice the length of one of its legs, so ΔFGH must be a 30-60-90 right triangle, meaning $x = \sqrt{3x}$.

$$x^2 + 5^2 = 10^2$$
$$x^2 + 25 = 100$$
$$x^2 = 75$$
$$x = \sqrt{75}$$
$$x = \sqrt{25}\ \sqrt{3}$$
$$x = 5\sqrt{3}$$

7. B

SMARTPOINTS CATEGORY: RATES 📶

Pick numbers for h and d. Let $h = 2$ and $d = 3$; that is, suppose he paints two houses per day and he paints for three days, so in three days he can paint six houses. You multiply the rate (h) by the number of days (d). The only answer choice that equals 6 when $h = 2$ and $d = 3$ is choice (B).

8. 4.5

SMARTPOINTS CATEGORY: PERCENTS 📶

25 percent of 25 percent means $(.25)(.25)$, so $(.25)(.25)(72) = 4.5$.

9. B

SMARTPOINTS CATEGORY: EQUATIONS 📶

When you add the two equations, the x's cancel out and you find that $2y = 6$, so $y = 3$.

10. C

SMARTPOINTS CATEGORY: TRIANGLES 📶

Angle BCA is supplementary to the angle marked 150°, so angle $BCA = 180° - 150° = 30°$. Because the sum of interior angles of a triangle is 180°, angle A + angle B + angle $BCA = 180°$, so angle $B = 180° - 60° - 30° = 90°$. So triangle ABC is a 30-60-90 right triangle, and its sides are in the ratio $1:\sqrt{3}:2$. The side opposite the 30°, AB, which we know has length 4, must be half the length of the hypotenuse, AC. Therefore, $AC = 8$, and that's answer choice (C).

11. 0

SMARTPOINTS CATEGORY: DIVISIBILITY 📶

If there's no remainder when n is divided by 12, then n is a multiple of 12, as is $2n$. Anything that's a multiple of 12 is a multiple of factors of 12, so $2n$ is a multiple of 6. Thus, the remainder is 0 when $2n$ is divided by 6. Picking numbers highlights this. Say n is 24. $2n$ is 48, and there's a remainder of 0 when 48 is divided by 6.

12. B

SMARTPOINTS CATEGORY: AVERAGES 📶

Bart has $80 and spent $35 on two gifts; therefore, he has $45 left to spend on the remaining three. So:

$$x = \frac{\$45}{3}$$

$$x = \$15$$

13. E

SMARTPOINTS CATEGORY: RATIOS

The parts are the number of homeowners (5) and the number of renters (3). The whole is the total (homeowners + renters).

$$\frac{\text{Part}}{\text{Whole}} = \frac{\text{Homeowners}}{\text{Homeowners} + \text{Renters}} = \frac{5}{5+3} = \frac{5}{8}$$

Because there are 24 people in the group, $\frac{5}{8} = \frac{x}{24}$, making $x = 15$.

14. E

SMARTPOINTS CATEGORY: RATES

Pick numbers for p, w, and x that work well in the problem. Let $p = 3$ and let $w = 100$. So there are three pages with 100 words per page, or 300 words total. Say he types five words a minute, so $x = 5$. Therefore, he types 5×60, or 300 words an hour. It takes him one hour to type the paper.

The only answer choice that equals 1 when $p = 3$, $w = 100$, and $x = 5$ is choice (E).

15. 80

SMARTPOINTS CATEGORY: PERCENTS

You need to solve for the whole, so identify the part and the percent. If 85 percent planned to attend and only 65 percent did, 20 percent failed to attend, and you know that 16 students failed to attend.

$$\text{Percent} \times \text{Whole} = \text{Part}$$

$$\frac{20}{100} \times \text{Whole} = 16$$

$$\text{Whole} = 16 \times \frac{100}{20}$$

$$\text{Whole} = 80$$

16. 15

SMARTPOINTS CATEGORY: TRIANGLES

Draw a diagram. Because RS isn't parallel to either axis, the way to compute its length is to create a right triangle with legs that are parallel to the axes, so their lengths are easy to find. If the triangle formed is not a special triangle, we can then use the Pythagorean theorem to find the length of RS.

Ready for Test Day | 10 Basic Math Concepts | Practice | **Answers and Explanations** | Chapter Highlights

Because S has a y-coordinate of 12, it's 12 units above the x-axis, so the length of ST must be 12. Also, because T is the same number of units to the right of the y-axis as S, given by the x-coordinate of 9, the distance from the origin to T must be 9. So we have a right triangle with legs of 9 and 12. You should recognize this as a multiple of the 3-4-5 triangle. $9 = 3 \times 3$; $12 = 3 \times 4$; so the hypotenuse RS must be 3×5, or 15.

17. 5

SMARTPOINTS CATEGORY: EQUATIONS

Adding the two equations, you find that $5a + 5b = 25$. Dividing by 5 shows that $a + b = 5$.

18. E

SMARTPOINTS CATEGORY: FUNCTIONS

Start in the parentheses and work out: $(3 \heartsuit 5) = 3(3 - 5) = 3(-2) = -6$; $4 \heartsuit (-6) = 4 [4 - (-6)] = 4(10) = 40$.

19. 10

SMARTPOINTS CATEGORY: PERMUTATIONS AND COMBINATIONS

Be careful not to count each handshake twice. Call the five people A, B, C, D, and E. We can pair them off like this:

A with B, C, D, and E (four handshakes)

B with C, D, and E (three more—note that we leave out A because the handshake between A and B is already counted)

C with D and E (two more)

D with E (one more)

The total is $4 + 3 + 2 + 1$, or 10 handshakes.

20. B

SMARTPOINTS CATEGORY: COMPLEX FIGURES

Draw in diagonal *QS* and you will notice that it is also a diameter of the circle.

Because the area of the square is 4, its sides must each be 2. Think of the diagonal as dividing the square into two isosceles right triangles. Therefore, the diagonal $= 2\sqrt{2} =$ the diameter; the radius is half this amount, or $\sqrt{2}$.

21. D

SMARTPOINTS CATEGORY: AVERAGES

Average × Number of Terms = Sum of Terms. The sum of all five numbers is $8 \times 5 = 40$. The sum of two of these numbers is $(-6) \times 2 = -12$. So the difference of these two sums, $40 - (-12) = 52$, is the sum of the other numbers.

22. D

SMARTPOINTS CATEGORY: RATES

Let $x = 4$. That means that he drove 120 miles in four hours, so his speed was $\dfrac{120 \text{ miles}}{4 \text{ hours}}$, or 30 miles per hour. Because 20 minutes $= \dfrac{1}{3}$ of an hour, the distance he traveled in the first 20 minutes is $\dfrac{1}{3}$ hours $\times$ 30 miles per hour $= 10$ miles. The only answer choice that equals 10 when $x = 4$ is choice (D).

23. D

SMARTPOINTS CATEGORY: FUNCTIONS

Plug in 12 for c and 3 for d: $\dfrac{12 - 3}{12} = \dfrac{9}{12} = \dfrac{3}{4}$.

24. C
SMARTPOINTS CATEGORY: RATIOS

The $\dfrac{\text{Part}}{\text{Whole}}$ ratio of advertisements (16) to total pages (28) in Magazine A is $\dfrac{16}{28}$, or $\dfrac{4}{7}$. Magazine B has the same ratio, so if there are 35 pages in Magazine B, $\dfrac{4}{7} \times 35$—or 20 pages—are advertisements.

Therefore, there are four more pages of advertisements in Magazine B than in Magazine A.

25. E
SMARTPOINTS CATEGORY: DIVISIBILITY

The sequence contains seven terms: R, O, Y, G, B, I, and V. So V will be every seventh bead, that is, the 7th, 14th, 28th, 35th beads, and so on. Another way of saying this is that all the multiples of 7 will always be V. Y is three beyond V, so it's three beyond a multiple of 7. (E) is the only choice that's three more than a multiple of 7.

26. C
SMARTPOINTS CATEGORY: EQUATIONS

Multiply the first equation by 2, then subtract the first equation from the second to eliminate the ms and find that $5n = 5$, or $n = 1$:

$$2m + 3n = 15$$
$$\underline{-2m + 2n = -10}$$
$$5n = 5$$
$$n = 1$$

Plugging this value for n into the first equation shows that $m = 6$:

$$m - n = 5$$
$$m - 1 = 5$$
$$m = 6$$

So $m + n = 7$:
$$m + n = 6 + 1 = 7$$

Choice (C) is correct.

27. C

SMARTPOINTS CATEGORY: PERCENTS

We want to solve for the original price, the Whole. The percent markdown is 25 percent, so $48 is 75 percent of the whole.

$$\text{Percent} \times \text{Whole} = \text{Part}$$

$$75 \text{ percent} \times \text{original price} = \$48$$

$$\text{original price} = \frac{\$48}{0.75} = \$64$$

28. D

SMARTPOINTS CATEGORY: TRIANGLES

To find the area you need to know the base and height. If the perimeter is 16, then $AB + BC + AC = 16$, that is, $AB = 16 - 5 - 6 = 5$. Because $AB = BC$, this is an isosceles triangle. If you drop a line from vertex B to AC, it will divide the base in half. This divides up the triangle into two smaller right triangles:

These right triangles each have one leg of 3 and a hypotenuse of 5; therefore, they are 3-4-5 right triangles. The missing leg (which is also the height of triangle ABC) must have a length of 4. We now know that the base of ABC is 6 and the height is 4, so the area is $\frac{1}{2} \times 6 \times 4$, or 12, answer choice (D).

29. C

SMARTPOINTS CATEGORY: COMPLEX FIGURES

The perimeter of the shaded region is $BC + AB + AE +$ arc EC. The quarter circle has its center at D, and point C lies on the circle, so side DC is a radius of the circle and equals 4.

Opposite sides of a rectangle are equal, so *AB* is also 4.

The perimeter of the rectangle is 20, and because the two short sides account for 8, the two longer sides must account for 12, making *BC* and *AD* each 6. To find *AE*, subtract the length of *ED*, another radius of length 4, from the length of *AD*, which is 6; *AE* = 2.

Because arc *EC* is a quarter circle, the length of the arc *EC* is $\frac{1}{4}$ of the circumference of a whole circle with radius 4: $\frac{1}{4} \times 2\pi r = \frac{1}{4} \times 8\pi = 2\pi$. So the perimeter of the shaded region is $6 + 4 + 2 + 2\pi = 12 + 2\pi$.

30. C

SMARTPOINTS CATEGORY: FUNCTIONS

Plug in on both sides of the equation:

$$\frac{9-4}{9} = \frac{15-k}{15}$$

$$\frac{5}{9} = \frac{15-k}{15}$$

Cross-multiply and solve for *k*:

$$75 = 135 - 9k$$

$$-60 = -9k$$

$$\frac{-60}{-9} = k$$

$$\frac{20}{3} = k$$

31. C

SMARTPOINTS CATEGORY: PERMUTATIONS AND COMBINATIONS

To find the number, let's call the three items they can purchase A, B, and C. The possibilities are as follows:

All three order the same thing: AAA, BBB, CCC

Two order the same thing: AAB, AAC, BBA, BBC, CCA, CCB

All three order something different: ABC

There are ten different ways the three items could be ordered.

IF YOU LEARN ONLY ONE THING IN THIS CHAPTER . . .

1. **WHAT ARE THE TEN MOST TESTED BASIC MATH CONCEPTS AND WHAT METHODS CAN I USE TO SOLVE EACH?**

- **Divisibility**—Pick a number for the variable.

- **Averages**—Use the average formula, and work with the sum.

- **Ratios**—Identify the parts and the whole.

- **Rates**—Pick numbers for the variables to make the relationship between units clear.

- **Percents**—Make sure you know which whole to plug in.

- **Permutations and Combinations**—Be systematic and organized when listing possible combinations.

- **Equations**—Combine equations by adding or subtracting them to cancel out all but one variable.

- **Functions**—Use the symbols as a map of where to plug in numbers.

- **Triangles**—Know the predefined ratios for special triangles.

- **Complex Figures**—Find the parts that the different figures have in common.

Ready for Test Day | 10 Basic Math Concepts | Practice | Answers and Explanations | **Chapter Highlights**

CHAPTER 13: ADVANCED MATH CONCEPTS

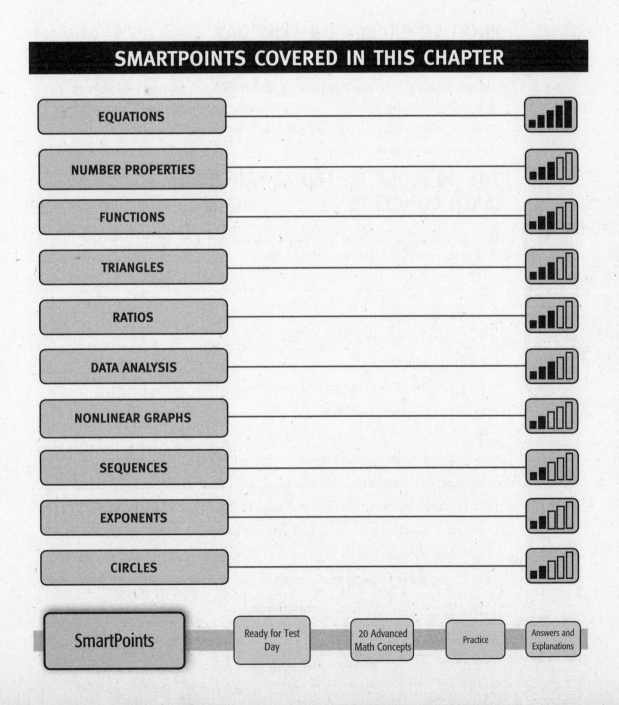

SMARTPOINTS COVERED IN THIS CHAPTER

- EQUATIONS
- NUMBER PROPERTIES
- FUNCTIONS
- TRIANGLES
- RATIOS
- DATA ANALYSIS
- NONLINEAR GRAPHS
- SEQUENCES
- EXPONENTS
- CIRCLES

SmartPoints → Ready for Test Day → 20 Advanced Math Concepts → Practice → Answers and Explanations

WHAT TO EXPECT ON TEST DAY

In this chapter, we review the advanced math concepts tested on the SAT. This list is extensive and may seem overwhelming. But remember, your goal should not be to memorize each concept and method, but rather to familiarize yourself with the review of each concept so you will know what to expect on Test Day.

THE 20 MOST TESTED ADVANCED MATH CONCEPTS

The SAT covers the following advanced math topics:

1. Sequences involving exponential growth
2. Sets
3. Absolute value
4. Rational equations and inequalities
5. Radical equations
6. Manipulation with integer and rational exponents
7. Direct and inverse variation
8. Function notation and evaluation
9. Concepts of domain and range
10. Functions as models
11. Linear functions—equations and graphs
12. Quadratic functions—equations and graphs
13. Geometric notation
14. Problems in which trigonometry can be used as an alternative method of solution

EXPERT TUTOR TIP

If math isn't your thing, don't worry. The ideas in this chapter should help you know what's coming, so you're not surprised on Test Day!

SmartPoints | Ready for Test Day | **20 Advanced Math Concepts** | Practice | Answers and Explanations

15. Properties of tangent lines

16. Coordinate geometry

17. Qualitative behavior of graphs and functions

18. Transformations and their effect on graphs of functions

19. Data interpretation, scatterplots, and matrices

20. Geometric probability

As in chapter 12, the techniques we give for solving these problems will work with both types of SAT Math questions: regular math and Grid-in questions.

 # SEQUENCES

Problems that test sequences are fairly common on the SAT. One advanced variety that you may see on Test Day is sequences involving exponential growth. The name sounds like a mouthful, but relax: sequences involving exponential growth, also known as geometric sequences, are a tough but manageable area of SAT Math.

> **PERFECT SCORE TIP**
>
> " For sequence questions, always double-check the formula with the problem to make sure that you're counting the terms correctly. "

GEOMETRIC SEQUENCES

A geometric sequence of numbers is simply one in which a constant ratio exists between consecutive terms.

Questions about geometric sequences are likely to hinge on this formula:

If r is the ratio between consecutive terms, a_1 is the first term, and a_n is the nth term, then $a_n = a_1 r^{n-1}$.

RATIOS AND CONSECUTIVE TERMS

Remember that if r is the ratio between consecutive terms, a_1 is the first term, and a_n is the nth term, then $a_n = a_1 r^{n-1}$. Most questions concerning geometric sequences will involve this formula.

Now take a look at how the SAT might ask a question about geometric sequences.

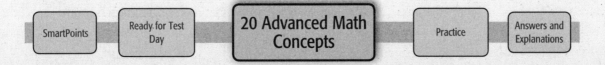

If the first term in a geometric sequence is 4, and the fifth term is 64, what is the eighth term?

(A) 512
(B) 864
(C) 1,245
(D) 13,404
(E) 22,682

First, use the formula to solve for r:

$$64 = 4r^4$$

$$16 = r^4$$

$$r = 2$$

Now, using $r = 2$, solve for a_8:

$$a_8 = 4(2)^7$$

$$a_8 = 512$$

The correct answer is (A).

 SETS

Most questions about geometric sequences are likely to appear in the middle or end of an SAT Math section because such questions tend to be hard for most students. Sets, on the other hand, are slightly easier and are more likely to show up in the beginning or middle of a section.

TERMS AND CONDITIONS

Knowing the definitions of the terms used is the key to solving problems involving sets:

- **Elements** or **members** are the things in a set.

- A **union** of sets, sometimes expressed with the symbol ∪, is the set of elements that are in *either* or *both* of the different sets you start with. The *union set* is what you get when you merge sets.

  - For example, if Set A = {1, 2} and Set B = {3, 4}, then A ∪ B {1, 2, 3, 4}.

- The intersection of sets, sometimes expressed with the symbol ∩, is the set of elements *common* to the sets you start with.

  - For example, if Set A = {1, 2, 3} and Set B = {3, 4, 5}, then A ∩ B = {3}.

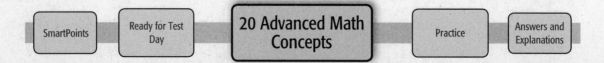

Try to work through the following example.

If Set *R* contains 6 distinct numbers and Set *S* contains 5 distinct letters, how many elements are in the union of the two sets?

(A) 1
(B) 5
(C) 6
(D) 8
(E) 11

In this question, because Set *R* and Set *S* contain different kinds of elements, no element is in both sets. So the union set of *S* and *R*—$S \cup R$—contains everything in each: $6 + 5 = 11$. The correct answer is (E).

> **EXPERT TUTOR TIP**
>
> " Sets are like trains. The *union* of sets is like two trains moving together for connection. The *intersection* of sets is like one end of a train dropping onto the end of another one. "

UNION AND INTERSECTION

> Think of the **union** of sets as what you get when you merge the sets.
>
> Think of the **intersection** of sets as the overlap of the sets.

 ## NUMBER PROPERTIES

The SAT will test your knowledge on a wide variety of concepts that relate to number properties. One advanced concept that you'll see on Test Day is absolute value. The absolute value of a number is the distance between that number and zero on the number line.

ABSOLUTE VALUES—ALWAYS POSITIVE

> Because absolute value is a distance, it is *always* positive.

The absolute value of 7 is 7; this is expressed as $|7| = 7$. Similarly, the absolute value of −7 is 7: $|-7| = 7$. Every positive number is the absolute value of two numbers: itself and its negative counterpart. The following diagram helps to illustrate this point.

As you'll see in the following example, the SAT sometimes connects the concept of absolute value to the concept of inequalities.

If $|r + 7| < 2$, which of the following statements are true?

I. $r < -9$

II. $r < -5$

III. $r > -9$

(A) I only

(B) II only

(C) III only

(D) I and II only

(E) II and III only

You can solve this problem algebraically, as shown below, or you can think about what the inequality would look like on a number line. You can express $|r + 7| < 2$ as *the difference between r and −7 is less than* 2 and determine that *r* must be between −5 and −9:

$$r + 7 < 2 \text{ and } -r - 7 < 2$$
$$r < -5 \text{ and } -r < 9$$
$$r < -5 \text{ and } r > -9$$

The correct answer here is (E).

📊 QUADRATIC EQUATIONS

Quadratic equations on the SAT can involve two advanced concepts: rational equations and quadratic functions. A rational equation is one that contains at least one fraction in which the numerator and denominator are polynomials. Rational equations follow the same rules as simpler looking equations, and they are just as susceptible to Kaplan strategies, such as picking numbers, as the following illustration shows.

For all values of *x* not equal to −2 or 3, $\dfrac{x^4 - 5x^3 - 2x^2 + 24x}{x^2 - x - 6}$ is equal to

(A) $x^2 - 4x$

(B) $x^2 - 5x - 2$

(C) $x + 24$

(D) x

(E) $x - 4$

PICKING NUMBERS FOR ADVANCED EQUATIONS

Picking numbers works just as well for advanced equations as it does for easier ones. Use this strategy to your advantage!

Say $x = 2$:

$$\frac{2^4 - 5(2^3) - 2(2^2) + 24(2)}{2^2 - 2 - 6} = \frac{16 - 5(8) - 2(4) + 24(2)}{4 - 2 - 6} = \frac{16 - 40 - 8 + 48}{-4} = \frac{16}{-4} = -4$$

Now find the choice that has a value of -4 when $x = 2$. Only (A) works:

$2^2 - 4(2) = 4 - 8 = -4$. So (A) is the correct answer.

Quadratic functions are closely related to linear functions. A quadratic function is one that takes the form $f(x) = ax^2 + bx + c$. Rather than take the form of a straight line as, you'll recall, a linear function does, the graph of a quadratic function is a parabola.

As the following question illustrates, a quadratic function question could be similar to a quadratic equations question.

If $x^2 - 7x + 12 = 0$, what is the sum of the two possible values of x?

(A) -4

(B) -1

(C) 3

(D) 4

(E) 7

Factor:

$$x^2 - 7x + 12 = 0$$
$$(x - 4)(x - 3) = 0$$
$$x = 4 \text{ or } x = 3$$
$$4 + 3 = 7$$

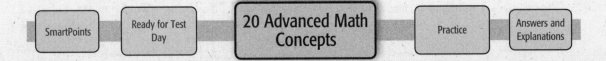

SmartPoints · Ready for Test Day · **20 Advanced Math Concepts** · Practice · Answers and Explanations

You should have come up with (E) as the correct answer.

 EQUATIONS

The SAT contains many types of equations, with radical equations being one of the more popular advanced concepts.

Radical equations have at least one variable under a radical sign. Like rational equations, they follow the same rules as other kinds of algebraic equations, so solve them accordingly.

The last step is what makes them unique: often, you must square both sides of the equation.

Look at the following example.

If $4 - \sqrt{n} = -1$, what is the value of n?

(A) 3
(B) 5
(C) 9
(D) 25
(E) 81

Apply the same algebraic steps here as you would in any other question involving an equation, isolating the variable step-by-step. Just remember to square both sides of the equation as your last step. (Notice that (B) is a trap for test takers who forget to do so. We will cover math traps in more detail in the next chapter.)

$$4 - \sqrt{n} = -1$$
$$5 = \sqrt{n}$$
$$(5)^2 = (\sqrt{n})^2$$
$$25 = n$$

Answer choice (D) is correct.

 EXPONENTS

Not every exponent on the SAT is a positive integer. Numbers can be raised to a fractional or negative exponent. Although such numbers follow their own special rules, they adhere to the same general rules of exponents with which you've probably worked before.

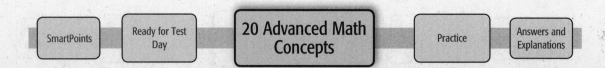

SmartPoints | Ready for Test Day | **20 Advanced Math Concepts** | Practice | Answers and Explanations

If $x = \dfrac{1}{4}$, $x^{-4} =$

(A) $\dfrac{-1}{256}$

(B) $\dfrac{-1}{16}$

(C) 4

(D) 16

(E) 256

A NOTE ON EXPONENTIAL EQUIVALENTS

$$x^{-a} = \frac{1}{x^a}$$

$$x^{\frac{p}{q}} = \sqrt[q]{x^p}$$

To find the value of a number raised to a negative power, simply rewrite the number, without the negative sign in front of the exponent, as the bottom of a fraction with 1 as the numerator of the fraction: $3^{-2} = \dfrac{1}{3^2} = \dfrac{1}{9}$.

In this case:

$$x^{-4} = \frac{1}{x^4} = \frac{1}{\left(\frac{1}{4}\right)^4} = \frac{1}{\left(\frac{1}{256}\right)} = 256, \text{ or answer choice (E).}$$

 ## RATIOS

On the SAT, some of the most advanced ratio concepts tested involve *direct* and *inverse* *variation*.

In **direct variation**, $y = kx$, where k is a nonzero constant. In direct variation, the variable y changes directly as x does.

- If a unit of Currency A is worth 2 units of Currency B, then $A = 2B$.
- If the number of units of B were to double, the number of units of A would double, and so on for halving, tripling, etc.

In **inverse variation**, $xy = k$, where x and y are variables and k is a constant.

- A famous inverse relationship is *rate* × *time* = *distance*. Imagine having to cover a distance of 24 miles. If you were to travel at 12 miles per hour, you'd need 2

PERFECT SCORE TIP

" For variation problems, I found it easier to apply the rate equation as an analogy and figure out how things varied together in each question. "

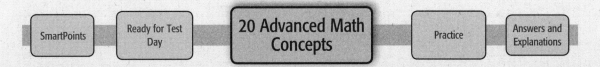
SmartPoints | Ready for Test Day | **20 Advanced Math Concepts** | Practice | Answers and Explanations

hours. But if you were to cut your rate in half, you would have to double your time.

The following is an example of direct variation.

If the length of a sea turtle is directly proportional to its age, and a 2-year-old sea turtle is 3 inches long, how many feet long is an 80-year-old sea turtle?

(A) 10

(B) 12

(C) 100

(D) 120

(E) 144

Relate the length of the turtle to its age. Use the equation to find the length of an 80-year-old sea turtle in inches; then convert from inches to feet. Because length is directly proportional to age, you can represent their relationship as $l = ka$, where l is length, a is age, and k is a constant:

$$3 = k(2)$$
$$1.5 = k$$
$$l = 1.5(80) = 120 \text{ inches} = 10 \text{ feet}$$

(A) is the correct answer.

 FUNCTIONS

A few questions on Test Day will probably focus on functions and use standard function notation such as $f(x)$. Evaluating a function sounds fancy, but it mostly involves substitution of numbers for variables—a skill you should already be familiar with.

> **PERFECT SCORE TIP**
>
> ❝ I wrote out all of my work for compositions of functions. It made it easier to figure out where I went wrong if I didn't think my answer was correct. ❞

FUNCTION NOTATION AND EVALUATION

Function Notation and Evaluation questions usually appear on the test, so know how to handle them.

- **Function notation** is the standard way to write numbers down in relation to the operations needed. The order follows the mnemonic **PEMDAS**.

- **Evaluation** involves substitution of numbers for variables, a skill you should already be familiar with.

SmartPoints   Ready for Test Day   **20 Advanced Math Concepts**   Practice   Answers and Explanations

For example, to evaluate the function $f(x) = 5x + 1$ for $f(3)$, replace x with 3 and simplify: $f(3) = 5(3) + 1 = 15 + 1 = 16$.

The example below presents a slightly more complex variation: a composition of functions. $h(g(a))$ requires you to first evaluate $g(a)$, and then apply h to the result.

If $g(a) = (a + 4)^2$ and $h(b) = 2b - 7$, then what is the value of $h(g(2))$?

(A) 1
(B) 36
(C) 45
(D) 65
(E) 79

Follow the order of operations:

$$g(2) = (2 + 4)^2 = 6^2 = 36$$

$$h(36) = 2(36) - 7 = 72 - 7 = 65$$

The correct answer is choice (D).

DOMAIN AND RANGE

- The **domain** of a function is the set of values for which the function is defined. For example, the domain of $f(x) = \dfrac{1}{1 - x^2}$ is all values of x except 1 and -1, because for those values, the denominator has a value of 0 and the fraction is therefore undefined.

- The **range** of a function is the set of outputs or results of the function. For example, the range of $f(x) = x^2$ is all numbers greater than or equal to zero because x^2 cannot be negative. Try the following sample question.

If $f(a) = a^2 + 7$ for all real values of a, which of the following is a possible value of $f(a)$?

(A) -2
(B) 0
(C) $\sqrt{5}$
(D) $\sqrt{7}$
(E) $100\sqrt{3}$

If a is a real number, then a^2 must be positive or equal to zero. Think about how this limits the range of $f(a)$: If $a = 0$, then $f(a) = 7$. All other values result in a higher value of $f(a)$. Only (E) is greater than 7 and is the correct answer.

> **PERFECT SCORE TIP**
>
> " The trickiest domain and range questions for me were the ones that dealt with radicals and absolute values. I plugged in numbers or graphed the functions on my calculator to make sure that I had the correct domain and range. "

SmartPoints · Ready for Test Day · **20 Advanced Math Concepts** · Practice · Answers and Explanations

FUNCTIONS AS MODELS

The SAT might challenge your ability to relate functional relationships to real-life situations.

For example, consider the question below, in which you're asked to interpret data about the relationship between the selling price of a car and the number of cars that sell at that price.

A NOTE ON FUNCTIONS

The **domain** of a function is the set of values for which the function is defined. The **range** of a function is the set of possible values of the function.

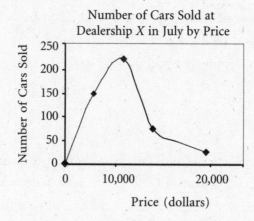

Number of Cars Sold at
Dealership *X* in July by Price

The above graph represents the number of cars sold at Dealership *X* in July. If the dealer wants to sell the maximum number of cars possible in August, at what price should he set the cars, based on his sales in July?

(A) 5,000

(B) 10,000

(C) 15,000

(D) 20,000

(E) 22,500

READ GRAPHS CAREFULLY

Make sure to read your graphs carefully, knowing what each axis represents. If you are not careful, you may choose the incorrect answer that is meant as a trap.

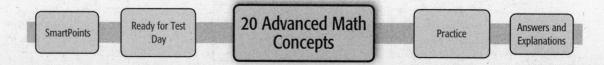

SmartPoints | Ready for Test Day | **20 Advanced Math Concepts** | Practice | Answers and Explanations

Use the graph of July to figure out which price point sold the most cars. The peak value is $10,000, which sold 225 cars. Based on this information, the dealer should price cars at $10,000 in August and hope to sell the maximum number of cars that he can in that month. Answer choice (B) is correct.

LINEAR FUNCTIONS—EQUATIONS AND GRAPHS

You'll most likely see a question or two on the SAT involving equations and graphs of linear functions.

A **linear function** is simply an equation whose graph is a straight line. The following question is an example of what could appear on the SAT.

> Which of the following equations describes a line perpendicular to the line $y = 7x + 49$?
>
> (A) $y = -7x - 49$
>
> (B) $y = -\dfrac{1}{7}x + 10$
>
> (C) $y = \dfrac{1}{7}x + 7$
>
> (D) $y = 7x - 49$
>
> (E) $y = 7x + 14$

> **PERFECT SCORE TIP**
>
> " Make sure to look at what quadratic equation questions are actually asking. If you don't need to factor or expand the equation, don't waste your time. "

If two lines are perpendicular, then the slope of one is the negative reciprocal of the slope of the other.

These lines are written in the form $y = mx + b$, where m is the slope and b is the y-intercept, or the value of y when $x = 0$.

In this case, the negative reciprocal of 7 is $-\dfrac{1}{7}$. The only equation with this slope is (B), the correct answer.

SLOPES: PERPENDICULAR AND PARALLEL LINES

- The slopes of **perpendicular** lines are **negative** reciprocals.
- The slopes of **parallel** lines are **equal**.

 TRIANGLES

Triangles are quite common on the SAT and acing these problems requires knowledge of two advanced concepts—**geometric notation** and **Pythagorean triplets.**

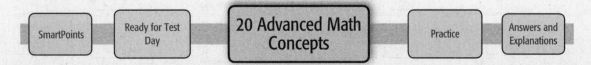

SmartPoints | Ready for Test Day | **20 Advanced Math Concepts** | Practice | Answers and Explanations

You should expect SAT geometry questions to use the symbols $\leftrightarrow$, —, and $\cong$.

$\leftrightarrow$ signifies a line. $\overline{XY}$ is the line that passes through points X and Y.

— signifies a line segment: $\overline{XY}$ is the line segment whose endpoints are X and Y.

$\cong$ symbolizes congruence. If two triangles are congruent, they coincide exactly when superimposed. You may want to think of two congruent figures as identical twins.

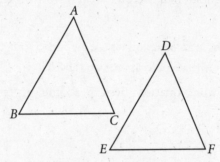

Note: Figure not drawn to scale.

$\angle CAB \cong \angle FDE$ and $\angle ABC \cong \angle DEF$. Which of the following must be true?

   I. $\triangle ABC \cong \triangle DEF$

  II. Triangles ABC and DEF are similar.

 III. $\overline{AB} = \overline{DE}$

(A) II only

(B) III only

(C) I and III

(D) II and III

(E) I, II, and III

When a figure is not drawn to scale, it is most likely drawn in a misleading way. The figure above certainly looks as though ABC and DEF are identical and that all their parts are congruent, but you can't assume that based on the information in the problem.

WATCH THE SCALE

Even though a figure on the SAT may seem to be a certain size, if the text says "Figure not drawn to scale," one part of the drawing could be much smaller or larger than the other. Be careful.

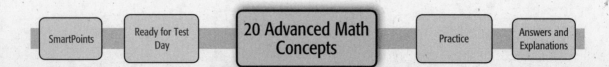

You may want to draw your own diagrams to think about some of the different possibilities. All we know about these triangles is that they have two pairs of corresponding angles that are congruent. Therefore, the third angle of each triangle must also be congruent.

This tells us that the triangles are similar because their angles are the same. However, we know nothing about the lengths of the sides—one triangle could be much smaller than the other; thus, choice (A) is the correct answer.

KNOW TRIANGLE RELATIONSHIPS

Now more than ever, the SAT will reward test takers who recall the special relationships in 45-45-90 and 30-60-90 right triangles:

THE ISOSCELES RIGHT TRIANGLE
(Note the side ratio—$1:1:\sqrt{2}$)

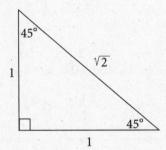

> **PERFECT SCORE TIP**
>
> "Memorizing special right triangles is definitely worth the effort. They come up frequently in geometry problems, so don't waste time working out all the sides and angles for every question."

THE 30-60-90 RIGHT TRIANGLE
(Note the side ratio—$1:\sqrt{3}:2$, and which side is opposite which angle.)

Try the following question.

What is the total area of the figure above?

To find the area of a triangle, you need its height and the length of its base. Think about the information presented in the figure. What other data can you derive from it? The triangle on the left is a special triangle with side lengths of 3, 4, and 5. (You could also find the missing side using the Pythagorean theorem.) The triangle on the right is a 45-45-90 triangle, so its base must also equal 4. The total area of the figure is then $\frac{1}{2}(3+4)(4) = 14$.

 ## CIRCLES

Properties of circles are tested fairly often on the SAT. On some of the tougher questions, you will be expected to know how to deal with tangent lines.

When a line is tangent to a circle, it is perpendicular to the radius that it intersects. Look at the following example.

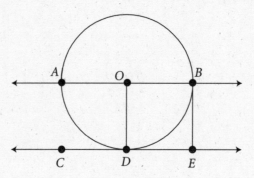

In the figure above, $\overline{AB}$ is a diameter of the circle, and $\overline{CE}$ is tangent to the circle at point D. $\overline{AB}$ is parallel to $\overline{CE}$. If the area of quadrilateral $OBED$ is 16 cm², what is the area of the circle whose center is at O?

(A)   4 cm²

(B)   4π cm²

(C)   8π cm²

(D) 16π cm²

(E) 256 cm²

A circle in a problem often means you'll need the radius at some point. To figure out how to get that from the area of quadrilateral $OBED$, you'll need the rest of the information in the question stem.

Because there's a circle in this problem, you can be sure you'll need the radius at some point. To figure out how to get that from the area of quadrilateral $OBED$, you'll need to use the rest of the information in the question stem.

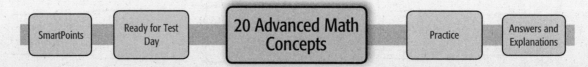

It may be helpful to add a few angles to the figure—for instance, because $\overline{CE}$ is tangent to the circle at point D, it is perpendicular to the radius of the circle at that point.

The information given in the first two sentences of the question stem tells you that $\overline{OD}$ is perpendicular to $\overline{CE}$ and therefore also to $\overline{AB}$.

$\overline{OD}$ and $\overline{OB}$ are both radii of the circle, so quadrilateral $OBED$ is a square.

The area of $OBED$ is 16, so each side has a length of 4.

This is also the radius of the circle. $4^2\pi = 16\pi$ is the area of the circle, so you should have chosen answer (D).

 ## COORDINATE PLANES

Coordinate geometry questions on the SAT tend to focus on the properties of straight lines.

The equation of a straight line is $y = mx + b$, where y and x are the infinite number of coordinated (x, y) pairs that fall on the line. Variable b is the y-intercept, or the value of y when $x = 0$.

Variable m is the slope of the line and is expressed $\dfrac{\Delta Y}{\Delta X}$, or $\dfrac{y_2 - y_1}{x_2 - x_1}$.

> **PERFECT SCORE TIP**
>
> ❝ Knowing midpoint and slope equations was really useful. Being able to plug in numbers quickly for coordinate geometry problems was a huge time-saver! ❞

SLOPE

The slope or steepness of a line is the change in *y*-values in relation to the change in corresponding *x*-values.

- **Positive slopes** tilt upward to the **right**.
- **Negative slopes** tilt downward to the **right**.
- A **horizontal line** has a slope of **zero**.
- A **vertical line** has an **undefined slope**.
- **Parallel lines** have **equal slopes**.
- **Perpendicular lines** have **negative reciprocal slopes**.

As the question below illustrates, the SAT may also ask you to identify the midpoint of a line segment or the distance between two points.

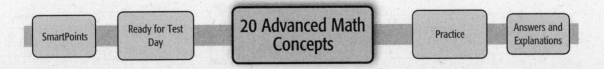

If point P is at $(8, 10)$ and point Q is at $(0, 4)$, what is the midpoint of PQ?

(A) $(0, 10)$

(B) $(4, 2)$

(C) $(4, 5)$

(D) $(4, 7)$

(E) $(9, 2)$

FINDING THE MIDPOINT

The midpoint of a line segment with endpoints (x_1, y_1) and (x_2, y_2) is really just the average of its *x*-values and *y*-values.

To find it, plug the two sets of points into the following expression:

$$\left(\frac{x_1 + x_2}{2}, \frac{y_1 + y_2}{2} \right)$$

PERFECT SCORE TIP

❝ When dealing with graphs, use the fact that you can write in your test booklet to your advantage. It can help you uncover key info like the number of intersections between two functions or the maximum value on a graph. ❞

Now plug in the numbers from the question.

$$x = \frac{8 + 0}{2} = \frac{8}{2} = 4$$

$$y = \frac{10 + 4}{2} = \frac{14}{2} = 7$$

The midpoint is $(4, 7)$, or choice (D).

 ## NONLINEAR GRAPHS

The SAT will likely ask you to show an understanding of a general or particular property of a complex graph, such as the one in the example problem below.

SmartPoints | Ready for Test Day | **20 Advanced Math Concepts** | Practice | Answers and Explanations

The figure shows the graph of $f(x)$. At how many values of x does $f(x)$ equal 4?

(A) 0

(B) 1

(C) 2

(D) 3

(E) 4

The value of $f(x)$ is measured on the y-axis. Find 4 on the y-axis, and then see how many points on the graph have a y-value of 4. The points are approximately $(3, 4)$, $(4.7, 4)$, and $(5.4, 4)$. So your answer here is 3, or choice (D).

TRANSFORMATIONS

A **transformation** is an alteration in a function. An SAT question, such as the following might present a graph and ask you to identify a specific transformation.

COMMON TRANSFORMATIONS ON THE SAT

- $f(x) + n$ shifts the graph of $f(x)$ n units **up**
- $f(x) - n$ shifts the graph of $f(x)$ n units **down**
- $f(x + n)$ shifts the graph of $f(x)$ n units **left**
- $f(x - n)$ shifts the graph of $f(x)$ n units **right**

The figure above shows the graph of the function $r(x)$. Which of the following figures shows the graph of the function $r(x - 2)$?

(A)

(B)

(C)

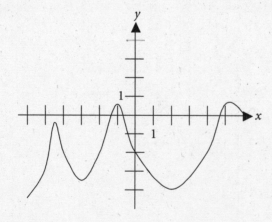

SmartPoints | Ready for Test Day | **20 Advanced Math Concepts** | Practice | Answers and Explanations

(D)

(E)

The graph of $r(x-2)$ will look like the graph of $r(x)$ shifted two units to the right. You can check this by plugging in a few points. For example, $r(-1) = 2.5$, so $r(1-2)$ should equal 2.5. This is only true of answer (E).

 ## DATA ANALYSIS

Some SAT questions focus on the test taker's ability to interpret, evaluate, and draw conclusions from data presented in matrices or, like those below, in scatterplots.

SmartPoints | Ready for Test Day | **20 Advanced Math Concepts** | Practice | Answers and Explanations

Which of the following equations best fits these points?

(A) $y = 3x + 2$

(B) $y = 3x - 2$

(C) $y = 2x + 3$

(D) $y = 2x - 3$

(E) $y = x - 3$

Try to figure out what sort of line would fit these points.

- What should the slope be?

- What should the y-intercept be? Remember that the standard equation for a line is in the form $y = mx + b$, where m is the slope and b is the y-intercept.

If you think visually, you might want to try sketching the line described by each answer choice to see which one fits the closest to the points on the graph.

If you're more comfortable working with numbers, you could try plugging a few points from the graph into each possible equation to see which one works.

The y-intercept of this graph is at -3.

The slope is around 2 because the graph is raised about 2 units for every 1 unit it moves along the x-axis.

The correct answer to this question is (D).

 # PROBABILITY

Probability problems involve determining the chance that something might happen. A common way for the SAT to make these problems seem tougher is to throw geometry into the mix.

Geometric probability questions are those geometry questions that contain a final step in which you're asked to calculate a probability. At this final stage, use the formula

$$\text{probability} = \frac{\text{desired outcome}}{\text{possible outcomes}}.$$ Try this formula on the following question.

What is the probability that a point selected at random from the interior of the figure will fall within the shaded region?

(A) $\dfrac{\sqrt{3}}{13}$

(B) $\dfrac{3}{13}$

(C) $\dfrac{6}{13}$

(D) $\dfrac{1}{3}$

(E) $\dfrac{1}{2}$

The probability that a randomly selected point will fall into the shaded region is equal to the area of the shaded region divided by the area of the entire figure.

The figure is made up of three 30-60-90 triangles, so you can calculate the ratio of the lengths of the bases and heights of the various triangles and then find their areas.

This will be easier if you pick a number to be the length of the base of the smallest triangle.

The lengths of the sides of a 30-60-90 triangle are in the ratio $x: x\sqrt{3}:2x$.

If the length of the smallest triangle is 1, its height is $\sqrt{3}$. This is also the length of the base of the middle triangle.

The height of the middle triangle is $\sqrt{3} \times \sqrt{3} = 3$, which is also the length of the base of the largest triangle.

The height of the largest triangle is $3\sqrt{3}$.

$$\text{Area of smallest triangle: } \frac{1}{2}(1)(\sqrt{3}) = \frac{\sqrt{3}}{2}$$

$$\text{Area of middle triangle: } \frac{1}{2}(\sqrt{3})(3) = \frac{3\sqrt{3}}{2}$$

$$\text{Area of largest triangle: } \frac{1}{2}(3)(3\sqrt{3}) = \frac{9\sqrt{3}}{2}$$

PERFECT SCORE TIP

❝ Geometric probability was harder for me if I used variables. Picking easy numbers made the calculations much easier because I didn't have to worry about an *x* or *y* canceling out in the end. ❞

SmartPoints | Ready for Test Day | **20 Advanced Math Concepts** | Practice | Answers and Explanations

Probability that a point will lie in the shaded region: $\dfrac{\dfrac{3\sqrt{3}}{2}}{\dfrac{\sqrt{3}}{2}+\dfrac{3\sqrt{3}}{2}+\dfrac{9\sqrt{3}}{2}}=\dfrac{\dfrac{3\sqrt{3}}{2}}{\dfrac{13\sqrt{3}}{2}}=\dfrac{3}{13}$

Use the techniques and knowledge you just gained to work through the practice set. Be sure to go over the concepts that you struggled with.

PRACTICE

We have labeled the following questions by the math concept they test. If you get stumped, go back to the appropriate part of this chapter and refresh your memory on how to solve that kind of problem.

SEQUENCES

1. A scientist is running an experiment with two species of bacteria that grow exponentially. If species A doubles in population every two days, species B doubles in population every five days, and each species began the experiment with a population of 50 bacteria, what will the difference be between the populations of the two species after ten days?

   (A)   200
   (B)   800
   (C) 1,200
   (D) 1,400
   (E) 1,500

SETS

2. If Set $A = \{2, 3, 5, 7, 10\}$ and Set $B = \{3, 4, 5, 6, 7\}$, how many elements are in the intersection of the two sets?

   (A) 2
   (B) 3
   (C) 5
   (D) 7
   (E) 10

NUMBER PROPERTIES

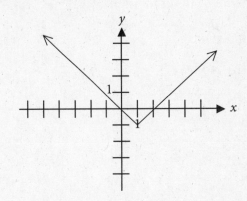

3. Which of the following equations best represents the graph?

   (A) $y = |x|$
   (B) $y = |x| - 1$
   (C) $y = |x - 1|$
   (D) $y = |x - 1| - 1$
   (E) $y = |x - 2|$

QUADRATIC EQUATIONS

4. If $\dfrac{x^3 - 4x}{x^3 - 5x^2 + 6x} = 0$, and $x \neq 0, 2,$ or 3, what is the value of x?

   (A) −3
   (B) −2
   (C) 0
   (D) 1
   (E) 4

EQUATIONS

5. If $\sqrt{x + 2y} - 2 = 15$, what is the value of y in terms of x?

    (A) $\dfrac{289 - x}{2}$

    (B) $289 - x$

    (C) $\dfrac{17 - x}{2}$

    (D) $17 - x$

    (E) 289

EXPONENTS

6. What is the value of $4^{\frac{1}{2}} + 4^{\frac{3}{2}}$?

    (A) 4

    (B) 8

    (C) 10

    (D) 16

    (E) 64

RATIOS

7. The rate at which a certain balloon travels is inversely proportional to the amount of weight attached to it. If the balloon travels at 10 inches per second when there is a 2-gram weight attached to it, approximately how much weight must be attached to the balloon for it to travel 18 inches per second?

    (A) 0.4 grams

    (B) 1.0 gram

    (C) 1.1 grams

    (D) 3.6 grams

    (E) 10.0 grams

FUNCTIONS

8. If $f(x) = \dfrac{(x^2 - 9)}{(x + 3)}$, what is the value of $f(-4)$?

    (A) -7

    (B) $-\dfrac{1}{4}$

    (C) 0

    (D) $\dfrac{1}{4}$

    (E) 7

DOMAIN AND RANGE

9. If $g(x) = 2 - \sqrt{x - 7}$, and $g(x)$ is a real number, which of the following cannot be the value of x?

    (A) 4

    (B) 7

    (C) 11

    (D) 102

    (E) 496

FUNCTIONS AS MODELS

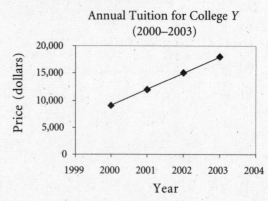

Annual Tuition for College Y (2000–2003)

10. The graph represents the annual tuition for college Y from 2000–2003. Based on the graph, what was most likely the tuition for college Y in 1999?

   (A) $6,000

   (B) $9,000

   (C) $15,000

   (D) $18,000

   (E) $21,000

FUNCTIONS

11. The graph shows the function $g(x)$. What is the value of $g(0)$?

   (A) −1

   (B) $-\dfrac{1}{2}$

   (C) 0

   (D) 1

   (E) 3

QUADRATIC EQUATIONS

12. Which of the following equations best describes the curve?

   (A) $y = x^2 + 4$

   (B) $y = x^2 - 1$

   (C) $y = -x^2 + 4$

   (D) $y = -x^2 + 1$

   (E) $y = -x^2 - 1$

TRIANGLES

13. In the figure above, $\triangle ABC \cong \triangle EFD$. What is the area of $\triangle ABC$?

   (A) 6

   (B) 7.5

   (C) $6\sqrt{2}$

   (D) $6\sqrt{3}$

   (E) 12

Problems in Which Trigonometry Can Be Used as an Alternative Method of Solution

14. In the figure, $\triangle ABC \cong \triangle EFD$, what is the value of x?

(A) 3

(B) 4

(C) 5

(D) 6

(E) 7

Circles

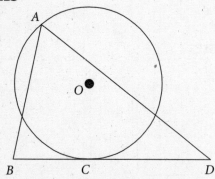

Note: Figure not drawn to scale.

15. In the figure, $\overline{BD}$ is 8 units long and tangent to the circle at point C. $\overline{AC}$ is a diameter of the circle. If the circumference of the circle is 6π, what is the area of $\triangle ABD$?

(A) 9

(B) 12

(C) 24

(D) 9π

(E) 10π

Coordinate Planes

16. If point R is $(2, 4)$ and point S is $(7, 7)$, what is the length of $\overline{RS}$?

(A) 2

(B) $\sqrt{7}$

(C) $\sqrt{34}$

(D) 9

(E) $\sqrt{202}$

Nonlinear Graphs

17. The figure above shows the graph of $g(x)$. What is the largest value of $g(x)$ shown in this figure?

(A) −2

(B) 2

(C) 4

(D) 6

(E) 6.5

Nonlinear Graphs

SmartPoints | Ready for Test Day | 20 Advanced Math Concepts | Practice | Answers and Explanations

18. The figure above shows the graph of the function $h(x)$. Which of the following figures shows the graph of the function $h(x+1)$?

DATA ANALYSIS

19. Which of the following equations best fits these points?

    (A) $y = \dfrac{1}{2}x$

    (B) $y = \dfrac{1}{2}x + 4$

    (C) $y = x$

    (D) $y = 2x - 4$

    (E) $y = 2x$

PROBABILITY

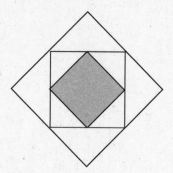

20. The figure above shows a square inscribed in a square inscribed in another square. What is the probability that a point selected at random from the interior of the largest figure will fall within the shaded region?

    (A) $\dfrac{1}{5}$

    (B) $\dfrac{1}{4}$

    (C) $\dfrac{1}{3}$

    (D) $\dfrac{4}{9}$

    (E) $\dfrac{1}{2}$

ANSWERS AND EXPLANATIONS

1. D
SMARTPOINTS CATEGORY: SEQUENCES

Species A doubles every two days and species B doubles every 5 days, so in 10 days, species A will double $10 \div 2 = 5$ times and species B will double $10 \div 5 = 2$ times. After 10 days from an initial population of 50 in each species, species A will have $50 \times 2^5 = 50 \times 32 = 1600$ population, while species B will have $50 \times 2^2 = 50 \times 4 = 200$ population. Their difference is $1600 - 200 = 1400$, or choice (D).

2. B
SMARTPOINTS CATEGORY: SETS

Focus on the overlap of the sets, which share three numbers: 3, 5, and 7. The correct answer is 3, choice (B).

3. D
SMARTPOINTS CATEGORY: NUMBER PROPERTIES

If you're not sure what these transformations of the graph look like, try plugging a few points from the graph into each equation to see which one is correct.

The point $(1, -1)$ immediately eliminates (A), (C), and (E) because the absolute value of a quantity cannot be negative.

(B) evaluates to $-1 = |1| - 1$, which is a false statement.

This leaves (D), the correct answer: $|1 - 1| - 1 = 0 - 1 = -1$.

4. B
SMARTPOINTS CATEGORY: QUADRATIC EQUATIONS

In general, try to simplify problems with complex rational equations like this by factoring the numerator and denominator to see whether any parts cancel out. In this case, you need only to focus on the numerator. You know the fraction has a value of zero, so the numerator must equal zero:

$$x^3 - 4x = 0$$
$$x(x^2 - 4) = 0$$
$$x(x - 2)(x + 2) = 0$$
$$x = 0, 2, \text{ or } -2$$

The question stem states that $x \neq 0$ or 2, so the answer must be $x = -2$, choice (B).

Ready for Test Day | 20 Advanced Math Concepts | Practice | **Answers and Explanations** | Chapter Highlights

5. A

SMARTPOINTS CATEGORY: EQUATIONS

$$\sqrt{x+2y} - 2 = 15$$

$$\sqrt{x+2y} = 17$$

$$(\sqrt{x+2y})^2 = 17^2$$

$$x + 2y = 289$$

$$2y = 289 - x$$

$$y = \frac{289 - x}{2}$$

The correct answer is (A). This is an example designed to illustrate that squaring both sides is not always the last step.

6. C

SMARTPOINTS CATEGORY: EXPONENTS

If x is a positive real number and a is a nonzero integer, then $x^{\frac{1}{a}} = \sqrt[a]{n}$. So $4^{\frac{1}{2}} = \sqrt[2]{4} = 2$. If p and q are integers, then $x^{\frac{p}{q}} = \sqrt[q]{x^p}$. So $4^{\frac{3}{2}} = \sqrt[2]{4^3} = \sqrt{64} = 8$. Therefore, $2 + 8 = 10$, and answer choice (C) is correct.

7. C

SMARTPOINTS CATEGORY: RATIOS

To find the exact amount of weight required, set up a relationship between the height of the balloon and the weight attached to it. Because these quantities vary inversely, you can express that relationship as $h = \dfrac{k}{w}$, where h is the rate of travel of the balloon, w is the weight attached to it, and k is a constant. First, use the given values of h and w to find k, and then use the equation to find the amount of weight required to make the balloon travel at 18 inches per second.

$$10 = \frac{k}{2}$$

$$k = 20$$

$$18 = \frac{20}{w}$$

$w = \dfrac{20}{18} = \dfrac{10}{9} = 1.\overline{11}$, which is approximately 1.1, choice (C).

8. A

SMARTPOINTS CATEGORY: FUNCTIONS (NOTATION AND EVALUATION)

Substitute −4 wherever you see x:

$$f(x) = \frac{(x^2 - 9)}{(x + 3)}$$

$$f(-4) = \frac{[(-4)^2 - 9]}{(-4 + 3)}$$

$$f(-4) = \frac{(16 - 9)}{(-1)}$$

$$f(-4) = \frac{7}{-1}$$

$$f(-4) = -7, \text{ choice (A)}.$$

9. A

SMARTPOINTS CATEGORY: FUNCTIONS (CONCEPTS OF DOMAIN AND RANGE)

If $g(x)$ is a real number, then $\sqrt{x - 7}$ must be a real number. Therefore, $x - 7$ must be zero or a positive number: $x - 7 \geq 0$, and so $x \geq 7$. Any number less than 7, such as choice (A), is outside the domain of the function, which is why it is the correct answer.

10. A

SMARTPOINTS CATEGORY: FUNCTIONS (FUNCTIONS AS MODELS)

Making inferences from a linear graph can be difficult, but remember that you can write in your test booklet. Use a straight surface or your free hand to extend the line on the graph. By looking at the graph, we can see that each year the tuition of college Y increases. In 2000, tuition was $9,000. So we know that in 1999 it should be less than that. The only option is choice (A).

11. E

SMARTPOINTS CATEGORY: FUNCTIONS (LINEAR)

One question on Test Day might require you to evaluate the graph of a linear function, perhaps by indicating the value of y for a given value of x. This question essentially asks you to identify which value of y corresponds to an x-value of 0. Locate $x = 0$; then locate the corresponding y-value. In this case, that value is 3, or (E).

Ready for Test Day | 20 Advanced Math Concepts | Practice | **Answers and Explanations** | Chapter Highlights

12. D

SMARTPOINTS CATEGORY: FUNCTIONS (QUADRATIC)

If you encounter a question about the graph of a quadratic function, it's likely to ask you merely to evaluate a particular point on the graph or, as this question asked, to describe the graph as a whole.

Plug in some points from the graph into each equation to see which ones fit. Good points to test on this graph include $(0, 1)$ and $(1, 0)$. Tested in choice (D):

$$1 = -(0^2) + 1$$
$$0 = -(1^2) + 1$$

Both points work with $y = -x^2 + 1$, choice (D), so it is correct.

13. A

SMARTPOINTS CATEGORY: TRIANGLES (GEOMETRIC NOTATION)

Because the two triangles are congruent, you can combine the information given about each triangle. That is, because $DE = 3$, CA also equals 3.

These are 3-4-5 right triangles, so their height is 4.

The area of the triangle is $(3)(4) = 6$, so choice (A) is correct.

14. A

SMARTPOINTS CATEGORY: TRIANGLES

If two triangles are congruent, they are identical. Each angle or length in one triangle is equal to the corresponding angle or length in the other triangle. Combine the information in the two triangles to get the following triangle:

This is a 30-60-90 special triangle, so $x = \frac{1}{2}(6) = 3$, choice (A).

15. C

SMARTPOINTS CATEGORY: CIRCLES

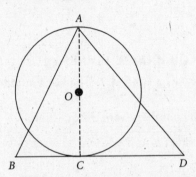

Note: Figure not drawn to scale.

When you see a figure that is not drawn to scale, you can often assume that it has been drawn to be deliberately misleading. Be careful not to assume anything from the apparent positions or lengths of any parts of the figure. Rely instead on the information in the question stem. You may wish to draw your own figure to incorporate that information. This figure includes a circle. Anytime you see a circle, you're going to want its radius at some point. How is the radius of the circle related to the triangle?

Using the circumference formula and the known circumference of the circle:

$$6\pi = 2\pi r$$
$$r = 3$$

The diagram below has been corrected to include the information in the question stem. Note that because $\overline{BD}$ is tangent to the circle at point C, it is perpendicular to $\overline{OC}$. Because $\overline{AC}$ is a diameter of the circle, it must pass through the center of the circle.

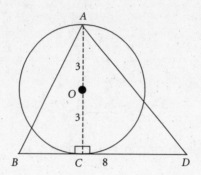

The area of a triangle is one half the length of the base times the height. The height of this triangle is $\overline{AC}$: $3 + 3 = 6$. The area is $\frac{1}{2}(8)(6) = 24$, choice (C).

16. C

SMARTPOINTS CATEGORY: COORDINATE PLANES

The distance between two points (x_1, y_1) and (x_2, y_2) can be found by using the distance formula:

$\sqrt{(x_2 - x_1)^2 + (y_2 - y_1)^2}$. Plug in the numbers from the question:

$$\sqrt{(7-2)^2 + (7-4)^2} = \sqrt{5^2 + 3^2} = \sqrt{25+9} = \sqrt{34}$$

The correct answer is choice (C).

17. C

SMARTPOINTS CATEGORY: NONLINEAR GRAPHS

The value of $g(x)$ is the y-value of the graph. Don't worry about how much of the x-axis is shown; it isn't relevant. The largest value of $g(x)$ shown in the figure is 4, at the points $(-5, 4)$ and $(6.5, 4)$, so (C) is the correct answer.

18. C

SMARTPOINTS CATEGORY: NONLINEAR GRAPHS

The graph of $h(x + 1)$ is the graph of $h(x)$ shifted one unit to the left. If you're not sure what that would look like, try comparing a few points from each graph:

$$h(3) = h(2 + 1) = 0$$
$$h(0) = h(-1 + 1) = 3$$

19. A

SMARTPOINTS CATEGORY: DATA ANALYSIS

Try to figure out what sort of line would fit these points. What should the slope be? What should the y-intercept be? A line through these points would cross the y-axis at or near 0. Its slope is positive but less than 1. Choice (A) fulfills both these criteria. You might want to check your answer by plugging a few points from the graph into the equation to make sure they work.

20. B

SMARTPOINTS CATEGORY: PROBABILITY

There are several different ways to approach this problem, but they all require some knowledge of triangles. The most important thing to notice about the figure is that all the triangles in it are 45-45-90 triangles. This allows you to either calculate the ratios between their sides or break them up further as shown below.

Adding two lines to this figure makes it much easier to work with.

Note that every triangle in this new figure is identical. At this point, you can count the number of shaded triangles and divide by the total number of triangles.

$\frac{4}{16} = \frac{1}{4}$, choice (B).

Ready for Test Day | 20 Advanced Math Concepts | Practice | **Answers and Explanations** | Chapter Highlights

IF YOU LEARN ONLY ONE THING IN THIS CHAPTER . . .

1. WHAT ARE THE 20 MOST TESTED ADVANCED MATH CONCEPTS AND WHAT METHODS CAN I USE TO SOLVE EACH?

- **Sequences**—If r is the ratio between consecutive terms, a_1 is the first term, and a_n is the nth term, then $a_n = a_1 r^{n-1}$.

- **Sets**—Think of the union of sets as what you get when you merge the sets. Think of the intersection of sets as the overlap of the sets.

- **Number Properties (Absolute Value)**—Absolute value is the distance of a number from zero on the number line.

- **Quadratic Equations (Rational Equations)**—When an expression looks especially complex, try to simplify it by factoring.

- **Quadratic Functions**—These functions take the shape of a parabola and the form $f(x) = ax^2 + bx + c$. Solve them like you would a quadratic equation.

- **Equations (Radical Equations)**—Remember that $\sqrt{3}$ refers only to the positive root of a number. If $\sqrt{25} = x$, then $x = 5$. But if $x^2 = 25$, then $x = \pm 5$.

- **Exponents**—$x^{-a} = \dfrac{1}{x^a}$ and $x^{\frac{p}{q}} = \sqrt[q]{x^p}$

- **Ratios (Direct and Inverse Variation)**—Direct variation is $y = kx$, where y changes as x does. Inverse variation is $xy = k$, where x and y change differently based on their relationship in the equation.

- **Functions (Notation and Evaluation)**—Evaluating functions is simply substituting numbers for the variables.

- **Functions (Domain and Range)**—The domain of a function is the set of values for which the function is defined. The range of a function is the set of possible values of the function.

- **Functions (Functions as Models)**—Be sure to understand the relationship and value of each part of a graph or chart.

- **Functions (Linear Functions)**—Equations and Graphs—Parallel lines have equal slopes. Perpendicular lines have negative reciprocal slopes.

- **Triangles (Geometric Notation)**—If two figures are similar, they have the same shape. If two figures are congruent, they're identical. Any two 45-45-90 triangles are similar, even

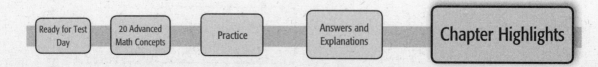
Ready for Test Day | 20 Advanced Math Concepts | Practice | Answers and Explanations | **Chapter Highlights**

though one might be much larger than the other. Only if they are identical in size as well as proportion are they congruent.

- **Triangles (Pythagorean Triplets)**—Know the special relationships between 45-45-90 and 30-60-90 right triangles.

- **Circles (Properties of Tangent Lines)**—The radius of a circle is perpendicular to a tangent line at the point of contact.

- **Coordinate Planes**—The midpoint of two points is simply the average of the x-values and the average of the y-values.

- **Nonlinear Graphs (Graphs and Functions)**—Know the values for the x-axis and y-axis.

- **Nonlinear Graphs (Transformations)**—A transformation is merely an adjustment to a function equation. Treat them similarly.

- **Data Analysis**—Sketch the shape given in the equation, and try plugging in some data points into that equation.

- **Probability (Geometric Probability)**—probability $= \dfrac{\text{desired outcome}}{\text{possible outcomes}}$

Ready for Test Day

20 Advanced Math Concepts

Practice

Answers and Explanations

Chapter Highlights

CHAPTER 14: HOW TO AVOID SAT MATH TRAPS

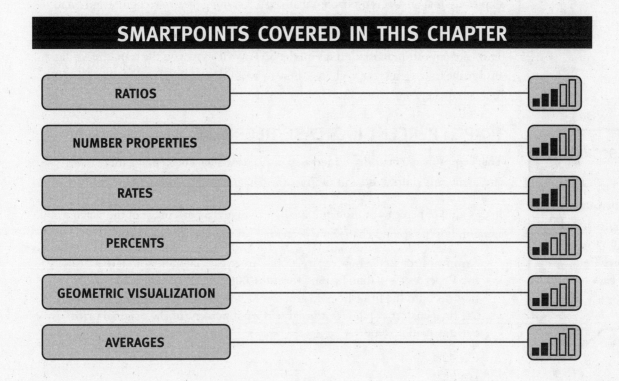

SMARTPOINTS COVERED IN THIS CHAPTER

RATIOS

NUMBER PROPERTIES

RATES

PERCENTS

GEOMETRIC VISUALIZATION

AVERAGES

SmartPoints

Ready for Test Day

10 Common Math Traps

Practice

Answers and Explanations

WHAT TO EXPECT ON TEST DAY

As we've mentioned several times, Math sets are arranged in order of difficulty, with the easiest problems coming first and the hardest problems coming last. Knowing this leads you, the test taker, to treat question #3 differently from question #14. This is where SAT math traps come into play.

THE TEN MOST COMMON MATH TRAPS AND HOW TO AVOID THEM

If you arrive at an answer choice to a hard Math problem without too much effort, be suspicious; that answer is probably a math trap. Learning how to recognize and avoid common SAT math traps will help you be more successful on the Math sections.

There are ten common math traps on the SAT. We'll show you the trap, the wrong answer the trap wants you to choose, how to avoid that answer, and how to solve the problem quickly and correctly.

TRAP 1: PERCENT INCREASE/DECREASE

The Trap: When a quantity is increased or decreased by a percentage more than once, you can't simply add and subtract the percentages to get the answer.

In this kind of percentage problem, the first change is a percentage of the starting amount, but the second change is a percentage of the new amount.

> Sammy purchased a new car in 2000. Three years later, he sold it to a dealer for 40 percent less than he paid for it in 2000. The dealer then added 20 percent onto the price he paid and resold it to another customer. The price the final customer paid for the car was what percent of the original price Sammy paid in 2000?
>
> (A) 40%
> (B) 60%
> (C) 72%
> (D) 80%
> (E) 88%

THE WRONG ANSWER

The increase/decrease percentage problems usually appear at the end of a section and invariably contain a trap. Most students will figure that taking away 40 percent

SmartPoints · Ready for Test Day · **10 Common Math Traps** · Practice · Answers and Explanations

and then adding 20 percent will give them an overall loss of 20 percent, and they'll pick choice (D), 80 percent, as the correct answer. Those students would be wrong.

AVOIDING THE TRAP

Don't blindly add and subtract percentages. They can only be added and subtracted when they are of the same amount. Also, multiple percent changes on the SAT will *never* result in the straight sum or difference of those changes.

$$50\% - 50\% \neq 0\%$$

FINDING THE RIGHT ANSWER

We know:

- The *40 percent less* that Sammy got for the car is 40 percent of his original price.

- The *20 percent* the dealer adds on is 20 percent of what the dealer paid, which is a much smaller amount.

- Adding 20 percent of that smaller amount is *not* the same thing as adding back 20 percent of the original price.

SOLVING THE PROBLEM FAST

Pick the number 100 to start with. In theory, you could pick any number, but because the question asks for the percent of change, 100 is the best number to work with.

Now you are ready to follow these steps:

Step 1. What is 40 percent of the $100 Sammy paid for the car? $40

Step 2. What did *Sammy* sell the car for? Luckily, each percent equals $1. Thus, $100 - 40 = 60$; Sammy sold the car for $60 (also the price the dealer paid).

Step 3. What did the *dealer* sell the car for? Figure what 20 percent of 60 is ($60 \times .20 = \$12$).

Note: This is different from 20 percent of $100, which would be $20.

Step 4. Because $60 + 12 = \$72$, the dealer received $72.

Step 5. Finally what percent of the starting price ($100) is $72? It's 72 percent, so the correct answer is choice (C).

> **PERFECT SCORE TIP**
>
> " On percentage problems, I frequently used my calculator (even though I wrote out all my work!) to plug in the numbers and percents and come up with my final answer. "

SmartPoints | Ready for Test Day | **10 Common Math Traps** | Practice | Answers and Explanations

TRAP 2: WEIGHTED AVERAGES

The Trap: You cannot combine averages of different quantities by taking the average of those original averages.

In an averages problem, if one value occurs more frequently than others, it is *weighted* more. Remember, the average formula calls for the sum of all the terms divided by the total number of terms.

> In a class of 27 plumbers, the average (arithmetic mean) score of the male plumbers on the final exam was 83. If the average score of the 15 female plumbers in the class was 92, what was the average of the whole class?
>
> (A) 86.2
> (B) 87.0
> (C) 87.5
> (D) 88.0
> (E) 88.2

THE WRONG ANSWER

Some students will rush in and simply average 83 and 92 to come up with 87.5 as the class average. Those students will be wrong.

AVOIDING THE TRAP

Don't just take the average of the averages; work with the sums.

FINDING THE RIGHT ANSWER

To find the combined average:

Step 1. To find each sum, multiply each average by the number of terms (plumbers) it represents. So calculate (female plumbers × average) or $(15 × 92)$ + (male plumbers × average) or $(12 × 83)$.

Step 2. Divide that number by the total number of plumbers, or 27.

Presenting this as a formula, you would have:

$$\text{Total class average} = \frac{\text{Sum of females' scores} + \text{Sum of males' scores}}{\text{Total number of students}}$$

SmartPoints | Ready for Test Day | **10 Common Math Traps** | Practice | Answers and Explanations

$$= \frac{(\text{\# of females' females' average score}) + (\text{\# of males' males' average score})}{\text{Total number of students}}$$

$$= \frac{15(92) + 12(83)}{27} = \frac{1,380 + 996}{27} = 88$$

So the class average is 88, answer choice (D).

Note: Notice how using a calculator helps in this problem.

TRAP 3: RATIO:RATIO:RATIO

The Trap: Parts of different ratios don't always refer to the same whole.

In the classic ratio trap, two different ratios each share a common part that is represented by two different numbers. However, the two ratios do not refer to the same whole, so they are not in proportion to each other.

To solve this type of problem, restate both ratios so that the numbers representing the common part (in this case *dimes*) are the same. Then all the parts will be in proportion and can be compared to each other.

> Mammo's coin collection consists of quarters, dimes, and nickels. If the ratio of the number of quarters to the number of dimes is 5:2, and the ratio of the number of dimes to the number of nickels is 3:4, what is the ratio of the number of quarters to the number of nickels?

(A) 5:4
(B) 7:5
(C) 10:6
(D) 12:7
(E) 15:8

THE WRONG ANSWER

If you chose 5:4 as the correct answer, you fell for the classic ratio trap.

AVOIDING THE TRAP

> Restate ratios so that the same number refers to the same quantity. Make sure the common quantity in both ratios has the same number in both.

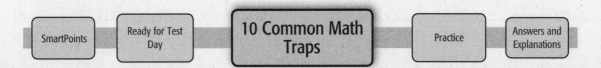

> **PERFECT SCORE TIP**
>
> 66 The easiest way for me to avoid trap answers was to turn ratios into actual numbers *and* jot them down. 99

FINDING THE RIGHT ANSWER

To find the ratio of quarters to nickels, restate both ratios so that the number of dimes is the same in both. You are given two ratios:

quarters to dimes = 5:2   dimes to nickels = 3:4

Step 1. Determine the number of dimes in the first ratio, or 2.

Step 2. Determine the number of dimes in the second ratio, or 3.

Step 3. To restate the ratios, find the least common multiple of 2 and 3, or 6.

Step 4. Restate the ratios with the number of dimes as 6:
Quarters to dimes using 6 is $(5 \times 3):(3 \times 2)$, or 15:6 (the same as 5:2).
Dimes to nickels using 6 is $(3 \times 2):(4 \times 2)$, or 6:8 (the same as 3:4).

Step 5. See that the ratio of quarters to dimes to nickels is 15:6:8.

The ratios are still in their original proportions, but now they can be compared easily because the same number in both represents dimes.

The ratio of quarters to nickels is 15:8, which is answer choice (E).

TRAP 4: "LEAST" AND "GREATEST"

The Trap: In questions that ask for the *least, minimum,* or *smallest* something, the choice offering the smallest number is rarely right.

In questions that ask for the *greatest, maximum,* or *largest* something, the choice offering the largest number is very rarely right.

What is the least positive integer that is divisible by both 2 and 5 and leaves a remainder of 3 when divided by 11?

(A) 30
(B) 32
(C) 33
(D) 70
(E) 80

THE WRONG ANSWER

(A) is the choice not to go for here.

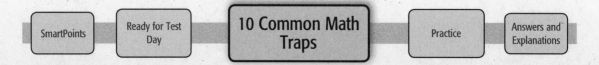

AVOIDING THE TRAP

Consider the constraints and requirements that the nature of the question has placed upon the possible answer. Don't leap to conclusions. In fact, if you ever need to guess on questions asking about the least number, the one place not to go is to the smallest choice and vice versa for questions asking about the largest number.

FINDING THE RIGHT ANSWER

Use an elimination process to find the answer:

Step 1. Eliminate all answers that aren't divisible by both 2 and 5—here choices (B) and (C).

Step 2. Subtract 3 from all the other number choices. Only choice (E), which yields 77, is divisible by 11.

TRAP 5: TRICKY WORDING IN PERCENT QUESTIONS

There is a big difference between *of, less than,* and *greater than* in the ordering of percent problems. They each mean different things.

Consider the following example:

What number is $33\frac{1}{3}\%$ less than 9?

THE WRONG ANSWER

Three.

To avoid confusion on Test Day:

- Think **multiply** when you **see** *of.*

- Think **add** when you see *greater than.*

- Think **subtract** when you see *less than.*

FINDING THE RIGHT ANSWER

$33\frac{1}{3}\%$ less than 9 means $9 - \left(\frac{1}{3}\right)(9) = 9 - 3 = 6.$

> **PERFECT SCORE TIP**
>
> " Whenever there's more than one piece of information given in problems dealing with "least" and "greatest" numbers, try using each piece individually to eliminate as many answer choices as possible. "

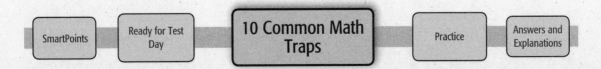

SmartPoints | Ready for Test Day | **10 Common Math Traps** | Practice | Answers and Explanations

TRAP 6: RATIO VERSUS QUANTITY

The Trap: You cannot simply add to or subtract from the parts of a ratio at will. Test takers unfamiliar with this rule would probably add 1 to 3 and to 4, coming up incorrectly with the ratio of 4:5.

> The ratio of two quantities is 3:4. If each of the quantities is increased by 1, what is the ratio of these two new quantities?
>
> (A) 9:16
> (B) 2:3
> (C) 3:4
> (D) 4:5
> (E) It cannot be determined from the information given.

THE WRONG ANSWER

(D) is a trap.

AVOIDING THE TRAP

Avoid this trap by remembering the rule that you can multiply or divide a ratio or part of a ratio, but you cannot add to or subtract from a ratio or part of a ratio.

FINDING THE RIGHT ANSWER

For students on the lookout for violations of the rule we've been discussing, this question means quick points.

Once you realize that the ratio of the new quantities depends on the actual original quantities—not simply their ratio—you'll quickly recognize that the answer cannot be determined from the information provided. The correct answer is (E).

SmartPoints — Ready for Test Day — **10 Common Math Traps** — Practice — Answers and Explanations

THE RATIO RULE

You can multiply or divide a ratio or part of a ratio:

- If the number of apples to oranges is 2:4 and you double the oranges, then the new ratio is 2:8.
- If instead you halve the number of oranges, then the new ratio is 2:2, or an equal number of each.
- However, you cannot add a fixed quantity to or remove one from a ratio without knowing the original quantity.

TRAP 7: NOT ALL NUMBERS ARE POSITIVE INTEGERS

The Trap: Not all numbers are positive integers. Don't forget there are negative numbers and fractions as well. This is important because negative numbers and fractions between 0 and 1 behave very differently from positive integers.

If $n \neq 0$, then which of the following must be true?

I. $n^2 > n$

II. $2n > n$

III. $n + 1 > n$

(A) I only

(B) II only

(C) III only

(D) I and III only

(E) I, II, and III

THE WRONG ANSWER

In the example above, if you considered only positive integers greater than 1 for the value of n, you would assume that all three statements were true. However, that is not the case.

> **PERFECT SCORE TIP**
>
> " When solving questions that are open-ended as to which number to choose, try many different types—positive and negative integers and fractions and zero. "

AVOIDING THE TRAP

When picking numbers for variables, consider fractions and negative numbers.

| SmartPoints | Ready for Test Day | **10 Common Math Traps** | Practice | Answers and Explanations |

FINDING THE RIGHT ANSWER

Here you are looking for *exceptions* to a statement, so look for instances when something might NOT be true.

Consider fractions and negative numbers in testing "must be true" questions:

- **Statement I:** You might assume that squaring a number will result in a larger number. But always? What happens if you square a *fraction between 0 and 1*? In fact, the result is quite different: $\frac{1}{2^2} = \frac{1}{4}$ and $(\frac{1}{10})^2 = 1/100$. Thus, you can eliminate choices (A), (D), and (E).

- **Statement II:** You might assume that multiplying a number by 2 will result in a larger number. Again, be careful. What happens if you multiply a *negative number* by 2? Your result is smaller than the original number. For example, $-3 \times 2 = -6$. Eliminate (B).

- **Statement III:** This is the only possibility left, so answer choice (C) is correct. But let's look at why: adding 1 to any number gives you a larger number as a result in any situation. For example, $5 + 1 = 6$, $\frac{1}{2} + 1 = 1\frac{1}{2}$, and $-7 + 1 = -6$.

Therefore, only Statement III must be true, so choice (C) is correct. If you didn't consider fractions or negative numbers, you would have fallen into the trap and answered the question incorrectly.

TRAP 8: HIDDEN INSTRUCTIONS

The Trap: A small clue, easily overlooked, can mean the difference between a right and wrong answer.

> At a certain restaurant, the hourly wage for a waiter is 20 percent more than the hourly wage for a dishwasher, and the hourly wage for a dishwasher is half as much as the hourly wage for a cook's assistant. If a cook's assistant earns $8.50 per hour, how much less than a cook's assistant does a waiter earn each hour?
>
> (A) $2.55
> (B) $3.40
> (C) $4.25
> (D) $5.10
> (E) $5.95

THE WRONG ANSWER

To solve this problem, you must find the hourly wage of the waiter. The cook's assistant earns $8.50 per hour. The dishwasher earns half of this—$4.25 per hour. The waiter earns 20 percent more than the dishwasher—$4.25 × 1.2 = $5.10. So the waiter earns $5.10 per hour, and your automatic reaction might be to fill in answer choice (D). But (D) is the wrong answer.

AVOIDING THE TRAP

Make sure you answer the question that's being asked. Watch out for hidden instructions.

FINDING THE RIGHT ANSWER

You have figured out that the waiter earns $5.10 per hour, and the cook's assistant earns $8.50 per hour.

To find out how much less the waiter earns than the cook's assistant, subtract the waiter's hourly wage from the cook's assistant's hourly wage. The correct answer is (B).

SPEED UP BY SLOWING DOWN

As you approach the end of a section and the clock begins to tick away, it can be extremely tempting to rush and start reading faster.

Don't make that mistake!

Reading faster will not only cause you to miss important words, it also will force you to reread things a second or third time, which wastes time rather than saving it.

Read it right by reading once—and carefully.

TRAP 9: AVERAGE RATES

The Trap: To get an average speed, you can't just average the rates.

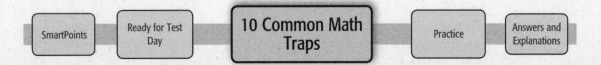

A car traveled from *A* to *B* at an average speed of 40 mph and then immediately traveled back from *B* to *A* at an average speed of 60 mph. What was the car's average speed for the roundtrip in miles per hour?

(A) 45

(B) 48

(C) 50

(D) 52

(E) 54

THE WRONG ANSWER

Do you see which answer choice looks too good to be true? The temptation is simply to add 40 and 60 and divide by two. The answer is *obviously* 50 (C). But 50 is wrong.

AVOIDING THE TRAP

You can solve almost any average rate problem with this general formula:

$$\text{Average Rate} = \frac{\text{Total Distance}}{\text{Total Time}}$$

Use the given information to figure out the total distance and the total time.

PERFECT SCORE TIP

" Picking numbers worked well for me when I came across average rate questions. I always approached them in a consistent and methodical way. "

FINDING THE RIGHT ANSWER

Pick a number for the total distance, if the total distance is not provided.

Step 1. Pick a number that's easy to work with. A good number to pick here would be 240 for the total distance because you can figure in your head the times for two 120-mile legs at 40 mph and 60 mph.

Step 2. Now plug *total distance = 240 miles* and *total time = 5 hours* into the general formula.

$$\text{Average Rate} = \frac{\text{Total Distance}}{\text{Total Time}} = \frac{240 \text{ miles}}{5 \text{ hours}} = 48 \text{ hour}$$

Correct answer: (B).

SmartPoints | Ready for Test Day | **10 Common Math Traps** | Practice | Answers and Explanations

TRAP 10: COUNTING NUMBERS

The Trap: Subtracting the first and last integers in a range will give you the difference of the two numbers. It won't give you the number of integers in that range.

> The tickets for a certain raffle are consecutively numbered. If Louis sold the tickets numbered from 75 to 148 inclusive, how many raffle tickets did he sell?
>
> (A) 71
> (B) 72
> (C) 73
> (D) 74
> (E) 75

THE WRONG ANSWER

If you subtract 75 from 148 and get 73 as the answer, you are wrong.

PERFECT SCORE TIP

❝ Look at your answer to avoid silly math mistakes. If it's clearly too big or too small, check your work or redo the problem. ❞

AVOIDING THE TRAP

Don't rush through a problem such as this. Take the time to see if either *inclusive* or *exclusive* is specified in the wording. These words are the key to finding the right answer.

FINDING THE RIGHT ANSWER

- To count the number of integers in a range *inclusive*, subtract then add 1.

- If you forget the rule, pick two small numbers that are close together, such as 1 and 4. Obviously, there are four integers from 1 to 4, inclusive. If you had subtracted 1 from 4, your remainder would have been 3.

- The word *inclusive* tells you to include the first and last numbers given. In this problem, subtract 75 from 148. The result is 73. Adding 1 to this difference gives you 74, or choice (D).

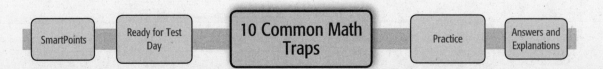

SmartPoints | Ready for Test Day | **10 Common Math Traps** | Practice | Answers and Explanations

PRACTICE

Directions: Identify the trap in each problem (and solve the problem correctly). Answers are found on page 340.

1. If x is 300 percent of 25 and y is 25 percent more than 40, then x is what percent of y? (Disregard the % sign when you grid your answer.)

2. In the figure above, what is the maximum number of nonoverlapping regions into which the shaded area can be divided using exactly two straight lines?

    (A) 3

    (B) 4

    (C) 5

    (D) 6

    (E) 7

3. A certain school event was open only to juniors and seniors. Half the number of juniors who had planned to attend actually attended. Double the number of seniors who had planned to attend actually attended. If the ratio of the number of juniors who had planned to attend to the number of seniors who had planned to attend was 4 to 5, then juniors were what fraction of attendees?

    (A) $\dfrac{1}{6}$

    (B) $\dfrac{1}{5}$

    (C) $\dfrac{4}{19}$

    (D) $\dfrac{4}{15}$

    (E) It cannot be determined from the information given.

4. If $p - q = 4$ and r is the number of integers less than p and greater than q, then which of the following could be true?

    I. $r = 3$

    II. $r = 4$

    III. $r = 5$

    (A) I only

    (B) II only

    (C) III only

    (D) I and II

    (E) I, II, and III

5. Pump 1 can drain a 400-gallon water tank in 1.2 hours. Pump 2 can drain the same tank in 1.8 hours. How many minutes longer than pump 1 would it take pump 2 to drain a 100-gallon tank?

   (A) 0.15
   (B) 1.2
   (C) 6
   (D) 9
   (E) 18

6. Volumes 12 through 30 of a certain encyclopedia are located on the bottom shelf of a bookcase. If the volumes of the encyclopedia are numbered consecutively, how many volumes of the encyclopedia are on the bottom shelf?

   (A) 17
   (B) 18
   (C) 19
   (D) 29
   (E) 30

7. A reservoir is at full capacity at the beginning of summer. By the first day of fall, the level in the reservoir is 30 percent below full capacity. Then during the fall, a period of heavy rains increases the level by 30 percent. After the rains, the reservoir is at what percent of its full capacity?

   (A) 60%
   (B) 85%
   (C) 91%
   (D) 95%
   (E) 100%

8. Two classes, one with 50 students and the other with 30, take the same exam. The combined average of both classes is 84.5. If the larger class averages 80, what is the average of the smaller class?

   (A) 87.2
   (B) 89.0
   (C) 92.0
   (D) 93.3
   (E) 94.5

9. In a pet shop, the ratio of puppies to kittens is 7:6, and the ratio of kittens to guinea pigs is 5:3. What is the ratio of puppies to guinea pigs?

   (A) 7:3
   (B) 6:5
   (C) 13:8
   (D) 21:11
   (E) 35:18

10. A typist typed the first n pages of a book, where $n > 0$, at an average rate of 12 pages per hour and typed the remaining n pages at an average rate of 20 pages per hour. What was the typist's average rate in pages per hour for the entire book?

   (A) 14
   (B) 15
   (C) 16
   (D) 17
   (E) 18

SmartPoints | Ready for Test Day | 10 Common Math Traps | Practice | Answers and Explanations

ANSWERS AND EXPLANATIONS

DID YOU FALL FOR THE TRAPS?

Each wrong answer represents one trap you need to work on. Go back and reread the section on that trap. Then look at the practice set's problem again. Do you see the trap now?

1. 150

SMARTPOINTS CATEGORY: PERCENTS

Trap Answer: 37.5 (Trap #5)

2. C

SMARTPOINTS CATEGORY: GEOMETRIC VISUALIZATION

Trap Answer: B (Trap #4)

3. A

SMARTPOINTS CATEGORY: RATIOS

Trap Answer: B (Trap #6)

4. D

SMARTPOINTS CATEGORY: NUMBER PROPERTIES

Trap Answer: A (Trap #7)

5. D

SMARTPOINTS CATEGORY: RATES

Trap Answer: A (Trap #8)

6. C

SMARTPOINTS CATEGORY: NUMBER PROPERTIES

Trap Answer: B (Trap #10)

7. C

SMARTPOINTS CATEGORY: PERCENTS

Trap Answer: E (Trap #1)

8. C

SMARTPOINTS CATEGORY: AVERAGES

Trap Answer: B (Trap #2)

9. E

SMARTPOINTS CATEGORY: RATIOS

Trap Answer: A (Trap #3)

10. B

SMARTPOINTS CATEGORY: RATES

Trap Answer: C (Trap #9)

IF YOU LEARN ONLY THREE THINGS IN THIS CHAPTER . . .

1. SECRETS OF SAT MATH TRAPS

- If an answer to a hard question comes too easily, you've probably fallen into a trap.

- Read the questions carefully, circling keywords that tell you what exactly the question requires of you (especially percentage and ratio questions).

- Know where you are in a section: the harder questions lie in the middle and end.

- Picking numbers and back solving can be helpful tools when a tricky choice is presented.

2. WHAT ARE THE MOST COMMON MATH TRAPS?

The SAT uses traps on harder math problems. The ten most common traps are:

- **Trap 1:** Percent Increase/Decrease

- **Trap 2:** Weighted Averages

- **Trap 3:** Ratio:Ratio:Ratio

- **Trap 4:** "Least" and "Greatest"

- **Trap 5:** Tricky Wording in Percent Questions

- **Trap 6:** Ratio versus Quantity

- **Trap 7:** Not All Numbers Are Positive Integers

- **Trap 8:** Hidden Instructions

- **Trap 9:** Average Rates

- **Trap 10:** Counting Numbers

3. WHAT SKILLS DO I NEED TO WORK AROUND TRICKY ANSWER CHOICES TO SOLVE THE PROBLEM?

- Picking numbers and back solving (discussed at length in chapter 11) are helpful tools when a tricky answer choice is presented.

Ready for Test Day | 10 Common Math Traps | Practice | Answers and Explanations | **Chapter Highlights**

Part Five

HOW TO PREPARE FOR TEST DAY

Chapter 15: Strategies for Test Day Success

You've worked through Kaplan's SAT program, and Test Day is fast approaching. If you haven't taken three out of four of your Practice Tests, take another one now. Link to the official test site and check for any late-breaking information. Prepare yourself for a positive SAT experience!

CHAPTER 15: STRATEGIES FOR TEST DAY SUCCESS

GET READY FOR TEST DAY

There's no need to panic or lose confidence as Test Day approaches. You've studied hard and Kaplan has provided you with all the tools you need to make your SAT experience a success. The following information will help you structure the crucial days right before, during, and after Test Day—to your best advantage.

BEFORE THE TEST

The week leading up to Test Day can be a stressful time for test takers. Students are often worried about how they're going to do on the exam and wonder what they should be doing to get ready.

Does this sound familiar? If so, then worry no more! Keep reading, and remember: Kaplan's got you covered!

SEVEN DAYS BEFORE THE TEST

- Take a full-length Practice Test under timed conditions. Approach the test strategically, actively, and confidently. Use the techniques and strategies you've learned in this book:

  - Circle and skip the questions you would omit on Test Day. You can go back later and try answering them, if there's time.

    Note: Analyze your omitting strategy now. This reduces the time you spend wondering about omitting on Test Day—streamlining these decisions leaves more time for answering the questions you do know.

  - Use the Answer Sheet provided to practice your bubbling techniques. Accuracy is very important.

> **PERFECT SCORE TIP**
>
> Whenever I took a complete practice test, it was really important for me to simulate test conditions as much as possible. I really recommend you do so as well!

Ready for Test Day | **Before the Test** | During the Test | After the Test

- Have a bottle of water, fruit, or an energy bar handy for your two timed breaks which usually occur after Sections 3 and 7.
- Wear a digital watch to help you keep track of the time.
- Read all the explanations of the questions you get wrong.
- Write down the types of questions you struggle with and go back to the relevant sections of the book to fine-tune these areas.

TWO DAYS BEFORE THE TEST

Go to your syllabus online to view the results of your practice tests. It's likely that you will see clear improvement, but don't worry too much about your scores or about whether you got any specific question right or wrong.

The practice tests don't count. But do flip through your answer keys to examine your performance on specific questions with an eye to how you might get through each one faster and better on the test to come.

THE NIGHT BEFORE THE TEST

Our advice is to not do any studying on this day. Get together an *SAT Kit* containing the following items:

- A calculator with fresh batteries
- A watch
- A few No. 2 pencils (pencils with slightly dull points fill the ovals better)
- Erasers
- Photo ID card (e.g., passport, driver's license, or student ID)
- Your admission ticket from ETS
- A snack—there are breaks, and you'll probably get hungry
- SAT Premier Program Study Sheet

Know exactly where you're going, exactly how you're getting there, and exactly how long it takes to get there. It's probably a good idea to visit your test center sometime before the day of the test so that you know what to expect—what the rooms are like, how the desks are set up, and so on.

Relax the night before the test. Do some relaxation and visualization techniques. Read a magazine, take a long hot shower, or watch something on TV. Get a good night's sleep. Go to bed early, and leave yourself extra time in the morning.

> **PERFECT SCORE TIP**
>
> " I didn't bring extra batteries for my calculator on Test Day, which was a mistake. Even though I didn't need them, another student's calculator ran out of batteries. Don't be that student! "

Ready for Test Day | **Before the Test** | During the Test | After the Test

THE MORNING OF THE TEST

First, wake up. After that:

- Eat breakfast. Make it something substantial but not anything too heavy or greasy.

- Don't drink a lot of coffee if you're not used to it. Bathroom breaks cut into your time, and too much caffeine may make you jittery.

- Dress in layers so that you can adjust to the temperature of the testing room.

- Read something. Warm up your brain with a newspaper or a magazine. You shouldn't let the SAT be the first thing you read that day.

- Be sure to get there early. Allow yourself extra time for traffic, mass transit delays, or detours.

DURING THE TEST

Don't be shaken. If you find your confidence slipping, remind yourself how well you've prepared. You know the structure of the test; you know the instructions; you've had practice with—and have learned strategies for—every question type.

If something goes really wrong, don't panic. If the test booklet is defective—two pages are stuck together or the ink has run—raise your hand, and tell the proctor you need a new book. If you accidentally misgrid your answer page or put the answers in the wrong section, raise your hand and tell the proctor. He or she might be able to arrange for you to regrid your test after it's over when it won't cost you any time.

Remember, don't think about which section is experimental. You never know for sure which section won't count. Besides, you can't work on any other section during that section's designated time slot.

> **EXPERT TUTOR TIP**
>
> " Try your hardest on every section of the SAT—because you won't be able to tell which section is experimental. "

AFTER THE TEST

Congratulate yourself!

Now, you might walk out of the SAT thinking that you blew it. This is a normal reaction. Lots of people—even the highest scorers—feel that way. You tend to remember the questions that stumped you, not the ones that you knew.

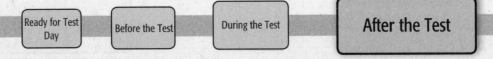

Ready for Test Day | Before the Test | During the Test | **After the Test**

WORRIED ABOUT YOUR SCORE?

You can always call ETS within 24 hours to find out about canceling your score, but there's usually no good reason to do so. Remember, colleges typically accept your highest SAT score, and no test experience is going to be perfect.

If you were distracted by a weird smell or a particularly loud test proctor this time around, next time you may be even more distracted by construction noise, a cold, or a particularly hot room. Carefully consider your performance before canceling your score.

PERFECT SCORE TIP

" After I finished the SAT, the last thing I wanted to do was think about it. I went out to dinner with my family that night, and got on with my life! "

However, we're positive that you performed well and scored your best on the exam because you followed the our SAT Premier Program. Be confident that you were prepared, and celebrate in the fact that the SAT is a distant memory.

If you want more help or just want to know more about the SAT, college admissions, or Kaplan prep courses for the SAT, give us a call at 1-800-KAP-TEST or visit us at www.kaptest.com. We're here to answer your questions and to help you in any way we can. Also, be sure to return one last time to your online syllabus and complete our survey. We're only as good as our successful students.

Ready for Test Day | Before the Test | During the Test | **After the Test**

Part Six

PRACTICE TESTS AND EXPLANATIONS

Before taking the following practice tests, find a quiet room where you can work uninterrupted. Make sure you have a comfortable desk and several No. 2 pencils. Use the answer sheets on the following pages to record your answers. (You can tear it out or photocopy it.)

Once you start each practice test, do not stop until you have finished. Remember, you may review any questions within a section, but you may not go back or forward a section.

When you have finished taking each practice test, you can go on to the section that follows Practice Test Four to calculate your scores.

Good luck!

SECTION 1
Time—25 Minutes
ESSAY

The essay gives you an opportunity to show how effectively you can develop and express ideas. You should, therefore, take care to develop your point of view, present your ideas logically and clearly, and use language precisely.

Your essay must be written in your Answer Grid Booklet—you will receive no other paper on which to write. You will have enough space if you write on every line, avoid wide margins, and keep your hand-writing to a reasonable size. Remember that people who are not familiar with your handwriting will read what you write. Try to write or print so that what you are writing is legible to those readers.

You have twenty-five minutes to write an essay on the topic assigned below.
DO NOT WRITE ON ANOTHER TOPIC. AN OFF-TOPIC ESSAY WILL RECEIVE A SCORE OF ZERO.

Think carefully about the issue presented in the following excerpt and the assignment below.

"Everything comes if a man will only wait."
—Benjamin Disraeli, *Tancred*

"Destiny is not a matter of chance, it is a matter of choice; it is not a thing to be waited for, it is a thing to be achieved."
—William Jennings Bryan, *Memoirs*

Assignment: Should we wait for good things to come, or is destiny not something we can wait for? Plan and write an essay in which you develop your point of view on this issue. Support your position with reasoning and examples taken from your reading, studies, experience, or observations.

DO NOT WRITE YOUR ESSAY IN YOUR TEST BOOK.
You will receive credit only for what you write in your Answer Grid Booklet.

Write your essay on separate sheets of paper.

GO ON TO THE NEXT PAGE ⟶

SECTION 2

Time—25 Minutes
24 Questions

Directions: For each of the following questions, choose the best answer and darken the corresponding oval on the answer sheet.

Each sentence below has one or two blanks, each blank indicating that something has been omitted. Beneath the sentence are five words or sets of words labeled A through E. Choose the word or set of words that, when inserted in the sentence, best fits the meaning of the sentence as a whole.

EXAMPLE:

Today's small, portable computers contrast markedly with the earliest electronic computers, which were -------.

(A) effective
(B) invented
(C) useful
(D) destructive
(E) enormous   Ⓐ Ⓑ Ⓒ Ⓓ ●

1. More insurers are limiting the sale of property insurance in coastal areas and other regions ------- natural disasters.

(A) safe from
(B) according to
(C) despite
(D) which include
(E) prone to

2. Roman legions ------- the mountain ------- of Masada for three years before they were able to seize it.

(A) dissembled . . . bastion
(B) assailed . . . symbol
(C) besieged . . . citadel
(D) surmounted . . . dwelling
(E) honed . . . stronghold

3. Unlike his calmer, more easygoing colleagues, the senator was -------, ready to quarrel at the slightest provocation.

(A) whimsical
(B) irascible
(C) gregarious
(D) ineffectual
(E) benign

4. Although historians have long thought of Genghis Khan as a ------- potentate, new research has shown he was ------- by many of his subjects.

(A) tyrannical . . . abhorred
(B) despotic . . . revered
(C) redundant . . . venerated
(D) jocular . . . esteemed
(E) peremptory . . . invoked

GO ON TO THE NEXT PAGE ⟩

5. Jill was ------- by her employees because she often ------- them for not working hard enough.

   (A) deified . . . goaded
   (B) loathed . . . berated
   (C) disregarded . . . eulogized
   (D) cherished . . . derided
   (E) execrated . . . lauded

6. Reconstructing the skeletons of extinct species like dinosaurs is ------- process that requires much patience and effort by paleontologists.

   (A) a nascent
   (B) an aberrant
   (C) a disheveled
   (D) a worthless
   (E) an exacting

7. Nearly ------- by disease and the destruction of their habitat, koalas are now found only in isolated parts of eucalyptus forests.

   (A) dispersed
   (B) compiled
   (C) decimated
   (D) infuriated
   (E) averted

8. Deep ideological ------- and internal power struggles ------- the government.

   (A) disputes . . . facilitated
   (B) similarities . . . protracted
   (C) distortions . . . accelerated
   (D) agreements . . . stymied
   (E) divisions . . . paralyzed

GO ON TO THE NEXT PAGE

<u>**Directions:**</u> The passages below are followed by questions based on their content; questions following a pair of related passages may also be based on the relationship between the paired passages. Answer the questions on the basis of what is <u>stated</u> or <u>implied</u> in the passages and in any introductory material that may be provided.

Questions 9–12 refer to the following passages.

Passage 1

Musicologists and linguists argue about the relationship between music and language. Prominent ethno musicologist Bruno Nettl has concluded that like language, music is a
(5) "series of symbols." However, music has traditionally been used purely to express emotions while language has also been used for more functional, prosaic tasks. This distinction was especially evident in the Romantic era of
(10) Western music, when many composers and critics felt that music could stand by itself to connote emotions without any extra-musical references.

Passage 2

The fundamental building blocks of both
(15) language and music are quite similar, as are the manners in which these components are combined to form a cohesive whole. In the same way that an entire piece of music can be divided into phrases, and further subdivided
(20) into specific notes, language can be subdivided into paragraphs, sentences, and words. A single note can have different meanings depending on the piece; a lone word can have different meanings depending on the context in the
(25) sentence. Words and notes are also similar in that they have little intrinsic meaning, but instead act as symbols to convey larger ideas.

9. The author of Passage 1 most likely cites the "Romantic era of Western music" (line 9) in order to establish that

(A) our modern perception of Romantic music is different from that held in the Romantic era

(B) unlike language, Romantic music is not used functionally

(C) composers of Romantic music always used music to express emotion

(D) in the Romantic era it was commonly thought that music alone could convey emotion

(E) music of the Romantic era is compromised because it contains no extra-musical references

10. In lines 11–12, the term "extra-musical" most nearly means

(A) especially musical

(B) nonmusical

(C) more than musical

(D) better than musical

(E) classically musical

11. In both passages, the authors state that music and language are

(A) symbols

(B) subdivided sections

(C) functional parts

(D) clues

(E) conveyers of emotion

GO ON TO THE NEXT PAGE ⇨

12. About which of the following statements would the author of Passage 1 and the author of Passage 2 most likely disagree?

(A) Music and language can both be subdivided into several parts.

(B) Although significantly similar, music and language have several fundamentally distinct aspects.

(C) A group of notes used in a musical composition has the same meaning in a piece by a different composer.

(D) Language is not an effective means to express emotions.

(E) The meaning of a particular word is solely dependent on context.

Questions 13–24 refer to the following passage.

In the following passage, a 19th-century American writer recalls his boyhood in a small town along the Mississippi River.

My father was a justice of the peace, and I supposed he possessed the power of life and death over all men and could hang anybody that offended him. This was distinction enough
(5) for me as a general thing; but the desire to be a steamboatman kept intruding, nevertheless. I first wanted to be a cabin boy so that I could come out with a white apron on and shake a tablecloth over the side, where all my old com-
(10) rades could see me. Later I thought I would rather be the deck hand who stood on the end of the stage plank with a coil of rope in his hand, because he was particularly conspicuous.

But these were only daydreams—too heav-
(15) enly to be contemplated as real possibilities. By and by one of the boys went away. He was not heard of for a long time. At last he turned up as an apprentice engineer or "striker" on a steamboat. This thing shook the bottom out of all my
(20) Sunday-school teachings. That boy had been notoriously worldly, and I had been just the reverse—yet he was exalted to this eminence, and I was left in obscurity and misery. There was nothing generous about this fellow in his
(25) greatness. He would always manage to have a rusty bolt to scrub while his boat was docked at our town, and he would sit on the inside guard and scrub it, where we could all see him and envy him and loathe him.
(30) He used all sorts of steamboat technicalities in his talk, as if he were so used to them that he forgot common people could not understand them. He would speak of the "labboard" side of a horse in an easy, natural way that would
(35) make you wish he was dead. And he was always talking about "St. Looy" like an old citizen. Two

GO ON TO THE NEXT PAGE ⟶

or three of the boys had long been persons of consideration among us because they had been to St. Louis once and had a vague general (40) knowledge of its wonders, but the day of their glory was over now. They lapsed into a humble silence and learned to disappear when the ruthless "cub" engineer approached. This fellow had money, too, and hair oil, and he wore a showy (45) brass watch chain, a leather belt, and used no suspenders. No girl could withstand his charms. He "cut out" every boy in the village. When his boat blew up at last, it diffused a tranquil contentment among us such as we had not known (50) for months. But when he came home the next week, alive, renowned, and appeared in church all battered up and bandaged, a shining hero, stared at and wondered over by everybody, it seemed to us that the partiality of Providence (55) for an undeserving reptile had reached a point where it was open to criticism.

   This creature's career could produce but one result, and it speedily followed. Boy after boy managed to get on the river. Four sons of the (60) chief merchant, and two sons of the county judge became pilots, the grandest position of all. But some of us could not get on the river—at least our parents would not let us.

   So by and by I ran away. I said I would (65) never come home again till I was a pilot and could return in glory. But somehow I could not manage it. I went meekly aboard a few of the boats that lay packed together like sardines at the long St. Louis wharf and very humbly (70) inquired for the pilots but got only a cold shoulder and short words from mates and clerks. I had to make the best of this sort of treatment for the time being, but I had comforting daydreams of a future when I should (75) be a great and honored pilot, with plenty of money, and could kill some of these mates and clerks and pay for them.

13. The author makes the statement that "I supposed he . . . offended him" (lines 1–4) primarily to suggest the

   (A) power held by a justice of the peace in a frontier town

   (B) naive view that he held of his father's importance

   (C) respect in which the townspeople held his father

   (D) possibility of miscarriages of justice on the American frontier

   (E) harsh environment in which he was brought up

14. As used in line 4, the word "distinction" most nearly means

   (A) difference

   (B) variation

   (C) prestige

   (D) desperation

   (E) clarity

15. The author decides that he would rather become a deck hand than a cabin boy (lines 7–12) because

   (A) the job offers higher wages

   (B) he believes that the work is easier

   (C) he wants to avoid seeing his older friends

   (D) deck hands often go on to become pilots

   (E) the job is more visible to passersby

GO ON TO THE NEXT PAGE

16. The author most likely mentions his "Sunday-school teachings" in lines 19–20 in order to emphasize

   (A) the influence of his early education in later life
   (B) his sense of injustice at the engineer's success
   (C) his disillusionment with longstanding religious beliefs
   (D) his determination to become an engineer at all costs
   (E) the unscrupulous nature of the engineer's character

17. The author most likely concludes that the engineer is not "generous" (line 24) because he

   (A) has no respect for religious beliefs
   (B) refuses to share his wages with friends
   (C) flaunts his new position in public
   (D) takes pride in material possessions
   (E) ignores the disappointment of other people's ambitions

18. The author most probably mentions the use of "steamboat technicalities" (line 30) in order to emphasize the engineer's

   (A) expertise after a few months on the job
   (B) fascination for trivial information
   (C) ignorance on most other subjects
   (D) desire to appear sophisticated
   (E) inability to communicate effectively

19. The word "consideration" in line 38 most nearly means

   (A) generosity
   (B) deliberation
   (C) contemplation
   (D) unselfishness
   (E) reputation

20. According to the passage, the "glory" of having visited St. Louis (lines 39–41) was over because

   (A) the boys' knowledge of St. Louis was much less detailed than the engineer's
   (B) St. Louis had changed so much that the boys' stories were no longer accurate
   (C) the boys realized that traveling to St. Louis was not a mark of sophistication
   (D) the engineer's account revealed that the boys' stories were lies
   (E) travel to St. Louis had become too commonplace to be envied

21. The author describes the engineer's appearance (lines 43–46) primarily in order to

   (A) suggest one reason why many people found the engineer impressive
   (B) convey the way steamboatmen typically dressed
   (C) emphasize the inadequacy of his own wardrobe
   (D) contrast the engineer's behavior with his appearance
   (E) indicate his admiration for fashionable clothes

GO ON TO THE NEXT PAGE ▷

22. In lines 50–56, the author's response to the engineer's survival is one of

   (A) thankfulness for what he believes is God's providence

   (B) astonishment at the engineer's miraculous escape

   (C) reflection on the occupational hazards of a steamboating career

   (D) outrage at his rival's undeserved good fortune

   (E) sympathy for the extent of the engineer's wounds

23. The major purpose of the passage is to

   (A) sketch the peaceful life of a frontier town

   (B) relate the events that led to a boy's first success in life

   (C) portray the unsophisticated ambitions of a boy

   (D) describe the characteristics of a small-town boaster

   (E) give a humorous portrayal of a boy's conflicts with his parents

24. At the end of the passage, the author reflects on

   (A) his new ambition to become either a mate or a clerk

   (B) the wisdom of seeking a job in which advancement is easier

   (C) the prospect of abandoning a hopeless search for fame

   (D) the impossibility of returning home and asking his parents' pardon

   (E) his determination to keep striving for success in a glorious career

IF YOU FINISH BEFORE TIME IS CALLED, YOU MAY CHECK YOUR WORK ON THIS SECTION ONLY. DO NOT TURN TO ANY OTHER SECTION IN THE TEST.   STOP

SECTION 3

Time—25 Minutes
20 Questions

Directions: For this section, solve each problem and decide which is the best of the choices given. Fill in the corresponding oval on the answer sheet. You may use any available space for scratchwork.

Notes:

(1) Calculator use is permitted.

(2) All numbers used are real numbers.

(3) Figures are provided for some problems. All figures are drawn to scale and lie in a plane UNLESS otherwise indicated.

(4) Unless otherwise specified, the domain of any function f is assumed to be the set of all real numbers x for which $f(x)$ is a real number.

Information

$A = \frac{1}{2}bh$ $\qquad$ $c^2 = a^2 + b^2$ $\qquad$ Special Right Triangles $\qquad$ $A = \pi r^2$ $\qquad$ $C = 2\pi r$ $\qquad$ $V = \ell wh$ $\qquad$ $V = \pi r^2 h$ $\qquad$ $A = \ell w$

The sum of the degree measures of the angles in a triangle is 180.
The number of degrees of arc in a circle is 360.
A straight angle has a degree measure of 180.

---

1. Which of the following must be equal to 30 percent of x?

   (A) $\dfrac{3x}{1,000}$

   (B) $\dfrac{3x}{100}$

   (C) $\dfrac{3x}{10}$

   (D) $3x$

   (E) $30x$

2. $(2 \times 10^4) + (5 \times 10^3) + (6 \times 10^2) + (4 \times 10^1) =$

   (A) 2,564

   (B) 20,564

   (C) 25,064

   (D) 25,604

   (E) 25,640

GO ON TO THE NEXT PAGE

3. On the number line shown above, the length of YZ is how much greater than the length of XY?

(A) 3
(B) 4
(C) 5
(D) 6
(E) 7

4. If $2^{x+1} = 16$, what is the value of x?

(A) 2
(B) 3
(C) 4
(D) 5
(E) 6

Note: Figure not drawn to scale.

5. In the figure above, what is the value of a?

(A) 50
(B) 55
(C) 60
(D) 65
(E) 70

6. A machine labels 150 bottles in 20 minutes. At this rate, how many minutes does it take to label 60 bottles?

(A) 2
(B) 4
(C) 6
(D) 8
(E) 10

7. If $x - 1$ is a multiple of 3, which of the following must be the next greater multiple of 3?

(A) x
(B) $x + 2$
(C) $x + 3$
(D) $3x$
(E) $3x - 3$

8. When x is divided by 5, the remainder is 4. When x is divided by 9, the remainder is 0. Which of the following is a possible value for x?

(A) 24
(B) 45
(C) 59
(D) 109
(E) 144

9. In triangle ABC, $AB = 6$, $BC = 12$, and $AC = x$. Which of the following cannot be a value of x?

(A) 6
(B) 7
(C) 8
(D) 9
(E) 10

GO ON TO THE NEXT PAGE

10. The average of 20, 70, and x is 40. If the average of 20, 70, x, and y is 50, then $y =$

    (A) 30
    (B) 60
    (C) 70
    (D) 80
    (E) 100

NUMBER OF BOOKS BORROWED
FROM MIDVILLE LIBRARY

11. According to the graph above, the number of books borrowed during the month of January was what fraction of the total number of books borrowed during the first six months of the year?

    (A) $\dfrac{1}{8}$

    (B) $\dfrac{1}{7}$

    (C) $\dfrac{1}{6}$

    (D) $\dfrac{3}{16}$

    (E) $\dfrac{5}{12}$

12. If 40 percent of r is equal to s, then which of the following is equal to 10 percent of r?

    (A) $4s$
    (B) $2s$
    (C) $\dfrac{s}{2}$
    (D) $\dfrac{s}{4}$
    (E) $\dfrac{s}{8}$

13. In the figure above, which of the following must be true?

    (A) $x + r = z + y$
    (B) $x + r = z - y$
    (C) $x - y = z + r$
    (D) $x - r = y - z$
    (E) $x + y = z + r$

14. If a *prifact* number is a nonprime integer such that each factor of the integer other than 1 and the integer itself is a prime number, which of the following is a *prifact* number?

    (A) 12
    (B) 18
    (C) 21
    (D) 24
    (E) 28

GO ON TO THE NEXT PAGE

15. If $3x + y = 14$, and x and y are positive integers, all of the following could be the value of $x + y$ EXCEPT

 (A)   4

 (B)   6

 (C)   8

 (D) 10

 (E) 12

16. A certain deck of cards contains r cards. After the cards are distributed evenly among s people, 8 cards are left over. In terms of r and s, how many cards did each person receive?

 (A) $\dfrac{s}{8 - r}$

 (B) $\dfrac{r - s}{8}$

 (C) $\dfrac{r - 8}{s}$

 (D) $s - 8r$

 (E) $rs - 8$

17. If d is an integer, which of the following CANNOT be an integer?

 (A) $\dfrac{d}{2}$

 (B) $\dfrac{\sqrt{d}}{2}$

 (C) $2d$

 (D) $d\sqrt{2}$

 (E) $d + 2$

18. In the figure above, the area of triangle ABC is 6. If $BC = CD$, what is the area of triangle ACD?

 (A)   6

 (B)   8

 (C)   9

 (D) 10

 (E) 12

GO ON TO THE NEXT PAGE

19. What is the minimum number of rectangular tiles, each 12 centimeters by 18 centimeters, needed to completely cover five flat rectangular surfaces, each 60 centimeters by 180 centimeters?

(A) 50
(B) 100
(C) 150
(D) 200
(E) 250

20. In the figure above, side *AB* of square *ABDE* is extended to point *C*. If *BC* = 8 and *CD* = 10, what is the perimeter of triangle *ACD*?

(A) $18 + 6\sqrt{2}$
(B) $24 + 6\sqrt{2}$
(C) $26 + 6\sqrt{2}$
(D) 30
(E) 36

SECTION 4

Time—25 Minutes
24 Questions

Directions: For each of the following questions, choose the best answer and darken the corresponding oval on the answer sheet.

Each sentence below has one or two blanks, each blank indicating that something has been omitted. Beneath the sentence are five words or sets of words labeled A through E. Choose the word or set of words that, when inserted in the sentence, best fits the meaning of the sentence as a whole.

EXAMPLE:

Today's small, portable computers contrast markedly with the earliest electronic computers, which were ------- .

(A) effective
(B) invented
(C) useful
(D) destructive
(E) enormous   Ⓐ Ⓑ Ⓒ Ⓓ ●

---

1. The rain is so rare and the land is so ------- that few of the men who work there see much ------ in farming.

    (A) plentiful . . . hope
    (B) barren . . . difficulty
    (C) productive . . . profit
    (D) infertile . . . future
    (E) dry . . . danger

2. The principal declared that the students were not simply ignoring the rules, but openly ------- them.

    (A) accepting
    (B) redressing
    (C) reviewing
    (D) flouting
    (E) discussing

3. Some critics believe that the ------- of modern art came with dadaism, while others insist that the movement was a ------- .

    (A) zenith . . . sham
    (B) pinnacle . . . triumph
    (C) decline . . . disaster
    (D) acceptance . . . success
    (E) originality . . . fiasco

4. She would never have believed that her article was so ------- were it not for the ------- of correspondence that followed its publication.

    (A) interesting . . . dearth
    (B) inflammatory . . . lack
    (C) controversial . . . spate
    (D) commonplace . . . influx
    (E) insignificant . . . volume

5. The writings of the philosopher Descartes are ------- ; many readers have difficulty following his complex, intricately woven arguments.

    (A) generic
    (B) trenchant
    (C) reflective
    (D) elongated
    (E) abstruse

GO ON TO THE NEXT PAGE ⟩

> **Directions:** The passages below are followed by questions based on their content; questions following a pair of related passages may also be based on the relationship between the paired passages. Answer the questions on the basis of what is <u>stated</u> or <u>implied</u> in the passages and in any introductory material that may be provided.

Questions 6–7 refer to the following passage.

One of the hazards of swimming in the ocean is an unexpected encounter with a jellyfish. Contact with the poison in a jellyfish's tentacles can result in sharp, lingering pain,
(5) or even death if the person stung is highly allergic. While everyone, including the jellyfish, would like to avoid these encounters, they are not uncommon. This is hardly surprising considering that jellyfish live in every ocean in
(10) the world and have done so for more than 650 million years. The animals are likely so widespread because of their extreme adaptability—they are quite hardy and can withstand a wide range of temperatures and conditions in
(15) their environment.

6. The author uses the phrase "including the jellyfish" (lines 6–7) in order to

   (A) introduce a small note of humor to an otherwise serious discussion
   (B) encourage the reader's sympathy for the jellyfish
   (C) ridicule humans' fear of jellyfish
   (D) emphasize the danger that jellyfish pose for swimmers
   (E) contrast the jellyfish's reaction to the encounter to that of humans

7. According to the passage, encounters between humans and jellyfish in the ocean are relatively common because jellyfish

   (A) are more than 650 million years old
   (B) live in all the world's oceans
   (C) are extremely robust
   (D) have poisonous tentacles
   (E) can endure a range of temperatures

GO ON TO THE NEXT PAGE

Questions 8–9 refer to the following passage.

Connecting the northern frontier of
Pakistan with Afghanistan, the Khyber Pass
is one of the most noteworthy mountain
passes in the world. At its narrowest point in
(5) the north, the pass is walled on either side by
precipitous cliffs up to 300 meters in height,
while the pass itself is only 3 meters wide.
Because it is only 53 kilometers long, the Pass
offers the best land route between India and
(10) Pakistan. This has led to a long and often violent history—conquering armies have used the
Khyber as an entry point for their invasions of
India, Pakistan, and Afghanistan. Today there
are two highways that snake their way through
(15) the Khyber pass, one for motor traffic and
another for traditional caravans.

8. Which of the following topics is NOT
    addressed by the passage?

    (A) the origin of the pass
    (B) the countries that border the pass
    (C) the length of the pass
    (D) the role of the pass in history
    (E) the uses of the pass today

9. In line 14, the word "snake" most directly
    emphasizes the

    (A) function of the Khyber Pass as a means
         to connect two points
    (B) danger of crossing the Khyber Pass
    (C) Khyber Pass as a direct route through the
         Hindu Kush mountains
    (D) relatively short length of the Khyber
         Pass
    (E) winding quality of the Khyber Pass

GO ON TO THE NEXT PAGE

Questions 10–16 refer to the following passage.

In this excerpt, a Nobel Prize–winning scientist discusses ways of thinking about extremely long periods of time.

There is one fact about the origin of life which is reasonably certain. Whenever and wherever it happened, it started a very long time ago, so long ago that it is extremely difficult to
(5) form any realistic idea of such vast stretches of time. The shortness of human life necessarily limits the span of direct personal recollection.

Human culture has given us the illusion that our memories go further back than that.
(10) Before writing was invented, the experience of earlier generations, embodied in stories, myths, and moral precepts to guide behavior, was passed down verbally or, to a lesser extent, in pictures, carvings, and statues. Writing
(15) has made more precise and more extensive the transmission of such information and, in recent times, photography has sharpened our images of the immediate past. Even so, we have difficulty in contemplating steadily
(20) the march of history, from the beginnings of civilization to the present day, in such a way that we can truly experience the slow passage of time. Our minds are not built to deal comfortably with periods as long as hundreds or
(25) thousands of years.

Yet when we come to consider the origin of life, the time scales we must deal with make the whole span of human history seem but the blink of an eyelid. There is no simple way to
(30) adjust one's thinking to such vast stretches of time. The immensity of time passed is beyond our ready comprehension. One can only construct an impression of it from indirect and incomplete descriptions, just as a blind man
(35) laboriously builds up, by touch and sound, a picture of his immediate surroundings.

The customary way to provide a convenient framework for one's thoughts is to compare the age of the universe with the length of a
(40) single earthly day. Perhaps a better comparison, along the same lines, would be to equate the age of our earth with a single week. On such a scale the age of the universe, since the Big Bang, would be about two or three weeks. The oldest
(45) macroscopic fossils (those from the start of the Cambrian* Period would have been alive just one day ago. Modern man would have appeared in the last 10 seconds and agriculture in the last one or two. Odysseus** would have lived only
(50) half a second before the present time.

Even this comparison hardly makes the longer time scale comprehensible to us. Another alternative is to draw a linear map of time, with the different events marked on
(55) it. The problem here is to make the line long enough to show our own experience on a reasonable scale, and yet short enough for convenient reproduction and examination. But perhaps the most vivid method is to compare
(60) time to the lines of print themselves. Let us make a 200-page book equal in length to the time from the start of the Cambrian to the present; that is, about 600 million years. Then each full page will represent roughly three mil-
(65) lion years, each line about ninety thousand years, and each letter or small space about fifteen hundred years. The origin of the earth would be about seven books ago and the origin of the universe (which has been dated only
(70) approximately) ten or so books before that. Almost the whole of recorded human history would be covered by the last two or three letters of the book.

If you now turn back the pages of the book,
(75) slowly reading *one letter at a time*—remember, each letter is fifteen hundred years—then this may convey to you something of the immense

GO ON TO THE NEXT PAGE ⇨

stretches of time we shall have to consider. On this scale the span of your own life would be (80) less than the width of a comma.

*Cambrian: the earliest period in the Paleozoic era, beginning about 600 million years ago.

**Odysseus: the most famous Greek hero of antiquity; he is the hero of Homer's *The Odyssey*, which describes the aftermath of the Trojan War (ca. 1200 B.C.).

10. The phrase "to a lesser extent" in line 13, indicates that before the invention of writing, the wisdom of earlier generations was

(A) rejected by recent generations when portrayed in pictures, carvings, or statues

(B) passed down orally, or not at all

(C) transmitted more frequently by spoken word than by other means

(D) based on illusory memories that turned fact into fiction

(E) more strongly grounded in science than in the arts

11. The author most likely describes the impact of writing (lines 14–16) in order to

(A) illustrate the limitations of the human memory

(B) provide an example of how cultures transmit information

(C) indicate how primitive preliterate cultures were

(D) refute an opinion about the origin of human civilization

(E) explain the difference between historical facts and myth

12. The word "ready" in line 32 most nearly means

(A) set

(B) agreeable

(C) immediate

(D) apt

(E) willing

13. The analogy of the "blind man" (line 34) is presented primarily to show that

(A) humans are unable to comprehend long periods of time

(B) myths and legends fail to give an accurate picture of the past

(C) human history is only a fraction of the time since life began

(D) humans refuse to learn the lessons of the past

(E) long periods of time can only be understood indirectly

14. In lines 42–46, the author mentions the Big Bang and the Cambrian Period in order to demonstrate which point?

(A) The age of the earth is best understood using the time scale of a week.

(B) Agriculture was a relatively late development in human history.

(C) No fossil record exists before the Cambrian Period.

(D) Convenient time scales do not adequately represent the age of the earth.

(E) The customary framework for thinking about the age of the universe should be discarded permanently.

GO ON TO THE NEXT PAGE

15. According to lines 53–58, one difficulty of using a linear representation of time is that

(A) linear representations of time do not meet accepted scientific standards of accuracy

(B) prehistoric eras overlap each other, making linear representation deceptive

(C) the more accurate the scale, the more difficult the map is to copy and study

(D) there are too many events to represent on a single line

(E) our knowledge of pre-Cambrian time is insufficient to construct an accurate linear map

16. The author of this passage discusses several kinds of time scales primarily in order to illustrate the

(A) difficulty of assigning precise dates to past events

(B) variety of choices faced by scientists investigating the origin of life

(C) evolution of efforts to comprehend the passage of history

(D) immensity of time since life began on earth

(E) development of the technology of communication

GO ON TO THE NEXT PAGE

Questions 17–24 refer to the following passage.

The following excerpt is from a speech delivered in 1873 by Susan B. Anthony, a leader in the women's rights movement of the 19th century.

Friends and fellow-citizens: I stand before you tonight under indictment for the alleged crime of having voted at the last Presidential election, without having a lawful right to vote.
(5) It shall be my work this evening to prove to you that in thus voting, I not only committed no crime, but, instead, simply exercised my citizen's rights, guaranteed to me and all United States citizens by the National Constitution,
(10) beyond the power of any State to deny.

The preamble of the Federal Constitution says: "We, the people of the United States, in order to form a more perfect union, establish justice, insure domestic tranquillity, provide
(15) for the common defense, promote the general welfare, and secure the blessings of liberty to ourselves and our posterity, do ordain and establish this Constitution for the United States of America."
(20) It was we, the people; not we, the white male citizens; nor yet we, the male citizens; but we, the whole people, who formed the Union. And we formed it, not to give the blessings of liberty, but to secure them; not to the half of
(25) ourselves and the half of our posterity, but to the whole people—
women as well as men. And it is a downright mockery to talk to women of their enjoyment of the blessings of liberty while they are denied
(30) the use of the only means of securing them provided by this democratic-republican government—the ballot.

For any State to make sex a qualification that must ever result in the disfranchisement* of
(35) one entire half of the people is a violation of the supreme law of the land. By it the blessings of liberty are forever withheld from women and their female posterity. To them this government

had no just powers derived from the consent of
(40) the governed. To them this government is not a democracy. It is not a republic. It is an odious aristocracy; a hateful oligarchy of sex; this oligarchy of sex, which makes father, brothers,
(45) husband, sons, the oligarchs over the mother and sisters, the wife and daughters of every household—which ordains all men sovereigns, all women subjects, carries dissension, discord and rebellion into every home of the nation.
(50) Webster, Worcester and Bouvier all define a citizen to be a person in the United States, entitled to vote and hold office.

The one question left to be settled now is: Are women persons? And I hardly believe any
(55) of our opponents will have the hardihood to say they are not. Being persons, then, women are citizens; and no State has a right to make any law, or to enforce any old law, that shall abridge their privileges or immunities. Hence,
(60) every discrimination against women in the constitutions and laws of the several States is today null and void, precisely as is every one against Negroes.

disfranchisement: to deprive of the right to vote.

17. The author addresses her "fellow citizens" (line 1) primarily in order to

(A) limit her intended audience to those who are citizens

(B) establish a spirit of good-natured cooperation

(C) irritate her audience, since they do not consider her a citizen

(D) introduce an important element of one of her main arguments

(E) make it clear that she intends to address only men

GO ON TO THE NEXT PAGE ▷

18. In the first paragraph, Anthony states that her action in voting was

    (A) illegal, but morally justified

    (B) the result of her keen interest in national politics

    (C) legal, if the Constitution is interpreted correctly

    (D) an illustration of the need for a women's rights movement

    (E) illegal, but worthy of leniency

19. Which best captures the meaning of the word "promote" in line 15?

    (A) further

    (B) organize

    (C) publicize

    (D) commend

    (E) motivate

20. By saying "we, the people . . . the whole people, who formed the Union" (lines 20–22), Anthony means that

    (A) the founders of the nation conspired to deprive women of their rights

    (B) some male citizens are still being denied basic rights

    (C) the role of women in the founding of the nation is generally ignored

    (D) society is endangered when women are deprived of basic rights

    (E) all people deserve to enjoy the rights guaranteed by the Constitution

21. By "the half of our posterity" (lines 24–25), Anthony means

    (A) the political legacy passed down from her era

    (B) future generations of male United States citizens

    (C) those who wish to enjoy the blessings of liberty

    (D) current and future opponents of the women's rights movement

    (E) future members of the democratic-republican government

22. In the fourth paragraph, lines 33–52, Anthony's argument rests mainly on the strategy of convincing her audience that

    (A) any state which denies women the vote undermines its status as a democracy

    (B) women deprived of the vote will eventually raise a rebellion

    (C) the nation will remain an aristocracy if the status of women does not change

    (D) women's rights issues should be debated in every home

    (E) even an aristocracy cannot survive without the consent of the governed

GO ON TO THE NEXT PAGE

23. The word "hardihood" in line 55 could best be replaced by

    (A) endurance
    (B) vitality
    (C) nerve
    (D) opportunity
    (E) stupidity

24. When Anthony warns that "no State . . . shall abridge their privileges" (lines 57–59), she means that

    (A) women should be allowed to live a life of privilege
    (B) women on trial cannot be forced to give up their immunity
    (C) every state should repeal its outdated laws
    (D) governments may not deprive citizens of their rights
    (E) the rights granted to women must be decided by the people, not the state

IF YOU FINISH BEFORE TIME IS CALLED, YOU MAY CHECK YOUR WORK ON THIS SECTION ONLY. DO NOT TURN TO ANY OTHER SECTION IN THE TEST.

STOP

SECTION 5

Time—25 Minutes
18 Questions

Directions: For this section, solve each problem and decide which is the best of the choices given. Fill in the corresponding oval on the answer sheet. You may use any available space for scratchwork.

Notes:

(1) Calculator use is permitted.

(2) All numbers used are real numbers.

(3) Figures are provided for some problems. All figures are drawn to scale and lie in a plane UNLESS otherwise indicated.

(4) Unless otherwise specified, the domain of any function f is assumed to be the set of all real numbers x for which $f(x)$ is a real number.

$A = \frac{1}{2}bh$ $c^2 = a^2 + b^2$ Special Right Triangles $A = \pi r^2$ $V = \ell wh$ $V = \pi r^2 h$ $A = \ell w$
$C = 2\pi r$

The sum of the degree measures of the angles in a triangle is 180.
The number of degrees of arc in a circle is 360.
A straight angle has a degree measure of 180.

1. If $100 + x = 100$, then $x =$

   (A) −100
   (B) −10
   (C)   0
   (D)   10
   (E) 100

2. Set X is the set of all odd numbers, and set Y is the set of all negative numbers. Which of the following represents the intersection of X and Y?

   (A) all odd numbers
   (B) all negative odd numbers
   (C) all negative numbers
   (D) all real numbers
   (E) all positive numbers

GO ON TO THE NEXT PAGE ⟹

3. If $x < y < 0$, which of the following is greater than $\frac{y}{x}$?

   (A) 0

   (B) $\frac{x}{y}$

   (C) $\frac{-x}{y}$

   (D) $\frac{-y}{x}$

   (E) $\frac{y}{2x}$

5. If $f(x) = \frac{(3x^2 - 9)}{(x + 1)}$, what is the value of $f(3)$?

   (A) $\frac{3}{2}$

   (B) 3

   (C) $\frac{9}{2}$

   (D) 6

   (E) 9

4. In the figure above, circular region D represents households with dogs, circular region C represents households with cats, and circular region F represents households with fish. What does the crosshatched region represent?

   (A) households with dogs, but no cats or fish

   (B) households with cats and fish, but no dogs

   (C) households with dogs, cats, and fish

   (D) households with dogs and cats, but no fish

   (E) households with dogs and fish, some of which may have cats

6. In the figure above, the length of CD is twice the length of AB. What is the value of h?

   (A) 2

   (B) 3

   (C) 4

   (D) 5

   (E) 6

GO ON TO THE NEXT PAGE

7. The percent decrease from 12 to 9 is equal to the percent decrease from 40 to what number?

(A)   3

(B)   10

(C)   25

(D)   30

(E)   36

8. For a group of x people, Joe ordered 5 pizza pies, each of which was cut into 12 slices. Each person was originally supposed to have an equal number of slices. However, 4 people did not want any pizza, so when the pizza was distributed among the remaining people, each of them received 4 more slices. Which of the following equations could be used to find x?

(A) $x^2 - 4x - 60 = 0$

(B) $x^2 - 4x + 60 = 0$

(C) $x^2 + 4x - 60 = 0$

(D) $x^2 + 4x + 60 = 0$

(E) $x^2 - 16x - 240 = 0$

GO ON TO THE NEXT PAGE

Directions: For Student-Produced Response questions 9–18, use the grids at the bottom of the answer sheet page on which you have answered questions 1–8.

Each of the remaining 10 questions requires you to solve the problem and enter your answer by marking the ovals in the special grid, as shown in the example below. You may use any available space for scratch work.

Answer: 1.25 or $\frac{5}{4}$ or 5/4

Write answer in boxes.

Grid-in result →

Either position is correct.

Fraction line
Decimal point

You may start your answers in any column, space permitting. Columns not needed should be left blank.

- It is recommended, though not required, that you write your answer in the boxes at the top of the columns. However, you will receive credit only for darkening the ovals correctly.

- Grid only one answer to a question, even though some problems have more than one correct answer.

- Darken no more than one oval in a column.

- No answers are negative.

- Mixed numbers cannot be gridded. For example: the number $1\frac{1}{4}$ must be gridded as 1.25 or 5/4.

(If | 1 | 1 | / | 4 | is gridded, it will be interpreted as $\frac{11}{4}$ not $1\frac{1}{4}$.)

- **Decimal Accuracy:** Decimal answers must be entered as accurately as possible. For example, if you obtain an answer such as 0.1666..., you should record the result as .166 or .167. **Less accurate values such as .16 or .17 are not acceptable.**

Acceptable ways to grid $\frac{1}{6}$ = .1666...

GO ON TO THE NEXT PAGE →

9. If $A = 2.54$ and $20B = A$, what is the value of B?

10. What is the perimeter of the figure shown above?

11. If $\frac{h}{3}$ and $\frac{h}{4}$ are integers, and if $75 < h < 100$, what is one possible value of h?

12. A retailer buys 16 shirts at \$4.50 each, and she sells all 16 shirts for \$6.75 each. If the retailer purchases more of these shirts at \$4.50 each, what is the greatest number of these shirts that she can buy with the profit she made on the 16 shirts?

13. Lines ℓ and m intersect at a point to form four angles. If one of the angles formed is 15 times as large as an adjacent angle, what is the measure, in degrees, of the smaller angle?

14. If $x = -4$ when $x^2 + 2xr + r^2 = 0$, what is the value of r?

15. Let $n \text{✳} = n^2 - n$ for all positive numbers n. What is the value of $\frac{1}{4}\text{✳} - \frac{1}{2}\text{✳}$?

16. What is the area of $\triangle ABC$ shown above?

17. If x is a factor of 8,100 and if x is an odd integer, what is the greatest possible value of x?

18. In a certain class, $\frac{1}{2}$ of the male students and $\frac{2}{3}$ of the female students speak French. If there are $\frac{3}{4}$ as many girls as boys in the class, what fraction of the entire class speaks French?

IF YOU FINISH BEFORE TIME IS CALLED, YOU MAY CHECK YOUR WORK ON THIS SECTION ONLY. DO NOT TURN TO ANY OTHER SECTION IN THE TEST.

STOP

SECTION 6
Time—25 Minutes
35 Questions

Directions: For each question in this section, select the best answer from among the choices given and fill in the corresponding oval on the answer sheet.

The following sentences test correctness and effectiveness of expression. Part of each sentence or the entire sentence is underlined; beneath each sentence are five ways of phrasing the underlined material. Choice A repeats the original phrasing; the other four choices are different. If you think the original phrasing produces a better sentence than any of the alternatives, select choice A; if not, select one of the other choices.

In making your selection, follow the requirements of standard written English; that is, pay attention to grammar, choice of words, sentence construction, and punctuation. Your selection should result in the most effective sentence—clear and precise, without awkwardness or ambiguity.

EXAMPLE:

Every apple in the baskets <u>are ripe and labeled according to the date it was picked</u>.

(A) are ripe and labeled according to the date it was picked
(B) is ripe and labeled according to the date it was picked
(C) are ripe and labeled according to the date they were picked
(D) is ripe and labeled according to the date they were picked
(E) are ripe and labeled as to the date it was picked

ANSWER:

Ⓐ ● Ⓒ Ⓓ Ⓔ

1. <u>Arranged as an event for funding a new wing for the art museum</u>, the museum's Board of Directors organized a fundraiser for the construction of one.

    (A) Arranged as an event to for funding a new wing for the art museum
    (B) Having been arranged as an event to fund a new wing for the art museum
    (C) A new wing for the art museum needed an event for funding
    (D) Although an event for funding a new wing for the art museum
    (E) Realizing that the art museum needed funding for a new wing

2. One of the most popular broadcasters on the evening news is a retired <u>politician; the one with nearly</u> as many fans is an executive recently retired from the film industry.

    (A) politician; the one with nearly
    (B) politician; near one with
    (C) politician, the one with nearly
    (D) politician, and also the one with near
    (E) politician; although the one with nearly

GO ON TO THE NEXT PAGE

3. Although the architects created a new earthquake-proof structural design, they <u>had refused to patent nor otherwise benefiting</u> from the design plans.

(A) had refused to patent nor otherwise benefiting

(B) had refused to patent or otherwise benefit

(C) refused to patent or otherwise benefit

(D) refuse to patent or otherwise benefit

(E) refused to patent or otherwise benefiting

4. Oscar Wilde was <u>almost as brilliant a novelist as he was at writing plays</u>.

(A) almost as brilliant a novelist as he was at writing plays

(B) almost brilliant at writing novels and plays

(C) almost equally brilliant, whether a novelist or a playwright

(D) almost as brilliant a novelist as he was a playwright

(E) a brilliant novelist, with almost as much brilliance as a playwright

5. Examining the sale offers in the catalogue, <u>the phrases</u> "while supplies last" and "get it while it's hot" are designed to encourage consumers to order the products immediately.

(A) the phrases

(B) the slogans

(C) one sees that the phrases

(D) although one saw the phrases

(E) one may have noticed phrases

6. <u>In professional soccer, players kick the ball sharply and accurately; however in other sports their technique is not quite so effective.</u>

(A) In professional soccer, players kick the ball sharply and accurately; however in other sports their technique is not quite so effective.

(B) Most professional soccer players kick the ball sharply and accurately, however in other sports their technique is not quite so effective.

(C) Although in other sports their technique is not quite so effective, most professional soccer players, however, kick the ball sharply and accurately.

(D) Most professional soccer players which kick the ball sharply and accurately do not have such effective technique in other sports.

(E) Most professional soccer players kick the ball sharply and accurately and in other sports their technique is not so effective.

7. The changing color of autumn leaves has a unique fascination for those people <u>which have an understanding of life cycles in them</u>.

(A) which have an understanding of life cycles in them

(B) who see the life cycles in them

(C) which have seen life cycles in them

(D) who understand that they have life cycles

(E) who see about them

GO ON TO THE NEXT PAGE ⟹

8. <u>The traffic rules were ignored by each of us,
   failing to appreciate their role in ensuring
   safety.</u>

   (A) The traffic rules were ignored by each
       of us, failing to appreciate their role in
       ensuring safety.

   (B) Each of us ignored traffic rules, because
       we failed to appreciate their role in
       ensuring safety.

   (C) Traffic rules, ignored by each of us, fail
       to appreciate their role in ensuring safety.

   (D) Failing to appreciate their role in ensur-
       ing safety, traffic rules were ignored by
       each of us.

   (E) Traffic rules ignored by each of us, fail-
       ing to appreciate their role in ensuring
       safety.

9. The meaning of his words was even more
   elusive in his own country than <u>either Europe
   or Latin America</u>.

   (A) either Europe or Latin America

   (B) either Europe or in Latin America

   (C) either in Europe or Latin America

   (D) in either Europe or in Latin America

   (E) in either Europe or Latin America

10. It was primarily when I visited the seashore
    that I felt nostalgic for my childhood home,
    <u>growing up on a small island</u>.

    (A) growing up on a small island

    (B) as I had grown up on a small island

    (C) as on a small island I grow up

    (D) which is on a small island

    (E) on a small island growing up

11. By 1975, 12 percent of the households with
    televisions were cable <u>subscribers, and
    established hundreds of cable stations there
    were</u>.

    (A) subscribers, and established hundreds of
        cable stations there were

    (B) subscribers, and hundreds of cable sta-
        tions were established

    (C) subscribers, and there were established
        hundreds of cable stations

    (D) subscribers plus hundreds of cable sta-
        tions established

    (E) subscribers and hundreds of cable
        stations

GO ON TO THE NEXT PAGE

Directions: The following sentences test your ability to recognize grammar and usage errors. Each sentence contains either a single error or no error at all. No sentence contains more than one error. The error, if there is one, is underlined and lettered. If the sentence contains an error, select the one underlined part that must be changed to make the sentence correct. If the sentence is correct, select choice E. In choosing answers, follow the requirements of standard written English.

EXAMPLE:

<u>Whenever</u> one is driving late at night, <u>you</u> must take extra precautions <u>against</u>
   A   B   C

falling asleep <u>at the wheel.</u> <u>No error</u>
             D   E

Ⓐ ● Ⓒ Ⓓ Ⓔ

---

12. <u>As Picasso</u> matured as a painter, his <u>use of</u> shapes
   A   B

   <u>became</u> bolder, more abstract, and
   C

   <u>they can astonish people.</u> <u>No error</u>
           D   E

13. The chemical plant is already <u>such a</u> danger that
                            A

   <u>it became</u> imperative <u>to find other ways</u> of
   B   C

   developing effective pesticides <u>for</u> use in gardens.
                              D

   <u>No error</u>
   E

14. <u>Due to</u> <u>their</u> recent rapid sales growth, retail
   A   B

   stores <u>are increasing</u> their <u>stock of</u> popular items.
            C   D

   <u>No error</u>
   E

15. The <u>lyric</u> novels of Virginia Woolf <u>which eerily</u>
      A   B

   <u>hint at</u> the despair <u>of her</u> later life. <u>No error</u>
   C   D   E

16. With <u>more than</u> 150 associated countries, the
        A

   United Nations owes <u>their</u> name <u>to a</u> worldwide
                       B   C

   membership <u>that oversees</u> international treaties
               D

   and human rights. <u>No error</u>
                   E

17. <u>Walking along</u> the empty boardwalk, I <u>could hear</u>
   A   B

   the lapping of water against the docks as <u>well as</u>
                                    C

   the sound of Jake and Kelsey talking softly

   <u>as he approached.</u> <u>No error</u>
   D   E

18. <u>At the stoplight,</u> Hiam, <u>impatient</u> to be home on
   A   B

   that <u>rainy</u> night, drummed his fingers
        C

   <u>at the wheel.</u> <u>No error</u>
   D   E

GO ON TO THE NEXT PAGE ⇨

19. If you <u>surround</u> the roots of your new rose with a
          A
    <u>generously</u> mixture of mulch and compost, you
          B
    <u>will provide</u> the roots the space to <u>grow</u> healthily.
          C   D
    <u>No error</u>
          E

20. Kelly <u>is proud of</u> <u>her</u> own abilities <u>to mediate</u>
              A   B   C
    disputes <u>more than</u> any of her other strengths.
                  D
    <u>No error</u>
          E

21. We <u>had drove</u> no more than fifty yards <u>from our</u>
           A   B
    parking spot when it <u>became apparent</u> that Shelly
                                C
    <u>had left</u> her purse behind at the steakhouse.
        D
    <u>No error</u>
          E

22. <u>Most of</u> the small country stores in the United
        A
    States <u>are</u> in isolated, thinly populated areas where
            B
    there are <u>hardly no</u> supermarkets <u>within easy</u>
                   C   D
    driving distance. <u>No error</u>
                           E

23. <u>Working with</u> the ease and skill of the true
        A
    professional, Lehrmann quickly outlined a <u>sketch</u>
                                                   B
    of the young <u>but</u> experienced skater who was
                     C
    <u>posing for</u> her. <u>No error</u>
        D   E

24. Many historians have <u>written about</u> the Roosevelt
                              A
    family, but <u>never before</u> <u>has</u> the characters of the
                     B   C
    family members been <u>so skillfully</u> evaluated.
                             D
    <u>No error</u>
        E

25. <u>No matter</u> how <u>attentive</u> Mark applies himself to
        A   B
    his studies, he <u>never seems</u> to get the grades he
                         C
    <u>needs</u> to make the Dean's List. <u>No error</u>
        D   E

26. There has always been a <u>great deal of</u> antipathy
                                 A
    between <u>Sarah and I</u> <u>because we</u> have opposing
                 B   C
    opinions <u>about which</u> we are very outspoken.
                  D
    <u>No error</u>
        E

27. The extraordinary breath control <u>used by</u> students
                                          A
    of meditation to control stress and pain levels <u>is</u> a
                                                        B
    <u>benefit</u> to both <u>their</u> physical and mental well-
        C   D
    being. <u>No error</u>
               E

GO ON TO THE NEXT PAGE ⟹

28. A scientist at the institute <u>indicated that</u> an
                                        A
<u>unusually high</u> percentage of <u>their</u> funding <u>comes</u>
        B   C   D
from money donated to it by private

philanthropists. <u>No error</u>
                        E

29. The candidate, John Kallan, is of an <u>undetermined</u>
                                                    A
age, <u>and</u> he <u>uses</u> this ambiguity <u>to his benefit</u>.
        B   C   D
<u>No error</u>
E

> **<u>Directions</u>:** The following passage is an early draft of an essay. Some parts of the passage need to be rewritten.
>
> Read the passage and select the best answer for each question that follows. Some questions are about particular sentences or parts of sentences and ask you to improve sentence structure or word choice. Other questions ask you to consider organization and development. In choosing answers, follow the conventions of standard written English.

Questions 30–35 are based on the following passage.

(1) There is a duality in ballet that most people don't see. (2) Most often, it is seen only as beautifully graceful.

(3) First, ballet is tough physically. (4) Because the human body is not designed for ballet. (5) Dancers must perform steps that come from ballet's five fundamental positions in which dancers rotate their hips and legs unnaturally. (6) This makes dancers walk funny (you can always recognize dancers by the way they walk with their feet turning out instead of facing forward). (7) Unfortunately, it also often results in permanent injury.

(8) Ballet companies' financial struggles creating fierce competition between dancers for a place in a professional company. (9) Dancers often live below the poverty line, particularly as most companies pay by the dance season, which can last for as little as twenty weeks out of the year, instead of by year. (10) In general, most people who spend years training for their jobs stay in the same career until they retire at 65. (11) Not being the case with dancers, as ballet careers hardly ever extend beyond the mid-thirties, even though the dancers have trained since they were 5 years old. (12) Few retired dancers continue as ballet teachers or choreographers. (13) The vast majority find themselves unemployed in their mid-thirties.

30. Which of the following sentences is best inserted at the end of the first paragraph, after sentence 2?

   (A) But in reality, ballet is grueling, painful, and competitive.

   (B) Yet few people really appreciate that fact.

   (C) Missing, however, the extreme athleticism it requires.

   (D) Many types of dance share this quality.

   (E) Not every ballet dancer, however, dances for this reason.

31. Which of the following is the best way to revise the underlined portions of sentences 4 and 5 (reproduced below) in order to combine the sentences?

Because the human body is not designed <u>for ballet. Dancers must perform</u> steps that come from ballet's five fundamental positions in which dancers rotate their hips and legs unnaturally.

   (A) for ballet, it is difficult for dancers to perform

   (B) for ballet; dancers must perform

   (C) for ballet, making it difficult for dancers to perform

   (D) for ballet, their difficulty in performing

   (E) for ballet; therefore dancers must perform

GO ON TO THE NEXT PAGE ⟩

32. Which is the best sentence to insert before sentence 8 to begin the third paragraph?

    (A) Second, ballet is tough financially.
    (B) Secondly, ballet is competitive.
    (C) Furthermore, ballet dancers struggle financially.
    (D) In addition, ballet companies are difficult employers.
    (E) This is not the worst consequence, however.

33. In context, which is the best version of the underlined portion of sentence 8 (reproduced below)?

    Ballet companies' financial struggles <u>creating fierce competition</u> between dancers for a place in a professional company.

    (A) (As it is now)
    (B) compiling to create fiercely
    (C) created their fierce competition
    (D) create fierce competition
    (E) had created a fierce competition

34. In context, which is the best version of the underlined portion of sentence 11 (reproduced below)?

    <u>Not being the case with</u> dancers, as ballet careers hardly ever extend beyond the mid-thirties, even though the dancers have trained since they were 5 years old.

    (A) (As it is now)
    (B) Which is not true of
    (C) That model does not apply to
    (D) But not so for
    (E) And so also for

35. Which of the following is the best way to combine sentences 12 and 13 (reproduced below)?

    Few retired dancers continue as ballet teachers or choreographers. The vast majority find themselves unemployed in their mid-thirties.

    (A) Although a few retired dancers continue as ballet teachers or choreographers, and the vast majority find themselves unemployed in their mid-thirties.
    (B) A few retired dancers continue as ballet teachers or choreographers, but the vast majority find themselves unemployed in their mid-thirties.
    (C) However, few retired dancers continued as ballet teachers or choreographers although the vast majority unemployed in their mid-thirties.
    (D) A few retired dancers continue as ballet teachers or choreographers, the vast majority find themselves unemployed in their mid-thirties.
    (E) Few retired dancers continued as ballet teachers or choreographers vastly the majority are found unemployed in their mid-thirties.

IF YOU FINISH BEFORE TIME IS CALLED, YOU MAY CHECK YOUR WORK ON THIS SECTION ONLY. DO NOT TURN TO ANY OTHER SECTION IN THE TEST.

SECTION 7

Time—20 Minutes
19 Questions

Directions: For each of the following questions, choose the best answer and darken the corresponding oval on the answer sheet.

Each sentence below has one or two blanks, each blank indicating that something has been omitted. Beneath the sentence are five words or sets of words labeled A through E. Choose the word or set of words that, when inserted in the sentence, best fits the meaning of the sentence as a whole.

EXAMPLE:

Today's small, portable computers contrast markedly with the earliest electronic computers, which were -------.

(A) effective
(B) invented
(C) useful
(D) destructive
(E) enormous

---

1. The prisoner was ------- even though he presented evidence clearly proving that he was nowhere near the scene of the crime.

   (A) abandoned
   (B) indicted
   (C) exculpated
   (D) exhumed
   (E) rescinded

2. Many biologists are critical of the film's ------- premise that dinosaurs might one day return.

   (A) scientific
   (B) tacit
   (C) speculative
   (D) unwitting
   (E) ambiguous

3. It is ------- that people so capable of treachery and brutality should also exhibit such a tremendous capacity for heroism.

   (A) unfortunate
   (B) explicable
   (C) paradoxical
   (D) distressing
   (E) appalling

4. To ------- the seasonal migration of caribou, engineers ------- the trans-Alaska pipeline in over 500 locations to allow large animals access through the pipeline corridor.

   (A) banish . . . buried
   (B) preserve . . . elevated
   (C) admire . . . razed
   (D) prevent . . . erected
   (E) enable . . . delivered

GO ON TO THE NEXT PAGE

5. Most people today think of licorice as candy; however, the ------- properties of the licorice root were once used to treat coughs, digestive problems, and insomnia.

    (A) somnolent
    (B) basic
    (C) sweet
    (D) indelible
    (E) medicinal

6. To ------- free education for children with special needs, parents have had to ------- legislation guaranteeing services and programs targeted to those children.

    (A) ensure . . . demand
    (B) prevent . . . pass
    (C) assert . . . console
    (D) alleviate . . . request
    (E) provide . . . veto

GO ON TO THE NEXT PAGE

> **Directions:** The passages below are followed by questions based on their content; questions following a pair of related passages may also be based on the relationship between the paired passages. Answer the questions on the basis of what is <u>stated</u> or <u>implied</u> in the passages and in any introductory material that may be provided.

Questions 7–19 refer to the following passages.

The controversy over the authorship of Shakespeare's plays began in the 18th century and continues to this day. Here, the author of Passage 1 embraces the proposal that Francis Bacon actually wrote the plays, while the author of Passage 2 defends the traditional attribution to Shakespeare himself.

Passage 1

Anyone with more than a superficial knowledge of Shakespeare's plays must necessarily entertain some doubt concerning their true authorship. Can scholars honestly accept the
(5) idea that such masterworks were written by a shadowy actor with limited formal education and a social position that can most charitably be called "humble"? Obviously, the author of the plays must have traveled widely, yet there
(10) is no record that Shakespeare ever left his native England. Even more obviously, the real author had to have intimate knowledge of life within royal courts and palaces, yet Shakespeare was a commoner, with little firsthand experi-
(15) ence of the aristocracy. No, common sense tells us that the plays must have been written by someone with substantial expertise in the law, the sciences, classics, foreign languages, and the fine arts—someone, in other words,
(20) like Shakespeare's eminent contemporary, Sir Francis Bacon.

The first person to suggest that Bacon was the actual author of the plays was Reverend James Wilmot. Writing in 1785, Wilmot argued
(25) that someone of Shakespeare's educational background could hardly have produced works of such erudition and insight. But a figure like Bacon, a scientist and polymath* of legendary stature, would certainly have known about,
(30) for instance, the circulation of the blood as alluded to in *Coriolanus*. And as an aristocrat, Bacon would have possessed the familiarity with court life required to produce *Love's Labour's Lost*.
(35) Delia Bacon (no relation to Sir Francis) was next to make the case for Francis Bacon's authorship. In 1856, in collaboration with Nathaniel Hawthorne, she insisted that it was ridiculous to look for the creator of *Hamlet*
(40) among "that dirty, doggish group of players, who come into the scene [of the play Hamlet] summoned like a pack of hounds to his service." Ultimately, she concluded that the plays were actually composed by a committee consisting
(45) of Bacon, Edmund Spenser, Walter Raleigh, and several others.

Still, some might wonder why Bacon, if indeed the plays were wholly or partly his work, would not put his own name on them.
(50) But consider the political climate of England in Elizabethan times. Given that it would have been politically and personally damaging for a man of Bacon's position to associate himself with such controversial plays, it is quite under-
(55) standable that Bacon would hire a lowly actor to take the credit—and the consequences.

But perhaps the most convincing evidence of all comes from the postscript of a 1624 letter sent to Bacon by Sir Tobie Matthew. "The
(60) most prodigious wit that I ever knew . . . is your lordship's name," Matthew wrote, "though he be known by another." That name, of course, was William Shakespeare.

*polymath—a person of wide and varied learning

GO ON TO THE NEXT PAGE ⟩

Passage 2

Over the years, there have been an astonish-
(65) ing number of persons put forth as the "true
author" of Shakespeare's plays. Some critics
have even gone so far as to claim that only a
"committee" could have possessed the abun-
dance of talent and energy necessary to produce
(70) Shakespeare's thirty-seven plays. Among the
individual figures most seriously promoted
as "the real Shakespeare" is Sir Francis Bacon.
Apparently, the fact that Bacon wrote most of
his own work in academic Latin does nothing to
(75) deter those who would crown him the premier
stylist in the English language.

Although the entire controversy reeks of
scholarly gamesplaying, the issue underlying
it is worth considering: how could an unedu-
(80) cated actor create such exquisite works? But
the answer to that is easy. Shakespeare's dramatic gifts had little to do with encyclopedic
knowledge, complex ideas, or a fluency with
great systems of thought. Rather, Shakespeare's
(85) genius was one of common sense and perceptive intuition—a genius that grows not out of
book-learning, but out of a deep understanding of human nature and a keen grasp of basic
emotions, passions, and jealousies.

(90) One of the most common arguments
advanced by skeptics is that the degree of
familiarity with the law exhibited in a *Hamlet*
or a *Merchant of Venice* can only have been
achieved by a lawyer or other man of affairs.
(95) The grasp of law evidenced in these plays, however, is not a detailed knowledge of formal law,
but a more general understanding of so-called
"country law." Shakespeare was a landowner —
an extraordinary achievement in itself for an
(100) ill-paid Elizabethan actor—and so would have
been knowledgeable about legal matters related
to the buying, selling, and renting of real estate.
Evidence of such a common understanding of
land regulations can be found, for instance, in
(105) the gravedigging scene of *Hamlet*.

So no elaborate theories of intrigue and
secret identity are necessary to explain the
accomplishment of William Shakespeare.
Scholars who have made a career of ferreting
(110) out "alternative bards" may be reluctant to
admit it, but literary genius can flower in any
socioeconomic bracket. Shakespeare, in short,
was Shakespeare—an observation that one
would have thought was obvious to everyone.

7. In Passage 1, line 3, "entertain" most nearly
means

(A) amuse
(B) harbor
(C) occupy
(D) cherish
(E) engage

8. In Passage 1, the author draws attention to
Shakespeare's social standing as a "commoner"
(line 14) in order to cast doubt on the
Elizabethan actor's

(A) aptitude for writing poetically
(B) knowledge of foreign places and habits
(C) ability to support himself by playwriting
(D) familiarity with life among persons of
high rank
(E) understanding of the problems of
government

GO ON TO THE NEXT PAGE ▷

9. *Coriolanus* and *Love's Labour's Lost* are mentioned in Passage 1, lines 31–34 as examples of works that

(A) only Francis Bacon could have written

(B) exhibit a deep understanding of human nature

(C) resemble works written by Francis Bacon under his own name

(D) portray a broad spectrum of Elizabethan society

(E) reveal expertise more likely held by Bacon than Shakespeare

10. In Passage 1, the quotation from Delia Bacon (lines 40–43) conveys a sense of

(A) disdain for the disreputable vulgarity of Elizabethan actors

(B) resentment at the way Shakespeare's characters were portrayed

(C) regret that conditions for Elizabethan actors were not better

(D) doubt that Shakespeare could actually have created such unsavory characters

(E) disappointment at the incompetence of Elizabethan actors

11. The author of Passage 1 maintains that Bacon did not put his own name on the plays attributed to Shakespeare because he

(A) regarded writing as an unsuitable occupation for an aristocrat

(B) wished to protect himself from the effects of controversy

(C) preferred being known as a scientist and politician rather than as a writer

(D) did not want to associate himself with lowly actors

(E) sought to avoid the attention that fame brings

12. In the first paragraph of Passage 2, the author calls into question Bacon's likely ability to

(A) write in a language with which he was unfamiliar

(B) make the transition between scientific writing and playwriting

(C) produce the poetic language evident in the plays

(D) cooperate with other members of a committee

(E) single-handedly create thirty-seven plays

13. The word "premier" in Passage 2, line 75 most nearly means

(A) earliest

(B) influential

(C) inaugural

(D) greatest

(E) original

GO ON TO THE NEXT PAGE ⟩

14. In Passage 2, line 82, the word "encyclopedic" most nearly means

   (A) technical
   (B) comprehensive
   (C) abridged
   (D) disciplined
   (E) specialized

15. The author of Passage 2, cites Shakespeare's status as a landowner in order to

   (A) prove that Shakespeare was a success as a playwright
   (B) refute the claim that Shakespeare had little knowledge of aristocratic life
   (C) prove that Shakespeare didn't depend solely on acting for his living
   (D) dispute the notion that Shakespeare was a commoner
   (E) account for Shakespeare's apparent knowledge of the law

16. In Passage 2, lines 110–111, the author maintains that literary genius

   (A) is not dependent on a writer's external circumstances
   (B) must be based on an inborn comprehension of human nature
   (C) is enhanced by the suffering that poverty brings
   (D) frequently goes unrecognized among those of modest means and position
   (E) can be stifled by too much book-learning and academic training

17. The author of Passage 2 would probably respond to the speculation in the fourth paragraph of Passage 1 by pointing out that

   (A) Shakespeare's plays would not have seemed particularly controversial to Elizabethan audiences
   (B) the extent and range of Bacon's learning has been generally exaggerated
   (C) such scenarios are farfetched and unnecessary if one correctly understands Shakespeare's genius
   (D) Bacon would not have had the knowledge of the lower classes required to produce the plays
   (E) the claim implies that Shakespeare was disreputable when in fact he was a respectable landowner

GO ON TO THE NEXT PAGE

18. The author of Passage 1 would probably respond to the skepticism expressed in Passage 2, lines 73–76 by making which of the following statements?

   (A) The similarities between English and Latin make it plausible that one person could write well in both languages.

   (B) Plays written in Latin would not have been likely to attract a wide audience in Elizabethan England.

   (C) The premier stylist in the English language is more likely to have been an eminent scholar than an uneducated actor.

   (D) Writing the plays in Latin would have shielded Bacon from much of the political damage he wanted to avoid.

   (E) The style of the plays is notable mostly for the clarity of thought behind the lines rather than their musicality or beauty.

19. In Passage 2, line 113, "observation" most nearly means

   (A) inspection

   (B) measurement

   (C) research

   (D) comment

   (E) memorandum

IF YOU FINISH BEFORE TIME IS CALLED, YOU MAY CHECK YOUR WORK ON THIS SECTION ONLY. DO NOT TURN TO ANY OTHER SECTION IN THE TEST. STOP

SECTION 8

Time—20 Minutes
16 Questions

Directions: For this section, solve each problem and decide which is the best of the choices given. Fill in the corresponding oval on the answer sheet. You may use any available space for scratchwork.

Notes:

(1) Calculator use is permitted.

(2) All numbers used are real numbers.

(3) Figures are provided for some problems. All figures are drawn to scale and lie in a plane UNLESS otherwise indicated.

(4) Unless otherwise specified, the domain of any function f is assumed to be the set of all real numbers x for which $f(x)$ is a real number.

$A = \frac{1}{2}bh$ $c^2 = a^2 + b^2$ Special Right Triangles $A = \pi r^2$ $C = 2\pi r$ $V = \ell wh$ $V = \pi r^2 h$ $A = \ell w$

The sum of the degree measures of the angles in a triangle is 180.
The number of degrees of arc in a circle is 360.
A straight angle has a degree measure of 180.

1. If $p = -2$ and $q = 3$, then $p^3 q^2 + p^2 q =$

    (A) -84
    (B) -60
    (C) 36
    (D) 60
    (E) 84

Note: Figure not drawn to scale.

2. In the figure above, B is the midpoint of AC, and D is the midpoint of CE. If $AB = 5$ and $BD = 8$, what is the length of DE?

    (A) 3
    (B) 4
    (C) 5
    (D) 6
    (E) 8

GO ON TO THE NEXT PAGE ⇨

N	P
2	7
4	13
6	19
8	25

3. Which of the following equations describes the relationship of each pair of numbers (N, P) in the table above?

(A) $P = N + 5$

(B) $P = 2N + 3$

(C) $P = 2N + 5$

(D) $P = 3N + 1$

(E) $P = 3N - 1$

Note: Figure not drawn to scale.

4. In the figure above, MQ is a straight line. If PM = PN, what is the value of x?

(A) 30

(B) 45

(C) 60

(D) 75

(E) 90

5. Marty has exactly five blue pens, six black pens, and four red pens in his knapsack. If he pulls out one pen at random from his knapsack, what is the probability that the pen is either red or black?

(A) $\dfrac{1}{5}$

(B) $\dfrac{1}{3}$

(C) $\dfrac{1}{2}$

(D) $\dfrac{2}{3}$

(E) $\dfrac{11}{15}$

6. Two hot dogs and a soda cost $3.25. If three hot dogs and a soda cost $4.50, what is the cost of two sodas?

(A) $0.75

(B) $1.25

(C) $1.50

(D) $2.50

(E) $3.00

7. In the figure above, if $\ell \parallel m$, which of the following must be equal to a?

(A) $b + c$

(B) $b + e$

(C) $c + d$

(D) $d + e$

(E) $d + f$

GO ON TO THE NEXT PAGE ⟹

8. A certain phone call costs 75 cents for the first three minutes plus 15 cents for each additional minute. If the call lasted x minutes and x is an integer greater than 3, which of the following expresses the cost of the call, in dollars?

(A) $0.75(3) + 0.15x$

(B) $0.75(3) + 0.15(x + 3)$

(C) $0.75 + 0.15(3 - x)$

(D) $0.75 + 0.15(x - 3)$

(E) $0.75 + 0.15x$

9. The figure above shows a piece of wire in the shape of a semicircle. If the piece of wire is bent to form a circle without any of the wire overlapping, what is the area of the circle?

(A) 6π

(B) 9π

(C) 12π

(D) 18π

(E) 36π

10. If $a^2 - a = 72$, and b and n are integers such that $b^n = a$, which of the following CANNOT be a value for b?

(A) -8

(B) -2

(C) 2

(D) 3

(E) 9

11. In the standard xy-coordinate plane, the midpoint of $\overline{XY}$ is $(3, 4)$. If the coordinates of point X are $(0, 2)$, what are the coordinates of point Y?

(A) $(3, 2)$

(B) $(4, 3)$

(C) $(6, 6)$

(D) $(7, 6)$

(E) $(8, 2)$

12. If $4\sqrt{2x} - 2 = 16$, then $x =$

(A) -4

(B) -2

(C) 8

(D) $\dfrac{81}{8}$

(E) $8\dfrac{1}{4}$

GO ON TO THE NEXT PAGE

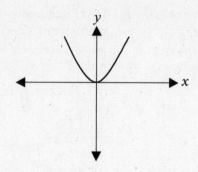

Note: Figure not drawn to scale.

13. If the above graph is $y = 3x^2$, which of the following is the graph of $y = -3x^2$?

(A)

(B)

(C)

(D)

(E)

14. What was the initial weight, in pounds, of a person who gained p pounds, then lost 8 pounds, and now weighs w pounds?

(A) $w + p + 8$

(B) $w + p - 8$

(C) $w - p + 8$

(D) $w - p - 8$

(E) $p - w - 8$

$0 = p - 8$

16. The ratio of x to y to z is 3 to 6 to 8. If $y = 24$, what is the value of $x + z$?

(A) 11

(B) 33

(C) 44

(D) 66

(E) 88

$w + 5 - 8$
$7 + 8 - 5$
$15 - 5$

15. If a cube has a surface area of $36n^2$ square feet, what is its volume in cubic feet, in terms of n?

(A) $n^3\sqrt{6}$

(B) $6n^3\sqrt{6}$

(C) $36n^3$

(D) $36n^3\sqrt{6}$

(E) $216n^3$

$\sqrt{6n^2}$

$12 + 32$

$n\sqrt{6}$

SECTION 9

Time—10 Minutes
14 Questions

Directions: For each question in this section, select the best answer from among the choices given and fill in the corresponding oval on the answer sheet.

The following sentences test correctness and effectiveness of expression. Part of each sentence or the entire sentence is underlined; beneath each sentence are five ways of phrasing the underlined material. Choice A repeats the original phrasing; the other four choices are different. If you think the original phrasing produces a better sentence than any of the alternatives, select choice A; if not, select one of the other choices.

In making your selection, follow the requirements of standard written English; that is, pay attention to grammar, choice of words, sentence construction, and punctuation. Your selection should result in the most effective sentence—clear and precise, without awkwardness or ambiguity.

EXAMPLE: ANSWER:

Every apple in the baskets <u>are ripe and labeled according to the date it was picked</u>.   Ⓐ ● Ⓒ Ⓓ Ⓔ

(A) are ripe and labeled according to the date it was picked
(B) is ripe and labeled according to the date it was picked
(C) are ripe and labeled according to the date they were picked
(D) is ripe and labeled according to the date they were picked
(E) are ripe and labeled as to the date it was picked

1. The dean stated that although the teacher shortage is partly due to low salaries, <u>they did not get resolved</u> when salaries increased.

  (A) they did not get resolved
  (B) there was no resolve
  (C) resolving there was not
  (D) they did not resolve
  (E) it did not get resolved

2. Animal behaviorists are researching how bats respond to abnormalities in their environments, detect light and sound, <u>and communicate with each other</u>.

  (A) and communicate with each other
  (B) and communicating with each other
  (C) and to communicate between each other
  (D) and how they communicate with each other
  (E) and communication amongst each other

GO ON TO THE NEXT PAGE ⇨

3. <u>The first truly American art movement, formed in the early nineteenth century by a group of landscape painters, called the Hudson River School.</u>

   (A) The first truly American art movement, formed in the early nineteenth century by a group of landscape painters, called the Hudson River School.

   (B) Formed in the early nineteenth century by a group of landscape painters was the first truly American art movement, called the Hudson River School.

   (C) Called the Hudson River School, it was formed in the early nineteenth century by a group of landscape painters, the first truly American art movement.

   (D) The first truly American art movement was formed in the early nineteenth century by a group of landscape painters called the Hudson River School.

   (E) By a group of landscape painters called the Hudson River School, the first truly American art movement was formed.

4. During the rainy season, a sloth's brown fur is usually covered wih a coat of green <u>algae, which helps</u> the sloth blend with its surroundings.

   (A) algae, which helps

   (B) algae for the purpose of helping

   (C) algae; helps

   (D) algae being that it helps

   (E) algae, helping it does

5. Many researchers contend that driving while talking on a cellular phone poses essentially the same risks <u>than if you drive</u> while intoxicated.

   (A) than if you drive

   (B) than to drive

   (C) as if one drives

   (D) as driving

   (D) as it does when driving

6. Before 1988, the corporation's board of directors included 153 <u>members, none of the members were women</u>.

   (A) members, none of the members were women

   (B) members; and no women

   (C) members, none of whom were women

   (D) members, and of the members not one of them was a woman

   (E) members; none of them being women

7. <u>The client was waiting for fifteen minutes when</u> the receptionist suddenly looked up from her work, noticed him, and informed him that his appointment had been canceled.

   (A) The client was waiting for fifteen minutes when

   (B) The client, having waited for fifteen minutes, when

   (C) Already the client was waiting for fifteen minutes when

   (D) When the client waited for fifteen minutes,

   (E) The client had been waiting for fifteen minutes when

GO ON TO THE NEXT PAGE ▷

8. Banquets are frequently thrown to honor guests in a Chinese <u>home, they often feature</u> shark fin as the main dish.

   (A) home, they often feature

   (B) home; often feature

   (C) home and often feature

   (D) home and they often feature

   (E) home, these often feature

9. <u>Many wealthy taxpayers pay</u> less than ten percent of their annual incomes to the government, some middle-income taxpayers pay a much larger percentage annually.

   (A) Many wealthy taxpayers pay

   (B) However, many wealthy taxpayers pay

   (C) With many wealthy taxpayers which pay

   (D) Many a wealthy taxpayer pays

   (E) Although many wealthy taxpayers pay

10. Mysteriously beautiful, the Nepalese shrine <u>inlaid with semiprecious stones</u> rare enough to honor the spiritual essence of the Buddha.

    (A) inlaid with semiprecious stones

    (B) inlaid with semiprecious stones which are

    (C) being inlaid with semiprecious stones that are

    (D) is inlaid with semiprecious stones

    (E) inlaid with semiprecious stones, these are

11. Most western European countries have decreased their consumption of fossil <u>fuels, a number of eastern European countries, however, have not done so</u>.

    (A) fuels, a number of eastern European countries, however, have not done so

    (B) fuels, however a number of eastern European countries have not done so

    (C) fuels, while on the other hand a number of eastern European countries have not done so

    (D) fuels; a number of eastern European countries, however, have not done so

    (E) fuels, a number, however, of eastern European countries have not done so

12. For reasons not fully understood, nearly all children on the island <u>gifted with musical ability</u> so strong they can master any instrument in hours.

    (A) gifted with musical ability

    (B) gifted with musical ability which is

    (C) are gifted with musical ability

    (D) being gifted with musical ability that is

    (E) are gifted with musical abilities, these are

GO ON TO THE NEXT PAGE

ANSWERS AND EXPLANATIONS

SECTION 1

6 ESSAY

I believe that a person's destiny is the result of hard work, not luck. One example that convinces me of this is someone I admire a lot, Michelle Kwan. I've read a lot about her and I know she has to work hard to keep in shape, develop routines, and to face the pressure of competition. She has also suffered some injuries, but she hasn't let them stop her from reaching her goals. Since the middle of the 1990s Michelle has won titles at World, National, and Olympic figure skating events. She is the only woman to lose a world title and then regain it two times. Michelle is able to acomplish all these things because she sets goals for herself and then works toward them with discipline and determination.

Probably if you have seen Michelle skate you have noticed that she always wears the same necklace. Its a Chinese good luck symbol that her grandmother gave her. Michelle will never part from it. But she wears it because of her deep feelings for her grandmother, not for luck. Even though its a good luck symbol, I don't think Michelle acomplished her goals by being lucky. Her hard work is what got her all the fame and medals.

So, as I said at the beginning, I believe that a person's destiny is the result of hard work, not luck. Since I believe this and I can see how Michelle's hard work has led to her sucess, I try to work hard, too. I set goals for myself and then put in the work that I need to, without expecting that success will be easy, or a gift from fate. Right now my goal is to get good grades and get into a good college.

GRADER'S COMMENTS

All essays are evaluated on four basic criteria: Topic, Support, Organization, and Language. Though it is on the short side for a 6 essay, it sticks to the topic throughout. The author supports the thesis quite well by explaining how hard work has actually resulted in achieving the goals that Kwan set for herself—a completely relevant and responsive example. This strong follow-through on an argument the writer feels strongly about raises the essay above mere technical competence.

This essay is highly organized. Paragraph 2, which could seem at first like a digression, is actually support for the author's thesis. The language is pretty good, though not exceptional. The vocabulary is straightforward and not challenging. There are a few grammatical and spelling errors, but not enough to mar the overall effect: paragraph 1, sentence 3 is not parallel. *Accomplish* and *success* are misspelled. *Its* is misused for *it's* twice.

4 ESSAY

I agree that people need to work hard for their destiny and not rely on luck. When I think of people who have worked hard to get their destiny, I always think of Abraham Lincoln. He started out very poor in a log cabin in Kentucky, but he became President of the United States. He did this because he worked very hard instead of hoping good things would just happen to him.

Lincoln didn't go to school too much because his father wanted him to work on the farm. Resulting from this, Lincoln had to teach himself law by reading law books on his own. He worked hard among the people of Illinois to get into Congress. In 1860 Lincoln was elected as the 16th President of the United States. This was a result of his hard work.

Lincoln is a great example of the statement above that destiny or fate is not dependent on luck, but rather is the result of planning and effort.

GRADER'S COMMENTS

All essays are evaluated on four basic criteria: Topic, Support, Organization, and Language. This essay is on the short side for a 4, but it sticks to the topic throughout. The essay is not very well developed. The author tends to repeat thoughts rather than develop them. He also does something that should be avoided—his final paragraph is almost entirely a repeat of the statement. This adds nothing to the author's reasoning, and uses too much of the very limited time to write. The author supports his thesis by explaining how Lincoln studied law and worked on his own. However, this is not filled in with any detail.

This essay is well organized, with each paragraph covering a separate idea. The meaning is always clear, but the author's language is sometimes below standard. For example, in paragraph 2, sentence 2 "Resulting from this" is not idiomatic. There are no misspellings in the essay.

1 ESSAY

For me its true that people have to work hard to get their destiny. Roger Clemons is the greatest pitcher ever and he works very hard. Someday I would like to be like Roger Clemons. I want to pitch in the majors. I practise real hard to get to do this.

On my last game I almost had a perfect no-hitter. To bad, though, that the last hitter got a single. But my coach said I did real good anyway and we did win the game. The score was 5 to 4.

In conclusion, I want to say again that as far as the statement above, I beleive its true.

GRADER'S COMMENTS

All essays are evaluated on four basic criteria: Topic, Support, Organization, and Language. This author starts out with promise. He states his opinion and then offers an example to support his opinion. Unfortunately, he digresses to discuss his desire to succeed as a pitcher and his baseball record. The essay offers little support for the author's opinion. While this essay is fairly well organized, it's mostly off topic.

The author's language is unsophisticated and, in some cases, substandard. There are grammatical and spelling errors that break the flow of thought: "My coach said I did real good. . ." *Its* is misused for *it's* twice. *Practice* and *believe* are misspelled. *To* is misused for *too*.

SECTION 2

1. E

It's easy enough to understand that insurers don't like to insure property in places where natural disasters are likely to happen. The term *prone to* in (E) means *having a tendency to*, so it is correct.

2. C

If it took Roman legions three years to seize Masada, we can predict that they spent a long time *surrounding or isolating* the mountain *fortress or stronghold* of Masada before they were finally able to take it. (C) is the best choice. (B) *assailed*, meaning *attacked*, would make sense in the first blank, and (E) *stronghold* and (A) *bastion* would fit, too. But (A), (B), and (E)'s second-position words don't make sense when plugged in.

3. B

If the senator was *unlike his calmer, more easygoing colleagues* and *ready to quarrel at the slightest provocation*, it's fair to infer that the senator was short-tempered or extremely irritable. The best choice is (B)—*irascible*.

4. B

You don't have to know that Genghis Khan was a violent dictator to get this question right. What's important to know is that the first word of the sentence, *although*, implies that the two blanks have to contain words that contrast with each other. (B) is the best choice—although historians had thought that Genghis Khan was a *despotic* potentate, new research shows that many of his subjects nevertheless *revered* him. Although (A) *tyrannical* is synonymous with *despotic,* (A)'s second-blank choice, *abhorred,* doesn't provide the predicted contrast. Choice (C) *venerated* doesn't really contrast with *redundant.* And in (E), it doesn't make sense to say that Khan's subjects *invoked* him despite his *peremptory* reputation.

5. B

The word *because* in the middle of the sentence lets us know that the words in the blanks will be consistent in meaning, which means that they will share the same type of charge. We can predict two positive words, like *Jill was appreciated by her employees because she often forgave* the fact that they were lazy, or two negative words like *Jill was disliked by her employees because she often scolded them* for being lazy. (B) matches the latter prediction—Jill was *loathed* by her employees because she often *berated* them for not working hard enough. No other choice besides (B) contains two like charges.

6. E

If *reconstructing the skeletons of extinct species like dinosaurs . . . requires much patience and effort by paleontologists,* we can predict that such an activity is a *painstaking or tough, demanding process.* (E) *exacting* is our best choice.

7. C

Because of disease and the destruction of their habitat, koalas are now found only in isolated parts of eucalyptus forests. The word in the blank must mean something like *killed off* or *destroyed,* since things like *disease and habitat destruction* are destructive processes. (C) is our best choice—*nearly decimated or wiped out by disease and habitat destruction,* koalas are now found only in isolated parts of eucalyptus forests. (A) *dispersed,* meaning *scattered,* may have been a little tempting, but there's no reason to assume that the koalas were scattered around the forests due to *disease and habitat destruction.*

8. E

Looking at the first blank first, if there were *internal power struggles* in the government, then it's likely that the government had something like *deep ideological differences or conflicts.* For the second blank, we can predict that these conflicts and power struggles harmed or crippled the government. Although choice (C)'s first-blank choice, *distortions,* sounds negative, like *differences or conflicts,* choices (A) and (E) make more sense. We can easily imagine *deep ideological disputes* or *deep ideological divisions* going hand in hand with *internal power struggles,* but it's hard to imagine ideological *distortions.* Now we can turn to (A)'s and (E)'s second-blank choices. (A) doesn't make sense given the context of the sentence—why would *deep ideological disputes and internal power struggles facilitate the government?* (E) is the best choice—*deep ideological divisions and internal power struggles paralyzed the government.*

MUSIC AND LANGUAGE PASSAGES

9. D

The author includes lines 8–13 as evidence that in the Romantic era, folks believed that music by itself could signify emotion (D). There is no evidence in the Passage 1 to support choice (A). While you know what the perception was during the Romantic era, the author doesn't mention the current perception, so you can't support this choice. Although the author states that language is used functionally as opposed to music, this claim is not made specifically for Romantic music in these lines, (B). (C) is too extreme—the author is not saying that Romantic music composers always used music to connote emotions. (E) expresses a negativity absent from the passage.

10. B

The prefix *extra* covers a lot of ground. Look at the context. The sentence is about music *standing by itself* so *extra-musical references* must be information from nonmusical sources. (A) is the common meaning. Nothing in the context suggests the author would consider them better than music (D), just different.

11. A

Both authors mention the symbolic nature of music and language (A). In Passage 1, the author says, . . .*Nettl has concluded that like language, music is a 'series of symbols.'* The author of Passage 2 says something similar in the last line of the passage. Only the author of Passage 2 compares both to subdivided sections, (B). Only the author of Passage 1 compares both to functional parts, (C). Clues are never mentioned, (D). (E) fits Passage 2 pretty well, but Passage 1 never links emotions and language.

12. B

Remember that the wrong answer here will be something that the authors agree on, or something that is not mentioned at all in one of the passages. Author 1 would agree with (B), whereas author 2 would disagree. Author 2 would agree with (A) and (E), but you don't know how author 1 would feel; she might agree, or she might disagree. Author 2 would probably disagree with (C) since context is so important, but there's no telling what author 1 would think about the statement. (D) is too extreme—you don't know that author 1 would agree with this.

THE TWAIN PASSAGE

This excerpt from Mark Twain's *Life on the Mississippi* should be amusing and easy to read. All the humor comes from the same technique—using deadpan, matter-of-fact language to describe the exaggerated daydreams and jealousies of a boy's life. The central point here is the author's envy of the engineer, and many of the questions focus on this. The author starts with his own glamorous ideas about steamboating, then spends most of the passage on the show-off engineer. The passage finishes with the author's own failure to find work as a pilot. The slightly old-fashioned style isn't hard to follow, but several questions focus on the author's figurative use of words.

13. B

The keyword in the sentence is *supposed*. Of course, a justice of the peace *doesn't* possess unlimited power, but because of inexperience, the author *supposed* he did. (B) accurately uses *naive* (inexperienced, gullible) to characterize the author's misconception. Three of the wrong choices assume that the father really *did* have unlimited powers and explain this in different ways—frontier justice (A and D) and public support (C). (E) mistakenly views the boy's description of his father as an indication that the boy's childhood environment was harsh.

14. C

Distinction has several meanings, including those in (A), (B), (C), and (E). The key to its use here is context: In the previous sentence the author is talking about his naive ideas of his father's great power. *Prestige,* (C), suggesting high status and honor, fits this context; the other three don't. (D) is not a meaning of *distinction* at all.

15. E

This question asks about the literal meaning of the sentence, but inference and context help, too. The sentence explains that the author wanted the job because a deck hand was *conspicuous*, or easily seen. The previous sentence stresses standing *where all my old comrades could see me*, so you can deduce that the author wants to be seen and admired in what he imagines is a glamorous profession (E). (A) and (B) invent advantages that are not mentioned and miss the humor by suggesting common-sense economic motivations. (C) assumes that if the author could be seen by his *old comrades* in the first job, he must want not to be seen by them in a different job; but this is false, since he'd be *conspicuous* in the second job, too. (D) brings in an ambition—becoming a pilot—that the author doesn't develop until the end of the passage.

16. B

Again, context helps you to figure out the answer to the question. The *Sunday-school* reference is explained in the next sentence. The engineer had been *worldly*—which is what Sunday-school probably taught students not to be—and the author had been *just the reverse*. In other words, the author followed his Sunday-school teachings and the engineer didn't—yet the engineer gets the glory. The underlying idea is that this was unjust, choice (B). (A) is never mentioned. (C) takes the Sunday-school reference literally and misses the humorous tone. (D) invents an ambition that the author never mentions; his reaction is pure envy, not frustrated ambition. (E) misconstrues the reference to the engineer as *worldly*; it means he didn't take Sunday-school seriously, not that he was *unscrupulous* (dishonest or crooked).

17. C

To get this question, you need to read the sentence that follows. The engineer was not generous because he sat about where *we all could see him and envy him*. The implication is that great people should be generous by not showing off or (C) *flaunting* their success. (A) refers to the Sunday-school comment, but that was about undeserved greatness, not lack of generosity. (B) and (D) interpret generous in the literal sense of not caring for money, but the author is using the word figuratively. (E) relates to the author's unfulfilled desire to work on a steamboat, but the engineer is not thinking about the author, he is just showing off.

18. D

The engineer does everything for the purpose of showing off. He talks the jargon of the trade to make himself look knowledgeable, or (D) sophisticated. Reading between the lines, we realize he's not an expert (A), and doesn't care about knowledge for its own sake (B). His (C) ignorance on other subjects is not mentioned; in fact, he has a working knowledge of St. Louis. (E) takes literally the phrase about how the engineer *forgot common people could not understand*—he couldn't communicate effectively. But the author says the engineer talked *as if* he forgot common people. In other words, he didn't fail to communicate, he chose not to, to impress others.

19. E

The first four choices are all common meanings of *consideration,* but the context makes it clear that the figurative use in (E) is meant. The boys had *consideration* because they knew something about St. Louis, but their glory is over because the engineer knows much more. Prestige, respect, or (E) *reputation* supplies the meaning that fits. Boys are not likely to have the qualities of *generosity, deliberation, contemplation,* or *unselfishness* as a result of knowing a little about St. Louis.

20. A

The context makes it clear that the engineer had, or at least seemed to have, much more familiarity with St. Louis than the other boys with their *vague knowledge*; their *glory* is ended because he can talk rings around them about St. Louis (A). There's no indication that (B) *St. Louis has changed* or that the boys had been lying—their knowledge was *vague*, not false (D). Reading between the lines, it's clear that travel to St. Louis was still rare enough to seem enviable (E). As for choice (C), the passage implies just the opposite.

21. A

With his *hair oil . . . showy brass watch chain, [and] leather belt*, the engineer was obviously out to impress (A). The next sentence confirms that, telling us *no girl could withstand his charms*. The author never says the young man's dress is typical (B). (C) and (E) are both wrong; the emphasis here is on the engineer's charms, not the author's wardrobe or fashion ideas. (D) won't work because the engineer's behavior is as showy and superficial as his clothes.

22. D

As often in these questions, wrong choices give flatfooted, literal interpretations where the author is being humorous. (A) misunderstands the reference to Providence—the author is criticizing Providence, not thanking it, because it has spared an *undeserving reptile*, the engineer. So the author feels resentment, or (D) *outrage,* because the engineer's good luck seems *undeserved.* Choice (B) sounds believable at first, but the passage doesn't emphasize the lucky escape—it focuses on people's sense that the engineer got better than he deserved. (C) and (E) are never mentioned.

23. C

The passage focuses on the author's ambition to work on a steamboat and his envy of the engineer. This makes (C) and (D) the strongest choices, so you need to decide between them. Looking at (D), the passage certainly emphasizes the engineer's *boastfulness,* but only within the framework of the author's dreams and ambitions (paragraphs 1 and 5) and the author's reactions to the engineer. So (C) describes the *whole* passage whereas (D) describes only the long central paragraphs. In a *major purpose/major focus* question, the answer that sums up the *whole* passage will be correct. The life of the town (A) is barely suggested. (B) is wrong because the passage's events don't end in success—although in reality, Mark Twain did go on to become a pilot. The author's *conflict with his parents* (E) is mentioned only briefly, toward the end of paragraph 4.

24. E

The last paragraph discusses the author's failed attempts to become a pilot and his daydreams that he will still become one, so (E) works best. Mates and clerks are mentioned as ignoring the author, but he never considers becoming either a mate or a clerk (A), looking for some other job (B), giving up his aim of being a pilot (C), or asking for his parents' forgiveness (D).

SECTION 3

1. C

Use the formula Percent × Whole = Part.

30 percent is $\frac{30}{100}$, or $\frac{3}{10}$. So $\frac{3}{10} \times x =$ part, and choice (C) is correct.

2. E

$2 \times 10^4 = 20{,}000$. $5 \times 10^3 = 5{,}000$. $6 \times 10^2 = 600$. $4 \times 10^1 = 40$. So the sum is 25,640.

3. A

Find the length of each segment, and then subtract the length of XY from the length of YZ. Y is at 3 on the number line and Z is at 8, so the length of YZ is $8 - 3 = 5$. X is at 1 on the number line and Y is at 3, so the length of XY is $3 - 1 = 2$. So the length of YZ is $5 - 2 = 3$ greater than the length of XY.

4. B

To find the value of x, you need to change 16 into a power of 2: $16 = 2^4$. Therefore, $2^{x+1} = 2^4$. So $x + 1 = 4$, or $x = 3$.

5. E

The number of degrees around a point is 360. Therefore:

$$90 + 30 + 2a + 30 + a = 360$$
$$150 + 3a = 360$$
$$3a = 210$$
$$a = 70$$

6. D

$$\frac{150 \text{ bottles}}{20 \text{ minutes}} = \frac{60 \text{ bottles}}{x \text{ minutes}}$$
$$150x = 1200$$
$$x = 8$$

7. B

To find the next multiple of 3, simply add 3 to the expression: $x - 1 + 3 = x + 2$, choice (B).

If this is unclear, pick a number for x. If $x = 4$, $4 - 1 = 3$; the next greatest multiple of 3 is 6. Plugging 4 for x into each answer choice, we find that only choice (B) gives us 6.

8. E

Since x leaves a remainder of 4 when divided by 5, it must end in either a 4 or a 9, so choice (B) can be eliminated. Since x leaves no remainder when divided by 9, it is evenly divisible by 9. Of the remaining choices, only 144 is divisible by 9.

9. A

The sum of the lengths of any two sides of a triangle must be greater than the length of the third side. So $AB + AC$ must be greater than BC; $6 + x > 12$. If $x = 6$, $6 + 6 = 12$ is not greater than 12, so x cannot equal 6.

10. D

Number of terms $\times$ average = sum of the terms. For the first group, $3 \times 40 = 120$, so the sum of 20, 70, and x is 120. For the second group, $4 \times 50 = 200$, so $20 + 70 + x + y = 200$. Since the sum of the first three terms is 120, $120 + y = 200$, $y = 80$.

11. A

Looking at the graph, you can see that the number of books borrowed in January was 300. To find the total number of books borrowed during the first six months of the year, add the values of each bar: $300 + 350 + 400 + 450 + 500 + 400 = 2,400$ books. So the number of books borrowed in January is $\frac{300}{2,400}$ or $\frac{1}{8}$ of the total number of books borrowed during the first six months of the year.

12. D

We're told that 40% of $r = s$. The value of 40% of r is 4 times the value of 10% of r, so 10% of $r = \frac{1}{4} \times s = \frac{s}{4}$.

An alternative method is to pick numbers. Since you're dealing with percents, let $r = 100$. 40% of $r = s$, so 40% of $100 = 40 = s$. You're asked which answer choice is equal to 10% of r; 10% of $100 = 10$. Now plug the value for s into the answer choices to see which ones give you 10:

(A) $4s = 4 \times 40 = 160$. Eliminate.

(B) $2s = 2 \times 40 = 80$. Eliminate.

(C) $\frac{s}{2} = \frac{40}{2} = 20$. Eliminate.

(D) $\frac{s}{4} = \frac{40}{4} = 10$. Works!

(E) $\frac{s}{8} = \frac{40}{8} = 5$. Eliminate.

Since (D) is the only choice that produces the desired result, it is the correct answer. But remember, when picking numbers you need to check all the answer choices; if more than one works, pick new numbers and plug them in until only one answer choice works.

13. D

The two overlapping triangles share a common angle, which we can label $p°$. Since the interior angles of any triangle add up to $180°$, we have two equations: $x + z + p = 180$ and $y + r + p = 180$. Subtracting p from both sides of each equation, we have $x + z = 180 - p$ and $y + r = 180 - p$. Since $x + z$ and $y + r$ both equal the same quantity, $x + z$ and $y + r$ must be equal to each other. Rearranging $x + z = y + r$, we get $x - r = y - z$, which matches choice (D).

14. C

Check the answer choices. If a number has even one factor (not including 1 and itself) that is not a prime number, eliminate that choice:

(A) 12: 4 is not prime. Eliminate.

(B) 18: 6 is not prime. Eliminate.

(C) 21: 3 and 7 are its only other factors, and both are prime. Correct!

(D) 24: 6 is not prime. Eliminate.

(E) 28: 4 is not prime. Eliminate.

15. A

Try different possible values for x and y, eliminating the incorrect answer choices. Since x is multiplied by 3, let's begin with the smallest positive integer value for x: 1. If $3(1) + y = 14$, then $y = 11$, and $x + y = 12$. So choice (E) is out.

If $3(2) + y = 14$, then $y = 8$, and $x + y = 10$. So choice (D) is out. If $3(3) + y = 14$, then $y = 5$, and $x + y = 8$. So choice (C) is also out. If you're really clever, you'll see at this point that answer choice (A) is impossible (which makes it the right choice). After all, the next smallest possible value of x is 4, and since x and y must both be positive integers, neither one can equal 0. (Zero is *not* positive—or negative.) So the sum of x and y must be greater than 4. (Sure enough, if $x = 4$, then $y = 2$, and $x + y = 6$, eliminating choice (B) as well.)

16. C

When the r cards are distributed, there are 8 left over, so the number of cards distributed is $r - 8$. Divide the number of cards distributed by the number of people. Since there are s people, each person gets $\dfrac{r - 8}{s}$ cards.

Another approach is to pick numbers. Let $r = 58$ and $s = 10$; if $58 - 8$ or 50 cards were distributed evenly among 10 people, each would receive 5 cards. Plug the values you picked for r and s into the answer choices to see which ones give you 5:

(A) $\dfrac{s}{8-r} = \dfrac{10}{8-58} = -\dfrac{1}{5}$. Eliminate.

(B) $\dfrac{r-s}{8} = \dfrac{58-10}{8} = 6$. Eliminate.

(C) $\dfrac{r-8}{s} = \dfrac{58-8}{10} = 5$. Works!

(D) $s - 8r = 10 - (8 \times 58) = -454$. Eliminate.

(E) $rs - 8 = (58 \times 10) - 8 = 572$. Eliminate.

Since (C) is the only answer choice that gives you 5, it is the correct answer. But be sure to check all the answer choices when picking numbers.

17. D

Check each answer choice to see which doesn't work:

(A) $\dfrac{d}{2}$: If d is an even integer, say 2, then $\dfrac{d}{2} = \dfrac{2}{2} = 1$ is an integer. Eliminate.

(B) $\dfrac{\sqrt{d}}{2}$: If d is a perfect square with an even square root, say $d = 4$, then $\dfrac{\sqrt{4}}{2} = \dfrac{2}{2} = 1$ is an integer. Eliminate.

(C) $2d$: This will always produce an even integer; if $d = 3$, $2d = 2 \times 3 = 6$ is an integer. Eliminate.

(D) $d\sqrt{2}$ CANNOT produce an integer. An integer would result if $\sqrt{2}$ is multiplied by another multiple of $\sqrt{2}$, which is impossible because d must be an integer. So (D) is correct.

Let's check (E) just to make sure.

(E) $d + 2$: This will always produce an integer; if $d = 5$,
$d + 2 = 5 + 2 = 7$ is an integer. Eliminate.

18. A

The area of a triangle $\frac{1}{2}$(base $\times$ height). Since the area of $\triangle ABC$ is 6, $\frac{1}{2}(AB \times BC) = 6$. If you consider CD as the base of $\triangle ACD$, you will notice that its height is represented by altitude AB. So the area of $\triangle ACD = \frac{1}{2}(CD \times AB)$. Since $CD = BC$, the area of $\triangle ACD$ can be expressed as $\frac{1}{2}(BC \times AB)$, which you know equals 6.

19. E

Each of the five surfaces is 60 by 180 centimeters, so tiles measuring 12 by 18 centimeters can be laid down in 5 rows of 10 to exactly cover one surface. There are 5 surfaces so $5 \times 5 \times 10 = 250$ tiles are needed.

20. B

The perimeter of triangle $ACD = AD + AB + BC + CD$. You are given the lengths of BC and CD, so you need to find the lengths of AD and AB. Angle DBC is a right angle because it is supplementary to angle DBA, one of the 4 right angles of square $ABDE$. Since right triangle DBC has sides of length 8 and 10, you should recognize it as a 6-8-10 right triangle (a multiple of the 3-4-5 right triangle) and realize that $BD = 6$. (If you didn't recognize this, you could have used the Pythagorean theorem to find the length of BD.) BD is also a side of the square, and since all sides of a square are equal, $AB = 6$.

So triangle DBA is an isosceles right triangle with sides in the ratio of $1:1:\sqrt{2}$. That means hypotenuse AD is equal to the length of a side times $\sqrt{2}$, so $AD = 6\sqrt{2}$. Now you can find the perimeter of triangle ACD: $6\sqrt{2} + 6 + 8 + 10 = 24 + 6\sqrt{2}$.

SECTION 4

1. D

The use of the word *and* tells us that we're looking for a word to fill the first blank which is consistent with *scarcity of rain*—a word like *dry*. We can, therefore, eliminate (A) and (C) at once. Since farming conditions are *bad*, our second blank should express the idea that there's no point in trying to work there. By that criterion, choices (B) and (E) can be eliminated. This leaves us with (D) *future*. (D)'s first word, *infertile*, also fits perfectly, so (D) is the correct answer.

2. D

The structural clue in this sentence is *not simply . . . but*, which suggests that the students were doing something even worse than ignoring the rules. The only word that fits here is *flouting*, choice (D).

3. A

The word *while* following the comma in the second part of the sentence tells us that there will be a contrast between what some critics believe about dadaism and what *others* "insist the movement was." The best choice is (A)—"some critics believe that the *zenith* of modern art came with dadaism, while others insist the movement was a *sham*." Other choices have single words that would make sense in one of the blanks, but none of the pairs except (A) expresses the contrast that is implied by the sentence.

4. C

In this question you are asked to make a logical connection between two parts of a sentence. It is clear that the content of the journalist's article either had no impact, in which case there was little or no response from the public, or it attracted a great deal of attention and was followed by a lot of correspondence. (C) is the correct answer. The author would never have thought her article was *controversial* were it not for the *spate* of correspondence. The other answer choices are wrong because they sound contradictory when plugged into the sentence. For example, in choice (A), if the article were *interesting,* one would expect it to be followed by a lot of correspondence— not by a *dearth,* or lack of it. In choice (D), if the article were *commonplace* (ordinary), why would an *influx* of letters follow its publication?

5. E

If many readers have difficulty following Descartes's complex, intricately woven arguments, then it's likely that his writings are something like *complicated, esoteric,* or *obscure.* The best choice is (E) *abstruse.*

JELLYFISH

6. A

Since it's clear that a jellyfish couldn't have any feelings about its encounter with humans, the author is apparently using this image to make the reader smile (A). (Even if you don't think it's funny, you should note that this is the author's intent.) The author doesn't ask us to feel sympathy for either the jellyfish or humans (B), and doesn't discuss whether or not humans are afraid of jellyfish (C). Although the author does discuss the danger of jellyfish, the quote in question doesn't accomplish that purpose. The passage never discusses how humans or jellyfish react to these encounters (E).

7. B

The third and fourth sentences contains the key to answering this question. You learn there that the relatively common encounters are not surprising because jellyfish *live in every ocean in the world* (B). (A), (C), (D), and (E) are all details from the passage, but none of them help to explain why encounters are so common.

KHYBER PASS

8. A

For this question, eliminate everything that *does* appear, and you'll be left with the answer. The passage answers (B) (Pakistan and Afghanistan), (C) (53 kilometers), (D) (was used in several wars), and (E) (two roads pass through today). The origin of the pass (A), is never mentioned.

9. E

Function questions ask you to consider what a statement adds to the author's reasoning. To find the answer, consider what claim or argument the phrase relates to and what it adds to the author's argument. Here, the word *snake* implies a twisting, turning path, like a snake (E). Although the Khyber Pass connects two points, the word *snake* implies a winding path (A). Although crossing the Khyber Pass may be dangerous (B), that doesn't follow from the word *snake*. (C) is the opposite of what you're looking for; the word implies that the pass is anything but direct. (D) comes from the wrong part of the passage. The short length of the Khyber Pass is mentioned earlier in the passage, but this is not why the author stated that the path *snakes*.

THE TIME PASSAGE

Next up is a fairly abstract science passage. This particular passage is perhaps a little bit harder than the ones you're going to encounter on the test—but don't be intimidated by the subject matter. Even if your passage is written by a Nobel Prize–winner, it's going to contain ideas that you can relate to and probably some ideas that you've seen before. The topic of the passage is how difficult it is to comprehend long stretches of time. Paragraph 2 tells us that our minds aren't built to handle the idea of thousands of years passing. We have some conception of the past through the art, writing, and photography of previous generations, but the scale of longer time periods eludes us. Paragraphs 4 and 5 attempt to bridge this gap by providing a few everyday yardsticks; the time the human race has been around is compared to a few seconds in a week, or a few letters in a book. Essentially, that's all you need to take from your first reading of the passage; you can come back to the details later.

10. C

Before writing, we're told, the wisdom of generations was passed down in two ways—verbally, and *to a lesser extent*, in pictures, carvings, and statues. This means that the wisdom of the past was transmitted less frequently by nonverbal means and thus (C) *more frequently by the spoken word than by other means*. Choices (A) and (B) *distort* this idea. Nowhere are we told that wisdom was rejected, and since spoken words *and* pictures were both used, it was obviously not an all or nothing proposition. (E) doesn't make much sense. How could there be an emphasis on science before writing existed? (D), finally, makes no sense at all—the author never says that all ancient wisdom was fiction.

11. B

This is a Little Picture question asking about the purpose of a detail. The question asks why the author discusses the impact of writing. Looking at the lines around the line reference given, we're told that writing has made the transmission of information about the past a lot more precise and extensive. Pictures and photography are also mentioned as ways in which the experience of the past has been passed down. So choice (B) is correct here—writing is mentioned as an *example* of how cultures record knowledge about the past. (A) is a distortion—the author is showing us something about the past, not why we remember hardly anything. He never implies any criticism of preliterate cultures, so choice (C) is out too. Choices (D) and (E) are wrong because the author never mentions them in the context referred to or in the whole passage.

12. C

Another Vocabulary-in-Context question. The word *ready* can mean several things—choices (A), (C), (D), and (E) are all possible meanings. In this context, however, it most nearly means *immediate,* choice (C). In the sentence before the cited line, the author says *there is no simple way* to understand vast stretches of time. In the sentence following the cited line, the author compares the way we understand time to the way a blind man *laboriously* constructs a picture of his surroundings. This implies that our understanding of time is a difficult and time-consuming task, not something we can do *readily* or *immediately.*

13. E

Another question asking about the *purpose behind* part of the author is argument. Give the context a quick scan. Once again, the author's talking about how difficult it is to understand vast stretches of time. We're told that it's like a blind man building up a sensory picture of his surroundings. This is an *indirect* process, so choice (E) is right. Choice (C) is dealt with later in paragraph 4, so you can eliminate it right away. (A) is too sweeping. The author never says that human beings are *completely unable to comprehend time.* (B) and (D) have nothing to do with the passage.

14. A

Inference skills are required here. What is the author's underlying point in mentioning the Big Bang and the Cambrian Period? The author *introduces* this discussion in the cited passage by saying that *a week* provides a better yardstick for the age of the earth than a day. The Big Bang and the Cambrian Period are used as examples to support this point. So (A) is right—it's the point about the time scale that the author's trying to demonstrate. Choices (D) and (E) both distort the point in different ways. The author is not suggesting that the time scale of a day should be totally abandoned—just that the week is a better scale. The development of (B) *agriculture* is another supporting example like the Big Bang and the Cambrian Period, but it's not the author's central point here. Finally, *fossils* have nothing to do with the question at hand, so (C) is easily eliminated.

15. C

A more straightforward comprehension question this time. When we go back to the lines referred to, we're told about the problem with linear maps: When you produce one that's big enough to show us on it, the map becomes too big to study and reproduce conveniently. (C) gets the right paraphrase here. Notice especially the match up in synonyms for *convenient reproduction* and *examination.* (A), (B), and (E) aren't supported here—there's nothing about *overlapping* periods, *scientific standards,* or ignorance about *pre-Cambrian times* in the passage. (D) doesn't address the problem. The question is about getting our human experience on the map.

16. D

What's the overall point the author is trying to prove? The big picture is that life started on Earth so long ago that it is difficult for us to comprehend. Everything that follows is meant to illustrate this point, including the time scales. Don't let the material confuse you. The point is (D)—*the immensity of time* since the origin of *life.* (C) is tricky to reject because it's an aspect of the larger argument, but it's not the whole point. The other wrong choices mention issues that the author hardly touches on. In paragraphs 4–6, the author's *not* concerned with getting dates right (A), the question of how life actually began (B), or the (E) development of communication.

THE SUSAN B. ANTHONY PASSAGE

This humanities passage is from a speech by Susan B. Anthony, a 19th-century women's rights leader. Anthony admits at the outset that she was recently charged with the *crime* of voting. Her intention is to prove that her vote was no crime, but rather the exercise of her constitutional rights, which no state should be allowed to impinge upon. This generates the passage's big idea: that Anthony—and by extension all women—should be allowed to vote. You may have found Anthony's style a little dated or confusing. Don't worry; the questions will help you focus on specific details.

17. D

To answer this question, you have to consider the entire context of the speech. Anthony reasons that all citizens automatically have the right to the vote, so the word is a part of her principal argument, and her audience would recognize that as soon as the word was spoken. Since she wants to persuade her audience on an issue of great importance to her, she wouldn't be starting out by trying to irritate or offend them (C). But the other choices don't reflect the context at all.

18. C

The important thing here is to see what exactly Anthony is saying. The question stem is keyed to the first paragraph. In the second sentence she states that she *not only committed no crime, but . . . simply exercised my citizen's rights, guaranteed me . . . by the National Constitution.* The words *no crime* are the first important clue. You can immediately rule out (A) and (E) because they say she believes the act was illegal. The second part of the line discusses the Constitution, so (C) is clearly a restatement of her argument. (B) and (D) both make sense, but she does not state these points in the first paragraph. Therefore, they are wrong.

19. A

The most common meaning of *promote* is to move up to a higher position, rank, or job. This doesn't make sense, though, in the phrase *promote the general welfare. General welfare* means the good of all people, so (A), *further*, makes the most sense. (B) *organize* and (C) *publicize* both could apply to the general welfare but not as well as (A). They refer more to promotion as you would do with a concert or sports event. (D) *commend* means *praise*, which seems silly in the context given, as does (E) *motivate*.

> **Hint:** In Vocabulary-in-Context questions, the right answer is usually not the most common meaning of the given word. Be sure to reread the context.

20. E

Anthony points out that no subgroup was excluded by the wording of the preamble of the Constitution. . . . *we formed it . . . to secure* [*the blessings of liberty*]; *not to the half of ourselves . . . but to . . . women as well as men.* Therefore, (E) is correct. *All people deserve to enjoy the rights of the Constitution.* Anthony never claims that the Founding Fathers plotted to deny women their rights (A). (B) is incorrect because the author's concern is women's rights and not rights of any other group. Although *some male citizens may still be denied basic rights,* (B) goes against the gist of what is being said. (C) is like (A) in that it's a claim Anthony never makes. Finally, though (D) is a point that Anthony does make, she doesn't make it until the next paragraph.

21. B

We're still looking at the same part of the passage. Look at the structure of the quoted sentence: *We didn't do it only for X, but for X and Y. Posterity* means *future generations,* which would include men and women. So the *X,* the *half of our posterity,* refers to the posterity of those who already enjoy the blessings of liberty. In other words, men. (B) is the right choice. (A) has nothing to do with what Anthony is discussing. Since the construction of the sentence makes it clear that the *half of our posterity* is not the whole of those who want to vote, (C) is out. There's no way of saying that one-half of the people are and will be opponents of women's rights, so (D) is wrong. (E) wrongly suggests that in the future, one half of the country's population will be members of government.

22. A

Reread the keyed paragraph. Anthony is saying that a state that prohibits women from voting violates federal law—the Constitution. Therefore, it becomes *an odious aristocracy, a hateful oligarchy.* Neither of these things is a democracy. (A) is the correct answer. Anthony mentions rebellion, but she doesn't mean the kind of violent rebellion (B) talks about. (C) is wrong because of the word *remain*. The nation is not and never has been an aristocracy. (D) plays off the same sentence as (B) does, but instead of going too far, it doesn't go far enough. Anthony wants the laws against women voting repealed; she doesn't want them merely discussed. (E) is totally wrong because at no point is Anthony arguing that an aristocracy should be preserved.

23. C

You might readily associate *hardihood* with (A) *endurance* and (B) *vitality*, but a quick check back in context shows you these aren't correct. Anthony says she doesn't believe her opponents would have the ---- to say women aren't *persons*. Saying such an offensive thing would take a lot of *nerve*, choice (C). It might also take a lot of *stupidity* (E), but that's too strong a word, considering Anthony's diplomatic tone.

24. D

The stem keys you to the second to last sentence of the passage. *Abridge* means *deprive*, so Anthony is saying that no state can deprive citizens of their rights. (D) states exactly this. In (A), *privilege* means *luxury*, but voting is a basic right, not a luxury. (B) comes out of nowhere; there's no discussion of courts in this passage. (C) plays off Anthony's reference to *any old law*. She's not talking about *any* outdated laws in this passage; she means any law *that prohibits women from voting*. Anthony never addresses how the laws will be changed, but only that they must be changed, so (E) is out.

SECTION 5

1. C

Subtract 100 from both sides of the equation to find $x = 0$.

2. B

The intersection of X and Y is the set of elements common to X (odds) and to Y (negatives).

3. B

If x and y are both negative numbers and x is less than y, then $\frac{y}{x}$ is a number greater than zero and less than one. For example, assume that $x = -2$ and $y = -1$. Then $\frac{y}{x} = \frac{1}{2}$. Since $\frac{y}{x}$ must be a positive number, we know that is it greater than zero, so (A) is incorrect. (C) and (D) are also incorrect, as they are negative and therefore smaller than the positive $\frac{y}{x}$. (E) would be exactly half of

$\frac{y}{x}$ and is therefore smaller and incorrect. The only remaining option is (B), which is larger than $\frac{y}{x}$.

(Returning to our earlier example, $\frac{x}{y}$ would be 2, which is larger than $\frac{1}{2}$.)

4. D

The small region in the middle represents households with dogs, cats, and fish. The crosshatched region includes all households with dogs and cats except those that also have fish.

5. C

Like many questions about functions, this one looks complex but really just boils down to straightforward substitution. Plug in 3 wherever you see x:

$$f(x) = \frac{(3x^2 - 9)}{(x + 1)}$$

$$f(3) = \frac{(3(3)^2 - 9)}{(3 + 1)}$$

$$f(3) = \frac{(3(9) - 9)}{4}$$

$$f(3) = \frac{(27 - 9)}{4}$$

$$f(3) = \frac{18}{4}$$

$$f(3) = \frac{9}{2}$$

6. D

First, we need to find the length of the line segment AB. It is a vertical line stretching from $(-2, 2)$ to $(-2, -2)$, so its length is $2 - (-2) = 4$. CD is twice this length, so it is $4 \times 2 = 8$ units long. CD stretches from $(-3, 1)$ to $(h, 1)$, so it is a horizontal line. If it is 8 units long, $h - (-3) = 8$. Subtract 3 from each side of this equation to get $h = 5$.

7. D

Percent change is actual change over original amount. The change from 12 to 9 is 3. The amount being changed from is 12, so $\frac{3}{12}$, or 25% is the percent decrease. 25% of 40 is $40(.25) = 10$, so the percent decrease from 40 to $40 - 10 = 30$ is the same as the percent decrease from 12 to 9. Another way to solve this problem is to set up a proportion: $\frac{12}{9} = \frac{40}{x}$, where x is the number we are looking for. Cross–multiply to find $12x = 360$, then divide by 12 to find $x = 30$.

8. A

There are $5 \times 12 = 60$ slices of pizza. If these are equally distributed among x people, each person gets $\frac{60}{x}$ slices of pizza. When the same number of slices are distributed among four fewer people, each person got $\frac{60}{x} + 4$ slices of pizza. You can also describe this number of slices as $\frac{60}{x-4}$. So you have an equation you can use to find x: $\frac{60}{x} + 4 = \frac{60}{x-4}$. This looks nothing like the answer choices, so you'll have to play with it a bit. Multiply both sides by x to get $60 + 4x = \frac{60x}{x-4}$, then multiply both sides by $x - 4$ to get $(x-4)(60 + 4x) = 60x$. Distribute and simplify to get $60x + 4x^2 - 240 - 16x = 60x$, $4x^2 - 16x - 240 = 0$, and $x^2 - 4x - 60 = 0$.

9. .127

If $A = 2.54$ and $20B = A$, then $20B = 2.54$. So $B = \frac{2.54}{20}$ or .127.

10. 9.5 or $\frac{19}{2}$

The perimeter of the figure is equal to the sum of the lengths of its sides: $2 + 1\frac{1}{3} + 1\frac{1}{2} + 1\frac{2}{3} + 3 = 9\frac{1}{2}$, which is $\frac{19}{2}$ expressed as an improper fraction, or 9.5 expressed as a decimal.

11. 84 or 96

If $\frac{h}{3}$ and $\frac{h}{4}$ are both integers, then h must be a multiple of 3×4, or 12. Since it's given that h is between 75 and 100, h must be 84 or 96.

12. 8

The profit made by the retailer on the shirts is equal to the difference between the selling price and the cost for each shirt multiplied by the number of shirts: $(\$6.75 - \$4.50) \times 16 = \$2.25 \times 16 = \$36.00$ profit. To find the number of $4.50 shirts that can be bought for $36.00, you need to divide $36.00 by $4.50, and $\frac{36}{4.5} = 8$.

13. $\frac{45}{4}$ or 11.2 or 11.3

Draw a diagram and label it according to the given information:

Let the smaller angle measure $x°$. Since the other angle formed is 15 times as large, label it $(15x)°$. Notice that these two angles are supplementary, that is, they add up to $180°$. Therefore:

$$x + 15x = 180$$

$$16x = 180$$

$$x = \frac{45}{4}$$

So the smaller angle is $\frac{45}{4}$ degrees, which can also be gridded in decimal form as 11.2 or 11.3.

14. 4

Before you plug in -4 for x, you should factor the given equation:

$$x^2 + 2xr + r^2 = 0$$

$$(x + r)(x + r) = 0$$

$$(x + r)^2 = 0$$

Now plug in -4 for x to solve for r: $(-4 + r)^2 = 0$, $-4 + r = 0$, and $r = 4$.

15. $\frac{1}{16}$ or .062 or .063

Plug the values into the given definition:

$$\frac{1}{4} \ast = \left(\frac{1}{4}\right)^2 - \frac{1}{4}$$

$$= \frac{1}{16} - \frac{1}{4}$$

$$= \frac{1}{16} - \frac{4}{16}$$

$$= \frac{-3}{16}$$

$$\frac{1}{2} \ast = \left(\frac{1}{2}\right)^2 - \frac{1}{2}$$

$$= \frac{1}{4} - \frac{1}{2}$$

$$= \frac{1}{4} - \frac{2}{4}$$

$$= \frac{-1}{4}$$

So:

$$\frac{1}{4} \text{✱} - \frac{1}{2} \text{✱} = \frac{-3}{16} - \left(\frac{-1}{4}\right)$$

$$= \frac{-3}{16} - \left(-\frac{4}{16}\right)$$

$$= \frac{1}{16}$$

This can also be gridded as .062 or .063.

16. $\frac{1}{8}$ **or .125**

You should recognize that right $\triangle ABC$ is a 45-45-90 triangle, with side lengths in a ratio of $1:1:\sqrt{2}$. Therefore, the length of the two equal legs AB and AC is $\frac{1}{2}$.

To find the area of the triangle, plug the values of the base and height (the lengths of the two equal legs) into the area formula:

Area of a triangle $= \frac{1}{2}(\text{base} \times \text{height})$

$$= \frac{1}{2}\left(\frac{1}{2}\right)^2$$

$$= \frac{1}{2}\left(\frac{1}{4}\right)$$

$$= \frac{1}{8}, \text{ or } .125$$

17. 2,025

You're given that x is a factor of 8,100 and it's an odd integer. To find the greatest possible value of x, begin factoring 8,100 by using its smallest prime factor, 2, as one of the factors. Continue factoring out a 2 from the remaining factors until you find an odd one as shown below:

8,100

$2 \times 4,050$

$2 \times 2 \times 2,025$

Since 2,025 is odd, you can stop factoring; it is the greatest odd factor of 8,100.

18. $\frac{4}{7}$ **or .571**

Translate the problem into math: Let b = number of boys; let g = number of girls. So $b + g$ = total number of students in the class.

$\frac{1}{2}$ of the boys speak French, so $\frac{1}{2}b$ = the number of boys who speak French.

$\frac{2}{3}$ of the girls speak French, so $\frac{2}{3}g$ = the number of girls who speak French.

Therefore, $\frac{1}{2}b + \frac{2}{3}g$ = total French speakers.

So the fraction of the class that speaks French

$$= \frac{\frac{1}{2}b + \frac{2}{3}g}{b + g}$$

Since there are $\frac{3}{4}$ as many girls as boys in the class, $g = \frac{3}{4}b$. Plug in $\frac{3}{4}b$ for g into the fraction above.

Fraction of the class that speaks French:

$$= \frac{\frac{1}{2}b + \frac{2}{3}\left(\frac{3}{4}b\right)}{b + \frac{3}{4}b}$$

$$= \frac{\frac{1}{2}b + \frac{1}{2}b}{\frac{7}{4}b}$$

$$= \frac{b}{\frac{7}{4}b}$$

$$= \frac{4}{7} \text{ or .571}$$

SECTION 6

1. E

The introductory phrase doesn't modify the correct noun. The fundraiser is *arranged as an event*, not the Board of Directors. Also, the words *for funding* repeat information provided in the main clause. You need an introductory phrase that modifies the correct noun—the museum's Board of Directors. Only (E) does that. (B) and (D) don't correct the modification problem. (C) creates a run-on with a comma splice.

2. A

Don't forget that about 20 percent of Sentence Correction questions are correct as written. This sentence correctly uses a semicolon to connect two independent clauses, but (B) changes the meaning. (C) is a run-on sentence with a comma splice. (D) is a complete sentence because it adds the conjunction *and*, but it is wordy and incorrectly changes *nearly* to *near*. (E) should use a comma because it adds *although*, which subordinates the second clause.

3. C

Pay close attention to the sequence of events. The architects first made the design plans, then refused to copyright or benefit from them. The action *refused to patent* happened after, not before, the plans had been made, requiring the simple past tense. (C) and (E) make that change but only (C) makes *patent* and *benefit* parallel. (B) keeps the past perfect tense. (D) uses the present tense, even though the entire sentence is in the past.

4. D

The comparison between Wilde's novel writing and play writing must be logical. (C), (D), and (E) correctly compare *novelist* and *playwright*. However, only (D) retains the original meaning. (C) doesn't show that Wilde is a more brilliant playwright than novelist. (E) reverses the meaning, making him a more brilliant novelist than playwright. (B) changes the meaning as well, making Wilde *almost brilliant*.

5. C

The introductory phrase doesn't modify the correct noun. You need a subject that can logically examine the sale offers. (C), (D) and (E) provide that subject (*one*). Only (C) uses the present tense. (D) and (E) switch to the past tense. (D) also illogically uses the contrasting transition word *although*; (E) incorrectly omits *the* from *the phrases*. (B) doesn't address the modification problem.

6. A

This sentence is correct as written. (A) is your answer. (B) is incorrect because *however*, when used as a conjunction between two independent clauses, must be preceded by a semicolon. (C) is redundant, using two conjunctions *although* and *however*. (D) uses the relative pronoun *which* instead of *who* to refer to people. (E) loses the contrast between the two clauses (indicated by *however* in the original sentence).

7. B

The sentence uses the pronoun *which* to refer to people and includes the wordy intervening phrase *which have an understanding of*. (B) correctly changes *which* to *who* and makes the sentence more concise. (D) and (E) also use *who* but (D) introduces the ambiguous pronoun *they*, which could refer to the people or the leaves and (E) omits the fact that people understand the life cycles in leaves. (C) doesn't correct the original pronoun problem.

8. B

Be sure you understand the logic of the sentence: the traffic rules are the *they* and their role was not appreciated. (B) puts all these ideas into clear order by introducing the transition word *because* instead of relying on a modifier. (C) distorts the meaning of the sentence. (D) creates a misplaced modifier problem—the traffic rules fail to appreciate their role. (E) is a fragment, with no verb in an independent clause.

9. E

There are two pairs of parallel structures: *even more elusive in . . . . than in* and *either . . . . or*. In the original sentence the first pair is not parallel. (D) and (E) correctly add *in* to make the phrases *in his own country* and *in Europe or Latin America* parallel, but (D) introduces a new error by repeating *in*. (B) and (C) do not correct the parallel problem.

10. B

My old home is not *growing up*. There is a modification problem. (B) and (C) correct the modification problem by adding the transition word *as* but only (B) doesn't introduce new errors. (C) uses the present tense *grow up* and inserts a preposition at the end of the sentence. (D) loses the idea that the author grew up on the island. (E) doesn't correct the modification problem.

11. B

The use of *there were* in the sentence is very awkward, which rules out (A) and (C). (D) and (E) do not have logical sentence structures. (B) is the only choice that makes sense and has good sentence structure.

12. D

The pronoun *they* doesn't clearly refer to anything and *they can astonish people* is not parallel to *bolder* and *more abstract*. (D) should be changed to *astonishing*. The phrases *as Picasso* (A) and *use of* (B) are idiomatically correct. The verb *became* (C) is correctly in the past tense.

13. B

The sentence begins in present tense, but then changes to past tense. This must be incorrect. The chemical plant *is* a danger, at the present moment. *It became imperative* is past tense, which does not agree with the rest of the sentence. It should be changed to *it has become imperative*. Note that you could also simply substitute *is* to form *it is imperative*. *Such a* (A) is standard written English, as is *to find other ways* (C). *For* (D) is the correct preposition for *garden*.

14. B

The main clause of this sentence contains two plural nouns: *retail stores* and *popular items*. The pronoun *their* might refer to either, and must be clarified. The transition phrase *due to* (A) establishes a cause in the first clause and a logical result in the second clause. The verb *are increasing* (C) is correctly in the present tense. *Stock of* (D) uses the correct preposition.

15. B

This is a sentence fragment; we need a verb. The phrase *which eerily hint at* in (B) and (C) should read *eerily hint at*, adding a verb and creating a complete sentence. The adjective *lyric* (A) agrees with the noun *novels*. The adverb *eerily* (B) agrees with the correct verb *hint at*. The phrase *of her later life* (D) is idiomatically correct.

16. B

The pronoun *their* refers to the United Nations. Because the United Nations is a singular proper noun, the correct pronoun is *its*. (B) is incorrect. (A) correctly uses the comparative form and *than* is idiomatically correct. (C) is the correct preposition with owes. (D) correctly uses *that* and the present tense.

17. D

Each pronoun in a sentence should agree in gender and number with the word or words to which it refers. You will note that (A) is an appropriate modifier for the subject *I*. (B) is an appropriate verb tense. (C) is a correct idiom. (D) is the right answer. In this phrase, the pronoun refers to *Jake and Kelsey* and therefore it should be the plural *they*.

18. D

Be sure that each word means precisely what the writer intended to say. (A) is an appropriate phrase modifying the subject *Hiam*. (B) is an adjective, also appropriately modifying *Hiam*. (C) is another adjective, here correctly modifying the noun *night*. (D) uses the wrong preposition for the intended meaning; the writers meant *on* or *against*.

19. B

Adverbs and adjectives can be easily mixed-up. Check the sentence again to be sure there is no confusion. (A) uses the correct verb tense and the verb agrees with the subject *you*. (B) shows an adverb used in place of an adjective *generous*. Therefore, (B) is the right answer. (C) shows a correct verb tense and (D) shows an idiom used correctly to mean *flourish*.

20. D

Does the subordinate clause fit within the context of the sentence? (A) uses the correct verb tense, and the verb agrees with the subject *Kelly*. (B) shows the correct feminine singular pronoun, referring to *Kelly*. (C) shows the correct infinitive form of the verb *mediate*.

21. A

Irregular verbs do not follow the usual pattern in their past tense forms. Check the sentence carefully to be sure that the verbs are written correctly. (A) is the correct tense for an action that occurred before the action in the second part of the sentence: *became apparent*. However, it uses an incorrect past participle of the verb *drive*. The correct form is *driven*. (B) uses the correct preposition *from*. (C) is the correct verb tense and idiomatic expression. (D) is appropriate tense for another action that was completed before the action in the prior clause.

22. C

Check sentences for common usage errors. *Hardly no* is a double negative. You need to replace *no* with *any* to fix it.

23. E

Don't hyper-correct the sentences. All the elements in this sentence are correct.

24. C

Look for subjects that follow verbs—a common SAT trap. The verb *has* precedes its subject—*characters*. Because *characters* is plural, the verb has to be changed to the plural *have*.

25. B

Remember that adverbs modify verbs and adjectives modify nouns, adverbs and other adjectives. *Attentive* is an adjective, but it is modifying the verb *applies* so it has to be changed to the adverb *attentively*.

26. B

Know the difference between when to use nouns in the subjective case and the objective case. Any noun or pronoun that is part of a prepositional phrase must be in the objective case. Here the prepositional phrase is between *Sarah and I*. This is incorrect because *I* is a subjective case noun. To correct this sentence you need to change *I* to *me*.

27. E

Don't be distracted by phrases and clauses that come between a subject and its verb. The verb *used* and the preposition *by* (A) are used correctly. The subject *control* and its verb *is* (B) agree. *Benefit* (C), which means *aid* or *advantage*, is correctly used in this sentence. The pronoun *their* (D) agrees with its antecedent *students*.

28. C

Let the parts of the sentence not underlined help you identify the errors that are underlined. The pronoun *it* is used at the end of the sentence to refer to *the institute*, but the other pronoun that refers to *the institute*, in (C), is *their*. You need to make the pronouns consistent and correct. *The institute* is a collective noun, which means it's made up of many people, but is treated in a sentence as a single entity, so any pronouns that refer to it should be singular.

29. A

This sentence confuses *undetermined* (which means not decided) with indeterminate. You can see that this makes no sense. The word needed is *indeterminate* which means you can't tell his age by looking at him. Notice how this meaning works well with the rest of the sentence—he takes advantage of the ambiguity or uncertainty about his age. (B) The conjunction *and*, which indicates additional, related information is correctly used. (C) The present tense is correct since it expresses something that the candidate does regularly. (D) is the correct preposition in this context.

30. A

The passage begins by stating that ballet has a *duality* and the second sentences introduces the most common view of ballet. What follows should be a sentence that identifies the contrast suggested by the first sentence: the idea that ballet is *grueling, painful, and competitive*, as expressed in (A). This also gives a more clear transition to paragraphs 2 and 3, which talk about the difficulties of dancing. Although it starts appropriately with a contrast word, (B) goes off track; it even seems to contradict sentence 2. (C) is a fragment; it can't be correct even though it seems to follow the right line of reasoning. (D) and (E), like (B), go off the logical track. These would be digressions in this passage, which focuses only on the qualities of ballet.

31. A

To combine these two sentences we must first determine their relationship. It is a causal relationship—because of the first clause (the human body is not designed for ballet) it is difficult for dancers to do the second clause (perform ballet steps). (A) correctly establishes this relationship and creates a complete sentence. (B) and (E) incorrectly use a semicolon to connect a dependent and an independent clause. (C) combines the sentences into one big fragment by adding the gerund *making*. (D) is also a fragment and introduces another error—*their* is an ambiguous pronoun.

32. A

To determine what sentence should begin paragraph 3, we must understand the passage's organization. Paragraph 1 introduces the topic. Paragraph 2 describes the first negative aspect of ballet (physical injury). Paragraph 3 describes the second negative aspect (financial problems). (A) both indicates that paragraph 3 is the second aspect and that the paragraph relates to financial problems. The sentence is also identical in construction to the first sentence of paragraph 2. (B) changes *second* to *secondly* and only mentions a part of paragraph 3, not the entire subject. (C) and (D) use transition words that do not indicate that this is the second portion of the passage. (E) incorrectly indicates that the financial consequences are worse than the physical—the author never makes such a comparison.

33. D

As it is now, the sentence is a fragment; we need a subject and verb in an independent clause. (D) replaces the gerund *creating* with the present tense *create*. This works in context because the rest of the paragraph is in present tense. (B) simply substitutes the gerund *compiling* for the gerund *creating*. The sentence is still a fragment. (C) and (E) are incorrectly in the past tense; (C) uses the pronoun *they*, which would mean that the financial struggles were competitive instead of the dancers; and (E) changes the meaning to one competition.

34. B

Look at the context of sentence 11—how does it relate to sentence 10? Sentence 11 contrasts dancers' experience with that of *most people*. (D) uses the contrasting transition word *but* and also makes sentence 11, which was a fragment, a complete sentence. (B) has the right intention—it contrasts the two sentences—but the pronoun *which* makes sentence 11 a dependent clause (on sentence 10) instead of a sentence. (C) is incorrect because sentence 10 doesn't give us a *model*, just a fact. (E) incorrectly uses the transition word *and*.

35. B

What is the relationship of this pair of sentences to what came before? We've been told in sentences 10 and 11 that people in most occupations retire at 65, but that isn't true of dancing. Now we're told a few dancers continue in related careers, but most are simply unemployed. Sentence 12 continues what preceded it, but contrasts with sentence 13. (B) captures this best. (A) confuses the contrast between these two sentences by offering transition words suggesting both contrast (*although*) and continuity (*and*). (C) offers too many contrast words and needlessly changes tense. (D) is a run-on sentence. (E) also changes tense and distorts some of the meaning.

SECTION 7

1. B

The phrase *even though* indicates contrast. So, *even though* the prisoner "presented evidence clearly proving that he was nowhere near the scene of the crime," he was *indicted* or formally charged with committing the crime.

2. C

A *premise* is a proposition which is used as the basis for an argument—or a story. If scientists are critical of the premise for a movie, we can infer that they are so because they consider it to be unscientific, without basis in fact, or *speculative*. (C) is therefore the correct answer. (A) is wrong, because if the premise, or underlying argument, were *scientific* then it would hardly be open to criticism by scientists. (B) is wrong because there's no reason to think that the theme of the return of the dinosaurs is unexpressed in the movie.

3. C

In this sentence we find a description of two contradictory characteristics that exist in the same group of people. On the one hand, they are brutal; on the other, they are heroic. Such an occurrence is termed a *paradox* and therefore (C) *paradoxical* is the correct answer. Choices (A), (D), and (E) are wrong; it is *unfortunate, distressing,* and *appalling* that they are brutal—but not that they are heroic.

4. B

The second part of the sentence tells you that the engineers did something that allowed the movement of animals around the pipeline. You can, therefore, predict that this action would *help* the seasonal migration of caribou. This prediction eliminates choices (A) and (D) for the first blank. (B) and (E) both fit the first blank nicely. When you try the second blank, (B) describes how the pipeline could be designed to accommodate the passage of animals. (D) refers not to the pipeline but to the oil *delivered* through the pipeline. (C) does not fit either blank. Be sure not to misread *razed* ("demolished, leveled to the ground"), as *raised*.

5. E

The word *however* signals a contrast between licorice as candy and its use in earlier times when licorice root was used to treat a variety of medical problems. A good prediction for the blank would be *medical* or *healing*. (E) matches the prediction. (A) is too narrow because licorice root treated conditions other than insomnia. (C) describes candy but not medicine. The remaining choices do not match the prediction. Be sure not to misread *indelible* as *inedible* ("unfit to be eaten").

6. A

In this sentence, parents are doing something to legislation that guarantees programs and services. The first part of the sentence tells you that education is one of those services. You're looking for a word like *assure* in the first blank. (A) and (E) work for the first blank. Now look at the second blank. (A) works well. (E) would deny education to the children and can, therefore, be eliminated. To ensure free education for children with special needs, parents have had to demand legislation guaranteeing services and programs targeted to those children. (A) works for both blanks.

THE SHAKESPEARE PASSAGES

These paired passages present two opposing arguments on a single subject, the subject here being *Who Really Wrote Shakespeare's Plays?* The author of the first passage maintains that Francis Bacon actually wrote the plays, basing that conclusion on the assertion that Shakespeare didn't have the education and social experience necessary to create such sophisticated plays. The author of the second passage takes issue with that, claiming that Shakespeare's genius grew out of a deep understanding of human nature rather than any wide learning or arcane knowledge.

7. B

Here we're asked the definition of the word *entertain* in line 3, where it is used in the phrase *entertain some doubt*. Well, when you entertain doubt, or entertain an idea, you are holding it in your head. You are *harboring* it, in the sense of *to harbor* as *to be host to*. So choice (B) is correct. The other choices are all acceptable dictionary definitions of the verb *entertain*, but none fits the context as well as choice (B) does. (A) *amuse* is a common synonym for *entertain*, but how does one amuse doubt? (C) *occupy* and (E) *engage* are closer, but they don't fit the sentence either. One's *mind* is occupied or engaged, but the doubt itself is not occupied or engaged. Meanwhile, (D) *cherish* adds a sense of valuing the entertained thing, as if it were something desirable.

8. D

The author claims that the person who actually wrote the plays must have had *intimate knowledge of life within royal courts and palaces*, but that Shakespeare was just a commoner, without that kind of *firsthand experience* of the aristocracy. He wants to cast doubt on Shakespeare's *familiarity with the life of [aristocrats],* or choice (D). Shakespeare's ability to (A) *write poetically* and his (C) *ability to support himself as a playwright* never come up in Passage 1. The *knowledge of foreign places* mentioned in (B) does come up, but being a commoner is not necessarily related to Shakespeare's apparent lack of travel. Choice (E) is the closest wrong choice, since the aristocracy was the *government* in Elizabethan England, but the issue is his knowledge of all aspects of aristocratic life.

9. E

Two Shakespearian plays—*Coriolanus* and *Love's Labour's Lost*—are mentioned in lines 31–34 in connection with the allegedly specialized knowledge they contain. They support the point that the educated aristocrat Bacon was a more likely author than was the undereducated commoner Shakespeare. (E) answers the question best. Choice (A) is a clever wrong choice, but it's too extreme. The author's not trying to prove that *only* Bacon could have written these plays, just that Bacon was far more likely than Shakespeare to have written them. The *deep understanding of human nature* mentioned in (B) is something brought up in Passage 2, not Passage 1. The author is not comparing the two plays to *works written by Bacon,* as (C) claims. And (D) is wrong since nothing about society is mentioned with regard to *Coriolanus*. Also, it's not the *broad spectrum of society* the author alludes to with regard to *Love's Labour's Lost,* but rather the knowledge of just the upper range of society.

10. A

It's clear that Ms. Bacon is looking down on actors, of which Shakespeare was one, regarding them with the *disdain* expressed in correct choice (A). She's not *resentful* at how the *characters are portrayed,* choice (B), since she's talking about the characters themselves and what they tell us about real-life actors. Given her opinion of actors, she certainly doesn't *regret that their conditions weren't better,* choice (C). (D) is closer, but it's a distortion. She never doubts that anyone could *create such characters;* she doubts that the author of the plays could *be like* such a character. Finally, in (E), there's no evidence in the quote that Ms. Bacon thinks the actors are inept at their art, just that they are vulgar and lowly persons.

11. B

This question sends you back to paragraph 4 of Passage 1, where Bacon's preference for anonymity is explained. The author claims that, because the plays were controversial, Bacon felt that associating himself with them would have been politically and personally damaging. So, *he wished to protect himself from the effects of controversy,* choice (B). (A) is wrong because Bacon did publish a lot of writing under his own name. (C) is plausible, but it's not the reason given in paragraph 4 or anywhere else in the first passage. (D) tries to confuse us by introducing the subject of *lowly actors* from the preceding paragraph, and (E) is a fabrication since we know that Bacon was already famous from his other writings.

12. C

This question takes us to the first paragraph of Passage 2, where the emphasis is on language ability. The author doubts that Bacon, a writer primarily of academic Latin, would have had the ability to produce the exalted English in which the plays were written. That makes (C) the best answer. (A) is a distortion. Just because Bacon wrote most of his own work in another language doesn't mean that he was *unfamiliar* with English. (B)'s emphasis on the difficult switch from *scientific writing* to *writing plays* is close, but language rather than the type of writing is the focus. There's no reason to surmise that the author doubts Bacon's ability to *cooperate* on a *committee,* choice (D). Finally, (E) is wrong because there is no evidence in the first paragraph that the author has doubts about Bacon's ability to produce that amount of work.

13. D

This question asks about *premier* as it is used in the phrase *premier stylist in the English language.* The author definitely wants to indicate the sublime language of the plays here, so *premier* is being used in the sense of *of the first rank*, or, as choice (D) has it, *greatest.* (A), (C), and (E) all play on the sense of premier as *first in sequence* (*inaugural,* by the way, means *marking the commencement or beginning*), but the author is not referring here to *when* Shakespeare wrote. He's writing about how *well* Shakespeare wrote. On the other hand, (B) *influential* misses on two counts—first, it's not a definition of *premier* in any context, and second, the issue of influence on other writers is not brought up here.

14. B

This question concerns the adjective *encyclopedic* in Passage 2, line 82, where it's used to modify the noun *knowledge.* The author says that Shakespeare's genius was one of common sense and perceptive intuition, not encyclopedic knowledge, which is related to great book-learning. So the knowledge described as *encyclopedic* is wide-ranging and in-depth—*comprehensive,* in other words, choice (B). (A) *technical* is close to the sense of the context, but it's not a synonym of *encyclopedic,* so it really won't work here. (C) won't work either, since *abridged* (meaning *condensed*) cannot describe the kind of exhaustive knowledge the author is describing here. While it may take discipline to gain encyclopedic knowledge, *encyclopedic* itself cannot be defined as *disciplined,* so cut (D). Finally, (E) *specialized* isn't quite right, since it implies a narrowness of focus.

15. E

The reference to Shakespeare's status as a landowner comes in the third paragraph of Passage 2, where it is brought up to show that Shakespeare would have been *knowledgeable about legal matters related to . . . real estate.* That makes (E) the best answer, *legal matters* being equivalent to *the law*. (A) is interesting, since the author does say that owning land was quite an accomplishment for a playwright, but it has nothing to do with his knowledge of the law. (B) is off, since owning land doesn't make one automatically friendly with the highborn set. (C) is wrong, because Shakespeare's financial state is just a side issue; it's not the point of bringing up Shakespeare's landowning status. And (D) doesn't fit, since no one doubts that Shakespeare was a commoner.

16. A

This question directs us to Passage 2, lines 110–111, where the author claims that literary genius *can flower in any socioeconomic bracket.* That implies that genius has little to do with a person's social and financial position—or, as correct choice (A) has it—genius doesn't depend *on a writer's external circumstances.* (B) fails by bringing in the notion of *comprehension of human nature* from elsewhere in the passage. (C) is a common cliché, but there's no evidence here that the author felt that Shakespeare's genius was *enhanced by poverty.* In fact, this author implies that Shakespeare wasn't even all that poor. (D) may be a true statement, but recognition of genius isn't really under discussion here; it's the simple existence of genius. (E) is a distortion; the author claims that at least one kind of genius does not *stem* from *book-learning and academic training,* but that doesn't mean that those things would *stifle literary genius.*

17. C

Go back to the fourth paragraph of Passage 1, where our first author claims that Bacon may have *hired a lowly actor* like Shakespeare to put his name to the plays and take the heat of controversy. How would our second author respond to this claim? The second author, remember, writes in the concluding paragraph of Passage 2 that *no elaborate theories of intrigue and secret identity are necessary to explain the accomplishment of William Shakespeare.* Surely author 2 would regard the *scenario* described in Passage 1 as just this kind of *unnecessary* theory, so (C) is the best guess for how author 2 would react. As for choice (A), author 2 may or may not agree that the plays were *controversial* in their time, so (A) won't work. (B) gets the thrust of author 2's argument wrong. Author 2 denigrates the notion that Bacon wrote the plays *not* by arguing that Bacon wasn't a great scholar, but by arguing that it didn't require a great scholar to write the plays. (D) tries to turn author 1's argument on its head. A nice idea, perhaps, but author 2 shows no hint of doing anything of the kind. (E) brings up the notion of Shakespeare's social *respectability*, which really isn't of much concern to author 2.

18. C

What would be author 1's reaction to author 2's skepticism that Bacon, the author of Latin treatises, could be the "premier stylist in the English language"? Well, author 1's repeated assertions of Bacon's scholarly genius and Shakespeare's lack of education are both reflected in choice (C), which makes it a good bet as the correct answer. (A)'s mention of the *similarities between Latin and English* is enough to kill this choice, since author 1 mentions no such similarities in the passage. (B) is a true statement, perhaps, but it doesn't really address the issue. (D) is fairly nonsensical, since it would weaken author 1's entire theory about why Bacon hired Shakespeare. Finally, (E) makes a good point, but again, there is no hint of this sentiment in author 1's statements.

19. D

Always check back to the passage to figure out the meaning of a Vocabulary-in-Context word. Here, the word *observation* refers to the phrase that *Shakespeare, in short, was Shakespeare*—a jokey comment on the author's part. None of the other choices fits the context of an informal remark, so (D) is correct here.

SECTION 8

1. B

Plug in −2 for p and 3 for q: $p^3q^2 + p^2q = (-2)^3 3^2 + (-2)^2 3 = (-8)(9) + 4(3)$, or $(-72) + 12 = -60$. (Note that a negative number raised to an even power becomes positive, but raised to an odd power stays negative.)

2. A

Keep track of the lengths you know on the diagram. B is the midpoint of AC so $AB = BC$. Since $AB = 5$, $BC = 5$. $BD = 8$, so $BC + CD = 8$. $BC = 5$, so $5 + CD = 8$, $CD = 3$. D is the midpoint of CE, so $CD = DE = 3$.

3. D

Try each answer choice until you find one that works for all of the pairs of numbers.

Choice (A), $P = N + 5$ works for 2 and 7, but not for 4 and 13.

Choice (B), $P = 2N + 3$ also works for 2 and 7, but not for 4 and 13.

Choice (C), $P = 2N + 5$, doesn't work for 2 and 7.

Choice (D), $P = 3N + 1$, works for all four pairs of numbers, so that's the answer.

4. A

$\angle PNM$ is supplementary to $\angle PNQ$, so $\angle PNM + 105° = 180°$, and $\angle PNM = 75°$. Since $PM = PN$, triangle MPN is an isosceles and $\angle PMN = \angle PNM = 75°$. The interior angles of a triangle sum to $180°$, so $75 + 75 + x = 180$, and $x = 30$.

5. D

Probability is defined as the number of desired events divided by the total number of possible events. There are $5 + 6 + 4 = 15$ pens in the knapsack. If he pulls out 1 pen, there are 15 different pens he might pick, or 15 possible outcomes. The desired outcome is that the pen be either red or black. The group of acceptable pens consists of $4 + 6$, or 10 pens. So the probability that one of these pens will be picked is 10 of 15, or $\frac{10}{15}$, which we can reduce to $\frac{2}{3}$.

6. C

Pick variables for the two items and translate the given information into algebraic equations. Let $h =$ the price of a hot dog and $s =$ the price of a soda. The first statement is translated as $2h + s = 3.25, and the second as $3h + s = 4.50. If you subtract the first equation from the second, the s is eliminated so you can solve for h:

$$3h + s = $4.50$$
$$\underline{-(2h + s = $3.25)}$$
$$h = $1.25$$

Plug this value for h into the first equation to solve for s:

$$2($1.25) + s = $3.25$$
$$$2.50 + s = $3.25$$
$$s = $0.75$$

So two sodas would cost $2 \times $0.75 = 1.50.

7. C

$a = f$, since all the obtuse angles formed when two parallel lines are cut by a transversal are equal. f is an exterior angle of the small triangle containing angles c, d, and e, so it is equal to the sum of the two nonadjacent interior angles, c and d. Since $a = f$ and $f = c + d$, $a = c + d$, answer choice (C).

8. D

The first 3 minutes of the phone call cost 75 cents or 0.75 dollars. If the entire call lasted x minutes, the rest of the call lasted $x - 3$ minutes. Each minute after the first 3 cost 15 cents or $0.15, so the rest of the call cost $0.15(x - 3)$. Thus, the cost of the entire call is $0.75 + 0.15(x - 3)$ dollars.

If this isn't clear, pick numbers. Let $x = 5$. The first 3 minutes cost $0.75 and the additional $5 - 3 = 2$ minutes are $0.15 each. So the entire call costs $0.75 + 2(\$0.15) = \$1.05$. Plug 5 for x into all the answer choices to see which ones give you 1.05:

(A) $0.75(3) + 0.15x = 2.25 + 0.15(5) = 2.25 + 0.75 = 3.00$. Eliminate.

(B) $0.75(3) + 0.15(x + 3) = 2.25 + 0.15(5 + 3) = 2.25 + 1.20 = 3.45$. Eliminate.

(C) $0.75 + 0.15(3 - x) = 0.75 + 0.15(3 - 5) = 0.75 - 0.30 = 0.45$. Eliminate.

(D) $0.75 + 0.15(x - 3) = 0.75 + 0.15(5 - 3) = 0.75 + 0.30 = 1.05$. Works!

(E) $0.75 + 0.15(5) = 0.75 + 0.75 = 1.50$. Eliminate.

The only choice that yields the desired result is (D), so it must be correct.

9. B

Before you can find the area of the circle, you need to find the length of the wire. The wire is in the shape of a semicircle with diameter 12. Since circumference $= \pi d$, the length of a semicircle is half of that, $\frac{\pi d}{2}$. So the length of the wire is $\frac{\pi(12)}{2}$, or 6π. When this wire is bent to form a circle, the circumference of this circle will equal 6π. So the length of the circle's diameter must equal 6, and the radius must be 3. Now you can find the area of the circle:

$$\text{Area} = \pi r^2$$

$$= \pi(3)^2$$

$$= 9\pi$$

10. C

If $a^2 - a = 72$, then $a^2 - a - 72 = 0$. Factoring this quadratic equation: $(a - 9)(a + 8) = 0$. So $a - 9 = 0$ or $a + 8 = 0$, and $a = 9$ or $a = -8$. b to the nth power equals a, so b must be a root of either 9 or -8. Look through the answer choices to find the choice that is not a root of either 9 or -8:

(A) $(-8)^1 = -8$, so this can be a value for b.

(B) $(-2)^3 = -8$, so this can be a value for b.

(C) $2^3 = 8$, not -8, so this *cannot* be a value for b.

(D) $3^2 = 9$, so this can be a value for b.

(E) $9^1 = 9$, so this can be a value for b.

So (C) is the only answer choice that cannot be a value for b.

11. C

The most efficient way to answer this question is to use

the midpoint formula: the midpoint of points (x_1, y_1) and (x_2, y_2) is $\left(\dfrac{x_1 + x_2}{2}, \dfrac{y_1 + y_2}{2} \right)$. You'll use the formula more skillfully if, rather than merely memorize it, you think about what it means, namely, that the midpoint of two points is merely the average of their x- and y-coordinates:

$$\left(\frac{(0 + x_2)}{2} = 3, \frac{(2 + y_2)}{2} = 4 \right)$$

$$(x_2 = 6, y_2 = 6)$$

12. D

$$4\sqrt{2x} - 2 = 16$$

$$4\sqrt{2x} = 18$$

$$\sqrt{2x} = \frac{18}{4}$$

$$\left(\sqrt{2x} \right)^2 = \left(\frac{18}{4} \right)^2$$

$$x = \frac{18 \times 18}{4 \times 4 \times 2} = \frac{9 \times 9}{2 \times 2 \times 2} = \frac{81}{8}$$

13. E

If you can't visualize a graph, plug points in and graph it yourself. If doing so is helpful, use your calculator.

Plug in 2 for x:

$$y = -3x^2$$

$$y = -3(2)^2$$

$y = -3(4)$

$y = -12$

Eliminate (A) and (B).

Plug in -2 for x:

$y = -3x^2$

$y = -3(-2)^2$

$y = -3(4)$

$y = -12$

Eliminate (C) and (D), leaving only (E).

14. C

Think backward. If the person now weighs w pounds, then his or her weight before losing 8 pounds was 8 pounds more than w, or $w + 8$. The person's weight before gaining p pounds was $w + 8 - p$, which can also be written as $w - p + 8$.

15. B

The surface area of a cube is $6e^2$, where $e = $ the length of an edge of the cube. Since the surface area is $36n^2$:

$$6e^2 = 36n^2$$

$$e^2 = 6n^2$$

$$e = n\sqrt{6}$$

The volume of a cube is e^3. To solve for the volume in terms of n, plug in the value for an edge that you just found: Volume $= e^3 = (n\sqrt{6})^3 = 6n^3\sqrt{6}$, answer choice (B).

16. C

Since the ratio of x to y to z is 3:6:8, if $y = 24$ or 4×6, x and z must also be multiplied by 4 for the ratio to hold. So $x = 4 \times 3 = 12$ and $z = 4 \times 8 = 32$, and $x + z = 44$.

SECTION 9

1. E

The pronoun in the sentence must correspond with *teacher shortage* (not *salaries*). Therefore, the pronoun should be *it*. (E) is the only answer choice with this pronoun.

2. A

Items in a series must have the same structure, which is the case for the original sentence. The other answer choices break the parallelism.

3. D

(A) is a run-on, so it cannot be correct. (B), (C), and (E) are awkward and confusing. Be wary of sentences with nonessential clauses separated by commas. (D) has the cleanest structure and is the best answer choice.

4. A

(C) does not use a semicolon correctly. (B), (D), and (E) all unnecessarily add extra words. Be suspicious of answer choices that make the sentence more complex.

5. D

Idiomatically, *the same* should be followed by the preposition *as*, not *than*. There is also a problem of parallelism here; the two things being compared should be in the same grammatical form. Since *talking* is a gerund, the thing it's being compared to should also be a gerund: *driving*.

6. C

This run-on sentence is best corrected by (C), which is grammatically correct and doesn't include extra verbiage. (B) and (E) use the semicolon improperly, and (D) is wordy.

7. E

The sentence is unclear because it doesn't use the correct sequence of tenses. Since the client had already been waiting for fifteen minutes *before* the moment when the receptionist looked up, the first verb must be in the past perfect: *had been waiting*.

8. C

This run-on sentence is a comma splice. A good prediction is to exchange the comma for a semicolon. (B) does this, but (B) also removes *they* and with it the second independent clause. (C) is the only choice with correct sentence structure.

9. E

Because the second part of the sentence is an independent clause, the underlined portion must be altered to create a dependent clause. (C) and (E) do this, but (E) is clearer and better constructed.

10. D

(D) is the only answer choice that creates a complete sentence. Also, the words *rare enough to honor the spiritual essence of the Buddha* is descriptive of *stones*. Therefore, (D) makes sense.

11. D

The two independent clauses in this sentence must be separated by either a semicolon or a coordinating conjunction. (D) uses the semicolon correctly, so it is correct. (C) is close to being correct, but the nonessential information *on the other hand* needs to be set apart with commas.

12. C

The original sentence does not contain a verb. (C) and (E) insert *are* to create a working verb structure. However, (E) incorrectly creates a dependent clause with *these are*.

13. B

The word *that* at the beginning of the sentence makes this sentence incomplete. Simply removing *that*, as in (B), makes the sentence correct.

14. D

The coordinating conjunction *but* makes this sentence incorrect. (D) removes the word to make an independent clause that makes sense with *although* at the beginning of the sentence.

SAT PRACTICE TEST TWO ANSWER SHEET

Remove (or photcopy) the answer sheet and use it to complete the practice test. See the answer key following the test when finished.

Start with number 1 for each section. If a section has fewer questions than answer spaces, leave the extra spaces blank.

SECTION

1

Section 1 is the writing section's essay component.
Lined pages on which you will write your essay can be found in that section.

SECTION

2

1. Ⓐ Ⓑ Ⓒ Ⓓ Ⓔ   11. Ⓐ Ⓑ Ⓒ Ⓓ Ⓔ   21. Ⓐ Ⓑ Ⓒ Ⓓ Ⓔ   31. Ⓐ Ⓑ Ⓒ Ⓓ Ⓔ
2. Ⓐ Ⓑ Ⓒ Ⓓ Ⓔ   12. Ⓐ Ⓑ Ⓒ Ⓓ Ⓔ   22. Ⓐ Ⓑ Ⓒ Ⓓ Ⓔ   32. Ⓐ Ⓑ Ⓒ Ⓓ Ⓔ
3. Ⓐ Ⓑ Ⓒ Ⓓ Ⓔ   13. Ⓐ Ⓑ Ⓒ Ⓓ Ⓔ   23. Ⓐ Ⓑ Ⓒ Ⓓ Ⓔ   33. Ⓐ Ⓑ Ⓒ Ⓓ Ⓔ
4. Ⓐ Ⓑ Ⓒ Ⓓ Ⓔ   14. Ⓐ Ⓑ Ⓒ Ⓓ Ⓔ   24. Ⓐ Ⓑ Ⓒ Ⓓ Ⓔ   34. Ⓐ Ⓑ Ⓒ Ⓓ Ⓔ
5. Ⓐ Ⓑ Ⓒ Ⓓ Ⓔ   15. Ⓐ Ⓑ Ⓒ Ⓓ Ⓔ   25. Ⓐ Ⓑ Ⓒ Ⓓ Ⓔ   35. Ⓐ Ⓑ Ⓒ Ⓓ Ⓔ
6. Ⓐ Ⓑ Ⓒ Ⓓ Ⓔ   16. Ⓐ Ⓑ Ⓒ Ⓓ Ⓔ   26. Ⓐ Ⓑ Ⓒ Ⓓ Ⓔ   36. Ⓐ Ⓑ Ⓒ Ⓓ Ⓔ
7. Ⓐ Ⓑ Ⓒ Ⓓ Ⓔ   17. Ⓐ Ⓑ Ⓒ Ⓓ Ⓔ   27. Ⓐ Ⓑ Ⓒ Ⓓ Ⓔ   37. Ⓐ Ⓑ Ⓒ Ⓓ Ⓔ
8. Ⓐ Ⓑ Ⓒ Ⓓ Ⓔ   18. Ⓐ Ⓑ Ⓒ Ⓓ Ⓔ   28. Ⓐ Ⓑ Ⓒ Ⓓ Ⓔ   38. Ⓐ Ⓑ Ⓒ Ⓓ Ⓔ
9. Ⓐ Ⓑ Ⓒ Ⓓ Ⓔ   19. Ⓐ Ⓑ Ⓒ Ⓓ Ⓔ   29. Ⓐ Ⓑ Ⓒ Ⓓ Ⓔ   39. Ⓐ Ⓑ Ⓒ Ⓓ Ⓔ
10. Ⓐ Ⓑ Ⓒ Ⓓ Ⓔ   20. Ⓐ Ⓑ Ⓒ Ⓓ Ⓔ   30. Ⓐ Ⓑ Ⓒ Ⓓ Ⓔ   40. Ⓐ Ⓑ Ⓒ Ⓓ Ⓔ

☐ # right in Section 2

☐ # wrong in Section 2

SECTION

3

1. Ⓐ Ⓑ Ⓒ Ⓓ Ⓔ   11. Ⓐ Ⓑ Ⓒ Ⓓ Ⓔ   21. Ⓐ Ⓑ Ⓒ Ⓓ Ⓔ   31. Ⓐ Ⓑ Ⓒ Ⓓ Ⓔ
2. Ⓐ Ⓑ Ⓒ Ⓓ Ⓔ   12. Ⓐ Ⓑ Ⓒ Ⓓ Ⓔ   22. Ⓐ Ⓑ Ⓒ Ⓓ Ⓔ   32. Ⓐ Ⓑ Ⓒ Ⓓ Ⓔ
3. Ⓐ Ⓑ Ⓒ Ⓓ Ⓔ   13. Ⓐ Ⓑ Ⓒ Ⓓ Ⓔ   23. Ⓐ Ⓑ Ⓒ Ⓓ Ⓔ   33. Ⓐ Ⓑ Ⓒ Ⓓ Ⓔ
4. Ⓐ Ⓑ Ⓒ Ⓓ Ⓔ   14. Ⓐ Ⓑ Ⓒ Ⓓ Ⓔ   24. Ⓐ Ⓑ Ⓒ Ⓓ Ⓔ   34. Ⓐ Ⓑ Ⓒ Ⓓ Ⓔ
5. Ⓐ Ⓑ Ⓒ Ⓓ Ⓔ   15. Ⓐ Ⓑ Ⓒ Ⓓ Ⓔ   25. Ⓐ Ⓑ Ⓒ Ⓓ Ⓔ   35. Ⓐ Ⓑ Ⓒ Ⓓ Ⓔ
6. Ⓐ Ⓑ Ⓒ Ⓓ Ⓔ   16. Ⓐ Ⓑ Ⓒ Ⓓ Ⓔ   26. Ⓐ Ⓑ Ⓒ Ⓓ Ⓔ   36. Ⓐ Ⓑ Ⓒ Ⓓ Ⓔ
7. Ⓐ Ⓑ Ⓒ Ⓓ Ⓔ   17. Ⓐ Ⓑ Ⓒ Ⓓ Ⓔ   27. Ⓐ Ⓑ Ⓒ Ⓓ Ⓔ   37. Ⓐ Ⓑ Ⓒ Ⓓ Ⓔ
8. Ⓐ Ⓑ Ⓒ Ⓓ Ⓔ   18. Ⓐ Ⓑ Ⓒ Ⓓ Ⓔ   28. Ⓐ Ⓑ Ⓒ Ⓓ Ⓔ   38. Ⓐ Ⓑ Ⓒ Ⓓ Ⓔ
9. Ⓐ Ⓑ Ⓒ Ⓓ Ⓔ   19. Ⓐ Ⓑ Ⓒ Ⓓ Ⓔ   29. Ⓐ Ⓑ Ⓒ Ⓓ Ⓔ   39. Ⓐ Ⓑ Ⓒ Ⓓ Ⓔ
10. Ⓐ Ⓑ Ⓒ Ⓓ Ⓔ   20. Ⓐ Ⓑ Ⓒ Ⓓ Ⓔ   30. Ⓐ Ⓑ Ⓒ Ⓓ Ⓔ   40. Ⓐ Ⓑ Ⓒ Ⓓ Ⓔ

☐ # right in Section 3

☐ # wrong in Section 3

Remove (or photocopy) this answer sheet and use it to complete the practice test.

Start with number 1 for each section. If a section has fewer questions than answer spaces, leave the extra spaces blank.

SECTION

4

1. Ⓐ Ⓑ Ⓒ Ⓓ Ⓔ   11. Ⓐ Ⓑ Ⓒ Ⓓ Ⓔ   21. Ⓐ Ⓑ Ⓒ Ⓓ Ⓔ   31. Ⓐ Ⓑ Ⓒ Ⓓ Ⓔ
2. Ⓐ Ⓑ Ⓒ Ⓓ Ⓔ   12. Ⓐ Ⓑ Ⓒ Ⓓ Ⓔ   22. Ⓐ Ⓑ Ⓒ Ⓓ Ⓔ   32. Ⓐ Ⓑ Ⓒ Ⓓ Ⓔ
3. Ⓐ Ⓑ Ⓒ Ⓓ Ⓔ   13. Ⓐ Ⓑ Ⓒ Ⓓ Ⓔ   23. Ⓐ Ⓑ Ⓒ Ⓓ Ⓔ   33. Ⓐ Ⓑ Ⓒ Ⓓ Ⓔ
4. Ⓐ Ⓑ Ⓒ Ⓓ Ⓔ   14. Ⓐ Ⓑ Ⓒ Ⓓ Ⓔ   24. Ⓐ Ⓑ Ⓒ Ⓓ Ⓔ   34. Ⓐ Ⓑ Ⓒ Ⓓ Ⓔ
5. Ⓐ Ⓑ Ⓒ Ⓓ Ⓔ   15. Ⓐ Ⓑ Ⓒ Ⓓ Ⓔ   25. Ⓐ Ⓑ Ⓒ Ⓓ Ⓔ   35. Ⓐ Ⓑ Ⓒ Ⓓ Ⓔ

right in Section 4

6. Ⓐ Ⓑ Ⓒ Ⓓ Ⓔ   16. Ⓐ Ⓑ Ⓒ Ⓓ Ⓔ   26. Ⓐ Ⓑ Ⓒ Ⓓ Ⓔ   36. Ⓐ Ⓑ Ⓒ Ⓓ Ⓔ
7. Ⓐ Ⓑ Ⓒ Ⓓ Ⓔ   17. Ⓐ Ⓑ Ⓒ Ⓓ Ⓔ   27. Ⓐ Ⓑ Ⓒ Ⓓ Ⓔ   37. Ⓐ Ⓑ Ⓒ Ⓓ Ⓔ
8. Ⓐ Ⓑ Ⓒ Ⓓ Ⓔ   18. Ⓐ Ⓑ Ⓒ Ⓓ Ⓔ   28. Ⓐ Ⓑ Ⓒ Ⓓ Ⓔ   38. Ⓐ Ⓑ Ⓒ Ⓓ Ⓔ
9. Ⓐ Ⓑ Ⓒ Ⓓ Ⓔ   19. Ⓐ Ⓑ Ⓒ Ⓓ Ⓔ   29. Ⓐ Ⓑ Ⓒ Ⓓ Ⓔ   39. Ⓐ Ⓑ Ⓒ Ⓓ Ⓔ

wrong in Section 4

10. Ⓐ Ⓑ Ⓒ Ⓓ Ⓔ   20. Ⓐ Ⓑ Ⓒ Ⓓ Ⓔ   30. Ⓐ Ⓑ Ⓒ Ⓓ Ⓔ   40. Ⓐ Ⓑ Ⓒ Ⓓ Ⓔ

If section 4 of your test book contains math questions that are not multiple choice, continue to item 9 below. Otherwise, continue to item 9 above.

9.   10.   11.   12.   13.

14.   15.   16.   17.   18.

Remove (or photocopy) this answer sheet and use it to complete the practice test.

Start with number 1 for each section. If a section has fewer questions than answer spaces, leave the extra spaces blank.

SECTION

5

1. A B C D E	11. A B C D E	21. A B C D E	31. A B C D E
2. A B C D E	12. A B C D E	22. A B C D E	32. A B C D E
3. A B C D E	13. A B C D E	23. A B C D E	33. A B C D E
4. A B C D E	14. A B C D E	24. A B C D E	34. A B C D E
5. A B C D E	15. A B C D E	25. A B C D E	35. A B C D E
6. A B C D E	16. A B C D E	26. A B C D E	36. A B C D E
7. A B C D E	17. A B C D E	27. A B C D E	37. A B C D E
8. A B C D E	18. A B C D E	28. A B C D E	38. A B C D E
9. A B C D E	19. A B C D E	29. A B C D E	39. A B C D E
10. A B C D E	20. A B C D E	30. A B C D E	40. A B C D E

right in Section 5

wrong in Section 5

SECTION

6

1. A B C D E	11. A B C D E	21. A B C D E	31. A B C D E
2. A B C D E	12. A B C D E	22. A B C D E	32. A B C D E
3. A B C D E	13. A B C D E	23. A B C D E	33. A B C D E
4. A B C D E	14. A B C D E	24. A B C D E	34. A B C D E
5. A B C D E	15. A B C D E	25. A B C D E	35. A B C D E
6. A B C D E	16. A B C D E	26. A B C D E	36. A B C D E
7. A B C D E	17. A B C D E	27. A B C D E	37. A B C D E
8. A B C D E	18. A B C D E	28. A B C D E	38. A B C D E
9. A B C D E	19. A B C D E	29. A B C D E	39. A B C D E
10. A B C D E	20. A B C D E	30. A B C D E	40. A B C D E

right in Section 6

wrong in Section 6

SECTION

7

1. A B C D E	11. A B C D E	21. A B C D E	31. A B C D E
2. A B C D E	12. A B C D E	22. A B C D E	32. A B C D E
3. A B C D E	13. A B C D E	23. A B C D E	33. A B C D E
4. A B C D E	14. A B C D E	24. A B C D E	34. A B C D E
5. A B C D E	15. A B C D E	25. A B C D E	35. A B C D E
6. A B C D E	16. A B C D E	26. A B C D E	36. A B C D E
7. A B C D E	17. A B C D E	27. A B C D E	37. A B C D E
8. A B C D E	18. A B C D E	28. A B C D E	38. A B C D E
9. A B C D E	19. A B C D E	29. A B C D E	39. A B C D E
10. A B C D E	20. A B C D E	30. A B C D E	40. A B C D E

right in Section 7

wrong in Section 7

Remove (or photocopy) this answer sheet and use it to complete the practice test.

Start with number 1 for each section. If a section has fewer questions than answer spaces, leave the extra spaces blank.

SECTION

8

1. Ⓐ Ⓑ Ⓒ Ⓓ Ⓔ	11. Ⓐ Ⓑ Ⓒ Ⓓ Ⓔ	21. Ⓐ Ⓑ Ⓒ Ⓓ Ⓔ	31. Ⓐ Ⓑ Ⓒ Ⓓ Ⓔ
2. Ⓐ Ⓑ Ⓒ Ⓓ Ⓔ	12. Ⓐ Ⓑ Ⓒ Ⓓ Ⓔ	22. Ⓐ Ⓑ Ⓒ Ⓓ Ⓔ	32. Ⓐ Ⓑ Ⓒ Ⓓ Ⓔ
3. Ⓐ Ⓑ Ⓒ Ⓓ Ⓔ	13. Ⓐ Ⓑ Ⓒ Ⓓ Ⓔ	23. Ⓐ Ⓑ Ⓒ Ⓓ Ⓔ	33. Ⓐ Ⓑ Ⓒ Ⓓ Ⓔ
4. Ⓐ Ⓑ Ⓒ Ⓓ Ⓔ	14. Ⓐ Ⓑ Ⓒ Ⓓ Ⓔ	24. Ⓐ Ⓑ Ⓒ Ⓓ Ⓔ	34. Ⓐ Ⓑ Ⓒ Ⓓ Ⓔ
5. Ⓐ Ⓑ Ⓒ Ⓓ Ⓔ	15. Ⓐ Ⓑ Ⓒ Ⓓ Ⓔ	25. Ⓐ Ⓑ Ⓒ Ⓓ Ⓔ	35. Ⓐ Ⓑ Ⓒ Ⓓ Ⓔ
6. Ⓐ Ⓑ Ⓒ Ⓓ Ⓔ	16. Ⓐ Ⓑ Ⓒ Ⓓ Ⓔ	26. Ⓐ Ⓑ Ⓒ Ⓓ Ⓔ	36. Ⓐ Ⓑ Ⓒ Ⓓ Ⓔ
7. Ⓐ Ⓑ Ⓒ Ⓓ Ⓔ	17. Ⓐ Ⓑ Ⓒ Ⓓ Ⓔ	27. Ⓐ Ⓑ Ⓒ Ⓓ Ⓔ	37. Ⓐ Ⓑ Ⓒ Ⓓ Ⓔ
8. Ⓐ Ⓑ Ⓒ Ⓓ Ⓔ	18. Ⓐ Ⓑ Ⓒ Ⓓ Ⓔ	28. Ⓐ Ⓑ Ⓒ Ⓓ Ⓔ	38. Ⓐ Ⓑ Ⓒ Ⓓ Ⓔ
9. Ⓐ Ⓑ Ⓒ Ⓓ Ⓔ	19. Ⓐ Ⓑ Ⓒ Ⓓ Ⓔ	29. Ⓐ Ⓑ Ⓒ Ⓓ Ⓔ	39. Ⓐ Ⓑ Ⓒ Ⓓ Ⓔ
10. Ⓐ Ⓑ Ⓒ Ⓓ Ⓔ	20. Ⓐ Ⓑ Ⓒ Ⓓ Ⓔ	30. Ⓐ Ⓑ Ⓒ Ⓓ Ⓔ	40. Ⓐ Ⓑ Ⓒ Ⓓ Ⓔ

☐ # right in Section 8

☐ # wrong in Section 8

SECTION

9

1. Ⓐ Ⓑ Ⓒ Ⓓ Ⓔ	11. Ⓐ Ⓑ Ⓒ Ⓓ Ⓔ	21. Ⓐ Ⓑ Ⓒ Ⓓ Ⓔ	31. Ⓐ Ⓑ Ⓒ Ⓓ Ⓔ
2. Ⓐ Ⓑ Ⓒ Ⓓ Ⓔ	12. Ⓐ Ⓑ Ⓒ Ⓓ Ⓔ	22. Ⓐ Ⓑ Ⓒ Ⓓ Ⓔ	32. Ⓐ Ⓑ Ⓒ Ⓓ Ⓔ
3. Ⓐ Ⓑ Ⓒ Ⓓ Ⓔ	13. Ⓐ Ⓑ Ⓒ Ⓓ Ⓔ	23. Ⓐ Ⓑ Ⓒ Ⓓ Ⓔ	33. Ⓐ Ⓑ Ⓒ Ⓓ Ⓔ
4. Ⓐ Ⓑ Ⓒ Ⓓ Ⓔ	14. Ⓐ Ⓑ Ⓒ Ⓓ Ⓔ	24. Ⓐ Ⓑ Ⓒ Ⓓ Ⓔ	34. Ⓐ Ⓑ Ⓒ Ⓓ Ⓔ
5. Ⓐ Ⓑ Ⓒ Ⓓ Ⓔ	15. Ⓐ Ⓑ Ⓒ Ⓓ Ⓔ	25. Ⓐ Ⓑ Ⓒ Ⓓ Ⓔ	35. Ⓐ Ⓑ Ⓒ Ⓓ Ⓔ
6. Ⓐ Ⓑ Ⓒ Ⓓ Ⓔ	16. Ⓐ Ⓑ Ⓒ Ⓓ Ⓔ	26. Ⓐ Ⓑ Ⓒ Ⓓ Ⓔ	36. Ⓐ Ⓑ Ⓒ Ⓓ Ⓔ
7. Ⓐ Ⓑ Ⓒ Ⓓ Ⓔ	17. Ⓐ Ⓑ Ⓒ Ⓓ Ⓔ	27. Ⓐ Ⓑ Ⓒ Ⓓ Ⓔ	37. Ⓐ Ⓑ Ⓒ Ⓓ Ⓔ
8. Ⓐ Ⓑ Ⓒ Ⓓ Ⓔ	18. Ⓐ Ⓑ Ⓒ Ⓓ Ⓔ	28. Ⓐ Ⓑ Ⓒ Ⓓ Ⓔ	38. Ⓐ Ⓑ Ⓒ Ⓓ Ⓔ
9. Ⓐ Ⓑ Ⓒ Ⓓ Ⓔ	19. Ⓐ Ⓑ Ⓒ Ⓓ Ⓔ	29. Ⓐ Ⓑ Ⓒ Ⓓ Ⓔ	39. Ⓐ Ⓑ Ⓒ Ⓓ Ⓔ
10. Ⓐ Ⓑ Ⓒ Ⓓ Ⓔ	20. Ⓐ Ⓑ Ⓒ Ⓓ Ⓔ	30. Ⓐ Ⓑ Ⓒ Ⓓ Ⓔ	40. Ⓐ Ⓑ Ⓒ Ⓓ Ⓔ

☐ # right in Section 9

☐ # wrong in Section 9

SECTION 1
Time—25 Minutes
ESSAY

The essay gives you an opportunity to show how effectively you can develop and express ideas. You should, therefore, take care to develop your point of view, present your ideas logically and clearly, and use language precisely.

Your essay must be written in your Answer Grid Booklet—you will receive no other paper on which to write. You will have enough space if you write on every line, avoid wide margins, and keep your handwriting to a reasonable size. Remember that people who are not familiar with your handwriting will read what you write. Try to write or print so that what you are writing is legible to those readers.

You have twenty-five minutes to write an essay on the topic assigned below.
DO NOT WRITE ON ANOTHER TOPIC. AN OFF-TOPIC ESSAY WILL RECEIVE A SCORE OF ZERO.

Think carefully about the issue presented in the following excerpt and the assignment below.

> "Life without memory is no life at all, just as an intelligence without the possibility of expression is not really an intelligence. Our memory is our coherence, our reason, our feeling, even our action. Without it, we are nothing."
> –Luis Buñuel, *An Unspeakable Betrayal*
>
> "Many a man fails to become a thinker for the sole reason that his memory is too good."
>
> –Friedrich Nietzsche, *Maxims*

Assignment: Is memory as central as Buñuel believes, or does it merely hold us back? Plan and write an essay in which you develop your point of view on this issue. Support your position with reasoning and examples taken from your reading, studies, experience, or observations.

DO NOT WRITE YOUR ESSAY IN YOUR TEST BOOK.
You will receive credit only for what you write in your Answer Grid Booklet.

Write your essays on separate sheets of paper.

SECTION 2

Time—25 Minutes
20 Questions

Directions: For this section, solve each problem and decide which is the best of the choices given. Fill in the corresponding oval on the answer sheet. You may use any available space for scratchwork.

Notes:

(1) Calculator use is permitted.

(2) All numbers used are real numbers.

(3) Figures are provided for some problems. All figures are drawn to scale and lie in a plane UNLESS otherwise indicated.

(4) Unless otherwise specified, the domain of any function f is assumed to be the set of all real numbers x for which $f(x)$ is a real number.

$A = \frac{1}{2}bh$ $c^2 = a^2 + b^2$ Special Right Triangles $A = \pi r^2$ $V = \ell wh$ $V = \pi r^2 h$ $A = \ell w$
$C = 2\pi r$

The sum of the degree measures of the angles in a triangle is 180.
The number of degrees of arc in a circle is 360.
A straight angle has a degree measure of 180.

1. $\left(\dfrac{1}{5} + \dfrac{1}{3}\right) \div \dfrac{1}{2} =$

(A) $\dfrac{1}{8}$

(B) $\dfrac{1}{4}$

(C) $\dfrac{4}{15}$

(D) $\dfrac{1}{2}$

(E) $\dfrac{16}{15}$

2. What is the value of $x^2 - 2x$ when $x = -2$?

(A) -8

(B) -4

(C) 0

(D) 4

(E) 8

3. Vito read 96 pages in 2 hours and 40 minutes. What was Vito's average rate of pages per hour?

(A) 24

(B) 30

(C) 36

(D) 42

(E) 48

GO ON TO THE NEXT PAGE

4. For how many integer values of x will $\frac{7}{x}$ be greater than $\frac{1}{4}$ and less than $\frac{1}{3}$?

(A) 6
(B) 7
(C) 12
(D) 28
(E) Infinitely many

5. What is the average (arithmetic mean) of $2x + 5$, $5x - 6$, and $-4x + 2$?

(A) $x + \frac{1}{3}$

(B) $x + 1$

(C) $3x + \frac{1}{3}$

(D) $3x + 3$

(E) $3x + 3\frac{1}{3}$

6. In a group of 25 students, 16 are female. What percent of the group is female?

(A) 16%
(B) 40%
(C) 60%
(D) 64%
(E) 75%

7. In the triangle above, what is the degree measure of angle B?

(A) 45
(B) 60
(C) 65
(D) 75
(E) 80

8. For all $x \neq 0$, $\dfrac{x^2 + x^2 + x^2}{x^2} =$

(A) 3
(B) $3x$
(C) x^2
(D) x^3
(E) x^4

9. The equation $x^2 = 5x - 4$ has how many distinct real solutions?

(A) 0
(B) 1
(C) 2
(D) 3
(E) Infinitely many

GO ON TO THE NEXT PAGE

10. Which of the following sets of numbers has the property that the sum of any two numbers in the set is also a number in the set?

    I. The set of even integers
    II. The set of odd integers
    III. The set of prime numbers

(A) I only
(B) III only
(C) I and II only
(D) I and III only
(E) I, II, and III

11. Martin's average (arithmetic mean) score after 4 tests is 89. What score on the 5th test would bring Martin's average up to exactly 90?

(A) 90
(B) 91
(C) 92
(D) 93
(E) 94

12. The price s of a sweater is reduced by 25% for a sale. After the sale, the reduced price is increased by 20%. Which of the following represents the final price of the sweater?

(A) .80s
(B) .85s
(C) .90s
(D) .95s
(E) 1.05s

13. How many distinct prime factors does the number 36 have?

(A) 2
(B) 3
(C) 4
(D) 5
(E) 6

14. If the area of a triangle is 36 and its base is 9, what is the length of the altitude to that base?

(A) 2
(B) 4
(C) 6
(D) 8
(E) 12

15. Let a ♣ be defined for all positive integers a by the equation $a ♣ = \dfrac{a}{4} - \dfrac{a}{6}$. If $x ♣ = 3$, what is the value of x?

(A) 18
(B) 28
(C) 36
(D) 40
(E) 54

16. Joan has q quarters, d dimes, n nickels, and no other coins in her pocket. Which of the following represents the total number of coins in Joan's pocket?

(A) $q + d + n$
(B) $5q + 2d + n$
(C) .25q + .10d + .05n
(D) $(25 + 10 + 5)(q + d + n)$
(E) $25q + 10d + 5n$

GO ON TO THE NEXT PAGE ⇨

17. Which of the following is an equation for the graph above?

(A) $y = -2x + 1$

(B) $y = x + 1$

(C) $y = x + 2$

(D) $y = 2x + 1$

(E) $y = 2x + 2$

18. If an integer is divisible by 6 and by 9, then the integer must be divisible by which of the following?

   I. 12
   II. 18
   III. 36

(A) I only

(B) II only

(C) I and II only

(D) II and III only

(E) I, II, and III

19. A wooden cube with volume 64 is sliced in half horizontally. The two halves are then glued together to form a rectangular solid which is not a cube. What is the surface area of this new solid?

(A) 48

(B) 56

(C) 96

(D) 112

(E) 128

20. In $\triangle PRS$ above, RT is the altitude to side PS, and QS is the altitude to side PR. If $RT = 7$, $PR = 8$, and $QS = 9$, what is the length of PS?

(A) $5\frac{1}{7}$

(B) $6\frac{2}{9}$

(C) $7\frac{7}{8}$

(D) $10\frac{2}{7}$

(E) $13\frac{4}{9}$

IF YOU FINISH BEFORE TIME IS CALLED, YOU MAY CHECK YOUR WORK ON THIS SECTION ONLY. DO NOT TURN TO ANY OTHER SECTION IN THE TEST.

STOP

SECTION 3

Time—25 Minutes
24 Questions

Directions: For each of the following questions, choose the best answer and darken the corresponding oval on the answer sheet.

Each sentence below has one or two blanks, each blank indicating that something has been omitted. Beneath the sentence are five words or sets of words labeled A through E. Choose the word or set of words that, when inserted in the sentence, best fits the meaning of the sentence as a whole.

EXAMPLE:

Today's small, portable computers contrast markedly with the earliest electronic computers, which were --------.

(A) effective
(B) invented
(C) useful
(D) destructive
(E) enormous   Ⓐ Ⓑ Ⓒ Ⓓ ●

1. Finding an old movie poster that is still-------- usually proves difficult because such posters were meant to be used and then--------.

   (A) recognizable . . . returned
   (B) relevant . . . discarded
   (C) intact . . . destroyed
   (D) immaculate . . . restored
   (E) displayed . . . maintained

2. The Kemp's Ridley turtle, long considered one of the most--------creatures of the sea, finally appears to be making some headway in its battle against extinction.

   (A) elusive
   (B) prevalent
   (C) combative
   (D) voracious
   (E) imperiled

3. Before the invention of the tape recorder, quotes from an interview were rarely--------; journalists usually paraphrased the words of their subject.

   (A) verbatim
   (B) misconstrued
   (C) pragmatic
   (D) extensive
   (E) plagiarized

4. Batchelor's reputation as---------novelist encouraged hopes that his political thriller would offer more --------characterizations than are usually found in the genre.

   (A) a serious . . . subtle
   (B) a maturing . . . sweeping
   (C) a prolific . . . accurate
   (D) an accomplished . . . fictional
   (E) a reclusive . . . authentic

5. Aristotle espoused a---------biological model in which all extant species are unchanging and eternal and no new species ever come into existence.

   (A) paradoxical
   (B) morbid
   (C) static
   (D) holistic
   (E) homogeneous

GO ON TO THE NEXT PAGE ⟶

6. The agency's failure to---------policies that it has acknowledged are flawed is a potent demonstration of its---------approach to correcting its problems.

   (A) support . . . ambiguous
   (B) institute . . . earnest
   (C) rescind . . . lackadaisical
   (D) amend . . . devoted
   (E) chasten . . . meticulous

7. The inconsistency of the educational policies adopted by various schools across the state has been greatly---------by the rapid turnover of school superintendents.

   (A) counteracted
   (B) stabilized
   (C) criticized
   (D) exacerbated
   (E) understated

8. The journalist's claim of---------is belied by her record of contributing to the campaign funds of only one party's candidates.

   (A) innocence
   (B) corruption
   (C) impartiality
   (D) affluence
   (E) loyalty

GO ON TO THE NEXT PAGE

Directions: The passages below are followed by questions based on their content; questions following a pair of related passages may also be based on the relationship between the paired passages. Answer the questions on the basis of what is <u>stated</u> or <u>implied</u> in the passages and in any introductory material that may be provided.

Questions 9–12 refer to the following passage.

Passage 1

Recently, a disturbing practice has developed among book publishers. They have hired contemporary authors to write sequels to the novels of long-dead authors. If these sequels
(5) were being written for the works of relatively untalented or unknown authors, then no one would pay much attention. Unfortunately, this has not been the case. One author wrote a sequel to Margaret Mitchell's *Gone with the*
(10) Wind, for example. It's clear that these sequels are written in order to entice an author's or a literary work's fans to spend money. Since these counterfeits can never equal the original, however, disappointment is the only possible
(15) outcome for the reader.

Passage 2

What unalloyed delight for those who have read all of Sir Arthur Conan Doyle's stories of Sherlock Holmes to discover Nicholas Meyer's 1989 novel, *The Seven Percent Solution*. In
(20) it, the violin-playing detective and his faithful sidekick, Dr. Watson, roam the moors in search of evil-doers. Once again, readers can get lost in the cozy, yet often terrifying world of Victorian England. While Meyer's
(25) style, informed as it is by modern civilization and sensibilities, is not Sir Arthur's, the book nonetheless contains many pleasures for the avid Sherlockian. One can only hope that Meyer will continue to write novels about
(30) Watson and Holmes so that devoted followers will get lasting pleasure from reading them.

9. The author of Passage 1 would most likely agree with which of the following statements?

(A) It is easier to write a sequel to the work of an unknown author than it is to write a sequel to the work of a famous author.

(B) Modern sequels to old works should be regarded as pale imitations of the originals.

(C) Although many modern sequels to older books are of poor quality, *The Seven Percent Solution* is an exception to that rule.

(D) The works of Margaret Mitchell have caused indignation among many readers.

(E) Readers who buy sequels rarely read the original works on which the sequels are based.

10. The author of Passage 1 most likely regards Margaret Mitchell as an author

(A) who is well-known

(B) who wrote only one novel

(C) whose skills are comparable to those of Sir Arthur Conan Doyle

(D) whose book is more famous than its author

(E) who will disappoint her readers

GO ON TO THE NEXT PAGE ⇨

11. In Passage 2, line 16, the word "unalloyed" most nearly means

    (A) metallic
    (B) effervescent
    (C) plentiful
    (D) pure
    (E) bland

12. The author of Passage 2 would most likely respond to the contention that "disappointment is the only possible outcome for the reader" (Passage 1, lines 14–15) of sequels by

    (A) reconsidering his own thesis
    (B) countering that *The Seven Percent Solution* is superior to the sequel to *Gone with the Wind*
    (C) mocking the author's rigid views in Passage 1
    (D) agreeing that while some readers will be disappointed, some will be very pleased
    (E) emphasizing the pleasure an ardent fan gets from reading a sequel to the work of an admired author

GO ON TO THE NEXT PAGE

Questions 13–24 refer to the following passage.

The following passage is an excerpt from a book about wolves, written by a self-taught naturalist who studied them in the wild.

My precautions against disturbing the wolves were superfluous. It had required me a week to get their measure, but they must have taken mine at our first meeting; and while there
(5) was nothing disdainful in their evident assessment of me, they managed to ignore my presence, and indeed my very existence, with a thoroughness which was somehow disconcerting.
(10) Quite by accident I had pitched my tent within ten yards of one of the major paths used by the wolves when they were going to, or coming from, their hunting paths to the westward; and only a few hours after I had
(15) taken up my residence one of the wolves came back from a trip and discovered me and my tent.

He was at the end of a hard night's work and was clearly tired and anxious to go home
(20) to bed. He came over a small rise fifty yards from me with his head down, his eyes half-closed, and a preoccupied air about him. Far from being the preternaturally alert and suspicious beast of fiction, this wolf was so self-
(25) engrossed that he came straight on to within fifteen yards of me, and might have gone right past the tent without seeing it at all, had I not banged an elbow against the teakettle, making a resounding clank. The wolf's head
(30) came up and his eyes opened wide, but he did not stop or falter in his pace. One brief, side-long glance was all he vouchsafed to me as he continued on his way.

By the time this happened, I had learned a
(35) great deal about my wolfish neighbors, and one of the facts which had emerged was that they were not nomadic roamers, as is almost universally believed, but were settled beasts and the possessors of a large permanent estate
(40) with very definite boundaries. The territory owned by my wolf family comprised more than a hundred square miles, bounded on one side by a river but otherwise not delimited by geographical features. Nevertheless there were
(45) boundaries, clearly indicated in wolfish fashion.

Once a week, more or less, the clan made the rounds of the family lands and freshened up the boundary markers—a sort of lupine* beating of the bounds. This careful attention
(50) to property rights was perhaps made necessary by the presence of two other wolf families whose lands abutted on ours, although I never discovered any evidence of bickering or disagreements between the owners of the vari-
(55) ous adjoining estates. I suspect, therefore, that it was more of a ritual activity.

In any event, once I had become aware of this strong feeling of property among the wolves, I decided to use this knowledge to
(60) make them at least recognize my existence. One evening, after they had gone off for their regular nightly hunt, I staked out a property claim of my own, embracing perhaps three acres, with the tent at the middle, and including a
(65) hundred yard long section of the wolves' path. This took most of the night and required frequent returns to the tent to consume copious quantities of tea; but before dawn brought the hunters home, the task was done and I retired,
(70) somewhat exhausted, to observe the results.

I had not long to wait. At 0814 hours, according to my wolf log, the leading male of the clan appeared over the ridge behind me, padding homeward with his usual air of
(75) preoccupation. As usual, he did not deign to look at the tent; but when he reached the point where my property line intersected the trail, he stopped as abruptly as if he had run into an invisible wall. His attitude of fatigue vanished
(80) and was replaced by one of bewilderment. Cautiously he extended his nose and sniffed at one of my marked bushes. After a minute of complete indecision he backed away a

few yards and sat down. And then, finally, he
(85) looked directly at the tent and me. It was a
long, considering sort of look.

Having achieved my object—that of forcing
at least one of the wolves to take cognizance
of my existence—I now began to wonder if,
(90) in my ignorance, I had transgressed some
unknown wolf law of major importance and
would have to pay for my temerity. I found
myself regretting the absence of a weapon as
the look I was getting became longer, more
(95) thoughtful, and still more intent. In an effort
to break the impasse I loudly cleared my throat
and turned my back on the wolf to indicate as
clearly as possible that I found his continued
scrutiny impolite, if not actually offensive.
(100) He appeared to take the hint. Briskly, and
with an air of decision, he turned his attention away from me and began a systematic
tour of the area, sniffing each boundary
marker once or twice, and carefully placing
(105) his mark on the outside of each clump of
grass or stone. In fifteen minutes he rejoined
the path at the point where it left my property
and trotted off towards his home, leaving me
with a good deal to occupy my thoughts.

lupine: relating to wolves

13. According to the author, why were his
precautions against disturbing the wolves
"superfluous" (line 2)?

(A) It was several weeks before he encountered his first wolf.

(B) Other wild animals posed a greater
threat to his safety.

(C) The wolves noticed him but were not
interested in harming him.

(D) He was not bothered by the wolves until
he started interfering with them.

(E) The wolves were unable to detect him
because of their poor eyesight.

14. The author mentions the wolves'
"assessment" of him (line 6) in order to

(A) account for their strange behavior
towards him

(B) convey his initial fear of being attacked

(C) emphasize his ignorance on first
encountering them

(D) indicate the need for precautions
against disturbing them

(E) suggest his courage in an unfamiliar
situation

15. In the third paragraph, the author is primarily
surprised to find that the wolf

(A) is traveling alone

(B) lacks the energy to respond

(C) is hunting at night

(D) is not more on its guard

(E) does not attack him

16. In line 19, the word "anxious" most nearly
means

(A) distressed

(B) afraid

(C) eager

(D) uneasy

(E) worried

17. In line 38, the word "settled" most nearly
means

(A) decided

(B) resolute

(C) stable

(D) inflexible

(E) confident

GO ON TO THE NEXT PAGE ⟶

18. Lines 34–40 provide

    (A) a contradiction of popular myth

    (B) an explanation of a paradox

    (C) a rebuttal of established facts

    (D) an exception to a general rule

    (E) a summary of conclusions

19. The author suggests that boundary marking was a "ritual activity" (line 56) because

    (A) the wolves marked their boundaries at regular intervals

    (B) no disputes over territory ever seemed to occur

    (C) the boundaries were marked by geographical features

    (D) the boundaries were marked at the same time each week

    (E) the whole family of wolves participated in the activity

20. Which of the following discoveries would most weaken the author's thesis concerning the wolves' "strong feeling of property" (line 58)?

    (A) Disputes over boundaries are a frequent occurrence.

    (B) Wolf territories are typically around one hundred square miles in area.

    (C) Wolf families often wander from place to place to find food.

    (D) Territorial conflicts between wolves and human beings are rare.

    (E) Wolves are generally alert when encountering other animals.

21. The author most likely mentions an "invisible wall" (line 79) in order to emphasize

    (A) his delight in attracting the wolf's attention

    (B) the wolf's annoyance at encountering a challenge

    (C) the high speed at which the wolf was traveling

    (D) the sudden manner in which the wolf stopped

    (E) the wolf's exhaustion after a night of hunting

22. The wolf's first reaction on encountering the author's property marking is one of

    (A) combativeness

    (B) confusion

    (C) anxiety

    (D) wariness

    (E) dread

23. In line 92, "temerity" means

    (A) discourtesy

    (B) rashness

    (C) courage

    (D) anger

    (E) discretion

24. The author turns his back on the wolf (line 97) primarily in order to

    (A) demonstrate his power over the wolf

    (B) bring about some change in the situation

    (C) compel the wolf to recognize his existence

    (D) look for a suitable weapon

    (E) avoid the wolf's hypnotic gaze

IF YOU FINISH BEFORE TIME IS CALLED, YOU MAY CHECK YOUR WORK ON THIS SECTION ONLY. DO NOT TURN TO ANY OTHER SECTION IN THE TEST.

SECTION 4

Time—25 Minutes

18 Questions

Directions: For this section, solve each problem and decide which is the best of the choices given. Fill in the corresponding oval on the answer sheet. You may use any available space for scratchwork.

Notes:

(1) Calculator use is permitted.

(2) All numbers used are real numbers.

(3) Figures are provided for some problems. All figures are drawn to scale and lie in a plane UNLESS otherwise indicated.

(4) Unless otherwise specified, the domain of any function f is assumed to be the set of all real numbers x for which $f(x)$ is a real number.

Information

$A = \frac{1}{2}bh$ $c^2 = a^2 + b^2$ Special Right Triangles $A = \pi r^2$ $V = \ell wh$ $V = \pi r^2 h$ $A = \ell w$

$C = 2\pi r$

The sum of the degree measures of the angles in a triangle is 180.

The number of degrees of arc in a circle is 360.

A straight angle has a degree measure of 180.

---

1. If $r = 3$ and $s = 1$, then $r^2 - 2s =$

   (A) 2

   (B) 4

   (C) 6

   (D) 7

   (E) 9

2. Which of the following equations best describes the line shown in the graph above?

   (A) $y = -2x + 6$

   (B) $y = \frac{1}{2}x + 6$

   (C) $y = -2x + 3$

   (D) $y = \frac{-1}{2}x + 3$

   (E) $y = 2x + 3$

GO ON TO THE NEXT PAGE

3. If q is 4 less than r and r is 6 more than s, what is the value of q when $s = 2$?

(A) −8

(B) −4

(C) −2

(D) 4

(E) 8

4. On a certain planet, if each year has 9 months and each month has 15 days, how many full years have passed after 700 days on this planet?

(A) 1

(B) 2

(C) 3

(D) 5

(E) 7

5. If $f(x) = x^2$ for all real values of x, which of the following is *not* a possible value of $f(x)$?

   I. −4

   II. 0

   III. 2.3

(A) I only

(B) II only

(C) III only

(D) I and II only

(E) II and III only

Questions 6–8 refer to the following table, which shows the amount of trash collected by 30 participants in a litter cleanup drive.

Trash Collected in Litter Cleanup Drive

Pieces of trash	10	15	20	25	30
Number of participants	12	9	4	4	1

6. What is the mode of the number of pieces of trash collected by the participants in the litter cleanup drive?

(A) 10

(B) 15

(C) 20

(D) 25

(E) 30

7. The goal of the litter cleanup drive was to collect 500 pieces of trash. What percent of this goal did the 30 participants achieve?

(A) 8%

(B) 20%

(C) 56%

(D) 93%

(E) 100%

8. What was the average amount of trash collected by the 30 participants in the litter cleanup drive?

(A) Between 10 and 11 pieces

(B) Between 11 and 12 pieces

(C) Between 15 and 16 pieces

(D) Between 19 and 20 pieces

(E) Between 20 and 21 pieces

GO ON TO THE NEXT PAGE

Directions: For Student-Produced Response questions 9–18, use the grids at the bottom of the answer sheet page on which you have answered questions 1–8.

Each of the remaining 10 questions requires you to solve the problem and enter your answer by marking the ovals in the special grid, as shown in the example below. You may use any available space for scratch work.

Answer: 1.25 or $\frac{5}{4}$ or 5/4

Write answer in boxes.

Grid-in result →

Fraction line
Decimal point

You may start your answers in any column, space permitting. Columns not needed should be left blank.

Either position is correct.

- It is recommended, though not required, that you write your answer in the boxes at the top of the columns. However, you will receive credit only for darkening the ovals correctly.

- Grid only one answer to a question, even though some problems have more than one correct answer.

- Darken no more than one oval in a column.

- No answers are negative.

- Mixed numbers cannot be gridded. For example: the number $1\frac{1}{4}$ must be gridded as 1.25 or 5/4.

(If $\boxed{1\,|\,1\,|\,/\,|\,4}$ is gridded, it will be interpreted as $\frac{11}{4}$ not $1\frac{1}{4}$.)

- **Decimal Accuracy:** Decimal answers must be entered as accurately as possible. For example, if you obtain an answer such as 0.1666..., you should record the result as .166 or .167. **Less accurate values such as .16 or .17 are not acceptable.**

Acceptable ways to grid $\frac{1}{6}$ = .1666...

10. What is $\frac{1}{4}$ percent of 16?

9. In the figure above, if line p is parallel to line q, what is the value of y?

GO ON TO THE NEXT PAGE ⟩

$$\frac{3}{a}, \frac{5}{a}, \frac{14}{a}$$

11. Each of the fractions above is in its simplest reduced form, and a is an integer greater than 1 and less than 50. Grid-in one possible value of a.

12. If there are 36 men and 24 women in a group, women make up what fraction of the entire group?

16. What is the area of the triangle in the figure above?

13. What is the value of $\frac{3s+5}{4}$ when $s = 9$?

17. A square is divided in half to form two congruent rectangles, each with perimeter 24. What is the area of the original square?

14. If the positive integer x leaves a remainder of 2 when divided by 6, what will the remainder be when $x + 8$ is divided by 6?

18. The formula for converting a Fahrenheit temperature reading to a Celsius temperature reading is $C = \frac{5}{9}(F - 32)$, where C is the reading in degrees Celsius and F is the reading in degrees Fahrenheit. What is the Fahrenheit equivalent to a reading of 95° Celsius?

15. Pat deposited 15% of last week's take-home pay into a savings account. If she deposited $37.50, what was last week's take-home pay?

IF YOU FINISH BEFORE TIME IS CALLED, YOU MAY CHECK YOUR WORK ON THIS SECTION ONLY. DO NOT TURN TO ANY OTHER SECTION IN THE TEST.

STOP

SECTION 5
Time—25 Minutes
35 Questions

Directions: For each question in this section, select the best answer from among the choices given and fill in the corresponding oval on the answer sheet.

The following sentences test correctness and effectiveness of expression. Part of each sentence or the entire sentence is underlined; beneath each sentence are five ways of phrasing the underlined material. Choice A repeats the original phrasing; the other four choices are different. If you think the original phrasing produces a better sentence than any of the alternatives, select choice A; if not, select one of the other choices.

In making your selection, follow the requirements of standard written English; that is, pay attention to grammar, choice of words, sentence construction, and punctuation. Your selection should result in the most effective sentence—clear and precise, without awkwardness or ambiguity.

EXAMPLE: ANSWER:

Every apple in the baskets <u>are ripe and labeled according to the date it was picked</u>.   Ⓐ ● Ⓒ Ⓓ Ⓔ

(A) are ripe and labeled according to the date it was picked
(B) is ripe and labeled according to the date it was picked
(C) are ripe and labeled according to the date they were picked
(D) is ripe and labeled according to the date they were picked
(E) are ripe and labeled as to the date it was picked

1. Trekking into the deep, inactive crater, we suddenly realized that all outside sound <u>blocked by the dense rock walls</u> of the volcano.

   (A) blocked by the dense rock walls
   (B) blocked as a result of the dense rock walls
   (C) was blocked by the dense rock walls
   (D) was blocking the dense rock walls
   (E) was going to be blocking the dense and rocky walls

2. Tessa, after several lengthy phone conversations <u>who occupied most of her afternoon</u>, confirmed debate practice, an African dance class, and a part-time babysitting job.

   (A) who occupied most of her afternoon
   (B) whom occupied most of her afternoon
   (C) that occupied most afternoons
   (D) which occupied most of her afternoon
   (E) which became her afternoon occupation

3. <u>Perhaps no person was most crucial</u> to the success of the film *On the Waterfront* than the young actor Marlon Brando, who mesmerized audiences with his talent.

   (A) Perhaps no person was most crucial
   (B) Perhaps no person was crucialer
   (C) Perhaps every person was more crucial
   (D) Perhaps the most crucial person
   (E) Perhaps no person was more crucial

4. During the Renaissance, artists such as Michelangelo and Fra Angelico, <u>who have worked</u> for the Church, did not have to search far for subject matter.

   (A) who have worked
   (B) which worked
   (C) who worked
   (D) who worked mostly
   (E) who have always worked

GO ON TO THE NEXT PAGE ⇨

5. As we waited for the Haunted House ride to begin, we heard strange sounds that seemed to be <u>neither of human or mechanical origin</u>.

   (A) neither of human or mechanical origin
   (B) neither of human nor mechanical origin
   (C) either of human nor mechanical origin
   (D) neither of human nor was it mechanical in origin
   (E) either of human origin or that of mechanical

6. Artists during World War I created performances and paintings that reflected the chaos of war, the anxiety of the people, and <u>they showed the irrational behavior that was escalating</u> in the cities of Europe.

   (A) they showed the irrational behavior that was escalating
   (B) the irrational behavior that is escalating
   (C) they showed the irrational escalation of behavior
   (D) the irrational behavior that was escalating
   (E) the irrational behavior that should have been escalating

7. Known as one of the group of existential French writers, Simone Weil is respected as much for her philosophical ideas <u>as she was for her writing</u>.

   (A) as she was for her writing
   (B) as she was for writing them down
   (C) as she is for having written
   (D) and she was for her writing
   (E) as she is for her writing

8. The professor, after distributing samples of igneous rock, explained that this type of rock is formed under intense heat and pressure <u>deep down there within the crust of the earth</u>.

   (A) deep down there within the crust of the earth
   (B) deep within earth's crust
   (C) deeper down there within the crust of earth
   (D) deep within the earth

   (E) deep down there within the earth's crust

9. Three women in the booth of the Swan Diner <u>were angrily discussing the terms of the lease, and arguing about</u> the level of commitment expected from each of them.

   (A) were angrily discussing the terms of the lease, and arguing about
   (B) were angrily discussing the terms of the lease, but they argued about
   (C) were discussing angrily the terms of the lease, and arguing for
   (D) was angrily discussing the terms of the lease, and arguing with
   (E) had been angrily in discussion about the terms of the lease, and arguing about

10. Although talent may be a crucial element on the road to fame, it will be <u>difficult to get very far</u> without a highly developed work ethic.

    (A) difficult to get very far
    (B) difficult to travel there
    (C) hard to get going
    (D) difficult to get farther
    (E) difficult to become well known

11. Unlike a root canal, which is the preferred method for saving a diseased tooth, <u>chewing problems can result from extraction</u>.

    (A) chewing problems can result from extraction
    (B) problems with chewing can result from an extraction
    (C) an extraction is resulting in chewing problems
    (D) an extraction can result in chewing problems
    (E) an extraction is the result of chewing problems

GO ON TO THE NEXT PAGE →

Directions: The following sentences test your ability to recognize grammar and usage errors. Each sentence contains either a single error or no error at all. No sentence contains more than one error. The error, if there is one, is underlined and lettered. If the sentence contains an error, select the one underlined part that must be changed to make the sentence correct. If the sentence is correct, select choice E. In choosing answers, follow the requirements of standard written English.

EXAMPLE:

<u>Whenever</u> one is driving late at night, <u>you</u> must take extra precautions <u>against</u>
   A   B   C

falling asleep <u>at the wheel</u>. <u>No error</u>
               D   E

(A) ● (C) (D) (E)

---

12. In the <u>original</u> Star Trek series, the crew <u>defied</u> the
          A   B
laws <u>of nature</u>, because they could breathe as
     C
easily on other planets <u>as humans</u> could breathe
                        D
on earth. <u>No error</u>
          E

13. Thomas <u>was</u> so proud of his <u>younger</u> brother,
       A   B
<u>who was graduating</u> <u>from</u> college last month.
        C   D
<u>No error</u>
  E

14. <u>Outside the barn</u>, a commotion <u>involving</u> three
     A   B
hens and a rooster <u>woke</u> the twins, who were
              C
sleeping <u>deep</u>. <u>No error</u>
     D   E

15. <u>When</u> we <u>looked</u> at the photograph of the
    A   B
lightning bolt hitting the tree, we noticed a
<u>more smaller</u> bolt of electricity also <u>emanating</u>
    C   D
from the ground. <u>No error</u>
              E

16. Our Monthly Club seasonal fruits are <u>such a</u>
                            A
popular gift item that it <u>has become</u> necessary
                B
<u>to find ways</u> to accelerate the growth of <u>its trees</u>.
    C   D
<u>No error</u>
  E

GO ON TO THE NEXT PAGE ⇒

17. He could have easily <u>completed</u> the <u>unusually</u> long
                         A   B
    and complicated assignment before it was due, if

    only <u>he had started</u> it <u>earlier</u> in the week. <u>No error</u>
          C   D   E

18. Concerned <u>about</u> the playoff game <u>on</u> Saturday,
               A   B
    each of the team members <u>spent</u> most of the
                              C
    week practicing <u>their</u> plays. <u>No error</u>
                     D   E

19. Studies indicate that the environment in schools

    <u>where</u> there are <u>less</u> adults on staff <u>is</u> often not
     A   B   C
    conducive <u>to</u> learning. <u>No error</u>
               D   E

20. At breakfast, Dad asked <u>Hilary and I</u> if we <u>wanted</u>
                             A   B
    to attend <u>my cousin Noah's</u> university
               C
    graduation ceremony in Nebraska <u>next spring</u>.
                                     D
    <u>No error</u>
     E

21. Only after the water in the river had <u>rose</u>
                                           A
    <u>to dangerous</u> levels <u>did</u> the governor order the
     B   C
    <u>evacuation of</u> the city. <u>No error</u>
     D   E

22. The list of concert-goers <u>who waited</u> hours for
                               A
    the entrance of their favorite music group,

    <u>include</u> <u>more than</u> one hundred fans from
     B   C
    European countries, <u>who</u> traveled long
                         D
    distances for the show. <u>No error</u>
                             E

23. Because the university's math department was

    reconsidering <u>its</u> degree requirements it
                   A
    <u>announced</u> that the schedule of classes <u>would be</u>
     B   C
    delayed for an <u>indecisive</u> period. <u>No error</u>
                    D   E

24. Grant Parson's new book <u>is</u> more a
                             A
    compilation of stories <u>than like</u> a novel;
                            B
    characters and plot lines <u>appear</u> <u>and</u> disappear
                               C
    <u>from chapter to</u> chapter. <u>No error</u>
     D   E

25. If one <u>is interested</u> <u>in learning</u> <u>even more</u> about
            A   B   C
    Eleanor and Franklin Roosevelt, <u>you</u> should
                                     D
    read Goodwin's biography of the couple.

    <u>No error</u>
     E

GO ON TO THE NEXT PAGE

26. Learning stations <u>in</u> elementary school
                      A

   classrooms <u>allow</u> students to personalize <u>their</u>
              B   C

   education by reading extracurricular books

   that <u>interests</u> them. <u>No error</u>
        D   E

27. The guidance counselor's recommendation

   <u>included</u> a plan <u>where</u> each student was <u>to visit</u>
   A   B   C

   colleges <u>throughout</u> the spring of junior year.
            D

   <u>No error</u>
   E

28. <u>From 1607 until</u> 1698, Jamestown, now an
    A

   <u>excavation site</u> in Virginia, was the capital of the
   B

   state; <u>however</u>, by 1750 it <u>will be</u> privately
          C   D

   owned. <u>No error</u>
          E

29. Throughout history, <u>both literary scholars</u>
                        A

   as well as Greek historians <u>have been obsessed</u>
                               B

   <u>with discovering</u> if the lost city of Atlantis,
   C

   <u>described</u> by Plato, is real or mythological.
   D

   <u>No error</u>
   E

GO ON TO THE NEXT PAGE

Directions: The following passage is an early draft of an essay. Some parts of the passage need to be rewritten.

Read the passage and select the best answer for each question that follows. Some questions are about particular sentences or parts of sentences and ask you to improve sentence structure or word choice. Other questions ask you to consider organization and development. In choosing answers, follow the conventions of standard written English.

Questions 30–35 are based on the following passage.

(1) Most people seem to find the winter season dreary. (2) It is true that it is cold and snows a lot. (3) But I don't see this as bleak; I see it as beautiful. (4) Winter is my favorite season of the year for three reasons.

(5) First, I think white snow and icicles all around are magical and make winter exceptional. (6) The snow puts a beautiful blanket on the outdoors, with a certain shimmer and shine. (7) Most days, when it doesn't snow, are very bright and sunny, not bleak.

(8) Second, winter weather provides them with the opportunity for so many activities. (9) It allows us to ski down mountains, skate on frozen ponds, and sled down hills. (10) When we complain that Americans don't exercise enough, people are saying that they don't take advantage of the outdoors. (11) But winter sport are the perfect opportunity to exercise outdoors.

(12) Third, winter weather allows families to gather together and connect. (13) On winter nights my family, is always enjoying a fire in the fireplace, hot chocolate, and board games. (14) And throughout the evening we can look outside and see the beautiful white snow fall on the trees and the ground. (15) The winter weather makes us more aware of the protection our home provides, and of the companionship we can provide each other, than the rest of the year.

30. Which sentence would be most appropriate to follow sentence 1?

(A) They see it as cold, snowy, and bleak.

(B) There are three months in winter.

(C) I think they are right.

(D) People prefer the warmth of summer.

(E) In winter they don't get enough exercise.

31. In context, which is the best way to revise and combine the underlined portions of sentences 8 and 9 (reproduced below)?

Second, <u>winter weather provides them with the opportunity for so many activities. It allows us to</u> ski down mountains, skate on frozen ponds, sled down hills.

(A) winter weather provides them with the opportunity for so many activities, allowing us to

(B) winter weather provides the opportunity for so many activities, allowing people to

(C) providing the opportunity for so many activities, in winter weather it is allowed to

(D) winter weather provides many activities and allows them to

(E) winter weather is the opportunity for so many activities, it allows them to

---

GO ON TO THE NEXT PAGE ⟹

32. Which of the following is the best version of the underlined portion of sentence 10 (reproduced below)?

    When we complain that Americans don't exercise enough, people are saying that they don't take advantage of the outdoors.

    (A) (As it is now)

    (B) In fact, Americans don't exercise enough; we however

    (C) Therefore, by our complaints that Americans don't exercise enough, people

    (D) However, when Americans don't exercise enough, it is because people,

    (E) When people complain that Americans don't exercise enough, they

33. In context, which of the following revisions is necessary in sentence 13 (reproduced below)?

    On winter nights my family, for instance, is always enjoying a fire in the fireplace, hot chocolate, and board games.

    (A) Replace "and board games" with "and playing board games."

    (B) Replace "is always" with "are always."

    (C) Replace "is always enjoying" with "always enjoys."

    (D) Replace "on" with "during."

    (E) Replace "for instance" with "as an example."

34. Which of the following is the best version of the underlined portion of sentence 15 (reproduced below)?

    The winter weather makes us more aware of the protection our home provides, and of the companionship we can provide each other, than the rest of the year.

    (A) (As it is now)

    (B) than the rest of the year of the protection of our home and companionship of our family

    (C) of the protection and companionship which is provided by our home and family than the rest of the year

    (D) than we are during the rest of the year of the protection our home provides, and of the companionship we can provide each other

    (E) of home protection and companionship than we are during the rest of the year

35. Which of the following would make the most logical final sentence for the essay?

    (A) However, in the summertime I can't enjoy hot beverages.

    (B) The snow even seems to magnify the sunlight.

    (C) Most people prefer the spring or autumn months.

    (D) Increased outdoor activity improves both mental and physical health.

    (E) Winter deserves a better reputation.

IF YOU FINISH BEFORE TIME IS CALLED, YOU MAY CHECK YOUR WORK ON THIS SECTION ONLY. DO NOT TURN TO ANY OTHER SECTION IN THE TEST.

SECTION 6

Time—25 Minutes
24 Questions

Directions: For each of the following questions, choose the best answer and darken the corresponding ovalon the answer sheet.

Each sentence below has one or two blanks, each blank indicating that something has been omitted. Beneath the sentence are five words or sets of words labeled A through E. Choose the word or set of words that, when inserted in the sentence, best fits the meaning of the sentence as a whole.

EXAMPLE:

Today's small, portable computers contrast markedly with the earliest electronic computers, which were -------.

(A) effective
(B) invented
(C) useful
(D) destructive
(E) enormous   Ⓐ Ⓑ Ⓒ Ⓓ ●

1. The band has courted controversy before in order to get attention, and the ------- lyrics on their new album demonstrate that they found the strategy -------.

   (A) sedate . . . plausible
   (B) vacuous . . . rewarding
   (C) belligerent . . . counterproductive
   (D) scandalous . . . effective
   (E) provocative . . . comparable

2. James Joyce regarded ------- as central to the creative process, which is evident in the numerous scribbled edits that cover even his supposedly final drafts.

   (A) contrivance
   (B) revision
   (C) inspiration
   (D) obsession
   (E) disavowal

3. Fans who believe that the players' motivations are not ------- would be ------- to learn that they now charge for their signatures.

   (A) self-serving . . . vindicated
   (B) venal . . . chagrined
   (C) altruistic . . . unsurprised
   (D) atypical . . . disillusioned
   (E) tainted . . . gratified

4. Though the film ostensibly deals with the theme of -------, the director seems to have been more interested in its absence—in isolation and the longing for connection.

   (A) reliance
   (B) fraternity
   (C) socialism
   (D) privation
   (E) levity

5. Everything the candidate said publicly was -------; he manipulated the media in order to present the image he wanted.

   (A) incendiary
   (B) calculated
   (C) facetious
   (D) scrupulous
   (E) impromptu

GO ON TO THE NEXT PAGE

Directions: The passages below are followed by questions based on their content; questions following a pair of related passages may also be based on the relationship between the paired passages. Answer the questions on the basis of what is <u>stated</u> or <u>implied</u> in the passages and in any introductory material that may be provided.

Questions 6–7 refer to the following passage.

The discovery of helium required the combined efforts of several scientists. Pierre-Jules Cesar Janssen first obtained evidence for the existence of helium during a solar eclipse in
(5) 1868 when he detected a new yellow line on his spectroscope while observing the sun. This experiment was repeated by Norman Lockyer who concluded that no known element produced such a line. However, other scientists
(10) were dubious, finding it unlikely that an element existed only on the sun. Then, in 1895, William Ramsay discovered helium on Earth after treating clevite, a uranium mineral, with mineral acids. After isolating the resulting gas,
(15) Ramsay sent samples to William Crookes and Norman Lockyer who identified it conclusively as the missing element helium.

6. The passage indicates that Ramsay's chief contribution to the discovery of helium was to

(A) prove the validity of Janssen's experiment
(B) find helium in uranium minerals
(C) identify the element discovered by Crookes as helium
(D) detect helium on the sun without using a spectroscope
(E) discover that helium naturally occurs on Earth

7. The author of the passage suggests that the results of the work of Janssen and Lockyer were

(A) repeated incorrectly by other scientists
(B) thought by others to be the result of flawed methodologies
(C) met with skepticism by other scientists
(D) only valid during solar eclipses
(E) obtained using outdated equipment

Questions 8–9 refer to the following passage.

July 19: Loretta arrives tomorrow, and I'll pick her up at the airport. We'll spend the week exploring the city together, but first we'll visit Grandmama. It's been years since
(5) Loretta has seen her. The rift that began for reasons lost in the mists of family lore has continued to this day. I'll wager that Loretta can't even remember why she and Grandmama haven't spoken in all this time.
(10) The truth is, I think that Grandmama is angry with Uncle Martin, not his daughter. Now she seems ready for reconciliation—perhaps this is because she's getting older.

8. Based on the passage, the reason that Loretta and Grandmama have not seen each other in years is most likely

(A) due to Grandmama's treatment of Uncle Martin
(B) the sole purpose of Loretta's visit to the city
(C) the impetus for their reunion
(D) that Loretta has been too busy to visit
(E) forgotten by both of them

9. In line 5, "rift" is best understood as meaning

(A) motion
(B) break
(C) revelry
(D) clarity
(E) discussion

GO ON TO THE NEXT PAGE ⟩

Questions 10–16 refer to the following passage.

The following passage is from a discussion of the origin of the Cold War between the United States and the Soviet Union.

Revisionist historians maintain that it was within the power of the United States, in the years during and immediately after the Second World War, to prevent the Cold War with
(5) the Soviet Union. Revisionists suggest that the prospect of impending conflict with the Soviets could have been avoided in several ways. The U.S. could have officially recognized the new Soviet sphere of influence in
(10) Eastern Europe instead of continuing to call for self-determination in those countries. A much-needed reconstruction loan could have helped the Soviets recover from the war. The Americans could have sought to assuage Soviet
(15) fears by giving up the U.S. monopoly of the atomic bomb and turning the weapons over to an international agency (with the stipulation that future nuclear powers do the same).

This criticism of the post-war American
(20) course of action fails to take into account the political realities in America at the time and unfairly condemns the American policy-makers who did consider each of these alternatives and found them to be unworkable.
(25) Recognition of a Soviet Eastern Europe was out of the question. Roosevelt had promised self-determination to the Eastern European countries, and the American people, having come to expect this, were furious when Stalin
(30) began to shape his spheres of influence in the region. The President was in particular acutely conscious of the millions of Polish-Americans who would be voting in the upcoming election.
(35) Negotiations had indeed been conducted by the administration with the Soviets about a reconstruction loan, but the Congress refused to approve it unless the Soviets made enormous concessions tantamount to restruc-
(40) turing their system and withdrawing from Eastern Europe. This, of course, made Soviet

rejection of the loan a foregone conclusion. As for giving up the bomb—the elected officials in Washington would have been in deep trou-
(45) ble with their constituents had that plan been carried out. Polls showed that 82 per-cent of the American people understood that other nations would develop bombs eventu-ally, but that 85 percent thought that the U.S.
(50) should retain exclusive possession of the weap-on. Policy-makers have to abide by certain constraints in deciding what is acceptable and what is not. They, and not historians, are in the best position to perceive those constraints and
(55) make the decisions.

Revisionist historians tend to eschew this type of political explanation of America's sup-posed failure to reach a peaceful settlement with the Soviets in favor of an economic read-
(60) ing of events. They point to the fact that in the early post-war years, American businessmen and government officials cooperated to expand American foreign trade vigorously and to exploit investment opportunities in many for-
(65) eign countries. In order to sustain the lucrative expansion, revisionists assert, American poli-cy-makers were obliged to maintain an "Open Door" foreign policy, the object of which was to keep all potential trade opportunities open.
(70) Since the Soviets could jeopardize such oppor-tunities in Eastern Europe and elsewhere, they had to be opposed. Hence, the Cold War. But if American policy-makers were simply pawns in an economic game of expansionist capital-
(75) ism, as the revisionists seem to think, why do the revisionists hold them responsible for not attempting to reach an accord with the Soviets? The policy-makers, swept up by a tidal wave of capitalism, clearly had little control
(80) and little choice in the matter.

Even if American officials had been free and willing to make conciliatory gestures toward the Soviets, the Cold War would not have been prevented. Overtures of friend-
(85) ship would not have been reciprocated (as far as we can judge; information on the inner

GO ON TO THE NEXT PAGE ⟶

workings of the Kremlin during that time
is scanty). Soviet expert George F. Kennan
concluded that Russian hostility could not
(90) be dampened by any effort on the part of the
United States. The political and ideological
differences were too great, and the Soviets
had too long a history of distrust of for-
eigners—exacerbated at the time by Stalin's
(95) rampant paranoia, which infected his government—to embark on a process of establishing trust and peace with the United States,
though it was in their interest to do so.

10. The primary purpose of the passage is to

(A) explode a popular myth

(B) criticize historical figures

(C) refute an argument

(D) analyze an era

(E) reconcile opposing views

11. In line 8, the word "recognized" most nearly means

(A) identified

(B) noticed

(C) acknowledged

(D) distinguished

(E) remembered

12. The author refers to the Polish-Americans
(lines 33–34) chiefly to illustrate that

(A) the president had an excellent rapport
with ethnic minorities

(B) immigrants had fled from Eastern
European countries to escape communism

(C) giving up the idea of East European self-
determination would have been costly in
political terms

(D) the Poles could enjoy self-determination
only in America

(E) the political landscape of the United
States had changed considerably since
the president was elected

13. A fundamental assumption underlying the
author's argument in the second and third
paragraphs is that

(A) the Soviets were largely to blame for the
failure of conciliatory U.S. initiatives

(B) the American public was very well-
informed about the incipient Cold War
situation

(C) none of the proposed alternatives would
have had its intended effect

(D) the American public was overwhelmingly opposed to seeking peace with the
Soviets

(E) the government could not have been
expected to ignore public opinion

14. The phrase "certain constraints" in lines 51–52
most likely refers to the

(A) etiquette of international diplomacy

(B) danger of leaked information about
atomic bombs

(C) views of the electorate

(D) potential reaction of the enemy

(E) difficulty of carrying out a policy initiative

GO ON TO THE NEXT PAGE

15. Which statement best summarizes the revisionist argument concerning the origin of the Cold War (lines 56–72)?

(A) The United States started the Cold War in order to have a military cover for illegal trading activities.

(B) The Soviets were oblivious to the negative impact they had on the American economy.

(C) The economic advantage of recognizing Soviet Europe outweighed the disadvantage of an angry public.

(D) America could trade and invest with foreign countries only if it agreed to oppose the Soviet Union.

(E) American economic interests abroad would have been threatened by any Soviet expansion.

16. The question at the end of the fourth paragraph (lines 72–79) serves to

(A) point out an inconsistency in a position

(B) outline an area that requires further research

(C) contrast two different historical interpretations

(D) sum up a cynical view of post-war economic activity

(E) restate the central issue of the passage

GO ON TO THE NEXT PAGE

Questions 17–24 refer to the following passage.

*James Weldon Johnson was a poet, diplomat, composer,
and historian of black culture who wrote around the
turn of the century. In this narrative passage, Johnson
recalls his first experience of hearing rag-time jazz.*

When I had somewhat collected my senses, I
realized that in a large back room into which
the main room opened, there was a young
fellow singing a song, accompanied on the
(5) piano by a short, thickset black man. After
each verse, he did some dance steps, which
brought forth great applause and a shower
of small coins at his feet. After the singer had
responded to a rousing encore, the stout man
(10) at the piano began to run his fingers up and
down the keyboard. This he did in a manner which indicated that he was a master of a
good deal of technique. Then he began to play;
and such playing! I stopped talking to listen. It
(15) was music of a kind I had never heard before.
It was music that demanded physical response,
patting of the feet, drumming of the fingers,
or nodding of the head in time with the beat.
The dissonant harmonies, the audacious reso-
(20) lutions, often consisting of an abrupt jump
from one key to another, the intricate rhythms
in which the accents fell in the most unexpected places, but in which the beat was never lost,
produced a most curious effect . . .
(25) This was rag-time music, then a novelty in
New York, and just growing to be a rage, which
has not yet subsided. It was originated in the
questionable resorts about Memphis and St.
Louis by Negro piano-players who knew no
(30) more of the theory of music than they did of
the theory of the universe, but were guided by
natural musical instinct and talent. It made its
way to Chicago, where it was popular some
time before it reached New York. These players
(35) often improvised simple and, at times, vulgar
words to fit the melodies. This was the beginning of the rag-time song . . .
American musicians, instead of investigating rag-time, attempt to ignore it, or dismiss

(40) it with a contemptuous word. But that has
always been the course of scholasticism in
every branch of art. Whatever new thing
the *people* like is pooh-poohed; whatever is
popular is spoken of as not worth the while.
(45) The fact is, nothing great or enduring, especially in music, has ever sprung full-fledged
and unprecedented from the brain of any
master; the best that he gives to the world he
gathers from the hearts of the people, and
(50) runs it through the alembic* of his genius. In
spite of the bans which musicians and music
teachers have placed upon it, the people still
demand and enjoy rag-time. One thing cannot
be denied; it is music which possesses at least
(55) one strong element of greatness: it appeals
universally; not only the American, but the
English, the French, and even the German
people find delight in it. In fact, there is not a
corner of the civilized world in which it is not
(60) known, and this proves its originality; for if it
were an imitation, the people of Europe, any-
how, would not have found it a novelty . . .
I became so interested in both the music
and the player that I left the table where I was
(65) sitting, and made my way through the hall
into the back room, where I could see as well
as hear. I talked to the piano player between
the musical numbers and found out that he
was just a natural musician, never having
(70) taken a lesson in his life. Not only could he
play almost anything he heard, but he could
accompany singers in songs he had never
heard. He had, by ear alone, composed some
pieces, several of which he played over for me;
(75) each of them was properly proportioned and
balanced. I began to wonder what this man
with such a lavish natural endowment would
have done had he been trained. Perhaps he
wouldn't have done anything at all; he might
(80) have become, at best, a mediocre imitator of
the great masters in what they have already
done to a finish, or one of the modern inno-
vators who strive after originality by seeing
how cleverly they can dodge about through

GO ON TO THE NEXT PAGE ⟩

(85) the rules of harmony and at the same time avoid melody. It is certain that he would not have been so delightful as he was in rag-time.

alembic: scientific apparatus used in the process of distillation

17. In relating his initial impression of rag-time music to the reader, the narrator makes use of

    (A) comparison with the improvisations of classical music

    (B) reference to the audience's appreciative applause

    (C) description of the music's compelling rhythmic effect

    (D) evocation of poignant visual images

    (E) allusion to several popular contemporary tunes

18. In the first paragraph, the narrator portrays rag-time as a type of music that

    (A) would be a challenge to play for even the most proficient musician

    (B) satisfied the narrator's expectations regarding the genre

    (C) violated all of the accepted rules governing musical composition

    (D) made up for a lack of melody with a seductive rhythm

    (E) contained several surprises for the discerning listener

19. In line 28, "questionable" most nearly means

    (A) disreputable

    (B) ambiguous

    (C) doubtful

    (D) approachable

    (E) unconfirmed

20. The narrator's perspective during the second and third paragraphs is that of

    (A) an impartial historian of events in the recent past

    (B) a mesmerized spectator of a musical spectacle

    (C) a knowledgeable critic of the contemporary musical scene

    (D) a commentator reflecting on a unique experience

    (E) an adult reminiscing fondly about his youth

21. The discussion in the third paragraph of the refusal of American musicians to investigate rag-time suggests that they

    (A) have little or no interest in pleasing people with their music

    (B) need to be made aware of the popularity of rag-time in Europe

    (C) are misguided in their conservative and condescending attitude

    (D) attack rag-time for being merely an imitation of an existing style

    (E) know that it would be difficult to refine rag-time as a musical form

22. Which statement best summarizes the author's argument in the third paragraph?

    (A) Any type of music that is extremely popular should be considered great.

    (B) The two criteria for musical greatness are popularity and originality.

    (C) Music that has become popular overseas cannot be ignored by American musicians.

    (D) Rag-time must be taken up by a musical master and purified to earn critical acclaim.

    (E) Mass appeal in music can be a sign of greatness rather than a stigma.

GO ON TO THE NEXT PAGE ⟹

23. The statement in lines 78–79 ("Perhaps he wouldn't have done anything at all") is best interpreted as conveying

   (A) doubt about the depth of the piano player's skill

   (B) understanding that no amount of talent can compensate for a lack of discipline

   (C) cynicism about the likelihood that a man can live up to his potential

   (D) a recognition that the piano player might have wasted his talent

   (E) frustration at the impossibility of knowing what might have been

24. The author's view (lines 78–88) about the rag-time piano player's lack of formal training can best be summarized as which of the following?

   (A) The piano player's natural talent had allowed him to develop technically to the point where formal training would have been superfluous.

   (B) Formal lessons would have impaired the piano player's native ability to play and compose by ear alone.

   (C) More would have been lost than gained if the piano player had been given formal lessons.

   (D) The piano player's potential to be a truly innovative rag-time artist had been squandered because he had not been formally trained.

   (E) Although dazzling when improvising rag-time, the piano player could never have been more than mediocre as a classical pianist.

IF YOU FINISH BEFORE TIME IS CALLED, YOU MAY CHECK YOUR WORK ON THIS SECTION ONLY. DO NOT TURN TO ANY OTHER SECTION IN THE TEST.   STOP

SECTION 7
Time—20 Minutes
16 Questions

Directions: For this section, solve each problem and decide which is the best of the choices given. Fill in the corresponding oval on the answer sheet. You may use any available space for scratchwork.

Notes:

(1) Calculator use is permitted.
(2) All numbers used are real numbers.
(3) Figures are provided for some problems. All figures are drawn to scale and lie in a plane UNLESS otherwise indicated.
(4) Unless otherwise specified, the domain of any function f is assumed to be the set of all real numbers x for which $f(x)$ is a real number.

$A = \frac{1}{2}bh$ $c^2 = a^2 + b^2$ Special Right Triangles $A = \pi r^2$ $V = \ell wh$ $V = \pi r^2 h$ $A = \ell w$
$C = 2\pi r$

The sum of the degree measures of the angles in a triangle is 180.
The number of degrees of arc in a circle is 360.
A straight angle has a degree measure of 180.

1. For all values of x, $(3x + 4)(4x - 3) =$

    (A) $7x + 1$
    (B) $7x - 12$
    (C) $12x^2 - 12$
    (D) $12x^2 - 25x - 12$
    (E) $12x^2 + 7x - 12$

2. In a certain set of numbers, the ratio of integers to nonintegers is 2:3. What percent of the numbers in the set are integers?

    (A) 20%
    (B) $33\frac{1}{3}\%$
    (C) 40%
    (D) 60%
    (E) $66\frac{2}{3}\%$

3. If $xyz \neq 0$, which of the following is equivalent to $\dfrac{x^2 y^3 z^4}{(xyz^2)^2}$?

    (A) $\dfrac{1}{y}$
    (B) $\dfrac{1}{z}$
    (C) y
    (D) $\dfrac{x}{yz}$
    (E) xyz

GO ON TO THE NEXT PAGE

4. When the positive integer p is divided by 7, the remainder is 5. What is the remainder when $5p$ is divided by 7?

   (A) 0
   (B) 1
   (C) 2
   (D) 3
   (E) 4

5. What is the y-intercept of the line with the equation $2x - 3y = 18$?

   (A) −9
   (B) −6
   (C) −3
   (D) 6
   (E) 9

6. Jan types at an average rate of 12 pages per hour. At that rate, how long will it take Jan to type 100 pages?

   (A) 8 hours and 3 minutes
   (B) 8 hours and 15 minutes
   (C) 8 hours and 20 minutes
   (D) 8 hours and 30 minutes
   (E) 8 hours and $33\frac{1}{3}$ minutes

7. In the figure above, AB is perpendicular to BC. The lengths of AB and BC are given in terms of x. Which of the following represents the area of $\triangle ABC$ for all $x > 1$?

   (A) x
   (B) $2x$
   (C) x^2
   (D) $x^2 - 1$
   (E) $\dfrac{x^2 - 1}{2}$

8. If Jim and Bill have less than 15 dollars between them, and Bill has 4 dollars, which of the following could be the number of dollars that Jim has?

   I. 10
   II. 11
   III. 15

   (A) I only
   (B) II only
   (C) I and II only
   (D) II and III only
   (E) I, II, and III

GO ON TO THE NEXT PAGE

9. Angelo makes x dollars for y hours of work. Sarah makes the same amount of money for 1 less hour of work. Which of the following expressions represents the positive difference between the two people's hourly wage?

(A) $\dfrac{x}{y-1} - \dfrac{x}{y}$

(B) $\dfrac{x}{y} - \dfrac{x}{y-1}$

(C) $\dfrac{x}{y-1} + \dfrac{x}{y}$

(D) $\dfrac{y-1}{x} - \dfrac{y}{x}$

(E) $\dfrac{y}{x} - \dfrac{y-1}{x}$

10. Erica has 8 squares of felt, each with area 16. For a certain craft project she cuts the largest circle possible from each square of felt. What is the combined area of the excess felt left over after cutting out all the circles?

(A) $4(4-\pi)$

(B) $8(4-\pi)$

(C) $8(\pi-2)$

(D) $32(4-\pi)$

(E) $16(16-\pi)$

11. In the sequence $2, 6, 18, x, 162 \ldots$, what is the most likely value of x?

(A) 36

(B) 48

(C) 54

(D) 81

(E) 98

12. What is the remainder when $5x^3 - 2x^2 + x + 1$ is divided by $x - 3$?

(A) -121

(B) -60

(C) 65

(D) 120

(E) 121

13. In the diagram above, the circle's center is at point O. $\overline{AC}$ is tangent to the circle at point B, which is the midpoint of $\overline{AC}$. If $AC = 4$ and the area of the circle is 4π, what is the length of $\overline{AO}$?

(A) 2

(B) $2\sqrt{2}$

(C) 3

(D) 4

(E) $4\sqrt{2}$

GO ON TO THE NEXT PAGE

Average Annual Cost of
Auto Insurance (2000–2003)

14. The graph above represents the average annual
cost of automobile insurance in a certain state
from 2000 to 2003. Assuming that the cost of
insurance increases at the same average
(arithmetic mean) rate depicted in the graph,
what is the expected cost of automobile
insurance in 2004?

(A) $200
(B) $550
(C) $875
(D) $1,000
(E) $1,500

15. Which of the following expressions describes
the indicated values on the number line
above?

(A) $x \le 1$
(B) $x \ge 1$
(C) $|x| \le 1$
(D) $|x| \ge 1$
(E) $x \ge |1|$

16. There are 3 routes from Bay City to
Riverville. There are 4 routes from Riverville
to Straitstown. There are 3 routes from
Straitstown to Frog Pond. If a driver must pass
through Riverville and Straitstown exactly
once, how many possible ways are there to go
from Bay City to Frog Pond?

(A)   6
(B)   10
(C)   12
(D)   24
(E)   36

SECTION 8

Time—20 Minutes
19 Questions

> **Directions:** For each of the following questions, choose the best answer and darken the corresponding oval on the answer sheet.

Each sentence below has one or two blanks, each blank indicating that something has been omitted. Beneath the sentence are five words or sets of words labeled A through E. Choose the word or set of words that, when inserted in the sentence, best fits the meaning of the sentence as a whole.

EXAMPLE:

Today's small, portable computers contrast markedly with the earliest electronic computers, which were -------.

(A) effective
(B) invented
(C) useful
(D) destructive
(E) enormous   Ⓐ Ⓑ Ⓒ Ⓓ ●

1. Although sub-Saharan Africa encompasses a large number of ------- cultures, its music is often considered an essentially ------- mass.

   (A) disparate . . . homogeneous
   (B) impoverished . . . inimitable
   (C) warring . . . concrete
   (D) interwoven . . . distinctive
   (E) proud . . . languid

2. His face was -------, his features pulled downward by the weight of heavy thoughts.

   (A) morose
   (B) onerous
   (C) contorted
   (D) ossified
   (E) inscrutable

3. The unfortunate demise of the protagonist in the final scene of the movie ------- all possibility of a sequel.

   (A) entertained
   (B) dissembled
   (C) raised
   (D) exacerbated
   (E) precluded

4. The repeated breakdown of negotiations only -------- the view that the two sides were not truly committed to the goal of --------- a military confrontation.

   (A) established . . . escalating
   (B) undermined . . . avoiding
   (C) distorted . . . financing
   (D) strengthened . . . initiating
   (E) reinforced . . . averting

5. Duncan was a modest and cooperative worker; he demonstrated none of his colleague's ------.

   (A) geniality
   (B) influence
   (C) arrogance
   (D) reluctance
   (E) humility

6. When the election results were announced, the victorious candidate's exhilaration temporarily ------- the recognition of the forthcoming ------- to improve the economic climate of the city.

   (A) accepted . . . promise
   (B) illuminated . . . campaign
   (C) admitted . . . hostility
   (D) eclipsed . . . struggle
   (E) blocked . . . inauguration

GO ON TO THE NEXT PAGE ⟹

Directions: The passages below are followed by questions based on their content; questions following a pair of related passages may also be based on the relationship between the paired passages. Answer the questions on the basis of what is <u>stated</u> or <u>implied</u> in the passages and in any introductory material that may be provided.

Questions 7–19 refer to the following passages.

These passages present two critics' perspectives on the topic of design museums.

Passage 1

City museums are places where people can learn about various cultures by studying objects of particular historical or artistic value. The increasingly popular "design museums"
(5) that are opening today perform quite a different function. Unlike most city museums, the design museum displays and assesses objects that are readily available to the general public. These museums place ignored household
(10) appliances under spotlights, breaking down the barriers between commerce and creative invention.

Critics have argued that design museums are often manipulated to serve as advertise-
(15) ments for new industrial technology. But their role is not simply a matter of merchandis-ing—it is the honoring of impressive, innova-tive products. The difference between the win-dow of a department store and the showcase
(20) in a design museum is that the first tries to sell you something, while the second informs you of the success of the attempt.

One advantage that the design museum has over other civic museums is that design
(25) museums are places where people feel familiar with the exhibits. Unlike the average art gal-lery patron, design museum visitors rarely feel intimidated or disoriented. Partly this is because design museums clearly illustrate how and why
(30) mass-produced consumer objects work and look as they do and show how design contrib-utes to the quality of our lives. For example, an exhibit involving a particular design of chair would not simply explain how it functions as a
(35) chair. It would also demonstrate how its various features combine to produce an artistic effect or redefine our manner of performing the basic act of being seated. The purpose of such an exhibit would be to present these concepts in ways that
(40) challenge, stimulate, and inform the viewer. An art gallery exhibit, on the other hand, would provide very little information about the chair and charge the visitor with understanding the exhibit on some abstract level.

(45) Within the past decade, several new design museums have opened their doors. Each of these museums has responded in totally original ways to the public's growing interest in the field. London's Design Museum, for
(50) instance, displays a collection of mass-pro-duced objects ranging from Zippo lighters to electric typewriters to a show of Norwegian sardine-tin labels. The options open to cura-tors of design museums seem far less rigor-
(55) ous, conventionalized, and pre-programmed than those applying to curators in charge of public galleries of paintings and sculpture. The humorous aspects of our society are bet-ter represented in the display of postmodern
(60) playthings or quirky Japanese vacuum clean-ers in pastel colors than in an exhibition of Impressionist landscapes.

Passage 2

The short histories of some of the leading technical and design museums make clear an
(65) underlying difficulty in this area. The tendency everywhere today is to begin with present machines and technological processes and to show how they operate and the scientific principles on which they are based without
(70) paying much attention to their historical development, to say nothing of the society

GO ON TO THE NEXT PAGE

that produced them. Only a few of the oldest,
largest and best-supported museums collect
historical industrial objects. Most science cent-
(75) ers put more emphasis on mock-ups, graphs,
and multimedia devices. This approach of "pre-
sentism" often leads the museum to drop all attempts at study and research; if industry is called
upon to design and build the exhibits, curators
(80) may be entirely dispensed with, so that impartial
and scientific study disappears, and emphasis is
placed on the idea that progress automatically
follows technology.

Industrialization and the machine have, of
(85) course, brought much progress; a large portion
of humankind no longer works from sun-up
to sundown to obtain the bare necessities of
life. But industrialization also creates problems—harm to the environment and ecology,
(90) neglect of social, cultural, and humanistic values, depletion of resources, and even threats of
human extinction. Thus, progress needs to be
considered critically—from a wider social and
humanitarian point of view. Unfortunately,
(95) most museums of science and technology glorify machines. Displayed in pristine condition,
elegantly painted or polished, they can make
the observer forget the noise, dirt, danger,
and frustration of machine-tending. Mines,
(100) whether coal, iron, or salt, are a favorite museum display but only infrequently is there even
a hint of the dirt, the damp, the smell, the low
headroom, or the crippling and destructive
accidents that sometimes occur in industry.
(105) Machinery also ought to be operated to be
meaningful. Consequently, it should not be
shown in sculptured repose but in full, often
clattering, action. This kind of operation is
difficult to obtain, and few museums can com-
(110) mand the imagination, ingenuity, and manual
dexterity it requires. Problems also arise in
providing adequate safety devices for both the
public and the machine operators. These, then,
are some of the underlying problems of the
(115) technical museum—problems not solved by
the usual push buttons, cranks, or multimedia

gimmicks. Yet attendance figures show that
technical museums outdraw all the others;
the public possesses lively curiosity and a real
(120) desire to understand science and technology.

7. In Passage 1, line 8, the word "readily"
    most nearly means

    (A) easily
    (B) willingly
    (C) instantly
    (D) cheaply
    (E) constantly

8. The author of Passage 1 refers to objects
    displayed in design museums as "ignored"
    (line 9) to emphasize that these objects were

    (A) unsuccessful commercially
    (B) generally unused in the household
    (C) never the subject of conversation in the
        household
    (D) allowed to fall into disrepair
    (E) not treated as objects of beauty

9. In lines 18–22, the author of Passage 1
    suggests that design museums are different
    from store windows in that

    (A) design museums display more
        technologically advanced products
    (B) store window displays are not created
        with as much concern to the visual qual-
        ity of the display
    (C) design museums are not concerned
        with the commercial aspects of a success-
        ful product
    (D) design museums focus on highlighting
        the artistic qualities that help sell products
    (E) the objects in store displays are more
        commercially successful than those in
        design museums

GO ON TO THE NEXT PAGE

10. From Passage 1, lines 23–28, it can be inferred that the author believes that most museum visitors

(A) are hostile toward the concept of abstract art

(B) prefer to have a context in which to understand museum exhibits

(C) are confused when faced with complex technological exhibits

(D) are unfamiliar with the exhibits in design museums

(E) undervalue the artistic worth of household items

11. The third paragraph of Passage 1 suggests that one important difference between design museums and the art galleries is

(A) the low price of admission at design museums

(B) the amount of information presented with design museum exhibits

(C) the intelligence of the average museum visitor

(D) that art galleries feature exhibits that have artistic merit

(E) the contribution that design museums make to our quality of life

12. In Passage 1, line 53, the word "options" most likely refers to the ability of curators of design museums to

(A) afford large collections of exhibits

(B) attract a wide range of visitors

(C) put together unconventional collections

(D) feature rare objects that interest the public

(E) satisfy their own personal whims in planning exhibitions

13. In Passage 1, line 62, the author most likely mentions "Impressionist landscapes" in order to

(A) provide an example of a typical design museum exhibit

(B) compare postmodern exhibits to 19th century art

(C) point out a decline in the sophistication of the museum-going public

(D) refute the notion that postmodern art is whimsical

(E) emphasize the contrast between two different types of exhibits

14. Which of the following best describes the "underlying difficulty" mentioned in line 65 of Passage 2?

(A) Design museums rarely mention the historical origin of objects they display.

(B) Industrial involvement often forces curators out of their jobs.

(C) Design museums appropriate technology that is essential for study and research.

(D) Technology almost never leads to progress.

(E) Industry places too much emphasis on impartial research.

15. The author of Passage 2 most likely mentions "harm to the environment and ecology" (line 89) in order to

(A) encourage a critical response to the technological age

(B) discourage the reader from visiting technology museums

(C) describe the hazardous conditions in coal, iron, and salt mines

(D) dissuade museum visitors from operating the machinery on display

(E) praise museums that present an accurate depiction of technology

GO ON TO THE NEXT PAGE

16. The author uses the phrase "sculptured repose" (Passage 2, line 107) in order to

    (A) condemn the curators of design museums for poor planning

    (B) illustrate the greatest problem inherent in design museums

    (C) present an idealized vision of a type of exhibit

    (D) describe the unrealistic way in which machinery is generally displayed

    (E) compare the shape of a machine to a work of art

17. The word "command" (Passage 2, line 109) most nearly means

    (A) oversee

    (B) direct

    (C) control

    (D) summon

    (E) order

18. The author of Passage 2 would probably object to the statement in Passage 1 that design "contributes to the quality of our lives" (lines 31–32) on the grounds that

    (A) technical innovation has historically posed threats to our physical and social well-being

    (B) the general public would benefit more from visiting art galleries

    (C) machinery that is not shown in action is meaningless to the viewer

    (D) industry has made a negligible contribution to human progress

    (E) few people have a genuine interest in the impact of science and technology

19. The authors of both passages would probably agree that

    (A) machinery is only enjoyable to watch when it is moving

    (B) most people are curious about the factors behind the design of everyday objects

    (C) the public places a higher value on packaging than it does on quality

    (D) the very technology that is displayed in the museums is likely to cost curators their jobs

    (E) design museums are flawed because they fail to accurately portray the environmental problems that technology sometimes causes

IF YOU FINISH BEFORE TIME IS CALLED, YOU MAY CHECK YOUR WORK ON THIS SECTION ONLY. DO NOT TURN TO ANY OTHER SECTION IN THE TEST.   STOP

SECTION 9

Time—10 Minutes
14 Questions

Directions: For each question in this section, select the best answer from among the choices given and fill in the corresponding oval on the answer sheet.

The following sentences test correctness and effectiveness of expression. Part of each sentence or the entire sentence is underlined; beneath each sentence are five ways of phrasing the underlined material. Choice A repeats the original phrasing; the other four choices are different. If you think the original phrasing produces a better sentence than any of the alternatives, select choice A; if not, select one of the other choices.

In making your selection, follow the requirements of standard written English; that is, pay attention to grammar, choice of words, sentence construction, and punctuation. Your selection should result in the most effective sentence—clear and precise, without awkwardness or ambiguity.

EXAMPLE:

Every apple in the baskets <u>are ripe and labeled according to the date it was picked</u>.

ANSWER:
(A) ● (C) (D) (E)

(A) are ripe and labeled according to the date it was picked
(B) is ripe and labeled according to the date it was picked
(C) are ripe and labeled according to the date they were picked
(D) is ripe and labeled according to the date they were picked
(E) are ripe and labeled as to the date it was picked

---

1. A spokesman for the car company boasted that the new model was lightweight, effective, <u>and virtually indistinguishable from the expensive model commonly used in movies</u>.

   (A) and virtually indistinguishable from the expensive model commonly used in movies

   (B) and the expensive model commonly used in movies could not distinguish it

   (C) and virtually indistinguishable by the expensive model commonly used in movies

   (D) and had gone virtually indistinguished by the expensive model commonly used in movies

   (E) and the expensive model commonly used in movies virtually unable to distinguish it

2. <u>Because the polar ice caps are melting, therefore many</u> scientists and environmentalists fear that several small island nations will be completely covered by water in only a few decades.

   (A) Because the polar ice caps are melting, therefore many

   (B) Because the polar ice caps are melting, many

   (C) The polar ice caps are melting, therefore many

   (D) Because the polar ice caps are melting; many

   (E) The polar ice caps are melting; and many

GO ON TO THE NEXT PAGE

3. One of the great literary artists of the nineteenth <u>century was Gustave Flaubert known for his obsession with the writer's craft</u>.

   (A) century was Gustave Flaubert known for his obsession with the writer's craft

   (B) century, Gustave Flaubert's obsession with the writer's craft was well known

   (C) century, Gustave Flaubert was known for his obsession with the writer's craft

   (D) century, Gustave Flaubert, known for his obsession with the writer's craft

   (E) century was Gustave Flaubert: known for his obsession with the writer's craft

4. David Hockney created <u>images and they converge</u> the art of photography with the craft of collages, giving his works a cubist effect.

   (A) images and they converge

   (B) images, being the convergence of

   (C) images, they converge

   (D) images that converge

   (E) images, and converging in them

5. The dean of students argued that although the university's professors have raised students' interest in continuing in academia, <u>the failure is in their not preparing</u> the students for the real world outside of textbooks and calculators.

   (A) the failure is in their not preparing

   (B) the failure they have is in their not preparing

   (C) they failed not to prepare

   (D) they have failed to prepare

   (E) failing in their preparation of

6. The amount of water used by Americans can be reduced by turning off faucets when not in use, decreasing time spent in showers, <u>and running washing machines</u> less frequently.

   (A) and running washing machines

   (B) and if they run washing machines

   (C) also by running washing machines

   (D) and washing machines being run

   (E) and if there ran washing machines

GO ON TO THE NEXT PAGE

7. Having exceptionally clear waters and active underwater life, the directors chose Cozumel as a prospective site for their next documentary on scuba diving.

   (A) Having exceptionally clear waters and active underwater life, the directors chose Cozumel

   (B) Directors who chose Cozumel for its exceptionally clear waters and active underwater life seeing it

   (C) Cozumel's exceptionally clear waters and active underwater life led to its choice by directors

   (D) Because its waters are clear and it has active underwater life, directors chose Cozumel

   (E) Based on its clear waters and active underwater life, Cozumel, which was chosen by directors,

8. Several of Salvador Dali's paintings were inspired by his wife, featured beauty, grace, and femininity.

   (A) paintings were inspired by his wife, featured

   (B) paintings had their inspiration from his wife, with features

   (C) paintings, inspired by his wife, featured

   (D) paintings, which were inspired by his wife, and which featured

   (E) paintings, being inspired by his wife, featuring

9. The fire, once close to destroying another forest, had trickled to a small flame.

   (A) The fire, once close to destroying another forest, had

   (B) The fire was once close to destroying another forest, it had

   (C) The fire that once having been close to destroying another forest had

   (D) The fire, because it was once close to destroying a forest, had

   (E) The fire was once close to destroying a forest, and it had

10. Michael Ondaatje collected the anecdotes and memories of his family in Ceylon, his native country, and these are stories that are told in his memoir.

    (A) these are stories that are told

    (B) the telling of these stories is

    (C) these stories having been told

    (D) his telling of these stories

    (E) told these stories

11. The idea that women should not vote or express their political opinions prevailed in nineteenth-century America.

(A) The idea that women should not vote or express their political opinions prevailed in nineteenth-century America.

(B) The idea that prevailed about women during nineteenth-century America was that of not voting and not expressing their political opinions.

(C) During most of nineteenth-century America, they had a prevalent idea that women should not vote or express political opinions.

(D) Prevalent as the idea during nineteenth-century America was for women to not vote or express their political opinions.

(E) Prevalent during nineteenth-century America, they thought that women should not vote or express political opinions.

12. The peace conference that was being mediated by the president, but now the countries are adamantly refusing to compromise their positions.

(A) The peace conference that was being mediated by the president, but now the countries are adamantly refusing to compromise their positions.

(B) The president had mediated the peace conference, but the countries are now adamantly refusing to compromise their positions.

(C) The peace conference was mediated by the president, and so now the countries are adamantly refusing to compromise their positions.

(D) Though the president mediated the peace conference, the countries now adamantly refusing to compromise their beliefs.

(E) Now adamantly refusing to compromise their beliefs, the president mediated the peace conference.

GO ON TO THE NEXT PAGE

13. For many an inspirational writer, <u>being free to create is more important</u> than having a lot of money.

   (A) being free to create is more important

   (B) having freedom of creation is more important

   (C) there is more importance in the freedom to create

   (D) freedom to create has more importance

   (E) to have the freedom to create is more important

14. Although Internet traffic often occurs during the evening hours, <u>causing it to delay connection no more</u> than two minutes.

   (A) causing it to delay connection no more

   (B) and yet it delays connection no more

   (C) it does not delay connection more

   (D) and it does not delay connection more

   (E) yet causing it to delay no more

IF YOU FINISH BEFORE TIME IS CALLED, YOU MAY CHECK YOUR WORK ON THIS SECTION ONLY. DO NOT TURN TO ANY OTHER SECTION IN THE TEST.

STOP

Practice Test Two: **Answer Key**

SECTION 1

Essay

SECTION 2

1. E
2. E
3. C
4. A
5. A
6. D
7. C
8. A
9. C
10. A
11. E
12. C
13. A
14. D
15. C
16. A
17. E
18. B
19. D
20. D

SECTION 3

1. C
2. E
3. A
4. A
5. C
6. C
7. D
8. C
9. B

10. A
11. D
12. E
13. C
14. A
15. D
16. C
17. C
18. A
19. B
20. C
21. D
22. B
23. B
24. B

SECTION 4

1. D
2. D
3. D
4. D
5. A
6. A
7. D
8. C
9. 115
10. .04
11. 11, 13, 17, 19, 23, 29, 31, 37, 41, 43, or 47
12. 2/5 or .4
13. 8
14. 4
15. 250
16. 9

17. 64
18. 203

SECTION 5

1. C
2. D
3. E
4. C
5. B
6. D
7. E
8. B
9. A
10. A
11. D
12. E
13. C
14. D
15. C
16. D
17. E
18. D
19. B
20. A
21. A
22. B
23. D
24. B
25. D
26. D
27. B
28. D
29. A
30. A
31. B

32. E
33. C
34. D
35. E

SECTION 6

1. D
2. B
3. B
4. B
5. B
6. E
7. C
8. E
9. B
10. C
11. C
12. C
13. E
14. C
15. E
16. A
17. C
18. E
19. A
20. C
21. C
22. E
23. D
24. C

SECTION 7

1. E
2. C
3. C
4. E

5. B
6. C
7. E
8. A
9. A
10. D
11. C
12. E
13. B
14. E
15. D
16. E

SECTION 8

1. A
2. A
3. E
4. E
5. C
6. D
7. A
8. E
9. D
10. B
11. B
12. C
13. E
14. A
15. A
16. D
17. D
18. A
19. B

SECTION 9

1. A
2. B
3. C
4. D
5. D
6. A
7. C
8. C
9. A
10. E
11. A
12. B
13. A
14. C

ANSWERS AND EXPLANATIONS

SECTION 1

6 ESSAY

Luis Buñuel hits truth with this statement, bringing up one of the human condition's greatest dilemmas. I think that without memory, we would know nothing, absorb nothing, feel nothing, and be nothing. The only reason humans care about anything, feel anything, or are anything, is because of memories from their own lives.

Memories play a large role in shaping our societies, because we learn from the events of history, and we even shape our governments based on the ideas of ancient Greeks.

And most importantly, memories are exactly what make us individuals. For example, our childhood shapes who we are for our whole lives, from things as vital as the thinking process, to things as trivial as eating habits and music taste. We have to remember words in order to speak and we have to remember how to walk as well as the names and faces of our parents.

I have found that love, hate, anger, happiness, sadness, are all caused by remembering what just happened to us. And these emotions would mean nothing if we forgot them an instant after we had them, because they would seem to never existed. Even the greatest suffering would mean nothing if we forgot it seconds later, and if I fell in love with someone, but I forgot about them a second later, it would mean absolutely nothing to me. It's just like the "If a tree falls in the forest and no one sees it, does it make a sound" dilemma. If we experience something and forget it instantly, we can never know and will never know if it existed.

Memory is vital to human existence. In fact, it is human existence. To quote Luis Buñuel,
. . . Memory is our coherence, our reason . . . Without it we are nothing.

GRADER'S COMMENTS

The essay is scored based on four basic criteria: Topic, Support, Organization, and Language. This essay does well on all counts, so it has earned a 6. It demonstrates an especially strong grasp of the writing assignment, earning high points for topic, support, and organization. The author states a thesis in paragraph 1, and then provides specific, relevant examples in each paragraph that support the idea of memory shaping the individual life. The examples are explained clearly and follow logically.

The writing stays on track, using the writer's previous knowledge to discuss the topic comfortably. The writer uses key phrases such as *and most importantly, for example,* and *I have found* to link and explain connected ideas. Vocabulary is strong (*dilemmas,* and *absorb* for example). The brief discussion of philosophy in the fourth paragraph shows the writer's attempt to connect the argument to literature. The closing paragraph sums up the writer's opinion. The opening sentence of the fourth paragraph is unnecessarily passive but this does not detract from the overall high quality of the essay.

4 ESSAY

Without memory, we are basically nothing. For instance, during the war in 2003, if we had remembered that Saddam Hussein hadn't cooperated last time, we could have gone in and removed him without the hassle of waiting for the weapons inspectors and things might have gone easier.

Another is example is to eat chocolate. Everyone knows that it tastes good. But I would never buy chocolate if I didn't remember how it tasted. In history, as well, such as the French revolution, memory is also vital. The French would not have fought for their freedom in the Revolution unless they remembered what freedom was like or what it would be like as well. Also, scientists wouldn't be able to make new discoveries without the memory, because how else would they remember complicated formulas or even their experiments? They wouldn't. Also, I remember that when I was about three years old, I burned my hand on the stove, and because then I have not placed my hand on a hot stove again. if I had no memory, I would still be burning myself. I believe people learn from their mistakes and this is because of memory.

There is another experience that tells me memory is vital. My grandfather had Alscizmers's disease. He completely lost his memory and didn't even recognize my mother, his own daughter. And this was disturbing because she was his own daughter. My mother said it was like her dad had disappeared completely because he has no memory. He also forgot how to brush his teeth and asked the same question over and over again. It was the opposite of when I burned myself. So memory is vital to human life, and so I agree with Bunuel's idea.

GRADER'S COMMENTS

The essay is scored based on four basic criteria: Topic, Support, Organization, and Language. This author attempted with some success to fulfill the assignment, and the arguments make sense overall. However, no one idea is sufficiently developed and many opinions are lacking supporting examples. The essay presents several logical arguments in the third paragraph, but organization is lacking. The final argument is the most successful as it shows the writer's understanding of the essay topic. However the organization is confused and this detracts from the strength of the argument.

The language and vocabulary in the essay could be improved. Phrases like *as well, and how else* and *this is because of* distract the reader from the author's meaning. The tone of the question and answer in the third paragraph is not appropriate for the essay. Many sentences could have been written with more clarity.

Overall, the essay looks like the writer is able to think about difficult issues but unable to express his or her ideas clearly. It would have been a better essay if the writer had spent a few minutes reviewing the completed essay to clarify sentences, add supporting ideas, and improve the vocabulary.

1 ESSAY

I remember songs in my head all the time and there is nothing I can do about it. My favorite songs are not the ones I remember but more than likely some advertisement I heard on the way to school this morning. It seems like things are like that. You have to remember so. Everyone does and then if we didn't remember things we wouldn't really have much thoughts or people who live wouldn't really have very much reasons to make decesions.

Once my fish died and when the fish buried, we didn't like the part when the fish didn't remind us of things. It was sad, like when Roger moved to Dallas. But memory is a funny thing, the way you can't control it or nothing when you really want to.

GRADER'S COMMENTS

The essay is scored based on four basic criteria: Topic, Support, Organization, and Language. In this essay, the author mentions memory, but does not answer the assignment. Nearly every sentence has a grammatical error (*there is nothing I can do about it, we didn't like the part when the fish didn't remind us*) and there are many spelling errors. The story about remembering songs might have been used to create an argument about memory, but the story about the fish makes no sense. The essay lacks a thesis statement and a closing summary. It might have been a better essay if the writer had focused on one story and developed a single basic argument about how memory shapes our lives.

SECTION 2

1. E

Do what's in parentheses first:

$$\left(\frac{1}{5} + \frac{1}{3}\right) \div \frac{1}{2} = \left(\frac{3}{15} + \frac{5}{15}\right) \div \frac{1}{2}$$

$$= \frac{8}{15} \div \frac{1}{2}$$

Then, to divide fractions, invert the one after the division sign and multiply:

$$\frac{8}{15} \div \frac{1}{2} = \frac{8}{15} \times \frac{2}{1} = \frac{16}{15}$$

2. E

Plug in $x = -2$ and see what you get:

$$x^2 - 2x = (-2)^2 - 2(-2)$$

$$= 4 - (-4)$$

$$= 4 + 4$$

$$= 8$$

3. C

To get Vito's rate in pages per hour, take the 96 pages and

divide by the time in hours. The time is given as "2 hours and 40 minutes." Forty minutes is $\frac{2}{3}$ of

an hour, so you can express Vito's time as $2\frac{2}{3}$ hours, or $\frac{8}{3}$ hours:

$$\text{Pages per hour} = \frac{96 \text{ pages}}{\frac{8}{3}} \text{ hours}$$

$$= 96 \times \frac{3}{8} = 36$$

4. A

For $\frac{7}{x}$ to be greater than $\frac{1}{4}$, the denominator x has to be less than 4 times the numerator, or 28.

And for $\frac{7}{x}$ to be less than $\frac{1}{3}$, the denominator x has to be greater than 3 times the numerator, or

21. Thus, x could be any of the integers 22 through 27, of which there are 6.

5. A

To find the average of three numbers—even if they're algebraic expressions—add them up and divide by 3:

$$\text{Average} = \frac{(2x+5)+(5x-6)+(-4x+2)}{3}$$

$$= \frac{3x+1}{3}$$

$$= x + \frac{1}{3}$$

6. D

$$\text{Percent} \times \text{Whole} = \text{Part:}$$

$$(\text{Percent}) \times 25 = 16$$

$$\text{Percent} = \frac{16}{25} \times 100\% = 64\%$$

7. C

The measures of the interior angles of a triangle add up to 180, so add the two *given* measures and subtract the sum from 180. The difference will be the measure of the third angle:

$$45 + 70 = 115$$
$$180 - 115 = 65$$

8. A

$$\frac{x^2 + x^2 + x^2}{x^2} = \frac{3x^2}{x^2} = 3$$

9. C

To solve a quadratic equation, put it in the "$ax^2 + bx + c = 0$" form, factor the left side (if you can), and set each factor equal to 0 separately to get the two solutions. To solve $x^2 = 5x - 4$, first, rewrite it as $x^2 - 5x + 4 = 0$. Then factor the left side:

$$x^2 - 5x + 4 = 0$$
$$(x-1)(x-4) = 0$$
$$x = 1 \text{ or } 4$$

10. A

Picking numbers is the easiest, fastest way to do this problem. Choose a pair of numbers from each set and add them together. If you are unable to prove immediately that a set does not have the property described in the question stem, you may want to choose another pair. In set I, if we add 2 and 4, we get 6. Adding 12 and 8 gives us 20. Adding −2 and 8 gives us 6. Since each sum is a member of the set of even integers, set I seems to be true. For set II, adding 3 and 5 yields 8, which is not an odd integer. Therefore, II is not true. Finally, if we add two primes, say 2 and 3, we get 5. That example is true. If we add 3 and 5, however, we get 8, and 8 is not a prime number. Therefore, only set I has the property, and the answer is (A).

11. E

The best way to deal with changing averages is to use the sum. Use the old average to figure out the total of the first 4 scores:

Sum of first 4 scores = (4)(89) = 356

Use the new average to figure out the total he needs after the 5th score:

Sum of 5 scores = (5)(90) = 450

To get his sum from 356 to 450, Martin needs to score 450 − 356 = 94.

12. C

Don't fall for the trap choice (D): You can't add or subtract percents of different wholes. Let the original price $s = 100$. Reducing s by 25% gives you a sale price of $75. This price is then increased by 20%, so the final price is $90. Since $s = 100$, it's easy to see that this is equal to choice (C), $.90s$.

13. A

The prime factorization of 36 is $2 \times 2 \times 3 \times 3$. That factorization includes 2 distinct prime factors, 2 and 3.

14. D

The area of a triangle is equal to one-half the base times the height:

$$\text{Area} = \frac{1}{2}(\text{base})(\text{height})$$

$$36 = \frac{1}{2}(9)(\text{height})$$

$$36 = \frac{9}{2}h$$

$$h = \frac{2}{9} \times 36 = 8$$

15. C

According to the definition, $x \clubsuit = \frac{x}{4} - \frac{x}{6}$. Set that equal to 3 and solve for x:

$$\frac{x}{4} - \frac{x}{6} = 3$$
$$12\left(\frac{x}{4} - \frac{x}{6}\right) = 12(3)$$
$$3x - 2x = 36$$
$$x = 36$$

16. A

Read carefully. This question's a lot easier than you might think at first. It's asking for the total number of coins, not the total value. q quarters, d dimes, and n nickels add up to a total of $q + d + n$ coins.

17. E

Use the points where the line crosses the axes—$(-1, 0)$ and $(0, 2)$—to find the slope:

$$\text{Slope} = \frac{y_2 - y_1}{x_2 - x_1} = \frac{2 - 0}{0 - (-1)} = 2$$

The y-intercept is 2. Now plug $m = 2$ and $b = 2$ into the slope-intercept equation form:

$$y = mx + b$$
$$y = 2x + 2$$

18. B

An integer that's divisible by 6 has at least one 2 and one 3 in its prime factorization. An integer that's divisible by 9 has at least two 3s in its prime factorization. Therefore, an integer that's divisible by both 6 and 9 has at least one 2 and two 3s in its prime factorization. That means it is divisible by 2 and 3: $2 \times 3 = 6$, $3 \times 3 = 9$, and $2 \times 3 \times 3 = 18$. It's not necessarily divisible by 12 or 36, each of which includes two 2s in its prime factorization.

You could also do this one by picking numbers. Think of a common multiple of 6 and 9 and use it to eliminate some options. $6 \times 9 = 54$ is an obvious common multiple—and it's not divisible by 12 or 36, but it is divisible by 18. The least common multiple of 6 and 9 is 18, which is also divisible by 18. It looks like every common multiple of 6 and 9 is also a multiple of 18.

19. D

The volume of a cube is equal to an edge cubed, so $e^3 = 64$, and each edge of the cube has length 4. If the cube is sliced horizontally in two, each of the resulting solids will have two sides of length 4 and one of length 2. So when they are glued together, the resulting figure will have one edge of length 2, one of length 4, and one of length 4 + 4 or 8.

The surface area is the sum of the areas of the solid's six faces. The top and bottom each have area $8 \times 4 = 32$, the front and back each have area $8 \times 2 = 16$, and each side has area $4 \times 2 = 8$. So the surface area of the new solid is $2(32) + 2(16) + 2(8) = 64 + 32 + 16 = 112$.

20. D

The area of a triangle is equal to one-half the base times the height. You can use any of the 3 sides of a triangle for the base—each side has a height to go along with it. It doesn't make any difference which base-height pair you use—a triangle has the same area no matter how you figure it. Thus, one-half times *PR* times *QS* will be the same as one-half times *PS* times *RT*:

$$\frac{1}{2}(PR)(QS) = \frac{1}{2}(PS)(RT)$$

$$\frac{1}{2}(8)(9) = \frac{1}{2}(PS)(7)$$

$$(8)(9) = (PS)(7)$$

$$PS = \frac{72}{7} = 10\frac{2}{7}$$

SECTION 3

1. C

The phrase *proves difficult* is a clue: the two missing words have to be nearly opposite in meaning. Choice (C) is correct, because few posters would be *intact* if they were meant to be *destroyed*. None of the other choices makes sense: being (A) *returned* would not stop something from being *recognizable*, being (B) *discarded* would not necessarily stop something from being *relevant*, and so on.

2. E

The phrases *long considered* and *finally* suggest contrast. The missing word is probably the opposite of *making some headway in its battle against extinction*. (E) *imperiled, in danger*, is the best answer. (A) *elusive* means *hard to find*; (B) *prevalent* means *common*; (C) *combative* means *eager to fight*; (D) *voracious* means *having a huge appetite*.

3. A

The sentence sets up a contrast between the situation before the invention of the tape recorder and the situation after. We need a word that's the opposite of *paraphrased*, which means *expressed in different words*. The answer is *verbatim, word-for-word*.

4. A

The phrase *encouraged hopes* suggests that the two missing words will be somewhat related in meaning. Choice (A) is the best answer, because we expect a *serious* novelist to use *subtle* characterizations. The other choices make less sense; in fact, it's not clear what (C) *accurate*, (D) *fictional*, or (E) *authentic* characterizations would be. (C) *prolific* means *highly productive*; (D) *accomplished* means *skillful, experienced*; (E) *reclusive* means *unsociable*.

5. C

Words like *unchanging* and *eternal* provide a definition of the missing word, (C) *static*. (D) *holistic* means *functioning as a whole*, and (E) *homogeneous* means *all of one kind*; neither word implies species being unchanging and no new species coming into existence.

6. C

The phrase *failure to* establishes the negative tone of the sentence. An agency ought to *fix* or *get rid of* flawed policies. Possible answers for the first blank are (C) *rescind* or *remove, cancel*, and (D) *amend* or *fix*. Failure to do this is a bad thing, so we need a negative word for the second blank. The best choice is *lackadaisical, careless, sloppy*.

7. D

Rapid turnover would tend to increase *inconsistency*, so we need a word that means *increased* or *worsened*. *Exacerbated* means *made worse*.

8. C

What claim would be *belied* or contradicted by a record of contributing to only one party? A claim of *impartiality*, of not favoring one side over the other.

BOOK SEQUELS

9. B

When asked for information about one author, eliminate choices that discuss the other author. Be sure that you have each author's position clear in your mind before you tackle the questions. The author of Passage 1 is hostile to the idea of sequels, so you should look for an answer that reflects this attitude. (B) fits well and follows directly from the last sentence. The author of Passage 1 is not concerned with the ease of writing a sequel (A)—she considers all sequels a bad idea. Author 1 never discusses *The Seven Percent Solution*, so (C) is out. Although the author is indignant, you don't have any information that other readers feel that way. (E) is actually the opposite of the truth, since the author states that sequels are written to entice readers of the original books.

10. A

The author uses Margaret Mitchell as an example of a group of authors who've had sequels written to their books. The author states that if the authors and the books that are the subjects of sequels were untalented or unknown, this practice wouldn't be so bad. But, the author goes on to state, that's not the case. From this, you can infer that the author regards Margaret Mitchell as talented or well-known (A). While the author mentions only one novel, *Gone with the Wind*, you can't infer that Mitchell only wrote one book (B). The passage doesn't discuss the relative skills of the authors she mentions (C), or the relative fame of the author and her book (D). (E) might be tempting for the unwary test taker; the passage says that the authors of sequels, rather than of the original books, will disappoint readers.

11. D

Always read the context in which the vocabulary word appears—the context for this word is: *What unalloyed delight for those who have read . . .* You can tell immediately that the adjective unalloyed must have a positive connotation, since it modifies a positive noun—delight. It wouldn't make sense to say, *awful delight,* or *unpleasant delight.* Even something neutral won't work with delight, *middling delight,* or *moderate delight,* for example. Since delight means high satisfaction or great pleasure, you need an adjective of equal intensity to modify it. Therefore, you can eliminate all negative or neutral words, like (A) and (E). (B), (C), and (D) are all positive, but (D) is the best match here. *Unalloyed* means not mixed with anything else. (You might be familiar with the term *alloy* to refer to a blend of metals.) So, unalloyed means pure.

12. E

Remember, author 1 is against sequels; author 2 contends that fans will be delighted that there's a sequel to Arthur Conan Doyle's Sherlock Holmes stories. So author 2 would almost certainly disagree with author 1's comments that sequels are always disappointing. (E) captures this by noting the delight that readers will get when they read a sequel to a book they love. You don't have any reason to believe that author 1 will change her mind (A), or even concede that some readers will be disappointed (D). Since author 2 never discusses *Gone with the Wind*, there's no support for (B). Finally, you can rule out (C) since the tone is so extreme.

THE WOLVES PASSAGE

This Science passage is written by a naturalist who recounts how he went into the wilderness and, through trial and error experimentation and observation, learned some new and surprising things about the way wolves live. For example, wolves are a lot less suspicious and aggressive than people think they are, and contrary to popular belief, wolf families are not nomadic—they live and stay in territories with very definite boundaries.

13. C

In the first paragraph, the author explains how the wolves were aware of his presence but ignored him. That's why the author's precautions were superfluous. (C) basically paraphrases that idea: the author's precautions were unnecessary because the wolves weren't interested in him. (A) doesn't work because the author never really says how long it was before he encountered the wolves. (B) is out because the author never mentions any wild animals other than wolves. Contrary to (D), even after the author interfered with the wolves' boundaries, they never bothered him. (E) is out because it's never suggested that the wolves have poor eyesight.

14. A

The author's basic point in paragraph 1 is that he was surprised at the way the wolves behaved toward him: they sized him up quickly right at the beginning and, from then on, ignored him. He found this behavior disconcerting, or *strange*, as (A) puts it. (B) sounds exaggerated—the author never really suggests that he was fearful of attack. With (C), the author says that he took longer to assess the wolves than they took to assess him, but his basic point is not to emphasize his own ignorance. (D) doesn't work because the wolves left the author alone—precautions weren't necessary. (E), like (B), isn't suggested—that the author thinks he has a lot of courage.

15. D

In paragraph 3, the author describes how the wolf was so preoccupied that he came within 15 yards of his tent without seeing it. It wasn't until the author made noise that the wolf suddenly became aware of its surroundings. (D) paraphrases this idea: that the wolf was not *on its guard*—it was self-absorbed. The author expresses no surprise about the wolf traveling alone (A) or hunting at night (C). As for (B), the point is not that the wolf lacks energy—it does respond when the author startles it. (E) is out because the author doesn't really mention any fear of attack.

16. C

The first sentence of paragraph 3 describes the wolf as *anxious to go home to bed*. The idea is that he was *eager* to get home (C). *Distressed* (A), *afraid* (B), *uneasy* (D), and *worried* (E) are other definitions of anxious, but they don't fit the idea in the sentence.

17. C

In paragraph 4, the author explains that one of the things he learned is that, contrary to popular belief, the wolves were *settled beasts* rather than *nomadic hunters*. The idea, in other words, is that the wolves were *stable*—they had established homes. *Decided* (A) and *resolute* (B) are other meanings of *settled*, but they don't work in the sentence. Neither *inflexible* (D) nor *confident* (E) fits when plugged in.

18. A

The idea at the beginning of paragraph 4 is that the wolves, contrary to what people generally think, are not nomadic. (A) catches the idea: the author is countering a popular myth or belief about the behavior of wolves. (B) is tricky, but there's really no paradox or ambiguity: the idea is that the wolves are NOT nomadic. (C) is tricky too, but the passage never says that the idea that wolves are nomadic is an established fact. As for (D), there's no indication that what the author observed—that the wolves live in established territories—is an exception to a general rule. (E) doesn't work because there's really no summary of any conclusions in the quoted lines. (A) is the best choice.

19. B

In the middle of paragraph 5, the author describes how the wolf family regularly made the rounds of their lands and *freshened up the boundary markers*. He guessed that this was done because there were other wolves living in adjacent areas, although he never saw any sign of trouble between the neighboring wolf families. Then you get the quoted idea: since he never witnessed any disputes, he figured that it was all basically a ritual activity. (B) catches the idea. The idea that the activity was a ritual isn't related to the fact that it was repeated (A), that the boundaries were marked by geographic features (C), that they were marked at the same time each week (D)—that's never suggested—or that the whole family participated (E). The wrong choices miss the point.

20. C

One of the author's discoveries is that the wolves live in territories with clearly marked boundaries. So, contrary to what most people think, they aren't nomadic—they don't travel endlessly from place to place looking for food and sleeping in new areas. The idea in (C), if it were true, would contradict or weaken that idea. The idea in (A) would strengthen the thesis—if there were disputes over boundaries, that would suggest that the wolves are protective of their territory. The idea in (B)—the particular size of the wolves' territory—is irrelevant—it doesn't really relate to the question. (D) is tricky, but it doesn't work: the author finds that the wolves are territorial even though they actually don't have conflicts with their neighbors. The idea in (E) is irrelevant: the passage never discusses whether or not wolves are alert when encountering other animals.

21. D

The phrase *invisible wall* occurs in paragraph 7, and the point is that the wolf, who was plodding home as preoccupied as usual, was suddenly stopped in its tracks when it encountered the spot where the author had left his own markings. So the idea about the invisible wall is that the wolf was stopped suddenly (D), as if it had suddenly banged up against it. The idea of an invisible wall has nothing to do with delight in getting the wolf's attention (A), annoyance on the part of the wolf (B), high speed (C)—the wolf was *padding*, not running—or exhaustion after a night of hunting (E).

22. B

In the very same sentence in paragraph 7, the author says that the wolf, upon finding the author's marks, immediately became bewildered. (B) restates that. The passage says nothing about *combativeness* (A), *anxiety* (C), *wariness* (D), or *dread* (E).

23. B

Temerity is a tough vocabulary word—it means *impetuousness* or *rashness* (B). But you really didn't have to know that definition to pick the right answer. All you have to do with Vocabulary-in-Context questions is plug in each of the answer choices, and eliminate the ones that don't fit the sentence's meaning. If you do that here, none of the other choices works. With (A), it's not that the author's being discourteous. That sounds strange. Rather, he's being too bold—only (B) makes sense. Remember, if you're stumped with any hard question, work backward by eliminating any wrong choices you can—and then guess.

24. B

At the end of paragraph 8, the author states that he turned his back on the wolf *in an effort to break the impasse*. In other words, he did it to bring about a change in the situation (B). Nothing suggests that he did it to show his power over the wolf (A); make the wolf recognize his existence (C)—the wolf already did; look for a weapon (D); or avoid the wolf's *hypnotic* gaze (E).

SECTION 4

1. D

This is a straightforward substitution problem. Plug in the given values and remember your order of operations (PEMDAS): $3^2 - 2(1) = 9 - 2(1) = 9 - 2 = 7$.

2. D

The answer choices are given in the form $y = mx + b$,

where m is the slope and b is the y-intercept. The y-intercept is clearly 3, so the answer must be (C),

(D), or (E). You can either estimate the slope by looking at the graph, or calculate it. To calculate it,

you first need the x and y values of two points on the graph, for instance (0, 3) and (6, 0). $\frac{0-3}{6-0} =$

$\frac{-3}{6} = \frac{-1}{2}$, so the slope of the graph must be $\frac{-1}{2}$.

3. D

First translate the question into a system of equations. $q = r - 4$ and $r = 6 + s$. Now plug $s = 2$ into
the second equation to get $r = 6 + 2 = 8$, and plug this into the first equation to find $q = 8 - 4 = 4$.

4. D

Each month has 15 days, so 700 days is $\frac{700}{15}$ months. Each year has 9 months, so $\frac{700}{15}$ months is

$\frac{\frac{700}{15}}{9} = \frac{700}{135} = 5\frac{5}{27}$. This means 5 full years have gone by.

5. A

The square of a positive number is positive. The square of a negative number is positive. The
square of zero is zero. Therefore, statement I, which presents a negative number, cannot be the
square of any real number x. I cannot be the value of $f(x)$ for any real value of x. II is the result of
$f(0)$. III is the result of $f(\pm\sqrt{2.3})$.

6. A

The mode is the number that appears most often in a set of data. The largest number of people
who collected the same amount of trash was the 12 people who collected 10 pieces of trash, so 10 is
the mode of this set of data.

7. D

The total amount of trash collected by the 30 participants was $12(10) + 9(15) + 4(20) + 4(25) +$
$1(30) = 120 + 135 + 80 + 100 + 30 = 465$ pieces of trash. The goal of the drive was to collect 500
pieces of trash, so we need to figure out what percent 465 is of 500. $\frac{465}{500} = .93$, so the participants
reached 93% of the goal.

8. C

The total amount of trash collected by the 30 participants was $12(10) + 9(15) + 4(20) + 4(25) + 1(30) = 120 + 135 + 80 + 100 + 30 = 465$ pieces of trash. Since there were 30 participants, the average amount of trash collected by each one was $\frac{465}{30} = 15.5$ pieces.

9. 115

Since lines p and q are parallel, we can use the rule about alternate interior angles to fill in the following:

Since the angle marked $y°$ is adjacent and supplementary to a 65° angle, $y = 180 - 65 = 115$.

10. 04

Be careful. The question is not asking: "What is $\frac{1}{4}$ of 16?" It's asking: "What is $\frac{1}{4}$ *percent* of 16?" One-fourth of 1 percent is 0.25%, or 0.0025:

$$\frac{1}{4}\% \text{ of } 16 = 0.0025 \times 16 = .04$$

11. 11, 13, 17, 19, 23, 29, 31, 37, 41, 43, or 47

In order for each of these fractions to be in its simplest form, a would have to be a number that has no prime factors in common with 3, 5, or 14. So find a value between 2 and 50 that fits that description. Your best bet is to use a prime number, such as 11. That's one of 11 acceptable answers.

12. $\frac{2}{5}$ or .4

If there are 36 men and 24 women in the group, then the total number of group members is 60. The women make up $\frac{24}{60}$ of the group. Since this fraction cannot be gridded, reduce it or turn it into a decimal. To reduce it, divide both the numerator and denominator by 12, and you end up with $\frac{2}{5}$. To turn it into a decimal, divide 60 into 24, and you end up with .4.

13. 8

To evaluate this expression when $s = 9$, simply plug 9 in for s. Substituting 9 into the expression yields:

$$\frac{3(9) + 5}{4} = \frac{27 + 5}{4} = \frac{32}{4} = 8$$

14. 4

The easiest way to get the answer here is to pick numbers. Pick a number for x that has a remainder of 2 when divided by 6, such as 8. Increase the number you picked by 8. In this case, $8 + 8 = 16$. Now divide 16 by 6, which gives you 2 remainder 4. Therefore, the answer is 4.

15. 250

$$\text{Percent} \times \text{Whole} = \text{Part:}$$
$$(15\%) \times (\text{take-home pay}) = \$37.50$$
$$(0.15) \times (\text{take-home pay}) = \$37.50$$
$$\text{take-home pay} = \frac{\$37.50}{0.15} = \$250.00$$

16. 9

The area of a triangle is equal to one-half the base times the height. Here the base (along the x-axis) is 6 and the height (perpendicular to the base—i.e., parallel to the y-axis) is 3, so the area is $\frac{1}{2}bh = \frac{1}{2}$ (6)(3) = 9.

17. 64

You cannot find the area of the square without finding the length of a side, so use the information you are given about the rectangles to find the length of the square's sides. Since the rectangles have the same dimensions, we know that the side of the square must be twice the length of the shorter side of either rectangle. The side of the square must also be the longer side of either rectangle. Call the length of a side of the square, which is also the length of a longer side of either rectangle, x. Then the shorter side of either rectangle is $\frac{x}{2}$. Now use the formula for the perimeter:

$$P = 2l + 2w$$

For either rectangle, you have

$$24 = 2x + 2\left(\frac{x}{2}\right)$$
$$24 = 2x + x$$
$$24 = 3x$$
$$8 = x$$

To find the area of the square, simply multiply 8 by 8. The answer is 64.

18. 203

This looks like a physics question, but in fact it's just a "plug-in-the-number-and-see-what-you-get" question. Be sure you plug 95 in for C (not F):

$$C = \frac{5}{9}(F - 32)$$

$$95 = \frac{5}{9}(F - 32)$$

$$\frac{9}{5} \times 95 = F - 32$$

$$F - 32 = 172$$

$$F = 171 + 32 = 203$$

SECTION 5

1. C

In this sentence the subject *sound* lacks a verb. The word *blocked* is not a verb; it's the past participle of the verb, which is used as an adjective. Look for choices that offer, *was blocked.* (B) keeps the original problem. It also unnecessarily changes the preposition *by* to the longer *as a result of.* In general, the SAT prefers sentences that are more concise. (C) matches your prediction. (D) gives you *was*, but makes a mess of the meaning of the sentence. (E) has the same problem as (D), even though it's expressed a little differently.

2. D

Here, the pronoun *who* is incorrectly used to refer to phone conversations. For this clause, look for choices that replace *who* with *which.* (C), (D), and (E) are all possibilities. (B) uses *whom* which should refer to people, incorrectly. (C) uses *that* but changes the meaning of the sentence. (D) matches your prediction. (E) changes the meaning of the sentence.

3. E

Because the error in this sentence occurs before you have enough information to know it is wrong, a majority of students get this type of question wrong. The comparative adjective *more* is used to compare two people, places, or things; *most* is used to compare more than two. Here, you are comparing Brando to any other person on the set individually. (E) matches the prediction. (B) tries to form the comparative by adding the suffix *-er* to crucial. This is incorrect. (C) changes the meaning of the sentence. (D) is grammatically incorrect and distorts the meaning.

4. C

Be sure that each verb tense is the appropriate choice in the context of the sentence. Because this sentence talks about the Renaissance, which is long over, it requires simple past tenses. Look for a choice that provides it. (B) uses the incorrect pronoun to refer to people. You need the correct form of *who*. (C) This choice provides the simple past tense that you were looking for. (D) changes the meaning of the sentence. (E) has a similar problem to (D).

5. B

Remember that *neither . . . nor* and *either . . . or* work in pairs. In this sentence you have *neither . . . or*, so you need to find a choice that gives you *neither . . . nor*. Two choices start with *neither*—(B) and (D). (B) correctly pairs *neither . . . nor* and maintains the meaning of the sentence. (D) correctly pairs *neither . . . nor*, but it adds unnecessary wordiness. While (E) gives you *either . . . or*, when you read it into the sentence you see that it makes the sentence grammatically incorrect. In (C), the incorrect pairing of *either . . . nor* makes this an easy choice to eliminate.

6. D

In this sentence you have a series that should be written the same way to maintain parallelism—*the chaos of war, the anxiety of the people*, and *the irrational behavior*. Look for that parallel structure among the choices. (B) corrects the parallelism but adds the incorrect present tense verb *is*. Because choice (C) maintains the incorrect, *they showed*, you know it's wrong. It also changes the meaning of the sentence, because here it's the escalation and not the behavior that is irrational. Choice (D) does what you predicted you'd need—it fixes the parallelism problem while keeping the meaning of the sentence intact. (E) uses an incorrect verb tense.

7. E

In this sentence the comparison is between *is respected . . . as she was*. You need to find a choice that changes *was* to *is*. Only (C) and (E) make this change. (C) uses the passive voice which should be avoided, if possible, in the SAT Writing section. (B), in addition to not correcting the error, slightly changes the meaning of the sentence. (D) maintains *was*, and destroys the comparison by changing *as* to *and*.

8. B

Be on the lookout for words and phrases that are acceptable in speech but not in writing. The expression, *deep down there* is too colloquial for written English. (B) eliminates the colloquialism and also cleans up the possessive to make it less wordy. (C) uses the incorrect comparative form of the adjective. (D) changes the meaning of the sentence. (E) cleans up the possessive, but doesn't correct the colloquialism.

9. A

If you think there are no errors in a sentence, there's at least a 20 percent chance that you're right. Check the sentence for common errors if you're not sure—subject-verb, pronoun agreement, parallelism, logical comparisons. If this all checks out, choose (A). (B) substitutes the incorrect conjunction, *but*, for the correct one. It also incorrectly changes the past progressive tense to the simple past. (C) changes the correct preposition, *about*, to *for*. (D) The subject, *three women*, is plural so you need the plural verb, *were*, not *was*. (E) uses the wrong verb tense and changes the meaning of the sentence by changing *discussing* to *in discussion*.

10. A

Be sure that idioms are expressed clearly and precisely. In (B), *there* is used without any proper antecedent—what place is referred to? (C) expresses a different idea. (D) makes no sense; what is *farther* a comparison to? (E) also expresses a different meaning.

11. D

This sentence meant to compare two dental procedures—root canal and extraction, instead it compares root canals to chewing problems. Only (C), (D), and (E) correctly begin with *an extraction*, eliminating (A) and (B). (B) is also wordy. (C) uses the incorrect verb tense. (D) is what you were looking for. (E) reverses the cause/effect—an extraction can lead to chewing problems according to the original sentence. This choice has chewing problems leading to an extraction.

12. E

What are the possible issues? An adjective, a past-tense verb, a prepositional phrase, and a phrase completing a comparison are underlined. (A) uses an appropriate adjective to describe the noun *series*. (B) is a verb that agrees in tense and number with its subject. (C) uses the idiomatically correct preposition. (D) correctly completes the comparison begun with *as easily*. Therefore, (E) is the right answer: no error.

13. C

You have a clear indication of time in this sentence—last month. Make sure that the verb or verbs that refer to this event are in the simple past tense. (D) is in the progressive past tense and needs to be changed to the simple past—*graduated*. (A) uses the correct, simple past tense form of the verb. (B) is the correct comparative form of the adjective. (D) is the correct preposition to use with *graduate*.

14. D

The adjective *deep* is incorrectly used to modify *sleeping*. Remember adjectives modify nouns and adverbs modify verbs, adjectives, and other adverbs. (A) is an idiomatically correct prepositional phrase that explains where the commotion took place. (B) is correctly used to indicate that the hens and the rooster were part of an ongoing ruckus. In (C), the past tense verb, *woke* is correct.

15. C

The general rule for forming comparatives is to use *more* if the adjective has more than one syllable, and the suffix *-er* if the adjective has one syllable. In this sentence (C) does both things—it places *more* in front of *small* and adds the suffix *-er* to it. Because *small* has one syllable, the correct comparative form is *smaller*. In (A), *when* is used correctly to refer to time. (B) correctly uses the past tense form of the verb *to look*. (D) is a good vocabulary word, correctly used. It means *to come forth*.

16. D

Note that the subject is *fruits* not *item*. The singular pronoun *its* incorrectly refers to the plural subject *fruits*. *Its* should be *their*. (A) is idiomatically correct. (B) is in the correct tense, and in (C) *necessary* correctly takes the preposition *to*.

17. E

The sentence is correct as written. In (A), *completed* is the correct form to complete the verb *could have completed*. (B) correctly modifies the adjective *long*. (C) is in the correct tense because it happened before *he might have succeeded*. (D) is the correct form of the adverb, modifying *started*.

18. D

The pronoun *their* is plural, but it refers to the pronoun *each* which is singular. If you were correcting this sentence, you would replace *their* with *his* or *her* depending on who is on the team. In (A), *about* is one of the prepositions that can be used with *concerned*. In (B), the preposition *on* is used correctly. In (C), the past tense verb correctly expresses the time indicated in the sentence.

19. B

Use *fewer* for countable nouns and *less* for uncountable nouns. *Adults* is a countable noun, so (B) is incorrect. (A) is the correct adverb. (C) agrees with the singular subject, *environment*. (D) The preposition *to* is correctly used with *conducive*.

20. A

(A) is a compound object using a noun, *Hilary*, and a pronoun, *I*. Read the sentence without *Hilary*. You would never say: *Dad asked I* so you need the objective pronoun, *me*. (B) uses the correct simple past tense. (C) uses the possessive correctly. (D) is idiomatically correct.

21. A

This sentence needs a verb in the past perfect tense, to indicate that an action was completed at some point in the past before something else happened. Here the water rose and then governor ordered the evacuation. The correct form of the irregular verb *rise* is *had risen*. (B) is idiomatically correct usage. (C) is correctly the past tense, (D) is idiomatically correct.

22. B

The phrase and clause *of concert-goers who waited hours for the entrance of their favorite music group* comes between the subject and verb. The singular subject *list* needs a singular verb and so (B) should be *includes*. (A) is the right relative pronoun to refer to people correctly uses the past tense. (C) is idiomatically correct and *who* (D) is the correct pronoun.

23. D

Make sure that all underlined words are used correctly. In this sentence the author meant to use *indeterminate* or *undetermined* which mean *not yet decided*. Instead he used *indecisive* which means *uncertain* or *vague*. (A) is the correct possessive pronoun to refer to the university. (B) is correctly the past tense. (C) is the correct verb form.

24. B

Remember that certain words go together. For example, *not only . . . but also; more . . . than*. The addition of *like* is incorrect and it has to be omitted to make this sentence correct. (A) is correct in the present singular tense. (C) is the right conjunction. (D) is idiomatically correct.

25. D

The sentence begins with the impersonal pronoun *one* and then switches to the personal pronoun *you*. You have to change *you* to *one* for consistency. (A) is correctly in the present progressive. (B) uses the idiomatically correct preposition. (C) is idiomatically correct.

26. D

Make sure all subjects and verbs agree. *Books* is plural, so *interests* needs to be changed to *interest* to agree with the plural subject. Don't be confused by the relative pronoun *that*. (A) is the right preposition. (B) is correctly the present tense. (C) is the right plural pronoun to refer to *students*.

27. B

If you're not sure there's an error, check each underlined part of the sentence. The adverb *where* means *in what place*. A plan is not a place, so you need to change *where* to *in which* to make this sentence correct. (A) is appropriately in the past tense. (C) is idiomatically correct. (D) is the right preposition.

28. D

Each verb must accurately express time. Something that happened in 1750 needs a past tense verb. In this sentence, the verb *will be* is the future tense. (A) idiomatically expresses the time period. (B) uses the correct words. (C) is an appropriate transition word.

29. A

If you find two elements in the sentence that are expressing the same thought, you need to eliminate one of them. In this sentence *both* and *as well as* are saying the same thing, creating a redundancy. You need to eliminate one and the only one that is underlined is *both* (A). (B) is correctly in the perfect tense, since it is an ongoing obsession. (C) uses the idiomatically correct preposition. (D) is properly in the past tense.

30. A

To determine what logically follows the first sentence, read through the first paragraph to see what ideas are introduced. The paragraph goes on to describe how winter is viewed by some as cold, snowy, and bleak. (A) introduces this. (B) is true, but irrelevant here. (C) is opposite in meaning to the passage; the author clearly likes winter. (D) is out of scope; the author never states what season people prefer. And, this sentence doesn't introduce the ideas that follow in the paragraph. (E) brings in an idea from paragraph 3 which is out of place here.

31. B

To combine the sentences, you must determine their relationship. (B) combines the sentences by subordinating the second clause and replacing the ambiguous pronouns *them* and *us*. (A) doesn't correct the ambiguity or the inconsistency between *them* and *us*. (C) badly distorts the meaning. (D) omits the idea that the *opportunity* for activity is provided. (E) is a run-on sentence with a comma splice.

32. E

Sentence 10 starts with the pronoun *we* and then switches to *people*. (E) correctly uses *people* as the subject of the sentence. (B) changes the meaning by stating a fact instead of stating that people *complain* about this fact. (C) inserts the transition word *therefore* which incorrectly sets up a causal relationship with sentence 9. (D) incorrectly sets up a causal relationship within sentence 10.

33. C

Paragraph 4 generally uses present tense, but sentence 13 uses present progressive. (C) correctly uses the present tense. (A) eliminates the parallelism in the list of nouns (*a fire, hot chocolate,* and *board games*). (B) is incorrect—*family* is a singular noun. (D) and (E) make unnecessary changes.

34. D

The original sentence is unclear about what is being compared: how aware we are in winter compared to how aware we are the rest of the year. (D) clarifies this by moving the *than . . . closer* to *more . . .* and by adding *we are during* to complete the second half of that thought. (B) starts to correct the problem, but *protection of our home* is ambiguous. (C) mixes the ideas of protection and companionship together, making them less clear. (E) is another partial correction, but it loses part of the original meaning.

35. E

The essay claims most other people don't appreciate winter as much as they should, and details three reasons why the writer prefers winter. (E) is a logical conclusion to this reasoning. (A) is a change of subject. (B) might be added in the second paragraph, but not here, where evening snowfall is discussed. (C) could be appropriate close to the first sentence, and (D) in the third paragraph.

SECTION 6

1. D

The word in the first blank has to be similar in meaning to *controversy*: (C) *belligerent*, (D) *scandalous*, and (E) *provocative* would fit. The band wouldn't do this if they didn't find that the strategy worked, so (B) *rewarding* and (D) *effective* fit for the second blank. Only (D) fits for both blanks.

2. B

The correct answer is implied by *numerous scribbled edits that cover even his supposed final drafts*. In other words, Joyce attached great importance to (B) *revision*.

3. B

The key is that the players *now charge for their signatures*. Either the fans who believe that the players are not *greedy* would be *surprised* or *disappointed*, or the fans who believe that the players are not *ungreedy* would be *confirmed*. Choice (B) fits the former prediction.

4. B

The words *though* and *absence* indicate contrast, so the missing word has to be nearly opposite in meaning to *isolation and the longing for connection. Fraternity*—brotherhood or fellowship—is the best choice. Choice (D) may be tempting, but the term *socialism* refers to a specific set of political and economic doctrines, not just to any sort of society.

5. B

The part of the sentence after the semicolon basically defines the missing word. The word is *calculated*, consciously planned. (A) *incendiary* means *inflaming*, (C) *facetious* means *joking*, (D) *scrupulous* means *honest*, (E) *impromptu* means *unplanned*.

DISCOVERY OF HELIUM

6. E

Ramsay appears toward the middle of the passage after the author mentions that scientists doubted that helium exists only on the sun. Since Ramsay's experiment with naturally occurring Earth minerals occurs in the next sentence, the correct answer will probably be something that cites discovering helium on Earth, and (E) fits this well. The wrong answers here all misuse details from other parts of the passage. Ramsay did not repeat Janssen's experiment, Lockyer did (A). Ramsay's chief contribution was to find helium on Earth; the fact that it was found in uranium minerals is secondary to this larger concern (B). Ramsay did not identify the gas as being helium, Crookes did (C). Finally. Ramsay was not involved with detecting helium on the sun; Janssen and Lockyer were (D).

7. C

The passage states that Janssen and Lockyer observed the sun using their spectroscopes and discovered a new yellow line that belonged to an unknown element. Reading the next sentence reveals that Janssen and Lockyer's work was doubted by many other scientists (C). Watch out for incorrectly used details: Lockyer repeated Janssen's experiment, but it is not stated that other scientists repeated the experiment incorrectly (A). Other scientists were skeptical, but this doesn't mean they thought the methodology behind the experiments was unsound (B); for example, perhaps they thought the results were interpreted incorrectly. Although it is mentioned that Janssen did his experiment during a solar eclipse, the author does not mention that this was necessary for the experiment (D). (E) is pretty far out-of-scope; using outdated equipment is never mentioned in the passage.

LORETTA'S VISIT

8. E

In the fourth sentence, we learn that the reasons for their separation is *lost in the mists of family lore*. In other words, no one knows the original cause of the estrangement (E). The author doesn't tell us how Grandmama treated Uncle Martin (A). (B) is too extreme, since Loretta is also visiting the city to spend time exploring it with the author. The author doesn't tell us what led to the impending reunion between Loretta and Grandmama (C), or anything about how busy Loretta is (D).

9. B

The context for this word is: *The rift that began for reasons lost in the mists of family lore has continued to this day.* Reading the sentence following this one is helpful: *I'll wager that Loretta can't even remember why she and Grandmama haven't spoken in all this time.* So there's been a *break* in relations between Grandmama and Loretta (B). A *motion* (A) between the two doesn't make sense. *Revelry* (C) and *clarity* (D) are both too positive for this situation. *Discussion* also doesn't fit for people that are angry with one another.

THE COLD WAR PASSAGE

The author of this passage has one overarching strategy: Set up the arguments of the revisionist historians and then knock them down. Paragraph 1 explains the things that, according to the revisionists, could have been done to avoid the Cold War, which are 1) the U.S. could have just accepted Soviet domination in Eastern Europe, 2) the U.S. could have given them money for reconstruction, and 3) the U.S. could have given up its monopoly of the bomb. Paragraphs 2 and 3 outline the author's refutation of these arguments; he concentrates on the American political atmosphere as the main reason that the revisionists' ideas were not really workable at the time. Revisionists, he then asserts in paragraph 4, would reject this politics-based argument and claim instead that it was the economic situation that forced American policy-makers to oppose the Soviets. The author of course then knocks down this new argument; it is contradictory, he says, to say that American officials were caught in an economic tide and then to blame them for not doing things differently. The author concludes in the final paragraph by stating that there was essentially no way, given the climate in the Soviet Union, that the Cold War could have been avoided.

10. C

As we noted above, the author of this passage is primarily engaged in setting up and knocking down the arguments of the revisionist historians of the Cold War. This makes (C) correct and (E) wrong (the author is definitely not interested in reconciling his view with that of the revisionists). (A) is wrong because the ideas of the revisionists are not, as far as we know, a popular myth. (B) is out because the author is defending historical figures—the policy makers—for what they did, not criticizing them. (D) is too neutral a choice for this passage; the author does engage in analysis of the era of the beginning of the Cold War, but his purpose is to do far more than just analyze events. He wants to poke holes in revisionist theories.

11. C

When revisionists say that the U.S. could have *recognized* the Soviet influence in Eastern Europe, they mean that the U.S. could have formally *acknowledged* this Soviet presence. (C) is correct.

12. C

Look back to the second half of the second paragraph. The author says there that Roosevelt could never have recognized a Soviet Eastern Europe because the American people did not like the idea of the Soviets holding sway in that region. In particular, the president would have lost the votes of the Polish-Americans who, you can infer, did not want the Soviets controlling their *old country*. (C) spells out this point. Each of the other choices is a misreading of the context of the sentence about the Polish-American voters.

13. E

In the second and third paragraphs, the author refutes the suggestions of the revisionists primarily by saying that the policy-makers couldn't do what was necessary to avoid the Cold War because the American people were against it. The assumption the author makes is that the policy-makers *could not have been expected to ignore public opinion* (E). The author never says in the second and third paragraphs that the Soviets were to blame for failed U.S. peace initiatives (A), or that none of the alternatives would work (C)—what he does say, in a later paragraph, is that if peace initiatives had not run aground due to American politics, then they would have run aground due to the Soviet climate. The author also does not say in the second and third paragraphs that the American public was *well-informed* (B) or *overwhelmingly opposed to seeking peace* (D); all we know is that they opposed Soviet influence in Eastern Europe as well as the idea of giving up the atom bomb monopoly.

14. C

This question is closely linked to the previous one. The author refers to the *certain constraints* at the end of the third paragraph, in the midst of the discussion on the impact of public opinion on the policy-makers. From context, then, you know that the constraints the author is talking about are the opinions of the people—in other words, *the views of the electorate* (C). If you didn't put the sentence about *constraints* in context, any of the other choices might have looked appealing.

15. E

This question centers on the fourth paragraph, which is where the author explains the revisionists' view that American policy-makers decided to oppose the Soviet Union because Soviet expansion could jeopardize U.S. trade and investment opportunities in Eastern Europe and elsewhere. (E) captures this idea. The author says nothing about illegal trading activities (A), nor does he indicate whether or not the Soviets knew about the negative impact they could have on the American economy (B). (C) is out because the Soviet Union was not recognized by the United States, so this could not possibly have had anything to do with the origin of the Cold War. (D) is wrong because there is no evidence in the paragraph to support it.

16. A

The author poses the question in order to show that there is a problem with the revisionists' economic interpretation of the Cold War: you can't blame the policy-makers if they didn't have any control. Thus, the question serves to *point out an inconsistency* (A) in the revisionists' position. (D) might be tempting since the revisionists' view is pretty cynical, but the author is questioning that view here, not summing it up.

THE JAMES WELDON JOHNSON PASSAGE

Johnson, the author of this autobiographical piece, does not just describe the experience he had watching the piano-player playing rag-time; he also uses the scene as a jumping-off point from which to comment on the origin of rag-time (second paragraph), to disparage American musicians for refusing to accept rag-time (third paragraph), and to speculate on what the piano player could have amounted to under different circumstances (fourth paragraph).

17. C

The author's initial impression of rag-time can be found in the first paragraph. He emphasizes how the beat demanded a physical response and meshed with the *dissonant harmonies*, etc., to produce a *curious effect*. (C) is the correct answer. The only other choice that has anything to do with the first paragraph is (B). (B) is wrong because the audience is said to have applauded the singer's dance steps, not the rag-time music.

18. E

Let's go through the choices one-by-one, keeping in mind that we're focusing exclusively on the first paragraph. Although the piano player is *master of a good deal of technique*, choice (A) is too extreme to be correct. We know nothing in the first paragraph of the author's expectations of rag-time, so (B) is out too. (C), (D), and (E) are different interpretations of the author's description of the piano player's playing. While it is certainly true that rag-time has dissonant harmonies and jumps from one key to another, you cannot infer from this that rag-time violates every rule of musical composition (C) or that it has no melody at all (D). (E) is correct since the narrator notes that *the accents fell in the most unexpected places*.

19. A

In the context of the phrase *questionable resorts about Memphis and St. Louis*, the word questionable means *disreputable* (A).

20. C

Choice (B) might have jumped right out at you since the narrator's perspective in paragraph 1 is that of a mesmerized spectator, but his perspective in paragraphs 2 and 3 changes. He steps back from the description of his first encounter with rag-time and begins to discuss rag-time's history, appeal, and impact on the contemporary musical scene. Therefore, (C) is the correct answer. (A) is wrong because the author is not impartial; he thinks highly of rag-time. Watching rag-time playing is not a *unique experience*, which eliminates (D). As for (E), the narrator says nothing about his youth in the second and third paragraphs.

21. C

The narrator argues in the third paragraph that rag-time should not be ignored or dismissed by American musicians just because it is popular. All great music, he states, comes from the hearts of the people. In other words, he is saying that the *conservative and condescending attitude* of the American musicians is misguided (C). There is no evidence in the third paragraph to support any of the other choices. (B) is perhaps the most tempting since the author talks in the third paragraph about rag-time's popularity in Europe, but it seems as though American musicians do know about rag-time's popularity and find it distasteful.

22. E

This question is a follow-up on the previous one. As we've said, the author's argument in the third paragraph is that music should not be dismissed by serious musicians just because it happens to be popular. (E) paraphrases this idea. (A) stretches the author's argument way too far. (B) is wrong because the author does not try to establish criteria for musical greatness. (C) focuses too narrowly on the author's mention of the fact that rag-time was popular abroad. (D) is clearly wrong since rag-time gained popularity even though it had not been *taken up by a musical master*.

23. D

The narrator poses to himself the question about what might have become of the piano player had he been properly trained and then answers himself by saying *perhaps he wouldn't have done anything at all*. The narrator goes on to say that even if the piano player achieved some success as an imitator of the greats or as an innovator, he still would not have been as *delightful* as he was playing rag-time. Thus, the statement that *perhaps he wouldn't have done anything at all* can best be interpreted as a *recognition that the piano player might have wasted his talent* (D) had he been formally trained.

(A) and (B) are wrong because the narrator thinks highly of the piano player's skill even if that skill is not genius-level or particularly disciplined. (C) and (E) are both far too broad and too negative to be the correct answer.

24. C

The correct answer here is going to be a paraphrase of the idea that no matter how far the piano player would have gone if trained, he would not have been as delightful as he was as a rag-time player. (C) is the choice you're looking for. (E) is the most tempting wrong answer since the author's statements at the end of the passage can easily be misconstrued to mean that the piano player could never have been more than mediocre as a classical artist. However, *never* is too strong a word here—the narrator is not, and cannot be, as sure as that—so this choice is wrong.

SECTION 7

1. E
Use FOIL:
$$(3x + 4)(4x - 3)$$
$$= (3x \times 4x) + [3x \times (-3)] + (4 \times 4x) + [4 \times (-3)]$$
$$= 12x^2 - 9x + 16x - 12$$
$$= 12x^2 + 7x - 12$$

2. C
When you know that the given parts add up to the whole, then you can turn a part-to-part ratio into two part-to-whole ratios—put each term of the ratio over the sum of the terms. In this case, since all the numbers in the set must be either integers or nonintegers, the parts do add up to the whole. The sum of the terms in the ratio 2:3 is 5, so the two part-to-whole ratios are 2:5 and 3:5.

$$\frac{\text{integers}}{\text{numbers}} = \frac{2}{5}(100\%) = \frac{200\%}{5} = 40\%$$

3. C
Get rid of the parentheses in the denominator, and then cancel factors the numerator and denominator have in common:
$$\frac{x^2 y^3 z^4}{(xyz^2)^2} = \frac{x^2 y^3 z^4}{x^2 y^2 z^4}$$
$$= \frac{x^2}{x^2} \times \frac{y^3}{y^2} \times \frac{z^4}{z^4}$$
$$= y$$

4. E

If p divided by 7 leaves a remainder of 5, you can say that $p = 7n + 5$, where n represents some integer. Multiply both sides by 5 to get $5p = 35n + 25$. The remainder when you divide 7 into $35n$ is 0. The reminder when you divide 7 into 25 is 4, so the remainder when you divide $5p$ by 7 is $0 + 4 = 4$.

For most people this one's a lot easier to do by picking numbers. Think of an example for p and try it out. p could be 12, for example, because when you divide 12 by 7, the remainder is 5. (p could also be 19, 26, 33, or any of infinitely many more possibilities.) Now multiply your chosen p by 5: $12 \times 5 = 60$. Divide 60 by 7 and see what the remainder is: 60 by $7 = 8$, remainder 4.

5. B

To find the y-intercept of a line from its equation, put the equation in slope-intercept form:

$$2x - 3y = 18$$
$$-3y = -2x + 18$$
$$y = \frac{2}{3}x - 6$$

In this form, the y-intercept is what comes after the x. In this case, it's -6.

6. C

Set up a proportion:

$$\frac{12 \text{ pages}}{1 \text{ hour}} = \frac{100 \text{ pages}}{x \text{ hours}}$$
$$12x = 100$$
$$x = \frac{100}{12} = 8\frac{1}{3}$$

One-third of an hour is $\frac{1}{3}$ of 60 minutes, or 20 minutes. So $8\frac{1}{3}$ hours is 8 hours and 20 minutes.

7. E

With a right triangle you can use the two legs as the base and the height to figure out the area. Here, the two leg lengths are expressed algebraically. Just plug the two expressions in for b and h in the triangle area formula:

$$\text{Area} = \frac{1}{2}(x - 1)(x + 1)$$
$$= \frac{1}{2}(x^2 - 1) = \frac{x^2 - 1}{2}$$

8. A

The easiest way to do this problem is to subtract Bill's money from the total of the money that Jim and Bill have. Doing this gives you $15 - 4 = 11$. However, the problem states that they have LESS THAN 15 dollars. Therefore, Jim must have less than 11 dollars. Of I, II, and III, the only value that is less than 11 is I, so the answer must be (A).

To solve this problem algebraically, set up an inequality where J is Jim's money and B is Bill's money:

$$J + B < 15 \text{ where } B = 4$$
$$J + 4 < 15$$
$$J < 11$$

Again, be wary of the fact that this is an inequality, NOT an equation.

9. A

Pick numbers for x and y. For instance, say that Angelo makes $20 for working 5 hours and Sarah makes $20 for working 4 hours. In this case, Angelo makes $4 per hour and Sarah makes $5. The difference between their wages is $1 per hour. Now plug 20 in for x and 5 in for y in each of the answer choices. Which ones give you a result of 1? Only (A), which is the answer.

10. D

A square with area 16 has sides of length 4. Therefore, the largest circle that could possibly be cut from such a square would have a diameter of 4.

Such a circle would have a radius of 2, making its area 4π. So the amount of felt left after cutting such a circle from one of the squares of felt would be $16 - 4\pi$, or $4(4 - \pi)$. There are 8 such squares, so the total area of the leftover felt is $8 \times 4(4 - \pi) = 32(4 - \pi)$.

11. C

When you see a question like this one on test day, look for patterns in the differences between terms. Is each term a result of adding some number to the previous term? Is each term a result of multiplying the previous term by some number? In this case, each term is the result of multiplying the previous term by 3.

$$x = 18(3) = 54$$

You can check this result by comparing it to later terms:

$54(3) = 162$

12. E

$$
\begin{array}{r}
5x^2 + 13x + 40 \\
x - 3 \overline{)5x^3 - 2x^2 + x + 1} \\
\underline{-(5x^3 - 15x^2)} \\
13x^2 + x \\
\underline{-(13x^2 - 39x)} \\
40x + 1 \\
\underline{-(40x - 120)} \\
121
\end{array}
$$

13. B

This problem requires you to put together several different pieces of information. If you don't see all the steps you need to follow at first, just write down what information you can get from the problem and that may help you figure out what to do next. Since B is the midpoint of $\overline{AC}$, which is 4 units long, $\overline{AB}$ and $\overline{BC}$ are each 2 units long. Since the area of the circle is $4\pi = \pi r^2 = \pi 2^2$, its radius is 2. $\overline{BO}$ is a radius of the circle, so it is 2 units long. $\overline{AC}$ is tangent to the circle at point B, so $\angle OBA$ is 90 degrees. The following diagram summarizes this information:

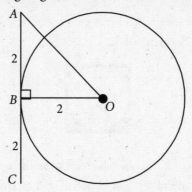

Since BO and AB both equal 2 and $\angle ABO$ is 90 degrees, triangle ABO is a 45-45-90 special triangle, and $AO = 2\sqrt{2}$

14. E

Learning how to interpret a graph can be challenging. Practice this skill before test day, so you have mastered it by then. Each year, the cost increases. In 2003, insurance was $1,200. So you know that in 2004 it should be more; the only option is (E).

15. D

Be sure not to be tempted by answers that are partly right. $x \geq 1$ describes the right half of the values on the number line but leaves out the left half. The selected values on the number line consist of 1, everything greater than 1, −1, and everything less than −1. The easiest way to describe this set is that the absolute value of x, or its distance from zero on the number line, is greater than or equal to 1. This can be written in mathematical notation as $|x| \geq 1$.

16. E

In order to find the number of possibilities, multiply the number of possibilities in each step. In other words, there are 3 routes from Bay City to Riverville and 4 routes from Riverville to Straitstown. There are 3 more routes from Straitstown to Frog Pond, so there are $12 \times 3 = 36$ total routes from Bay City to Frog Pond.

SECTION 8

1. A

The word *although* indicates contrast, and the words *large number* and *mass* provide a clue to what's missing. We need something that means *different* for the first blank, and something that means *the same* for the second blank. This is basically what *disparate* and *homogeneous* mean.

2. A

We need something here that goes with *heavy thoughts. Morose*, or *gloomy*, is the best choice.

3. E

The *demise* or death of the protagonist presumably *eliminated* all possibility of a sequel. That's what *precluded* means.

4. E

Repeated breakdown of negotiations would tend to *support* or *reinforce* the view that the sides *were not truly committed to preventing* or *averting* a military confrontation. In (A) and (D), *established* and *strengthened* fit the first blank, but *escalating* and *initiating* are wrong for the second. In (B), *avoiding* fits the second blank, but *undermined* is wrong for the first.

5. C

The sentence contrasts Duncan with his coworker. You can, therefore, predict that the colleague is neither *modest* nor *cooperative*. (C) meaning "proud contempt for others," matches the prediction.

(A) meaning "pleasantness, friendliness" and (E) meaning "the quality of being humble," have the wrong charge. You could use those words to describe Duncan perhaps, but not the colleague. The remaining two choices do not contrast with the modest and cooperative qualities of Duncan.

6. D

Start with the second blank where you are looking for a word to suggest the effort needed to improve the economic climate. (B) and (D) both fit. (A) may be tempting because the candidate may very well have made a *promise* about the economic climate before the election. You do not, however, recognize a forthcoming ("approaching, upcoming") *promise*. Note that an *inauguration* ("formal acceptance into office) may be forthcoming for the candidate, but it will not improve the economic climate. (C) is too extreme for the second blank. Now look at the first blank for (B) and (D). The candidate's exhilaration ("joy, elation") temporarily *illuminated* ("clarified, brought to light") or *eclipsed* ("surpassed, outshone") the recognition of the coming effort. (D) is the best fit.

THE DESIGN MUSEUMS PASSAGES

Passage 1: The position of the author of this passage starts to become clear in the second paragraph: she likes design museums and is willing to defend them against critics. She thinks design museums are not just advertisements for new technology but places where new products can be honored. Design museums, she asserts, are comfortable for visitors because the exhibits provide a lot of information about the objects displayed—information you wouldn't get in an art gallery. Another advantage of design museums, she says, is that their curators have more freedom than do the curators of public art galleries.

Passage 2: Author 2 does not hold technical and design museums in the same high regard as author 1 does. Author 2 complains about several things: 1) technical museums concentrate on present technology and ignore historical study and research; 2) they glorify machines and industrialization when these things do harm as well as good; and 3) they do not (and cannot safely and imaginatively) show machinery in action. Author 2 does admit at the very end, however, that the public has shown a healthy curiosity about science and technology.

7. A

To say that something is *readily available to the general public* is to say that it is *easily* available. (A) is the correct answer.

8. E

Although the question is not Vocab-in-Context, you must still be careful not to assume the word is used in its most common sense. Look at the context. Since these appliances are in design museums, they must have been very popular and successful. It's only as "design" that they have been ignored.

(C) might have been tempting, but it's not to the point and outside the scope. People may or may not have had conversations about, say, a toaster—it's never mentioned. But the conversations might have been about how well it worked, or how little it cost, not about its design attributes—the focus of the passage.

9. D

Author 1 says that department store windows try to sell you something whereas design exhibits try to give you an appreciation of the aesthetic value of something. (D) paraphrases this idea. (A), (B), and (E) can be readily eliminated. Be careful with (C), though. Even though design museums focus on the artistic qualities of products, it does not automatically follow from this that design museums are not concerned at all with the commercial aspects of a successful product. (C) is wrong.

10. B

In the third paragraph of Passage 1, the author argues that design museums make visitors feel comfortable because the exhibits illustrate the purpose behind the look and function of the displayed object; art gallery exhibits, by contrast, provide no such information. From this argument you can infer that author 1 thinks that visitors want to be informed about the object they are viewing. This makes (B) correct. There is no evidence to support any of the other choices, all of which are misreadings of paragraph 3. (A) can be eliminated as soon as you see *hostile toward . . . abstract art*. (C) and (D) contradict the author, who says that visitors are not confused by technological exhibits since they are familiar and informative. (E) is an unwarranted inference based on the author's statement that design exhibits point out the artistic qualities of the displayed items; you cannot conclude from this that most museum visitors undervalue the artistic worth of household items.

11. B

Since you just reviewed paragraph 3 for the last question, the answer to this one should jump right out at you. The difference between a design museum exhibit and an art gallery exhibit is that a design museum exhibit provides you with information about the object being displayed, whereas the art gallery exhibit does not. (B) is correct. None of the other choices has any basis in the passage.

12. C

After mentioning the collection of Zippo lighters, etc., in London's Design Museum, author 1 says that curators of design museums have options that are far less rigorous, conventionalized, and pre-programmed than those open to curators of art galleries. This is a fancy way of saying that the curators of design museums have more freedom to put together unconventional collections (C).

(E) is the tempting wrong answer to this question. It's wrong because it goes too far: the design curators have freedom, but not, as far as we know, the freedom to satisfy *their own personal whims*.

13. E

In the very last sentence of Passage 1, the author says that design museums (*the display of postmodern playthings or quirky Japanese vacuum cleaners*) are better able to represent humor than art galleries (*an exhibition of Impressionist landscapes*). The author is emphasizing the contrast between design museum and art gallery exhibits (E). (B) is the trickiest wrong answer. It misses the point of the last sentence because the author is not comparing *postmodern playthings* with Impressionist art; she is comparing the different ways these two things are exhibited.

14. A

The answer to this question will be the choice that summarizes paragraph 1. Since the author spends paragraph 1 complaining that design museums ignore the historical aspect of technology, choice (A) is the best answer. (B) focuses too narrowly on the last part of the paragraph, where the author says that since industry builds the exhibits, curators may be dispensed with. This is not the underlying difficulty referred to at the beginning of the paragraph. The other choices have nothing to do with the first paragraph.

15. A

Author 2's point in the second paragraph is that industrialization and *progress* have not been all good and should be considered critically, but technology museums just glorify them. He mentions industrialization's harm to the environment and ecology to support this point and to encourage a *critical response* to technology, so (A) is correct. (B) is wrong because it's too negative, even for this author. (C) is a distortion of a detail at the end of the second paragraph, whereas (D) is a distorted idea from the third paragraph. (E) is out because author 2 doesn't do any praising in the second paragraph.

16. D

Put the phrase in context. Author 2 says that displayed machinery should be in action, not in *sculptured repose*, as is the case with the machinery in technology museums. To author 2, you can infer, the *sculptured repose* is meaningless and *unrealistic* (D). (A) is out because the author is not condemning the curators for poor planning; in fact, the author admits that displaying operating machinery would be extremely difficult. (B) can be eliminated because it's too extreme. The author never says which—if any—of the problems he discusses is the *greatest problem*. (C) and (E) miss the author's point and the context in which the phrase *sculptured repose* is found.

17. D

Choices (A), (B), (C), and (E) are common synonyms for *command*, but none of them works in the context of the phrase *command the imagination, ingenuity, and manual dexterity it requires*. Only choice (D) can do the job.

18. A

Predict the answer to the question before you go looking through the choices. You know that author 2 thinks that technology has had a lot of negative consequences, so you can assume that he would point this out in response to author 1's optimistic statement. This makes (A) the best answer. We don't know what author 2's position on art galleries is, so (B) is out. (C) comes from Passage 2 but is irrelevant to the question asked in the stem. (D) and (E) contradict specific things author 2 says in the course of his passage.

19. B

In questions like this one, wrong answer choices are often statements that one author, but not both, would agree with. For example, author 2 would probably agree with choice (A) and would definitely agree with (D) and (E), but author 1 would most likely not agree with any of these three. That narrows the field to (B) and (C). (C) is a very general statement that really has no basis in either passage. (B), on the other hand, is an idea that can be found in both passages, so it is the correct answer.

SECTION 9

1. A

The sentence is correct and conforms to the rules of parallelism; all three items in the list are adjectives describing the new model.

2. B

There is an error of subordination here. To express the causal relationship between melting ice caps and flooding of islands, you need only one conjunction: *because* or *therefore*. To have both is redundant. (Furthermore, the word *therefore* should be preceded by a semicolon, not a comma.)

3. C

This sentence fragment is best corrected by moving the verb *was* and inserting a comma after the introductory phrase describing *Flaubert*.

4. D

In order for (A) to be grammatically correct, a comma is needed before the coordinating conjunction *and*. (C) adds the comma but takes away the conjunction, so it is incorrect. (B) and (E) are extremely awkward. (D) is the clearest and most concise answer

5. D

Eliminate the excessively wordy answer choices—(A), (B), and (E). (C) might be tempting, but *failed* not creates a double negative. (D) is correct because it is clear and concise; (D) also continues the structure established in the first part of the sentence: *have raised . . . have failed.*

6. A

Make sure that all three items in the series are parallel. The first two begin with gerunds (verbs ending in -*ing*), so (A) is correct. Do not be confused by the word *washing*. It is part of the noun *washing machine* and cannot be called upon to function in any other way in this sentence

7. C

First, eliminate any answer choices that begin with misplaced modifiers. (A) and (D) both say the *directors* have *exceptionally clear waters and active underwater life*. Next, eliminate answer choices that do not create complete sentences. (B) and (E) are long sentence fragments. (C) is correct because it is the only choice with grammatically correct structure.

8. C

(A) is a run-on; the phrase beginning with *featured* makes the sentence incorrect. (B) is nonsensical—the phrase *with features beauty* makes it incorrect. The remaining answer choices set apart the nonessential information with commas, so look for the choice that does this best. That choice is (C)—it is the clearest (and shortest).

9. A

(A) is the clearest answer choice because it sets apart the nonessential information with commas. (D) also uses this structure, but it unnecessarily adds *because it was*. The other answer choices are wordy.

10. E

Eliminate the answer choices that change the underlined portion to an incomplete sentence—(C) and (D). The other answer choices are technically correct, but (E) is the clearest and most concise.

11. A

(C) and (E) have vague pronouns with the word *they*. (B) is very awkward with the words *that* and *not* repeated. (D) is also awkward because of the word *as* toward the beginning of the sentence. (A), the original sentence, is the most concise answer choice.

12. B

Some of the answer choices violate the rules of independent and dependent clauses. For example, (A) uses a comma and coordinating conjunction, calling for two independent clauses. However, the first clause is dependent because of the word *that*. In (D), the first clause is dependent, so the second should be independent, but it is not. (E) introduces a misplaced modifier, and (C) has an illogical connection between the two clauses. (B) has correct structure and makes the most sense.

13. A

The correct answer will have to be parallel with *having a lot of money*. In other words, the underlined portion should contain a gerund (a word ending in *-ing*). The only answer choices with this structure are (A) and (B). (A) is much clearer and more concise, so it is the correct answer.

14. C

The introductory phrase is a dependent clause, so the underlined portion must create an independent clause. The word *causing* in (A) and (E) does not make an independent clause, so eliminate these choices. (B) and (D) insert the coordinating conjunction *and*, which is incorrect when connecting a dependent clause and an independent clause. (The coordinating conjunction and comma are only used for connecting two independent clauses.) (C) is the only answer choice to set up a correct independent clause.

SAT Practice Test Three
Answer Sheet

Remove (or photocopy) the answer sheet and use it to complete the practice test. See the answer key following the test when finished.

Start with number 1 for each section. If a section has fewer questions than answer spaces, leave the extra spaces blank.

SECTION

1

Section 1 is the writing section's essay component.
Lined pages on which you will write your essay can be found in that section.

SECTION

2

1. Ⓐ Ⓑ Ⓒ Ⓓ Ⓔ	11. Ⓐ Ⓑ Ⓒ Ⓓ Ⓔ	21. Ⓐ Ⓑ Ⓒ Ⓓ Ⓔ	31. Ⓐ Ⓑ Ⓒ Ⓓ Ⓔ
2. Ⓐ Ⓑ Ⓒ Ⓓ Ⓔ	12. Ⓐ Ⓑ Ⓒ Ⓓ Ⓔ	22. Ⓐ Ⓑ Ⓒ Ⓓ Ⓔ	32. Ⓐ Ⓑ Ⓒ Ⓓ Ⓔ
3. Ⓐ Ⓑ Ⓒ Ⓓ Ⓔ	13. Ⓐ Ⓑ Ⓒ Ⓓ Ⓔ	23. Ⓐ Ⓑ Ⓒ Ⓓ Ⓔ	33. Ⓐ Ⓑ Ⓒ Ⓓ Ⓔ
4. Ⓐ Ⓑ Ⓒ Ⓓ Ⓔ	14. Ⓐ Ⓑ Ⓒ Ⓓ Ⓔ	24. Ⓐ Ⓑ Ⓒ Ⓓ Ⓔ	34. Ⓐ Ⓑ Ⓒ Ⓓ Ⓔ
5. Ⓐ Ⓑ Ⓒ Ⓓ Ⓔ	15. Ⓐ Ⓑ Ⓒ Ⓓ Ⓔ	25. Ⓐ Ⓑ Ⓒ Ⓓ Ⓔ	35. Ⓐ Ⓑ Ⓒ Ⓓ Ⓔ
6. Ⓐ Ⓑ Ⓒ Ⓓ Ⓔ	16. Ⓐ Ⓑ Ⓒ Ⓓ Ⓔ	26. Ⓐ Ⓑ Ⓒ Ⓓ Ⓔ	36. Ⓐ Ⓑ Ⓒ Ⓓ Ⓔ
7. Ⓐ Ⓑ Ⓒ Ⓓ Ⓔ	17. Ⓐ Ⓑ Ⓒ Ⓓ Ⓔ	27. Ⓐ Ⓑ Ⓒ Ⓓ Ⓔ	37. Ⓐ Ⓑ Ⓒ Ⓓ Ⓔ
8. Ⓐ Ⓑ Ⓒ Ⓓ Ⓔ	18. Ⓐ Ⓑ Ⓒ Ⓓ Ⓔ	28. Ⓐ Ⓑ Ⓒ Ⓓ Ⓔ	38. Ⓐ Ⓑ Ⓒ Ⓓ Ⓔ
9. Ⓐ Ⓑ Ⓒ Ⓓ Ⓔ	19. Ⓐ Ⓑ Ⓒ Ⓓ Ⓔ	29. Ⓐ Ⓑ Ⓒ Ⓓ Ⓔ	39. Ⓐ Ⓑ Ⓒ Ⓓ Ⓔ
10. Ⓐ Ⓑ Ⓒ Ⓓ Ⓔ	20. Ⓐ Ⓑ Ⓒ Ⓓ Ⓔ	30. Ⓐ Ⓑ Ⓒ Ⓓ Ⓔ	40. Ⓐ Ⓑ Ⓒ Ⓓ Ⓔ

☐ # right in Section 2

☐ # wrong in Section 2

SECTION

3

1. Ⓐ Ⓑ Ⓒ Ⓓ Ⓔ	11. Ⓐ Ⓑ Ⓒ Ⓓ Ⓔ	21. Ⓐ Ⓑ Ⓒ Ⓓ Ⓔ	31. Ⓐ Ⓑ Ⓒ Ⓓ Ⓔ
2. Ⓐ Ⓑ Ⓒ Ⓓ Ⓔ	12. Ⓐ Ⓑ Ⓒ Ⓓ Ⓔ	22. Ⓐ Ⓑ Ⓒ Ⓓ Ⓔ	32. Ⓐ Ⓑ Ⓒ Ⓓ Ⓔ
3. Ⓐ Ⓑ Ⓒ Ⓓ Ⓔ	13. Ⓐ Ⓑ Ⓒ Ⓓ Ⓔ	23. Ⓐ Ⓑ Ⓒ Ⓓ Ⓔ	33. Ⓐ Ⓑ Ⓒ Ⓓ Ⓔ
4. Ⓐ Ⓑ Ⓒ Ⓓ Ⓔ	14. Ⓐ Ⓑ Ⓒ Ⓓ Ⓔ	24. Ⓐ Ⓑ Ⓒ Ⓓ Ⓔ	34. Ⓐ Ⓑ Ⓒ Ⓓ Ⓔ
5. Ⓐ Ⓑ Ⓒ Ⓓ Ⓔ	15. Ⓐ Ⓑ Ⓒ Ⓓ Ⓔ	25. Ⓐ Ⓑ Ⓒ Ⓓ Ⓔ	35. Ⓐ Ⓑ Ⓒ Ⓓ Ⓔ
6. Ⓐ Ⓑ Ⓒ Ⓓ Ⓔ	16. Ⓐ Ⓑ Ⓒ Ⓓ Ⓔ	26. Ⓐ Ⓑ Ⓒ Ⓓ Ⓔ	36. Ⓐ Ⓑ Ⓒ Ⓓ Ⓔ
7. Ⓐ Ⓑ Ⓒ Ⓓ Ⓔ	17. Ⓐ Ⓑ Ⓒ Ⓓ Ⓔ	27. Ⓐ Ⓑ Ⓒ Ⓓ Ⓔ	37. Ⓐ Ⓑ Ⓒ Ⓓ Ⓔ
8. Ⓐ Ⓑ Ⓒ Ⓓ Ⓔ	18. Ⓐ Ⓑ Ⓒ Ⓓ Ⓔ	28. Ⓐ Ⓑ Ⓒ Ⓓ Ⓔ	38. Ⓐ Ⓑ Ⓒ Ⓓ Ⓔ
9. Ⓐ Ⓑ Ⓒ Ⓓ Ⓔ	19. Ⓐ Ⓑ Ⓒ Ⓓ Ⓔ	29. Ⓐ Ⓑ Ⓒ Ⓓ Ⓔ	39. Ⓐ Ⓑ Ⓒ Ⓓ Ⓔ
10. Ⓐ Ⓑ Ⓒ Ⓓ Ⓔ	20. Ⓐ Ⓑ Ⓒ Ⓓ Ⓔ	30. Ⓐ Ⓑ Ⓒ Ⓓ Ⓔ	40. Ⓐ Ⓑ Ⓒ Ⓓ Ⓔ

☐ # right in Section 3

☐ # wrong in Section 3

Remove (or photocopy) this answer sheet and use it to complete the practice test.

Start with number 1 for each section. If a section has fewer questions than answer spaces, leave the extra spaces blank.

SECTION 4

1. Ⓐ Ⓑ Ⓒ Ⓓ Ⓔ   11. Ⓐ Ⓑ Ⓒ Ⓓ Ⓔ   21. Ⓐ Ⓑ Ⓒ Ⓓ Ⓔ   31. Ⓐ Ⓑ Ⓒ Ⓓ Ⓔ
2. Ⓐ Ⓑ Ⓒ Ⓓ Ⓔ   12. Ⓐ Ⓑ Ⓒ Ⓓ Ⓔ   22. Ⓐ Ⓑ Ⓒ Ⓓ Ⓔ   32. Ⓐ Ⓑ Ⓒ Ⓓ Ⓔ
3. Ⓐ Ⓑ Ⓒ Ⓓ Ⓔ   13. Ⓐ Ⓑ Ⓒ Ⓓ Ⓔ   23. Ⓐ Ⓑ Ⓒ Ⓓ Ⓔ   33. Ⓐ Ⓑ Ⓒ Ⓓ Ⓔ
4. Ⓐ Ⓑ Ⓒ Ⓓ Ⓔ   14. Ⓐ Ⓑ Ⓒ Ⓓ Ⓔ   24. Ⓐ Ⓑ Ⓒ Ⓓ Ⓔ   34. Ⓐ Ⓑ Ⓒ Ⓓ Ⓔ
5. Ⓐ Ⓑ Ⓒ Ⓓ Ⓔ   15. Ⓐ Ⓑ Ⓒ Ⓓ Ⓔ   25. Ⓐ Ⓑ Ⓒ Ⓓ Ⓔ   35. Ⓐ Ⓑ Ⓒ Ⓓ Ⓔ
6. Ⓐ Ⓑ Ⓒ Ⓓ Ⓔ   16. Ⓐ Ⓑ Ⓒ Ⓓ Ⓔ   26. Ⓐ Ⓑ Ⓒ Ⓓ Ⓔ   36. Ⓐ Ⓑ Ⓒ Ⓓ Ⓔ
7. Ⓐ Ⓑ Ⓒ Ⓓ Ⓔ   17. Ⓐ Ⓑ Ⓒ Ⓓ Ⓔ   27. Ⓐ Ⓑ Ⓒ Ⓓ Ⓔ   37. Ⓐ Ⓑ Ⓒ Ⓓ Ⓔ
8. Ⓐ Ⓑ Ⓒ Ⓓ Ⓔ   18. Ⓐ Ⓑ Ⓒ Ⓓ Ⓔ   28. Ⓐ Ⓑ Ⓒ Ⓓ Ⓔ   38. Ⓐ Ⓑ Ⓒ Ⓓ Ⓔ
9. Ⓐ Ⓑ Ⓒ Ⓓ Ⓔ   19. Ⓐ Ⓑ Ⓒ Ⓓ Ⓔ   29. Ⓐ Ⓑ Ⓒ Ⓓ Ⓔ   39. Ⓐ Ⓑ Ⓒ Ⓓ Ⓔ
10. Ⓐ Ⓑ Ⓒ Ⓓ Ⓔ   20. Ⓐ Ⓑ Ⓒ Ⓓ Ⓔ   30. Ⓐ Ⓑ Ⓒ Ⓓ Ⓔ   40. Ⓐ Ⓑ Ⓒ Ⓓ Ⓔ

right in Section 4

wrong in Section 4

SECTION 5

1. Ⓐ Ⓑ Ⓒ Ⓓ Ⓔ   11. Ⓐ Ⓑ Ⓒ Ⓓ Ⓔ   21. Ⓐ Ⓑ Ⓒ Ⓓ Ⓔ   31. Ⓐ Ⓑ Ⓒ Ⓓ Ⓔ
2. Ⓐ Ⓑ Ⓒ Ⓓ Ⓔ   12. Ⓐ Ⓑ Ⓒ Ⓓ Ⓔ   22. Ⓐ Ⓑ Ⓒ Ⓓ Ⓔ   32. Ⓐ Ⓑ Ⓒ Ⓓ Ⓔ
3. Ⓐ Ⓑ Ⓒ Ⓓ Ⓔ   13. Ⓐ Ⓑ Ⓒ Ⓓ Ⓔ   23. Ⓐ Ⓑ Ⓒ Ⓓ Ⓔ   33. Ⓐ Ⓑ Ⓒ Ⓓ Ⓔ
4. Ⓐ Ⓑ Ⓒ Ⓓ Ⓔ   14. Ⓐ Ⓑ Ⓒ Ⓓ Ⓔ   24. Ⓐ Ⓑ Ⓒ Ⓓ Ⓔ   34. Ⓐ Ⓑ Ⓒ Ⓓ Ⓔ
5. Ⓐ Ⓑ Ⓒ Ⓓ Ⓔ   15. Ⓐ Ⓑ Ⓒ Ⓓ Ⓔ   25. Ⓐ Ⓑ Ⓒ Ⓓ Ⓔ   35. Ⓐ Ⓑ Ⓒ Ⓓ Ⓔ
6. Ⓐ Ⓑ Ⓒ Ⓓ Ⓔ   16. Ⓐ Ⓑ Ⓒ Ⓓ Ⓔ   26. Ⓐ Ⓑ Ⓒ Ⓓ Ⓔ   36. Ⓐ Ⓑ Ⓒ Ⓓ Ⓔ
7. Ⓐ Ⓑ Ⓒ Ⓓ Ⓔ   17. Ⓐ Ⓑ Ⓒ Ⓓ Ⓔ   27. Ⓐ Ⓑ Ⓒ Ⓓ Ⓔ   37. Ⓐ Ⓑ Ⓒ Ⓓ Ⓔ
8. Ⓐ Ⓑ Ⓒ Ⓓ Ⓔ   18. Ⓐ Ⓑ Ⓒ Ⓓ Ⓔ   28. Ⓐ Ⓑ Ⓒ Ⓓ Ⓔ   38. Ⓐ Ⓑ Ⓒ Ⓓ Ⓔ
9. Ⓐ Ⓑ Ⓒ Ⓓ Ⓔ   19. Ⓐ Ⓑ Ⓒ Ⓓ Ⓔ   29. Ⓐ Ⓑ Ⓒ Ⓓ Ⓔ   39. Ⓐ Ⓑ Ⓒ Ⓓ Ⓔ
10. Ⓐ Ⓑ Ⓒ Ⓓ Ⓔ   20. Ⓐ Ⓑ Ⓒ Ⓓ Ⓔ   30. Ⓐ Ⓑ Ⓒ Ⓓ Ⓔ   40. Ⓐ Ⓑ Ⓒ Ⓓ Ⓔ

right in Section 5

wrong in Section 5

If section 5 of your test book contains math questions that are not multiple choice, continue to item 9 below. Otherwise, continue to item 9 above.

9.   10.   11.   12.   13.

14.   15.   16.   17.   18.

Remove (or photocopy) this answer sheet and use it to complete the practice test.

Start with number 1 for each section. If a section has fewer questions than answer spaces, leave the extra spaces blank.

SECTION

6

1. Ⓐ Ⓑ Ⓒ Ⓓ Ⓔ 11. Ⓐ Ⓑ Ⓒ Ⓓ Ⓔ 21. Ⓐ Ⓑ Ⓒ Ⓓ Ⓔ 31. Ⓐ Ⓑ Ⓒ Ⓓ Ⓔ
2. Ⓐ Ⓑ Ⓒ Ⓓ Ⓔ 12. Ⓐ Ⓑ Ⓒ Ⓓ Ⓔ 22. Ⓐ Ⓑ Ⓒ Ⓓ Ⓔ 32. Ⓐ Ⓑ Ⓒ Ⓓ Ⓔ
3. Ⓐ Ⓑ Ⓒ Ⓓ Ⓔ 13. Ⓐ Ⓑ Ⓒ Ⓓ Ⓔ 23. Ⓐ Ⓑ Ⓒ Ⓓ Ⓔ 33. Ⓐ Ⓑ Ⓒ Ⓓ Ⓔ
4. Ⓐ Ⓑ Ⓒ Ⓓ Ⓔ 14. Ⓐ Ⓑ Ⓒ Ⓓ Ⓔ 24. Ⓐ Ⓑ Ⓒ Ⓓ Ⓔ 34. Ⓐ Ⓑ Ⓒ Ⓓ Ⓔ
5. Ⓐ Ⓑ Ⓒ Ⓓ Ⓔ 15. Ⓐ Ⓑ Ⓒ Ⓓ Ⓔ 25. Ⓐ Ⓑ Ⓒ Ⓓ Ⓔ 35. Ⓐ Ⓑ Ⓒ Ⓓ Ⓔ
6. Ⓐ Ⓑ Ⓒ Ⓓ Ⓔ 16. Ⓐ Ⓑ Ⓒ Ⓓ Ⓔ 26. Ⓐ Ⓑ Ⓒ Ⓓ Ⓔ 36. Ⓐ Ⓑ Ⓒ Ⓓ Ⓔ
7. Ⓐ Ⓑ Ⓒ Ⓓ Ⓔ 17. Ⓐ Ⓑ Ⓒ Ⓓ Ⓔ 27. Ⓐ Ⓑ Ⓒ Ⓓ Ⓔ 37. Ⓐ Ⓑ Ⓒ Ⓓ Ⓔ
8. Ⓐ Ⓑ Ⓒ Ⓓ Ⓔ 18. Ⓐ Ⓑ Ⓒ Ⓓ Ⓔ 28. Ⓐ Ⓑ Ⓒ Ⓓ Ⓔ 38. Ⓐ Ⓑ Ⓒ Ⓓ Ⓔ
9. Ⓐ Ⓑ Ⓒ Ⓓ Ⓔ 19. Ⓐ Ⓑ Ⓒ Ⓓ Ⓔ 29. Ⓐ Ⓑ Ⓒ Ⓓ Ⓔ 39. Ⓐ Ⓑ Ⓒ Ⓓ Ⓔ
10. Ⓐ Ⓑ Ⓒ Ⓓ Ⓔ 20. Ⓐ Ⓑ Ⓒ Ⓓ Ⓔ 30. Ⓐ Ⓑ Ⓒ Ⓓ Ⓔ 40. Ⓐ Ⓑ Ⓒ Ⓓ Ⓔ

☐ # right in Section 6

☐ # wrong in Section 6

SECTION

7

1. Ⓐ Ⓑ Ⓒ Ⓓ Ⓔ 11. Ⓐ Ⓑ Ⓒ Ⓓ Ⓔ 21. Ⓐ Ⓑ Ⓒ Ⓓ Ⓔ 31. Ⓐ Ⓑ Ⓒ Ⓓ Ⓔ
2. Ⓐ Ⓑ Ⓒ Ⓓ Ⓔ 12. Ⓐ Ⓑ Ⓒ Ⓓ Ⓔ 22. Ⓐ Ⓑ Ⓒ Ⓓ Ⓔ 32. Ⓐ Ⓑ Ⓒ Ⓓ Ⓔ
3. Ⓐ Ⓑ Ⓒ Ⓓ Ⓔ 13. Ⓐ Ⓑ Ⓒ Ⓓ Ⓔ 23. Ⓐ Ⓑ Ⓒ Ⓓ Ⓔ 33. Ⓐ Ⓑ Ⓒ Ⓓ Ⓔ
4. Ⓐ Ⓑ Ⓒ Ⓓ Ⓔ 14. Ⓐ Ⓑ Ⓒ Ⓓ Ⓔ 24. Ⓐ Ⓑ Ⓒ Ⓓ Ⓔ 34. Ⓐ Ⓑ Ⓒ Ⓓ Ⓔ
5. Ⓐ Ⓑ Ⓒ Ⓓ Ⓔ 15. Ⓐ Ⓑ Ⓒ Ⓓ Ⓔ 25. Ⓐ Ⓑ Ⓒ Ⓓ Ⓔ 35. Ⓐ Ⓑ Ⓒ Ⓓ Ⓔ
6. Ⓐ Ⓑ Ⓒ Ⓓ Ⓔ 16. Ⓐ Ⓑ Ⓒ Ⓓ Ⓔ 26. Ⓐ Ⓑ Ⓒ Ⓓ Ⓔ 36. Ⓐ Ⓑ Ⓒ Ⓓ Ⓔ
7. Ⓐ Ⓑ Ⓒ Ⓓ Ⓔ 17. Ⓐ Ⓑ Ⓒ Ⓓ Ⓔ 27. Ⓐ Ⓑ Ⓒ Ⓓ Ⓔ 37. Ⓐ Ⓑ Ⓒ Ⓓ Ⓔ
8. Ⓐ Ⓑ Ⓒ Ⓓ Ⓔ 18. Ⓐ Ⓑ Ⓒ Ⓓ Ⓔ 28. Ⓐ Ⓑ Ⓒ Ⓓ Ⓔ 38. Ⓐ Ⓑ Ⓒ Ⓓ Ⓔ
9. Ⓐ Ⓑ Ⓒ Ⓓ Ⓔ 19. Ⓐ Ⓑ Ⓒ Ⓓ Ⓔ 29. Ⓐ Ⓑ Ⓒ Ⓓ Ⓔ 39. Ⓐ Ⓑ Ⓒ Ⓓ Ⓔ
10. Ⓐ Ⓑ Ⓒ Ⓓ Ⓔ 20. Ⓐ Ⓑ Ⓒ Ⓓ Ⓔ 30. Ⓐ Ⓑ Ⓒ Ⓓ Ⓔ 40. Ⓐ Ⓑ Ⓒ Ⓓ Ⓔ

☐ # right in Section 7

☐ # wrong in Section 7

SECTION

8

1. Ⓐ Ⓑ Ⓒ Ⓓ Ⓔ 11. Ⓐ Ⓑ Ⓒ Ⓓ Ⓔ 21. Ⓐ Ⓑ Ⓒ Ⓓ Ⓔ 31. Ⓐ Ⓑ Ⓒ Ⓓ Ⓔ
2. Ⓐ Ⓑ Ⓒ Ⓓ Ⓔ 12. Ⓐ Ⓑ Ⓒ Ⓓ Ⓔ 22. Ⓐ Ⓑ Ⓒ Ⓓ Ⓔ 32. Ⓐ Ⓑ Ⓒ Ⓓ Ⓔ
3. Ⓐ Ⓑ Ⓒ Ⓓ Ⓔ 13. Ⓐ Ⓑ Ⓒ Ⓓ Ⓔ 23. Ⓐ Ⓑ Ⓒ Ⓓ Ⓔ 33. Ⓐ Ⓑ Ⓒ Ⓓ Ⓔ
4. Ⓐ Ⓑ Ⓒ Ⓓ Ⓔ 14. Ⓐ Ⓑ Ⓒ Ⓓ Ⓔ 24. Ⓐ Ⓑ Ⓒ Ⓓ Ⓔ 34. Ⓐ Ⓑ Ⓒ Ⓓ Ⓔ
5. Ⓐ Ⓑ Ⓒ Ⓓ Ⓔ 15. Ⓐ Ⓑ Ⓒ Ⓓ Ⓔ 25. Ⓐ Ⓑ Ⓒ Ⓓ Ⓔ 35. Ⓐ Ⓑ Ⓒ Ⓓ Ⓔ
6. Ⓐ Ⓑ Ⓒ Ⓓ Ⓔ 16. Ⓐ Ⓑ Ⓒ Ⓓ Ⓔ 26. Ⓐ Ⓑ Ⓒ Ⓓ Ⓔ 36. Ⓐ Ⓑ Ⓒ Ⓓ Ⓔ
7. Ⓐ Ⓑ Ⓒ Ⓓ Ⓔ 17. Ⓐ Ⓑ Ⓒ Ⓓ Ⓔ 27. Ⓐ Ⓑ Ⓒ Ⓓ Ⓔ 37. Ⓐ Ⓑ Ⓒ Ⓓ Ⓔ
8. Ⓐ Ⓑ Ⓒ Ⓓ Ⓔ 18. Ⓐ Ⓑ Ⓒ Ⓓ Ⓔ 28. Ⓐ Ⓑ Ⓒ Ⓓ Ⓔ 38. Ⓐ Ⓑ Ⓒ Ⓓ Ⓔ
9. Ⓐ Ⓑ Ⓒ Ⓓ Ⓔ 19. Ⓐ Ⓑ Ⓒ Ⓓ Ⓔ 29. Ⓐ Ⓑ Ⓒ Ⓓ Ⓔ 39. Ⓐ Ⓑ Ⓒ Ⓓ Ⓔ
10. Ⓐ Ⓑ Ⓒ Ⓓ Ⓔ 20. Ⓐ Ⓑ Ⓒ Ⓓ Ⓔ 30. Ⓐ Ⓑ Ⓒ Ⓓ Ⓔ 40. Ⓐ Ⓑ Ⓒ Ⓓ Ⓔ

☐ # right in Section 8

☐ # wrong in Section 8

Remove (or photocopy) this answer sheet and use it to complete the practice test.

Start with number 1 for each section. If a section has fewer questions than answer spaces, leave the extra spaces blank.

SECTION

9

1. Ⓐ Ⓑ Ⓒ Ⓓ Ⓔ	11. Ⓐ Ⓑ Ⓒ Ⓓ Ⓔ	21. Ⓐ Ⓑ Ⓒ Ⓓ Ⓔ	31. Ⓐ Ⓑ Ⓒ Ⓓ Ⓔ
2. Ⓐ Ⓑ Ⓒ Ⓓ Ⓔ	12. Ⓐ Ⓑ Ⓒ Ⓓ Ⓔ	22. Ⓐ Ⓑ Ⓒ Ⓓ Ⓔ	32. Ⓐ Ⓑ Ⓒ Ⓓ Ⓔ
3. Ⓐ Ⓑ Ⓒ Ⓓ Ⓔ	13. Ⓐ Ⓑ Ⓒ Ⓓ Ⓔ	23. Ⓐ Ⓑ Ⓒ Ⓓ Ⓔ	33. Ⓐ Ⓑ Ⓒ Ⓓ Ⓔ
4. Ⓐ Ⓑ Ⓒ Ⓓ Ⓔ	14. Ⓐ Ⓑ Ⓒ Ⓓ Ⓔ	24. Ⓐ Ⓑ Ⓒ Ⓓ Ⓔ	34. Ⓐ Ⓑ Ⓒ Ⓓ Ⓔ
5. Ⓐ Ⓑ Ⓒ Ⓓ Ⓔ	15. Ⓐ Ⓑ Ⓒ Ⓓ Ⓔ	25. Ⓐ Ⓑ Ⓒ Ⓓ Ⓔ	35. Ⓐ Ⓑ Ⓒ Ⓓ Ⓔ
6. Ⓐ Ⓑ Ⓒ Ⓓ Ⓔ	16. Ⓐ Ⓑ Ⓒ Ⓓ Ⓔ	26. Ⓐ Ⓑ Ⓒ Ⓓ Ⓔ	36. Ⓐ Ⓑ Ⓒ Ⓓ Ⓔ
7. Ⓐ Ⓑ Ⓒ Ⓓ Ⓔ	17. Ⓐ Ⓑ Ⓒ Ⓓ Ⓔ	27. Ⓐ Ⓑ Ⓒ Ⓓ Ⓔ	37. Ⓐ Ⓑ Ⓒ Ⓓ Ⓔ
8. Ⓐ Ⓑ Ⓒ Ⓓ Ⓔ	18. Ⓐ Ⓑ Ⓒ Ⓓ Ⓔ	28. Ⓐ Ⓑ Ⓒ Ⓓ Ⓔ	38. Ⓐ Ⓑ Ⓒ Ⓓ Ⓔ
9. Ⓐ Ⓑ Ⓒ Ⓓ Ⓔ	19. Ⓐ Ⓑ Ⓒ Ⓓ Ⓔ	29. Ⓐ Ⓑ Ⓒ Ⓓ Ⓔ	39. Ⓐ Ⓑ Ⓒ Ⓓ Ⓔ
10. Ⓐ Ⓑ Ⓒ Ⓓ Ⓔ	20. Ⓐ Ⓑ Ⓒ Ⓓ Ⓔ	30. Ⓐ Ⓑ Ⓒ Ⓓ Ⓔ	40. Ⓐ Ⓑ Ⓒ Ⓓ Ⓔ

right in
Section 9

wrong in
Section 9

Practice Test Three

SECTION 1
Time—25 Minutes
ESSAY

The essay gives you an opportunity to show how effectively you can develop and express ideas. You should, therefore, take care to develop your point of view, present your ideas logically and clearly, and use language precisely.

Your essay must be written in your Answer Grid Booklet—you will receive no other paper on which to write. You will have enough space if you write on every line, avoid wide margins, and keep your handwriting to a reasonable size. Remember that people who are not familiar with your handwriting will read what you write. Try to write or print so that what you are writing is legible to those readers.

You have twenty-five minutes to write an essay on the topic assigned below.
DO NOT WRITE ON ANOTHER TOPIC. AN OFF-TOPIC ESSAY WILL RECEIVE A SCORE OF ZERO.

Think carefully about the issue presented in the following excerpt and the assignment below.

> "Nothing in the world can take the place of persistence. Talent will not; nothing is more common than unsuccessful men with talent. Genius will not; unrewarded genius is almost a proverb. Education will not; the world is full of educated derelicts. Persistence and determination are omnipotent. The slogan, "Press on!" has solved and always will solve the problems of the human race."
>
> –Calvin Coolidge, *Autobiography*

Assignment: Do you agree that persistence is the major factor in success, and that talent, genius, and education play, at best, secondary roles? Plan and write an essay in which you develop your point of view on this issue. Support your position with reasoning and examples taken from your reading, studies, experience, or observations.

DO NOT WRITE YOUR ESSAY IN YOUR TEST BOOK.
You will receive credit only for what you write in your Answer Grid Booklet.

Write your essays on separate sheets of paper.

GO ON TO THE NEXT PAGE

SECTION 2
Time—25 Minutes
24 Questions

Directions: For each of the following questions, choose the best answer and darken the corresponding oval on the answer sheet.

Each sentence below has one or two blanks, each blank indicating that something has been omitted. Beneath the sentence are five words or sets of words labeled A through E. Choose the word or set of words that, when inserted in the sentence, best fits the meaning of the sentence as a whole.

EXAMPLE:

Today's small, portable computers contrast markedly with the earliest electronic computers, which were -------.

(A) effective
(B) invented
(C) useful
(D) destructive
(E) enormous   Ⓐ Ⓑ Ⓒ Ⓓ ●

1. Despite their fierce appearance, caymans are rarely -------, and will not attack humans unless provoked.

(A) extinct
(B) timid
(C) domesticated
(D) amphibious
(E) aggressive

2. Some historians claim that the concept of courtly love is a ------- that dates from the age of chivalry, while others believe it has more ------- origins.

(A) relic . . . simultaneous
(B) notion . . . ancient
(C) memento . . . discovered
(D) period . . . documented
(E) doctrine . . . amorous

3. In Shakespeare's day, ------- theater audiences would often throw fruits and vegetables at actors who failed to live up to their expectations.

(A) doting
(B) ravenous
(C) jingoistic
(D) boisterous
(E) stagnant

4. Although they physically resemble each other, the brothers could not be more ------- temperamentally; while the one is quiet and circumspect, the other is brash and--------.

(A) inimical . . . timid
(B) passionate . . . superficial
(C) dissimilar . . . audacious
(D) different . . . forgiving
(E) alike . . . respectful

GO ON TO THE NEXT PAGE

5. The retreat of Napoleon's army from Moscow quickly turned into a rout, as French soldiers, already ------- in the snow were ------- by Russian troops.

(A) replenishing . . . ravaged

(B) pursuing . . . joined

(C) sinking . . . camouflaged

(D) floundering . . . assaulted

(E) tottering . . . upbraided

6. The Morgan Library in New York provides a ------- environment in which scholars work amidst costly tapestries, paintings, stained-glass windows, and hand-crafted furniture.

(A) realistic

(B) frugal

(C) sumptuous

(D) friendly

(E) practical

7. The lecturer's frustration was only ------- by the audience's ------- to talk during her presentation.

(A) compounded . . . propensity

(B) alleviated . . . invitation

(C) soothed . . . authorization

(D) increased . . . inability

(E) supplanted . . . desire

8. The proposal to build a nuclear power plant was the most ------- issue ever to come up at a council meeting; it is astonishing, therefore, that the members' vote was unanimous.

(A) popular

(B) contentious

(C) concise

(D) exorbitant

(E) inconsequential

GO ON TO THE NEXT PAGE

Directions: The passages below are followed by questions based on their content; questions following a pair of related passages may also be based on the relationship between the paired passages. Answer the questions on the basis of what is <u>stated</u> or <u>implied</u> in the passages and in any introductory material that may be provided.

Questions 9–10 refer to the following passage.

While it is often helpful to think of humans as simply another successful type of mammal, a vital distinction remains. When a pride of lions enjoys a surfeit of food, they are likely to
(5) hunt quickly, eat all they can, then spend the remainder of the day sleeping. When people enjoy such easy living, we see a markedly different pattern—our big brains cause us to be restless, and we engage in play. This takes the
(10) form of art, philosophy, science, even government. So the intelligence and curiosity that allowed early humans to develop agriculture, and thus a caloric surplus, also led to the use of that surplus as a foundation for culture.

9. The author most likely cites the behavior of lions in order to

(A) provide an example of an even more successful mammalian species

(B) question the efficiency of the lion's feeding behavior

(C) provide a contrast to the image of humans as industrious and resourceful

(D) help illustrate the distinguishing characteristic of humans that led to the development of culture

(E) explore the range of hunting behaviors in different successful species

10. The final sentence ("So, the intelligence . . . for culture") primarily serves to

(A) illustrate the significance of a distinction

(B) counter a likely objection

(C) provide an alternative explanation

(D) suggest future implications of a phenomenon

(E) condone a future investigation

Questions 11–12 refer to the following passage.

Eugene O'Neill is truly a playwright of ideas, ideas that speak to a fundamental aspect of humanity. Many of O'Neill's plays are set firmly on American soil at a particular
(5) time in history, and it is easy to imagine that since the characters on stage are American, the only viable audience for such a play must be American as well. While a logical conclusion, this does not allow for the consistently
(10) strong record of production of O'Neill plays in Europe. His plays encompass ideas relevant to everyone, not just Americans.

11. The "logical conclusion" (line 8) is contradicted by O'Neill's

(A) primarily American audiences

(B) knowledge of American humanity

(C) mastery of playwriting

(D) authentically American characters

(E) popularity in Europe

12. Which of the following, if true, would most seriously undermine the conclusion of the passage?

(A) O'Neill's plays, once popular in American theaters, are rarely performed there today.

(B) In order to be a successful playwright, it is important to cultivate a specific and loyal following.

(C) When O'Neill's plays are staged in Europe, they are generally performed in English.

(D) The audiences attending O'Neill's plays in Europe are, for the most part, Americans traveling or living in Europe.

(E) O'Neill never traveled to Europe.

GO ON TO THE NEXT PAGE ⟶

Questions 13–24 refer to the following passage.

In the following passage, a famous zoologist discusses the origins of the domesticated animal.

The relationship between humans and animals dates back to the misty morning of history. The caves of southern France and northern Spain are full of wonderful depictions
(5) of animals. Early African petroglyphs depict recognizable mammals and so does much American Indian art. But long before art, we have evidence of the closeness of humans and animals. The bones of dogs lie next to those of
(10) humans in the excavated villages of northern Israel and elsewhere. This unity of death is terribly appropriate. It marks a relationship that is the most ancient of all, one that dates back at least to the Mesolithic Era.* With the
(15) dog, the hunter acquired a companion and ally very early on, before agriculture, and long before the horses and the cat. The companion animals were followed by food animals, and then by those that provided enhanced speed
(20) and range, and those that worked for us.

How did it all come about? A dog of some kind was almost inevitable. Consider its essence: a social carnivore, hunting larger animals across the broad plains it shared with
(25) our ancestors. Because of its pack structure it is susceptible to domination by, and attachment to, a pack leader—the top dog. Its young are born into the world dependent, rearable, without too much skill, and best of all, they
(30) form bonds with the rearers. Dogs have a set of appeasement behaviors that elicit affective reactions from even the most hardened and unsophisticated humans. Puppies share with human babies the power to transform cynics
(35) into cooing softies. Furthermore, the animal has a sense of smell and hearing several times more acute than our own, great advantages to a hunting companion and intrusion detector. The dog's defense behavior makes it an
(40) instinctive guard animal.

No wonder the dog was first and remains so close to us. In general, however, something else was probably important in narrowing the list—the candidates had to be camp followers
(45) or cohabitants. When humankind ceased to be continually nomadic, when we put down roots and established semi-permanent habitations, hut clusters, and finally villages, we created an instant, rich food supply for guilds
(50) of opportunistic feeders. Even today, many birds and mammals parasitize our wastes and feed from our stores. They do so because their wild behaviors provide the mechanisms for opportunistic exploitation. A striking example
(55) occurred in Britain during the 1940s and '50s. In those days, milk was delivered to the homeowners' doorstep in glass bottles with aluminum foil caps. Rich cream topped the milk, the paradise before homogenization. A chicka-
(60) dee known as the blue tit learned to puncture the cap and drink the cream. The behavior soon spread among the tits, and soon milk bottles were being raided in the early morning throughout Britain. If the birds had been so
(65) specialized that they only fed in deep forest, it never would have happened. But these were forest-edge opportunists, pioneers rather than conservatives. It is from animals of this ilk that we find our allies and our foes.
(70) Returning to the question of how it all came about, my instincts tell me that we first domesticated those individual animals that were orphaned by our hunting ancestors. In my years in the tropics, I have seen many wild
(75) animals raised by simple people in their houses. The animals were there, without thought of utility or gain, mainly because the hunter in the family had brought the orphaned baby back for his wife and children. In Panama it
(80) was often a beautiful small, spotted cat that bounced friskily out of a peasant's kitchen to

GO ON TO THE NEXT PAGE

play at my feet. The steps from the
home-raised wolfling to the domestic dog
probably took countless generations. I bet it
(85) started with affection and curiosity. Only later
did it become useful.

When we consider that there are more
than 55 million domestic cats and 50 million
dogs in this country, and that they support
(90) an industry larger than the total economy
of medieval Europe, we must recognize the
strength of the ancient bond.

Without the "aid" of goats, sheep, pigs, cattle, and horses we would never have reached
(95) our present population densities. Our parasiti-
zation of some species and symbiosis
with others made civilization possible. That
civilization, in turn, is increasingly causing
the extinction of many animals and plant
(100) species—an ironic paradox indeed.

*Mesolithic Era: the Middle Stone Age, between
8,000 and 3,000 years B.C.*

13. The author most likely describes the
archeological discoveries mentioned in lines
9–11 as "terribly appropriate" because

(A) dogs were always buried next to their
owners in the Mesolithic Era

(B) few animals were of religious significance
in prehistoric cultures

(C) they illustrate the role of dogs on a typical hunting expedition

(D) our relationship with dogs goes back farther than with any other animal

(E) they indicate the terrible speed of natural
disasters

14. According to the first paragraph, the first
animals that humans had a close relationship
with were those that

(A) acted as companions

(B) provided a source of food

(C) helped develop agriculture

(D) enabled humans to travel farther

(E) raided our food supply

15. According to the author, why was some kind
of dog "inevitable" (line 22) as a companion
animal for humans?

(A) It survived by maintaining its
independence.

(B) It was stronger than other large animals.

(C) It shared its prey with our ancestors.

(D) It was friendly to other carnivores.

(E) It was suited for human domination.

16. In line 23, "essence" means

(A) history

(B) nature

(C) scent

(D) success

(E) aggression

17. Judging from lines 31–32, "affective reactions"
most probably means

(A) callous decisions

(B) rational judgements

(C) emotional responses

(D) juvenile behavior

(E) cynical comments

GO ON TO THE NEXT PAGE

18. The author most likely compares puppies with human babies in lines 33–35 in order to

    (A) criticize an uncaring attitude toward animals

    (B) point out ways in which animals dominate humans

    (C) support the idea that dogs form bonds with their owners

    (D) dispel some misconceptions about the innocence of puppies

    (E) show how rewarding the ownership of a dog can be

19. In lines 43–44, "the list" most likely refers to the

    (A) types of birds that scavenge human food supplies

    (B) number of animals that developed relationships with humans

    (C) group of species that are able to communicate with dogs

    (D) variety of attributes that make dogs good hunters

    (E) range of animals depicted in cave paintings

20. The author most likely discusses the case of the British blue tit (lines 59–64) in order to

    (A) highlight a waste of valuable food supplies

    (B) indicate the quality of milk before homogenization

    (C) explain how unpredictable animal behavior can be

    (D) point out the disadvantages of living in rural areas

    (E) provide one example of an opportunistic feeder

21. In line 68, "animals of this ilk" refers to animals that are

    (A) good companions

    (B) forest inhabitants

    (C) adaptable feeders

    (D) efficient hunters

    (E) persistent pests

GO ON TO THE NEXT PAGE ▷

22. The author most likely describes his experience in the tropics (lines 73–82) in order to

    (A) portray the simple life led by a hunter's family

    (B) show how useful animals can be in isolated places

    (C) underline the effort involved in training a wild animal

    (D) illustrate how the first domesticated animals were created

    (E) indicate the curious nature of the domestic cat

23. In line 93, the use of "aid" in quotation marks emphasizes the point that

    (A) the animals' help was involuntary

    (B) population levels are dangerously high

    (C) the contribution of animals is rarely recognized

    (D) many animals benefited from the relationship

    (E) livestock animals are not as loyal as dogs

24. Which of the following best describes the "ironic paradox" mentioned in line 100?

    (A) More money is now spent on domestic animals than on animal livestock.

    (B) Pet ownership will become impractical if population density continues to increase.

    (C) The pet care industry in the U.S. today is larger than the total economy of medieval Europe.

    (D) Many parasitical species have a beneficial effect on the human population.

    (E) Human civilization is currently making extinct many of the other life forms that enabled it to grow.

SECTION 3

Time—25 Minutes
20 Questions

Directions: For this section, solve each problem and decide which is the best of the choices given. Fill in the corresponding oval on the answer sheet. You may use any available space for scratchwork.

Notes:

(1) Calculator use is permitted.

(2) All numbers used are real numbers.

(3) Figures are provided for some problems. All figures are drawn to scale and lie in a plane UNLESS otherwise indicated.

(4) Unless otherwise specified, the domain of any function f is assumed to be the set of all real numbers x for which $f(x)$ is a real number.

$A = \frac{1}{2}bh$ $\quad c^2 = a^2 + b^2$ $\quad$ Special Right Triangles $\quad A = \pi r^2$ $\quad C = 2\pi r$ $\quad V = \ell wh$ $\quad V = \pi r^2 h$ $\quad A = \ell w$

The sum of the degree measures of the angles in a triangle is 180.
The number of degrees of arc in a circle is 360.
A straight angle has a degree measure of 180.

1. If $2(x + y) = 8 + 2y$, then $x =$

   (A) 1
   (B) 2
   (C) 3
   (D) 4
   (E) 8

2. On the number line above, what is the distance from point B to the midpoint of AC?

   (A) 1
   (B) 2
   (C) 3
   (D) 4
   (E) 5

GO ON TO THE NEXT PAGE

3. A certain machine caps 5 bottles every 2 seconds. At this rate, how many bottles will be capped in 1 minute?

   (A) 10
   (B) 75
   (C) 150
   (D) 225
   (E) 300

4. If $2n + 3 = 5$, then $4n =$

   (A) 1
   (B) 2
   (C) 4
   (D) 8
   (E) 16

5. If $a + b < 5$, and $a - b > 6$, which of the following pairs could be the values of a and b?

   (A) (1, 3)
   (B) (3, –2)
   (C) (4, –2)
   (D) (4, –3)
   (E) (5, –1)

Note: Figure not drawn to scale.

6. In the triangle if the measure of angle B is 60 degrees, then what is the value of y?

   (A) 24
   (B) 26
   (C) 28
   (D) 30
   (E) 32

7. In a certain building, there are 10 floors and the number of rooms on each floor is R. If each room has exactly C chairs, which of the following gives the total number of chairs in the building?

   (A) $10R + C$
   (B) $10R + 10C$
   (C) $\dfrac{10}{RC}$
   (D) $10RC$
   (E) $100RC$

8. If a "sump" number is defined as one in which the sum of the digits of the number is greater than the product of the digits of the same number, which of the following is a "sump" number?

   (A) 123
   (B) 234
   (C) 332
   (D) 411
   (E) 521

9. If 4 percent of r is 6.2, then 20 percent of $r =$

   (A) 25
   (B) 26
   (C) 30
   (D) 31
   (E) 35

GO ON TO THE NEXT PAGE

10. At a certain school, if the ratio of teachers to students is 1 to 10, which of the following could be the total number of teachers and students?

    (A)   100

    (B)   121

    (C)   144

    (D)   222

    (E)   1,011

11. If $x \wedge y$ is defined by the expression $(x - y)^x + (x + y)^y$, what is the value of $4 \wedge 2$?

    (A) 16

    (B) 20

    (C) 28

    (D) 44

    (E) 52

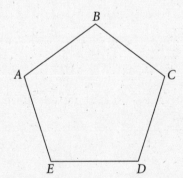

12. In pentagon *ABCDE* shown above, each side is 1 centimeter. If a particle starts at point *A* and travels clockwise 723 centimeters along *ABCDE*, the particle will stop on which point?

    (A) *A*

    (B) *B*

    (C) *C*

    (D) *D*

    (E) *E*

13. Which of the following values of *s* would yield the smallest value for $4 + \dfrac{1}{s}$?

    (A) $\dfrac{1}{4}$

    (B) $\dfrac{1}{2}$

    (C) 1

    (D) 2

    (E) 4

14. The first and seventh terms in a sequence are 1 and 365 respectively. If each term after the first in the sequence is formed by multiplying the preceding term by 3 and subtracting 1, what is the sixth term?

    (A)   40

    (B)   41

    (C)   121

    (D)   122

    (E)   123

15. If an integer is randomly chosen from the first 50 positive integers, what is the probability that an integer with a digit of 3 is selected?

    (A) $\dfrac{7}{25}$

    (B) $\dfrac{3}{10}$

    (C) $\dfrac{8}{25}$

    (D) $\dfrac{2}{5}$

    (E) $\dfrac{3}{5}$

GO ON TO THE NEXT PAGE

16. In a certain triangle, the measure of the largest angle is 40 degrees more than the measure of the middle-sized angle. If the measure of the smallest angle is 20 degrees, what is the degree measure of the largest angle?

   (A) 60
   (B) 80
   (C) 100
   (D) 120
   (E) 160

18. In a coordinate plane, if points $A(p, 3)$ and $B(6, p)$ lie on a line with a slope of 2, what is the value of p?

   (A) 1
   (B) 2
   (C) 3
   (D) 4
   (E) 5

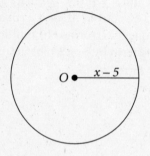

17. In the circle with center O above, for what value of x does the circle have a circumference of 20π?

   (A)   5
   (B) 10
   (C) 15
   (D) 20
   (E) 25

GO ON TO THE NEXT PAGE

19. In the coordinate plane above, points $P(0, 6)$, $Q(1, 4)$, and $C(3, 0)$ are on line ℓ. What is the sum of the areas of the shaded triangular regions?

(A) $\dfrac{7}{2}$

(B) 4

(C) $\dfrac{9}{2}$

(D) 5

(E) $\dfrac{11}{2}$

n cubes

20. In the figure above, there is a total of n cubes, each with an edge of 1 inch, stacked directly on top of each other. If $n > 1$, what is the total surface area, in square inches, of the resulting solid, in terms of n?

(A) $2n$

(B) $2n^2 + 2$

(C) $4n + 2$

(D) $4n^2$

(E) $5n$

IF YOU FINISH BEFORE TIME IS CALLED, YOU MAY CHECK YOUR WORK ON THIS SECTION ONLY. DO NOT TURN TO ANY OTHER SECTION IN THE TEST.

STOP

SECTION 4
Time—25 Minutes
24 Questions

Directions: For each of the following questions, choose the best answer and darken the corresponding oval on the answer sheet.

Each sentence below has one or two blanks, each blank indicating that something has been omitted. Beneath the sentence are five words or sets of words labeled A through E. Choose the word or set of words that, when inserted in the sentence, <u>best</u> fits the meaning of the sentence as a whole.

EXAMPLE:

Today's small, portable computers contrast markedly with the earliest electronic computers, which were -------.

(A) effective

(B) invented

(C) useful

(D) destructive

(E) enormous   Ⓐ Ⓑ Ⓒ Ⓓ ●

1. Ozone in the upper layers of Earth's atmosphere is beneficial, ------- animal and plant life from dangerous ultraviolet radiation.

   (A) reflecting

   (B) withdrawing

   (C) displacing

   (D) thwarting

   (E) protecting

2. While George Balanchine's choreography stayed within a classical context, he challenged convention by recombining ballet idioms in ------- ways.

   (A) unexpected

   (B) familiar

   (C) redundant

   (D) naive

   (E) awkward

3. All of today's navel oranges are ------- of a single mutant tree that began bearing seedless fruit 200 years ago.

   (A) progenitors

   (B) combinations

   (C) descendants

   (D) conglomerations

   (E) spores

GO ON TO THE NEXT PAGE

4. Because he consumed ------- quantities of food and drink at feasts given in his honor, King Henry VIII was considered a ------- by his subjects.

   (A) enormous . . . glutton

   (B) prodigious . . . peer

   (C) minute . . . luminary

   (D) unhealthy . . . fraud

   (E) unknown . . . dolt

5. The prime minister ordered the cabinet to stay on as ------- administration until a new government could be formed.

   (A) an interim

   (B) a political

   (C) an invalid

   (D) a premature

   (E) a civilian

GO ON TO THE NEXT PAGE

Directions: The passages below are followed by questions based on their content; questions following a pair of related passages may also be based on the relationship between the paired passages. Answer the questions on the basis of what is <u>stated</u> or <u>implied</u> in the passages and in any introductory material that may be provided.

Questions 6–9 refer to the following passages.

Passage 1

Miles Davis, though noteworthy as a jazz trumpet player, can best be understood instead as the ultimate musical iconoclast—a constant defier of popular and critical expec-
(5) tations. He first came to prominence as the young trumpeter in Charlie Parker's quintet in the late 1940s. In the early 50s, however, Davis led his own band in a completely different direction, using elaborate and original
(10) arrangements to explore a cool, subdued sound more in keeping with Davis's own personality. Characteristically, Davis soon abandoned this increasingly popular sound, pioneering the less harmonically sophisticated
(15) "modal" movement. Each decade brought more surprises, as Davis was at the forefront of free jazz, Fusion, and electronic instrumentation.

Passage 2

Great art often comes from limitations, and
(20) one can find no better example of this maxim than jazz great Miles Davis. Davis entered the jazz world when bebop music was at its peak. This style, pioneered by alto saxophonist Charlie Parker, demanded acrobatic facility,
(25) as soloists improvised dizzying melodies at break-neck speeds. Davis, though supremely expressive, didn't have the range or technique to play convincingly in this style. Rather than giving up, or continuing his career as a sec-
(30) ond-rate footnote, Davis evolved a unique style in which a few well-chosen notes were surrounded by artful silences that spoke volumes.

6. The author of Passage 1 most likely uses the word "characteristically" (line 12) in order to convey that

(A) like many artists, Davis creatively overcame technical limitations to create original art

(B) Davis's development of the new "modal" sound was part of a larger pattern of innovation

(C) Davis's inability to dedicate himself to a single style of jazz compromised his ultimate contribution to the art form

(D) Davis's skill as an instrumentalist is secondary to his role as a stylistic pioneer

(E) the modal movement, like Davis's other innovations, occurred about a decade after his previous stylistic advance

7. As used in Passage 2, line 30, "footnote" most nearly means

(A) unexpressive technician

(B) bibliographic citation

(C) unskilled artist

(D) stylistic innovator

(E) incidental participant

GO ON TO THE NEXT PAGE ⇨

8. Which of the following is most like Davis's "unique style" as described in Passage 2, lines 30–33?

   (A) a writer who explores poetry, short stories, and novels over the course of her career

   (B) a chef who carefully selects ingredients to create a balanced flavor

   (C) a photographer who purposely leaves his subject unfocused

   (D) a painter who uses a simple background to highlight her subject

   (E) a playwright who writes fast-paced, witty dialogue to advance the play's plot

9. The author of Passage 1 would most likely regard the description of Davis's departure from "bebop music" described in Passage 2, as

   (A) illustrative of Davis's ability to overcome technical obstacles

   (B) an example of limitations facilitating artistic progress

   (C) characteristic of Davis's stylistic innovations

   (D) a surprising though important development in Davis's career

   (E) the most significant of Davis's contributions to jazz music

Questions 10–17 refer to the following passage.

The passage below is adapted from a short story set in the wilderness of Alaska.

Day had broken cold and gray, exceedingly cold and gray, when the man turned away from the main Yukon trail and climbed the high earth-bank, where a dim and lit-
(5) tle-traveled trail led eastward through the spruce timberland. It was a steep bank, and he paused for breath at the top, excusing the act to himself by looking at his watch. It was nine o'clock. There was no hint of sun, though
(10) there was not a cloud in the sky. It was a clear day, and yet there seemed an intangible pall over the face of things that made the day dark. This fact did not worry the man.

In fact, all this—the dim trail, the absence
(15) of sun from the sky, the tremendous cold, and the strangeness and weirdness of it all—made no impression on the man. It was not because he was used to it. He was a newcomer in the land, and this was his first winter. The trou-
(20) ble was that he was without imagination. He was young and quick and alert in the things of life, but only in the things, and not in the significances. It was fifty degrees below zero, he judged. That impressed him as being cold
(25) and uncomfortable, but it did not lead him to meditate upon his frailty as a creature of temperature, and upon human frailty in general, able only to live within narrow limits of heat and cold; and from there on it did not
(30) lead him to the conjectural field of immortality and humanity's place in the universe. Fifty degrees below zero stood for a bite of frost that hurt and that must be guarded against. Nothing more than that entered his head.
(35) He plunged in among the trees with determination. The trail was faint. A foot of snow had fallen since the last sled had passed, and

GO ON TO THE NEXT PAGE

he was glad he was traveling light. In fact, he
carried nothing but the lunch wrapped in his
(40) handkerchief. He was surprised, however, at
the cold. It certainly was cold, he concluded,
as he rubbed his numb nose and cheekbones
with his mittened hand. He was bearded, but
that did not protect the high cheekbones and
(45) the eager nose that thrust itself aggressively
into the frosty air.

　　At his heels walked a dog, a big native husky,
gray-coated, without any visible or tempera-
mental difference from its close relative, the
(50) wild wolf. The animal was depressed by the
tremendous cold. It knew that it was no time
for traveling. Its instinct told it a truer tale
than was told by the man's judgment. In reality, it was not merely colder than fifty below
(55) zero; it was colder than sixty below, than
seventy below. It was seventy-five below zero.
The dog knew nothing of thermometers.
Possibly in its brain there was no sharp consciousness of a condition of very cold such as
(60) was in the human brain. But the brute had its
instinct. It experienced a vague but menac-
ing apprehension that subdued it and made it
slink along at the man's heels, and that made
it question every unusual movement of the
man as if expecting him to go into camp or to
(65) seek shelter somewhere and build a fire. The
dog had learned fire, and it wanted fire, or else
to burrow under the snow and
cuddle its warmth away from the air.

10. By using the phrase "excusing the act to
himself" (lines 7–8), the author suggests that
the man

(A) is annoyed that it is already nine o'clock
in the morning

(B) distrusts his own intuitive reactions to
things

(C) finds fault with others more readily than
with himself

(D) doubts that the time of day has any real
bearing on things

(E) dislikes admitting to personal weaknesses

11. The author identifies the man as "a newcomer
in the land" (line 18) most likely in order to
suggest that the man was

(A) excited at being in a new place with
many opportunities

(B) nervous about being alone in an unfamiliar place

(C) lacking in knowledge and experience
about the things around him

(D) trying hard to forget something in his
past

(E) unsure about why he chose to come to
the new place

12. In lines 26–27, the phrase "a creature of
temperature" refers to

(A) the man's preference for cold climates

(B) the innate human ability to judge
temperature

(C) the fact that one's personality is shaped
by the environment

(D) the human body's physical vulnerability
in extreme climates

(E) the man's unfamiliarity with wilderness
survival techniques

GO ON TO THE NEXT PAGE ⇒

13. Judging from lines 20–31, the man does not see that

   (A) he should appreciate the immense beauty of nature
   (B) humans cannot survive in the Alaskan wilderness
   (C) there is no way to accurately judge the temperature
   (D) the extreme cold could potentially be fatal
   (E) he has undertaken to do something which most people could not

14. The man's opinion of the temperature (lines 31–34) reveals which aspect of his character?

   (A) determination to succeed against all odds
   (B) lack of concern about personal welfare
   (C) pragmatic approach to travel
   (D) absence of insight and understanding
   (E) apprehension about the extreme cold

15. In lines 50–60, by discussing the dog's reaction to the "tremendous cold," the author suggests that

   (A) animal instinct can prove to be superior to human intelligence
   (B) animals can judge temperature more accurately than humans can
   (C) humans are ill-equipped to survive in the wilderness
   (D) there is little difference between animal instinct and human judgment
   (E) animals and humans have different reactions to extreme temperatures

16. The statement "the dog knew nothing of thermometers" (line 57) means that

   (A) dogs need not be as concerned about temperature as humans do
   (B) the dog's awareness of its environment is on a different level from the man's
   (C) a dog's mental faculties are not very well developed
   (D) the dog's experience of humans had been rather limited
   (E) the dog could not rely on the technological devices that the man could

17. Which of the following best explains why the dog would "question every unusual movement of the man" (line 64)?

   (A) The dog senses that it cannot rely on the man for survival.
   (B) The man is beginning to be visibly affected by the cold.
   (C) The dog recognizes the need for protection from the cold.
   (D) The dog worries that the man intends to leave it behind.
   (E) The dog understands that the man does not realize how cold it is.

GO ON TO THE NEXT PAGE

Questions 18–24 refer to the following passage.

The social science passage below was adapted from an article written by a health scientist.

For people in Southeast Asian refugee families, the experience of aging in America is very different from what they had expected for their second half of life. Older Southeast Asian
(5) refugees must cope with their rapidly acculturating younger family members, while taking on new roles and expectations in a foreign culture.

Many Southeast Asian immigrants are
(10) surprised to find that by American standards, they are not even considered elderly. Migration to a new culture often changes the definition of life stages. In the traditional Hmong culture of Vietnam, one can become
(15) an elder at 35 years of age when one becomes a grandparent. With grandparent status, elder Hmong can retire and expect their children to take financial responsibility for the family. Retiring at 35, of course, is not common in
(20) the United States.

There is a strong influence of Confucianism in traditional Vietnamese society. Confucianism, an ancient system of moral and religious thought, fosters strong filial
(25) piety and respect for family elders. In many Southeast Asian societies, age roles are hierarchical, with strict rules for social interaction. In America, however, because older refugees lack facility with the English language and
(30) knowledge of American culture, their credibility decreases when advising younger family members about important decisions. As younger family members take on primary roles as family mediators with American insti-
(35) tutions—schools, legal systems, and social service agencies, for example—the leadership position of elders within the family is gradually eroded.

Refugee elders must also cope with differ-
(40) ences in gender roles in the United States.

Even before migration, traditional gender roles were changing in Southeast Asia. During the Vietnam War, when men of military age were away, women took responsibility for
(45) tasks normally divided along gender lines. When Vietnamese families came to this country, these changes became more pronounced. There were more employment opportunities for younger refugees and middle-aged refugee
(50) women because their expectations often fit with the lower status jobs that were among the few opportunities open to refugees. Many middle-aged women and younger refugees of both sexes became family breadwinners. This
(55) was a radical change for middle-aged men, who had been the major breadwinners of the family.

Although the pattern for long-term adaptation of middle-aged and older Southeast
(60) Asian refugees is still unknown, there are indications that the outlook for women is problematic. Many older women provide household and childcare services in order to allow younger family members to hold jobs
(65) or go to school. While these women are helping younger family members to succeed in America, they themselves are often isolated at home and cut off from learning English or other new skills, or becoming more familiar
(70) with American society. Thus, after the immigrant family passes through the early stages of meeting basic survival needs, older women may find that they are strangers in their own families as well as in their new country.

GO ON TO THE NEXT PAGE ⟩

18. The major purpose of the passage is to discuss

   (A) the reasons why Southeast Asian people move to the United States

   (B) educational challenges facing young refugees in America today

   (C) problems that elderly Southeast Asian people encounter in America

   (D) the influence of Confucianism in Southeast Asian cultures

   (E) changing gender relationships in Southeast Asian refugee families

19. In lines 4–6, "older Southeast Asian refugees must cope with their rapidly acculturating younger family members" refers to

   (A) middle-aged men's embarrassment at not being the principal breadwinner

   (B) middle-aged women's isolation in the home

   (C) the high crime rate among younger refugees

   (D) younger refugees' better educational and social opportunities in America

   (E) the tendency of younger refugees to join non-Asian gangs

20. The author mentions "the traditional Hmong culture" (lines 13–14) in order to

   (A) show that social expectations may vary greatly from one country to another

   (B) suggest the lessening importance of traditional values in Vietnamese society

   (C) indicate that modern Vietnam encompasses a number of ancient cultures

   (D) illustrate the growing influence of Confucianism in Vietnamese society

   (E) compare the religious beliefs of the Vietnamese to those of other Southeast Asian peoples

21. The author uses the term "family mediators" (line 34) to mean the

   (A) traditional role of elders in Vietnamese families

   (B) responsibilities which young refugees assume in a new country

   (C) help that newly arrived refugees get from friends who migrated earlier

   (D) professional help available to refugee families in U.S. communities

   (E) benefits that American society derives from immigrant people

22. The word "pronounced" in line 47 most nearly means

   (A) delivered

   (B) noticeable

   (C) famous

   (D) acceptable

   (E) declared

23. The phrase "radical change" (line 55) refers to the fact that

   (A) older refugees find that retirement ages are very different in America

   (B) women filled men's jobs during the Vietnam War

   (C) the education of their children is considered crucial by refugee parents

   (D) refugee men are often displaced as primary income earners in their families

   (E) it is difficult for young refugees of both sexes to find jobs in America

GO ON TO THE NEXT PAGE ⇨

24. The author's point about the problematic long-term outlook for refugee women is made primarily through

(A) personal recollection
(B) historical discussion
(C) case study analysis
(D) philosophical commentary
(E) informed speculation

SECTION 5

Time—25 Minutes
18 Questions

Directions: For this section, solve each problem and decide which is the best of the choices given. Fill in the corresponding oval on the answer sheet. You may use any available space for scratchwork.

Notes:

(1) Calculator use is permitted.

(2) All numbers used are real numbers.

(3) Figures are provided for some problems. All figures are drawn to scale and lie in a plane UNLESS otherwise indicated.

(4) Unless otherwise specified, the domain of any function f is assumed to be the set of all real numbers x for which $f(x)$ is a real number.

$A = \frac{1}{2}bh$ $\qquad$ $c^2 = a^2 + b^2$ $\qquad$ Special Right Triangles $\qquad$ $A = \pi r^2$ $\qquad$ $C = 2\pi r$ $\qquad$ $V = \ell wh$ $\qquad$ $V = \pi r^2 h$ $\qquad$ $A = \ell w$

The sum of the degree measures of the angles in a triangle is 180.
The number of degrees of arc in a circle is 360.
A straight angle has a degree measure of 180.

---

1. If $r = 3$, then $(r^2 - 2)(4 + r) =$

   (A)   5
   (B)   7
   (C)   49
   (D)   77
   (E)   91

2. If $f(x) = x^2 + x$, what is the value of $f(3)$?

   (A)   0
   (B)   3
   (C)   6
   (D)   9
   (E)   12

3. If Set A is the set of prime numbers between 10 and 20, Set B is the set of integers between -10 and 15, and Set C is the intersection of Set A and Set B, then how many elements does Set C contain?

   (A)   2
   (B)   4
   (C)   25
   (D)   29
   (E)   30

GO ON TO THE NEXT PAGE

4. What is the greatest prime factor of 87?

(A)   3
(B)   17
(C)   29
(D)   43
(E)   87

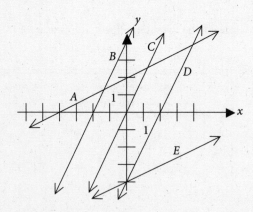

5. The graph above shows five lines, lettered A through E. Which of these lines can be represented as $y = 2x - 4$?

(A) A
(B) B
(C) C
(D) D
(E) E

6. The statement $(y - 3)^2 = (y + 1)^2$ is true for which of the following values of y?

(A) −1 only
(B) 1 only
(C) 3 and 1
(D) −3 and −1
(E) $\sqrt{3}$ only

7. A circular frame with a width of 2 inches surrounds a circular photo with a diameter of 8 inches. Assuming that the area of the frame does not overlap the area of the photo, what is the area of the frame?

(A) 4π
(B) 12π
(C) 16π
(D) 20π
(E) 36π

8. A business is owned by 4 women and 1 man, each of whom owns an equal share. If one of the women sells $\frac{1}{2}$ of her share to the man, and another woman keeps $\frac{1}{4}$ of her share and sells the rest to the man, what fraction of the business will the man own?

(A) $\frac{1}{3}$
(B) $\frac{9}{20}$
(C) $\frac{11}{20}$
(D) $\frac{2}{3}$
(E) $\frac{4}{5}$

9. If $y = 2$, then $(5 - y)(y + 3) =$

GO ON TO THE NEXT PAGE

Directions: For Student-Produced Response questions 9–18, use the grids at the bottom of the answer sheet page on which you have answered questions 1–8.

Each of the remaining 10 questions requires you to solve the problem and enter your answer by marking the ovals in the special grid, as shown in the example below. You may use any available space for scratch work.

Answer: 1.25 or $\frac{5}{4}$ or 5/4

Write answer in boxes. →

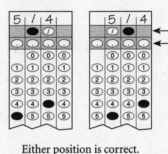

← Fraction line
← Decimal point

Grid-in result →

Either position is correct.

You may start your answers in any column, space permitting. Columns not needed should be left blank.

- It is recommended, though not required, that you write your answer in the boxes at the top of the columns. However, you will receive credit only for darkening the ovals correctly.

- Grid only one answer to a question, even though some problems have more than one correct answer.

- Darken no more than one oval in a column.

- No answers are negative.

- Mixed numbers cannot be gridded. For example: the number $1\frac{1}{4}$ must be gridded as 1.25 or 5/4.

(If ⬚1⬚1⬚/⬚4 is gridded, it will be interpreted as $\frac{11}{4}$ not $1\frac{1}{4}$.)

- Decimal Accuracy: Decimal answers must be entered as accurately as possible. For example, if you obtain an answer such as 0.1666…, you should record the result as .166 or .167. **Less accurate values such as .16 or .17 are not acceptable.**

Acceptable ways to grid $\frac{1}{6}$ = .1666…

10. At a certain car rental company, the daily rental rate for a midsize car is $18.99. If the weekly rental rate for the same car is $123.50, how much money, in dollars, is saved by renting this car by the week instead of renting daily for seven days? (Exclude the $ when gridding your answer.)

Note: Figure not drawn to scale.

11. In the figure above, $AB = 4$, $BC = 5$, and $DC = 12$. If point E lies somewhere between points A and B on line segment AB, what is one possible length of DE?

12. If $\frac{3}{4}$ of a cup of a certain drink mix is needed for every 2 quarts of water, how many cups of this drink mix is needed for 10 quarts of water?

13. In the figure above, what is the value of x?

Note: Figure not drawn to scale.

14. On the number line above, what is one possible value for y?

GO ON TO THE NEXT PAGE

15. Melanie drove at an average rate of 40 miles per hour for two hours and then increased her average rate by 25% for the next 3 hours. Her average rate of speed for the 5 hours was *t* miles per hour. What is the value of *t*?

16. At a convention of 500 dealers, each dealer sold coins or stamps or both. If 127 dealers sold both coins and stamps, and 198 dealers sold *only* stamps, how many dealers sold only coins?

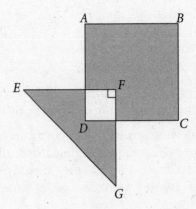

Note: Figure not drawn to scale.

17. In the figure above, square *ABCD* and right triangle *EFG* overlap to form a smaller square. The length of each side of the smaller square is 2. If $AB = EF = FG = 6$, what is the sum of the areas of the shaded regions?

$$\begin{array}{r} NR \\ +RN \\ \hline ABC \end{array}$$

18. The addition problem above is correct. If *N*, *R*, *A*, *B*, and *C* are different digits, what is the greatest possible value of $B + C$?

IF YOU FINISH BEFORE TIME IS CALLED, YOU MAY CHECK YOUR WORK ON THIS SECTION ONLY. DO NOT TURN TO ANY OTHER SECTION IN THE TEST.

STOP

SECTION 6
Time—25 Minutes
35 Questions

Directions: For each question in this section, select the best answer from among the choices given and fill in the corresponding oval on the answer sheet.

The following sentences test correctness and effectiveness of expression. Part of each sentence or the entire sentence is underlined; beneath each sentence are five ways of phrasing the underlined material. Choice A repeats the original phrasing; the other four choices are different. If you think the original phrasing produces a better sentence than any of the alternatives, select choice A; if not, select one of the other choices.

In making your selection, follow the requirements of standard written English; that is, pay attention to grammar, choice of words, sentence construction, and punctuation. Your selection should result in the most effective sentence—clear and precise, without awkwardness or ambiguity.

EXAMPLE: ANSWER:

Every apple in the baskets <u>are ripe and labeled according to the date it was picked</u>. Ⓐ ● Ⓒ Ⓓ Ⓔ

(A) are ripe and labeled according to the date it was picked
(B) is ripe and labeled according to the date it was picked
(C) are ripe and labeled according to the date they were picked
(D) is ripe and labeled according to the date they were picked
(E) are ripe and labeled as to the date it was picked

1. By the time I graduate from college three years from now, my brother <u>has practiced</u> law for five years.

   (A) has practiced
   (B) has been practicing
   (C) will have been practicing
   (D) would have practiced
   (E) is practicing

2. The historians at the university who are researching the Napoleonic Wars from the Russian <u>perspective includes more than two professors who emigrated from Russia</u> to the United States.

   (A) perspective includes more than two professors who emigrated from Russia
   (B) perspective included more than two professors who emigrated from Russia
   (C) perspective include more than two professors who emigrated from Russia
   (D) perspective include more than two professors whom emigrated from Russia
   (E) perspective includes at least two professors who emigrated from Russia

GO ON TO THE NEXT PAGE

3. In her Comparative Literature class, Nancy enjoyed reading Marcel Proust's groundbreaking novel, <u>which she considered to be more brilliant than the other writers we read</u>.

(A) which she considered to be more brilliant than the other writers we read

(B) whom she considered to have been more brilliant than the other writers we read

(C) which she considered to be more brilliant than the other novels we read

(D) which she considered to be brilliant opposed to the other novels we read

(E) whom she considered to be more brilliant than the other novels we read

4. Many people <u>watching the baseball series seen the hometown hero arriving</u> at the stadium before the game.

(A) watching the baseball series seen the hometown hero arriving

(B) watching the baseball series saw the hometown hero arriving

(C) who watch the baseball series seen the hometown hero arriving

(D) watching the baseball series saw the hometown hero have arrived

(E) who watch the baseball series seen the hometown hero arrived

5. The oxygen tank's increased capacity allows divers <u>to discover new species that congregate and feed close to</u> the bottom of the ocean.

(A) to discover new species that congregate and feed close to

(B) to have discovered new species that congregate and feed close to

(C) to discover new species that congregate in and feed close to

(D) to discover new species that congregate in and feed from close to

(E) to discover new species who congregate and feed close to

6. The referee halted play in an effort <u>at avoiding serious altercations in the stadium between fans of</u> the opposing teams.

(A) at avoiding serious altercations in the stadium between fans of

(B) at avoiding a serious altercation in the stadium between fans of

(C) to avoid serious altercations in the stadium between fans of

(D) to avoid serious altercations in the stadium between fans on

(E) to avoid serious altercations between fans in the stadium of

7. <u>Primarily a strategy to attract the votes of the elderly</u>, the social security adjustment carried great weight among the entire voting public of the day.

(A) Primarily a strategy to attract the votes of the elderly

(B) Primarily a strategy of attracting the votes of the elderly

(C) Primarily the strategy to attract the votes of the elders

(D) Primarily strategic to attracting the votes of the elderly

(E) Primarily elderly voters' votes were attracted

GO ON TO THE NEXT PAGE

8. A group of experts researching the bizarre occurrences theorized that the configuration of bright lights <u>were rather unusual but probably due to optical illusion.</u>

(A) were rather unusual but probably due to optical illusion

(B) were hardly unusual but probably due to optical illusion

(C) were rather unusual and probably due to optical illusion

(D) was rather unusual but probably due to optical illusion

(E) was rather unusual probably due to optical illusion

9. The school's new retro rock-and-roll band has drawn such huge crowds that an entirely new team has been hired <u>to determine new methods of providing security for their concerts.</u>

(A) to determine new methods of providing security for their concerts

(B) to determine new methods of providing security for its concerts

(C) to determine new methods for providing security for its concerts

(D) to determining new methods for providing security for their concerts

(E) to be determining new methods of providing security for their concerts

10. <u>If the concert had begun later, the conductor might have succeeded in giving the difficult last-minute corrections for the symphony to the orchestra.</u>

(A) If the concert had begun later, the conductor might have succeeded in giving the difficult last-minute corrections for the symphony to the orchestra.

(B) If the concert had began later, the conductor might have succeeded in giving the difficult last-minute corrections for the symphony to the orchestra.

(C) If the concert had begun later, the conductor will succeed in giving last-minute corrections to the difficult orchestra for the symphony.

(D) If the concert had begun afterwards, the conductor might have succeeded in having given last-minute corrections for the difficult symphony to the orchestra.

(E) If the concert had begun later, the orchestra would have succeeded in having difficulty last-minute corrections for the symphony from the conductor.

11. Igor Stravinsky created innovative musical <u>works and they superimposed</u> beautiful melodies over discordant harmonies.

(A) works and they superimposed

(B) works, which superimposing

(C) works, they superimposed

(D) works that superimposed

(E) works, and superimposed

GO ON TO THE NEXT PAGE

Directions: The following sentences test your ability to recognize grammar and usage errors. Each sentence contains either a single error or no error at all. No sentence contains more than one error. The error, if there is one, is underlined and lettered. If the sentence contains an error, select the one underlined part that must be changed to make the sentence correct. If the sentence is correct, select choice E. In choosing answers, follow the requirements of standard written English.

EXAMPLE:

Whenever one is driving late at night, you must take extra precautions against
   A   B   C

falling asleep at the wheel. No error
           D   E

---

12. The great blue heron, perhaps the most elegant species among birds, live in most parts of the
                       A   B
United States, at home in wetland habitats
           C
in both inland and coastal regions. No error
    D   E

13. At the football stadium, Susan liked watching
                           A
the home team's pre-game warm-ups, which
                             B
she considered more interesting than the
              C
visiting team. No error
    D   E

14. By tracing the source of artifacts found in
    A
Europe, researchers determined that the
                  B
pattern of Viking settlements were generally
                       C   D
similar, but varied in response to different
climates. No error
       E

15. The cake recipe actually called for a generous
              A
amount of sugar, and Chad used a sugar
              B
substitute instead since he wanted to lower
              C   D
the cake's calorie count. No error
              E

16. Although Luther Burbank conducted
    A   B
experiments that led to many new or
improved plants, such as the blight-resistant
              C
potato, his attempt to develop
                D
a spineless cactus was not a success. No error
                        E

17. They were relieved when monsoons carried
   A   B   C
rain from the southern seas and replenished
                    D
India's drought-stricken water supply.

No error
  E

GO ON TO THE NEXT PAGE

18. All of the children <u>waiting</u> for the school
        A
    bus <u>seen</u> the crossing guard <u>walking out</u> into
        B   C
    the street <u>to stop traffic</u>. <u>No error</u>
                    D   E

19. Arthur Miller's moral viewpoint allows him

    <u>to produce</u> plays <u>that</u> uniquely and
        A   B
    dramatically <u>expresses</u> the damaging effect
                    C
    modern life <u>has had</u> on Americans. <u>No error</u>
                    D   E

20. <u>While</u> many small children <u>claim hearing</u>
        A   B
    Santa and his reindeer on the roof, few teen-

    agers believe that <u>such a person</u> <u>truly</u> exists.
                            C   D
    <u>No error</u>
        E

21. This week, the company <u>initiated</u> Hawaiian
                                A
    Shirt Day in an attempt <u>at creating</u> a higher
                                B
    degree <u>of team spirit</u> <u>in the office</u>. <u>No error</u>
                C   D   E

22. <u>As</u> Shirin Abadi <u>was awarded</u> the Nobel Peace
        A   B
    Prize, many of her colleagues <u>praised</u> her
                                        C
    exceptional efforts <u>about</u> democracy
                            D
    and human rights in Iran. <u>No error</u>
                                    E

23. Although the San Francisco Earthquake

    <u>in the spring</u> of 1906 <u>was leveling</u> many
        A   B
    buildings, the subsequent <u>series of fires</u>
                                    C
    actually <u>destroyed</u> most of the city. <u>No error</u>
                D   E

24. The quarterback, after his startling <u>failure to</u>
                                            A
    throw a complete pass, <u>went about</u>
                                B
    <u>absolute shamefaced</u> and was available to
        C
    <u>only a few</u> of his teammates. <u>No error</u>
        D   E

25. <u>While</u> the effect of disease-causing agents on
        A
    cigarette smokers <u>has been known</u> for years,
                            B
    only recently <u>has</u> the damaging effects of
                        C
    cigarette smoke on second-hand smokers

    <u>become</u> widely recognized. <u>No error</u>
        D   E

26. The FBI <u>maintains</u> strict <u>requirements for</u>
                A   B
    citizens when <u>they are</u> <u>interested in</u> joining
                        C   D
    the Bureau. <u>No error</u>
                    E

GO ON TO THE NEXT PAGE

27. <u>Although</u> James Joyce, Samuel Beckett, and
    A
Seamus Deane <u>drew on similar</u> aspects of
           B
Irish culture in their novels, Beckett

<u>was more abstract</u> in his interpretations.
C   D
<u>No error</u>
  E

28. José Limón, <u>assuredly</u> one of the today's
           A
<u>most inventive</u> modern dance
   B
choreographers, <u>brought</u> to the stage a star
            C
tling <u>approach to</u> movement and musicality.
    D
<u>No error</u>
  E

29. Among the great moments in twentieth

century history, the toppling of the Berlin

Wall by East Germans <u>are</u> <u>probably seen</u> by
            A   B
<u>them</u> as one of the <u>most felicitous</u>. <u>No error</u>
C   D   E

GO ON TO THE NEXT PAGE

Directions: The following passage is an early draft of an essay. Some parts of the passage need to be rewritten.

Read the passage and select the best answer for each question that follows. Some questions are about particular sentences or parts of sentences and ask you to improve sentence structure or word choice. Other questions ask you to consider organization and development. In choosing answers, follow the conventions of standard written English.

Questions 30–35 refer to the following passage.

(1) When I visited England last year, I wanted to attend a football match (football in England is what is called soccer in the U.S.). (2) My mother wouldn't let me. (3) She tells me, "The fans are much too violent." (4) I really wanted to go so I did some research on English fans' violence.

(5) Through my research I realized that my mother would never let me go to a game. (6) But beyond that, I felt sad that hooliganism was such a reality in the English game. (7) They cause riots, and innocent football fans are sometimes injured by them when football-related fights get out of control.

(8) England had tried all sorts of remedies to stop the violence, but they couldn't stop hooliganism from increasing. (9) The officials tried creating lists of people banned from stadiums. (10) At international matches some known hooligans weren't even allowed into the country. (11) Some say that the older generation of hooligans was teaching the younger. (12) It is just human nature and crowd mentality. (13) But there was an argument that rang even more true for me: poverty was an underlying cause. (14) Economic data indicating that the football teams with the highest rate of violence were situated in the poorest areas.

30. In context, which is the best version of the underlined portion of sentence 3 (reproduced below)?

She tells me, "The fans are much too violent."

(A) (As it is now)
(B) My mother tells me,
(C) This was because she tells me,
(D) She told me,
(E) She suggested:

31. In context, which is the best version of the underlined portion of sentence 7 (reproduced below)?

They cause riots, and innocent football fans are sometimes injured by them when football-related fights get out of control.

(A) (As it is now)
(B) They caused riots and innocent football fans were sometimes injured by them
(C) Causing riots and injuring innocent football fans, the hooligans caused problems
(D) The hooligans cause riots and sometimes injure innocent football fans
(E) Innocent football fans sometimes cause riots and are injured

GO ON TO THE NEXT PAGE ⇒

32. In context, which of the following words are the most logical to insert at the beginning of sentence 12 (reproduced below)?

    It is just human nature and crowd mentality.

    (A) I see that
    (B) They say that
    (C) Others say that
    (D) However,
    (E) As a result,

33. In context, which is the best version of the underlined portion of sentence 14 (reproduced below)?

    Economic data indicating that the football teams with the highest rate of violence were situated in the poorest areas.

    (A) (As it is now)
    (B) seeming to indicate that the football teams
    (C) are indicating that the football teams
    (D) indicated that the football teams
    (E) had indicated that the football teams

34. Which of the following best describes the relationship between sentences 13 and 14?

    (A) Sentence 14 provides the conclusion supported by evidence in sentence 13.
    (B) Sentence 14 adds to information reported in sentence 13.
    (C) Sentence 14 poses an argument that contradicts the point made in sentence 13.
    (D) Sentence 14 provides supporting evidence for the conclusion in sentence 13.
    (E) Sentence 14 concludes that the theory proposed in sentence 13 is wrong.

35. Where is the best place to insert the following sentence?

    Instead of just punishing acts of hooliganism, England should attack its source, poverty.

    (A) After sentence 5
    (B) After sentence 7
    (C) After sentence 9
    (D) After sentence 12
    (E) After sentence 14

IF YOU FINISH BEFORE TIME IS CALLED, YOU MAY CHECK YOUR WORK ON THIS SECTION ONLY. DO NOT TURN TO ANY OTHER SECTION IN THE TEST. STOP

SECTION 7

Time—20 Minutes
19 Questions

Directions: For each of the following questions, choose the best answer and darken the corresponding oval on the answer sheet.

Each sentence below has one or two blanks, each blank indicating that something has been omitted. Beneath the sentence are five words or sets of words labeled A through E. Choose the word or set of words that, when inserted in the sentence, best fits the meaning of the sentence as a whole.

EXAMPLE:

Today's small, portable computers contrast markedly with the earliest electronic computers, which were -------.

(A) effective
(B) invented
(C) useful
(D) destructive
(E) enormous

1. The itinerary set by their travel agent included so many stops in ------- amount of time that they received only the most ------- impressions of places visited.

   (A) a limited . . . lasting
   (B) a brief . . . cursory
   (C) a generous . . . favorable
   (D) a sufficient . . . fleeting
   (E) an unnecessary . . . preliminary

2. Many formerly ------- peoples have moved into ------- settlements as urban areas have encroached upon their land.

   (A) roving . . . vulnerable
   (B) despondent . . . stable
   (C) transitory . . . covert
   (D) fervid . . . enduring
   (E) nomadic . . . permanent

3. The ------- effect of the sleeping tablets was so ------- that she still felt groggy the next day.

   (A) toxic . . . erratic
   (B) soporific . . . pronounced
   (C) salubrious . . . dependable
   (D) pharmaceutical . . . peculiar
   (E) stimulating . . . unreliable

GO ON TO THE NEXT PAGE

4. For many years Davis had difficulty in accepting those who were in positions of authority; in fact, when he was in high school his teachers described him as a ------- student.

(A) compliant

(B) slothful

(C) conscientious

(D) model

(E) recalcitrant

5. Although the actress had lived in a large city all her life, she was such a ------- performer that she became the virtual ------- of the humble farm girl she portrayed in the play.

(A) versatile . . . opposite

(B) melodramatic . . . understudy

(C) natural . . . nemesis

(D) consummate . . . incarnation

(E) drab . . . caricature

6. The chairman ------- the decision of the board members, describing it as a ------- of every worthy ideal that the organization had hitherto upheld.

(A) defended . . . denial

(B) lamented . . . negation

(C) criticized . . . fulfillment

(D) endorsed . . . renunciation

(E) applauded . . . repudiation

GO ON TO THE NEXT PAGE

Directions: The passages below are followed by questions based on their content; questions following a pair of related passages may also be based on the relationship between the paired passages. Answer the questions on the basis of what is <u>stated</u> or <u>implied</u> in the passages and in any introductory material that may be provided.

Questions 7–19 refer to the following passages.

The two excerpts below are from speeches that were made by outstanding American leaders of the nineteenth century. The first excerpt is from Thomas Jefferson's first Inaugural Address in 1801; the second was delivered by Frederick Douglass during the Fourth of July celebration in Rochester, New York, in 1852.

Passage 1

Let us then, with courage and confidence, pursue our own federal and republican principles; our attachment to union and representative government. Kindly separated by nature
(5) and a wide ocean from the exterminating havoc of one quarter of the globe; too high-minded to endure the degradation of others, possessing a chosen country, with room enough for our descendants to the thousandth
(10) and thousandth generation, entertaining a due sense of our equal right to the use of our own faculties, to the acquisition of our own industry, to honor and confidence from our fellow-citizens, resulting not from birth, but
(15) from our actions and their sense of them, enlightened by a benign religion, professed in deed and practiced in various forms, yet all of them inculcating honesty, truth, temperance, gratitude, and the love of man . . . Still
(20) one thing more, fellow citizens, a wise and frugal government, which shall restrain men from injuring one another, shall leave them otherwise free to regulate their own pursuits of industry and improvement, and shall not
(25) take from the mouth of labor the bread it has earned. This is the sum of good government; and this is necessary to close the circle of our felicities.

About to enter, fellow citizens, upon the
(30) exercise of duties which comprehend everything dear and valuable to you, it is proper you should understand what I deem the essential principles of our government, and consequently, those which ought to shape its
(35) administration. I will compress them within the narrowest compass they will bear, stating the general principle, but not all its limitations. Equal and exact justice to all men, of whatever state or persuasion, religious or
(40) political . . .

Passage 2

I say it with a sad sense of disparity between us. I am not included within the pale of this glorious anniversary! Your high independence only reveals the immeasurable distance
(45) between us. The blessings in which you this day rejoice are not enjoyed in common. The rich inheritance of justice, liberty, prosperity, and independence bequeathed by your fathers is shared by you, not by me. The sunlight that
(50) brought life and healing to you has brought stripes and death to me. This Fourth of July is yours, not mine. You may rejoice, I must mourn. To drag a man in fetters into the grand illuminated temple of liberty, and call
(55) upon him to join you in joyous anthems, were inhuman mockery and sacrilegious irony. Do you mean, citizens, to mock me by asking me to speak today?
(60)   . . . Fellow citizens, above your national, tumultuous joy, I hear the mournful wail of millions, whose chains, heavy and grievous

GO ON TO THE NEXT PAGE ⟹

yesterday, are today rendered more intolerable
by the jubilant shouts that reach them. If I do
(65) forget, if I do not remember those bleeding
children of sorrow this day, "may my right
hand forget her cunning, and may my tongue
cleave to the roof of my mouth!" To forget
them, to pass lightly over their wrongs, and to
(70) chime in with the popular theme, would be
treason most scandalous and shocking, and
would make me a reproach before God and
the world. My subject, then, fellow citizens, is
"American Slavery . . ."

(75)   . . . Would you have me argue that man
is entitled to liberty? That he is the rightful
owner of his own body? You have already
declared it. Must I argue the wrongfulness of
slavery? Is that a question for republicans? Is
(80) it to be settled by the rules of logic and argu-
mentation, as a matter beset with great difficulty, involving a doubtful application of the
principle of justice, hard to understand? . . .
    . . . What to the American slave is your
(85) Fourth of July? I answer, a day that reveals
more to him than all other days of the year,
the gross injustice and cruelty to which he
is the constant victim. To him your celebration is a sham; your boasted liberty an unholy
(90) license; your national greatness, swelling van-
ity; your sounds of rejoicing are empty and
heartless; your denunciation of tyrants, brass-
fronted impudence; your shouts of liberty and
equality, hollow mockery; your prayers and
(95) hymns, your sermons and thanksgivings, with
all your religious parade and solemnity, are to
him mere bombast, fraud, deception, impiety,
and hypocrisy—a thin veil to cover up crimes
which would disgrace a nation of savages.
(100) There is not a nation of the earth guilty of
practices more shocking and bloody than are
the people of the United States at this very
hour.

7. By "our equal right . . . to honor and confidence
from our fellow-citizens, resulting not from
birth, but from our actions and their sense of
them" (Passage 1, lines 11–15), Jefferson means
that

   (A) members of all nations are welcome to
       come to America
   (B) citizens have the right to demand respect
       from each other
   (C) citizens should judge each other by their
       accomplishments rather than their ances-
       try
   (D) one can build trust by doing things for
       others
   (E) one should rely not only on one's family
       but also on other citizens

8. In Passage 1, line 30, the word "comprehend"
most nearly means

   (A) include
   (B) understand
   (C) perceive
   (D) outline
   (E) realize

GO ON TO THE NEXT PAGE ⇨

9. By "I will compress them within the narrowest compass they will bear" Passage 1, (lines 35–36), Jefferson means that

(A) he intends to limit the role of government

(B) those who oppose justice will be imprisoned

(C) the general principles of government have boundaries

(D) he will speak concisely about the principles of government

(E) government bureaucracy has become too inflated

10. The word "persuasion" in Passage 1, line 39 most nearly means

(A) enticement

(B) influence

(C) cajolery

(D) authority

(E) opinion

11. The statement "To drag a man ... sacrilegious irony" Passage 2, (lines 53–56) conveys a sense of

(A) indignation at the hypocrisy of Fourth of July celebrations

(B) sorrow over the way the slaves had been treated

(C) anger that slavery had not yet been abolished

(D) disbelief that Fourth of July celebrations could even take place

(E) amazement that slaves were being forced to join in the celebration

12. In Passage 2, the references to the "mournful wail" and the "jubilant shouts" (lines 61–64) serve to

(A) remind the audience of difficulties in the past that have been overcome

(B) indicate the importance of commemorating the Fourth of July

(C) warn that the future of the country looks deceptively bright

(D) emphasize the different outlooks of two groups in the country

(E) suggest that some are faced with an unsolvable problem

13. In Passage 2, line 71, the author uses the word "treason" to refer to the act of

(A) rebelling against authority

(B) betraying the needs of a social group

(C) renouncing one's own principles

(D) expressing unpopular views

(E) acting upon irrational impulses

14. The author of Passage 2 most likely describes "American Slavery" as "my subject" (lines 73–74) in order to

(A) underline an unexpected new direction in his argument

(B) indicate the broad historical scope of his address

(C) emphasize his intent to discuss an apparent contradiction

(D) highlight the answer to a problem facing the United States

(E) underscore his eagerness to learn more about the topic of slavery

GO ON TO THE NEXT PAGE

15. In lines 92–93 of Passage 2, the phrase "brass-fronted impudence" is primarily used to convey the author's

(A) outrage at the contrast between political speeches and social reality

(B) exasperation at the many obstacles to racial equality

(C) resentment at the number of people excluded from July Fourth celebrations

(D) belief that resistance to authority is ultimately futile

(E) anger at the acts of tyrants throughout the world

16. The author of Passage 1 would most likely react to the questions at the beginning of the third paragraph of Passage 2 (lines 75–83) by commenting that

(A) a nation's political ideals are not always consistent with its actions

(B) the doctrine of equality is necessary for good government

(C) political views must be expressed through the proper democratic channels

(D) the goal of liberty for all may not be practical to attain

(E) the degradation of others must sometimes be endured

17. The author of Passage 2 would most likely react to the general principle of government in the last sentence of Passage 1 by pointing out that

(A) this general principle is hopelessly naive

(B) the real situation strongly contradicts this principle

(C) experience has proven this principle to be unattainable

(D) this principle is meaningless because it is vaguely worded

(E) the government never intended to adhere to this principle

18. Which statement is best supported by a comparison of the excerpts from the two speeches?

(A) Both excerpts denounce the degradation of some men and women in America.

(B) The purpose of both excerpts is to urge citizens to critically evaluate themselves.

(C) Both excerpts emphasize the necessity of justice for all citizens.

(D) Both excerpts argue that slavery is a violation of human rights.

(E) Both excerpts present a hopeful vision of the future.

19. The attitudes expressed in Passage 1 and Passage 2 toward equality in the United States might best be described as

(A) cautious versus angry

(B) disappointed versus adulated

(C) optimistic versus critical

(D) hopeful versus promising

(E) indulgent versus prudent

IF YOU FINISH BEFORE TIME IS CALLED, YOU MAY CHECK YOUR WORK ON THIS SECTION ONLY. DO NOT TURN TO ANY OTHER SECTION IN THE TEST.

SECTION 8
Time—20 Minutes
16 Questions

Directions: For this section, solve each problem and decide which is the best of the choices given. Fill in the corresponding oval on the answer sheet. You may use any available space for scratchwork.

Notes:

(1) Calculator use is permitted.

(2) All numbers used are real numbers.

(3) Figures are provided for some problems. All figures are drawn to scale and lie in a plane UNLESS otherwise indicated.

(4) Unless otherwise specified, the domain of any function f is assumed to be the set of all real numbers x for which $f(x)$ is a real number.

$A = \frac{1}{2}bh$ $c^2 = a^2 + b^2$ Special Right Triangles $A = \pi r^2$ $V = \ell wh$ $V = \pi r^2 h$ $A = \ell w$
$C = 2\pi r$

The sum of the degree measures of the angles in a triangle is 180.
The number of degrees of arc in a circle is 360.
A straight angle has a degree measure of 180.

1. According to the graph above, April sales accounted for approximately what percent of the total sales?

    (A) $12\frac{1}{2}$

    (B) 25

    (C) $37\frac{1}{2}$

    (D) 50

    (E) 60

2. If xy is negative, which of the following CANNOT be negative?

    (A) $y - x$

    (B) $x - y$

    (C) $x^2 y$

    (D) xy^2

    (E) $x^2 y^2$

GO ON TO THE NEXT PAGE

3. If 1 bora = 2 fedis and 1 fedi = 3 glecks, how many boras are equal to 48 glecks?

(A) 4

(B) 8

(C) 16

(D) 48

(E) 96

4. A college class is made up of f freshman and s sophomores. If 5 freshman drop this class, then the number of sophomores in the class is 3 times the number of freshman. Which of the following equations represents s in terms of f?

(A) $s = \dfrac{f-5}{3}$

(B) $s = \dfrac{f+5}{3}$

(C) $s = 3(f-5)$

(D) $s = 3(f+5)$

(E) $s = 5(f-3)$

5. In the figure above, if the perimeter of triangle ABC is 4 more than the perimeter of triangle ACD, what is the perimeter of quadrilateral $ABCD$?

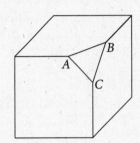

6. The figure above shows a cube-shaped stone with edges of 3 centimeters. Points A, B, and C are on three different edges of the cube, each 1 centimeter away from the same vertex. A jeweler slices off the corner with a straight cut through A, B, and C, as shown, and slices pieces of the same size off all the other corners of the stone. What is the total number of faces on the resulting stone?

(A)   7

(B) 10

(C) 12

(D) 14

(E) 16

GO ON TO THE NEXT PAGE

7. What is the average of the first 30 positive integers?

    (A) 14
    (B) 14.5
    (C) 15
    (D) 15.5
    (E) 16

Note: Figure not drawn to scale.

8. What is the area of the figure above?

    (A)   96
    (B) 102
    (C) 104
    (D) 108
    (E) 110

9. Sixty cookies were to be equally distributed to x campers. When 8 campers did not want the cookies, the other campers each received 2 more cookies. Which of the following equations could be used to find the number of campers x?

    (A) $x^2 - 8x - 240 = 0$
    (B) $x^2 - 8x + 240 = 0$
    (C) $x^2 + 8x - 240 = 0$
    (D) $x^2 + 8x + 240 = 0$
    (E) $x^2 - 4x - 120 = 0$

10. If 6 students are eligible for 2 scholarships worth $1,000 each how many different combinations of 2 students winning the 2 scholarships are possible?

    (A)   6
    (B)   9
    (C) 12
    (D) 15
    (E) 30

11. If $q \neq 0$ and $q = q^{-2}$, what is the value of q?

    (A) -1
    (B) 0
    (C) $\dfrac{1}{2}$
    (D) 1
    (E) 2

Price of One Can	Projected Number of Cans Sold
$0.75	10,000
$0.80	9,000
$0.85	8,000
$0.90	7,000
$0.95	6,000
$1.00	5,000

GO ON TO THE NEXT PAGE

12. The previous chart describes how many cans of a new soft drink a company expects to sell at a number of possible prices per can. Which of the following equations best describes the relationship shown in the chart, where n indicates the number of cans sold and p represents the price in dollars of one can?

(A) $n = -20{,}000p - 25{,}000$

(B) $n = -20{,}000p + 25{,}000$

(C) $n = -200p - 250$

(D) $n = 200p + 250$

(E) $n = 20{,}000p - 25{,}000$

13. Which of the following equations best describes the curve shown in the graph?

(A) $y = x$

(B) $y = x^2$

(C) $y = x^3$

(D) $y = \sqrt{x}$

(E) $y = \frac{1}{2}x$

14. In a game, all tokens of the same color are worth the same number of points. If one player won 4 green tokens and 8 yellow tokens for a total score of 48 points, and another player won 6 green tokens and 4 yellow tokens for a total score of 32 points, how many points is a yellow token worth?

(A) 2

(B) 4

(C) 5

(D) 8

(E) 10

15. Pablo has c grams of cherries. He uses 30 percent of the cherries to make muffins, each of which requires m grams of cherries. He uses the rest of the cherries to make preserves, each pint of which requires p grams of cherries. Which of the following describes the number of pints of preserves Pablo can make?

(A) $\dfrac{3c}{10m}$

(B) $\dfrac{3c}{10p}$

(C) $\dfrac{7c}{10p}$

(D) $\dfrac{7c}{10m}$

(E) $\dfrac{3cp}{10}$

GO ON TO THE NEXT PAGE

16. At a fruit stand, the price of one pound of
cherries is twice the price of one pound of
grapes. If 32 pounds of cherries and 8 pounds
of grapes were sold and sales totaled $90.00,
how much more money was made on the
cherries than on the grapes?

(A) $75.00

(B) $70.00

(C) $65.00

(D) $60.00

(E) $55.00

IF YOU FINISH BEFORE TIME IS CALLED, YOU MAY CHECK YOUR WORK ON
THIS SECTION ONLY. DO NOT TURN TO ANY OTHER SECTION IN THE TEST.

STOP

SECTION 9

Time—10 Minutes
14 Questions

Directions: For each question in this section, select the best answer from among the choices given and fill in the corresponding oval on the answer sheet.

The following sentences test correctness and effectiveness of expression. Part of each sentence or the entire sentence is underlined; beneath each sentence are five ways of phrasing the underlined material. Choice A repeats the original phrasing; the other four choices are different. If you think the original phrasing produces a better sentence than any of the alternatives, select choice A; if not, select one of the other choices.

In making your selection, follow the requirements of standard written English; that is, pay attention to grammar, choice of words, sentence construction, and punctuation. Your selection should result in the most effective sentence—clear and precise, without awkwardness or ambiguity.

EXAMPLE: ANSWER:

Every apple in the baskets <u>are ripe and labeled according to the date it was picked</u>.   Ⓐ ● Ⓒ Ⓓ Ⓔ

(A) are ripe and labeled according to the date it was picked
(B) is ripe and labeled according to the date it was picked
(C) are ripe and labeled according to the date they were picked
(D) is ripe and labeled according to the date they were picked
(E) are ripe and labeled as to the date it was picked

1. Lost items can be found <u>at the admissions booth they can be picked up until one hour after the museum's closing</u>.

    (A) at the admissions booth they can be picked up until one hour after the museum's closing

    (B) at the admissions booth; they can be picked up until one hour after the museum's closing

    (C) until one hour after the museum's closing, they can be picked up at the admissions booth

    (D) and that can be picked up at the admissions booth until one hour after the museum's closing

    (E) at the admissions booth, until one hour after the museum's closing is when they can be picked up

2. By utilizing cacophony and inconsistent rhythms, <u>the shock value of postmodern music was raised by Webern to a higher level</u> than ever before.

    (A) the shock value of postmodern music was raised by Webern to a higher level

    (B) Webern raised the shock value of postmodern music to a higher level

    (C) a higher level of postmodern music was reached by Webern

    (D) postmodern music's shock value was raised to a higher level by Webern

    (E) Webern's postmodern music shock value rose to a higher level

GO ON TO THE NEXT PAGE

3. The electric fan was an ingenious invention for keeping people cool during the <u>summer; it was</u> popular only briefly, however, until the air conditioner made it old-fashioned.

    (A) summer; it was popular only briefly, however

    (B) summer, for it was popular only briefly, however

    (C) summer; however, popular only briefly

    (D) summer, having been popular only briefly

    (E) summer, but was popular only briefly

4. Even the play's most tragic characters are delivered with a comic touch, <u>this dramatic effect</u> <u>results in a very unconventional story.</u>

    (A) this dramatic effect results in a very unconventional story

    (B) with this dramatic effect resulting in a very unconventional story

    (C) and a very unconventional story being the result of this dramatic effect

    (D) and this dramatic effect results in a very unconventional story

    (E) a very unconventional story results from this dramatic effect

5. The strict training schedule allowed the marathon runner to eventually run for 20 miles <u>and she could scale</u> steep hills without stopping for rest.

    (A) and she could scale

    (B) as well as scale

    (C) so she could scale

    (D) and a scaling

    (E) and to scale

6. Joseph Campbell espoused definitive ideas about the art of storytelling and <u>the heroes</u> <u>and villains were defined</u> through his work.

    (A) the heroes and villains were defined

    (B) the heroes and villains were defined by him

    (C) had defined the heroes and villains

    (D) defined the heroes and villains

    (E) the definition of the heroes and villains

7. In the past, many renowned singers wrote their own songs, <u>a trademark of originality</u> <u>that is</u> now rarely found.

    (A) a trademark of originality that is now rarely found

    (B) inasmuch as they displayed trademark of originality, it is now rarely found

    (C) this found rarely now in displaying their trademarks of originality

    (D) a trademark that is now rarely found in displaying their originality

    (E) which is now rarely found and it displays a trademark of originality

8. Thomas Jefferson was known as a brilliant <u>politician and he was also known as an</u> <u>accomplished architect.</u>

    (A) politician and he was also known as an accomplished architect

    (B) politician, and he was also an accomplished architect

    (C) politician; also he was known as an accomplished architect

    (D) politician and, furthermore, he was known as an accomplished architect

    (E) politician and an accomplished architect

GO ON TO THE NEXT PAGE ⇨

9. <u>Although liquor companies are now introducing low-alcohol and alcohol-free beverages, litigation against distillers continues to increase year after year.</u>

(A) Although liquor companies are now introducing low-alcohol and alcohol-free beverages, litigation against distillers continues to increase year after year.

(B) Litigation against distillers year after year continues to increase even though liquor companies are now introducing low-alcohol and alcohol-free beverages.

(C) Although introducing low-alcohol and alcohol-free beverages are liquor companies now, litigation against distillers continues to increase year after year.

(D) Increasing year after year, liquor companies are now introducing low-alcohol and alcohol-free beverages, but litigation against distillers continues.

(E) Liquor companies are now introducing low-alcohol and alcohol-free beverages, litigation against distillers continues to increase year after year.

10. The domestic <u>cat of which there are more than 40 breeds</u>, is a member of the feline family.

(A) cat of which there are more than 40 breeds

(B) cat, of which there are more than 40 breeds

(C) cat to which there belongs more than 40 breeds

(D) cat, which there are more than 40 breeds of

(E) cat, of which more than 40 breeds in existence

11. The Nobel Foundation <u>was established in 1900; since then</u> it has awarded prizes for achievements in literature and science.

(A) was established in 1900; since then

(B) was established in 1900, since then

(C) was established in 1900, then

(D) established in 1900; since then

(E) was established in 1900; and since then

12. Women are not rejecting the idea of raising children, but <u>many taking jobs</u> as well.

(A) many taking jobs

(B) many are taking jobs

(C) jobs are taken by many of them

(D) jobs are being taken

(E) many having taken jobs

GO ON TO THE NEXT PAGE

13. Changing over from a military to a peace-time economy means producing tractors rather than tanks, radios rather than rifles, and <u>to produce running shoes rather than combat boots</u>.

(A) to produce running shoes rather than combat boots

(B) to the production of running shoes rather than combat boots

(C) running shoes rather than combat boots

(D) replacing combat boots with running shoes

(E) to running shoes rather combat boots

14. The protest movement's impact will depend on both how many people it touches and <u>its durability</u>.

(A) its durability

(B) is it going to endure

(C) if it has durability

(D) how long it endures

(E) the movement's ability to endure

IF YOU FINISH BEFORE TIME IS CALLED, YOU MAY CHECK YOUR WORK ON THIS SECTION ONLY. DO NOT TURN TO ANY OTHER SECTION IN THE TEST.

STOP

Practice Test Three: **Answer Key**

SECTION 1

Essay

SECTION 2

1. E
2. B
3. D
4. C
5. D
6. C
7. A
8. B
9. D
10. A
11. E
12. D
13. D
14. A
15. E
16. B
17. C
18. C
19. B
20. E
21. C
22. D
23. A
24. E

SECTION 3

1. D
2. A
3. C

4. C
5. D
6. A
7. D
8. D
9. D
10. B
11. E
12. D
13. E
14. D
15. A
16. C
17. C
18. E
19. D
20. C

SECTION 4

1. E
2. A
3. C
4. A
5. A
6. B
7. E
8. D
9. C
10. E
11. C
12. D
13. D
14. D

15. A
16. B
17. C
18. C
19. D
20. A
21. B
22. B
23. D
24. E

SECTION 5

1. C
2. A
3. A
4. C
5. D
6. B
7. D
8. B
9. 15
10. 9.43
11. $13 <$ length < 15
12. 15/4 or 3.75
13. 166
14. $0.5 < y < 0.625$
15. 46
16. 175
17. 46
18. 11

SECTION 6

1. C
2. C
3. C
4. B
5. A
6. C
7. A
8. D
9. B
10. A
11. D
12. A
13. D
14. C
15. B
16. E
17. A
18. B
19. C
20. B
21. B
22. D
23. B
24. C
25. C
26. E
27. D
28. E
29. A
30. D
31. D
32. C

33. D
34. D
35. E

SECTION 7

1. B
2. E
3. B
4. E
5. D
6. B
7. C
8. A
9. D
10. E
11. A
12. D
13. B
14. C
15. A
16. B
17. B
18. C
19. C

SECTION 8

1. D
2. E
3. B
4. C
5. E
6. D
7. D

8. B
9. A
10. D
11. D
12. B
13. B
14. C
15. C
16. B

SECTION 9

1. B
2. B
3. A
4. D
5. E
6. D
7. A
8. E
9. A
10. B
11. A
12. B
13. C
14. D

ANSWERS AND EXPLANATIONS

SECTION 1

6 ESSAY

The first time I encountered a thought similar to the one expressed above by Calvin Coolidge was when I read a quote by Benjamin Franklin: "Energy and persistence conquer all things." The truth that Franklin expressed continues to affect me. I agree, therefore, that persistence is the major factor in someone's success. In fact, I know it's true because I've witnessed it first hand.

When I was 10 years old, my mother was in a car accident that left her a paraplegic; she is paralyzed from the waist down. I have watched her struggle from that day to this to reclaim a normal life and to be a mother to me and a wife to my father. She has come so far because she never gives up. She is a model of persistence. After the initial trauma she suffered from the accident faded she had to begin a long period of training to strengthen her upper body and to gain whatever strength she could in her legs. It was hard work. I used to go with her to the training room in the hospital and watch her sweat through the routines the therapist gave her.

Even today, almost 7 years since the accident, she trains three times a week. She also had to learn to use a wheelchair and how to drive a car using hand controls. She had to re-learn things she knew how to do before the accident like cooking and gardening. In fact, she had to learn how to do almost everything all over again, and she did.

I once asked her how she did all this and she said she did it because she was grateful that she survived the accident and could still be part of my father's and my life. So, Coolidge was right, and so was Franklin; persistence pays off. My mother is persistent and I'm so proud of her and so happy that her persistence means that she is still part of my life.

GRADER'S COMMENTS

All essays are evaluated on four basic criteria: Topic, Support, Organization, and Language. This is a strongly written essay in which the writer sticks to the assigned topic and develops it in a creative way. She has a stirring story to tell and she tells it very well. She never strays from her main idea which is that persistence pays off and her mother is living proof of that. The author's clear recounting of her mother's heroic actions since the accident offers much support for her thesis.

The essay has an interesting and strong organization. The first paragraph offers another quote that is similar to the statement given. The author whets the reader's appetite by not jumping immediately into her main point. The last sentence keeps the reader's interest going. The remaining three paragraphs support her thesis.

The essay exhibits a high degree of skill with language. Both the sentence structure and the vocabulary indicate that the essay is written by an adept writer. The sentence structure is varied and even long, complex sentences are correctly punctuated. This is particularly apparent throughout the second paragraph. Some words that indicate the author's solid vocabulary: reclaim; initial; trauma; encountered; witnessed; factor.

4 ESSAY

I think that Pres. Coolidge is right. It seems to me that if your persistent you do well in life. An example I can think of is Albert Einstein who said something like 99% of genius was hard work and the remaining 1% was because you are a genius. This shows that Einstein agreed that you need more persistence than genius to succeed. Of course, Albert Einstein was a genius, too, but as the quote above says a lot of geniuses don't get rewarded. Einstein is famous because he was a persistent genius.

When Einstein was young he failed some math tests and he didn't always get great grades. He didn't let this stop him, though. He knew he wanted to be a mathematician and a physics professor and he worked hard to get to these goals. His persistence paid off. He became a teacher and later he won the Nobel Prize.

Later on Einstein came to America where he taught at Princeton University. In this way he fulfilled his dream of being a teacher of physics and mathematics. This was what he said he wanted to do when he was young and he did it because he persisted until he reached his goal. I believe that his persistence more than his genius is what brought Einstein the things he wanted.

In conclusion, Einstein is a great example of why I agree with Calvin Coolidge that persistence is the most important quality a person can have to be successful.

GRADER'S COMMENTS

All essays are evaluated on four basic criteria: Topic, Support, Organization, and Language. This writer sticks to the topic, agreeing with the quote. The writer's use of Einstein's life is great support for his agreement. Note, however: the writer misattributes the quote about genius. Thomas Edison actually said that, not Einstein. But the essay is not testing for content; a mistake like this won't hurt the score.

The essay is well organized with an introduction, body, and conclusion. The writer's use of "In conclusion" in the last paragraph helps the sense of organization. Using words and phrases that indicate to the reader what your intentions are is a good technique for SAT essays.

The writer's language is generally good, though not very challenging. He makes a common error in the second sentence of the first paragraph—using "your" when he meant "you're." He also should not have abbreviated "President."

2 ESSAY

It's good to be persistent as the statement above says. I seen this many times. For example, my brother was not very good at basketball but he kept on shooting hoops in our backyard and after a while he got better he made the team. He not good enough to be on the varsity but he plays intrmurels.

I think persistent is important but I also think being a genius is pretty cool. I'd like to be a genius but I guess its not gonna happen. I guess I will have to just be persistent and see if that works. I think it will because as I said above I agree with the statement of Calvin Coolidge.

GRADER'S COMMENTS

All essays are evaluated on four basic criteria: Topic, Support, Organization, and Language. The author starts out pretty strongly by agreeing with the statement and using her brother as an example. However, she strays in the first part of the second paragraph and then returns to the topic at the end. The development of the topic is rudimentary. This contributed to her loss of points. The writer's example is good support for her opinion. She doesn't, however, develop her support enough. The essay meanders on and off topic, making the organization too loose.

The writer's language is generally below standard. There are grammatical and spelling errors. The grammar is particularly poor. There are numerous verb tense errors, run-on sentences, and slang words. Here's a sampling: "I seen" instead of "I've seen;" "He not good enough" instead of "He's not good enough;" "persistent" for "persistence;" "gonna" instead of "going to." The second sentence of the first paragraph is a long run-on. *Intramurals* and *important* are misspelled.

SECTION 2

1. E

Despite is our first clue word, signaling a contrast coming up. Despite their fierce appearance, caymans are actually rarely -------, to the point at which they won't attack humans unless provoked. So for the blank we need a word that means the same as *fierce*. The closest word here is choice (E), *aggressive.* Choice (B) was the exact opposite of what we wanted. Choice (C), *domesticated,* means tame and usually refers to animals treated as house pets.

2. B

There are two different schools of thought competing in this sentence. One group believes one thing *while* another believes something else. So, clearly we want words that help create a sense of the opposition between these two viewpoints. Let's start with the second blank. One group argues that courtly love *dates from the age of chivalry.* In other words, they think it's a fairly old idea, dating back from the days of knights and fair maidens. Another group thinks something else though, so they must feel it's either an even older idea or a more recent idea. A quick check through the answer choices for the second blank leads us to choice (B) *ancient. Notion,* or idea, fits quite nicely into the first blank, fitting with the word *concept* in the first half of the sentence.

3. D

Here we want a word that would describe the sort of people who might throw fruits and vegetables at those whose performance dissatisfied them. People like this are surely not *doting* (A), overindulgent or excessively fond, nor are they *ravenous* (B), or extremely hungry. If they were hungry, they'd eat the food instead of throwing it at the stage. There's nothing to imply that the audience is (C) *jingoistic,* or excessively nationalistic. However, the audience might certainly be described as (D) *boisterous,* or rowdy. (E) *stagnant* means dead or lifeless, which is illogical in the blank.

4. C

Although two brothers look alike, they could not be more ------- in terms of their personalities. *Not alike* or *different* or some such word must go into this first blank, something that helps convey that they look alike, but their behavior is not alike. The semicolon is our hint that the information following it will be more or less in line with what preceded it. So, *while* one is circumspect, or cautious, the other is brash, or the opposite of cautious. For this second blank, you should predict something that means the opposite of quiet, something that's sort of synonymous with brash. The best answer is choice (C), because *dissimilar* fits our prediction for the first blank, while *audacious* means bold—it's kind of a synonym for brash. (A) *inimical* is related to the word *enemy. Inimical* means hostile.

5. D

Napoleon's army was hightailing it out of Moscow. The retreat *quickly turned into a rout*, a state of wild confusion, a disastrous defeat. Why did it turn into an even bigger defeat? Probably because the French were stuck or struggling in the snow—if they were doing well traveling through snow, it's unlikely they'd end up being such big losers. Then, something was done to them by Russian troops. Well, if you know that Napoleon's army was routed by the opposing side, then it seems that we want a second-blank word that means something like *clobbered*. Choices (A) and (D) come close to that prediction. *Ravage* means to violently destroy. Now, going back to the first blank, we know we want something that implies the troops were stuck or struggling in the snow. Only choice (D) fits both blanks: the retreat of Napoleon's army turned into a rout as French troops, already *floundering* in the snow, were *assaulted* by Russian soldiers. To flounder is to struggle awkwardly and stumble about. In (A), *replenishing* in the snow sounds a bit weird—*replenishing* means replacing something that was used up. In (E), *tottering* means walking unsteadily, and *upbraided* means scolded or reprimanded—a little mild-mannered for our purposes here.

6. C

The word that will fill in the blank is defined here in the sentence—we want a word that describes an environment composed of tapestries, paintings, stained glass windows, and hand-crafted furniture. A quick survey of the answer choices leads us to choice (C), because *sumptuous* means costly or lavish, particularly with regard to furnishings and decor. While you might have been tempted to think that *friendly* in choice (D) was a plausible answer, it's hard to say to sure that an environment filled with rich, arty items is a *friendly* environment. For some people, such surroundings might be quite intimidating. *Frugal*, in choice (B), means thrifty or careful with money, which is quite the opposite of what we wanted here.

7. A

In this question, a lecturer is frustrated by something her audience has done. This frustration was only ------- by some connection between the audience and talking. It sounds like the lecturer was frustrated by her audience's desire or tendency to talk during her presentation. Lecturers want to be heard; an audience's inability or lack of desire to talk would not frustrate a lecturer. So, for the second blank, we want something like desire—choice (A) *propensity*, or tendency, and choice (E) *desire* could work. (C) makes no sense. What's an audience's *authorization*? To choose between (A) and (E), let's look at the second blank. (E) *supplanted*, or replaced, is illogical. So (A)'s got to be correct. In fact, it makes the most sense: the lecturer's frustration was *compounded*, or increased, by the audience's *propensity*, or tendency, to talk.

8. B

There's something about the issue of the nuclear power plant that makes it surprising the council all voted in agreement. If it was shocking that there was agreement, the issue must have been divisive or controversial. The answer here is (B), because *contentious* means causing controversy and disagreement. *Concise* in (C) means brief and to the point, while *exorbitant* in (D) means extravagant or excessive.

HUMANS VS. OTHER MAMMALS

9. D

The author says that there's a difference between humans and other mammals, and uses the lions to illustrate this point. Lions sit around or nap after they eat a lot. People get bored and do stuff. Why is this important? Because this led to the ultimate development of culture. (C) and (D) both look okay, but only (D) includes the author's larger point about culture. Also, the language of (C) is not quite in keeping with the tone of the passage. *Industrious* means hardworking, but the actions of people are described as play, not work. (A) is the opposite of what you're looking for—the author seems to regard the achievements of humans as pretty positive, and so wouldn't think that lions are more successful. The author never introduces the idea of efficiency (B). (E) is too broad; the passage focuses on what animals and humans do after they eat, and never discusses the hunting that precedes the eating.

10. A

The general purpose of the passage is to explain something, so look for this direction. (A) and (C) both look feasible. On further consideration, (C) doesn't quite work, since only one thesis is presented—the author is not providing an *alternative* to anything. (A), however, fits well. The author shows a *distinction* between the behavior of people and other mammals, and then shows the *significance* of this distinction (it led to culture). (B) is off base, since the author never indicates that there might be an objection to the thesis. (D) and (E) are out of the scope of the passage—what will (or should) happen in the future is never discussed.

EUGENE O'NEILL

11. E

First, you need to identify the *logical conclusion*—O'Neill's plays are very American, so the audience must also be American. The author then goes on to say that this is not true. The plays are also quite popular in Europe. This matches (E) quite well. (A) actually expresses the opposite of what you're looking for. It describes the *logical conclusion* rather than the contradiction of that conclusion. (B) is a distortion of several ideas in the passage, but does nothing to contradict the *logical assumption*. (C) is in keeping with the tone of the passage, but is also not offered as a contradiction of the *logical assumption.* (D) is a detail from the passage, but appears earlier, and doesn't disprove the assumption that Americans are the sole audience of O'Neill's plays.

12. D

The conclusion of the passage is that O'Neill's plays are relevant to everyone, including non-Americans, and we know this because the plays are popular with Europeans. (D) weakens the argument, because if it's mostly Americans going to the European performances, then there's no evidence that the plays are popular with non-Americans. (A) is out of scope, since the passage discusses European, not American productions. (B) could be tempting if you thought that O'Neill didn't have an American audience, and so couldn't be considered a successful playwright. This is going too far however, since there's no evidence that O'Neill is not also popular in America. (C) doesn't hurt the author's conclusion, since the plays could still be popular with non-Americans when performed in English. There's no reason that O'Neill couldn't be popular with Europeans, even if he'd never gone to Europe himself, so (E) doesn't affect the conclusion.

DOMESTICATED ANIMALS

If you're an animal lover you might enjoy this passage. Actually, it's not a bad passage, but it's long, so be sure to keep up a good pace. You should aim at getting the main points of paragraphs and moving on. Basically, the author says that the dog was the first domesticated animal, which makes sense because of the dog's nature (it comes from a pack and likes to have a leader; puppies are cute and trainable; and it has better senses of hearing and smell than humans do, which makes it a valuable hunting companion). Then the author wonders how domestication occurred, which sends him off on a tangent about animals that *parasitize* human wastes or food stores. He speculates that domestication began because baby animals were cute—only later did domesticated animals actually become useful. He concludes that it's ironic that human civilization is destroying many species, since our learning to live with them is what made civilization possible.

13. D

The *archaeological discoveries* mentioned in the question stem are human and dog bones lying next to each other in ancient burial sites. The reason the author feels it's *terribly appropriate* that these bones are found together comes a few lines later, when he says *it marks a relationship that is the most ancient of all.* (D) paraphrases that idea. You can see from this how important it is to read a few lines before and after the line reference in the stem. The author says nothing about burial habits in the Mesolithic Era (A), or the religious significance of animals in prehistoric cultures (B). He says nothing about *natural disasters* (E) either. He does mention hunting (C), but the bone finds are not *appropriate* because they *illustrate the role of dogs in hunting expeditions.* (D) is the only possibility.

14. A

The end of paragraph 1 provides the answer. The author says that the dog was the first domesticated animal because it served as *a companion and an ally* (A). Only *after* domesticating animals as companions did humans domesticate *food animals* (B) and then *those that provide enhanced speed and range* (D) and then those that helped us farm (C). The key thing is to see that all these other types of domesticated animals came after animals were domesticated as companions.

15. E

The line reference takes you to the beginning of paragraph 2. The author says that having a dog as a companion animal was almost *inevitable*, and then lists several reasons why. One of these is that the dog *is susceptible to domination by, and attachment to, a pack leader—the top dog*. The implication is that humans formed bonds with dogs because they could dominate them (E). None of the other choices gives characteristics that make sense in answer to the question.

16. B

As with all Vocabulary-in-Context questions, you should go back to the sentence to see how the word is used. The author asks us to consider the *essence* of the dog in order to understand why it became a companion. He then lists several of the dog's characteristics that made it easy to domesticate. In other words, we're looking at the dog's *nature* (B). The only other choice that might seem to make sense in this context is (A) *history*—but what follows the line *consider its essence* is not a history; rather, it's a list of characteristics that make up the dog's nature.

17. C

This is definitely a question you need to return to the passage to answer. Back in the second paragraph, the author lists the characteristics that made dogs *inevitable* companions for humans. In addition to being born dependent and forming bonds with their rearers, dogs *have a set of appeasement behaviors* that elicit *affective reactions* from even the most *hardened* humans. The author goes on to talk about puppies transforming *cynics* into *cooing softies*. Even if you weren't sure what *appeasement behaviors* were, you can see the gist of the author's point here: humans form bonds with dogs largely because dogs are cute and loveable. So would it make sense if *affective reactions* were *callous* (A), *rational* (B), or *cynical* (E)? No. (D) goes too far. The author isn't saying humans become childish around dogs, but that dogs arouse human emotions. (C) is the best answer.

18. C

The easiest way to understand the point of a comparison is to understand the context. What's the author saying in these lines? He's trying to show why it was inevitable that dogs became human companions. One reason is that dogs form bonds with their owners (C). That's the only reason he compares puppies with babies—to show how emotional people get about dogs. The author's point has nothing to do with *criticizing an uncaring attitude* (A), so that can't be the point of his comparing puppies and babies. The same is true for the rest of the choices, so (C) is correct.

19. B

Again, go back to the passage. Notice that the start of paragraph 3 actually refers back to the end of the *first* paragraph. Paragraph 1 ended with the author listing the dog as the first domesticated animal, followed by food animals, work animals, etc. Paragraph 2 talks about *why* the dog came first. So when paragraph 3 begins with *no wonder the dog was first*, it's referring to the dog's status as the first domesticated animal. Similarly, *the list* refers to other domesticated animals, or *the number of animals that developed relationships with humans* (B). The author hasn't yet mentioned *birds that scavenge human food supplies*, and when he does, he only mentions one, not many *types* (A). The passage never mentions species that are able to communicate with dogs (C), or the variety of attributes that make dogs good hunters (D). Finally, if you chose (E), you were losing track of the author's main points. Read over the first three paragraphs to see what's going on, and give a closer reading next time.

20. E

This question might seem more complicated than it really is. If you were confused by the digression the author made to talk about the blue tit, taking a look at the choices first probably would've saved you time. (A), (B), and (D) are fairly easy to eliminate—they have nothing to do with any of the author's main points. Good—now that you've eliminated three choices, you can always guess. But first let's go back to the passage. In line 46 the author mentions *opportunistic feeders*. He goes on, saying *even today, many birds . . . feed from our stores*. So (E) must be right; the blue tit is an example of an opportunistic feeder. The question doesn't go any more into depth than that, so you're done.

21. C

This is a clear reference question. Go back to the lines you're given to see what kind of animals are being referred to. You have to read above a little to find the answer. The author has just finished describing the blue tit as an example of an opportunistic feeder. He reinforces the idea that the tit is an animal that feeds when and where it can by saying, *If all birds had been so specialized that they only fed in deep forest, it never would have happened.* In other words, they are *not* so specialized—they'll eat wherever they find a food source (C). The author isn't talking here about companion animals (A). *Forest inhabitants* (B) is too broad. (D) is out because the birds are not hunting, they're feeding. And the point about the birds is not to give an example of *persistent pests* (E).

22. D

Go back to the passage to see in what context the author discusses his experiences in the tropics. At the beginning of paragraph 4, the author says that he thinks that the very first domesticated animals were orphaned as a result of hunting. He then tells how, in the tropics, he saw many instances of wild animals raised in homes of hunters. So his experiences illustrate his theory about how *the first domesticated animals were created* (D). None of the other choices relate to the author's argument here (or anywhere in the passage).

23. A

This one's a little tricky—if you thought so, you should've jumped ahead and come back later if you had time. Remember, reading questions don't go from easy to hard, so the next one could be easier. Check out the line *aid* is in to see what's going on. The author says that without domesticated animals—goats, sheep, pigs, cattle, and horses—we never would've achieved civilization. These animals helped or *aided* us—but they didn't have much choice in the matter. We dominated them, and then used them for food or labor. That's why *aid* is in quotes, and (A) is correct. The passage never says *population levels are dangerously high* (B). (C) is a better possibility— but it's not a point the author makes; you're inferring too much if you chose (C). It's not clear that animals benefited at all from domestication (D). (E) is really far-out, not supported by the passage.

24. E

The *ironic paradox* is found in the last four lines of the passage. The author says our living with other species—using them for food and labor—is what made our civilization possible. It is ironic then, that our civilization is presently wiping out many plant and animal species (E). Nowhere does the author say anything about (A) or (B). With (C), the author does talk about the pet care industry in the final paragraph, but not to say its size is *ironic*. His point is just to show how big it is. (D) twists the author's point. It's by being parasites on other species that humans benefit, not the other way around.

SECTION 3

1. D

We want the value of x. Let's begin by distributing the 2 over the terms inside the parentheses on the left side of the equation. This gives us $2x + 2y = 8 + 2y$. Subtracting $2y$ from both sides results in $2x = 8$. Dividing both sides by 2 gives us $x = 4$.

2. A

Since point A is at 1 on the number line and point C is at 7, the distance between them is $7 - 1$, or 6. Half the distance from A to C is $\frac{1}{2}$ of 6, or 3, and 3 units from either point A or point C is 4, since $1 + 3 = 4$ and $7 - 3 = 4$. Therefore, the point at 4 on the number line is the midpoint of AC, since a midpoint by definition divides a line in half. Point B is at 3 and the midpoint of AC is at 4, so the distance between them is 1, answer choice (A).

3. C

The machine caps 5 bottles every 2 seconds, and we want to know how many bottles it caps in 1 minute, or 60 seconds. Multiplying 2 seconds by 30 gives you 60 seconds. If the machine caps 5 bottles in 2 seconds, how many bottles does it cap in 30 times 2 seconds? 30×5, or 150 bottles, is answer choice (C).

4. C

All you have to do here is solve the equation, but instead of solving it for n, you have to solve it for $4n$. If $2n + 3 = 5$, then you can subtract 3 from both sides of the equation to get $2n = 2$. Multiplying both sides of this equation by 2 gives you $4n = 4$, choice (C).

5. D

The easiest way to do this problem is just to backsolve. Since each pair of numbers in the answer choices represents possible values of a and b, just add up each a and b to see if $a + b < 5$, and subtract each b from each a to see if $a - b > 6$. If you do this, you'll find that in all 5 cases $a + b < 5$, but in only 1 case, in choice (D), is $a - b > 6$. In choice (D), $a + b = 4 + (-3) = 1$ and $a - b = 4 - (-3) = 7$.

If you think about the properties of negative and positive numbers (drawing a number line can help) you'll probably realize that the only way $a - b$ could be larger than $a + b$ is if b is a negative number, but that would only eliminate choice (A). In some problems your knowledge of math only helps you a little bit. In those cases you just have to play with the given answer choices in order to solve.

6. A

In the figure angle B is labeled $(2x - 4)°$ and in the question stem you're told that angle B measures 60°. So $2x - 4 = 60$, and $x = 32$. That means that angle A, which is labeled $(3x)°$, must measure 3×32, or 96°. Since the three angles of a triangle must add up to 180°, $60° + 96° + y° = 180°$, and $y = 24$.

7. D

This one is easier if you plug in numbers for C and R. Suppose R is 2. Then there would be 2 rooms on each floor, and since there are 10 floors in the building, there would be 2×10 or 20 rooms altogether. If $C = 3$, then there are 3 chairs in each room. Since there are 20 rooms and 3 chairs per room there are $20 \times 3 = 60$ chairs altogether. Which answer choices are 60 when R is 2 and C is 3? Only $10RC$, choice (D).

You don't have to plug in numbers here if you think about the units of each variable. There are 10 floors, R rooms per floor, and C chairs per room. If you multiply 10 floors by $R \frac{\text{rooms}}{\text{floor}}$, the unit "floors" will cancel out, leaving you with $10R$ rooms, and if you multiply $10R$ rooms by $C \frac{\text{chairs}}{\text{room}}$, the unit "rooms" will cancel out, leaving $10RC$ chairs in the building, again choice (D).

8. D

Here you have a strange word, "sump", which describes a number that has a certain relationship between the sum and the product of its digits. To solve this one, just find the sum and the product of the digits for each answer choice. You're told that for a "sump" number, the sum should be greater than the product. Choice (D), 411, has a sum of 6 and a product of 4, so that's the one you're looking for.

9. D

In this question, if you think about the relationship between the information you're given and the information you have to find, it becomes very easy. You're given 4% of a number and you have to find 20% of that same number. 4% of r is just a certain fraction, $\frac{4}{100}$ to be exact, times r; and 20% of r is just $\frac{20}{100}$ times r. That means that 20% of r is 5 times as great as 4% of r, since $\frac{4}{100}$ times 5 is $\frac{20}{100}$. So if you're given that 4% of r is 6.2, then 20% of r must be 5 times 6.2, or 31, choice (D). You could also have figured out the value of r and then found 20% of that value, but this takes a bit longer. 4% of r is the same as 4% times r, or $.04r$. If $.04r = 6.2$, then $r = \frac{6.2}{.04} = 155$, and 20% of 155 is $.2 \times 155 = 31$, choice (D) again.

10. B

The ratio of teachers to students is 1 to 10, so there might be only 1 teacher and 10 students, or there might be 50 teachers and 500 students, or just about any number of teachers and students that are in the ratio 1 to 10. That means that the teachers and the students can be divided into groups of 11: one teacher and 10 students in each group. Think of it as a school with a large number of classrooms, all with 1 teacher and 10 students, for a total of 11 people in each room. So, the total number of teachers and students in the school must be a multiple of 11. If you look at the answer choices, you'll notice that 121, choice (B), is the only multiple of 11, so (B) must be correct.

11. E

Since x and y with a funny symbol between them is equal to $(x-y)^x + (x+y)^y$, to find 4 and 2 with a funny symbol between them just plug 4 in for x and 2 in for y. That gives you $(4-2)^4 + (4+2)^2$, or $2^4 + 6^2$, or $16 + 36$, or 52, answer choice (E).

12. D

If the particle travels from A to B to C to D to E and then back to A it has traveled 5 centimeters, since each side of the pentagon measures 1 centimeter. If it goes all the way around the pentagon again it's traveled another 5 centimeters, for a total of 10 centimeters. In fact, every time the particle makes a complete revolution around the pentagon (from point A back to point A again) it travels an additional 5 centimeters. So if the number of centimeters the particle has traveled is a multiple of 5, the particle must be at point A. The number 723 is 3 more than a multiple of 5. If the particle had gone 720 centimeters it would be at point A; since it has gone 3 more centimeters it must be at point D, answer choice (D).

13. E

When would $4 + \frac{1}{s}$ have the smallest possible value? Certainly if s, and its reciprocal $\frac{1}{s}$, were negative, $4 + \frac{1}{s}$ would be smaller than 4, since adding a negative number is like subtracting a positive number. However, none of the answer choices is negative, so $4 + \frac{1}{s}$ will be greater than 4. However, it will be as small as possible when $\frac{1}{s}$ is as small as possible. If you look at the answer choices, you can find the values for $\frac{1}{s}$. If $s = \frac{1}{4}$, then $\frac{1}{s} = 4$, etc. If you do that you'll probably notice that as s gets larger its reciprocal gets smaller, so $\frac{1}{s}$ is smallest when s is largest, in this case when $s = 4$, choice (E).

14. D

Since you're looking for the sixth term of the sequence, let's call the sixth term x. Every term in this sequence is formed by multiplying the previous term by 3 and then subtracting 1, so the seventh term must be formed by multiplying the sixth term, x, by 3 and then subtracting 1; in other words, the seventh term is equal to $3x - 1$. Since the seventh term is 365, $365 = 3x - 1$, and you can solve for x to get $x = 122$, choice (D).

15. A

If an integer is chosen randomly from the first 50 integers the probability of choosing any particular number is 1 divided by 50, and the probability of choosing an integer with a digit of 3 is the number of integers with a digit of 3 divided by 50. The integers 3, 13, 23, 30, 31, 32, 33, 34, 35, 36, 37, 38, 39, and 43 are the only integers with 3's in them, for a total of 14 different integers, so the probability is $\frac{14}{50}$, or $\frac{7}{25}$, choice (A).

16. C

Let's call the degree measure of the largest angle x. Since the degree measure of the middle-sized angle is 40 degrees less than the degree measure of the largest angle, the degree measure of the middle-sized angle is $x - 40$. We also know that the smallest angle is 20 degrees. We know that the sum of the measures of the three interior angles of any triangle is 180 degrees. So we can write an equation for our triangle: $x + (x - 40) + 20 = 180$.

Now let's solve for x:

$$x + x - 40 + 20 = 180$$
$$2x - 20 = 180$$
$$2x = 200$$
$$x = 100$$

17. C

The diagram tells you that the radius of the circle is $x - 5$ and the question stem tells you that the circumference of the circle is 20π. Since the circumference of a circle is 2π times the radius, 20π must equal 2π times $(x - 5)$, which gives you the equation $20\pi = 2\pi(x - 5)$. Solving this equation gives you $x = 15$, answer choice (C).

18. E

The slope of a line is defined as the change in the y-coordinate divided by the change in the x-coordinate. As you go from point A to point B, the x-coordinate goes from p to 6 and the y-coordinate goes from 3 to p, so the change in the x-coordinate is $6 - p$ and the change in the y-coordinate is $p - 3$. You can make this into an equation: $\frac{p-3}{6-p} = 2$, and solve this equation for p. That would give you $p = 5$, choice (E). You could also plug the 5 possible values for p into the expression $\frac{p-3}{6-p}$ to see which one gives you 2 as a result. Either way, choice (E) is correct.

19. D

In order to find the areas of the shaded triangles, you have to find the coordinates of all the vertices of the triangles. You know where points P, Q, and C are in the coordinate plane, but what about the rest of them? Well, first of all let's label all the other points that are vertices of the triangles. The triangle on top has two labeled vertices, P and Q. The third vertex of that triangle is on the y-axis between P and the origin. Let's call it point A. The other triangle has vertices Q, C, and an unlabeled point that is also the upper right-hand corner of the rectangle. Call that point B. Points A and B are both on the same horizontal line that point Q is on, so all three points must have the same y-coordinate of 4. The x-coordinate of point A is 0 since it is on the y-axis, and the x-coordinate of B must be 3, the same as point C's x-coordinate, since points B and C lie on the same vertical line. So point A's coordinates are $(0, 4)$ and point B's coordinates are $(3, 4)$. Since triangles PQA and QBC are right triangles, we just need to know the lengths of their legs in order to find their areas. In the coordinate plane, the length of a horizontal line segment is the difference of the x-coordinates of its endpoints and the length of a vertical line segment is the difference of the y-coordinates of its endpoints. So, the length of PA is $6 - 4$, or 2, and the length of AQ is $1 - 0$, or 1, so the area of triangle PQA is $\frac{1}{2} \times 2 \times 1 = 1$. The length of QB is $3 - 1$, or 2, and the length of BC is $4 - 0$, or 4, so the area of triangle QBC is $\frac{1}{2} \times 2 \times 4 = 4$. The sum of those areas is $1 + 4 = 5$, answer choice (D).

20. C

No matter what the value of n is, this figure will be a rectangular solid. All rectangular solids have six faces. You just have to figure out the area of each of the six faces. The face on the bottom, which is the face up against the table or whatever this stack of cubes is sitting on, is a square, and it will have an area of 1 square inch, since the edge of each cube has a length of 1 inch. The face on the top of the stack of cubes is also a square and it will also have a surface area of 1 square inch. The other four faces making up the stack are identical rectangles, each with dimensions of 1 inch by n inches. So the area of one of these rectangles is $1 \times n$ or n square inches and these four identical rectangular faces have a total area of $4 \times n$ or $4n$ square inches. So the total surface area of the solid is the sum of the areas of the square top, the square bottom, and the four identical rectangular faces, which is $1 + 1 + 4n$ or $4n + 2$ square inches.

If you found that confusing, it might be easier just to pick a value for n. Suppose $n = 4$ and there are 4 cubes, as in the figure shown. Then just add up the areas of the faces of the stack in the figure, but don't forget the faces that aren't shown in the drawing. Since each face of each cube has an area of 1, in square inches, the figure shown has an area of 4 in the front plus 4 on the right side plus 4 on the left side (not shown in the drawing) plus 4 in the back (not shown in the drawing) plus 1 on the top and finally 1 on the bottom (not shown in the drawing), for a total of 18. Only choice (C) has a value of 18 when $n = 4$, so choice (C) must be correct.

SECTION 4

1. E

The key here is the word *beneficial*, or helpful. If you don't know *beneficial*, a knowledge of word roots would help you. *Beneficial* contains the root BENE, meaning good, which indicates to you that it's a positive word. Well, if in one breath we are told that the ozone layer is positive, and in the next, that it does something for plant and animal life relating to dangerous ultraviolet radiation, we know we need a fairly positive word in the blank. The only choice that fits this requirement is choice (E) *protecting*. (D), *thwarting*, means impeding or preventing.

2. A

While is our tip-off that this sentence will in some way contain a contrast. While George Balanchine's choreography stayed within a classical context, he challenged convention by recombining ballet idioms. (If you don't know exactly what this means, it doesn't matter—you just need to grasp that this is how he challenged convention.) He's challenging convention by recombining typical ballet moves or whatever in some ---- way. The word in the blank must mean something like unconventional. The best choice here is (A), *unexpected*. Choice (C), *redundant*, means needlessly repetitive or excessive.

3. C

All of today's navel oranges have some common relationship to a single mutant tree that produced seedless fruit 200 years ago. They must all be descended from this one mutant. So the word in the blank must mean *descended from*. Choice (C), *descendants*, jumps out as the correct choice. *Progenitors*, in choice (A) is meant to fool you since it has something to do with genetics. If you break *progenitor* down, *PRO* means *for* or *before* while the GENUS root is related to the word *gene*. So, *progenitors* are ancestors—people (or things) which are related but came before—like grandparents. *Progenitors* are the opposite of descendants. Choice (E) was another word trap—just because *spores* have something to do with plants doesn't mean this is right. A *spore* is a reproductive body found in simpler forms of life. But you don't need to know biology to figure this one out. Just use your reasoning skills. While a seed could be a spore, it makes no sense to say that all of today's navel oranges are the actual *spores* of a 200-year-old tree. But it is more plausible that this one tree produced a number of seeds, which in turn produced more of their own seeds, and so on.

4. A

In this sentence, there's a relationship between the quantities of food and drink Henry VIII consumed, and the type of person he was seen as. Either he consumed minimal quantities of food and drink, and was considered a spartan of sorts, or he consumed large amounts, and was considered a pig. Well, choice (A) is the only one that fits either one of these predictions. A *glutton* is one who overindulges in the consumption of food and drink. This option is the only one that fits, where there's a connection between the type of person his subjects saw him as, and the amount of food and drink he scarfed up. (C)'s first word, *minute,* or very small, fits okay, but a *luminary,* a famous or important person, doesn't. Consuming small quantities of food wouldn't make someone famous. In (B), *prodigious* means either extraordinary or enormous, while a *peer* is an equal, or a member of nobility.

5. A

You want a vocabulary word that means something like *transition* or *temporary*—some word that describes a government that no longer is in power, but is staying in power just until a new government is ready to take over the reins. Choice (A), *interim,* means temporary or provisional, so this is the answer. INTER is a root you should know—it means between.

MILES DAVIS

6. B

Author 1's point is that Davis was a musical innovator. So, when the author says that Davis's change of musical direction was *characteristic*, she's making the point that this change was typical of Davis's innovation. That matches (B) quite well. (A) is the thesis of Passage 2, not Passage 1. (C) is far too negative; author 1 thinks that the stylistic innovation was a positive attribute. (D) is a paraphrase of the first sentence, but that occurs earlier and is unrelated to the word *characteristically*. (E) is too literal. The author says that *each decade brought more surprises*, but that doesn't mean the innovations were spaced ten years apart, and it certainly doesn't follow from the word *characteristically*.

7. E

Davis couldn't play in Charlie Parker's style very well, so he created a new one to avoid becoming a *second-rate footnote.* The term *footnote* usually means a note at the bottom of the page that supplements the body of a test. Here, it refers to a person who is not the main focus, an unimportant person (E).

The author says that Davis was *supremely expressive,* so the author wouldn't think that he was in danger of becoming *unexpressive* (A). (B) is a literal meaning of footnote, but doesn't refer to a person. Even though Davis was not as technically skilled as Parker, it seems unlikely that the author would refer to him as *unskilled* (C). (D) is the opposite of what you're looking for; Davis became a *stylistic innovator* in order to avoid being a *footnote.*

8. D

Right after the phrase *unique style*, the author offers a description: *a few well-chosen notes were surrounded by artful silences that spoke volumes*. So, you're looking for a description of someone who uses a little to say a lot. That matches (D) pretty well. The painter is surrounding her subject with empty space in the same way that Davis surrounded his notes with silence.

(A) might fit well with the description in Passage 1 of Davis as a stylistic innovator, but the question is asking about Passage 2, not Passage 1. (B) is not too bad, since we do get the sense that Davis carefully selected his notes, but (B) doesn't convey the sense that the chef was as spare as Davis. (Maybe the chef uses tons of different ingredients.) If anything, Davis was more focused than his predecessors, so (C) doesn't fit here. (E) sounds more like the description of the highly technical Parker than the spare and elegant Davis, so it's the opposite of what you're looking for.

9. C

Author 1 characterizes Davis as an innovator, so he would see Davis's development of a new style as typical of his entire career. That's right in line with (C).

(A) and (B) both fit pretty well with Passage 2, but author 1 never discusses technique or technical limitations, so they don't work for this question. (D) is half right, because author 1 does think the development is important, but the word *surprising* makes this the opposite of what you're looking for. The development was typical, not *surprising*. There's no real evidence that author 1 would think this particular innovation was more important that the many others described in Passage 1 (E).

To Build a Fire Passage

This fiction passage shouldn't pose too many problems: it's short, clear, and straightforward. If you enjoy reading fiction, be careful not to relax too much while reading the passage—you may slow down and lose time. Save pleasure reading for when you're not taking the SAT! The passage describes a man and a dog entering a little-traveled path in Alaska. A comparison is set up between the man, who *lacks imagination* and isn't alarmed by the extreme cold, and his dog who, going on instinct, is alarmed.

10. E

Review the beginning of the passage to see what *act* the man is *excusing to himself*. It turns out he stopped because he was out of breath, but doesn't want to admit it (to himself, since he's alone), so he plays it off by looking at his watch. That makes choice (E) correct. He shows no reaction to what time it is (A). You may have been confused by choice (B) because the narrator (later in the passage) implies that the dog's instincts are more accurate than the man's. However, the man never shows distrust of himself (B). You're overinterpreting if you chose (C)—there's no evidence in the passage to support this inference. The point of the man's *excusing the act to himself* has nothing to do with *the time of day* (D); it has to do with him not admitting why he stopped in the first place.

11. C

Watch for the tone in the lines around the quote—it'll help you eliminate choices. For example, does the man seem at all *excited*? No, so (A) is out. He also doesn't seem *nervous* (B), although by the end of the passage there's an ominous feeling of danger in the air. (C) is right because it's a straightforward description of what's going on. There's no evidence in the passage to support choice (D). (E) is similarly wrong—there's no discussion of why the man is in the wilderness. Remember, most inferences (or *suggestions*, as the question phrases it) are very mild, and are always supported by the passage.

12. D

Reread the lines the quote appears in. The man's being a creature of temperature is the same *frailty* that all humans have: we're *able only to live within narrow limits of heat and cold*. In other words, if it's too cold, we'll freeze to death. Choice (D) is correct. *A creature of temperature* does not imply the man prefers cold climates (A), because *temperature* includes hot and cold. The author shows later in the passage how wrong the man's judgment of the temperature is, so (B) is unlikely. There's no discussion of *personality being shaped by the environment* (C). The man may or may not know wilderness survival techniques (E), but in any case, that's not what *a creature of temperature* refers to.

13. D

This question refers you to a big chunk of text, so save time by scanning the choices before you go to the passage. Choice (A) implies the wrong thing. This wilderness must be immensely beautiful, but whether the man notices it or not is not the point. The point is the judgment the man makes about the temperature. (B) overstates the case. The author isn't flatly declaring, *humans can't survive in the Alaskan wilderness*. Instead, he's describing a man who is underestimating the potential danger. That makes (D) correct. Just because this character can't judge the temperature accurately doesn't mean *there's no way to accurately judge the temperature* (C). There's no evidence that *most people could not do* what this guy is doing, even though it's obviously a difficult thing (E).

14. D

All of paragraph 2 leads up to the four lines you're sent to for this question. After a discussion of the potential danger extreme temperatures pose to humans, the paragraph concludes by saying none of this entered the man's head. In other words, he lacks *insight and understanding* (D). The man thinks the cold *must be guarded against*, so (B) can't be right. At the same time, (A) is too strong—the man doesn't even acknowledge that there are *odds* to succeed against. (C) is too general. *Apprehension* in (E) means *fearfulness*, which we've already seen the man lacks.

15. A

Again, you have a lot of lines to review, so save time by scanning the answer choices before you check the passage. It's in these lines that the author introduces the dog and its *instinct*—which tells it to take shelter from the cold. Correct. Choice (A) restates what's in lines 50–60. The dog isn't judging the temperature (B), it's just reacting to an instinct of danger. Choice (C) is an inference that goes too far—it's too general for these lines. (D) contradicts the point the author's making. (E) is partially true, but it captures only a small part of what the author suggests.

16. B

This question doesn't require too much interpretation, so don't go digging for difficult answers. The passage says that the dog *knew nothing of thermometers*, but that it *had its instinct*. In other words, it didn't read the temperature with a device as humans do, and it didn't need to—it knew instinctively how cold it was. The answer is (B)—the dog's awareness of its environment is different from the man's. Nothing implies that dogs *need not be concerned about temperature* (A); the point is that they perceive it differently than people do. (C) is too negative. Although the author calls the dog a *brute* at one point, it is done with respect, since the dog's instincts prove to be more valuable than the man's intelligence. (D) is too literal, and the point is not that the dog *could not rely on technological devices* (E), but that the dog has no need of them.

17. C

Reread the lines at the end of the passage to see what's going on. We've seen that the dog fears the cold, and the end of the passage describes the dog watching the man for a sign that they are heading for protection (C). Choices (A) and (E) miss the mark because the author never says that the dog recognizes the man's mistaken estimation of the cold. There is also no sign that the man is being visibly affected by the cold (B). Choice (D) invents something not found in the passage.

ELDERLY ASIANS PASSAGE

This is a passage about Southeast Asian immigrants' experience of aging in America. This passage may be a little dry, but it's not complex. The discussion focuses on the problems older immigrants have when they come to America. These include: different standards of what's considered *elderly*, not getting the kind of respect they would in their homelands, dealing with different gender roles, and elderly women being isolated in the home and becoming estranged from their families. Don't worry about any more detail than this until you get to the questions.

18. C

Remember this strategy for dealing with main idea questions: look for an answer that's not too broad or too narrow, but that encompasses the whole passage. In this case, (A) is too broad. From the first paragraph, you know that the focus is more specific than *the reasons why Southeast Asian people move to the United States.* This helps you eliminate (B) as well: from the start you're told the passage is concerned with the problems of the elderly, not the young. (C) covers the whole passage, and is correct. (D) picks up on a detail—Confucianism—and expands it beyond the scope of the passage. And (E) is just one topic discussed in the passage, not the focus of it.

19. D

Even if the word *acculturating* was unfamiliar to you, the rest of the passage should have made it clear that the differences between generations, once the family came to America, had to do with differences in language ability, different cultural attitudes toward and definitions of age, better employment opportunities, and obstacles to older refugees mixing in their new society. The closest answer to capturing all that is (D). (A) and (B) are too narrow, focusing on single issues that affect only a portion of the refugees, while this quotation applies generally to older refugees. (C) and (E) are out of the scope of the passage.

20. A

Review paragraph 2 to understand why the author mentions the *traditional Hmong culture.* There, the author says that American and Asian cultures define *elderly* differently. In the Hmong culture, people become elders and retire at 35; obviously, in American culture, this is not the case. So Hmong culture is mentioned to illustrate the paragraph's main point—that *social expectations vary greatly from one country to another* (A). There's no mention of traditional values in Vietnamese society *lessening* (B). No other ancient cultures are mentioned in paragraph 2, so (C) is out. (D) is out because Confucianism isn't mentioned until paragraph 3. Likewise, no other Southeast Asian peoples are mentioned (E).

21. B

Go back to the line in which *family mediators* appears. This part of paragraph 3 says that younger members of immigrant families deal with schools and other institutions because they have better English language skills than older family members. So being a *family mediator* is a responsibility that young refugees assume in a new country (B). (A) might've confused you because a hasty reading of the passage makes it sound like this is a role older people used to fill—but in fact, it's not. The passage really says that in the traditional culture there are strict rules for social interaction based on age, which the new role of "family mediator" gradually erodes. The passage says nothing about getting help from friends (C) or professionals (D). The author doesn't write about the benefits American society derives from immigrant people (E).

22. B

After rereading the line that *pronounced* is in, the first thing you should do is eliminate the obvious choice. In this case, that's (E), *declared*. The author uses *pronounced* to mean (B) *noticeable*. Gender roles changed somewhat in Southeast Asia during the Vietnam War, but they changed even more drastically for families that emigrated to the United States. None of the other choices fits this context. The author doesn't imply that these changes became more *acceptable* (D); she implies that they happened out of necessity and says they were a *radical change*.

23. D

The *radical change* the author refers to is the fact that women often become the main source of income in immigrant families in the Unites States. This is a major change in gender roles, because in Southeast Asia men were usually the breadwinners. (D) is correct. (A) is an unlikely answer because retirement ages were discussed back in paragraph 2. (B) might've been tempting, because the Vietnam War is mentioned in paragraph 4, along with the answer. But the author says that while gender roles are changing in Southeast Asia due to the Vietnam War, the *radical change* occurs when families emigrate. Education (C) is not discussed in these lines. (E) is out because the author says there are more jobs for younger refugees, not that it's hard for young refugees to find them.

24. E

When you're not given a line reference, it makes sense to look in the passage where the previous question left off because Critical Reading questions are ordered sequentially. So that takes you to the last paragraph, which is indeed where the author makes a point about the *long-term outlook for refugee women*. The author starts off by saying that although the long-term outlook is *unknown*, there are *indications* about it. Now look at the choices. There's no evidence that this is a *personal recollection* (A), or a *historical discussion* (B). No specific *case* is mentioned or analyzed (C). The author isn't being *philosophical* (D); if anything, she's being as scientific as possible, given the lack of data. That leaves (E), *informed speculation*. Since the author is knowledgeable about the subject matter, but has to go on *indications* to make her final point, (E) is the best answer.

SECTION 5

1. C

This is a straightforward substitution problem, but be sure to remember order of operations. First plug in 3 for r to get $(3^2 - 2)(4 + 3)$. Simplify the expressions within the parentheses to get $(9 - 2)(4 + 3)$, which is 7×7, or 49.

2. A

Work carefully and follow the order of operations, and problems like this one will be easy points.
$f(3) = 3^2 + 3 = 9 + 3 = 12$

3. A

The intersection of two sets consists of all the elements that are common to both sets. Be sure to read the question carefully; there are many different questions that could be asked about these sets. Set A consists of the numbers 11, 13, 17, and 19. Only two of these are also in Set B.

4. C

The factors of 87 are 1, 3, 29, and 87; 87 is a factor of 87, but it is not prime, so (E) is incorrect. 29 and 3 are both factors of 87 and prime, so the greater of these, (C), is correct.

5. D

In equations of the form $y = mx + b$, m represents the slope of the line and b represents the y-intercept of the line. The slope of a line is the rise over the run, or the difference between the values of y at two different points on the line over the difference between the values of x at those same points—a shorthand way of expressing this is $\frac{\Delta Y}{\Delta X}$. A good way to double-check your answer is to plug the values of x and y at some point on your chosen line into the equation to see if they work. You need to figure out which line in the figure changes two units in the y-direction for every one it changes in the x-direction. Lines B, C, and D all do this, so they all have a slope of 2. However, only line D also has the correct y-intercept, -4.

6. B

Back solving is a good strategy for this question. Plug in all the numbers in the choices for y, and see which ones work; -1 gives you $(-1 - 3)^2 = (-1 + 1)^2$, which simplifies to $(-4)^2 = (0)^2$ or $16 = 0$. This isn't true, so eliminate (A) and (D). 1 gives you $(1 - 3)^2 = (1 + 1)^2$, which is $(-2)^2 = (2)^2$ or $4 = 4$. This is true, so (B) or (C) must be the answer. Try 3: $(3 - 3)^2 = (3 + 1)^2$, $(0)^2 = (4)^2$ or $0 = 16$. This isn't true, so the answer must be (B).

7. D

First find the area of the frame and photo combined; then find the area of the photo alone. Then find the difference. Since we know that the diameter of the photo is 8, its radius must be 4, and the area of the photo is $\pi r^2 = \pi 4^2 = 16\pi$. We are given that the frame is 2 inches wide, so we can say that the radius of the frame and photo combined is $4 + 2 = 6$. So the area of the frame and photo combined must be $\pi r2 = \pi 62 = 36\pi$. Finally, to get the area of only the frame, we subtract the area of the photo from the area of the frame and photo combined, giving us $36\pi - 16\pi = 20\pi$.

8. B

Picking numbers makes this problem easier to work with. Rather than dealing with fractions of the business, say that there are 100 total shares. At the beginning of the problem, the 4 women each own 20 shares and the man owns 20 shares. One woman sells $\frac{1}{2}$ of her part of the business, 10 shares, to the man, and another woman sells $1 - \frac{1}{4} = \frac{3}{4}$ of her part of the business, $20(\frac{3}{4}) = 15$ shares to the man. Now the man owns $20 + 10 + 15 = 45$ shares out of the total 100 shares in the business. $\frac{45}{100} = \frac{9}{20}$, so the man now owns $\frac{9}{20}$ of the business.

9. 15

This is a simple plug-in, but make sure you write out every step so as to avoid a careless error. This is especially important in the Grid-ins. If $y = 2$, the expression $(5 - y)(y + 3)$ becomes $(5 - 2)(2 + 3)$. Remember to do the calculations inside the parentheses first. $5 - 2$ is 3 and $2 + 3$ is 5 so $(5 - 2)(2 + 3) = 3 \times 5 = 15$, so put 15 in the grid.

10. 9.43

If the daily rate is $18.99, then the price for a week, or 7 days, is $7 \times \$18.99 = \$132.93$. Since the weekly rate is less, only $123.50, you can save $\$132.93 - \$123.50 = \$9.43$ by renting at the weekly rate.

11. 13 < length < 15

The first thing to do is to put the numbers 4, 5, and 12 in the appropriate places in the figure. Now you should see that you have the lengths of 2 sides of triangle BCD. Since BCD is a right triangle, you can use the Pythagorean theorem to figure out the length of the hypotenuse, but if you've memorized the common Pythagorean triplets you don't have to do that—you'll immediately recognize that this is a 5-12-13 right triangle, and so the length of BD is 13. The length of AC is $4 + 5 = 9$, so the triangle ACD has legs of lengths 9 and 12. Again, you can use the Pythagorean theorem to find the length of the hypotenuse, but you should notice that ACD is a multiple of the 3-4-5 right triangle, and AD has length 15. If you draw in point E in the figure between A and B, you'll see that DE will be longer than BD but shorter than AD, or greater than 13 but less than 15. So any number between 13 and 15, such as 14, is a possible answer.

12. 15/4 or 3.75

If you need $\frac{3}{4}$ of a cup of drink mix for 2 quarts of water, then you need more than $\frac{3}{4}$ of a cup of drink mix for 10 quarts of water. How much more? Since $2 \times 5 = 10$, you have 5 times as much water, so you also need 5 times as much drink mix. $5 \times \frac{3}{4} = \frac{15}{4}$, so grid in $\frac{15}{4}$ (in the form of $\frac{15}{4}$).

13. 166

The sum of the three angles of the triangle must be 180°. One angle measures 31°, but you don't know the measures of the other two angles in the triangle. However, the interior angle of the triangle on top lies on a straight line with an angle measuring 45°, so that interior angle must measure $180° - 45° = 135°$. If 2 angles of a triangle measure 135° and 31°, then the third angle measures $180° - 135° - 31° = 14°$. The 14° angle lies on a straight line with the $x°$ angle, so $14° + x° = 180°$, and $x = 166$.

If you remembered that any exterior angle of a triangle has the same measure as the sum of the two opposite interior angles, you could have saved a few steps. Once you figure out that the top angle of the triangle is 135°, you know that $x° = 135° + 31°$, and therefore $x = 166$.

14. $0.5 < y < 0.625$

The only thing you know about y is that it is between $\frac{1}{2}$ and $\frac{5}{8}$. $\frac{1}{2}$ is the same as $\frac{4}{8}$, so y is between $\frac{4}{8}$ and $\frac{5}{8}$. You can't grid a fraction like $4\frac{1}{2} \over 8$, but you can change $\frac{4}{8}$ to $\frac{8}{16}$ and $\frac{5}{8}$ to $\frac{10}{16}$. That gives you an obvious value for y; since y is between $\frac{8}{16}$ and $\frac{10}{16}$, it could be $\frac{9}{16}$, so that's one possible number to grid in. You could also solve this question by converting $\frac{1}{2}$ and $\frac{5}{8}$ to decimals. If you convert $\frac{1}{2}$ to .5 and $\frac{5}{8}$ to .625, you can grid in any number greater .5 and less than .625. For example, you can grid in .6.

15. 46

The average rate of speed is the total distance traveled divided by the total hours traveled. Melanie drove at 40 miles per hour for 2 hours, for a total of 40×2 or 80 miles. If she increased her speed by 25%, then she increased her speed by 25% of 40, or 10, so her new speed was $40 + 10 = 50$. So, she drove at 50 miles per hour for the next 3 hours, for a total of $50 \times 3 = 150$ miles. She went 80 miles and then 150 miles, for a total of 230 miles, and she drove for 2 hours and then for 3 hours, for a total of 5 hours. Her average rate for the trip was 230 miles divided by 5 hours, or 46 miles per hour.

16. 175

There are three types of dealers at this convention—dealers who sell only stamps, dealers who sell only coins, and dealers who sell both stamps and coins. The total number of dealers is 500. You're given the number of two out of the three types of dealers—there are 127 that sell both stamps and coins, and 198 that sell only stamps. Since there are only three types of dealers, $127 + 198 +$ the number of dealers who sell only coins $= 500$, and so the number of dealers who sell only coins is $500 - 198 - 127 = 175$.

17. 46

Since the small square has a side of length 2, the area of the square must be 2^2, or 4. The larger square has a side of length 6, so its area is 6^2, or 36. The shaded part of square $ABCD$ is then $36 - 4$, or 32. The triangle is a right triangle with both legs of length 6, so the area of the triangle is $\frac{1}{2} \times 6 \times 6$, or 18. The shaded area of the triangle is then $18 - 4 = 14$. The total shaded area is $32 + 14$, or 46, so grid in 46.

18. 11

If N and R added up to a number less than 10, the problem would look different, something like:

$$\begin{array}{r} NR \\ \underline{RN} \\ XX \end{array}$$

Since it doesn't look like that, $N + R$ must be greater than 10. The best way to proceed from here is to try different pairs of numbers for R and N, and see what you get for B and C (keeping in mind that N, R, A, B, and C are different digits.) If you try setting either N or R equal to 9, you'll notice that you won't get different digits for all five variables. For example, if $R = 9$ and $N = 7$:

$$\begin{array}{r} 79 \\ \underline{97} \\ 176 \end{array}$$

Since there is always a 1 carried over into the tens' place, if $R = 9$ then the tens' column will add up to $9 + N + 1$, or $10 + N$. The sum $10 + N$ has the same units' digit as N, so B and N will be the same if $R = 9$. The same thing happens if $N = 9$, only R and B turn out to be the same. If you try the next largest combination of numbers for N and R, which is 7 and 8, B and C turn out to be 6 and 5, so $B + C = 11$. Any smaller values for N and R will result in smaller values for B and C, so the greatest possible value of $B + C$ is 11.

SECTION 6

1. C

This sentence tests your knowledge of the sequence of tenses. By the time the speaker graduates from college in the future, her brother *will have been* practicing law—you need the future perfect tense. (C) expresses the sequence correctly. All the remaining choices have incorrect tenses. (B) places this action in the past. (D) makes it inappropriately conditional. (E) places it in the present.

2. C

The intervening phrase and clause make it difficult to see that the subject and verb don't agree. The plural subject *historians* needs a plural verb, so *includes* should be *include*. (B) incorrectly changes *includes* to the past tense. (C) and (D) both correct this problem, but only (C) keeps the correct relative pronoun. (D) incorrectly changes the subjective *who* to the objective *whom*. (E) doesn't correct the subject-verb problem and changes the idiomatically correct *more than* to *at least*, which changes the meaning.

3. C

Nancy illogically compares Marcel Proust's novel with other writers. Nancy should compare Proust's novel with other novels, as in (C), (D), and (E). Only (C) makes that change without introducing new errors. (D) illogically changes the comparison *more brilliant* (which is correct because two things are compared) to *brilliant opposed to*. (E) changes the correct relative pronoun *which* to *whom*—perhaps thinking that the authors, not the books, are compared. (B) also introduces that mistake, and incorrectly changes the second clause to the past tense.

4. B

The past tense of the irregular verb *to see* is *saw*. (B) and (D) correct this problem, but (D) introduces another error by changing *arriving* to *have arrived*. (C) and (E) illogically change the correct *watching* to *who watch*. (C) also doesn't correct the original problem and (E) incorrectly changes *arriving* to *arrived*.

5. A

This sentence is correct as written. (B) illogically changes *to discover* to the past tense *to have discovered*. (C) incorrectly adds the preposition *in* (the species don't congregate in the floor). (D) needlessly adds the preposition *from*. (E) incorrectly changes *that* to *who*.

6. C

In this sentence we must sort through all the prepositions to see that *in an effort at avoiding* is not good, idiomatic English. The correct phrase is *in an effort to avoid*. (C), (D), and (E) all make this change. However, (D) and (E) distort the meaning. (D) is incorrect because fans are not on the team. (E) switches the phrases *in the stadium* and *between fans* which would mean that the altercations happen in more than one stadium.

7. A

Look through the answer choices: all except (E) focus on the phrase *a means to attract*. Is that idiomatically correct? Yes, *a strategy to attract* is correct. (B), (C), and (D) alter the phrase. (C) also changes the adjective *elderly* to *elder*. (E) rearranges the introductory phrase so that the votes incorrectly modify the social security adjustment.

8. D

The words *bright lights* interrupt the subject and verb, making the agreement problem difficult to see. The singular subject *configuration* agrees with the singular verb *was*. (D) and (E) make this change but (E) omits the transition word *but*. (B) and (C) don't address the agreement problem and (C) changes the contrasting transition word *but* to *and*.

9. B

The plural pronoun *their* actually refers to the singular subject *band*. (B) and (C) correctly change *their* to *its*. (C) incorrectly changes the preposition *of* to *for*. The expression *methods of providing* is idiomatically correct. Neither (D) nor (E) address the pronoun problem. They both also change the infinitive *to determine* to *to determining* which is not standard English.

10. A

This is a complex sentence, so break it down to see if it is correct. (B) changes *had begun* (which is correctly in the past perfect tense) to the incorrect form *had began*. (C) illogically puts the second clause in the future tense. (D) incorrectly changes *later* (which is good standard written English) to the illogical *afterwards*. (E) changes the subject of the sentence from the conductor to the orchestra, altering the meaning.

11. D

The sentence is a run-on. (B) and (C) are also run-ons. (E) fixes the run-on, but the comma is incorrect. (D) is clear and concise, and it is the correct answer.

12. A

It's especially important to check subject-verb agreement when a verb is separated from its subject. The subject is the singular *heron*, but the verb is the plural *live*. To correct this, you would change *live* to *lives*. *Most* (B) is correctly in the superlative form, since all parts of the United States are compared. (C) is a idiomatically correct. (D) uses *both* correctly with *and*.

13. D

Susan compares the home team's warm-ups to the visiting team. She should compare the warm-ups of both teams. (D) is your answer. The phrase *liked watching* in (A) is correctly in the past tense. (B) uses the correct relative pronoun. In (C), the phrase *more interesting* works because two things are compared.

14. C

The intervening phrase *of Viking settlements and lifestyles* interrupts the subject and verb. The singular subject *pattern* doesn't agree with the plural verb *were*. The phrase *by tracing* (A) is idiomatically correct. The verb *determined* (B) is correctly in the past tense. The adverb *generally* (D) correctly modifies the adjective *similar*.

15. B

This sentence sets up a contrast between what the recipe required and what Chad did. However, the conjunction *and* indicates an addition rather than a contrast and should be replaced with a word like *but*. In (A), *actually* is an adverb correctly used to modify the verb, and *called for* is an idiomatic expression meaning *needed in the circumstances*. (C) sets up the right causal relationship required by the meaning of the sentence. (D) is idiomatically correct.

16. E

Read all sentences carefully looking for common errors, but remember that about 20 percent will be error-free. (A) is the correct word to express the contrast that the sentence sets up. (B) is correctly the past tense. (C) is a phrase that indicates an example is being given. (D) is idiomatically correct after the verb *attempt*. (E) is the correct choice since this sentence is correct as written.

17. A

When there are underlined pronouns in a Usage question, check to see that they have clear antecedents. The pronoun *they* doesn't. You can guess that *they* are the people of India, but that would be only a guess since the sentence doesn't provide that information. (B) is correctly used here. In (C), the past tense verb is correct. In (D), the conjunction *and* correctly expresses a continuation of the idea that precedes it.

18. B

The action took place in the past, and should use the simple past tense *saw* instead of the past participle of the verb *to see* (*seen*). The verbs *waiting* (A) and *walking* (C) are in the correct form, and the phrase *to stop traffic* (D) is idiomatically correct.

19. C

The plural subject *plays* doesn't agree with the singular verb *expresses*. (C) should read *express*. The infinitive verb *to produce* (A) is correct. The phrases *that expresses* (B) and *has had* (D) are in the correct tense and idiomatically correct.

20. B

The phrase *claim hearing* is not idiomatically correct. (B) should read *claim to have heard*. The contrasting transition word *while* (A) is used appropriately as is the adverb *truly* (D). The phrase *such a person* is idiomatically correct.

21. B

The preposition *to* should follow the phrase *in an attempt*. The phrase *at creating* (B) should read *to create*. The verb initiated (A) is correctly in the present tense. The phrases *of team spirit* (C) and *in the office* (D) use the correct prepositions.

22. D

Did efforts *about* democracy sound correct when you read this sentence? Probably not. What you would need is something like *efforts on behalf of*. In (A), the adverb *as* is correctly used to modify the verb. In (B), the verb tense is correct—past perfect, which indicates that something happened before something else happened. Abadi got the Nobel Prize before her colleagues praised her. (C) correctly uses the simple past.

23. B

Be sure that the verbs in the sentence correctly express the time of the action. This sentence contains a clear indication of time—1906, which is in the past. Anything that happened in 1906 is done. The verb tenses should express this completeness. (B) should be in the simple past tense— *leveled*. (A) is idiomatically correct. (C) uses the right words and the correct preposition. (D) uses the correct tense—the simple past.

24. C

The phrase *absolute shamefaced* has an adjective modifying an adjective (*shamefaced*). The phrase should read *absolutely shamefaced*. The phrases *failure to* (A), *went about* (B), and *only a few* (D) are all idiomatically correct.

25. C

Reversing the sentence order can help you find the error. Does it make sense to say *the damaging effects of cigarette smoking has become recognized*? No. The plural subject *effects* takes the plural verb *have*, rather than *has* (C). The transition word *while* (A) correctly sets up a contrast. The verb *has been known* (B) is in the correct tense because it takes place before the second part of the sentence. Therefore, the past participle *become* (D) is also in the correct tense (you can also reverse the order to say *the damaging effects have become known*).

26. E

The sentence is correct as written. The verb *maintains* (A) agrees with the singular subject *FBI* and is correctly in the present tense. The prepositions *for* (B) and *in* (D) correctly follow *maintains* and *interested*, respectively. The pronoun *they* (C) clearly refers to *citizens*.

27. D

When three people are being compared, the superlative phrase *most* should be used. (D) should read *most abstract*, rather than *more abstract*. The phrase *in many ways* (A) is idiomatically correct. (B) is an idiomatically correct phrase, and *similar* is correctly used to modify *aspects*. The verb *was* (C) is correctly in the past tense.

28. E

The sentence is correct as written. (A) correctly uses the adverb. (B) correctly uses the superlative, since all choreographers are compared, and *inventive* correctly modifies the noun *choreographers*. (C) is correctly in the past tense and is the correct form of the irregular verb, and the noun *approach* takes the preposition *to* (D).

29. A

The plural noun *Germans* is close to the verb but is not the subject. The subject *toppling* is singular, and so (A) should be the singular *is*. The phrases *probably seen* (B) and *most felicitous* (D) are idiomatically correct, and the pronoun *them* (C) is correctly plural and in the objective case (*they* wouldn't work).

30. D

The paragraph is in the past tense but *she tells me* is present tense. The author is telling a story about what happened last year so the mother's action should be in past tense. (D) is correct. (B) and (C) don't address the tense issue. (B) unnecessarily substitutes *my mother* for *she* and (C) incorrectly uses the causal word *because*.

31. D

Sentence 7 introduces the ambiguous pronoun *they* and uses the passive voice. (D) correctly substitutes *the hooligans* for *they* and uses the present tense. (B) doesn't address the pronoun problem. (C) is redundant and uses the past tense. (E) substitutes the football fans, instead of the hooligans, for *they*.

32. C

The correct answer should clarify sentence 12's relationship with sentence 11. Sentence 11 offers one explanation offered by *some*. Sentence 12 is another possibility, and (C) indicates that. (A) is incorrect because there is no indication this is the author's opinion. (B) introduces the ambiguous pronoun *they*. (D) and (E) set up incorrect relationships: contrasting and causal, respectively.

33. D

Sentence 14 is a fragment, with no verb in an independent clause. (D) uses the past tense *indicated*, which agrees with the prior sentence. (B) is still a fragment. (C) incorrectly uses the present progressive tense and (E) incorrectly uses the past perfect tense.

34. D

In sentence 13, the words *one argument . . . rang . . . true* tell you the author is offering a conclusion. What is the conclusion? It's set off by the colon: *poverty was an underlying cause*. Sentence 14, adding data about the connection between poverty and violence, supports that conclusion.

35. E

The sentence offers a conclusion based on the economic data in sentence 14, so it should conclude the passage. (A) would interrupt the related ideas in sentences 5 and 6. (B) is too soon; the problem has just been introduced, but the ways England has tried to solve the problem haven't been discussed. (C) is still too early—poverty isn't mentioned again until sentence 13. (D) is incorrect because the next sentence begins with the contrasting transition word *but*; however, the inserted sentence and sentence 14 do not contrast.

SECTION 7

1. B

So many stops in some particular amount of time led to only the most ------- impression about the places the tour visited. There's a connection between the amount of time spent visiting, and the impression of the places visited. So the two words that will fill in the blanks here must be roughly synonymous. Only choice (B) works here. There were so many stops in such a *brief* amount of time that only a *cursory* (superficial or hasty) impression of places was gained. (D)'s second word fits the blank, but (D)'s first word, *sufficient*, isn't a rough synonym and doesn't fit. In (A), many stops probably wouldn't leave a *lasting* impression. Nor would a tour at breakneck speed necessarily leave (C) a *favorable* impression on travelers.

2. E

The peoples discussed in this sentence were formerly -------, but now they've lost their land. They're living in ------- settlements. So we need two adjectives that are roughly the opposite of each other. The answer here is (E). Peoples who were once *nomadic*, or roaming freely without a permanent home, have moved into *permanent* settlements as their land got swallowed up by growing cities. *Fervid*, in choice (D), means passionate.

3. B

For the first blank, we want something that describes sleeping tablets—rule out (E) right away, since *stimulating* is the one word here that most definitely would not describe sleeping tablets. For the second blank, we want a word that characterizes the effect of those sleeping tablets, an effect that resulted in a woman feeling groggy the day after taking them. Something like *strong* or *intense* would be good. The best choice here is (B), because *soporific* means sleep-inducing—what word could be better to describe sleeping pills? *Pronounced*, meaning unmistakable or obvious, fits closely with our prediction. *Salubrious* in choice (C) means healthful.

4. E

Here we want a vocabulary word meaning something like *unable to accept the authority of others*. Choice (A), *compliant*, means the exact opposite of this; a *compliant* person is one who bends easily to the will of others. (B) *slothful* means lazy. In choice (C), *conscientious* means responsible, hardly a word to describe Davis. (E) is correct because *recalcitrant* describes someone who refuses to obey authority.

5. D

Although tells us that there will be some sort of contrast with the fact that the actress has lived in a large city her whole life. The contrast will be that, despite her upbringing in a city, she still manages to be successful at portraying a humble farm girl. Therefore, she must be quite a good performer—the first blank will be a positive word, describing what a good actress she is. The second blank must be a word that explains how successfully she portrays the farm girl. The best choice here is (D), because a *consummate* actress is very skilled, while an *incarnation* is the embodiment of something or someone—you'd have to be a pretty good actress to become the embodiment of the character you're playing. In choice (C), *nemesis* means enemy.

6. B

Notice the word *hitherto* in this sentence. It means *previously*. The board members had previously upheld worthy ideals. This implies that they no longer do. For the second blank, then, we need a word like *rejection*: the board's recent decision must be a rejection of the previous worthy ideals. In the first blank, we need a word to describe what the chairman was doing as he described the board's decision so negatively. So the first blank must mean something like *criticized*. (C) fits in the first blank, but not in the second. Remember to try both words in the blanks! Choice (B) works with both blanks: to *lament* is to regret, while a *negation* is what it sounds like, a rejection. The chairman lamented the decision of the board, describing it as a *negation* of worthy ideals. This was the only choice with two negative words that fit the context. To *endorse*, in choice (D), is to offer one's support, while a *renunciation* is a giving up or casting off of something like values. Finally, in (E), a *repudiation* is similar to a *renunciation*—it is a denial or rejection of something or someone.

THE JEFFERSON/DOUGLASS PASSAGES

These two passages may seem hard because of their old-fashioned language. But the main points should be clear on a quick read-through. Jefferson emphasizes the natural and social riches of the United States (paragraph 1), supports the idea of limited government (end of paragraph 1), and states the principle of equal justice for all (paragraph 2). Douglass, speaking as an escaped slave, stresses that slaves do not have the freedoms celebrated on the Fourth of July. (If you don't remember who Douglass was, you may not catch the point of his speech until the end of paragraph 2, where it is stated directly. Always be patient—the drift of a passage often becomes clearer as you go along.) In paragraph 2, Douglass says that the case against slavery should not have to be argued, because freedom and liberty are basic American principles. In paragraph 3, he concludes that as long as slavery exists, the Fourth of July is a *sham*.

Before going to the questions it can be helpful to think for a second about how the two passages relate—an important paired-passage strategy. You should come up with something like: Jefferson is stating American principles, but Douglass is saying they haven't been applied in practice. In a double passage, you'll have several questions on passage 1, followed by several on passage 2, followed by some asking for comparisons. Since answering the questions is the priority, be sure to read the first passage, do the questions that relate to it, then read the second passage and answer the rest of the questions.

7. C

In the cited lines, Jefferson is saying that Americans feel entitled to respect, or *honor and confidence*, on the basis of *actions* rather than *birth*. (C) is a paraphrase of this idea. Remember that the United States didn't have a hereditary aristocracy like European countries—that's what Jefferson is talking about. (A), (D), and (E) bring in ideas not mentioned in the excerpt—immigration (A), mutual help (D), family (E). (B)'s idea of demanding respect is wrong; Jefferson feels respect has to be based on actions.

8. A

In this Vocabulary-in-Context question, choice (B) might've jumped out at you. But remember, the correct answer is probably not going to be the most common or familiar definition of the word, so don't be too hasty. Find the word in the passage and see how it's used there. In this case, Jefferson is talking about what his duties as president involve, or *include*. Choices (A), (C), and (E) give you other common synonyms for *comprehend*, but they don't fit the context. (D) does not mean "comprehend."

9. D

Again, look at the context. Read the rest of the sentence in question, and the sentence before it. This should clarify that Jefferson is about to state what he believes to be the essential principles of government. Further, he's going to state them in the most brief possible way, which is what choice (D) says. (A) and (C) refer to Jefferson's mention of *limitations*, but all Jefferson says is that he won't mention *limitations* or exceptions to the general principles. (B) is wrong because *them* in Jefferson's sentence refers to the principles of government, not to people who oppose the principles. Finally, Jefferson never mentions *bureaucracy*, choice (E).

10. E

Ignore the choices for the moment and look at the context: Jefferson is talking about equal justice for all, regardless of something religious or political. This suggests that Jefferson is talking about people's beliefs, creeds, opinions, or convictions. (E) gives you the word that fits this context. (A), (B), and (C) are all vocabulary-list meanings for *persuasion*, but they don't fit the context. *Authority* (D) is often seen as the opposite of persuasion; it has nothing to do with Jefferson's meaning here.

11. A

The next two questions take us through the Douglass excerpt. This one asks about paragraph 1, in which Douglass is contrasting the American celebration of independence and liberty with the bondage of slaves. The overall idea is that the celebrations are a *mockery* and an *irony* (line 56) because they don't apply to everyone. In other words, they are hypocritical (A). (B) and (C) refer to emotions Douglass undoubtedly feels, but is not expressing here. (D) is an idea he never expresses at all. (E) interprets *drag a man in fetters* (chains) literally—force a slave to attend. Don't go for a simple paraphrase like this. Go back and get the meaning in context. Douglass is speaking figuratively; he doesn't mean he's actually being dragged to the celebration in chains.

12. D

In the cited sentence, the *millions* who are wailing are the slaves, while the *shouts* come from Fourth of July celebrants. Douglass uses this contrast to emphasize the differences between the lives and attitudes of slaves and free Americans (D). (A) and (C) twist the meaning of Douglass's mention of *yesterday* and *today* in these lines. Choice (B) goes against Douglass's overall point, which is to point out the hypocrisy of Fourth of July celebrations. And while the problem of slavery is not yet solved, Douglass doesn't imply it is *unsolvable* (E).

13. B

Always put the detail in context by rereading the surrounding lines. Here, the author's referring to the *treason* of betraying the American slaves by failing to protest during July 4th celebrations. Douglass is saying that he'd be committing *treason* to them by not speaking out. So in this example, *treason* refers to acting against the needs of a social group, i.e., the slaves. (A) and (D) may have sounded tempting as common definitions of *treason*, but they don't express what the author means in this context.

14. C

Rereading the context, you can see that Douglass is emphasizing throughout paragraph 2 the contradiction between July 4th celebrations and the condition of the slaves. When he describes *American Slavery* as *my subject*, he's highlighting this paradox, and also describing what he's about to talk about next—literally outlining what the subject of the rest of his speech is. (A) is wrong because the topic of slavery is not unexpected—it's what Douglass has been discussing all along. (B) is wrong because Douglass isn't talking about slavery through the ages. (D) is wrong because Douglass suggests no immediate answer to the problem. Finally, there's no suggestion that Douglass has to learn more about his topic (E).

15. A

Again, put the detail in context—who or what is *impudent* here? Douglass is contrasting political speeches with the actual conditions that slaves endured, making (A) the correct answer. (B) is too general; (C) is off the point. (D) actually contradicts Douglass's explicit point of view. Finally, (E) is a distortion—according to the passage, it's the hypocritical speeches of politicians that railed against tyrants.

16. B

In passage 1, Jefferson deals with the themes of liberty and equality as the necessary principles of good government—he's describing these qualities as the bedrock of the Constitution. Based on passage 1, you can infer that he would respond to Douglass's questions about liberty in a similar manner—by agreeing that these are staples in any democracy. None of the other choices is consistent with any statement made in passage 1—remember, you've always got to find evidence for your answer in the passage.

17. B

The last three questions ask for comparisons. In this one, you're asked how Douglass would respond to Jefferson's stated principle, *equal and exact justice to all men*. Douglass gives the answer when he says slaves do not enjoy the liberties of other Americans (paragraph 1). So he would respond that the principle is not being carried out in reality (B). (A), (C), and (E) all imply that the principle is invalid. But Douglass's argument is that a principle that is valid in general isn't being followed for African Americans. (E) is a possible response, but (B) sums up Douglass's overall point better.

18. C

Since each of the answer choices uses the word *both*, you should be looking for a similarity between the speeches. Jefferson states a general principle; Douglass points out how it has been violated. The only point that both agree on is that equal justice is desirable, choice (C). Choices (A) and (D) describe Douglass's speech as a whole; (B) is implied in Douglass's final sentence—but Jefferson's speech never discusses these topics. (E), on the other hand, is true of Jefferson's speech, but not Douglass's.

19. C

Summarizing each passage's point of view, you'd probably argue that Jefferson was optimistic about equality in the United States (having just established the Constitution), but that Douglass was critical of United States standards on equality 50 years later. Choice (C) picks up this contrast. None of the other choices captures the appropriate positive/negative answer required.

SECTION 8

1. D

The graph shows you the sales of all the toys for the months April, May, and June. If you look at the sales for those 3 months, you'll see that the bar for April goes up to 40, the bar for May goes up to 10, and the bar for June goes up to 30. The title on the vertical axis says "Sales (in millions of dollars)" so that's what those numbers represent: $40 million in sales for April, $10 million for May, and $30 million for June, for a total of $40 + 10 + 30 = 80$ million dollars total in sales for those months. The total sales were $80 million and the April sales were $40 million, and you want to know what percent of the total the April sales were. Since it says "of the total," $80 million is the whole and the $40 million is the part, so using the formula *Percent × Whole = Part*, you get Percent $\times 80 = 40$, or Percent $= \frac{40}{80} = \frac{1}{2} = 50$, answer choice (D).

2. E

If you remembered that any number squared is positive, a quick look at the answer choices would tell you that choice (E), x^2y^2, will be positive for any nonzero values of x and y. If you didn't remember that you should make a note of it, since it's a very important concept. You can also solve this one by picking numbers. If xy is negative, then either x or y is negative and the other is positive since a negative times a positive equals a negative. Picking a couple of pairs of numbers for x and y will tell you that both $x - y$ and $y - x$ can be either positive or negative depending on the exact values of x and y; x^2y can be negative if y is negative and xy^2 can be negative if x is negative. However, any values you pick for x and y will give you a positive number for x^2y^2, so again choice (E) is correct.

3. B

Don't get confused by the strange words! They're just symbols for an unknown quantity, the same as the letters x and y, which we usually use as symbols for unknown quantities. If 1 fedi = 3 glecks, then multiplying both sides by 2 tells you that 2 fedis = 6 glecks. You're given that 1 bora = 2 fedis, so 1 bora must be equal to 6 glecks. Now that we know the relationship between boras and glecks (whatever they are), the rest is easy. 1 bora is equal to 6 glecks, so how many boras equal 48 glecks? Since $6 \times 8 = 48$, just multiply both sides of the equation 1 bora = 6 glecks by 8 to get 8 boras = 48 glecks. So the correct answer is 8, answer choice (B).

4. C

If algebra confuses you, try picking numbers. If $f = 10$ then there are 10 freshmen in the class. If 5 freshmen drop the class then there are $10 - 5 = 5$ freshmen left in the class. The number of sophomores is 3 times the number of freshmen left, or 3 times $5 = 15$. So there are 15 sophomores in the class and $s = 15$. Which of the answer choices work with $f = 10$ and $s = 15$? All you have to do is plug those numbers into the 5 choices and you'll find that only choice (C) works and is therefore correct.

To do it algebraically, just translate one step at a time. There are f freshmen in the class, but if 5 freshmen drop the class there are $f - 5$ freshmen left. The number of sophomores is 3 times the number of freshmen left, or 3 times $f - 5$, or $3(f - 5)$. So $s = 3(f - 5)$, answer choice (C).

5. E

The perimeter of triangle ABC is $AC + AB + 7$, and the perimeter of triangle ACD is $AC + 5 + 6$. You can combine that with the given information that the perimeter of triangle ABC is 4 more than the perimeter of triangle ACD to get $AC + AB + 7 = AC + 5 + 6 + 4$. Adding the numbers on the right side of the equation gives you $AC + AB + 7 = AC + 15$ and subtracting 7 from both sides gives you $AC + AB = AC + 8$. If you subtract AC from both sides you get $AB = 8$. That's all you need to find the perimeter of $ABCD$, which is $5 + 6 + 7 + 8$, or 26, answer choice (E).

6. D

Notice that at each corner of the cube, a triangular face like triangular face ABC is being made. How many corners are there? There are 8 corners; 4 of the corners are on the top and 4 of them are on the bottom. After all 8 triangular faces are made, a part of each of the original 6 faces of the cube remains. The total number of faces of the resulting stone must be $6 + 8$, or 14.

7. D

We want the average of the first 30 positive integers. Whenever we want the average of a group of evenly spaced numbers, we just have to take the average of the smallest number and the largest number. If you have difficulty seeing this, consider a simpler problem. Consider the average of 1, 2, 3, and 4. The average of 1, 2, 3, and 4 is $\frac{1 + 2 + 3 + 4}{4} = \frac{10}{4} = \frac{5}{2} = 2\frac{1}{2}$, using the average formula: $\text{Average} = \frac{\text{Sum of the terms}}{\text{Numbers of terms}}$. What happens if we just take the average of the smallest number, 1, and the largest number, 4? We get $\frac{1 + 4}{2} = \frac{5}{2} = 2\frac{1}{2}$, which is what we got by finding the average the other way. So the average of the first 30 positive integers is just the average of 1 and 30, which $\frac{1 + 30}{2} = \frac{31}{2} = 15\frac{1}{2}$. None of the answer choices is $15\frac{1}{2}$, but $15\frac{1}{2}$ is 15.5. The average is 15.5.

8. B

You may notice that the figure looks like a rectangle with a quadrilateral piece hanging off of it. That means that you can find the area of the figure by adding the area of the rectangle and the area of the quadrilateral. The quadrilateral piece can be divided into a rectangle and a triangle. It may help to draw in some dotted lines to represent this:

The larger rectangle on the top has length 10 and width 9. Since the vertical line segment on the right is labeled 12, the length of the part of that line that is not part of the larger rectangle must be $12 - 9$, or 3, so write that on your figure. The short horizontal line in the middle of the figure has length 4, the small rectangle on the bottom has length 2, and the entire figure has a top horizontal length of 10, so the dotted horizontal line that is a leg of the right triangle must have length $10 - 4 - 2$, or 4.

Now we've got the lengths of all the pieces of the figure:

The rectangle on the top has an area of $9 \times 10 = 90$. The small rectangle on the bottom right has length 3 and width 2, so its area is 6, and the triangle has legs 4 and 3, so its area is also 6. The total area of the figure is $90 + 6 + 6 = 102$, answer choice (B).

9. A

If 60 cookies are distributed among x campers, then each camper gets $\frac{60}{x}$ cookies. When the same number of cookies is divided among fewer campers, then each camper gets 2 more than $\frac{60}{x}$ cookies, or $\frac{60}{x} + 2$. This number of cookies per camper is also equal to 60 cookies divided by 8 less than the original number of campers, or $\frac{60}{x-8}$. This gives us the equation $\frac{60}{x} + 2 = \frac{60}{x-8}$. Unfortunately, this equation is not in the same form as the equations in the answer choices, so you'll have to do some algebra:

$$\frac{60}{x} + 2 = \frac{60}{x-8}$$

$$\frac{60 + 2x}{x} = \frac{60}{x-8}$$

$$(60 + 2x)(x - 8) = 60x$$

$$60x - 480 + 2x^2 - 16x = 60x$$

$$2x^2 - 16x - 480 = 0$$

$$x^2 - 8x - 240 = 0, \text{ answer choice (A)}.$$

10. D

All they're asking here is—how many different pairs can you make from a group of 6? Let's call the 6 students A, B, C, D, E, and F; A can be joined with the others to make the 5 pairs AB, AC, AD, AE, and AF. Since you've already paired A and B you don't have to do it again, so just pair B up with the rest of the group to get BC, BD, BE, and BF. That's 4 new pairs. C has already been matched up with A and B, so the new pairs that involve C are CD, CE, and CF, for 3 new pairs. There are only 2 new pairs left for D, DE, and DF, and finally 1 more, EF. So, there's a total of $5 + 4 + 3 + 2 + 1 = 15$, choice (D).

11. D

$q = q^{-2} = \frac{1}{q^2}$

If $q = \frac{1}{q^2}$, then $q^3 = 1$ and $q = 1$.

12. B

Back solving is a great way to answer this question. Pick a set of p and n from the chart; then, plug them in to each given equation to see whether the pair works. If you would rather see how the equation was derived, you can follow the steps below. On test day, follow whichever approach gets you to the answer faster. The relationship between n and p can be expressed in the form $n = -kp + b$, where k and b are constants. There is a negative sign before k to indicate that as the price increases, the number of expected sales decreases. Pick two points from the chart and insert those values of p and n into this equation, then solve for k and b:

First point:

$10,000 = -k(.75) + b$

Second point:

$5,000 = -k(1.00) + b$

$5,000 = -k + b$

$5,000 + k = b$

Substitute:

$10,000 = -k(.75) + 5,000 + k$

$5,000 = k - .75k$

$5,000 = .25k$

$20,000 = k$

$25,000 = b$

$n = -20,000p + 25,000$

13. B

It's a good idea to know what the graphs of common equations such as $y = x^2$ look like, but if you forget or would like to double-check your answer, you can plug the x and y values of a few points on the graph into the given equations to see which one works. Be careful of using points like (0, 0), as they may work for several (or in this case, all) of the answer choices. In this case, some useful points to check are $(-2, 4)$ and $(2, 4)$: $4 = (-2)^2$ and $4 = 2^2$.

14. C

Let g = number of green tokens, and y = number of yellow tokens. The scores given in the problem can be written as $4g + 8y = 48$ and $6g + 4y = 32$. Both sides of the first equation can be divided by 4 to get $g + 2y = 12$. Subtract $2y$ from both sides to find $g = 12 - 2y$. Substitute this into the second equation to get $6(12 - 2y) + 4y = 72 - 12y + 4y = 32$. Solving for y, you find that $40 = 8y$, and $y = 5$.

15. C

Since there are variables in the answer choices, picking numbers is a good strategy for solving this problem. Since the question deals with percentages, 100 is a good number to pick for c. Pablo uses 30% of 100 cherries, that is $100(.3) = 30$ grams of cherries to make muffins. You don't need to know how many grams of cherries it takes to make a muffin or how many muffins Pablo makes. All you need to know is how many grams of cherries are available to make preserves with. $100 - 30 = 70$ grams of cherries are available to make preserves with. If each pint of preserves requires 7 grams of cherries (that is, if $p = 7$), Pablo can make 10 pints of preserves. Plug $c = 100$ and $p = 7$ into the answer choices to see which yields 10. $\frac{7c}{10p} = \frac{7(100)}{10(7)} = \frac{700}{70} = 10$, so (C) is correct.

16. B

If C is the price of one pound of cherries and G is the price of one pound of grapes, then $C = 2G$. The total cost of 32 pounds of cherries and 8 pounds of grapes is $32C + 8G$, and is also equal to $90. You can use the equations $C = 2G$ and $32C + 8G = 90$ to solve for C and G. Plugging $2G$ for C into the equation $32C + 8G = 90$, we have $32(2G) + 8G = 90$, $64G + 8G = 90$, $72G = 90$, and $G = \frac{90}{72} = \frac{5}{4} = 1.25$. $C = 2G$, so $C = 2(1.25) = 2.50$. Since 32 pounds of cherries and 8 pounds of grapes were sold, $\$2.50 \times 32 = \$80$ were made on the cherries, and $\$1.25 \times 8 = \$10$ were made on the grapes. That means that $\$80 - \$10 = \$70$ more was made on the cherries than on the grapes, answer choice (B).

SECTION 9

1. B

This sentence is a run-on—the part beginning with *they* starts an entirely new sentence. Therefore, look for the answer choice that fixes the run-on. (B) does so by simply inserting a semicolon. The other answer choices are also run-ons.

2. B

All of the incorrect answer choices contain mis-placed modifiers. (A), (D), and (E) say the *shock value utilized cacophony*. (C) says *a higher level utilized cacophony*. Clearly, you want the sentence to say that Webern or Webern's music utilized cacophony— the only answer choice to accomplish this is (B).

3. A

The answer choices that utilize semicolons must have independent clauses on both sides of the semicolon. (A) is the only choice that meets the requirement. (D) and (E) exchange the semicolon for a comma, but they are both incorrect. (D) adds a tense shift with the words *having been*, and (E) incorrectly uses a coordinating conjunction and a comma to separate an independent clause and a dependent clause.

4. D

(A) and (E) are comma splices—two independent clauses separated only by a comma. (C) adds the coordinating conjunction *and*, but it also adds *being*, which makes the second clause dependent and incorrect. (B) becomes very awkward by adding *with*. (D) is the best choice because it simply fixes the comma splice by adding the coordinating conjunction *and*.

5. E

(A) and (C) are run-on sentences; a coordinating conjunction separates two independent clauses without a comma. Look for the answer choice that is parallel with to *eventually run*. That answer choice is (E) because of the word *scale*.

6. D

(A) and (B) are run-on sentences because they have two independent clauses separated by *and* but do not have a comma before that conjunction. (E) does not make sense because the verb *defined* was changed to a noun, *definition*. Between (C) and (D), (D) is correct. (C) adds the word *had*, indicating that the Campbell's definition of the heroes and villains happened before his espousal of definitive ideas. Without a broader context, this does not make sense. (D) is correct because it extends the simple past tense structure of *espoused* to *defined*.

7. A

Look for the simplest (and shortest) answer choice. As long as that choice is grammatically correct, you can be sure it is the correct answer. In this case, that choice is (A). The other answer choices are all too wordy or overly complex.

8. E

For (A) and (D) to be technically correct, there needs to be a comma before *and*, as in (B). However, (E) is the most clear and concise way of expressing the sentence. (C) uses the semicolon correctly, but there needs to be a comma after *also*.

9. A

The original sentence is the best choice because it has a dependent clause that is related to the complete independent clause. The other answer choices do not have as good sentence structure.

10. B

The phrase *of which there are more than 40 breeds* is nonessential information and should be set apart with commas on both sides. The words *of which* are correct in starting the phrase. The words *in existence* in (E) are unnecessary.

11. A

The semicolon is used correctly with two independent clauses on both sides of the punctuation mark. (B) and (C) are run-on sentences. (D) and (E) do not contain two independent clauses.

12. B

This sentence uses a *not . . . but* word pair, so it requires parallel blocks of words around each half of the pair. The first block is *are not rejecting*, so the second block must be *are taking*. Don't be misled because *are* and *rejecting* are separated by the word *not*. *Are* is still a helping verb that works together with *rejecting*.

13. C

This sentence presents a list of comparisons. All items in a list must have parallel construction. Only (C) gives the last comparison an appearance parallel to the previous two comparisons. The word *producing* could have been repeated in all three comparisons. But since it wasn't repeated in the second comparison, it can't be repeated in the third one either.

14. D

This sentence uses a *both . . . and* pair, so it requires parallel blocks of words following each half of the pair. Only (D) has a second block of words—*how long it endures*—similar to the first block—*how many people it touches*.

SAT Practice Test Four
Answer Sheet

Remove (or photcopy) the answer sheet and use it to complete the practice test. See the answer key following the test when finished.

Start with number 1 for each section. If a section has fewer questions than answer spaces, leave the extra spaces blank.

SECTION 1

Section 1 is the writing section's essay component.
Lined pages on which you will write your essay can be found in that section.

SECTION 2

1. Ⓐ Ⓑ Ⓒ Ⓓ Ⓔ	11. Ⓐ Ⓑ Ⓒ Ⓓ Ⓔ	21. Ⓐ Ⓑ Ⓒ Ⓓ Ⓔ	31. Ⓐ Ⓑ Ⓒ Ⓓ Ⓔ
2. Ⓐ Ⓑ Ⓒ Ⓓ Ⓔ	12. Ⓐ Ⓑ Ⓒ Ⓓ Ⓔ	22. Ⓐ Ⓑ Ⓒ Ⓓ Ⓔ	32. Ⓐ Ⓑ Ⓒ Ⓓ Ⓔ
3. Ⓐ Ⓑ Ⓒ Ⓓ Ⓔ	13. Ⓐ Ⓑ Ⓒ Ⓓ Ⓔ	23. Ⓐ Ⓑ Ⓒ Ⓓ Ⓔ	33. Ⓐ Ⓑ Ⓒ Ⓓ Ⓔ
4. Ⓐ Ⓑ Ⓒ Ⓓ Ⓔ	14. Ⓐ Ⓑ Ⓒ Ⓓ Ⓔ	24. Ⓐ Ⓑ Ⓒ Ⓓ Ⓔ	34. Ⓐ Ⓑ Ⓒ Ⓓ Ⓔ
5. Ⓐ Ⓑ Ⓒ Ⓓ Ⓔ	15. Ⓐ Ⓑ Ⓒ Ⓓ Ⓔ	25. Ⓐ Ⓑ Ⓒ Ⓓ Ⓔ	35. Ⓐ Ⓑ Ⓒ Ⓓ Ⓔ
6. Ⓐ Ⓑ Ⓒ Ⓓ Ⓔ	16. Ⓐ Ⓑ Ⓒ Ⓓ Ⓔ	26. Ⓐ Ⓑ Ⓒ Ⓓ Ⓔ	36. Ⓐ Ⓑ Ⓒ Ⓓ Ⓔ
7. Ⓐ Ⓑ Ⓒ Ⓓ Ⓔ	17. Ⓐ Ⓑ Ⓒ Ⓓ Ⓔ	27. Ⓐ Ⓑ Ⓒ Ⓓ Ⓔ	37. Ⓐ Ⓑ Ⓒ Ⓓ Ⓔ
8. Ⓐ Ⓑ Ⓒ Ⓓ Ⓔ	18. Ⓐ Ⓑ Ⓒ Ⓓ Ⓔ	28. Ⓐ Ⓑ Ⓒ Ⓓ Ⓔ	38. Ⓐ Ⓑ Ⓒ Ⓓ Ⓔ
9. Ⓐ Ⓑ Ⓒ Ⓓ Ⓔ	19. Ⓐ Ⓑ Ⓒ Ⓓ Ⓔ	29. Ⓐ Ⓑ Ⓒ Ⓓ Ⓔ	39. Ⓐ Ⓑ Ⓒ Ⓓ Ⓔ
10. Ⓐ Ⓑ Ⓒ Ⓓ Ⓔ	20. Ⓐ Ⓑ Ⓒ Ⓓ Ⓔ	30. Ⓐ Ⓑ Ⓒ Ⓓ Ⓔ	40. Ⓐ Ⓑ Ⓒ Ⓓ Ⓔ

☐ # right in Section 2

☐ # wrong in Section 2

SECTION 3

1. Ⓐ Ⓑ Ⓒ Ⓓ Ⓔ	11. Ⓐ Ⓑ Ⓒ Ⓓ Ⓔ	21. Ⓐ Ⓑ Ⓒ Ⓓ Ⓔ	31. Ⓐ Ⓑ Ⓒ Ⓓ Ⓔ
2. Ⓐ Ⓑ Ⓒ Ⓓ Ⓔ	12. Ⓐ Ⓑ Ⓒ Ⓓ Ⓔ	22. Ⓐ Ⓑ Ⓒ Ⓓ Ⓔ	32. Ⓐ Ⓑ Ⓒ Ⓓ Ⓔ
3. Ⓐ Ⓑ Ⓒ Ⓓ Ⓔ	13. Ⓐ Ⓑ Ⓒ Ⓓ Ⓔ	23. Ⓐ Ⓑ Ⓒ Ⓓ Ⓔ	33. Ⓐ Ⓑ Ⓒ Ⓓ Ⓔ
4. Ⓐ Ⓑ Ⓒ Ⓓ Ⓔ	14. Ⓐ Ⓑ Ⓒ Ⓓ Ⓔ	24. Ⓐ Ⓑ Ⓒ Ⓓ Ⓔ	34. Ⓐ Ⓑ Ⓒ Ⓓ Ⓔ
5. Ⓐ Ⓑ Ⓒ Ⓓ Ⓔ	15. Ⓐ Ⓑ Ⓒ Ⓓ Ⓔ	25. Ⓐ Ⓑ Ⓒ Ⓓ Ⓔ	35. Ⓐ Ⓑ Ⓒ Ⓓ Ⓔ
6. Ⓐ Ⓑ Ⓒ Ⓓ Ⓔ	16. Ⓐ Ⓑ Ⓒ Ⓓ Ⓔ	26. Ⓐ Ⓑ Ⓒ Ⓓ Ⓔ	36. Ⓐ Ⓑ Ⓒ Ⓓ Ⓔ
7. Ⓐ Ⓑ Ⓒ Ⓓ Ⓔ	17. Ⓐ Ⓑ Ⓒ Ⓓ Ⓔ	27. Ⓐ Ⓑ Ⓒ Ⓓ Ⓔ	37. Ⓐ Ⓑ Ⓒ Ⓓ Ⓔ
8. Ⓐ Ⓑ Ⓒ Ⓓ Ⓔ	18. Ⓐ Ⓑ Ⓒ Ⓓ Ⓔ	28. Ⓐ Ⓑ Ⓒ Ⓓ Ⓔ	38. Ⓐ Ⓑ Ⓒ Ⓓ Ⓔ
9. Ⓐ Ⓑ Ⓒ Ⓓ Ⓔ	19. Ⓐ Ⓑ Ⓒ Ⓓ Ⓔ	29. Ⓐ Ⓑ Ⓒ Ⓓ Ⓔ	39. Ⓐ Ⓑ Ⓒ Ⓓ Ⓔ
10. Ⓐ Ⓑ Ⓒ Ⓓ Ⓔ	20. Ⓐ Ⓑ Ⓒ Ⓓ Ⓔ	30. Ⓐ Ⓑ Ⓒ Ⓓ Ⓔ	40. Ⓐ Ⓑ Ⓒ Ⓓ Ⓔ

☐ # right in Section 3

☐ # wrong in Section 3

Remove (or photocopy) this answer sheet and use it to complete the practice test.

Start with number 1 for each section. If a section has fewer questions than answer spaces, leave the extra spaces blank.

SECTION 4

1. Ⓐ Ⓑ Ⓒ Ⓓ Ⓔ   11. Ⓐ Ⓑ Ⓒ Ⓓ Ⓔ   21. Ⓐ Ⓑ Ⓒ Ⓓ Ⓔ   31. Ⓐ Ⓑ Ⓒ Ⓓ Ⓔ
2. Ⓐ Ⓑ Ⓒ Ⓓ Ⓔ   12. Ⓐ Ⓑ Ⓒ Ⓓ Ⓔ   22. Ⓐ Ⓑ Ⓒ Ⓓ Ⓔ   32. Ⓐ Ⓑ Ⓒ Ⓓ Ⓔ
3. Ⓐ Ⓑ Ⓒ Ⓓ Ⓔ   13. Ⓐ Ⓑ Ⓒ Ⓓ Ⓔ   23. Ⓐ Ⓑ Ⓒ Ⓓ Ⓔ   33. Ⓐ Ⓑ Ⓒ Ⓓ Ⓔ   ☐ # right in Section 4
4. Ⓐ Ⓑ Ⓒ Ⓓ Ⓔ   14. Ⓐ Ⓑ Ⓒ Ⓓ Ⓔ   24. Ⓐ Ⓑ Ⓒ Ⓓ Ⓔ   34. Ⓐ Ⓑ Ⓒ Ⓓ Ⓔ
5. Ⓐ Ⓑ Ⓒ Ⓓ Ⓔ   15. Ⓐ Ⓑ Ⓒ Ⓓ Ⓔ   25. Ⓐ Ⓑ Ⓒ Ⓓ Ⓔ   35. Ⓐ Ⓑ Ⓒ Ⓓ Ⓔ
6. Ⓐ Ⓑ Ⓒ Ⓓ Ⓔ   16. Ⓐ Ⓑ Ⓒ Ⓓ Ⓔ   26. Ⓐ Ⓑ Ⓒ Ⓓ Ⓔ   36. Ⓐ Ⓑ Ⓒ Ⓓ Ⓔ
7. Ⓐ Ⓑ Ⓒ Ⓓ Ⓔ   17. Ⓐ Ⓑ Ⓒ Ⓓ Ⓔ   27. Ⓐ Ⓑ Ⓒ Ⓓ Ⓔ   37. Ⓐ Ⓑ Ⓒ Ⓓ Ⓔ   ☐ # wrong in Section 4
8. Ⓐ Ⓑ Ⓒ Ⓓ Ⓔ   18. Ⓐ Ⓑ Ⓒ Ⓓ Ⓔ   28. Ⓐ Ⓑ Ⓒ Ⓓ Ⓔ   38. Ⓐ Ⓑ Ⓒ Ⓓ Ⓔ
9. Ⓐ Ⓑ Ⓒ Ⓓ Ⓔ   19. Ⓐ Ⓑ Ⓒ Ⓓ Ⓔ   29. Ⓐ Ⓑ Ⓒ Ⓓ Ⓔ   39. Ⓐ Ⓑ Ⓒ Ⓓ Ⓔ
10. Ⓐ Ⓑ Ⓒ Ⓓ Ⓔ   20. Ⓐ Ⓑ Ⓒ Ⓓ Ⓔ   30. Ⓐ Ⓑ Ⓒ Ⓓ Ⓔ   40. Ⓐ Ⓑ Ⓒ Ⓓ Ⓔ

SECTION 5

1. Ⓐ Ⓑ Ⓒ Ⓓ Ⓔ   11. Ⓐ Ⓑ Ⓒ Ⓓ Ⓔ   21. Ⓐ Ⓑ Ⓒ Ⓓ Ⓔ   31. Ⓐ Ⓑ Ⓒ Ⓓ Ⓔ
2. Ⓐ Ⓑ Ⓒ Ⓓ Ⓔ   12. Ⓐ Ⓑ Ⓒ Ⓓ Ⓔ   22. Ⓐ Ⓑ Ⓒ Ⓓ Ⓔ   32. Ⓐ Ⓑ Ⓒ Ⓓ Ⓔ
3. Ⓐ Ⓑ Ⓒ Ⓓ Ⓔ   13. Ⓐ Ⓑ Ⓒ Ⓓ Ⓔ   23. Ⓐ Ⓑ Ⓒ Ⓓ Ⓔ   33. Ⓐ Ⓑ Ⓒ Ⓓ Ⓔ   ☐ # right in Section 5
4. Ⓐ Ⓑ Ⓒ Ⓓ Ⓔ   14. Ⓐ Ⓑ Ⓒ Ⓓ Ⓔ   24. Ⓐ Ⓑ Ⓒ Ⓓ Ⓔ   34. Ⓐ Ⓑ Ⓒ Ⓓ Ⓔ
5. Ⓐ Ⓑ Ⓒ Ⓓ Ⓔ   15. Ⓐ Ⓑ Ⓒ Ⓓ Ⓔ   25. Ⓐ Ⓑ Ⓒ Ⓓ Ⓔ   35. Ⓐ Ⓑ Ⓒ Ⓓ Ⓔ
6. Ⓐ Ⓑ Ⓒ Ⓓ Ⓔ   16. Ⓐ Ⓑ Ⓒ Ⓓ Ⓔ   26. Ⓐ Ⓑ Ⓒ Ⓓ Ⓔ   36. Ⓐ Ⓑ Ⓒ Ⓓ Ⓔ
7. Ⓐ Ⓑ Ⓒ Ⓓ Ⓔ   17. Ⓐ Ⓑ Ⓒ Ⓓ Ⓔ   27. Ⓐ Ⓑ Ⓒ Ⓓ Ⓔ   37. Ⓐ Ⓑ Ⓒ Ⓓ Ⓔ   ☐ # wrong in Section 5
8. Ⓐ Ⓑ Ⓒ Ⓓ Ⓔ   18. Ⓐ Ⓑ Ⓒ Ⓓ Ⓔ   28. Ⓐ Ⓑ Ⓒ Ⓓ Ⓔ   38. Ⓐ Ⓑ Ⓒ Ⓓ Ⓔ
9. Ⓐ Ⓑ Ⓒ Ⓓ Ⓔ   19. Ⓐ Ⓑ Ⓒ Ⓓ Ⓔ   29. Ⓐ Ⓑ Ⓒ Ⓓ Ⓔ   39. Ⓐ Ⓑ Ⓒ Ⓓ Ⓔ
10. Ⓐ Ⓑ Ⓒ Ⓓ Ⓔ   20. Ⓐ Ⓑ Ⓒ Ⓓ Ⓔ   30. Ⓐ Ⓑ Ⓒ Ⓓ Ⓔ   40. Ⓐ Ⓑ Ⓒ Ⓓ Ⓔ

If section 5 of your test book contains math questions that are not multiple choice, continue to item 9 below. Otherwise, continue to item 9 above.

Grid-in answer boxes numbered 9, 10, 11, 12, 13, 14, 15, 16, 17, 18.

Remove (or photocopy) this answer sheet and use it to complete the practice test.

Start with number 1 for each section. If a section has fewer questions than answer spaces, leave the extra spaces blank.

SECTION

6

1. Ⓐ Ⓑ Ⓒ Ⓓ Ⓔ   11. Ⓐ Ⓑ Ⓒ Ⓓ Ⓔ   21. Ⓐ Ⓑ Ⓒ Ⓓ Ⓔ   31. Ⓐ Ⓑ Ⓒ Ⓓ Ⓔ
2. Ⓐ Ⓑ Ⓒ Ⓓ Ⓔ   12. Ⓐ Ⓑ Ⓒ Ⓓ Ⓔ   22. Ⓐ Ⓑ Ⓒ Ⓓ Ⓔ   32. Ⓐ Ⓑ Ⓒ Ⓓ Ⓔ
3. Ⓐ Ⓑ Ⓒ Ⓓ Ⓔ   13. Ⓐ Ⓑ Ⓒ Ⓓ Ⓔ   23. Ⓐ Ⓑ Ⓒ Ⓓ Ⓔ   33. Ⓐ Ⓑ Ⓒ Ⓓ Ⓔ
4. Ⓐ Ⓑ Ⓒ Ⓓ Ⓔ   14. Ⓐ Ⓑ Ⓒ Ⓓ Ⓔ   24. Ⓐ Ⓑ Ⓒ Ⓓ Ⓔ   34. Ⓐ Ⓑ Ⓒ Ⓓ Ⓔ   # right in Section 6
5. Ⓐ Ⓑ Ⓒ Ⓓ Ⓔ   15. Ⓐ Ⓑ Ⓒ Ⓓ Ⓔ   25. Ⓐ Ⓑ Ⓒ Ⓓ Ⓔ   35. Ⓐ Ⓑ Ⓒ Ⓓ Ⓔ
6. Ⓐ Ⓑ Ⓒ Ⓓ Ⓔ   16. Ⓐ Ⓑ Ⓒ Ⓓ Ⓔ   26. Ⓐ Ⓑ Ⓒ Ⓓ Ⓔ   36. Ⓐ Ⓑ Ⓒ Ⓓ Ⓔ
7. Ⓐ Ⓑ Ⓒ Ⓓ Ⓔ   17. Ⓐ Ⓑ Ⓒ Ⓓ Ⓔ   27. Ⓐ Ⓑ Ⓒ Ⓓ Ⓔ   37. Ⓐ Ⓑ Ⓒ Ⓓ Ⓔ
8. Ⓐ Ⓑ Ⓒ Ⓓ Ⓔ   18. Ⓐ Ⓑ Ⓒ Ⓓ Ⓔ   28. Ⓐ Ⓑ Ⓒ Ⓓ Ⓔ   38. Ⓐ Ⓑ Ⓒ Ⓓ Ⓔ   # wrong in Section 6
9. Ⓐ Ⓑ Ⓒ Ⓓ Ⓔ   19. Ⓐ Ⓑ Ⓒ Ⓓ Ⓔ   29. Ⓐ Ⓑ Ⓒ Ⓓ Ⓔ   39. Ⓐ Ⓑ Ⓒ Ⓓ Ⓔ
10. Ⓐ Ⓑ Ⓒ Ⓓ Ⓔ   20. Ⓐ Ⓑ Ⓒ Ⓓ Ⓔ   30. Ⓐ Ⓑ Ⓒ Ⓓ Ⓔ   40. Ⓐ Ⓑ Ⓒ Ⓓ Ⓔ

SECTION

7

1. Ⓐ Ⓑ Ⓒ Ⓓ Ⓔ   11. Ⓐ Ⓑ Ⓒ Ⓓ Ⓔ   21. Ⓐ Ⓑ Ⓒ Ⓓ Ⓔ   31. Ⓐ Ⓑ Ⓒ Ⓓ Ⓔ
2. Ⓐ Ⓑ Ⓒ Ⓓ Ⓔ   12. Ⓐ Ⓑ Ⓒ Ⓓ Ⓔ   22. Ⓐ Ⓑ Ⓒ Ⓓ Ⓔ   32. Ⓐ Ⓑ Ⓒ Ⓓ Ⓔ
3. Ⓐ Ⓑ Ⓒ Ⓓ Ⓔ   13. Ⓐ Ⓑ Ⓒ Ⓓ Ⓔ   23. Ⓐ Ⓑ Ⓒ Ⓓ Ⓔ   33. Ⓐ Ⓑ Ⓒ Ⓓ Ⓔ
4. Ⓐ Ⓑ Ⓒ Ⓓ Ⓔ   14. Ⓐ Ⓑ Ⓒ Ⓓ Ⓔ   24. Ⓐ Ⓑ Ⓒ Ⓓ Ⓔ   34. Ⓐ Ⓑ Ⓒ Ⓓ Ⓔ   # right in Section 7
5. Ⓐ Ⓑ Ⓒ Ⓓ Ⓔ   15. Ⓐ Ⓑ Ⓒ Ⓓ Ⓔ   25. Ⓐ Ⓑ Ⓒ Ⓓ Ⓔ   35. Ⓐ Ⓑ Ⓒ Ⓓ Ⓔ
6. Ⓐ Ⓑ Ⓒ Ⓓ Ⓔ   16. Ⓐ Ⓑ Ⓒ Ⓓ Ⓔ   26. Ⓐ Ⓑ Ⓒ Ⓓ Ⓔ   36. Ⓐ Ⓑ Ⓒ Ⓓ Ⓔ
7. Ⓐ Ⓑ Ⓒ Ⓓ Ⓔ   17. Ⓐ Ⓑ Ⓒ Ⓓ Ⓔ   27. Ⓐ Ⓑ Ⓒ Ⓓ Ⓔ   37. Ⓐ Ⓑ Ⓒ Ⓓ Ⓔ
8. Ⓐ Ⓑ Ⓒ Ⓓ Ⓔ   18. Ⓐ Ⓑ Ⓒ Ⓓ Ⓔ   28. Ⓐ Ⓑ Ⓒ Ⓓ Ⓔ   38. Ⓐ Ⓑ Ⓒ Ⓓ Ⓔ   # wrong in Section 7
9. Ⓐ Ⓑ Ⓒ Ⓓ Ⓔ   19. Ⓐ Ⓑ Ⓒ Ⓓ Ⓔ   29. Ⓐ Ⓑ Ⓒ Ⓓ Ⓔ   39. Ⓐ Ⓑ Ⓒ Ⓓ Ⓔ
10. Ⓐ Ⓑ Ⓒ Ⓓ Ⓔ   20. Ⓐ Ⓑ Ⓒ Ⓓ Ⓔ   30. Ⓐ Ⓑ Ⓒ Ⓓ Ⓔ   40. Ⓐ Ⓑ Ⓒ Ⓓ Ⓔ

SECTION

8

1. Ⓐ Ⓑ Ⓒ Ⓓ Ⓔ   11. Ⓐ Ⓑ Ⓒ Ⓓ Ⓔ   21. Ⓐ Ⓑ Ⓒ Ⓓ Ⓔ   31. Ⓐ Ⓑ Ⓒ Ⓓ Ⓔ
2. Ⓐ Ⓑ Ⓒ Ⓓ Ⓔ   12. Ⓐ Ⓑ Ⓒ Ⓓ Ⓔ   22. Ⓐ Ⓑ Ⓒ Ⓓ Ⓔ   32. Ⓐ Ⓑ Ⓒ Ⓓ Ⓔ
3. Ⓐ Ⓑ Ⓒ Ⓓ Ⓔ   13. Ⓐ Ⓑ Ⓒ Ⓓ Ⓔ   23. Ⓐ Ⓑ Ⓒ Ⓓ Ⓔ   33. Ⓐ Ⓑ Ⓒ Ⓓ Ⓔ
4. Ⓐ Ⓑ Ⓒ Ⓓ Ⓔ   14. Ⓐ Ⓑ Ⓒ Ⓓ Ⓔ   24. Ⓐ Ⓑ Ⓒ Ⓓ Ⓔ   34. Ⓐ Ⓑ Ⓒ Ⓓ Ⓔ   # right in Section 8
5. Ⓐ Ⓑ Ⓒ Ⓓ Ⓔ   15. Ⓐ Ⓑ Ⓒ Ⓓ Ⓔ   25. Ⓐ Ⓑ Ⓒ Ⓓ Ⓔ   35. Ⓐ Ⓑ Ⓒ Ⓓ Ⓔ
6. Ⓐ Ⓑ Ⓒ Ⓓ Ⓔ   16. Ⓐ Ⓑ Ⓒ Ⓓ Ⓔ   26. Ⓐ Ⓑ Ⓒ Ⓓ Ⓔ   36. Ⓐ Ⓑ Ⓒ Ⓓ Ⓔ
7. Ⓐ Ⓑ Ⓒ Ⓓ Ⓔ   17. Ⓐ Ⓑ Ⓒ Ⓓ Ⓔ   27. Ⓐ Ⓑ Ⓒ Ⓓ Ⓔ   37. Ⓐ Ⓑ Ⓒ Ⓓ Ⓔ
8. Ⓐ Ⓑ Ⓒ Ⓓ Ⓔ   18. Ⓐ Ⓑ Ⓒ Ⓓ Ⓔ   28. Ⓐ Ⓑ Ⓒ Ⓓ Ⓔ   38. Ⓐ Ⓑ Ⓒ Ⓓ Ⓔ   # wrong in Section 8
9. Ⓐ Ⓑ Ⓒ Ⓓ Ⓔ   19. Ⓐ Ⓑ Ⓒ Ⓓ Ⓔ   29. Ⓐ Ⓑ Ⓒ Ⓓ Ⓔ   39. Ⓐ Ⓑ Ⓒ Ⓓ Ⓔ
10. Ⓐ Ⓑ Ⓒ Ⓓ Ⓔ   20. Ⓐ Ⓑ Ⓒ Ⓓ Ⓔ   30. Ⓐ Ⓑ Ⓒ Ⓓ Ⓔ   40. Ⓐ Ⓑ Ⓒ Ⓓ Ⓔ

Remove (or photocopy) this answer sheet and use it to complete the practice test.

Start with number 1 for each section. If a section has fewer questions than answer spaces, leave the extra spaces blank.

SECTION

9

1. Ⓐ Ⓑ Ⓒ Ⓓ Ⓔ	11. Ⓐ Ⓑ Ⓒ Ⓓ Ⓔ	21. Ⓐ Ⓑ Ⓒ Ⓓ Ⓔ	31. Ⓐ Ⓑ Ⓒ Ⓓ Ⓔ
2. Ⓐ Ⓑ Ⓒ Ⓓ Ⓔ	12. Ⓐ Ⓑ Ⓒ Ⓓ Ⓔ	22. Ⓐ Ⓑ Ⓒ Ⓓ Ⓔ	32. Ⓐ Ⓑ Ⓒ Ⓓ Ⓔ
3. Ⓐ Ⓑ Ⓒ Ⓓ Ⓔ	13. Ⓐ Ⓑ Ⓒ Ⓓ Ⓔ	23. Ⓐ Ⓑ Ⓒ Ⓓ Ⓔ	33. Ⓐ Ⓑ Ⓒ Ⓓ Ⓔ
4. Ⓐ Ⓑ Ⓒ Ⓓ Ⓔ	14. Ⓐ Ⓑ Ⓒ Ⓓ Ⓔ	24. Ⓐ Ⓑ Ⓒ Ⓓ Ⓔ	34. Ⓐ Ⓑ Ⓒ Ⓓ Ⓔ
5. Ⓐ Ⓑ Ⓒ Ⓓ Ⓔ	15. Ⓐ Ⓑ Ⓒ Ⓓ Ⓔ	25. Ⓐ Ⓑ Ⓒ Ⓓ Ⓔ	35. Ⓐ Ⓑ Ⓒ Ⓓ Ⓔ
6. Ⓐ Ⓑ Ⓒ Ⓓ Ⓔ	16. Ⓐ Ⓑ Ⓒ Ⓓ Ⓔ	26. Ⓐ Ⓑ Ⓒ Ⓓ Ⓔ	36. Ⓐ Ⓑ Ⓒ Ⓓ Ⓔ
7. Ⓐ Ⓑ Ⓒ Ⓓ Ⓔ	17. Ⓐ Ⓑ Ⓒ Ⓓ Ⓔ	27. Ⓐ Ⓑ Ⓒ Ⓓ Ⓔ	37. Ⓐ Ⓑ Ⓒ Ⓓ Ⓔ
8. Ⓐ Ⓑ Ⓒ Ⓓ Ⓔ	18. Ⓐ Ⓑ Ⓒ Ⓓ Ⓔ	28. Ⓐ Ⓑ Ⓒ Ⓓ Ⓔ	38. Ⓐ Ⓑ Ⓒ Ⓓ Ⓔ
9. Ⓐ Ⓑ Ⓒ Ⓓ Ⓔ	19. Ⓐ Ⓑ Ⓒ Ⓓ Ⓔ	29. Ⓐ Ⓑ Ⓒ Ⓓ Ⓔ	39. Ⓐ Ⓑ Ⓒ Ⓓ Ⓔ
10. Ⓐ Ⓑ Ⓒ Ⓓ Ⓔ	20. Ⓐ Ⓑ Ⓒ Ⓓ Ⓔ	30. Ⓐ Ⓑ Ⓒ Ⓓ Ⓔ	40. Ⓐ Ⓑ Ⓒ Ⓓ Ⓔ

right in
Section 9

wrong in
Section 9

Practice Test Four

SECTION 1
Time—25 Minutes
ESSAY

The essay gives you an opportunity to show how effectively you can develop and express ideas. You should, therefore, take care to develop your point of view, present your ideas logically and clearly, and use language precisely.

Your essay must be written in your Answer Grid Booklet—you will receive no other paper on which to write. You will have enough space if you write on every line, avoid wide margins, and keep your handwriting to a reasonable size. Remember that people who are not familiar with your handwriting will read what you write. Try to write or print so that what you are writing is legible to those readers.

You have twenty-five minutes to write an essay on the topic assigned below.
DO NOT WRITE ON ANOTHER TOPIC. AN OFF-TOPIC ESSAY WILL RECEIVE A SCORE OF ZERO.

Think carefully about the issue presented in the following excerpt and the assignment below.

> "I don't know the key to success, but the key to failure is to try to please everyone."
> –Bill Cosby

Assignment: Is trying to please people a way to achieve success or a route to failure? Plan and write an essay in which you develop your point of view on this issue. Support your position with reasoning and examples taken from your reading, studies, experience, or observations.

DO NOT WRITE YOUR ESSAY IN YOUR TEST BOOK.
You will receive credit only for what you write in your Answer Grid Booklet.

Write your essays on separate sheets of paper.

SECTION 2
Time—25 Minutes
20 Questions

Directions: For this section, solve each problem and decide which is the best of the choices given. Fill in the corresponding oval on the answer sheet. You may use any available space for scratchwork.

Notes:

(1) Calculator use is permitted.

(2) All numbers used are real numbers.

(3) Figures are provided for some problems. All figures are drawn to scale and lie in a plane UNLESS otherwise indicated.

(4) Unless otherwise specified, the domain of any function f is assumed to be the set of all real numbers x for which $f(x)$ is a real number.

$A = \frac{1}{2}bh$ $c^2 = a^2 + b^2$ Special Right Triangles $A = \pi r^2$ $C = 2\pi r$ $V = \ell wh$ $V = \pi r^2 h$ $A = \ell w$

The sum of the degree measures of the angles in a triangle is 180.
The number of degrees of arc in a circle is 360.
A straight angle has a degree measure of 180.

1. If $x^6 + 4 = x^6 + w$, then $w =$

   (A) -4
   (B) $-\sqrt[6]{4}$
   (C) $\sqrt[6]{4}$
   (D) 4
   (E) 4^6

2. Depending on the cycle, washing a load of clothes takes from 22 to 28 minutes. Drying takes an additional 20 to 30 minutes. What are the minimum and maximum total times to complete a load of laundry?

   (A) 22 minutes and 28 minutes
   (B) 28 minutes and 48 minutes
   (C) 28 minutes and 58 minutes
   (D) 42 minutes and 48 minutes
   (E) 42 minutes and 58 minutes

GO ON TO THE NEXT PAGE

3. If $\frac{a}{b} = 4$, $\frac{a}{c} = 8$, and $c = 9$, what is the value of b?

(A) 2

(B) 8

(C) 18

(D) 36

(E) 72

4. Between which two digits of 4567890 should a decimal point be placed so that the value of the resulting number is 4.567890×10^2?

(A) 5 and 6

(B) 6 and 7

(C) 7 and 8

(D) 8 and 9

(E) 9 and 0

5. Set A is the set of all prime numbers. Set B is the set of all numbers equal to a prime number plus 2. Which of the following are in the intersection of set A and set B?

   I. 2
   II. 4
   III. 5

(A) I only

(B) II only

(C) III only

(D) I and III only

(E) II and III only

Note: Figure not drawn to scale.

6. In the figure above, if $a = 7c$ and $b = 2c$, what is the value of c?

(A) 18

(B) 20

(C) 28

(D) 34

(E) 36

GO ON TO THE NEXT PAGE

7. After 21 kids were added to a class, there were 4 times as many students as before. How many kids were in the class before the addition?

(A) 3
(B) 7
(C) 11
(D) 14
(E) 17

8. In the figure above, $l \parallel m$. What is the value of q?

(A) 40°
(B) 50°
(C) 60°
(D) 70°
(E) 80°

9. The value of $3x + 9$ is how much more than the value of $3x - 2$?

(A) 7
(B) 11
(C) $3x + 7$
(D) $3x + 11$
(E) $6x + 7$

10. If $a < b < 0 < c$, which of the following must be true?

   I. $-b > -a$
   II. $a + c < b + c$
   III. $a + b < c$

(A) I only
(B) II only
(C) III only
(D) II and III only
(E) I, II, and III

11. If set C includes all numbers between 0 and 5, inclusive. Set D includes all numbers between 3 and 7, inclusive. Which of the following sets of inequalities correctly describes x, where x is the union of set C and set D?

(A) $0 \le x \le 3$
(B) $0 \le x \le 5$
(C) $0 \le x \le 7$
(D) $3 \le x \le 5$
(E) $3 \le x \le 7$

12. If $\dfrac{10}{a+b} = \dfrac{4}{a}, \dfrac{b^2}{18} = \dfrac{a}{2}$, and $ab \ne 0$, what is the value of b?

(A) 0
(B) 2
(C) 4
(D) 6
(E) 8

GO ON TO THE NEXT PAGE

13. If $c^{-\frac{1}{2}} = 3$, what is the value of c^2?

    (A) -9

    (B) -3

    (C) $\dfrac{1}{81}$

    (D) $\dfrac{1}{9}$

    (E) $\dfrac{1}{\sqrt{3}}$

14. Which of the following equations best describes the curve in the figure above?

    (A) $y = -2x^2$

    (B) $y = -x^2$

    (C) $y = |x|$

    (D) $y = \dfrac{1}{2}x^2$

    (E) $y = 2x^2$

Questions 15 and 16 refer to the following figure.

15. What is the area of triangle ABC?

    (A) 5

    (B) 6

    (C) 8

    (D) 9

    (E) 10

16. What is the perimeter of triangle ABC?

    (A) 10

    (B) 11

    (C) $10 + \sqrt{5}$

    (D) 13

    (E) $10 + 2\sqrt{5}$

GO ON TO THE NEXT PAGE

17. Which of the following represents the statement "When the sum of the squares of $2a$ and $3b$ are added to the difference between $8c$ and $7d$, the result is 3 more than e"?

   (A) $(2a)^2 + (3b)^2 + (8c - 7d) = e + 3$

   (B) $(2a)^2 + (3b)^2 + (8c - 7d) + 3 = e$

   (C) $(2a + 3b)^2 + (8c - 7d) + 3 = e$

   (D) $(2a + 3b)^2 + (8c - 7d) = e + 3$

   (E) $2a^2 + 3b^2 + (8c - 7d) + 3 = e$

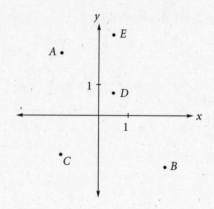

18. Line l has an undefined slope and contains the point $(-2, 3)$. Which of the following points is also on line l?

   (A) $(0, 3)$

   (B) $(5, 5)$

   (C) $(0, 0)$

   (D) $(3, -2)$

   (E) $(-2, 5)$

19. In the figure above, for which point (x, y) is the product xy the greatest?

   (A) A

   (B) B

   (C) C

   (D) D

   (E) E

20. If $a = 3n + 4$ and $b = 7 + 9n^2$, what is b in terms of a?

   (A) $a^2 + 8a + 23$

   (B) $a^2 - 8a + 23$

   (C) $9a^2 - 108a + 144$

   (D) $9a^2 - 108a + 148$

   (E) $9a^2 + 108a + 148$

SECTION 3

Time—25 Minutes

25 Questions

Directions: For each of the following questions, choose the best answer and darken the corresponding oval on the answer sheet.

Each sentence below has one or two blanks, each blank indicating that something has been omitted. Beneath the sentence are five words or sets of words labeled A through E. Choose the word or set of words that, when inserted in the sentence, <u>best</u> fits the meaning of the sentence as a whole.

Example:

Today's small, portable computers contrast markedly with the earliest electronic computers, which were -------.

(A) effective
(B) invented
(C) useful
(D) destructive
(E) enormous   Ⓐ Ⓑ Ⓒ Ⓓ ●

---

1. Leonardo Da Vinci was a ------- artist; he was a painter, sculptor, draftsman, architect, and inventor.

   (A) demonstrative
   (B) nebulous
   (C) meticulous
   (D) versatile
   (E) metaphoric

2. Although the class was told by their math teacher that the exercises in the chapter review were -------, the students knew that some questions on the exam would be the same as those found in the review.

   (A) pivotal
   (B) ritualistic
   (C) salient
   (D) supplementary
   (E) solemn

3. Renowned buildings such as "Fallingwater" and the eminent Solomon R. Guggenheim Museum in New York City ------- Frank Lloyd Wright as one of the most ------- architects of the 20th century.

   (A) buoyed . . . irrelevant
   (B) established . . . prominent
   (C) surrendered . . . prolific
   (D) decried . . . cynical
   (E) categorized . . . mundane

4. Although he was not particularly talented, his years of experience as a plumber at least solidified his status as a ------- of the profession.

   (A) novice
   (B) neighbor
   (C) interpreter
   (D) practitioner
   (E) detractor

GO ON TO THE NEXT PAGE

5. Known as a skilled mediator, Ms. Poole was able to ------- the couple's relationship by carefully ------- their numerous differences.

   (A) reinforce . . . strengthening
   (B) preserve . . . bridging
   (C) convey . . . widening
   (D) overcome . . . plugging
   (E) disregard . . . destroying

6. The ------- that plagued the once venerable institution was so entrenched and highly publicized that few imagined its reputation could ever be -------.

   (A) integrity . . . discredited
   (B) conviction . . . justified
   (C) corruption . . . redeemed
   (D) dignity . . . excused
   (E) degradation . . . convicted

7. The waiter performs his job with ------- and hopes that if he continues to work ------- he will eventually be promoted to maitre d'.

   (A) sagacity . . . unscrupulously
   (B) leniency . . . decorously
   (C) nonchalance . . . tenaciously
   (D) acrimony . . . cheerfully
   (E) ardor . . . assiduously

8. Even though we are supposed to be more evolved than animals, the human tendency toward ------- and egocentrism, shows that sometimes people can carry a narrow view of the universe.

   (A) irrationality
   (B) humanity
   (C) temerity
   (D) serendipity
   (E) anthropocentrism

GO ON TO THE NEXT PAGE

Directions: The passages below are followed by questions based on their content; questions following a pair of related passages may also be based on the relationship between the paired passages. Answer the questions on the basis of what is <u>stated</u> or <u>implied</u> in the passages and in any introductory material that may be provided.

Questions 9–10 refer to the following passage.

With my months of anticipation finally satisfied and the long-awaited bundle of fur fast asleep in my lap, I could not have then imagined the trials to come. Yet, by the time I
(5) arrived home from the breeder's with slightly scored shins and puppy urine coating my shoes, I had some idea. I suppose my mother had provided something of a warning with her constant refrain that came every time I crossed
(10) another day off my calendar: "Just make sure he stays your responsibility, not mine." But looking back, with that once tiny menace now a snoring beast asleep at my feet, I feel a hint of what must be parental satisfaction.

9. In line 6, "scored" most nearly means

(A) counted

(B) indented

(C) acquired

(D) scratched

(E) slashed

10. The author uses the words "snoring beast" (line 13) in order to

(A) suggest that her puppy grew to be too large

(B) imply that her once-energetic puppy is now rather lazy

(C) indicate that her decision to get a puppy was a mistake

(D) emphasize how much she has grown to love her puppy

(E) underscore how much her puppy has matured

Questions 11–12 refer to the following passage.

When the revolutionary American chocolate-maker Milton Hershey enthusiastically opened his first candy shop in Philadelphia at the age of 18, he knew little of the busi-
(5) ness, and his inexperience caused his endeavor to fold six years later. Nonetheless, getting his feet wet in the industry proved enough to keep him hooked on it, for he went on to work as an intern for a local caramel manu-
(10) facturer. There he learned that superior results could only be achieved when the freshest milk was used, and thus was born a lifelong dedication to quality ingredients upon which he would later build his chocolate empire.

11. As indicated in the first sentence of the passage, Milton Hershey was

(A) quite industrious

(B) something of a child prodigy

(C) an untalented entrepreneur

(D) a groundbreaking candy producer

(E) committed to using high-quality ingredients

GO ON TO THE NEXT PAGE

12. The passage implies that Hershey

(A) was the first to make candy from quality ingredients

(B) had a persisting interest in candy manufacturing

(C) tried to apply caramel-making techniques to chocolate production

(D) was well-suited for a career only in candy making

(E) had been fascinated by candy-making since early childhood

Questions 13–25 refer to the following passage.

The following passage is from a 2004 essay that discusses the decline in artistic awareness, appreciation, and taste in America.

While many of us express disdain at the declining condition of artistic awareness, let alone appreciation, in this country, we cannot honestly express surprise. This general

(5) decline in tastes has not escaped the commentary and analysis of cultural critics who have warned us that we may be turning into a nation of Philistines. These same critics have pointed to a pair of causes for this cul-

(10) tural decline. Perhaps, they note, the decline is due to the crumbling state of our educational system, or to the media's focus on pop culture and the general decline of taste this breeds. Nevertheless, this type of scholarly

(15) discussion about the roots of the decline, while relevant to sociological and cultural historical analysis, does nothing to solve the problem. Understanding the causes does not change the sad fact that the same coun-

(20) try that gave the world film noir, jazz, and abstract expressionism now mostly concerns itself with teen movies and boy bands. We must use our understanding and analysis of the causes to address the problem of artistic

(25) decline in America.

Before we can begin a discussion of artistic decline, we must first define the word "art," an endeavor that has proven problematic, especially after the introduction of modern art

(30) forms during the twentieth century. Indeed, some may argue that the entire debate about artistic decline in this country is flawed due to our exclusion of modern forms of art such as pop music. Many claim that such discus-

(35) sion can be seen as snobby, even culturally imperious. Without entering the debate on the validity of the post-modern conception of art as an idea, the question of "what is art" must be addressed. But it should be addressed

(40) expeditiously. Far too much time has been spent arguing over whether a teen movie is more or less art than Citizen Kane is, or whether the music of a boy band is more or less art than are the works of Sondheim. To

(45) be fair, society should not adopt an exclusionary definition or attitude. Indeed, history has proven that today's pop music can be tomorrow's great art in retrospect. Thus, we should accept all artistic endeavors as art. Individuals

(50) and critics should judge the quality of such endeavors. But this does not change the fact that today, people are unaware of and uneducated about the classics, or even about recent movements in art apart from cinema, televi-

(55) sion, and pop music.

Imagine a United States of America in which artistic education, and thus appreciation, flourishes, a place where parents read books on art and listen to classical music and

(60) opera, as well as pop music. Children observe these adult activities and mimic them. Parents read to their children and educate them. These parents also give their children art books, classical recordings, and plays as

(65) gifts. These parents underwrite, with their tax

GO ON TO THE NEXT PAGE ⇨

dollars, public art, public broadcasting, and community art groups. In school, students receive an education in art history, classical music, and opera. This curriculum can also
(70) include pop culture such as the music videos, teen movies, and pop music students enjoy in their free time. In fact, a better education in art will better equip them to judge the artistic merit of these newer, more trendy art forms,
(75) or at least place these art forms in historical context and analyze them as an outgrowth of societal and sociological trends—an important aspect of artistic knowledge that has been lost by the general public. When these
(80) children grow up, some may produce their own art, which would likely be higher in quality than the pop music and movies produced today. Imagine a land of such developed artistic production and taste! How can
(85) we achieve such a society?

Having noted that the proliferation of low quality art in pop culture can be addressed effectively by education, there remains one fundamental cause for the decline in artistic
(90) taste: the crumbling state of our educational system. The society dreamed of above can only be achieved by sustained efforts to improve the American educational system. Unfortunately, with tightening budgets due
(95) to increased levels of government debt, often the first programs cut are those that provide art and music classes. Often these cuts are viewed as easy ones by the public since they do not compromise the fundamentals sup-
(100) posedly required for an adequate education: reading, writing, history, science, and math. However, what the public often misses is that art, music, and culture are inextricably tied to literary and historical developments that
(105) themselves stem from changes in society and culture. A holistic approach to the arts would both redefine their role in education (thereby

subsuming the argument of those who want to focus on fundamentals) and improve the
(110) state of artistic education by teaching students in an intertextual and multidisciplinary manner. The first step in improving artistic awareness and taste in this country will be not only to reinstate and improve art, music,
(115) and other cultural classes but also to restructure the curriculum to provide a more holistic education in which art, music, and culture become a part of the fundamental education in history, literature, and society. This system
(120) would require more funding and most likely higher taxes. However, such an investment would pay dividends by ensuring a more educated populace, one which is better equipped to analyze its surroundings in an analytically
(125) balanced manner and one which appreciates all forms of human artistic endeavor.

13. According to the author, which endeavor has proven problematic?

(A) Improving the education system

(B) Making art seem relevant

(C) Defining the word "art"

(D) Deciding what students should learn in school

(E) Deciding whether or not to teach art

GO ON TO THE NEXT PAGE ⟹

14. In the second paragraph of the passage (lines 26–55), the author suggests that too much time has been spent

    (A) debating the artistic merits of so-called "classics"

    (B) debating the artistic merits of modern works

    (C) debating whether or not art education can be improved

    (D) debating whether or not a historical perspective should be used in art education

    (E) comparing the artistic merits of different works traditionally considered classics

15. The author mentions "film noir, jazz, and abstract expressionism" (lines 20–21) chiefly in order to

    (A) appeal to the reader's sense of nostalgia

    (B) introduce a historical parallel

    (C) examine the history of art

    (D) remind the reader how tastes change over time

    (E) suggest that current artistic works are inferior to older ones

16. In line 36, "imperious" most nearly means

    (A) imperative

    (B) arbitrary

    (C) regal

    (D) urgent

    (E) arrogant

17. According to the author, which important aspect of artistic knowledge has been lost by the general public?

    (A) the ability to place art works in a historical context

    (B) the ability to define the word "art"

    (C) the ability to produce art that rivals the classics

    (D) the ability to judge the merits of current art works

    (E) the ability to value all forms of art

18. In lines 56–65 ("Imagine . . . gifts"), the hypothetical United States described is noteworthy because

    (A) people have allowed new interests to develop

    (B) parents share their interest in and enjoyment of art

    (C) children learn about art in school

    (D) children and parents share many activities

    (E) artistic knowledge is viewed as a valuable skill

19. Lines 67–72 ("In school . . . time") present a model of education where students learn to

    (A) value artistic diversity over tradition

    (B) respect the views of all artists

    (C) reflect critically on the nature of artistic education

    (D) appreciate classic art works over contemporary ones

    (E) encounter art through a wide-ranging exploration

GO ON TO THE NEXT PAGE ⟩

20. The author includes the third paragraph (lines 56–85) primarily in order to

    (A) propose a vision of a utopian society

    (B) propose a vision of an artistically educated society

    (C) argue that pop culture leaves no lasting impact on society

    (D) observe that classic literature has great appeal for even reluctant students

    (E) indicate that contemporary and classical works are interchangeable

21. In lines 102–119 ("However . . . society"), the education illustrated is best described as

    (A) elitist

    (B) philanthropic

    (C) eclectic

    (D) comprehensive

    (E) rudimentary

22. In lines 112–119, the author describes an education system that would be

    (A) more expensive than the current system

    (B) more celebrated than the current system

    (C) more controversial than the current system

    (D) more interesting than the current system

    (E) more likely to inspire than the current system

23. The main purpose of the passage is to

    (A) shift the focus of a debate from causes to effects

    (B) outline a debate and support one side

    (C) present a problem and suggest a solution

    (D) revive a discredited idea that might be able to solve a current problem

    (E) promote certain kinds of art

24. In the hypothetical United States the author discusses, why does the author imply that children will grow up to produce art that may be higher in quality than the pop music and movies produced today?

    (A) They would not want to disappoint their parents.

    (B) Society would not accept low quality art.

    (C) Their education would provide them with more artistic knowledge.

    (D) They would have more free time to experiment with their art.

    (E) Critics would judge the merits of the art more harshly.

25. The author's attitude toward pop music is that

    (A) he admires it

    (B) he has no feelings about it

    (C) he is not a fan

    (D) he wants to see more pop-influenced education

    (E) he believes it is more important than classical music

IF YOU FINISH BEFORE TIME IS CALLED, YOU MAY CHECK YOUR WORK ON THIS SECTION ONLY. DO NOT TURN TO ANY OTHER SECTION IN THE TEST.

STOP

SECTION 4

Time—25 Minutes

35 Questions

Directions: For each question in this section, select the best answer from among the choices given and fill in the corresponding oval on the answer sheet.

The following sentences test correctness and effectiveness of expression. Part of each sentence or the entire sentence is underlined; beneath each sentence are five ways of phrasing the underlined material. Choice A repeats the original phrasing; the other four choices are different. If you think the original phrasing produces a better sentence than any of the alternatives, select choice A; if not, select one of the other choices.

In making your selection, follow the requirements of standard written English; that is, pay attention to grammar, choice of words, sentence construction, and punctuation. Your selection should result in the most effective sentence—clear and precise, without awkwardness or ambiguity.

EXAMPLE: ANSWER:

Every apple in the baskets <u>are ripe and labeled according to the date it was picked</u>.   Ⓐ ● Ⓒ Ⓓ Ⓔ

(A) are ripe and labeled according to the date it was picked
(B) is ripe and labeled according to the date it was picked
(C) are ripe and labeled according to the date they were picked
(D) is ripe and labeled according to the date they were picked
(E) are ripe and labeled as to the date it was picked

1. <u>Nora would like to fly to Egypt, but flying is unable to be afforded by her.</u>

   (A) Nora would like to fly to Egypt, but flying is unable to be afforded by her.

   (B) Nora would like to fly to Egypt, but she cannot afford to do so.

   (C) Nora would like to fly to Egypt, but she is unable to afford that.

   (D) Flying to Egypt is what Nora would like to do, but she cannot afford it.

   (E) Flying to Egypt appeals to Nora, but she cannot afford to buy the plane ticket.

2. The state of New Jersey <u>is one of the smallest states in the union, being also</u> the most densely populated.

   (A) is one of the smallest states in the union, being also

   (B) although one of the smallest states in the union, is

   (C) being one of the smallest states in the union makes it

   (D) which is one of the smallest states in the union, although it is

   (E) whose size is the smallest in the union, makes it

GO ON TO THE NEXT PAGE

3. The love story of Romeo and Juliet was the subject of a teen movie, being popular among high school students in the 90s.

    (A) The love story of Romeo and Juliet was the subject of a teen movie, being popular among high school students in the 90s.

    (B) The love story of Romeo and Juliet was popular among high school students in the 90s, where it is being made the subject of a teen movie.

    (C) The love story of Romeo and Juliet was popular among high school students in the 90s, when it was the subject of a teen movie.

    (D) Romeo and Juliet, whose love story was the subject of a popular teen movie among high school students in the 90s.

    (E) Being the subject of a teen movie, the love story of Romeo and Juliet having been popular among high school students in the 90s.

4. One consequence of the university's new bylaws is that they can no longer pay reduced wages to lecturers.

    (A) One consequence of the university's new bylaws is that they can no longer pay reduced wages to lecturers.

    (B) As a result of its new bylaws, the university can no longer pay reduced wages to lecturers.

    (C) One consequence of the university's new bylaws is that reduced wages to lecturers can no longer be paid by them.

    (D) The university's new bylaws result in their no longer being able to pay lecturers reduced wages.

    (E) One consequence of the university's new bylaws are that paying reduced wages to lecturers is no longer possible.

5. Photographer Andrea Valerai permitted only a few friends to view her work because her strict standards caused her to doubt that her pictures were worth looking at.

    (A) because her strict standards caused her to doubt

    (B) her standards being strict, she doubted

    (C) because of her standards being strict, which she doubted

    (D) from
    having strict standards causing her to doubt

    (E) having
    strict standards causing her doubting

6. It is hard for me to imagine that 100 years ago this area was undeveloped swamp land, but it has since become high-rise apartment buildings.

    (A) land, but it has since become high-rise apartment buildings

    (B) land, but it is now high-rise apartment buildings

    (C) land, and has since become high-rise apartment buildings

    (D) land that has since become high-rise apartment buildings

    (E) land, since becoming high-rise apartment buildings

GO ON TO THE NEXT PAGE

7. <u>Gorbachev started the opening of Soviet society, and he</u> was raised in the relative freedom of thought under Khrushchev.

   (A) Gorbachev started the opening of Soviet society, and he

   (B) Gorbachev, who started the opening of Soviet society,

   (C) Starting the opening of Soviet society was Gorbachev, and he

   (D) Gorbachev started the opening of Soviet society, and that is why he

   (E) A start of the opening of Soviet society, Gorbachev

8. The cost of attending college has been affected by an increase in scholarships and <u>because there has been a decrease in large alumni donations</u>.

   (A) because there has been a decrease in large alumni donations

   (B) because of the decrease in large alumni donations

   (C) by alumni who have decreased large donations

   (D) decreasing large alumni donations

   (E) a decrease in large alumni donations

9. Airlines such as Ryan Air and Easy Jet are able to find alternative, cheap landing strips <u>and are therefore able to pass savings on to their customers</u>.

   (A) and are therefore able to pass savings on to their customers

   (B) and savings are passed on as a result to their customers

   (C) so that their customers could have savings passed to them

   (D) so, therefore, savings would be gained by their customers

   (E) and therefore have savings gained in their customers

10. The first hand transplant was performed in 1998, made possible <u>by their fuller understanding of</u> immunobiology.

    (A) by their fuller understanding of

    (B) by their understanding more fully

    (C) by their more fully understanding

    (D) by a fuller understanding of

    (E) by its fuller understanding of

11. Some speedometers register <u>high speeds as</u> two hundred miles per hour, even though few cars will ever go faster than one hundred.

    (A) high speeds as

    (B) speeds as high as

    (C) speeds that are high

    (D) high speeds that are capable of exceeding

    (E) a speed as

GO ON TO THE NEXT PAGE

Directions: The following sentences test your ability to recognize grammar and usage errors. Each sentence contains either a single error or no error at all. No sentence contains more than one error. The error, if there is one, is underlined and lettered. If the sentence contains an error, select the one underlined part that must be changed to make the sentence correct. If the sentence is correct, select choice E. In choosing answers, follow the requirements of standard written English.

EXAMPLE:

<u>Whenever</u> one is driving late at night, <u>you</u> must take extra precautions <u>against</u>
   A   B   C

falling asleep <u>at the wheel</u>. <u>No error</u>
             D   E

Ⓐ ● Ⓒ Ⓓ Ⓔ

---

12. <u>That</u> the team with the worst record won the
   A
game <u>easily</u> using players <u>whom</u> had previously
       B   C
scored only two goals <u>came</u> as a shock to the
                      D
sportscasters. <u>No error</u>
             E

13. Acknowledging that her performance in class

   <u>was</u> not up to her usual standards, Stacy
   A
had worked to raise her test score average
   <u>had worked</u> <u>to raise</u> her test score average
      B   C
<u>for the third marking period</u>. <u>No error</u>
          D   E

14. <u>Although</u> he <u>knows</u> his own life was <u>in danger</u>,
     A   B   C
the Mayor insisted on going downtown to see

the site of the attack <u>for himself</u>. <u>No error</u>
                 D   E

15. The director was <u>annoyed by</u> Tom's inability
               A
<u>to learn</u> his lines, <u>because</u> his lack of preparation
   B   C
forced her to schedule an extra rehearsal

<u>for the next day</u>. <u>No error</u>
      D   E

16. The professor wanted <u>to be sure that</u> his
                 A
students <u>come</u> to class <u>on time</u>, so he posted a
       B   C
<u>schedule on</u> the Spanish department's bulletin
   D
board. <u>No error</u>
       E

17. Henley decorated her plain white kitchen walls

<u>with</u> colorful posters <u>because</u> she knew she
   A   B
<u>would enjoy</u> looking at the bright reds, blues,
   C
and yellows <u>every morning</u>. <u>No error</u>
          D   E

GO ON TO THE NEXT PAGE →

18. Paula, <u>who</u> loved <u>to see</u> new places but
         A   B
<u>had never enjoyed</u> flying, grew <u>increasing</u>
      C   D
nervous as the day of her first overseas

vacation approached. <u>No error</u>
                        E

19. In the <u>anticipatory</u> hush of the dark theater,
         A
we <u>could hear</u> the <u>rustling of</u> the costumes as
     B   C
the dancers took <u>their place</u> on the stage.
                D
<u>No error</u>
  E

20. The neighbors got <u>into their car</u> and <u>driving</u>
                A   B
off toward the main street as Katie <u>looked</u> out
                           C
the window, <u>sipping her hot chocolate.</u>
                D
<u>No error</u>
  E

21. The <u>heroine of</u> Dorothy Parker's short story
      A
"The Telephone Call" waits <u>feverishly</u> for the
                      B
telephone to ring, <u>refuses</u> to face her knowledge
              C
that the boy <u>will never call.</u> <u>No error</u>
            D   E

22. As we walked <u>through</u> the South Philadelphia
             A
neighborhood <u>known as</u> the Italian Market,
             B
a <u>number of</u> appetizing smells <u>greeting</u> our
    C   D
nostrils. <u>No error</u>
       E

23. Kyoko took <u>every opportunity</u> to practice
            A
<u>speaking</u> English, <u>even though</u> her friends
  B   C
<u>prefer</u> to speak Japanese together. <u>No error</u>
  D   E

24. The Berlin Wall, <u>which</u> became the <u>most potent</u>
              A   B
symbol <u>of the Cold War,</u> <u>constructed</u> in 1961.
      C   D
<u>No error</u>
  E

25. Larry McMurtry's <u>short</u> novel *The Last Picture*
               A
Show <u>perfectly</u> captures the atmosphere of a
      B
small Texas town <u>and</u> the loneliness
               C
<u>of its inhabitants.</u> <u>No error</u>
     D   E

26. Mrs. Ramsay told us that, since only one <u>slice of</u>
                                A
apple pie was left, <u>she</u> <u>would not be able</u> <u>to offer</u>
               B   C   D
us any desert. <u>No error</u>
           E

27. Today's student <u>frequently choose</u> a college
              A
degree program <u>that</u> <u>leads to</u> a <u>specific</u> career.
            B   C   D
<u>No error</u>
  E

GO ON TO THE NEXT PAGE ⇨

28. This Tibetan restaurant <u>serving</u> several
                            A
varieties stuffed dumplings <u>as well as</u> some
                                  B
<u>excellent</u> and hearty soups, unlike the
   C
restaurant <u>around the corner</u>. <u>No error</u>
                   D   E

29. In the 1950s, painters Jackson Pollock and

James Brooks <u>developed</u> <u>the idea of</u>
                  A   B
automatism: <u>to drip</u> and throwing paint
                 C
<u>spontaneously</u> across an unprimed canvas.
       D
<u>No error</u>
    E

GO ON TO THE NEXT PAGE

Directions: The following passage is an early draft of an essay. Some parts of the passage need to be rewritten.

Read the passage and select the best answer for each question that follows. Some questions are about particular sentences or parts of sentences and ask you to improve sentence structure or word choice. Other questions ask you to consider organization and development. In choosing answers, follow the conventions of standard written English.

---

(1) It is generally accepted as a theory among scientists that a change in atmospheric phenomena may signal pending changes to the Earth's climate. (2) Consequently, when NASA began to document increased sightings of noctilucent clouds in the latter half of the twentieth century, the agency institutes plans for a study to determine the cause, and to learn what effect, if any, this may have on future weather patterns.

(3) Noctilucent, or night-shining, clouds are virtually unknown to most people, even those that star-gaze on a regular basis. (4) This is because NCLs (as they are known in the scientific community) generally occur north of 50° latitude, above the polar region. (5) These clouds, however, are becoming increasingly visible in areas farther south. (6) In 1999, a dramatic display of NCLs appearing over Colorado and Utah, nearly 10° below the latitudes where scientists have come to expect them. (7) Sightings in Europe have also become more frequent in the past 50 years, for reasons that remain unclear.

(8) Ordinary clouds occur approximately 10 kilometers from the Earth's surface. (9) Noctilucent clouds are found at about 82 kilometers. (10) This is more than seven times higher than commercial airlines fly. (11) Although most scientists believe NCLs are formed of ice crystals, but some are convinced that they are composed of cosmic or volcanic dust. (12) This theory is most likely attributable to the fact that the first NCL sightings were documented following a large volcanic explosion in Indonesia.

30. In context, what is the best version of sentence 1 (reproduced below)?

It is generally accepted as a theory among scientists that a change in atmospheric phenomena may signal pending changes to the Earth's climate.

(A) (As it is now)

(B) Generally accepted by scientists as a theory, a change in atmospheric phenomena may signal pending changes to the Earth's climate.

(C) Scientists generally accepting the theory that a change in atmospheric phenomena may signal pending changes to the Earth's climate.

(D) Scientists generally accept the theory that a change in atmospheric phenomena may signal pending changes to the Earth's climate.

(E) Scientists, having generally accepted the theory that a change in atmospheric phenomena may signal pending changes to the Earth's climate.

GO ON TO THE NEXT PAGE

31. In context, what revision is required in sentence 2 (reproduced below)?

    Consequently, when NASA began to document increased sightings of noctilucent clouds in the latter half of the twentieth century, the agency institutes plans for a study to determine the cause, and to learn what effect, if any, this may have on future weather patterns.

    (A) Eliminate "Consequently."
    (B) Change "institutes" to "instituted."
    (C) Change "for a study" to "for studying."
    (D) Change "and" to "but."
    (E) Change "may have" to "may have had."

32. Which of the following is the best version of the underlined portion of sentence 3 (reproduced below)?

    Noctilucent, or night-shining, clouds are virtually unknown to <u>most people, even those that stargaze on a regular basis.</u>

    (A) (As it is now)
    (B) more people, even those that stargaze on a regular basis
    (C) most people, even them that stargaze on a regular basis
    (D) most people, even them who stargaze on a regular basis
    (E) most people, even those who stargaze on a regular basis

33. In context, which of the following is the best way to phrase the underlined portion of sentence 6 (reproduced below)?

    In 1999, <u>a dramatic display of NCLs appearing over Colorado and Utah</u>, nearly 10° below the latitudes where scientists have come to expect them.

    (A) (As it is now)
    (B) a dramatic display of NCLs appears over Colorado and Utah
    (C) a dramatic display of NCLs appeared over Colorado and Utah
    (D) appearing over Colorado and Utah was a dramatic display of NCLs
    (E) over Colorado and Utah there appeared a dramatic display of NCLs

GO ON TO THE NEXT PAGE →

34. Which of the following is the best way to combine sentences 8, 9, and 10 (reproduced below)?

    Ordinary clouds occur approximately 10 kilometers from the Earth's surface. Noctilucent clouds are found at about 82 kilometers. This is more than seven times higher than commercial airlines fly.

    (A) Ordinary clouds occur approximately 10 kilometers from the Earth's surface, noctilucent clouds are found at about 82 kilometers, and this is more than seven times higher than commercial airlines fly.

    (B) Ordinary clouds occur approximately 10 kilometers from the Earth's surface; while noctilucent clouds, being found at about 82 kilometers, which is more than seven times higher than commercial airlines fly.

    (C) Ordinary clouds occur approximately 10 kilometers from the Earth's surface, but noctilucent clouds are found at about 82 kilometers, which is more than seven times higher than commercial airlines fly.

    (D) Ordinary clouds occur approximately 10 kilometers from the Earth's surface, so noctilucent clouds are found at about 82 kilometer, which is more than seven times higher than commercial airlines fly.

    (E) Ordinary clouds occurring approximately 10 kilometers from the Earth's surface, and noctilucent clouds at about 82 kilometers, more than seven times higher than commercial airlines fly.

35. In context, what revision is necessary in sentence 11 (reproduced below)?

    Although most scientists believe NCLs are formed of ice crystals, but some are convinced that they are composed of cosmic or volcanic dust.

    (A) Eliminate "Although" and change "but" to "or."

    (B) Eliminate "Although" and change "but" to "because."

    (C) Change "but" to "or."

    (D) Change "but" to "while."

    (E) Eliminate "but."

IF YOU FINISH BEFORE TIME IS CALLED, YOU MAY CHECK YOUR WORK ON THIS SECTION ONLY. DO NOT TURN TO ANY OTHER SECTION IN THE TEST.

STOP

SECTION 5

Time—25 Minutes

18 Questions

Directions: For this section, solve each problem and decide which is the best of the choices given. Fill in the corresponding oval on the answer sheet. You may use any available space for scratchwork.

Notes:

(1) Calculator use is permitted.

(2) All numbers used are real numbers.

(3) Figures are provided for some problems. All figures are drawn to scale and lie in a plane UNLESS otherwise indicated.

(4) Unless otherwise specified, the domain of any function f is assumed to be the set of all real numbers x for which $f(x)$ is a real number.

$A = \frac{1}{2}bh$ $c^2 = a^2 + b^2$ Special Right Triangles $A = \pi r^2$ $C = 2\pi r$ $V = \ell wh$ $V = \pi r^2 h$ $A = \ell w$

The sum of the degree measures of the angles in a triangle is 180.

The number of degrees of arc in a circle is 360.

A straight angle has a degree measure of 180.

1. If $3\sqrt{x} - 31 = -13$, what is x?

   (A) 6
   (B) 18
   (C) 36
   (D) 49
   (E) 72

2. Find the value of x if $\frac{3x - 9}{2x + 7} = 8$.

   (A) −5
   (B) −3
   (C) 1
   (D) 4
   (E) 5

3. Points P and Q are on the standard xy-plane. P has coordinates $(-2, 4)$, and Q has coordinates $(5, -2)$. What is the distance between P and Q?

   (A) 4
   (B) 7
   (C) $3\sqrt{5}$
   (D) $\sqrt{13}$
   (E) $\sqrt{85}$

GO ON TO THE NEXT PAGE

4. For all u and v, let ∇ be defined by $u\nabla v = u - v + 2$. What is the value of $(2\nabla 3)\nabla 1$?

(A) 0

(B) 1

(C) 2

(D) 3

(E) 4

5. If a and b are multiples of 3, which of the following CANNOT also be a multiple of 3?

(A) $a + b$

(B) $a - b$

(C) $a + b + 1$

(D) ab

(E) $ab + 3$

6. If the length of one side of a triangle is 5, which of the following CANNOT be the lengths of the other two sides of the triangle?

(A) 3 and 3

(B) 3 and 5

(C) 7 and 8

(D) 7 and 3

(E) 7 and 12

7. If k and s are positive integers and the ratio of $2k$ to $6s$ is the same as the ratio of $6k + 5$ to $18s + 10$, which of the following must be true?

   I. $k = s$
  II. $k = 1.5$
 III. $k = 1.5s$

(A) None

(B) I only

(C) II only

(D) III only

(E) I and II

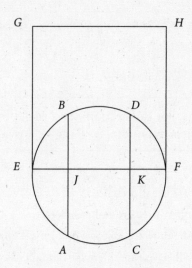

Note: Figure not drawn to scale.

8. In the figure above lines $\overline{BA}$ and $\overline{DC}$ have equal length, and are perpendicular to $\overline{EF}$, which passes through the center of the circle. If the area of square $GEFH$ is 81, and $JK = 5$, what is the length of EJ?

(A) 2

(B) 3

(C) 4

(D) 6

(E) 9

GO ON TO THE NEXT PAGE

Directions: For Student-Produced Response questions 9–18, use the grids at the bottom of the answer sheet page on which you have answered questions 1–8.

Each of the remaining 10 questions requires you to solve the problem and enter your answer by marking the ovals in the special grid, as shown in the example below. You may use any available space for scratchwork.

Answer: 1.25 or $\frac{5}{4}$ or 5/4

Write answer in boxes.

Grid-in result

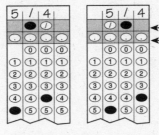

Fraction line
Decimal point

Either position is correct.

You may start your answers in any column, space permitting. Columns not needed should be left blank.

• It is recommended, though not required, that you write your answer in the boxes at the top of the columns. However, you will receive credit only for darkening the ovals correctly.

• Grid only one answer to a question, even though some problems have more than one correct answer.

• Darken no more than one oval in a column.

• No answers are negative.

• Mixed numbers cannot be gridded. For example: the number $1\frac{1}{4}$ must be gridded as 1.25 or 5/4.

(If $\boxed{1\,|\,1\,|\,/\,|\,4}$ is gridded, it will be interpreted as $\frac{11}{4}$ not $1\frac{1}{4}$.)

• Decimal Accuracy: Decimal answers must be entered as accurately as possible. For example, if you obtain an answer such as 0.1666…, you should record the result as .166 or .167. **Less accurate values such as .16 or .17 are not acceptable.**

Acceptable ways to grid $\frac{1}{6}$ = .1666…

GO ON TO THE NEXT PAGE

9. The figure above shows $f(x)$, a quadratic function. What is one solution of this function?

10. To borrow a single book from a lending library, Mr. Brown was charged $2 for 2 weeks, plus a fine of $.15 per day for every day he was late returning it. If he paid a total of $4.55, how many days did he have the book?

11. Points V, W, X, Y and Z lie on a line in that order. VW is twice as long as WX and XY is half as long as YZ. If the length of segment $\overline{WY}$ is 6, what is the length of segment $\overline{VZ}$?

$$-AA = AA$$

12. In the equation above, AA represents a positive, two-digit number in which both digits are the same. If the number that has been covered by the box is a positive, three-digit number that is divisible by 3, what is one possible value of the covered number?

13. Kelly has 25 pairs of pants and 32 shirts in her closet. If she wants to pick out an outfit consisting of a pair of pants and a shirt, how many different outfits could she wear?

14. The last Monday of a 31-day month must be at least how many days after the first Friday of the same month?

15. For positive integers a and b, let $a \sim b$ be defined by $a \sim b = a + (a-1) + (a-2) + \cdots + b$. For example, $9 \sim 4 = 9 + 8 + 7 + 6 + 5 + 4 = 39$. What is the value of $(100 \sim 5) - (98 \sim 3)$?

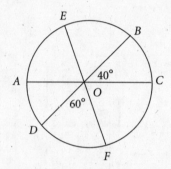

16. In the circle above, $\overline{AC}$, $\overline{BD}$, and $\overline{EF}$ pass through center O. The area of sector AOE is equal to what fraction of the total area of the circle?

17. In the figure above, what is the sum of y and z?

18. Tameka cleans her house every 7 days and does laundry every 5 days. In the next 315 days, how many times will she have to clean her house *and* do laundry on the same day?

SECTION 6

Time—25 Minutes

24 Questions

Directions: For each of the following questions, choose the best answer and darken the corresponding oval on the answer sheet.

Each sentence below has one or two blanks, each blank indicating that something has been omitted. Beneath the sentence are five words or sets of words labeled A through E. Choose the word or set of words that, when inserted in the sentence, <u>best</u> fits the meaning of the sentence as a whole.

EXAMPLE:

Today's small, portable computers contrast markedly with the earliest electronic computers, which were -------.

(A) effective
(B) invented
(C) useful
(D) destructive
(E) enormous

---

1. Jamal found the movie stubs lying on the counter to be ------- evidence that his friends had gone to the cinema without him; it was unquestionable that they had seen Spiderman.

   (A) immaterial
   (B) potential
   (C) incriminating
   (D) nominal
   (E) indisputable

2. When training for a marathon, runners prepare themselves for a challenge that is both ------- and mentally -------.

   (A) illusory . . . taxing
   (B) exaggerated . . . balanced
   (C) physically . . . demanding
   (D) appealing . . . indulgent
   (E) strenuous . . . dubious

3. Healthy lifestyle choices such as exercising regularly and maintaining a nutritious diet can promote ------- yet are often ------- by the busy lives people today lead.

   (A) extinction . . . enhanced
   (B) longevity . . . hampered
   (C) behavior . . . belied
   (D) mortality . . . bolstered
   (E) reproduction . . . confirmed

4. Despite his apparent ------- lifestyle, the old man was known to drink to excess when visited by friends.

   (A) temperate
   (B) laconic
   (C) duplicitous
   (D) aesthetic
   (E) voluble

5. Nostradamus gained a reputation for ------- as he accurately predicted events such as wars complete with descriptions of vehicles that were not invented until after the 16th century when he wrote about his presages.

   (A) prescience
   (B) sincerity
   (C) avarice
   (D) complicity
   (E) mendacity

GO ON TO THE NEXT PAGE ⇒

(corrected) ...until after the 16th century...

Directions: The passages below are followed by questions based on their content; questions following a pair of related passages may also be based on the relationship between the paired passages. Answer the questions on the basis of what is <u>stated</u> or <u>implied</u> in the passages and in any introductory material that may be provided.

Questions 6–9 refer to the following passages.

Passage 1

Acid rain clouds, formed by the release of gases from burning fossil fuels, join with existing weather patterns and eventually pour down toxic, highly acidic water droplets that
(5) can cause significant and often irreversible environmental damage. However, nuclear power and renewable energy technologies—those that take advantage of continuously-available resources such as the sea, sun,
(10) and various biofuels—can generate electricity without giving off the gases that contribute to acid rain, and there are even proven ways to effectively sequester the harmful gases generated by fossil fuel plants. Yet as acid
(15) rain continues to seriously damage countless waterways, forests, crops, and even to erode buildings, senselessly little is being done to take advantage of these new technologies.

Passage 2

While the world's most-developed nations
(20) have the luxury of squabbling over the political and environmental questions raised by those who actually have energy choices, the developing world usually has only one resource to turn to: coal. One of the cheap-
(25) est and most plentiful sources of energy in the world, coal is used to generate nearly 40 percent of the world's electricity. But when burned, coal releases large amounts of carbon dioxide—a gas that, when present in excess,
(30) can cause a whole host of serious respiratory diseases. So while wealthy nations can complain about global warming and acid rain, the rest of the world must struggle to cope with the immediate human damage caused by the
(35) only natural resource they can afford.

6. In Passage 1, the author's attitude toward the continuing presence of acid rain is best described as

   (A) astonishment that acid rain remains a problem in the developed world

   (B) frustration that the use of cleaner technologies is not more widespread

   (C) irritation that nothing is being done to curb the creation of acid rain

   (D) impatience towards plants that refuse to adopt experimental technologies

   (E) skepticism that irreversible damage is really being done to the environment

7. In Passage 2, the author characterizes "the world's most-developed nations" (line 19) as which of the following?

   (A) Insensitive

   (B) Responsible

   (C) Privileged

   (D) Reckless

   (E) Impoverished

GO ON TO THE NEXT PAGE ⇒

8. How would the author of Passage 2 most likely respond to the assertion in Passage 1 that "senselessly little" (line 17) is being done to take advantage of new and cleaner energy-generation technologies?

   (A) Wealthier nations have a responsibility to create opportunities for those less fortunate.

   (B) Most countries would adopt these technologies if they were affordable.

   (C) The environmental impact of an energy source is just as important as the cost of energy.

   (D) Environmental damage is less significant than damage to humans.

   (E) Not all countries can afford these technologies.

9. The authors of both passages agree that

   (A) clean energy technologies are more expensive than conventional methods

   (B) acid rain is a problem inevitably created by energy generation

   (C) the burning of fossil fuels can release harmful gases

   (D) the environmental debate over energy generation is only intensifying

   (E) the human and environmental impacts of energy generation are equally important

Questions 10–15 refer to the following passage.

When I accepted a volunteer position as a social worker at a domestic violence shelter in a developing nation, I imagined the position for which my university experience
(5) had prepared me. I envisioned conducting intake interviews and traipsing around from organization to organization seeking the legal, psychological, and financial support that the women would need to rebuild their
(10) lives. When I arrived, I felt as if I already had months of experience, experience garnered in the hypothetical situations I had invented and subsequently resolved single-handedly and seamlessly. I felt thoroughly prepared to
(15) tackle head-on the situation I assumed was waiting for me.

I arrived full of zeal, knocking at the shelter's door. Within moments, my reality made a sharp break from that which I had
(20) anticipated. The coordinator explained that the shelter's need for financial self-sufficiency had become obvious and acute. To address this, the center was planning to open a bakery. I immediately enthused about the project,
(25) making many references to the small enterprise case studies I had researched at the university. In response to my impassioned reply, the coordinator declared me in charge of the bakery and left in order to "get out of my
(30) way." At that moment, I was as prepared to bake bread as I was to run for political office. The bigger problem, however, was that I was completely unfamiliar with the for-profit business models necessary to run the bakery.
(35) I was out of my depth in a foreign river with only my coordinator's confidence to keep me afloat.

They say that necessity is the mother of invention. I soon found that it is also the
(40) mother of initiative. I began finding recipes and appropriating the expertise of friends.

GO ON TO THE NEXT PAGE ⇒

With their help making bread, balancing
books, printing pamphlets and making con-
tacts, the bakery was soon running smoothly
(45) and successfully. After a short time it became
a significant source of income for the house.

In addition to funds, baking bread provided
a natural environment in which to work with
and get to know the women of the shelter.
(50) Kneading dough side by side, I shared in the
camaraderie of the kitchen, treated to stories about their children and the towns and
jobs they had had to leave behind to ensure
their safety. Baking helped me develop strong
(55) relationships with the women and advanced
my understanding of their situations. It also
improved the women's self-esteem. Their ability to master a new skill gave them confidence
in themselves, and the fact that the bakery
(60) contributed to the upkeep of the house gave
the women, many of them newly single, a
sense of pride and the conviction that they
had the capability to support themselves.

Baking gave me the opportunity to work in
(65) a capacity I had not at all anticipated, but one
that proved very successful. I became a more
sensitive and skillful social worker, capable
of making a mean seven-grain loaf. Learning
to bake gave me as much newfound self-con-
(70) fidence as it gave the women, and I found
that sometimes quality social work can be as
simple as kneading dough.

10. The primary purpose of the passage is to show
how the author

   (A) was shocked by the discrepancy between
her earlier ideas about her work and the
reality she faced

   (B) discovered a talent her overly focused
mind had never allowed her to explore

   (C) broadened how she defined the scope of
her work

   (D) developed her abilities to orchestrate
a for-profit business enterprise

   (E) was abroad when she encountered and
overcame a challenging situation

11. The statement that the author arrived "full of
zeal" (line 17) indicates that she was

   (A) anxious and insecure

   (B) eager and interested

   (C) confident but uninformed

   (D) cheerful but exhausted

   (E) enthusiastic but incompetent

12. The author was initially enthusiastic about the
idea of the bakery because she

   (A) considered it from a theoretical point of
view

   (B) hoped to obtain a leadership position in
the bakery

   (C) wanted to demonstrate her baking
knowledge to her new coordinator

   (D) believed it would be a good way to build
the women's self-esteem

   (E) was a strong proponent of self-sufficiency projects for nonprofit organizations

GO ON TO THE NEXT PAGE ⇨

13. The comparison in lines 30–31 ("At that moment . . . political office") demonstrates the author's belief that

    (A) the bakery would never be a success

    (B) social workers should not be involved in either baking or politics

    (C) it was unfair of the coordinator to ask the author to run the bakery

    (D) similar skills were involved in both baking and politics

    (E) she was unqualified for a job baking bread

14. Lines 32–34 ("The bigger...models") suggest that the author believed that

    (A) learning the necessary business practices would be a more daunting challenge than learning to bake bread

    (B) good business practices are more important to running a successful bakery than is the quality of the bread

    (C) her coordinator's confidence in for-profit business models was misplaced

    (D) for-profit business models are significantly more complex than the nonprofit models with which she was familiar

    (E) her coordinator would be unwilling to help her

15. The last sentence ("Learning . . . dough") indicates that the author

    (A) lacked self-confidence just as much as the women with whom she worked

    (B) found that performing social work is surprisingly easy with no education

    (C) underestimated her own ability to learn new skills

    (D) discovered that social work is more effective when it includes tactile activities

    (E) derived a benefit from her work while helping others

GO ON TO THE NEXT PAGE

Questions 16–24 refer to the following passage.

This passage discusses some recreational options and reasons for making good use of leisure time.

Recreation is a vital aspect of human life, because it provides one with opportunities to recreate oneself. Recreation can be defined as the refreshment of mind or body through
(5) activity that stimulates or amuses. This definition invites one to both contemplate the myriad options for recreational activity and evaluate these options for their potential to enrich one's life and enhance personal growth
(10) and development.

The modern economic system has freed people from the necessity to relentlessly seek daily sustenance, and thus has augmented leisure, or recreational, time. Many choose
(15) to recreate by engaging in physical competition, namely sports. Former athletes cite their experiences in wrestling, tennis, football, or soccer by way of elucidating their successes in business, government, or academia. For
(20) instance, they commend coaches who taught them to gracefully handle conflict and disappointment; or they vividly recount a specific moment of competition that transformed their lives forever.

(25) Competition, proponents say, gives athletes a profound understanding of both their limits and their abilities. The ability to candidly analyze one's strengths and weaknesses confers resilience in the face of life's vicissitudes
(30) and thus the ability to overcome obstacles.

On the other hand, some athletes shun organized sports, preferring to test themselves physically without the element of competition. They may hike or bike, snowboard or ski, or run or
(35) ride alone or with companions. They contend that their bodies and spirits are best refreshed without the distraction of needless comparison with others.

Taking a different approach, many people
(40) engage in artistic and creative pursuits as a means of recreating themselves. In an academic environment of standardized testing, which directs minds down ever-narrowing avenues of thought, proponents of the arts
(45) point to the mental and emotional flexibility developed by creative activity. For example, art teaches one how to exercise the exquisite faculty of judgment in the absence of rules. It sets forth dilemmas to be resolved, dem-
(50) onstrating that every problem has more than one solution. Practitioners of the arts learn to swim in a turbulent sea of ambiguity and chance without the lifejacket of standard procedure; in other words, art prepares them for
(55) the exigencies of life.

Productive leisure activities amplify one's vocational efforts and increase chances of success. They enhance an understanding of one's place in the world. They facilitate full use
(60) of one's capacities and provide pleasure that enhances all of life's experiences.

16. The author's primary purpose in writing this passage is to

(A) describe the propensity of successful people for athletic participation

(B) compare the theoretical benefits of physical versus artistic activities

(C) convince the reader of the pleasurable nature of recreational pursuits

(D) promote the tangible and intangible benefits of productive leisure activities

(E) engage in speculation about the requisites for vocational success

GO ON TO THE NEXT PAGE

17. The author's statement that "the modern economic system has freed people from the necessity to relentlessly seek daily sustenance" (lines 11–13) suggests that increased leisure time is

    (A) always preferable to work
    (B) a consequence of shortened work days
    (C) becoming more scarce, and hence more valuable
    (D) closely related to democratic forms of government
    (E) ideally engaged in on a daily basis

18. According to the second paragraph of the passage, which of the following is a lifelong benefit of engaging in competition?

    (A) increased persistence in surmounting difficulties
    (B) heightened sensitivity to inherent lack of ability
    (C) the capacity to always prevail in life's struggles
    (D) a lifelong engagement with physical activity
    (E) gratitude to those who help one, such as coaches

19. The concept of "competition" is mentioned in line 14 for which of the following reasons?

    (A) to strengthen the case for competition as an element of proper recreation
    (B) to distract the reader from the importance of comparative physical activities
    (C) to acknowledge that enjoyment is more important than competition in recreation
    (D) to contend that athletics without competition is meaningless
    (E) to emphasize that the benefits of physical recreation do not necessarily have to include competition

20. According to the passage, advantages of recreational pursuit of the arts include which of the following?

    I. Tolerance of uncertainty
    II. Ability to exercise independent judgment in unanticipated situations
    III. Appreciation of aesthetic presentation

    (A) I only
    (B) II only
    (C) I and II only
    (D) II and III only
    (E) I, II and III

21. In line 55 "exigencies" most nearly means

    (A) crises
    (B) waves
    (C) situations
    (D) motivations
    (E) rules

GO ON TO THE NEXT PAGE

22. The author's statement about standardized testing in schools "direct[ing] minds down ever-narrowing avenues of thought" suggests a conviction that such testing is

    (A) necessary
    (B) irrelevant
    (C) limiting
    (D) productive
    (E) creative

23. The author of this passage is primarily interested in which of the following aspects of recreation?

    (A) Its benefits for society at large
    (B) The physical and emotional flexibility it confers
    (C) Its role as requisite for vocational success
    (D) Its benefits for the whole life of the individual
    (E) Its ubiquitous position in the human psyche

24. The author uses the metaphor "learn to swim in a turbulent sea of ambiguity and chance without the lifejacket of standard procedure" (lines 51–54) for what purpose?

    (A) To show that artists know how to swim
    (B) To show that artists live according to strict rules
    (C) To show that artists and athletes see the world the same way
    (D) To show that artists live without boundaries
    (E) To show the need for a life jacket

IF YOU FINISH BEFORE TIME IS CALLED, YOU MAY CHECK YOUR WORK ON THIS SECTION ONLY. DO NOT TURN TO ANY OTHER SECTION IN THE TEST. STOP

SECTION 7

Time—20 Minutes
16 Questions

Directions: For this section, solve each problem and decide which is the best of the choices given. Fill in the corresponding oval on the answer sheet. You may use any available space for scratchwork.

Notes:

(1) Calculator use is permitted.

(2) All numbers used are real numbers.

(3) Figures are provided for some problems. All figures are drawn to scale and lie in a plane UNLESS otherwise indicated.

(4) Unless otherwise specified, the domain of any function f is assumed to be the set of all real numbers x for which $f(x)$ is a real number.

$A = \frac{1}{2}bh$ $c^2 = a^2 + b^2$ Special Right Triangles $A = \pi r^2$ $V = \ell wh$ $V = \pi r^2 h$ $A = \ell w$
                                                                     $C = 2\pi r$

The sum of the degree measures of the angles in a triangle is 180.
The number of degrees of arc in a circle is 360.
A straight angle has a degree measure of 180.

---

1. If $8a < 3b$ and $3b < 10c$, which of the following must be true?

    (A) $8a < 10c$
    (B) $10c < 8a$
    (C) $c < a$
    (D) $8a = 10c$
    (E) $8a + 1 = 10c$

Department	Number of Teams	Employees per Team
Development	1	4
Marketing	2	3
Accounting	3	2
Public Relations	5	5

2. The chart above shows the distribution of employees at a company into different teams in different departments. According to the chart, how many total employees are there?

    (A) 14
    (B) 25
    (C) 41
    (D) 84
    (E) 154

GO ON TO THE NEXT PAGE

3. If the average (arithmetic mean) of 7 numbers is greater than 7 and less than 12, which of the following could be the sum of the 7 numbers?

(A) 84

(B) 77

(C) 49

(D) 42

(E) 35

4. Carmel is spinning a basketball on his finger so that it turns around completely every 1.5 seconds. How many degrees does the logo on the ball turn in 10 seconds, assuming it is not on the spinning axis?

(A) 54°

(B) 240°

(C) 720°

(D) 2,160°

(E) 2,400°

Questions 5 and 6 refer to the following figure.

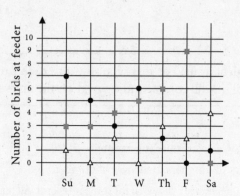

5. Joe kept a record of the birds that visited his backyard for one week. He set out three types of feeders and counted the number of birds that visited each feeder each day. In the graph above, each feeder is represented by a different colored dot. The black circles indicate the feeder with sunflower seeds. The gray squares represent the feeder with thistle seeds. The white triangles represent the feeder with suet. Approximately what percentage of the birds in Joe's yard on Thursday visited the suet feeder?

(A) 18%

(B) 27%

(C) 36%

(D) 48%

(E) 55%

6. On what day did the greatest number of birds eat sunflower seeds?

(A) Sunday

(B) Tuesday

(C) Wednesday

(D) Friday

(E) Saturday

GO ON TO THE NEXT PAGE

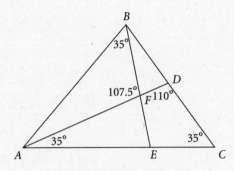

Note: Figure not drawn to scale.

7. In triangle ABC above, $\overline{AD}$ and $\overline{BE}$ are line segments. All of the following are isosceles triangles, EXCEPT

    (A) Triangle AFE
    (B) Triangle ABE
    (C) Triangle ADC
    (D) Triangle BFD
    (E) Triangle ABC

Questions 8–10 refer to the following sequence of steps.

Choose a number between 0 and 9.9.

Multiply the number from the previous step by 100.

Determine the smallest integer greater than or equal to the number obtained from the previous step.

Add 12 to the number found in the previous step.

Print the resulting number.

8. If 6.127 is the number chosen in step 1, what is the number printed in step 5?

    (A) 12
    (B) 74
    (C) 624
    (D) 624.7
    (E) 625

9. Which of the following could be a number printed in step 5 after steps 1 through 4 are performed?

    (A) −1
    (B) 10
    (C) 27.3
    (D) 674
    (E) 1,050

10. Which change, if any, could be made in the order of the steps without changing the number printed in step 5?

    (A) Only steps 2 and 3 could be switched.
    (B) Only steps 2 and 4 could be switched.
    (C) Only steps 3 and 4 could be switched.
    (D) Steps 2, 3, and 4 can be done in any order.
    (E) None of the above changes can be made.

11. If $x = 3^5$, which of the following expressions is equal to 3^{11}?

    (A) $243x$
    (B) $3x^2$
    (C) $9x^4$
    (D) $27x^3$
    (E) x^6

12. If $n - 3 = 7 + m$, what is the value of $2(n - m) + 4$?

    (A) 8
    (B) 12
    (C) 17
    (D) 24
    (E) 29

GO ON TO THE NEXT PAGE

13. If $x = -5$ satisfies the equation $x^2 + 3x + c = 0$, where c is a constant, what is another value of x that satisfies the equation?

(A) −2
(B) 2
(C) 5
(D) 7
(E) 10

14. The sum of three consecutive odd integers is 1,089. What is the greatest integer of the three?

(A) 185
(B) 299
(C) 317
(D) 365
(E) 423

15. Jan can mow her lawn in 60 minutes by herself. If she hires Wally to do it, he takes 30 minutes, while Peter can do it in 40 minutes. If Jan starts mowing the lawn for 15 minutes, then decides to hire Wally and Peter to help her finish, how long will it take (in hours), from when Jan started to when the three finished together?

(A) $\frac{1}{6}$ hours

(B) $\frac{5}{12}$ hours

(C) $\frac{7}{12}$ hours

(D) $\frac{3}{4}$ hours

(E) $\frac{5}{6}$ hours

Note: Figure not drawn to scale.

16. In the figure above, quadrilateral $ABDC$ has vertices A and B on line ℓ, point E is also on line ℓ, and the coordinates of B, D, and E are as indicated. What is the area of $ABDC$?

(A) $\frac{1}{2}$

(B) $\frac{4}{3}$

(C) $\frac{11}{3}$

(D) $\frac{22}{3}$

(E) $\frac{26}{3}$

IF YOU FINISH BEFORE TIME IS CALLED, YOU MAY CHECK YOUR WORK ON THIS SECTION ONLY. DO NOT TURN TO ANY OTHER SECTION IN THE TEST.

STOP

SECTION 8

Time—20 Minutes

18 Questions

Directions: For each of the following questions, choose the best answer and darken the corresponding oval on the answer sheet.

Each sentence below has one or two blanks, each blank indicating that something has been omitted. Beneath the sentence are five words or sets of words labeled A through E. Choose the word or set of words that, when inserted in the sentence, best fits the meaning of the sentence as a whole.

Example:

Today's small, portable computers contrast markedly with the earliest electronic computers, which were -------.

(A) effective

(B) invented

(C) useful

(D) destructive

(E) enormous   Ⓐ Ⓑ Ⓒ Ⓓ ⬤

---

1. ------ two doses of the Hepatitis A vaccine over a period of six to twelve months is ------- providing protection from the disease for ten years.

(A) Constraining . . . required for

(B) Distributing . . . unsuccessful in

(C) Reconstituting . . . instrumental in

(D) Administering . . . effective in

(E) Disseminating . . . unverified for

2. After all of the passengers were safely aboard lifeboats, the crew of the King Cruiser made every attempt to ------- what scuba diving equipment they could off of the ------- dive boat before it sank.

(A) qualify . . . obsolete

(B) salvage . . . floundering

(C) exacerbate . . . defunct

(D) revitalize . . . prosperous

(E) commandeer . . . lucrative

3. Many towns bordering two different countries have a heterogeneous population and can boast of a ------- of different foods that incorporate a ------- of various ingredients.

(A) multiplicity . . . variety

(B) proliferation . . . moderation

(C) ambivalence . . . focus

(D) dearth . . . depletion

(E) abridgment . . . imitation

4. Despite the markings that ranked the trail as moderately difficult, the hikers found the trek to be challenging as the path was -------; it meandered ceaselessly around the riverbank for miles.

(A) panoramic

(B) precipitous

(C) serpentine

(D) circumscribed

(E) retrograde

GO ON TO THE NEXT PAGE →

5. After the accident Jidapa's friends found that her behavior had changed drastically; once sprightly and friendly, she now seemed disheartened and unaffable, the ------- of her former self.

(A) remnant
(B) antithesis
(C) consequence
(D) extremity
(E) mainstay

6. The detectives knew they had to act punctiliously because any mistakes, even the slightest -------, would compromise the stakeout.

(A) query
(B) gibe
(C) gaffe
(D) tryst
(E) tribute

GO ON TO THE NEXT PAGE

Directions: The passages below are followed by questions based on their content; questions following a pair of related passages may also be based on the relationship between the paired passages. Answer the questions on the basis of what is <u>stated</u> or <u>implied</u> in the passages and in any introductory material that may be provided.

Questions 7–18 refer to the following passages.

The following passages represent two points of view about the future of cinema. The first is by a screenwriter arguing for a change in methodology. The second is by a film critic expressing his views on the changing world of film.

Passage 1

Ancient Greek drama, often cited as the crucible of all Western drama, consisted of three types of plays. Comedy was a form greatly affected by changing times and fash-
(5) ions; tragedy was inspired by mythology and history. The ancient Greeks believed that the dark and brooding form of tragedy required a "relief." Still common today, a relief is designed to be a moment of respite from the
(10) seriousness of the tragic theme. Satyr plays fulfilled that function in ancient Greece. Of these three forms, tragedy has received the most critical and scholarly attention in modern times. It is the Satyr play, however, that
(15) will capture the imagination of the rising generation.

A Satyr is a mythological creature—half-human and half-beast. This creature appears on stage in the Satyr plays as a character
(20) whose main function is to be part of the coterie of the god Dionysus, a central figure in the Greek theater. Even without the exact characters of Dionysus or the Satyrs, the ideas they embody can still be used in playwriting
(25) or screenwriting today. As ardent followers of their leader, the Satyrs in the plays display a curious mix of cowardice and boldness similar to what we see in Shakespeare's Falstaff.

The chorus is another dynamic element
(30) of the Satyr play that is full of potential. The chorus, sometimes dancing or singing, can be invisible to the central characters. In this mode, members of the chorus are free to engage the audience without interfering
(35) with the action of the play. At any moment, though, they can step into the world of the play and interact with the other characters. This fundamental boundary crossing is a central reason that this form lends itself to the
(40) modern cinema.

The Satyr form is widely ignored and has barely been acknowledged by critics and scholars. Screenwriters today persist in looking to tragic and comic forms for inspiration
(45) when there are volumes of untapped potential in the Satyr form. The example of the chorus, "unseen" by the central players at one moment and then jumping in to the center of the scene in the next, gives just a hint of what
(50) the Satyr form has to offer. If you seek an even more unpredictable inspiration, imagine the chorus jumping into the action singing and dancing.

Passage 2

Of the two primary forms of drama—com-
(55) edy and tragedy—comedy is the more promising form for the future of cinema. Comedy has always been the more stylistically forward form, because it looks to current events for topics and is quick to respond to trends.
(60) While some subject matter has been consistent over the centuries (for example, the lampooning of leaders or the misadventures

GO ON TO THE NEXT PAGE ⟩

of husbands and wives), the forms employed in comedy today can only be described as sophisticated. Tragedy, on the other hand, has (65) always looked to the past for subject matter and the form is consequently nostalgic.

In general, the forms of cinema have become predictable, to the point that the spoofing of some forms has become commonplace. (70) Modern filmmakers' overuse of a small number of narrative devices has produced a generation of moviegoers who are compelled by twists and turns. Jaded by their overexposure to form, they seek out the new and surpris-(75) ing. It is a difficult task indeed to surprise this generation of media-saturated spectators. But the comedic form has the requisite flexibility.

There is no limit to the ways in which comedy can transform and conform itself (80) to the requirements of any generation. This assertion is confirmed by the fact that even in ancient Greece, comedy responded to fashion and changing aesthetics. History has proven that comedy suits itself to all times and circumstances. The only theatri-(85) cal tradition to survive the fall of Rome was comic. Even in the darkest times, or perhaps especially in the darkest times, comedy shines on. The basic human need for comedy and comic relief is one thing that has forced the (90) form toward flexibility. Since people crave comedy, they do whatever they can, using form and structure, to create the kind of comedy they need at the time.

All of this is not to say that making comedy (95) is easy. Although the comic "form" is wildly loose, it is not the least bit forgiving. For this reason, the most impressive work is in the comic form. The discriminating viewer of today's cinema recognizes this fact and (100) rewards successful filmmakers with loyalty. Today's audience seeks variety, excitement, and surprise. The filmmakers most likely to succeed in this market will be those skilled in the comic form and willing to exploit all of its potential.

7. The overall tone of Passage 1 is

(A) muted
(B) strident
(C) whimsical
(D) grateful
(E) enthusiastic

8. As used in Passage 1, "engage" (line 34) most nearly means

(A) contract with
(B) propose marriage to
(C) hire
(D) lock together with
(E) hold the attention of

9. The statement that "there are volumes of untapped potential in the Satyr form" (lines 45–46) suggests that

(A) there are books of Satyr plays not yet translated
(B) numerous movies can be made about Greek drama
(C) many ideas in Satyr plays have not yet been explored
(D) the noise level in Satyr plays is extremely high
(E) there is dormant inspiration in music

GO ON TO THE NEXT PAGE ⟹

10. The author of Passage 1 refers to the chorus in the fourth paragraph primarily in order to

(A) prove the superiority of the comic form

(B) underline the variety and surprise provided by the Satyr form

(C) emphasize the importance of dancing to the future of cinema

(D) contrast the Satyr character with the chorus

(E) explain why the Satyr form is widely ignored

11. In lines 62–63, "the misadventures of husbands and wives" is an example of

(A) a consistent form of Greek comedy

(B) sophisticated subject matter for comedy

(C) nostalgic subject matter for tragedy

(D) traditional subject matter for comedy

(E) a typical Satyric plot

12. As used in Passage 2, the word "jaded" (line 74) most nearly means

(A) satisfied

(B) rocked

(C) conceited

(D) dulled

(E) surprised

13. In Passage 2, the main purpose of the third paragraph is to

(A) explain the flexibility of the comedic form

(B) emphasize the importance of ancient Greek civilization

(C) illustrate the tragedy of the fall of Rome

(D) correct a general misunderstanding about the rigidity of comedy

(E) illuminate the significance of intergenerational traditions

14. The word "form" (line 92) is in quotation marks primarily to

(A) emphasize that the author is using the exact definition of the word

(B) indicate that the structure of comedy is not as strict as the word suggests

(C) show that the author intended to use another word

(D) highlight the difference between theater and cinema

(E) refer the reader to a previously mentioned definition of the word

15. Both authors would most likely agree that

(A) ancient Greek theater is relevant to modern cinema

(B) comedy is one of the most resilient forms of drama

(C) tragedy is an irrelevant form in entertainment today

(D) Satyr plays represent a more adaptable form than comedy

(E) modern audiences are bored by the current cinema

GO ON TO THE NEXT PAGE

16. Both authors would most likely agree on the value of the

    (A) chorus
    (B) audience
    (C) critic
    (D) screenwriter
    (E) characters

17. The main idea of Passage 2 is that

    (A) comedy and tragedy are superior to the Satyr form
    (B) American cinema has become too predictable
    (C) comedy is superior to tragedy as a form of drama
    (D) the comic form has the greatest promise for reinvigorating cinema
    (E) American moviegoers are anxious for the release of high-quality comedies

18. The author of Passage 2 might respond to the reference to "Shakespeare's Falstaff" (line 28) in Passage 1 by

    (A) criticizing the misuse of such a famous character in support of an unknown art form
    (B) highlighting the added relevance given to Falstaff by comic aspects Shakespeare accords to him
    (C) contending that characters of Greek and Roman drama are more applicable than those of Elizabethan drama
    (D) arguing that Falstaff would make an excellent template for the hero of a Satyr play
    (E) citing Falstaff as an example of the sophistication of the comic form

IF YOU FINISH BEFORE TIME IS CALLED, YOU MAY CHECK YOUR WORK ON THIS SECTION ONLY. DO NOT TURN TO ANY OTHER SECTION IN THE TEST.

STOP

SECTION 9

Time—10 Minutes

14 Questions

Directions: For each question in this section, select the best answer from among the choices given and fill in the corresponding oval on the answer sheet.

The following sentences test correctness and effectiveness of expression. Part of each sentence or the entire sentence is underlined; beneath each sentence are five ways of phrasing the underlined material. Choice A repeats the original phrasing; the other four choices are different. If you think the original phrasing produces a better sentence than any of the alternatives, select choice A; if not, select one of the other choices.

In making your selection, follow the requirements of standard written English; that is, pay attention to grammar, choice of words, sentence construction, and punctuation. Your selection should result in the most effective sentence—clear and precise, without awkwardness or ambiguity.

EXAMPLE:

Every apple in the baskets <u>are ripe and labeled according to the date it was picked</u>.

(A) are ripe and labeled according to the date it was picked
(B) is ripe and labeled according to the date it was picked
(C) are ripe and labeled according to the date they were picked
(D) is ripe and labeled according to the date they were picked
(E) are ripe and labeled as to the date it was picked

ANSWER:

(A) ● (C) (D) (E)

---

1. For a hospital, a backup generator is <u>invaluable so that it</u> provides power in the event of an emergency that disrupts local electrical service.

    (A) invaluable so that it
    (B) invaluable because it
    (C) invaluable, although it
    (D) invaluable in order that
    (E) invaluable because they

2. In his press release, the actor <u>asserted that the media had unfairly biased</u> potential jurors before his trial had even begun.

    (A) asserted that the media had unfairly biased
    (B) asserted of how the media had unfairly biased
    (C) made an assertion of the media having unfairly biased
    (D) made an assertion that the media had unfairly biased
    (E) asserted that unfair bias had been made by the media of

GO ON TO THE NEXT PAGE ⇨

3. During the harvest, French <u>vineyards hiring many temporary workers</u>, a large percentage of whom come from Spain.

   (A) vineyards hiring many temporary workers

   (B) vineyards hires many temporary workers

   (C) vineyards hiring many workers who are temporary

   (D) vineyards hire many temporary workers

   (E) vineyards hire many people who work temporarily

4. <u>In most cases, in the election of a president, the results are determined by a small number of "swing states."</u>

   (A) In most cases, in the election of a president, the results are determined by a small number of "swing states."

   (B) Generally, the results of a president election are determined by a small number of "swing states" most of the time.

   (C) A few "swing states" decide the results of most presidential elections.

   (D) A presidential election, as to results, is most often determined by "swing states," of which there are a small number.

   (E) Presidential elections generally have a small number of "swing states" that determine their results.

5. Vocational and technical schools offer teenagers the opportunity to start working as electricians, plumbers, auto mechanics, <u>and other jobs</u> immediately after graduation

   (A) and other jobs

   (B) and as other jobs

   (C) and working in other jobs

   (D) and other careers

   (E) and in other jobs

6. In a police lineup, witnesses see several people, <u>there is one who is</u> the suspect.

   (A) there is one who is

   (B) because one is

   (C) one is

   (D) one of whom is

   (E) of which one is

7. In the 19th century, European politicians sought to establish a balance of power in the hope that <u>this had prevented war on the continent</u>.

   (A) this had prevented war on the continent

   (B) this would prevent war on the continent

   (C) war on the continent will be prevented

   (D) the continent will find war prevented

   (E) this will prevent war on the continent

GO ON TO THE NEXT PAGE ▷

8. The Vatican City is one of the most visited sites by tourists in Italy, since it is technically its own country.

    (A) The Vatican City is one of the most visited sites by tourists in Italy, since it is technically its own country.

    (B) The Vatican City, one of the most visited sites by tourists in Italy, is technically its own country.

    (C) Of the most visited sites by tourists in Italy, the Vatican City is technically its own country.

    (D) Since it is its own country, the Vatican City is technically one of the most visited sites by tourists in Italy.

    (E) Since it is technically its own country, one of the most visited sites by tourists in Italy is the Vatican City.

9. In the United States, a candidate must be 35 years old before you can run for president.

    (A) you can run

    (B) it can run

    (C) he or she can run

    (D) one runs

    (E) he or she is running

10. Among the most complex musical composition of the era, Chopin wrote his Etudes to be performed on the piano.

    (A) Chopin wrote his Etudes to be performed on the piano

    (B) the piano is what Chopin wrote his Etudes to be performed on

    (C) Chopin's Etudes, written to be performed on the piano

    (D) Chopin's Etudes were written to be performed on the piano

    (E) Chopin, having written his Etudes to be performed on the piano

11. The defendant's lawyer told the jury that he was sorry for the damage he had caused and the people he had hurt.

    (A) he was sorry for the damage he had caused and the people he had hurt

    (B) his client was sorry for the damage he had caused and the people he had hurt

    (C) given the damage caused and the people hurt, he was sorry

    (D) his client, sorry for the damage he had caused and the people he had hurt

    (E) the damage he had caused and the people he had hurt were what his client was sorry for

GO ON TO THE NEXT PAGE

12. <u>Although the first phase of construction was completed last month and the new wing has opened</u>, the hospital still suffers from a shortage of rooms.

   (A) Although the first phase of construction was completed last month and the new wing has opened

   (B) Although the new wing has opened, following the completion of the first phase of construction which occurred last month

   (C) The first phase of construction was completed last month and the new wing has opened

   (D) The first phase of construction was completed last month, resulting in the new wing being open but, even so

   (E) The first phase of construction, being completed last month, and the new wing has opened

13. When washing a car, rinse it to remove excess dirt, wipe it with a soapy sponge, and <u>then the car is dried with a clean cloth</u>.

   (A) then the car is dried with a clean cloth

   (B) dry it with a clean cloth

   (C) then drying it with a clean cloth

   (D) finally, it is dried with a clean cloth

   (E) as a final step, then, you dry the car with a clean cloth

14. <u>Images transmitted by email, sharper and clearer than fax, are</u> quickly making obsolete technologies that were once considered state-of-the-art.

   (A) Images transmitted by email, sharper and clearer than fax, are

   (B) Sharper and clearer than the fax, images transmitted by email are

   (C) Images transmitted by email, sharper and clearer than those transmitted by fax, are

   (D) Images transmitted by email, which are sharper and clearer than fax, are

   (E) Email transmission of images, sharper and clearer than the fax, are

---

IF YOU FINISH BEFORE TIME IS CALLED, YOU MAY CHECK YOUR WORK ON THIS SECTION ONLY. DO NOT TURN TO ANY OTHER SECTION IN THE TEST.   **STOP**

Practice Test Four: **Answer Key**

SECTION 1

Essay

SECTION 2

1. D
2. E
3. C
4. B
5. C
6. A
7. B
8. B
9. B
10. D
11. C
12. D
13. C
14. D
15. E
16. E
17. A
18. E
19. C
20. B

SECTION 3

1. D
2. D
3. B
4. D
5. B
6. C
7. E
8. E
9. D

10. E
11. D
12. B
13. C
14. B
15. E
16. E
17. A
18. B
19. E
20. B
21. D
22. A
23. C
24. C
25. C

SECTION 4

1. B
2. B
3. C
4. B
5. A
6. D
7. B
8. E
9. A
10. D
11. B
12. C
13. B
14. B
15. E
16. B
17. E

18. D
19. D
20. B
21. C
22. D
23. D
24. D
25. E
26. E
27. A
28. A
29. C
30. D
31. B
32. E
33. C
34. C
35. E

SECTION 5

1. C
2. A
3. E
4. C
5. C
6. E
7. D
8. A
9. 2
10. 31
11. 18
12. 132 or 198
13. 800
14. 24
15. 192

16. 8/36 or
    2/9
17. 235°
18. 9

SECTION 6

1. E
2. C
3. B
4. A
5. A
6. B
7. C
8. E
9. C
10. C
11. B
12. A
13. E
14. A
15. E
16. D
17. B
18. A
19. E
20. C
21. A
22. C
23. D
24. D

SECTION 7

1. A
2. C
3. B

4. E
5. B
6. A
7. D
8. E
9. D
10. C
11. B
12. D
13. B
14. D
15. B
16. E

SECTION 8

1. D
2. B
3. A
4. C
5. B
6. C
7. E
8. E
9. C
10. B
11. D
12. D
13. A
14. B
15. A
16. B
17. D
18. B

SECTION 9

1. B
2. A
3. D
4. C
5. E
6. D
7. B
8. B
9. C
10. D
11. B
12. A
13. B
14. C

ANSWERS AND EXPLANATIONS

SECTION 1

6 ESSAY

Most people are taught as children that it is important to do things to make other people happy. I remember how great I felt when I brought home the Valentine's Day card I made my mother in first grade. She was thrilled with the sparkly red heart and I was proud that my art project had made her so happy. This is just a small example of the positive reinforcement we receive when we make other people happy, but in the long run pleasing others can be have a negative effect on your life. If you are always guided by other people's desires, instead of discovering what makes you happy, you are more likely to fail than succeed.

I come from a football family, in a football town. My brother had been a star quarterback, and my whole family is very involved in the high school football team. My younger sister is a cheerleader; my mother works at the concession stand during games; and my father is good friends with the coach. I had played football since I was seven, and I was good enough to make the squad of our Division-A team. My parents were thrilled when I made the team in my sophomore year. My father took me aside to tell me how proud he was of me.

My decision to play football was completely motivated by my desire to please my family. What I really wanted to do was run for the cross country team. During football practice, I used to see the cross country team heading off on a long run and I felt so envious. I found the football drills boring, and I began to dread going to practice. During the season, the coach stopped playing me in games because he said I was not trying. He was right; my heart was not in the game. My father got very angry with the coach because he was not putting me in the games, and their friendship suffered. My grades even dropped because I found the situation with football so stressful.

At the end of the season I vowed that I would not play the following year. This summer when I told my parents that I was not going out for football they were not as upset as I thought they might be. I joined the cross country team and have started winning races. I look forward to practice and have made some great friends on the team. My grades are better than they have ever been. My parents still love football, and I discovered that their interest in the local team does not revolve around me. They go to games and cheer as loudly as ever. I even enjoy going to the games, when I don't have a race.

When I was guided by what I thought would make my parents happy, I made myself miserable. When I followed my own interests, I not only succeeded, I think my family is actually happier than when I was trying to please them. You have to seek your own happiness first, as you can only truly succeed at something that you enjoy. Then, as I discovered, you will probably find that the people you are most interested in pleasing will take pleasure in your success.

Grader's Comments

All essays are evaluated on four basic criteria: Topic, Support, Organization, and Language. This is a very well written essay. The writer shows that he understood the topic and took the time to think about it before beginning to write. He sticks to the topic and uses a personal experience to support his stance. His argument is well developed and strongly supported. He never leaves the main point of his example by wandering into another story. He further completes his argument by referencing back to his opening remarks about making people happy in the conclusion. Furthermore, the essay has strong organization and is interesting.

The language used by the writer is straightforward and mature. He does not slip into slang or use awkward language to impress the reader. His writing style and vocabulary use indicate that he is educated and capable of expressing his position in a constructive manner. He uses different structures of his sentences and paragraphs, and despite a few minor errors, stays in the same tense throughout the essay.

4 Essay

To borrow a phrase from President Lincoln, "You can make some of the people happy all the time, and you can make all the people happy some of the time, but you can't make all the people happy all the time." This is especially true in politics. This fall I volunteered on the campaign of a man who was running for mayor of my town. It was the first time I had volunteered on a campaign and I was really excited by what the candidate wanted to accomplish. I really believed in his ideas. For example, he wanted to add money to the school budget so we can have arts classes again. He also wanted to improve public transportation, which was important to me because I have to take the bus.

When the campaign started, the candidate was very idealistic. He was very committed to his ideas. Later into the campaign, however, he started to compromise in order to win more votes. He stopped emphasizing public transportation in his campaign when it seemed unpopular with voters.

He even backed away from his proposal for the school budget when it seemed that people weren't willing to support even the smallest increase in taxes. I was very disillusioned by his failure to stick by his ideas and principles. My candidate lost the mayoral race. I think his failure can be attributed to his attempt to please all the voters instead of sticking up for his own ideas.

Instead of trying to win people over to his platform, the candidate tried to accommodate everything all the voters wanted. Even though a politicians job is to represent the people, so in some ways, his or job is to make people happy, a politician has to stand for something otherwise nobody will vote for them. In politics, you cannot please everyone and if you try you will fail. To succeed in politics you have to stick by your own ideas and try to convince other people that you are right.

GRADER'S COMMENTS

All essays are evaluated on four basic criteria: Topic, Support, Organization, and Language. The writer begins by using a quote to express his position on the topic and to preface his argument. However, the writer misquotes Lincoln. But the essay is not about content, so this mistake does not affect the score. The writer uses an example that covers the topic and supports his position. His personal account of the way political success is attributed to the candidate's desire to please all of the voters speaks directly to the heart of the question. The essay is well organized, with an introduction, a body, and a conclusion.

The writer's language is good and mostly grammatically correct; however, the description is very basic and uninteresting. The tone is often very standard and conversational. He could have used more expressive terminology to help prove his point, and the conclusion is not as strong as it could be.

2 ESSAY

It is not easy to be successful. If you are not going to try, you will never be successfull. You have to do things your own way. One time I was friends with a bunch of girls who did everything together. We would call each other everynight to see who was going to where what the next day so we would not wear the same stuff. If everyone was going to the mall then there was no way you could say you were going to go to the do something else. These girls were really into clothes and makeup and jewelry. This was not the only things I was interested in but I went along with the other girls because I wanted to fit in. Then one time I wanted to join the drama club and the other girls said that drama club was not cool and they would never join drama club. I really wanted to be in the play but I didn't want to make my friends mad so I never tried out. When I went to see the play it looked like so much fun I was mad at myself for listening to my friends. When we moved to high school we were not friends as much just some girls stayed friends. Now I do plays and I think it is really fun and even played the lead roll last year. I learned that you shouldn't not do things because of what other people say and you do what you want and then you will be successful.

GRADER'S COMMENTS

All essays are evaluated on four basic criteria: Topic, Support, Organization, and Language. The writer is good about addressing the topic of the statement immediately in her opening sentence and using her friends as her example. However, the development of her example is not as descript as it needs to be, and her train of thought seems random and all over the place. The organization of the writer's thoughts is loose, and she never returns to her initial stance until the last sentence.

The writer's language is juvenile and against the principles of standard written English. She uses slang, such as "cool," and there are many spelling and diction errors. For example, she writes "where" when she meant "wear" and commits a double negative by using "shouldn't not." The last sentence is a run-on that goes nowhere.

SECTION 2

1. D

Don't over think this one—the x^6 is on each side and can be subtracted from both sides. Subtract x^6 from both sides to get $4 = w$.

2. E

To find the minimum total time, add the minimum times for each part; for the maximum total time, add the maximum times for each part.

Minimum = 22 + 20 = 42

Maximum = 28 + 30 = 58

3. C

Systematically solve for the variables until you have what you're looking for. Start with c, since it's defined in the question stem. Use c to find a, then a to find b.

$a = 8c = 8 \times 9 = 72$

$\dfrac{72}{b} = 4$

$72 = 4b$

$18 = b$

4. B

Convert the scientific notation into a simple number by multiplying it out. Then you can see where the decimal point should be.

$$4.567890 \times 10^2 = 4.567890 \times 100 = 456.7890$$

The decimal point should be between 6 and 7, choice (B).

5. C

The intersection of two sets consists of the elements that are in both sets. In this case, the intersection contains numbers which are both prime and equal to a prime number plus 2.

2 is prime, but is not equal to a prime number plus 2. It is only in set A.

4 is equal to a prime number (2) plus 2, but is not itself prime. It is only in set B.

5 is both prime and equal to a prime number (3) plus 2. Choice (C) is correct.

6. A

Whenever you see a triangle question about angles, remember that the sum of the interior angles of a triangle is 180 degrees.

$$a + b + c = 180$$
$$7c + 2c + c = 180$$
$$10c = 180$$
$$c = 18$$

7. B

Translate the words into algebra, and then let your algebra skills take you home!

Let x be the number of students at the beginning.

After the addition there are $x + 21$ students, which is 4 times x.

So: $\quad x + 21 = 4x$
$$21 = 3x$$
$$x = 7$$

8. B

Remember that you can always assume the diagram is drawn to scale, unless you're told otherwise. Use this to eliminate wrong answer choices if you get stuck.

Draw a third line parallel to *l* and *m*. Find the supplement of the given angles. The angle we want has been split into two angles, each of which is an alternate interior angle with one of the supplement, so $q = 30° + 20° = 50°$.

9. B

When you find the language confusing, try to put it in concrete terms. If you wanted to know how much more 9 was than 7, what would you do? You would subtract: $9 - 7 = 2$ more. So you need to subtract these two algebraic expressions.

$$(3x + 9) - (3x - 2) = 3x + 9 - 3x + 2 = 11$$

10. D

Remember that you can always plug in numbers for the variables (being careful to follow all the rules you are given).

I. When you multiply by a negative, the inequality flips. If $b > a$, then $-b < -a$. So this statement is always false.

II. If $a < b$, you can add c to both sides to get $a + c < b + c$. Always true.

III. a and b are negative, so their sum will be negative, while c is positive. So this statement will be always true.

11. C

The union of two sets includes all the elements that appear in either set. In this case, that means all the numbers between 0 and 5 and all the numbers between 3 and 7. You can combine these ranges and say that the union includes all the numbers between 0 and 7.

$0 \leq x \leq 7$ includes all the numbers between 0 and 7, including both 0 and 7.

12. D

When you see fractions set equal to each other, as in this problem, you should cross-multiply to make the equations easier to work with. Next, you should solve one equation for a in terms of b and plug this into the other equation. Then solve this new equation for b. If you have extra time, you might want to double-check your answer by plugging the values you found for a and b back into the original equations.

$$\frac{10}{a+b} = \frac{4}{a}$$

$$10a = 4(a+b) = 4a + 4b$$

$$6a = 4b$$

$$a = \frac{4b}{6} = \frac{2b}{3}$$

$$\frac{b^2}{18} = \frac{a}{2}$$

$$\frac{b^2}{18} = \frac{\left(\frac{2b}{3}\right)}{2}$$

$$2b^2 = \frac{36b}{3}$$

$$2b^2 = 12b$$

$$b^2 = 6b \qquad \text{(Note that you can divide by } b \text{ since you know } b \neq 0.)$$

$$b = 6$$

13. C

Most people find it easier to work with negative exponents if they are written as fractions. Once you've solved the given equation for c, don't forget to square it to find your answer!

$$c^{-\frac{1}{2}} = \frac{1}{\sqrt{c}} = 3$$

$$1 = 3\sqrt{c}$$

$$\frac{1}{3} = \sqrt{c}$$

$$\left(\frac{1}{3}\right)^2 = \frac{1^2}{3^2} = \frac{1}{9} = c$$

$$\left(\frac{1}{9}\right)^2 = \frac{1^2}{9^2} = \frac{1}{81} = c^2$$

14. D

If you're not familiar with transformations of x^2, you can try plugging some points from the graph into each equation to see which ones fit.

The point $(1, \frac{1}{2})$ is a great point to test—it only works for choice (D). (Even if you're not sure what the y-value of that point on the graph is, you can see that it is between 0 and 1. Choice (D) is the only equation that produces a y-value between 0 and 1 when $x = 1$.)

15. E

The area of a triangle is one-half the length of the base times the height. You need to find the base and height of this triangle. Since $\overline{AC}$ is a horizontal line (that is, A and C have the same y-coordinate) the length of the base is just the difference between the x-coordinates of A and C. The height is the vertical distance between B and the base. This is the difference between the y-coordinate of point B and the y-coordinate of the base.

Base: $7 - 2 = 5$

Height: $6 - 2 = 4$

Area: $\frac{1}{2}(5)(4) = 10$

16. E

The perimeter of this triangle is the sum of the lengths of its sides, $AB + BC + CA$. You can find these lengths by using the distance formula, $\sqrt{(x_1 - x_2)^2 + (y_1 - y_2)^2}$, or by sketching in the height of triangle ABC to create two right triangles, then using the Pythagorean theorem. In this case, both approaches take the same amount of time, so use whichever you prefer.

$$AB = \sqrt{(4-2)^2 + (6-2)^2}$$
$$= \sqrt{(2^2 + 4^2)} = \sqrt{(14+6)} = \sqrt{20} = 2\sqrt{5}$$
$$BC = \sqrt{(7-4)^2 + (2-6)^2}$$
$$= \sqrt{(3^2 + (-4)^2)} = \sqrt{9+16} = \sqrt{25} = 5$$

$CA = 7 - 2 = 5$ (Since this is a horizontal line, the distance between A and C is the difference between the x-coordinates of A and C. If you use the formula, you will get the same result.)

$$\text{Perimeter} = 2\sqrt{5} + 5 + 5 = 10 + 2\sqrt{5}$$

17. A

If you're stuck, focus on the differences between the answers; anything that's clearly wrong can be eliminated.

Squares of $2a$ and $3b$:

$(2a)^2$ and $(3b)^2$

Sum of those squares:

$(2a)^2 + (3b)^2$

Difference between $8c$ and $7d$:

$(8c - 7d)$

Sum of squares added to the difference:

$(2a)^2 + (9b)^2 + (8c - 7d)$

3 more than e:

$e + 3$

Sum is 3 more than e:

$(2a)^2 + (3b)^2 + (8c - 7d) = e + 3$

18. E

Remember, slope is $\dfrac{rise}{run}$ or $\dfrac{y_2 - y_1}{x_2 - x_1}$, so a slope of zero means the line is horizontal (rise = 0), and an undefined slope means the line is vertical (run = 0).

This line is vertical, so the x-coordinate stays the same. The only answer choice with the same x-coordinate is choice (E).

19. C

You should be able to immediately know where x and y are each positive and negative. Remember that a negative number times a negative number is positive.

The product will only be positive when either both coordinates are positive, or both are negative, so it must be C, D, or E. D clearly has a small product, so the answer is either C or E. Notice that E's x-coordinate is less than one, which means its product, xy, is less than y. C's x- and y-coordinates both have large values, more than making up for its y being slightly smaller than E's y (thinking in terms of absolute value, since the product gets rid of the negatives). Thus, C will have the largest product. You could also use your answer sheet as a ruler to estimate and confirm this.

20. B

You're looking for a way to get a and b in the same equation, without n. So solve for n in terms of a, and substitute it into the equation for b.

$a = 3n + 4$

$a - 4 = 3n$

$\dfrac{a - 4}{3} = n$

$b = 7 + 9n^2 = 7 + 9\,\dfrac{(a-4)^2}{3^2} = 7 + 9\,\dfrac{(a-4)^2}{9}$

$\qquad = 7 + (a - 4)^2 = 7 + a^2 - 8a + 16 = a^2 - 8a + 23$

SECTION 3

1. D

An artist who is proficient in many types of art forms is able to do many different things. Therefore, the prediction could be *adaptable* or maybe *talented*. Although artists tend to be *demonstrative* (A) or *uninhibited* or *unreserved*, the sentence does not describe the emotional aspect of Da Vinci's work. (B) does not match the prediction. Nothing is said to indicate that he was *unique* or *obscure*. The details of his artwork are not discussed here so there is no way of knowing if Da Vinci was *meticulous* (C), that is, *careful* or *thorough*. There is no indication whether his artwork was *metaphoric* (E) or more straightforward and literal. (D) means adaptable or flexible and matches the prediction.

2. D

We can assume that the questions on the exam will be required to be answered. Taking into consideration the contrast (exhibited by *although*) between the "required" exam and the word in the blank, a good prediction would be that the chapter review exercises are not required or additional questions. (A) can be eliminated because it is the opposite of the prediction. Only if the word *although* were eliminated and the word *and* was inserted after the blank would this word fit into the context of the sentence. If the students knew that these questions were to be found on the exam then doing the review may have already become *ritualistic* (B) for good students, but the teacher would not use this word to encourage the class to do extra studying. (C) doesn't make sense in the context of the question. (E) means "serious" but relates to demeanor or attitude, not to how the students are to treat the additional questions. (D) is the only answer that matches the prediction.

3. B

Start with the second blank. The architect of well-known, famous buildings must have been well-known and acclaimed himself. The prediction for the first blank must support Wright's becoming so distinguished; a word such as *proved* works. (A) Although *buoyed* works in the first blank, *irrelevant*, or inappropriate, is the opposite of the prediction for the second blank. *Surrendered* (C) has a negative connotation and is a bit extreme; buildings cannot surrender or give up a person as being either a good, bad, or prolific (productive) architect. Both words in (D) are negative; the predictions show they must be positive. (E), *categorized*, is not the best choice for the first blank, and *mundane*, or ordinary, does not fit as it is the opposite of the prediction. (B) is the best answer.

4. D

The words *at least* are important here. If he was *not particularly talented* as a plumber but had some *years of experience*, then he must have been working as a plumber and at the very least would have been considered a professional practicing the profession. Look for a word that refers to one who simply practices a profession. If he had "years of experience," he could not have been a *novice* (A). One cannot really be a *neighbor* (B) of a profession. Nothing in the sentence indicates that he was merely interpreting, as (C) suggests, or performing his job as a plumber in a way that expressed his particular feelings about the profession. Nothing in the sentence indicates that he *devalued* (E) or spoke negatively of the profession. (D) is the best answer.

5. B

Start with the second blank. As Ms. Poole is described as a *skilled mediator*, it would make sense that she found a way to "reconcile" or "resolve" their *numerous differences*. And if Ms. Poole were able to reconcile their differences, then she probably would have been able to save their relationship. Save and reconcile are great predictions for the two blanks. *Strengthening* (A) differences would not necessarily *reinforce* a relationship. *Widening* (C) their differences would not necessarily help Ms. Poole to express or give meaning to their relationship. *Plugging* (D) differences would not necessarily lead to a relationship being *overcome*. Again, *destroying* (E) numerous differences would not necessarily lead to their relationship being *disregarded* by Ms. Poole. (B) is the best choice.

6. C

If the first blank refers to a bad problem at the company, then it would follow that the company's positive reputation would be difficult to *restore*. Look for a choice that fills the first blank with a problem and the second with a word that means *restore*. *Integrity* (A) would not *plague* an institution. An institution with *conviction* (B) would not necessarily have trouble *justifying* its reputation. Whereas *dignity* (D) could potentially have a negative effect on an institution, such a quality would not necessarily make it difficult for that institution to *excuse* its reputation. *Degradation* (E) fits nicely into the first blank, but a reputation cannot really be *convicted*. (C) is the best answer.

7. E

If the waiter is hoping for a promotion, he is probably working hard and trying to smile about it. What words are synonyms for *hard work* and *a good attitude*? Anyone working *unscrupulously* (A) is surely on this way to getting fired. Approaching a job with *leniency* (B) is not really approaching it with a hard working ethic. If he approaches his job with *nonchalance* (C), then he's not working *tenaciously*. Having *acrimony* (D) or bitter feeling toward your job will not win you a promotion. (E) works. *Ardor* is a synonym for *strong enthusiasm*, and doing something *assiduously* is doing it *diligently*.

8. E

Think about the word *egocentrism*, which means to view one's own ego as a center. The fact that the blank is joined with egocentrism by *and* shows that the two words are linked in meaning. Look for a word that means something like human-centered. Although some would say that humans can display *irrationality* (A) at times, it does not mean the same thing as human-centered. A tendency toward humane acts does not match with egocentrism, thus (B) *humanity* is incorrect. To act with *temerity* (C) does not indicate a narrow view of the universe. (D), *serendipity*, would probably promote a larger or broader view of the universe. *Anthropocentrism*, (E), is a perfect fit. It puts humans at the center of the universe and works with egocentrism.

9. D

In the first two sentences of the passage, the author suggests that returning from the breeder's with *slightly scored shins* and *urine coating* her shoes gave her some idea of the trials to come. In this context, you can infer that *scored* refers to something negative that the puppy did to the author's shins, such as scratching them. (A) is a primary definition of the cited word and makes little sense in this context. (B) captures another meaning of scored—being grooved or gouged—but it's unclear what it would mean to say that shins were indented by the puppy. Whereas (C) is another meaning of the word, as in scoring a pair of basketball tickets, it makes no sense in this context. (E) This choice is too extreme given the author's use of the word *slightly*. (D) is the best choice.

10. E

The author says that her dog used to be a *tiny menace* but is now a *snoring beast*. This comparison emphasizes how much the once-troublesome small puppy has grown and calmed down, giving the author a sense of *parental satisfaction*. (A) is too extreme; the author indicates that her dog grew, but she does not suggest that the dog became *too* large. (B) does not match the positive tone of the sentence, and it undermines the statement that the author views her dog with pride or satisfaction. (C) is a distortion; the author's reference to *parental satisfaction* in the last sentence indicates that the dog has brought her some happiness. (D) is a misused detail; whereas the passage as a whole indicates that the author feels affection for her dog, the cited words themselves do not make this point. (E) is the best answer.

11. D

In the first sentence, the author refers to Hershey as a *revolutionary* chocolate-maker and suggests that he was enthusiastic, although his *inexperience* in the candy industry was the downfall of his first candy shop. You can expect the correct choice to match at least one of these characterizations. (A) is out of scope; this sentence does not say whether Hershey was particularly hardworking. (B) is a distortion; while the passage indicates that Hershey opened his own business when he was quite young, this information does not necessarily suggest he was exceptionally talented for his age. (C) is also a distortion; the passage describes Hershey as *inexperienced* but does not say that he lacked talent. (E) is an irrelevant detail; Hershey's commitment to using high-quality ingredients is mentioned in the last sentence, not the first. (D) is a good match for your prediction. *Groundbreaking* is a good synonym for *revolutionary*.

12. B

Go through the choices one by one, comparing each with the evidence found in the text. Aim to work quickly, but not so quickly that you compromise accuracy. (A) is a distortion; the passage indicates that Hershey acquired this dedication from another candy maker. (C) is out of scope; the passage indicates that Hershey learned to use quality ingredients from the caramel manufacturer, but it does not say that he tried to apply the *techniques* he learned there to chocolate-making. (D) is too extreme; whereas the passage suggests that Hershey was successful and that he was dedicated to the candy industry from a young age, it does not imply that he could *only* have succeeded at candy making. (E) is also out of scope; the passage only begins describing Hershey at age 18 and does not say whether his interest in candy-making originated in early childhood. (B) is the best choice; the author indicates that Hershey was *enthusiastic* about candy-making when he opened his shop at age 19 and that he was still *hooked on it* after his shop closed six years later.

13. C

Your notes should list something like "a discussion of defining art" as the purpose of paragraph 2; if not, skim for the words *endeavor* and *problematic*. Either way, you should find the first sentence of paragraph 2 mentioning: "Before we can begin a discussion of artistic decline, we must first define the word 'art,' an endeavor that has proven problematic." (A), (B), (C), and (D) are all distortions; the author discusses improving the education system (A) in later paragraphs, but the author never characterizes this as a *problematic endeavor*. The author discusses how education can make art more relevant (B) by linking it to historical and sociological developments, but the author never characterizes this as a *problematic endeavor*. Likewise, in later paragraphs, the author discusses what students should learn in school (D), but the author never characterizes this as a *problematic endeavor*. Finally, also in later paragraphs, the author discusses whether or not to teach art (E), but the author never characterizes this as a *problematic endeavor*. (C) is exactly as the passage states and is correct.

14. B

Since you are given the part of the passage from which you must draw the inference, skim paragraph 2 to find evidence of what the author characterizes as *too much time spent*. In lines 36–40 the author says that, "far too much time has been spent arguing over whether a teen movie is more or less art than *Citizen Kane,* or whether a boy band is more or less art than Sondheim." Now examine the answer choices by comparing them to this information and eliminating those that do not necessarily have to be true based on it. (A) is opposite; whereas the author discusses comparisons of "classics," the author does so in order to highlight the comparison of such classics to modern works, thereby judging the modern works' artistic merits. (C) and (D) are misused details; the author mentions them in later paragraphs. (E) is a distortion; the author never discusses comparisons of works traditionally considered classics to each other; the author discusses their comparison to newer works. (B) is the correct answer; the author states, "Far too much time has been spent arguing over whether a teen movie is more or less art than *Citizen Kane* is, or whether the music of a boy band is more or less art than the works of Sondheim are." Thus, the author implies that too much time has spent comparing modern works to more established works in order to judge the modern works' artistic merits.

15. E

Your task is to determine why the author included this detail in the passage. Your notes should tell you that the author uses most of paragraph 1 to bemoan or lament the decline of artistic appreciation and awareness in America. Since the author thinks that it is *sad* that America concerns itself with *teen movies and boy bands* then the author must think that film noir, jazz, and abstract expressionism are better. Thus, he must be mentioning them in order to draw a comparison and suggest their superiority. Look for that in the answer choices. (A) is a distortion; whereas the author does seem to be appealing to a sense of a lost golden age, the author uses that as part of the comparison to newer art to suggest their inferiority. (B) is opposite; far from making a historical parallel, this author suggests that newer works are inferior. (C) is out of scope; the author never examines the history of art. (D) is a misused detail; the author uses different details in a later paragraph to remind readers of this. (E) is just as we predicted.

16. E

The sentence in question states: "Many claim that our discussion can be seen as snobby, even culturally imperious." Since the author states that many people might think the discussion is *snobby* and then goes on to say *even culturally imperious* the author must be using imperious as a higher degree of the same meaning as snobby. (A), *imperative*, is not a higher degree of snobbery. (B) is opposite; when something is *arbitrary*, it is not carefully chosen which means that it cannot relay the meaning of snobbery. (C), *regal*, simply means elegant in a royal way. While this may be associated with snobbery, it does not convey the same meaning. (D), *urgent*, is a dictionary meaning of imperious but it makes no sense in the context of the original sentence. (E) is the answer; *arrogant* can be used as a higher degree of snobbery. When placed into the original sentence, it replaces imperious perfectly.

17. A

Both paragraphs 3 and 4 discuss aspects of artistic education. Skim for any language that might stand out of the text. In this case, the words "lost by the general public" should help you find the relevant detail in paragraph 3: " . . . a better education in art will better equip them to judge the artistic merit of these newer, more trendy art forms, or at least place these art forms in historical context and analyze them as an outgrowth of societal and sociological trends—an important aspect of artistic knowledge that has been lost by the general public." Now find the answer choice that matches an ability to place art works in a "historical context and analyze them as an outgrowth of societal and sociological trends."(B) is a misused detail; the definition of *art* is discussed earlier in the passage as a problematic endeavor for society, not an important aspect of artistic knowledge that has been lost. (C) is out of scope; the author never discusses the general public's ability to produce art that rivals the classics. (D) is a distortion; whereas the author does suggest ways the general public can better judge art works, the author never states that the general public has lost the ability to judge the merits of current art works. (E) is also a misused detail; the author discusses the value of all forms of art during the discussion of the definition of art. (A) is correct; this matches the first part of the author's detail.

18. B

Reread the lines in question in order to find evidence of what distinguishes the author's hypothetical United States. Parents read to their children and educate them. These parents also give their children art books, classical recordings, and plays as gifts." Now evaluate each answer choice, choosing the one that must be true based on the author's statements. (A) is out of scope; the author's statements deal with a new interest in art, not new interests in general. (C) is a misused detail; the author never mentions school in the piece of the paragraph mentioned by the question. (D) is out of scope; the author's statements discuss sharing enthusiasm for art, not other activities. (E) is a distortion; in the referenced lines, the author never alludes to the value of artistic skill. (B) is correct; the lines in question describe a country in which parents share their interests in and enjoyment of art with their children, so it must be true that this what the author finds distinguishing about this hypothetical country.

19. E

Since you are given specific line numbers, your first step should be to reread the relevant lines, which state that "in school, students receive in education in art history, classical music, and opera. This curriculum can also include pop-culture such as the music videos, teen movies, and pop music students enjoy in their free time." Now use this information to evaluate the answer choices, choosing the one that must describe such an educational model. (A), (B), (C), and (D) are all distortions; whereas the author's statements describe an education that examines a diverse body of art forms, the author never mentions which, if any, are valued (A) over others or whether or not the students would learn to respect (B) the views of all artists. In fact, a critical examination might lead students to disrespect the views of certain art or artists. The author's statements describe an education that reflects upon art forms, but the author never describes an education that reflects on the nature of art education (C). Likewise, the author describes an education that examines both classical and contemporary art (D), but the author never describes whether one would be valued over the other. (E) is correct; the author describes an education that explores both classical and contemporary art, including pop culture; such a model is wide-ranging in its exploration.

20. B

Your notes might indicate that in paragraph 3, the author advances a vision of an artistically educated society. If your notes do not indicate this, then simply revisit the paragraph by skimming it, and then evaluate what the author does in this paragraph. The author provides an example of a more artistically educated America. Thus, the author must have included the paragraph in order to propose or provide a vision of a more artistically educated society. (A) is a distortion; the author merely provides a vision of a more artistically educated society, not a utopian one. (C) and (D) are out of scope; in the third paragraph, the author never examines whether pop culture leaves a lasting impact on society (C), and the author never deals with classic literature and younger students (D). (E) is also a distortion; whereas the author proposes studying both, the author never states that contemporary and classical works are interchangeable. (B) is the best answer.

21. D

Use the line numbers to locate and reread the situation described by the author. The author states that since "art, music, and culture are inextricably tied to literary and historical developments which themselves stem from changes in society and culture," the educational system should focus on a more "holistic" approach that teaches "students in an intertextual and multidisciplinary manner." Find the answer choice that must be characteristic of this education. (A) and (B) are distortions; the author describes an artistic education, not an *elitist* one (A) or a charitable one (B). (C) is the opposite; *eclectic* means mixed together from various elements. This might seem true, but eclectic implies a mismatching of items. The author argues that literature, art, and history are not mismatched at all. (E) is also opposite; *rudimentary* means basic; the education described by the author goes beyond the basics and fundamentals by contextualizing art within other developments in society, thus creating an overarching education. (D) is correct; the author describes an education that takes an overarching view. *Comprehensive* characterizes this.

22. A

In lines 112–119, the author states that "this system would require more funding, and most likely higher taxes." Find the answer choice that must be true based on this information. (B), (C), (D), and (E) are all distortions; clearly, the author believes that the new system would be better, but the author's statements don't provide evidence that the new system would be more celebrated (B), *more controversial* (C), *more interesting* (D), or *more likely to inspire* (E) than the current system. (A) is correct; because the new system would require more funding and probably higher taxes, it must be true that the new system would be more expensive.

23. C

As you should have noted while reading the passage, the topic is the decline of artistic knowledge and appreciation in America. The author outlines causes for this decline then proposes a solution. Look for an answer choice that says something similar to this. (A) is a distortion; in the first paragraph, the author does shift the focus of the debate from analyzing causes to proposing solutions, but the author does not attempt to shift the focus of the debate from causes to effects. (B), (C) , and (D) are all out of scope; the author never supports a side in a debate (B), the author proposes a solution, nor does he revive a discredited idea (D), or promote certain types of art (E). The author promotes art education in general. (C) is the best answer.

24. C

Paragraph 3 contains the discussion of the author's hypothetical United States. Skim the passage for any facts regarding the production of higher quality art. The paragraph states that "when these children grow up, some may produce their own art, perhaps art that is higher in quality than the pop music and movies produced today." In a preceding line, the paragraph states that, "a better education in art will better equip them to judge the artistic merit of these newer, more trendy art forms, or at least place these art forms in historical context and analyze them as an outgrowth of societal and sociological trends . . ." Now compare each answer choice to this information. (A) is a distortion; the author never links parents to the production of better art. (B) is too extreme; the author presents a more artistically educated society, but the author never goes so far as to claim that this society would not accept lower quality art. (D) and (E) are also distortions; the author never mentions free time (D) or discusses how strictly critics would judge art in this hypothetical society (E). (C) is correct; the author presents children with better artistic educations, and then states that they would grow up to produce better art. Thus, their production of better art must stem from their artistic education.

25. C

In the first paragraph of the passage, the author states that the cultural decline in society has many causes, including "the media's focus on pop culture and the general decline of taste this breeds." (lines 12–13). It is clear from this statement and the continuing tone of the passage that the author does not think much of popular music, making (C) the best choice. (A) and (B) are out of scope; there is not evidence in the passage to support either statement, and quite the contrary, there is plenty of evidence against both (A) and (B). (D) and (E) are misused details. The author discusses education, but he believes society would benefit from a more artistic and classically geared music education, and this would eliminate the possibility of his feeling that pop music was more important than classical music.

SECTION 4

1. B

Although the passive voice will not always be incorrect on the SAT, when you see a passive structure, look for an active version among the answer choices. *Flying is unable to be afforded by her* is a passive (and much wordier) version of *she cannot afford to fly.* Since the first clause already mentions flying, *to do so* is an acceptable variation; (B) is correct. *That* in (C) and *it* in (D) do not have clear antecedents. (E) is unnecessarily wordy.

2. B

Transition words must express the correct relationship between ideas. As written, this sentence does not use an appropriate transition to express the contrast between ideas. (B) corrects this with the transition word *although.* (C) and (E) express a cause-and-effect relationship between the clauses that is inappropriate in context. (D) is a sentence fragment.

3. C

Sentences should be structured so that any modifying words or phrases clearly refer to one specific item. As written, this sentence does not make clear what was *popular among high school students in the 90s: the love story* or the *teen movie.* (C) clarifies the sentence's meaning. (B) introduces a verb tense that is incorrect in context. (D) and (E) are sentence fragments.

4. B

Pronouns must always have clear antecedents. Here, the only plural antecedent for the pronoun *they* is *bylaws,* but *bylaws* don't *pay . . . wages.* (B) clarifies that it is *the university* that can no longer *pay reduced wages.* The pronoun *them* in (C) has no logical antecedent. (D) is unnecessarily in the passive voice, and the pronoun *their* has no logical antecedent. The plural verb *are* in (E) does not agree with the singular subject *consequence.*

5. A

Be methodical in eliminating wrong answer choices, but if you don't spot an error, don't be afraid to choose (A). This sentence is correct as written. (B) creates a run-on sentence. (C) and (D) have incorrect grammatical structure. (E) is awkward and not very clear.

6. D

Transition words must express the correct relationship between clauses. The transition word *but* indicates contrast. In this sentence the second clause expands on the information presented in the first, so *but* is incorrect. (D) corrects this error with an appropriate transition word, *that*. (B) does not address the error. Neither the conjunction *and* in (C) or the transition word *since* in (D) express the correct relationship between the clauses.

7. B

Choose the most concise answer that does not introduce any additional errors. Although not technically a run-on, this sentence consists of two independent clauses with no indication of how they are related. By making the first clause dependent, (B) indicates the relative importance of the two ideas. (C) does not address the error. (D) creates a cause-and-effect relationship between the clauses that is not present in the original. (E) is awkward and loses some of the meaning of the original.

8. E

Items in a series, list, or compound noun or verb must be parallel in structure. The object of the preposition *by* is the compound *an increase . . . and because there has been a decrease.* (E) makes the second part of the compound parallel to the first. None of the other choices makes the items parallel.

9. A

If you don't find an error, don't be afraid to choose (A). This sentence is correct as written. (B) and (C) unnecessarily introduce the passive voice. (E) has grammatically incorrect structure.

10. D

A pronoun must have a clear antecedent, and agree with that antecedent in gender and number. The problem here is the pronoun *their*. We don't know to whom *their* refers, since the sentence has no plural nouns. (D) is the only choice that eliminates the pronoun. (B) and (C) do not address the error. (E) replaces *their* with the singular pronoun *its,* but the pronoun's antecedent is still unclear.

11. B

Certain idioms appear regularly on the SAT; learn their proper structure. This question tests your knowledge of the idiom that compares two nouns using *as*; the correct construction is *as (adjective) as*. Only (B) correctly completes the construction. (C) is grammatically incorrect, (D) is unnecessarily wordy, and (E) does not correct the error.

12. C

The pronoun *whom* is in the objective case and cannot be used as the subject of a verb. (C) should be in the subjective case (who) because it is the subject of the verb phrase *had . . . scored*. (A) correctly uses *that* as a conjunction. (To check this, you can reverse the sentence order: "The sportscasters were shocked *that* the team with the worst record won . . . ") The adverb in (B) correctly modifies the verb *won*. (D) is the appropriate verb tense in context.

13. B

The past perfect verb tense is only correct when used to refer to one completed action that precedes another. Since there is no other past action referred to in this sentence, (B) should simply be the past tense *worked*. The verb in (A) agrees with its singular subject *performance*. In (C), the infinitive *to raise* is appropriate in context. (D) is a correctly used prepositional phrase.

14. B

All verbs within a sentence must agree in tense, unless more than one time frame is referenced. The present tense verb in (B) is not consistent with the rest of the sentence; it should be *knew*. (A) correctly expresses the contrast between the two clauses in the sentence. (C) and (D) are properly used prepositional phrases.

15. E

The SAT writing sections will contain a total of five to eight sentences that contain no errors. (A) uses an appropriate preposition in context. (B) is a correct use of the infinitive verb tense. (C) correctly shows the cause-and-effect relationship between the two clauses. (D) is a properly used prepositional phrase.

16. B

Unless context indicates that more than one time frame is referenced in a sentence, verb tenses should remain consistent. Since the rest of the sentence is in the past tense, (B) should be as well. (A) is a correct idiomatic usage. (C) and (D) use appropriate prepositions.

17. E

If you don't spot an obvious error, check each answer choice in turn. (A) is an appropriate preposition in context. (B) shows the cause-and-effect relationship between the two clauses in the sentence. (C) is the correct verb tense in context. (D) properly uses an adjective to modify a noun.

18. D

Adjectives (including participles) can only be used to modify nouns and pronouns. In (D), the participle verb form *increasing* is an adjective used to modify the adjective *nervous*. Adjectives cannot be used to modify other adjectives, however; (D) should be *increasingly*. (A) is the proper relative pronoun to refer to a person. (B) is correct use of the infinitive. (C) is appropriate use of the past perfect tense, since it refers to an action completed before another stated past action (*grew . . . nervous*).

19. D

Related nouns in a sentence must agree in number. A plural number of *dancers* would have to take a plural number of *places*; the error is in (D). (A) properly uses an adjective to modify a noun. (B) is an appropriate verb phrase in context. (C) correctly uses the gerund *rustling* and the preposition *of*.

20. B

In a compound verb, the verbs must be in parallel form. The simple predicate of the main clause in this sentence is *got . . . and driving*; (B) should be *drove*. (A) is a correctly used prepositional phrase. The verb in (C) is consistent in tense with the rest of the sentence. (D) is a correctly placed modifying phrase.

21. C

The correct verb form for a modifying phrase is the gerund (*-ing*) form. The verb *refuses* in (C) has no subject; without a conjunction to make it part of the predicate of the main clause, it would have to be changed to *refusing* to create a grammatically correct sentence. (A) uses the proper preposition in context. In (B), the adverb is used correctly to modify the verb *waits*. (D) is a correct verb phrase to describe a future action.

22. D

A sentence requires an independent clause that expresses a complete thought. Both clauses of this sentence are subordinate. Changing the gerund form in (D) to *greeted* would make the second clause independent, correcting the error. (A) is an appropriate preposition in context. (B) and (C) are idiomatically correct phrases.

23. D

All verbs within a sentence must agree in tense, unless a verb is included in a phrase that implies a different time from the rest of the sentence. The present tense verb in (D) is inconsistent with the rest of the sentence; *preferred* would be the correct form here. (A) properly uses an adjective to modify a noun. In (B), the gerund is correctly used. (C) correctly expresses the contrast between the two clauses in the sentence.

24. D
Even a sentence with numerous nouns and verbs can be a fragment, if there is no independent clause. As written, this sentence is a fragment. Changing (D) to *was constructed* would remedy this. (A) is appropriate use of the relative pronoun *which*. In (B), the superlative form is used correctly, since presumably there are more than two symbols of the Cold War. (C) is a correctly used prepositional phrase.

25. E
Expect some sentences to be correct as written. (A) and (B) are proper usages of an adjective and an adverb, respectively. (C) is the correct conjunction in context. The prepositional phrase in (D) is used correctly.

26. E
If you don't spot an obvious error, check each choice in turn. (A) is correct idiomatic usage. The pronoun in (B) clearly refers to *Mrs. Ramsay*. (C) is an appropriate verb phrase in context. (D) is proper use of the infinitive.

27. A
Verbs must agree in number with their subject nouns. (A) correctly uses an adverb to modify a verb, but the plural verb form *choose* does not agree with its singular subject *student*. (B) is the appropriate relative pronoun in context. (C) is consistent verb tense use, and uses the correct preposition. (D) properly uses an adjective to modify a noun.

28. A
Make sure each sentence has an independent clause that expresses a complete thought. As written, this sentence is a fragment, since neither clause is independent. Changing (A) to *serves* would correct the error. (B) is an appropriate conjunction in context. (C) correctly uses an adjective to modify the noun *soups*. (D) is a properly used prepositional phrase.

29. C
In a compound verb construction, all verbs must be in parallel form. *To drip and throwing* is grammatically incorrect; (C) should read *dripping*. (A) is consistent verb tense usage. (B) is correct idiomatic usage. (D) properly uses an adverb to modify the compound verb.

30. D

By making *scientists* rather than *a theory* the subject, (D) puts the sentence in the active voice without changing its meaning. It also eliminates the pronoun *It*, which is used here with no antecedent. (B) eliminates the ambiguous pronoun, but does not address the passive problem. (C) and (E) correct the errors, but they are both sentence fragments.

31. B

Here, *institutes* is incorrectly in the present tense, since the sentence is talking about something that happened *in the latter half of the twentieth century.* (B) corrects the error. *Consequently,* in (A), correctly relates this sentence to the previous one. (C) is not idiomatically correct English. (D) misrepresents the relationship between the two ideas. (E) introduces a verb tense that's incorrect in context.

32. E

The relative pronoun *who* is used when referring to people; *that* and *which* are used for things. Since *people* is the noun the pronoun *that* is referring to here, the pronoun should be replaced with *who.* (E) does this, without introducing any additional errors. (B) misuses the comparative form *more.* (C) does not correct the error, and replaces the correct *those* with *them.* (D) corrects the error, but it also replaces *those* with *them*, which is incorrect.

33. C

As written, this sentence is a fragment, since neither of these clauses is independent. By changing the gerund (*-ing*) verb form, which can never be a predicate verb, to *appeared,* (C) corrects the error. (B) corrects the fragment error, but introduces an inappropriate verb tense. (D) does not address the error. (E) creates a complete sentence, but does so in the passive voice.

34. C

(C) combines the sentences, correctly using *but* to indicate the contrast between the first two clauses, and *while* to make the third clause subordinate. (A) merely strings the sentences together without relating their ideas. (B) misuses the semicolon splice, since the second clause is not independent. In (D), the transition word *so* indicates an inappropriate cause-and-effect relationship between the first and second clauses. (E) is a sentence fragment, with no predicate (main) verb in an independent clause.

35. E

The transition words *although* and *but* both indicate contrast, so having one in each clause is unnecessary. The sentence could be corrected by eliminating either of them, but only (E) does this without introducing any additional errors. (A) and (B) suggest eliminating *although,* but they also involving changing *but* to another transition word, which alters the relationship of the ideas in the sentence. (C) creates a run-on sentence with two subordinate clauses. (D) simply replaces the second contrast transition word with a different one, but doesn't address the problem.

SECTION 5

1. C

Radical equations are not difficult, even though they may look complicated. Just remember to follow each step carefully, and you'll get the correct answer every time. Also, remember that back solving is often a good strategy for attacking radical equations.

$$3\sqrt{x} - 31 = -13$$
$$3\sqrt{x} = 18$$
$$\sqrt{x} = 6$$
$$x = 36$$

2. A

Rational equations can be solved just like any other equation. Just remember to follow the order of operations carefully, and you can solve these equations easily.

$$\frac{3x - 9}{2x + 7} = 8$$
$$3x - 9 = 8(2x + 7)$$
$$3x - 9 = 16x + 56$$
$$-13x = 65$$
$$x = -5$$

3. E

This question is a simple application of the distance formula. Keep track of which points you're using for x_1 and x_2, as well as y_1 and y_2, and this will be an easy question.

Use P for (x_1, y_1), and Q for (x_2, y_2).

$$\text{Distance} = \sqrt{(x_1 - x_2)^2 + (y_1 - y_2)^2}$$

$$\sqrt{(-2 - 5)^2 + (4 - (-2))^2}$$

$$= \sqrt{(-7)^2 + 6^2} = \sqrt{49 + 36} = \sqrt{85}$$

4. C

Don't worry if you see a symbol you've never seen before—the operation will be defined in the problem. All you need to do is plug in the given values. Be sure to do anything in parentheses first.

$$2\nabla 3 = 2 - 3 + 2 = 1$$
$$1\nabla 1 = 1 - 1 + 2 = 2$$

5. C

You can use concrete numbers to get a handle on the situation.

Try $a = 6$ and $b = 3$:

(A) $a + b = 9$, eliminate.

(B) $a - b = 3$, eliminate.

(C) $a + b + 1 = 10$.

(D) $ab = 18$, eliminate.

(E) $ab + 3 = 21$, eliminate.

6. E

Any side of a triangle must be larger than the difference between than other two sides, and less than the sum of the other two sides. In choice (E), $12 = 5 + 7$, so the "triangle" would be totally flat.

7. D

Your task here is to translate English into math—what does "the ratio of $2k$ to $6s$" really mean?

The ratios described in the question can be written as:

$$\frac{2k}{6s} = \frac{6k+5}{18s+10}$$

Cross-multiply and simplify to get:

$$2k(18s+10) = 6s(6k+5)$$
$$36ks + 20k = 36ks + 30s$$
$$20k = 30s$$
$$k = 1.5s$$

You can see that statement I is never true, statement II is not necessarily true, and statement III must be true. If you're not sure about that, you can try plugging in numbers that fit each statement to see if they make the described ratios equivalent.

8. A

If two chords have equal length, they are the same distance from the center of the circle. Remember to add all the information from the question stem to the figure.

Because *GEFH* is a square, its area is equal to the length of a side squared:

$$81 = EF^2$$
$$9 = EF$$

Since the chords are the same distance from the center of the circle, $EJ = KF$.

$$EF = EJ + JK + KF$$
$$9 = 2(EJ) + 5$$
$$2 = EJ$$

9. 2

Remember that the solutions of a quadratic function are the values of x where the function equals zero. Where does this function equal zero?

The function equals zero at $x = 2$ and $x = -2$. Since you can't grid a negative number, grid in 2.

10. 31

You don't even have to turn this into algebra if you don't want to—just work backwards:

$2 for the first 14 days

$4.55 − $2 = $2.55 for the rest of the days

$\frac{\$2.55}{\$.15}$ = 17 additional days

17 + 14 = 31 days total

11. 18

Draw a diagram so you can see what's going on.

$\overline{WY} = 6 = a + b$ and $\overline{VZ} = 3a + 3b = 3(a + b) = 3(6) = 18$

12. 132 or 198

This question may look daunting, but we have two very useful pieces of information: $AA + AA$ is a 3-digit number that's divisible by 3, and it's also twice a 2-digit number where both digits are the same

$2(AA)$ = covered number

Knowing $2(AA)$ is 3 digits narrows the possibilities down to AA = 55, 66, 77, 88, or 99.

But it also must be divisible by 3, which we can only get from 66 or 99.

So the covered number is $2 \times 66 = 132$ or $2 \times 99 = 198$.

13. 800

Combinations are very similar to probabilities. How many ways can she make the first choice? How many ways can she make the second choice? Multiply these numbers to get the number of combinations.

$25 \times 32 = 800$

14. 24

Think about what has to happen for them to be as close together as possible—make the first Friday fall as late as possible.

The latest the first Friday can be is the 7th, which makes the last Friday the 28th and the last Monday the 31st. The last Monday falls $31 - 7 = 24$ days after the first Friday.

15. 192

Computing $(100 \sim 5)$ would take forever, so there must be an easier way. If a question on the SAT is taking a long time or you find yourself setting up an extremely complicated computation, you're probably missing a shortcut.

$$(100 \sim 5) = 100 + 99 + 98 + \cdots + 6 + 5$$

$$(98 \sim 3) = 98 + 97 + \cdots + 6 + 5 + 4 + 3$$

So when you subtract them, everything from 98 to 5 cancels out, leaving $100 + 99 - 4 - 3 = 192$.

16. $\dfrac{8}{36} = \dfrac{2}{9}$

Don't forget that the fraction of 360 degrees a sector has is also the fraction of the circle's area it contains, and the fraction of the circumference that its arc takes up. Don't stop too soon and grid the number of degrees in angle AOE—remember to make it a fraction.

$$EOB = DOF = 60°$$

$$AOE = 180° - (60° + 40°) = 80°$$

$$\frac{80°}{360°} = \frac{8}{36} = \frac{2}{9}$$

17. 235°

If you ever forget the formula for the number of degrees in a polygon, just divide it into triangles by drawing in some diagonals.

The sum of the interior angles in a polygon with n sides is $(n - 2) \times 180° = (6 - 2) \times 180° = 720°$. Or, as shown above, you can divide it into 4 triangles and deduce that the sum of the angles is $4 \times 180° = 720°$.

Since the known angles sum to $160° + 95° + 110° + 120° = 485°$, the remaining angles must sum to $720° - 485° = 235°$.

18. 9

She will clean the house on days 7, 14, 21 . . . (multiples of 7) and do laundry on days 5, 10, 15 . . . (multiples of 5). Think about what has to be true of days where both happen.

The least common multiple of 7 and 5 is 35. So every 35th day she will do both. This will happen $\frac{315}{35} = 9$ times.

SECTION 6

1. E

If it was *unquestionable* that his friends had seen Spiderman, then the evidence was *undeniable*, *uncontestable*, or *certain*. Look for an answer choice that matches this prediction. It may be helpful to break the answer choices apart by looking at their prefixes and suffixes. (A) is the opposite of the prediction; it means "not important." (B) is too weak; it suggests that the movie stubs are possible evidence that his friends had gone to the movies without him. Possible is not as certain as "no denying." Jamal's friends were not necessarily proven guilty. They had seen a movie, and did not do anything that was incriminating (C). (D) is the opposite of the prediction; *nominal* means "very small" or "insignificant." (E) is the answer. Break the word apart if you are unsure of its meaning; *indisputable* means "not disputable" or "not questionable."

2. C

At least one of the blanks must describe why marathons are challenging. Think of a prediction for the second blank. Marathons are mentally *draining* or *strenuous*. For the first blank, decide in what way marathons are primarily taxing; they are a challenge of fitness and bodily training. Although *taxing* or *difficult* works in the second blank, you can eliminate (A) based on the first blank. The challenge is not *illusory*, or imagined. Neither word in (B) fits. The challenge of running a very long race is not *exaggerated*, and describing a physical event as being *mentally balanced* does not make sense. Some runners may see the challenge as *appealing* (D), or interesting, but the process of preparing for a strenuous race is not in itself gratifying (although runners may feel a sense of satisfaction after the race has been completed). (E), *strenuous*, works in the first blank, but *mentally dubious* or doubtful does not work. Only (C) fits both blanks.

3. B

What is *promoted* by *healthy lifestyle choices*? The first blank describes the benefits of healthy choices and must contain a positive word. A good prediction is *increased health* or *longer lifespan*. The second blank must challenge this remark as busy lives reduce the time people have to exercise and eat right. For the second blank your prediction should be *prevented* or *challenged*. Both words in (A) are the opposite of the predictions. (C), *behavior*, is too general of a term. The blank is referring to the results of healthy behaviors, such as an increased lifespan. Although *belied* has a negative connotation, healthy lifestyles are not necessarily *contradicted* but rather challenged by busy lives. (D), *morality*, is positive but out of scope and *bolstered* or *supported* is the opposite of the prediction. (E) can be eliminated based on the second blank; it is the opposite of the prediction. *Reproduction* may be enhanced by healthy choices but this isn't what the sentence is discussing. (B) is the best choice.

4. A

What word describes someone who does not *drink to excess*? A good prediction would be someone who leads an *abstinent* or *self-restrained* lifestyle. (B), *laconic*, means brief or concise. The fact that the man is old and has therefore lived a long life is not what is being contrasted by the word in the blank. *Duplicitous*, (C), means deceitful; who was the old man deceiving? He would only be deceptive if he were trying to hide his drinking habits. (D) can mean either artistic or tasteful. Whether or not his lifestyle was *aesthetic* is not related to his drinking habits. Being *voluble*, (E), or talkative has nothing to do with drinking. (A) is the best choice.

5. A

The prediction should be a word that means Nostradamus had a knowledge of events before they occurred, such as *foresight*. Eliminate all answer choices that do not match this prediction. (B) Nostradamus became known for his predictions, not for honesty or *sincerity*. (C) is out of scope; nothing is said about Nostradamus being greedy. Be careful with (D); *complicity* does not mean *complicated*; it means involvement as an accomplice in a crime. (E) Because his predictions were accurate, Nostradamus was not being untruthful. (A) is the best choice.

6. B

What are the author's feelings or opinions about the fact that acid rain continues to exist despite the development of technologies that could eliminate it? An important clue comes in the final sentence, where the author uses the word *senselessly* to suggest that there seems to be no rational or understandable reason why the new technologies are not more widely used. (A) is a distortion; the author never expresses any *surprise* that acid rain continues to be a problem, and Passage 1 never mentions the *developed world* in particular. (C) is too extreme; the word *nothing* in this choice goes further than the author's *little*. (D) is out of scope; although the cleaner technologies are new, the passage does not state that they are experimental. (E) is opposite; the author states that acid rain can produce *often irreversible environmental damage*. (B) is the best choice.

7. C

The author of Passage 2 describes how the most-developed nations *have the luxury of squabbling over* questions that the poorer countries can't afford to consider, indicating that the wealthier nations have choices and advantages not shared by others. (A) is a distortion; that the author does not say whether developed nations are concerned about the energy choices available to poorer countries. (B) is out of scope; their degree of responsibility is not discussed in the passage. (D) is also a distortion; the passage does not mention any negative consequences resulting from blatant carelessness or the *squabbling* of developed nations. (E) is opposite; the author suggests that *less*-developed nations cannot afford cleaner fuels. (C) is the best answer.

8. E

The scope of Passage 2 is limited to the difference between the developed world—which has the *luxury of squabbling* over a variety of energy issues—and poorer nations, who are forced to deal with the human damage caused by the *only natural resource they can afford*. Therefore, the second author would probably reply that new and cleaner energy-generating technologies are not adopted by some countries because they can't afford them. (A) is out of scope; nowhere in Passage 2 does the author mention the responsibilities of wealthier nations. (B), (C), and (D) are distortions and are not supported by the text. (E) is the correct answer.

9. C

Passage 1 focuses on the fact that there are cleaner alternatives to the conventional burning of fossil fuels, whereas Passage 2 focuses on the fact that poorer nations are stuck with the cheaper (but more damaging) coal. However, although their emphases are different, both authors recognize the basic point that burning fossil fuels can be harmful. (A) is a distortion; only Passage 2 addresses the cost difference between clean and conventional technologies. (B) is too extreme; neither author makes such a strong statement, and the author of Passage 1 actually suggests that acid rain can be avoided. Both (D) and (E) are not supported by both passages.

10. C

The passage begins with a description of what the author envisioned doing in her work at the shelter: "conducting intake interviews and traipsing around from organization to organization seeking the legal, psychological, and financial support that the women would need." At the end of the passage, she relates how her unanticipated baking endeavor made her "a more sensitive and skillful social worker." You are looking for a choice that expresses her changed view of social work. (A) is too extreme; although the author's *reality* did differ from what she expected, the passage does not focus on her shock, but rather on how she responded to it. (B) is out of scope; the passage does not address the author's psychological constraints. (D) is a misused detail; although the bakery was for-profit, business abilities are not the focus of the passage. (E) is also a misused detail; the fact that the author was abroad in a *developing country* is not emphasized in the passage. (C) is correct; the author came to see social work as being more diverse than she originally envisioned.

11. B

The paragraph preceding the citation indicates that the author had spent a significant amount of time imagining her work and felt *thoroughly prepared*. It is thus likely that she arrived at the shelter with a positive, confident attitude. (A) is opposite; the last two sentences of the first paragraph indicate that the author felt self-assured. (C) is a misused detail; although she was uninformed about the actual content of her job, the author does not express this until later in the paragraph. (D) is also opposite; the author was energetic, not exhausted. (E) is a distortion; the author was not incompetent, only unprepared to run the bakery. (B) is the best choice.

12. A

The author's enthusiasm at the beginning of the second paragraph contrasts with her shock a few sentences later, when she discovers she will be in charge of the bakery. Her references to the *case studies* she researched reveal that she was initially enthusiastic about the *concept* of the bakery, not necessarily about her practical involvement in it. (B) is opposite; initially, the author felt *out of her depth* at being put in charge of the bakery. (C) and (D) are distortions; initially the author had little knowledge of baking (C), and the author only later found that the bakery *improved the women's self-esteem* (D). (E) is out of scope; the passage does not address the author's beliefs about such projects in general.

13. E

The author believed that starting the bakery presented a *problem*, and she never mentions any political experience or ambitions. We can infer that the author feels she is equally unsuited to perform either activity. (A) is too extreme; the fact that the author feels *unprepared* does not mean she thinks the bakery will *never* work. (B) is a distortion; although the author did not expect the bakery to be part of her job, this doesn't mean she believes it should not be. (C) and (D) are out of scope; the author's feelings about her coordinator are not discussed (C), and no connection is made between the skills necessary for politics and those needed for baking bread (D). (E) is correct. The comparison makes the author's lack of preparation clear.

14. A

Just before the cited sentence, the author relates one problem: she was unprepared to bake bread. In the cited sentence, the author relates a second problem: she was *completely unfamiliar with* for-profit business models. This second problem, she suggests, was the *bigger* one that might pose more of a challenge. (B) is a distortion; the author is discussing her own comparative lack of preparation for each activity, not the relative importance of each. (C) and (E) are misused details; the coordinator's confidence is mentioned in the *next* sentence, and the author does not express a belief that confidence in for-profit business models is misplaced (C), nor does the fact that the coordinator *left* the author does not mean she was unwilling to help, only that she did not (E). (D) is out of scope; the passage does not compare the relative complexity of for-profit and non-profit business models. (A) is the correct answer.

15. E
The author makes two points in this sentence: baking improved her self-confidence as well as that of the shelter residents, and simple activities can be helpful in social work. Look for a choice that picks up on one or both of these ideas. (A) and (B) are distortions; the women's self-confidence and the author's increased together, but this does not mean that their self-confidence levels were initially equal. Also, although social work can be *as simple as kneading dough*, this does not necessarily mean it is an easy profession for those who (unlike the author) have no education. (C) and (D) are out of scope; the author's prior expectations about learning new skills are not discussed, and (D) is too general because baking is the only hands-on activity discussed. (E) is the best answer. The *benefit* is increased self-confidence.

16. D
This passage has both introductory and concluding paragraphs. Reread those for an overview of the author's purpose. (A) is a misused detail; whereas the author says many successful people participate in athletics, it is not the purpose of the passage. (B) is a distortion; the author does not directly compare physical and artistic activities, nor is the passage theoretical in nature. (C) is a misused detail; pleasure is mentioned as a benefit of recreation but not as a major point of the passage. (E) is out of scope; the requisites for vocational success are not discussed in detail in this passage. (D) is the correct answer.

17. B
Limit your deliberations about meaning to the quoted clause and the sentence that contains it. (A), (D), and (E) are all out of scope; the author does not say that leisure time is preferable to work (A), does not refer to the democratic or any other form of government (D), and does not make a recommendation about frequency of recreational activities (E). (C) is opposite; the passage states that leisure time has been augmented or increased. (B) is the best answer.

18. A

Follow the logical chain of benefits mentioned in the second paragraph, to find the most important one. (B) is a distortion; this answer has a negative connotation that does not reflect either the question or the passage. (C) is too extreme; the word *always* exaggerates the expressed benefits of competition. (D) is out of scope; although this may be a true statement, it is not to be found in the passage. (E) is a misused detail; this relatively minor point is mentioned in passing. (A) is correct.

19. E

Match the tone of the answers to the tone of the words and sentences adjoining the word *competition*. (A) is opposite; note the words *without. . . competition* and, later in the paragraph, *needless comparison*. (B) is a distortion; the passage does not assign importance to comparative physical activities. (C) is a misused detail; whereas the author approves of enjoyment of recreation, the passage does not rank its importance. (D) is also opposite; this answer is basically a reworded version of (A) and should be eliminated for that reason alone. (E) is the best answer.

20. C

First, evaluate (for correctness) the advantage suggested after each roman numeral; then find the correct answer. (A) and (B) are limited; roman numeral I is correct but is not the only advantage mentioned in the passage, and roman numeral II is correct but is not the only advantage mentioned in the passage. (D) and (E) are out of scope; roman numerals I and II are correct, but aesthetic aspects of art are not mentioned in the passage. (C) is the best answer.

21. A

Carefully examine the context of the word, in this case, the comparison of life to a turbulent sea. (B) is a misused detail; the metaphor of the sea is not applicable in this part of the sentence. (C) is limited; *situations* is much too mild a term in this context of comparison to a sea where one might need a life jacket. (D) misconstrues the preceding metaphor of a turbulent sea. (E) counts on your being distracted by the previous mention of rules. (A) is the best answer.

22. C

Because the answer choices are adjectives, compare each one to the adjective in the quoted phrase. (A) is out of scope; the passage does not comment on the necessity of standardized testing. (B) is a misused detail; this answer could be justified by reference to the word *ever-narrowing*, but that is very different from *irrelevant*. (D) is also out of scope; the passage does not comment on whether or not standardized testing is productive. (E) is opposite; *ever-narrowing* is the opposite of *creative*, which implies expansive. (C) is the best answer.

23. D

Notice that each paragraph of the passage discusses positive aspects of productive leisure activities in terms of their benefits to individuals. (A) is opposite; the passage address the benefits of productive recreation for individuals, not for society. (B) is a misused detail; *emotional flexibility* is mentioned in connection with creative activity, but physical flexibility is not discussed. (C) and (E) are too extreme; the word *requisite* (C) means necessary, and this is an exaggeration of the author's position. Likewise, the word *ubiquitous* (E) means everywhere or always present, not a position taken by the author. (D) is the best choice.

24. D

The statement "learn to swim in a turbulent sea of ambiguity and chance without the lifejacket of standard procedure," is being used as a metaphor for the unorthodox world that artists often live in. The author is expressing the fact that those involved in this world often make decisions and have experiences that those who live by the normal societal standards may not have, which is the opposite of (B). (A) and (E) have nothing to do with the passage, and (C) is never supported by the author. (D) is the best choice that expresses this idea.

SECTION 7

1. A

If $a < b$ and $b < c$, then $a < c$.

$8a < 3b < 10c$, so $8a < 10c$

2. C

If a problem at the beginning of a section seems easy, it probably is. All you have to do is be careful that you don't make a silly arithmetic error.

Employees by division:

    Development $= 1 \times 4 = 4$

    Marketing $= 2 \times 3 = 6$

    Accounting $= 3 \times 2 = 6$

    Public Relations $= 5 \times 5 = 25$

    Overall total: $4 + 6 + 6 + 25 = 41$

3. B

You can rearrange the average formula to get whichever part you're missing.

For example, sum = (average) × (number of items).

$$7 < \frac{sum}{7} < 12$$
$$49 < sum < 84$$

4. E

We know that one revolution is 360°. Since this happens every 1.5 seconds, (A) and (B) are definitely too low.

The ball goes around $\frac{10}{1.5} = \frac{100}{15} = \frac{20}{3}$ times, for a total of $\frac{20}{3}(360°) = 2,400°$

5. B

You need to find the total number of birds in Joe's yard on Thursday and the number of those birds that were at the suet feeder. Divide the number of birds at the suet feeder by the total number of birds, then multiply by 100 to convert this fraction into a percent.

There were 3 birds at the suet feeder on Thursday, and $6 + 3 + 2 = 11$ total birds. $\frac{3}{11} \times 100\% = 27.\overline{27}\%$. The nearest answer choice is (B), 27%.

6. A

Sunflower seeds are represented by the black circles. Find the black circle that is highest on the *y*-axis, and look down to see what day it belongs to.

The greatest number of birds at the sunflower seed feeder was 7, on Sunday. Choice (A) is correct.

7. D

This problem is testing two concepts: the sum of the angles in a triangle is 180 degrees, and the definition of an isosceles triangle. Remember that if two sides of a triangle have the same length, the angles opposite them have the same measurement.

Use the facts that the interior angles of a triangle sum to 180 degrees and that angles along a line sum to 180 degrees to solve for the unknown angles, as in the figure above. Then you can see that *ABC*, *AFE*, *ADC*, and *ABE* are all isosceles; *BFD* is not.

8. E

This problem is designed to let you try out this procedure. Don't worry about having major insights—just plug in the given number and see what happens. This will help you gain the insight you need for the next two questions.

1. Choose 6.127

2. $6.127 \times 100 = 612.7$

3. The smallest integer greater than or equal to 612.7 is 613 (just round up)

4. $613 + 12 = 625$

5. Print 625

9. D

You can attack this by either trying to work backwards with each of the answers, or thinking about what kinds of results you can get from the procedure.

1. Choose a number 0–9.9

2. Result is between 0 and 990

3. Round up to nearest integer—now number is an integer between 0 and 990

4. Add 12—now number is an integer between 12 and 1002

5. Print the number from step 4

(A) Doesn't work because it's too small

(B) Doesn't work because it's too small

(C) Not an integer

(D) Correct

(E) Too large

10. C

Try plugging in a number into the reordered steps to see if you still get the same answer.

We can try 6.127 again (the number doesn't change in step 5, so we'll only show 1–4).

(A) Step 1. 6.127

Step 3. 7

Step 2. 700

Step 4. 712

This does not match with what we found in #8, so it does not work.

(B) Step 1. 6.127

Step 4. 18.127

Step 3. 19

Step 2. 1,900

This does not match with what we found in #8, so it does not work.

(C) Step 1. 6.127

Step 2. 612.7

Step 3. 624.7

Step 4. 625

This seems to work. Notice that since we're adding an integer, it doesn't matter whether we add first or round first.

(D) Doesn't work, since (A) and (B) don't work.

(E) Not true, since (C) works.

11. B

Don't waste time trying to write fancy expressions for 3^{11} in terms of x—just convert the answer choices into powers of 3.

(A) $243x = 3^5(3^5) = 3^{10}$

(B) $3x^2 = 3(3^5)^2 = 3(3^{10}) = 3^{11}$

(C) $9x^4 = 3^2(3^5)^4 = 3^2(3^{20}) = 3^{22}$

(D) $27x^3 = 3^3(3^5)^3 = 3^3(3^{15}) = 3^{18}$

(E) $x^6 = (3^5)^6 = 3^{30}$

12. D

In many cases you can't solve for the variables individually, but you can solve for some expression in terms of them.

$$n = 10 + m$$
$$n - m = 10$$
$$2(n - m) = 20$$
$$2(n - m) + 4 = 24$$

13. B

Use the value of x to solve for c; then find the other value by factoring:

$$(-5)^2 + 3(-5) + c = 0$$
$$25 - 15 + c = 0$$
$$c = -10$$
$$x^2 + 3x - 10 = 0$$
$$(x + 5)(x - 2) = 0$$
$$x = -5; x = 2$$

14. D

Always make sure you're answering the right question. All the good algebra in the world doesn't help if you grid in the smallest or middle number.

$$x + (x + 2) + (x + 4) = 1,089$$
$$3x + 6 = 1,089$$
$$3x = 1,083$$
$$x = 361$$
$$x + 2 = 363$$
$$x + 4 = 365$$
numbers are 361, 363, 365

15. B

Work methodically, using the rate formula. Don't be discouraged by a somewhat higher level of complexity—if you understand rates then this is simply more steps.

Their respective mowing rates are:

Jan: 1 hour per lawn or 1 lawn per hour

Wally: $\frac{1}{2}$ hours per lawn or 2 lawns per hour

Peter: $\frac{2}{3}$ hour per lawn or $\frac{3}{2}$ lawns per hour

Jan mows for $\frac{1}{4}$ hours at 1 lawn per hour, so she finishes

$\frac{1}{4} \times 1 = \frac{1}{4}$ of the lawn.

Together, the three mow $1 + 2 + \frac{3}{2} = \frac{9}{2}$ lawns per hour, or $\frac{2}{9}$ hours per lawn.

The final part takes $\frac{3}{4}$ lawn $\times \frac{2}{9}$ hour per lawn $= \frac{1}{6}$ hours.

So the total time is $\frac{1}{4} + \frac{1}{6} = \frac{5}{12}$ hours.

16. E

Use the slope of the line to find AB, then split the quadrilateral into a triangle and a rectangle

The slope of the line is $\frac{8-4}{6-0} = \frac{4}{6} = \frac{2}{3}$.

The coordinate of C is $(4, 3)$.

When we move from E to A, the x-coordinate changes by 4, so the y-coordinate changes by $4 \times \frac{2}{3} = \frac{8}{3}$, thus the coordinates of A are $(4, 4 + \frac{8}{3}) = (4, \frac{20}{3})$.

If you split the quadrilateral, the area of the triangle is

$\left(\frac{1}{2}\right) \times (2) \times \left(8 - \frac{20}{3}\right) = \left(\frac{1}{2}\right) \times (2) \times \left(\frac{4}{3}\right) = \frac{4}{3}$.

The area of the rectangle is $2 \times \left(\frac{20}{3} - 3\right) = 2 \times \frac{11}{3} = \frac{22}{3}$.

So the total area is $\frac{4}{3} + \frac{22}{3} = \frac{26}{3}$.

SECTION 8

1. D

Start with the first blank. Vaccines can either be given or not given. If your prediction for the first blank is *giving*, then the second blank should be positive in order to support this answer choice. A good prediction for the second blank would then be *successful* at providing protection. The first answer choice in (A) is the opposite of the prediction. *Unsuccessful in*, (B), is the opposite of the prediction for the second blank. *Reconstituting*, (C), or restoring, doses of the vaccine does not fit. Vaccines are not *restored* (although they may sometimes have to be re-administered). Both choices in (E) do not work; giving someone a dose of vaccine is not the same as *disseminating* or spreading it widely. *Unverified for* is the opposite of the prediction. (D) is the best answer.

2. B

Using the clue words to form a prediction for the blanks, the crew would be trying to *save* what equipment they could off of the *struggling* boat. The choices in (A) do not work. Although the boat may have been *obsolete* or *outdated*, this does not describe the manner in which it sank or even why it sank. The boat was *defunct*," (C), or no longer functioning, but the crew would not be *exacerbating* the equipment or making it worse. The words in (D) do not match the predictions; the crew would not try to *revitalize* or *invigorate* equipment, and a sinking dive boat is certainly not *prosperous*. The first choice in (E) is too extreme. *Commandeer* means more along the lines of seizing or confiscating and suggests taking against the will of someone else. *Lucrative* does not work in the second blank as it means profitable. (B) is the best choice.

3. A

Start with a prediction for the first blank. A word such as *variety* or *diversity* would work. The second blank should support the first with a word such as a *range* of various ingredients. The first choice in (B) can be eliminated because the sentence says nothing about the size of the population growing. A growing population would imply an increasing amount of different foods would come to exist; however, nothing about growth is mentioned. The second choice is the opposite of the prediction. The first choice in (C) is out of scope; the town wouldn't have *mixed feelings towards* different foods. The second choice doesn't match the prediction. (D) Both blanks do not work. *Dearth* or *scarcity* is the opposite of the prediction and nothing is said about a reduction of ingredients available caused by using them. (E) The first blank does not fit because nothing is said about either the population or the amount of food increasing or decreasing. The second blank does not work; towns would not boast of artificial ingredients. (A) is the best answer.

4. C

If the path *meandered . . . for miles* then it must have *winded* and *twisted* around the riverbank. (A) is out of scope; the hiking trail may have afforded *panoramic* or *scenic* views but this is not mentioned in the sentence. Sentence completion questions will never ask you for information that is not presented in the question stem. There is no indication that the trail was *precipitous*, (B), or steep. The trail did not necessarily *circumscribe*, (D), the river or follow it in a circular path; the sentence describes a river, not a pond. If you did not know the meaning of this word, break it apart; circles by nature are round, so to *circumscribe* something means to go around it. There is no indication that the path twisted back on itself or went backwards, as (E) suggests. (C) is the best answer.

5. B

Jidapa seemed to be the *opposite* of her former self. Check the answer choices to see if they match this prediction. (A) does not work. The sentence does not suggest that she became less of a certain way; she changed from behaving one way to acting quite the opposite. Her change in behavior was a result of the accident, but the sentence is comparing Jidapa to her former self and is not discussing the reasons for her change. Thus, (C) is incorrect. *The extremity of her former self*, (D), does not make sense. Read back answer choices into the sentence to make sure that they fit. Even if the word were *extreme*, the sentence does not suggest that she became an extreme version of her former self (i.e. more friendly or more sprightly). (E) does not fit; her behavior couldn't change to become *mainstay* or the *chief support* of herself. (B) is the best choice.

6. C

What words describe a type of *mistake*? The blank could read *blunder*. Eliminate any answer choices that don't match this prediction. You can eliminate (A) because the sentence is not referring to a possible dispute between the detectives. (B) means jeer or laugh at and does not match the prediction. A *tryst* is a pact made between lovers and has nothing to do with detectives working on a case, thus (D) is incorrect. A *tribute*, (E), or praise, cannot compromise a stakeout. (C) is the best choice.

7. E

Since the author is trying to convince or persuade the reader that the Satyr form is worthy of pursuit, you can expect the correct answer to have a positive charge. The author predicts that Satyr plays will *capture the imagination of the rising generation* and sees the chorus as a *dynamic element* that contributes to the *untapped potential* of the Satyr form. Together with the exclamation point ending the passage, this phrasing gives the passage a tone of *enthusiasm* or *excitement*. (A) is opposite; the tone is excited, not dull or faint. (B) is a distortion; the author's discussion does not have a harsh tone overall. (C) is also a distortion; although the last paragraph is somewhat playful, overall the passage does not have a carefree or impulsive tone. (D) is out of scope; what the author hopes for has not taken place. He has nothing to be *grateful* for. (E) is the best answer.

8. E

Read for context. The chorus dances and sings and although *invisible* to other characters, can *engage the audience without interfering* with the main action. Predict something like *draw the attention of the audience*. (A), (B), (C), and (D) are all out of scope and relate to another meaning of the word that doesn't make sense in context. (E) is the best answer choice.

9. C

The author's main point in the passage is that the Satyr form has not received as much attention as it deserves. The cited line supports this point by suggesting that screenwriters should seek inspiration in Satyr plays because these plays have *volumes of untapped potential*. Look for a choice that notes the unexplored possibilities in Satyr plays. (A) and (B) are out of scope; translations are not discussed in the passage (A), and possible *movies about Greek drama*, (B) are not mentioned. (D) is a distortion; in this context, volume is a matter of amount, not noise level. (E) is a misused detail; singing is mentioned elsewhere in the passage, but this is not related to the cited phrase.

10. B

The chorus is first mentioned in the third paragraph, but this question asks about the *fourth* paragraph. In the fourth paragraph, the author suggests that the chorus provides *a hint of what the Satyr form has to offer* and says that it can embody *unpredictable inspiration*. This functions to reinforce the description from the third paragraph of the chorus as a *dynamic element . . . that is full of potential*. Look for a choice that emphasizes the chorus's unpredictability or dynamic potential. (A) is opposite; the author is arguing that the Satyr form is worthy of more study. (C), (D), and (E) are misused details; the chorus dances, but this is not the point the author is making here (C), Satyrs, as creatures, are mentioned earlier in the passage, but this paragraph only mentions the Satyr *form* of drama (D), and although the author does say the form is *widely ignored*, the chorus is not mentioned in order to explain this fact (E). (B) is the best answer.

11. D

Along with *the lampooning of leaders*, *the misadventures of husbands and wives* is given as an example of subject matter for comedy that has been *consistent over the centuries*. Look for a choice that captures the long-term use of this subject matter. (A) is a distortion; whereas this may have been tempting, there is a distinction between *form* and *subject matter* that is important in this sentence and in the passage as a whole. Also, the consistency of use is not restricted to *Greek* comedy. (B) is also a distortion; again, this choice confuses form with subject matter. The form is described in the passage as sophisticated, not the *subject matter*. (C) is an example of subject matter for comedy, not tragedy. (E) is a misused detail; Satyr plays are discussed in Passage 1, not Passage 2. (D) is the best answer.

12. D

The gist of the paragraph is that, while moviegoers have become so used to common narrative devices that it's hard to surprise them, the comedic form is still flexible enough to do so. Since overexposure makes moviegoers *jaded* and unsurprised, you can infer that the word has a negative connotation. *Unsurprised* works fine as a prediction. (A) is opposite; this lacks the negative connotation required by the prediction. (B) is a distortion; this choice picks up on a similarity with jade, the mineral, but it is not the meaning in this passage. (C) is out of scope; this doesn't make sense in context. (E) is also opposite; moviegoers are *not* surprised by common narrative devices. (D) is the best answer.

13. A

The last sentence of the second paragraph leads you to anticipate more discussion of comedy's *flexibility*, which is exactly what you get in the third paragraph. Look for a choice that mentions the changeable or *flexible nature of comedy*. (B) is a misused detail; although the comedic form originally came from ancient Greece, the purpose of this paragraph isn't to emphasize the importance of ancient Greek civilization as a whole. (C) is also a misused detail; the author mentions the fall of Rome in order to point out that comedy survived the fall, not to talk about the fall itself. (D) is a distortion; the author's focus is on the flexibility of comedy, but the passage does not suggest that there is a *general misunderstanding* of comedy as rigid. (E) is out of scope; the paragraph is about the flexibility of comedy for many generations, not intergenerational traditions beyond the sphere of comedy. (A) is the best choice.

14. B

A form is a structure, model, or mode. To say that a form is *wildly loose* is to create a contradiction. So the author puts quotation marks around the word "form" to suggest that the word shouldn't be taken too literally. (A) is the opposite; if the author were using the exact definition, there would be no need for quotation marks. (C), (D), (E) are all distortions; if the author intended to use another word (C), presumably he would have; although the author discusses both theater and cinema (D), the quotation marks do not highlight a difference between them; and the author frequently uses the word earlier in the passage (E) but does not define it. (B) is the best answer.

15. A

The first author emphasizes the potential of Satyr plays, while the second author emphasizes the strengths of comedies. Despite these differences, however, both authors agree with the broad idea that current filmmakers and screenwriters can learn from the plays of antiquity. Even if this similarity doesn't occur to you right away, you can recognize it when you evaluate the choices. (B) is out of scope; the author of Passage 1 does not discuss comedy's flexibility or resilience as compared to other dramatic forms. (C) is too extreme; although neither author focuses on the potential value of tragedy, this choice is stronger than warranted by the text. (D) is also out of scope; the author of Passage 2 does not discuss Satyr plays. (E) is a distortion; both authors offer suggestions for making successful films, but they do not imply that audiences "are bored by the current cinema." (A) is correct; whereas the author of Passage 2 does not emphasize Greek theater as much as the first author does, he does reference it in the course of his argument.

16. B

Working by elimination is a good way to approach this question. The correct choice will be something discussed by both authors, and something both sees as valuable. The audience fits this bill. The first author describes the chorus's ability to *engage the audience* as a strength of Satyr plays, and the second author mentions how the audience *rewards successful filmmakers with loyalty*. (A) is out of scope; the *chorus* is not mentioned in Passage 2. (C) is a distortion; the first author only mentions critics briefly in a negative light, and the second author does not directly discuss critics at all. (D) and (E) are also out of scope; screenwriters (D) are mentioned in Passage 1, but the only job title mentioned in Passage 2 is that of filmmaker, and although this may initially seem tempting, a closer examination reveals that Passage 2 does not mention characters (E) at all. (B) is the best answer.

17. D

Sometimes the author will state the purpose right away, as in the first sentence here—"Of the two primary forms of drama . . . comedy is the more promising form for the future of cinema." The rest of the passage supports this thesis. Use this quote as your prediction. (A) is out of scope; Passage 2 does not discuss *the Satyr form*. (B) is a misused detail; whereas the author makes this point, it is not *the main idea* of the passage. (C) is too extreme; the author indicates that comedy is *more promising* for the cinema, not *superior* in every way. (E) is a distortion; this exaggerates points made in the text, and is hardly the author's main point. (D) is the best answer.

18. B

Passage 1 describes the *mix of cowardice and boldness* in Falstaff, but says little else. The author of Passage 2 is most concerned with advocating the comic form as the best way of breathing new life into the cinema. Look for a choice that incorporates that main idea in some way. (A) is out of scope; the author of Passage 2 does not comment on the Satyr form. (C) is a distortion; the author of Passage 2 does directly mention *Greek and Roman drama*, but says nothing about *Elizabethan drama*. (D) is also out of scope; the author of Passage 2 does not comment on Satyr plays. (E) is also a distortion; whereas the author of Passage 2 does mention *the sophistication of the comic form*, nothing indicates that Falstaff—based on the brief comment the first author makes about him—is *an example* of that sophistication. (B) is correct; this matches well with the main idea of Passage 2.

SECTION 9

1. B

This sentence presents a cause (providing emergency power) and its effect (being invaluable). *Because*, in (B), best reflects this relationship. The transitions in (C) and (D) do not properly relate the clauses. (E) uses a plural pronoun to refer to a singular antecedent, *generator*.

2. A

This sentence contains no error. The pronoun *of* in (B) is idiomatically incorrect with *assertive*. (C), (D), and (E) are unnecessarily wordy.

3. D

As written, this sentence as a fragment. (D) corrects this by replacing the gerund form with *hire*. The verb in (B) doesn't agree with its plural subject, *vineyards*. (C) does not address the error. (E) is unnecessarily wordy.

4. C

As written, this sentence is unnecessarily wordy. (C) is concise, yet contains all of the information in the original. Using both *generally* and *most of the time*, as (B) does, is redundant. (D) and (E) are both unnecessarily wordy.

5. E

Technical school graduates work *in other jobs*, not *as . . . other jobs*. (E) is the correct choice here. None of the other choices is in parallel form.

6. D

As written, this is a run-on sentence. (D) corrects this by making the second clause dependent. (B) implies a causation that doesn't exist in the original. (C) does not address the error. (E) incorrectly uses the pronoun *which* to refer to a person.

7. B

The past tense is not correct for a result that had not yet happened at the time. *In the hope* indicates that the result may or may not occur, so *would prevent* is the appropriate verb phrase here; the correct choice is (B). *Will prevent* would only be appropriate if the rest of the sentence were in the present tense, so (C), (D), and (E) are incorrect; additionally, (C) unnecessarily introduces the passive voice.

8. B

As written, this sentence indicates that the Vatican City is visited frequently because it is its own country. (B) clarifies the relationship between the ideas. (C) is incorrect grammatical structure, (D) changes the meaning of the original sentence, and (E) fails to address the error.

9. C

The pronoun *you* cannot be used with the antecedent *candidate*. (C) replaces *you* with the appropriate third-person pronouns. (B) uses *it* to refer to a person. (D) and (E) use verb tenses that are inappropriate in context.

10. D

As written, this sentence says that Chopin was *among the most complex musical composition of the era*. Both (C) and (D) place the correct noun, *etudes*, after the modifying phrase (a possessive, such as *Chopin's* here, functions as an adjective), but (C) creates a sentence fragment. In (B), the introductory phrase modifies *piano*. (E) does not address the error; additionally, it creates a sentence fragment.

11. B

In this sentence, *he* could refer to either the defendant or the lawyer. (B) and (D) both make it clear about who *was sorry*, but (D) creates a sentence fragment. (C) and (E) do not address the ambiguity issue.

12. A

This sentence is correct as written. (B) and (D) are unnecessarily wordy. (C) creates a run-on sentence. (E) is incorrect grammatical structure.

13. B

The first two verbs in the series are *rinse* and *wipe*; *dry* would be the correct form for the third verb. None of the other choices make the third verb parallel.

14. C

The sentence as written compares what is being transmitted, *images*, to a method of transmission, *fax*. (C) corrects this by using the pronoun *those* to refer to *images*. (B), (D), and (E) fail to address the error.